THE METAPHYSICS OF SIR WILLIAM HAMILTON,

COLLECTED, ARRANGED, AND ABRIDGED,

FOR THE USE OF COLLEGES AND PRIVATE STUDENTS.

BY

FRANCIS BOWEN,

ALFORD PROFESSOR OF MORAL PHILOSOPHY IN HARVARD COLLEGE.

BOSTON:

JOHN ALLYN, PUBLISHER,

LATE SEVER, FRANCIS, & CO.

1872.

SEVENTH THOUSAND.

PREFACE.

It is unfortunate that Sir William Hamilton did not undertake fully to digest his metaphysical opinions into system, and to publish them as one orderly and connected whole. He *had* a system, for he was eminently a methodical and self-consistent thinker; but it was built up piecemeal, and so given to the world, at various times, in successive articles in the Edinburgh Review; in copious notes, appendices, and other additions to these articles when they were republished as a volume of "Discussions," and again, when these "Discussions" passed to a second edition; in the Notes, and, still more at length, in the Supplementary Dissertations, to his ponderous edition of Reid; and finally, in the memoranda prepared at different times and for various purposes, which his English editors gathered up and annexed to the posthumous publication of his "Lectures on Metaphysics." While neither of these works furnishes an outline of his system as a whole, each one of them contains a statement, more or less complete, of his principal doctrines and arguments, so that, taken together, they abound in repetitions. Even the "Lectures," which afford the nearest approach to a full and systematic exposition of his opinions, besides laboring under the necessary disadvantage of a posthumous publication, never finally revised by the author for the press, and probably not even intended by him to be printed, were first written by him in great haste at the time (1836) of his original appointment to a Professorship in the University of Edinburgh, and seem to have received but few subsequent alterations or additions, though his opinions certainly underwent afterwards considerable development and modification.

As any course of instruction in the Philosophy of Mind

at the present day must be very imperfect which does not comprise a tolerably full view of Hamilton's Metaphysics, I have endeavored, in the present volume, to prepare a text-book which should contain, in his own language, the substance of all that he has written upon the subject. For this purpose, the "Lectures on Metaphysics" have been taken as the basis of the work; and I have freely abridged them by striking out the repetitions and redundancies in which they abound, and omitting also, in great part, the load of citations and references that they contain, as these are of inferior interest except to a student of the history of philosophy, or as marks of the stupendous erudition of the author. The space acquired by these abridgments has enabled me to interweave into the book, in their appropriate place and connection, all those portions of the "Discussions," and of the Notes and Dissertations supplementary to Reid, which seemed necessary either to elucidate and confirm the text, or to supplement it with the later and more fully expressed opinions of the author. These insertions, always distinguished by angular brackets [ ], and referred to the source whence they were drawn, are very numerous and considerable in amount; sometimes they are several pages long, others do not exceed in length a single paragraph, or even a single sentence. The author's language has invariably been preserved, and whereever a word or two had to be altered or supplied, to preserve the connection, the inserted words have been enclosed in brackets. The divisions between the Lectures, necessarily arbitrary, as the limits of a discourse of fixed length could not coincide with the natural division of the subject, have not been preserved in this edition. A chapter here often begins in the middle of a Lecture, and sometimes comprises two or more Lectures. A very few notes, critical or explanatory in character, are properly distinguished as supplied by the American Editor.

It has been a laborious, but not a disagreeable task, to examine and collate three bulky octavos, with a view thus to condense their substance into a single volume of moderate dimensions. I cannot promise that the work has been thoroughly, but only that it has been carefully, done.

CONTENTS.

CHAPTER VIII.

CHAPTER IX.

CHAPTER X.

CHAPTER XI.

CHAPTER XII.

CHAPTER XIII.

CHAPTER XIV.

CHAPTER XV.

CHAPTER XVI.

CHAPTER XVII.

CHAPTER XVIII.

CHAPTER XIX.

CHAPTER XX.

CHAPTER XXI.

CHAPTER XXII.

CHAPTER XXIII.

CHAPTER XXIV

CHAPTER XXV.

CHAPTER XXVI.

CHAPTER XXVII.

CHAPTER XXVIII.

HAMILTON'S METAPHYSICS.

CHAPTER I.

UTILITY OF THE STUDY OF PHILOSOPHY.

SOME things are valuable, finally, or for themselves, — these are ends; other things are valuable, not on their own account, but as conducive towards certain ulterior ends, — these are means. The value of ends is absolute, — the value of means is relative. Absolute value is properly called a *good*, — relative value is properly called a *utility*. Of goods, or absolute ends, there are for man but two, — perfection and happiness. By perfection is meant the full and harmonious development of all our faculties, corporeal and mental, intellectual and moral; by happiness, the complement of all the pleasures of which we are susceptible.

Now, I may state, though I cannot at present attempt to prove, that human perfection and human happiness coincide, and thus constitute, in reality, but a single end. For as, on the one hand, the perfection or full development of a power is in proportion to its capacity of free, vigorous, and continued action, so on the other, all pleasure is the concomitant of activity; its degree being in proportion as that activity is spontaneously intense, its prolongation in proportion as that activity is spontaneously continued; whereas, pain arises either from a faculty being restrained in its spontaneous tendency to action, or from being urged to a degree, or to a continuance, of energy beyond the limit to which it of itself freely tends. To promote our perfection is thus to promote our happiness; for to cultivate fully and harmoniously our various faculties, is simply to enable them, by exercise, to energize longer and stronger without painful effort; that is, to afford us a larger amount of a higher quality of enjoyment.

In considering the utility of a branch of knowledge, it behooves us, in the first place, to estimate its value as viewed simply in itself; and, in the second, its value as viewed in relation to other branches. Considered in itself, a science is valuable in proportion as its cultivation is immediately conducive to the mental improvement of the cultivator. This may be called its Absolute utility. In relation to others, a science is valuable in proportion as its study is necessary for the prosecution of other branches of knowledge. This may be called its Relative utility.

Absolute utility of two kinds — Subjective and Objective. — In the former point of view, that is, considered absolutely, or in itself, the philosophy of mind comprises two several utilities, according as it, 1°, Cultivates the mind or knowing subject, by calling its faculties into exercise; and, 2°, Furnishes the mind with a certain complement of truths or objects of knowledge. The former of these constitutes its Subjective, the latter its Objective utility. These utilities are not the same, nor do they even stand to each other in any necessary proportion. As an individual may possess an ample magazine of knowledge, and still be little better than an intellectual barbarian, so the utility of one science may be chiefly seen in affording a greater number of higher and more indisputable truths, — the utility of another in determining the faculties to a higher energy, and consequently to a higher education.

There are few, I believe, disposed to question the speculative dignity of mental science; but its practical utility is not unfrequently denied. To what, it is asked, is the science of mind conducive? What are its uses?

What is Practical Utility? — I am not one of those who think that the importance of a study is sufficiently established when its dignity is admitted; for, holding that knowledge is for the sake of man, and not man for the sake of knowledge, it is necessary, in order to vindicate its value, that every science should be able to show what are the advantages which it promises to confer upon its student. I, therefore, profess myself a utilitarian; and it is only on the special ground of its utility that I would claim for the philosophy of mind, what I regard as its peculiar and preëminent importance. But what is a utilitarian? Simply one who prefers the Useful to the Useless — and who does not? But what is the useful? That which is prized, not on its own account, but as conducive to the acquisition of something else, — the useful is, in short, only another word for a mean towards an end; for every mean is useful, and whatever is useful is a mean. Now the value of a mean is always in proportion to the value of its end; and the useful being a mean, it follows, that, of two utilities, the one which conduces to the more valuable end will be itself the more valuable utility.

So far there is no difference of opinion. All agree that the useful is a mean towards an end; and that, *cæteris paribus*, a mean towards a higher end constitutes a higher utility than a mean towards a lower. The only dispute that has arisen, or can possibly arise, in regard to the utility of means (supposing always their relative efficiency), is founded on the various views that may be entertained in regard to the existence and comparative importance of ends.

Two errors in the popular estimate of the comparative utility of human sciences. — Now the various opinions which prevail concerning the comparative utility of human sciences and studies, have all arisen from two errors.

The first of these consists in viewing man, not as an end *unto himself*, but merely as a mean organized for the sake of something *out of himself;* and, under this partial view of human destination, those branches of knowledge obtain exclusively the name of *useful*, which tend to qualify a human being to act the lowly part of a dexterous instrument. It has been the tendency of different ages, of different countries, of different ranks and conditions of society, to measure the utility of studies rather by one of these standards, than by both. Thus it was the bias of antiquity, when the moral and intellectual cultivation of the citizen was viewed as the great end of all political institutions, to appreciate all knowledge principally by the higher standard; on the contrary, it is unfortunately the bias of our modern civilization, since the accumulation (and not too the distribution) of riches in a country, has become the grand problem of the statesman, to appreciate it rather by the lower.

The second, and the more dangerous, of these errors consists in regarding the cultivation of our faculties as subordinate to the acquisition of knowledge, instead of regarding the possession of knowledge as subordinate to the cultivation of our faculties; and, in consequence of this error, those sciences which afford a greater number of more certain facts, have been deemed superior in utility to those which bestow a higher cultivation on the higher faculties of the mind.

Man an end unto himself. — As to the first of these errors, the fallacy is so palpable, that we may well wonder at its prevalence. It is manifest, indeed, that man, in so far as he is a mean for the glory of God, must be an end unto himself; for it is only in the accomplishment of his own perfection, that, as a creature, he can manifest the glory of his Creator. Though therefore man, by relation to God, be but a mean, for that very reason, in relation to all else is he an end. Wherefore, now speaking of him exclusively in his natural capacity and temporal relations, I say it is manifest that man is by nature necessarily an end to himself, — that his perfection and happiness constitute the goal of his activity, to which he tends, and ought to tend, when not diverted from this, his general and native destination, by peculiar and accidental circumstances. But it is equally evident, that, under the condition of society, individual men are, for the most part, to a greater or less degree, actually so diverted. To live, the individual must have the means of living; and these means (unless he already possess them) he must procure, — he must purchase. But purchase with what? With his services, *i. e.* — he must reduce himself to an instrument, — an instrument of utility to others; and the services of this instrument he must barter for those means of subsistence of which he is in want. In other words, he must exercise some trade, calling, or profession.

Thus, in the actualities of social life, each man, instead of being solely an end to himself, — instead of being able to make every thing subordinate to that full and harmonious development of his individual faculties, in which his full perfection and his true happiness consist, — is, in general, compelled to degrade himself into the mean or instrument towards the accomplishment of some end external to himself, and for the benefit of others.

Liberal and Professional Education. — Now the perfection of man as an end, and the perfection of man as a mean or instrument, are not only not the same; they are, in reality, generally opposed. And as these two perfections are different, so the training requisite for their acquisition is not identical, and has, accordingly, been distinguished by different names. The one is styled Liberal, the other Professional education, — the branches of knowledge cultivated for these purposes being called respectively liberal and professional, or liberal and lucrative, sciences. By the Germans, the latter are usually distinguished as the *Brodwissenschaften*, which we may translate, *The Bread and Butter Sciences.* A few of the professions, indeed, as requiring a higher development of the higher faculties, and involving, therefore, a greater or less amount of liberal education, have obtained the name of liberal professions. We must, however, recollect that this is only an accidental and a very partial exception. But though the full and harmonious development of our faculties be the high and natural destination of all, while the cultivation of any professional dexterity is only a contingency, though a contingency incumbent upon most, it has, however, happened that the paramount and universal end of man, — of man absolutely, — has been often ignorantly lost sight of, and the term *useful* appropriated exclusively to those acquirements which have a value only to man considered in his relative, lower, and accidental character of an instrument. But, because some have thus been led to appropriate the name of useful to those studies and objects of knowledge, which are conducive to the inferior end, it assuredly does not follow that those conducive to the higher have not a far preferable title to the name thus curiously denied to them. Even admitting, therefore, that the study of mind is of no immediate advantage in preparing the student for many of the subordinate parts in the mechanism of society, its utility cannot, on that account, be called in question, unless it be asserted that man "liveth by bread alone," and has no higher destination than that of the calling by which he earns his subsistence.

Knowledge and intellectual cultivation. — The second error to which I have adverted, reverses the relative subordination of knowledge and of intellectual cultivation. In refutation of this, I shall attempt briefly to show, *firstly*, that knowledge and intellectual cultivation are not identical; *secondly*, that knowledge is itself principally valuable as a mean of intellectual cultivation; and, *lastly*, that intellectual cultivation is more directly and effectually accomplished by the study of mind than by any other of our rational pursuits.

But to prevent misapprehension, I may premise what I mean by knowledge, and what by intellectual cultivation. By knowledge is understood the mere possession of truths; by intellectual cultivation, or intellectual development, the power, acquired through exercise by the higher faculties, of a more varied, vigorous and protracted activity.

In the first place, then, it will be requisite, I conceive, to say but little to show that knowledge and intellectual development are not only not the same, but stand in no necessary proportion to each other. This is manifest, if we consider the very different conditions under which these two qualities are acquired. The one condition under which all powers, and consequently the intellectual faculties, are developed, is exercise. The more intense and continuous the exercise, the more vigorously developed will be the power.

But a certain quantity of knowledge, — in other words, a certain amount of possessed truths, — does not suppose, as its condition, a corresponding sum of intellectual exercise. One truth requires much, another truth requires little, effort in acquisition; and, while the original discovery of a truth evolves perhaps a maximum of the highest quality of energy, the subsequent learning of that truth elicits probably but a minimum of the very lowest.

Is truth or mental exercise the superior end?—But, as it is evident that the possession of truths, and the development of the mind in which they are deposited, are not identical, I proceed, in the second place, to show that, considered as ends, and in relation to each other, the knowledge of truths is not supreme, but subordinate to the cultivation of the knowing mind. The question—Is Truth, or is the Mental Exercise in the pursuit of truth, the superior end?—this is perhaps the most curious theoretical, and certainly the most important practical, problem in the whole compass of philosophy. For, according to the solution at which we arrive, must we accord the higher or the lower rank to certain great departments of study; and, what is of more importance, the character of its solution, as it determines the aim, regulates from first to last the method, which an enlightened science of education must adopt.

But, however curious and important, this question has never, in so far as I am aware, been regularly discussed. Nay, what is still more remarkable, the erroneous alternative has been very generally assumed as true. The consequence of this has been, that sciences of far inferior, have been elevated above sciences of far superior, utility; while education has been systematically distorted,—though truth and nature have occasionally burst the shackles which a perverse theory had imposed. The reason of this is sufficiently obvious. At first sight, it seems even absurd to doubt that truth is more valuable than its pursuit; for is this not to say that the end is less important than the mean?—and on this superficial view is the prevalent misapprehension founded. A slight consideration will, however, expose the fallacy.

Practical and speculative Knowledge; their ends.—Knowledge is either practical or speculative. In practical knowledge it is evident that truth is not the ultimate end; for, in that case, knowledge is, *ex hypothesi*, for the sake of application. The knowledge of a moral, of a political, of a religious truth, is of value only as it affords the preliminary or condition of its exercise.

In speculative knowledge, on the other hand, there may indeed, at first sight, seem greater difficulty; but further reflection will prove that speculative truth is only pursued, and is only held of value, for the sake of intellectual activity: "Sordet cognita veritas" is a shrewd aphorism of Seneca. A truth, once known, falls into comparative insignificance. It is now prized less on its own account, than as opening up new ways to new activity, new suspense, new hopes, new discoveries, new self-gratulation. Every votary of science is wilfully ignorant of a thousand established facts, — of a thousand which he might make his own more easily than he could attempt the discovery of even one. But it is not knowledge, — it is not truth, — that he principally seeks; he seeks the exercise of his faculties and feelings; and, as in following after the one, he exerts a greater amount of pleasurable energy than in taking formal possession of the thousand, he disdains the certainty of the many, and prefers the chances of the one. Accordingly, the sciences always studied with keenest interest are those in a state of progress and uncertainty; absolute certainty and absolute completion would be the paralysis of any study; and the last worst calamity that could befall man, as he is at present constituted, would be that full and final possession of speculative truth, which he now vainly anticipates as the consummation of his intellectual happiness.

"Quæsivit cœlo lucem, ingemuitque reperta."

But what is true of science, is true, indeed, of all human activity. "In life," as the great Pascal observes, "we always believe that we are seeking repose, while, in reality, all that we ever seek is agitation." It is ever the contest that pleases us, and not the victory. Thus it is in play; thus it is in hunting thus it is in the search of truth; thus it is in life. The past does not interest, the present does not satisfy, the future alone is the object which engages us.

> "(Nullo votorum fine beati)
> Victuros agimus semper, nec vivimus unquam."

The question, I said, has never been regularly discussed, — probably because it lay in too narrow a compass; but no philosopher appears to have ever seriously proposed it to himself, who did not resolve it in contradiction to the ordinary opinion. A contradiction of this opinion is even involved in the very term Philosophy; and the man who first declared that he was not a σοφὸς, or possessor, but a φιλόσοφος, or seeker of truth, at once enounced the true end of human speculation, and embodied it in a significant name. Under the same conviction, Plato defines man "the hunter of truth," for science is a chase, and in a chase, the pursuit is always of greater value than the game.

"The intellect," says Aristotle, in one passage, "is perfected, not by knowledge, but by activity;" and in another, "The arts and sciences are powers, but every power exists only for the sake of action; the end of philosophy, therefore, is not knowledge, but the energy conversant about knowledge." The profoundest thinkers of modern times have emphatically testified to the same great principle. "If," says Malebranche, "I held truth captive in my hand, I should open my hand and let it fly, in order that I might again pursue and capture it." "Did the Almighty," says Lessing, "holding in his right hand *Truth*, and in his left *Search after Truth*, deign to tender me the one I might prefer, — in all humility, but without hesitation, I should request *Search after Truth*." [We *exist* only as we energize; *pleasure* is the reflex of unimpeded energy; energy is the *means* by which our faculties are developed; and a higher energy the *end* which their development proposes. In *action* is thus contained the existence, happiness, improvement, and perfection of our being; and knowledge is only precious, as it may afford a stimulus to the exercise of our powers, and the condition of their more complete activity. Speculative truth is, therefore, subordinate to speculation itself; and its value is directly measured by the quantity of energy which it occasions, — immediately in its discovery, — mediately through its consequences. Life to Endymion was not preferable to death

aloof from practice, a waking error is better than a sleeping truth. — Neither, in point of fact, is there found any proportion between the *possession* of truths, and the *development* of the mind in which they are deposited. Every *learner* in science is now familiar with more truths than Aristotle or Plato ever dreamt of knowing; yet, compared with the Stagirite or the Athenian, how few, even of our *masters* of modern science, rank higher than intellectual barbarians! Ancient Greece and modern Europe prove, indeed, that "the march of intellect" is no inseparable concomitant of "the march of science;" — that the cultivation of the individual is not to be rashly confounded with the progress of the species.] — *Discussions.*

Philosophy best entitled to be called useful. — But if speculative truth itself be only valuable as a mean of intellectual activity, those studies which determine the faculties to a more vigorous exertion, will, in every liberal sense, be better entitled, absolutely, to the name of useful, than those which, with a greater complement of more certain facts, awaken them to a less intense, and consequently to a less improving exercise. On this ground I would rest one of the preëminent utilities of mental philosophy. That it comprehends all the sublimest objects of our theoretical and moral interest; — that every (natural) conclusion concerning God, the soul, the present worth and the future destiny of man, is exclusively deduced from the philosophy of mind, will be at once admitted. But I do not at present found the importance on the paramount dignity of the pursuit. It is as the best gymnastic of the mind, — as a mean, principally, and almost exclusively, conducive to the highest education of our noblest powers, that I would vindicate to these speculations the necessity which has too frequently been denied them. By no other intellectual application is the mind thus reflected on itself, and its faculties aroused to such independent, vigorous, unwonted, and continued energy; — by none, therefore, are its best capacities so variously and intensely evolved. "By turning," says Burke, "the soul inward on itself, its forces are concentred, and are fitted for greater and stronger flights of science; and in this pursuit, whether we take or whether we lose our game, the chase is certainly of service."

These principles being established, it follows, that I must regard the main duty of a Professor to consist not simply in communicating information, but in doing this in such a manner, and with such an accompaniment of subsidiary means, that the information he conveys may be the occasion of awakening his pupils to a vigorous and varied exertion of their faculties. Self-activity is the indispensable condition of improvement; and education is only education, — that is, accomplishes its purpose, only by affording objects and supplying incitements to this spontaneous exertion. Strictly speaking, every one must educate himself. [All profitable study is a silent disputation — an intellectual gymnastic; and the most improving books are precisely those which most excite the reader, — to understand the author, to supply what he has omitted, and to canvass his facts and reasonings. To read passively, to learn, — is, in reality, not to learn at all. In study, implicit faith, belief upon authority, is worse even than, for a time, erroneous speculation. To read profitably, we should read the authors, not most in unison with, but most adverse to, our opinions; for whatever may be the case in the cure of bodies, *enantiopathy*, and not *homœopathy*, is the true medicine of minds. Accordingly, such sciences and such authors as present only unquestionable truths, determining a minimum of self-activity in the student, are, in a rational education, subjectively naught. Those sciences and authors, on the contrary, who constrain the student to independent thought, are, whatever may be their objective certainty, subjectively, educationally, best.] — *Discussions.*

But though the common duty of all academical instructors be the cultivation of the student, through the awakened exercise of his faculties, this is more especially incumbent on those to whom is intrusted the department of liberal education; for, in this department, the pupil is trained, not to any mere professional knowledge, but to the command and employment of his faculties in general. But, moreover, the same obligation is specially imposed upon a professor of intellectual philosophy by the peculiar nature of his subject, and the conditions under which alone it can be taught. The phænomena of the external world are so palpable and so easily described, that the experience of one observer suffices to render the facts he has witnessed intelligible and probable to all. The phænomena of the internal world, on the contrary, are not capable of being thus described: all that the prior observer can do, is to enable others to repeat his experience. In the science of mind, we can neither understand nor be convinced of any thing at second hand. Here testimony can impose no belief; and instruction is only instruction as it enables us to teach ourselves. A fact of consciousness, however accurately observed, however clearly described, and however great may be our confidence in the observer, is for us as zero, until we have observed and recognized it ourselves. Till that be done, we cannot realize its possibility, far less admit its truth. Thus it is that, in the philosophy of mind, instruction can do little more than point out the position in which the pupil ought to place himself, in order to verify, by his own experience, the facts which his instructor proposes to him as true. The instructor, therefore, proclaims, *οὐ φιλοσοφία, ἀλλὰ φιλοσοφεῖν*; he does not profess to teach *philosophy, but to philosophize.* It is this condition imposed upon the student of doing every thing himself, that renders the study of the mental sciences the most improving exercise of intellect.

Philosophy: its Objective utility. — I [have] endeavored to show that all knowledge is only for the sake of energy, and that even merely speculative truth is valuable only as it determines a greater quantity of higher power into activity. I [have] also endeavored to show that, on the standard of Subjective utility, philosophy is of all our studies the most useful; inasmuch as more than any other it exercises, and consequently develops to a higher degree, and in a more varied manner, our noblest faculties. I shall [now] confine myself to certain views of the importance of philosophy estimated by the standard of its Objective utility.

The human mind the noblest object of speculation. — Considered in itself, a knowledge of the human mind, whether we regard its speculative or its practical importance, is confessedly of all studies the highest and the most interesting. "On earth," says an ancient philosopher, "there is nothing great but man; in man, there is nothing great but mind." No other study fills and satisfies the soul like the study of itself. No other science presents an object to be compared in dignity, in absolute or in relative value, to that which human consciousness furnishes to its own contemplation. What is of all things the best, asked Chilon of the Oracle. "To know thyself," was the response. This is, in fact, the only science in which all are always interested; for, while each individual may have his favorite occupation, it still remains true of the species, that "the proper study of mankind is man." "For the world," says Sir Thomas Browne, "I count it not an inn, but an hospital; and a place not to live, but to die in. The world that I regard is myself; it is the microcosm of my own frame that I cast mine eye on; for the other, I use it but like my globe, and turn it round sometimes, for my recreation. . . . . The earth is a point, not only in respect of the heavens above us, but of that heavenly and celestial part within us. That mass of flesh that circumscribes me, limits not my mind. That surface that tells the heavens it hath an end, cannot persuade me I have any. . . . . Whilst I study to find how I am a microcosm, or little world, I find myself something more than the great. There is surely a piece of divinity in us; something that was before the elements, and owes no homage unto the sun. Nature tells me, I am the image of God, as well as Scripture. He that understands not thus much hath not his introduction or first lesson, and is yet to begin the alphabet of man."

Relation of Psychology to Theology. — But, though mind, considered in itself, be the noblest object of speculation which the created universe presents to the curiosity of man, it is under a certain relation that I would now attempt to illustrate its utility; for mind rises to its highest dignity when viewed as the object through which, and through which alone, our unassisted reason can ascend to the knowledge of a God. The Deity is not an object of immediate contemplation; as existing and in himself, he is beyond our reach; we can know him only mediately through his works, and are only warranted in assuming his existence as a certain kind of cause necessary to account for a certain state of things, of whose reality our faculties are supposed to inform us. The affirmation of a God being thus a regressive inference, from the existence of a special class of effects to the existence of a special character of cause, it is evident, that the whole argument hinges on the fact, — Does a state of things really exist such as is only possible through the agency of a Divine Cause? For if it can be shown that such a state of things does not really exist, then our inference to the kind of cause requisite to account for it is necessarily null.

Argument founded exclusively on the phænomena of mind. — This being understood, I now proceed to show that the class of phænomena which requires that kind of cause we denominate a Deity, is exclusively given in the phænomena of mind, — that the phænomena of matter, taken by themselves (you will observe the qualification, 'taken by themselves'), so far from warranting any inference to the existence of a God, would, on the contrary, ground even an argument to his negation, — that the study of the external world taken with, and in subordination to, that of the internal, not only loses its atheistic tendency, but, under such subservience, may be rendered conducive to the great conclusion, from which, if left to itself, it would dissuade us.

We must, first of all, then, consider what kind of cause it is which constitutes a Deity, and what kind of effects they are which allow us to infer that a Deity must be.

The notion of a God — what. — The notion of a God is not contained in the notion of a mere First Cause; for in the admission of a first cause, Atheist and Theist are at one. Neither is this notion completed by adding to a first cause the attribute of Omnipotence; for the atheist who holds matter or necessity to be the original principle of all that is, does not convert his blind force into a God, by merely affirming it to be all-powerful. It is not until the two great attributes of Intelligence and Virtue (and be it observed that virtue involves Liberty) — I say, it is not until the two attributes of intelligence and virtue or holiness are brought in, that the belief in a primary and omnipotent cause becomes the belief in a veritable Divinity. But these latter attributes are not more essential to the divine nature than are the former. For as original and infinite power does not of itself constitute a God, neither is a God constituted by intelligence and virtue, unless intelligence and goodness be themselves conjoined with this original and infinite power. For even a Creator, intelligent, and good, and powerful, would be no God, were he dependent for his intelligence and goodness and power on any higher principle. On this supposition, the perfections of the Creator are viewed as limited and derived. He is himself, therefore, only a dependency, — only a creature; and if a God there be, he must be sought for in that higher principle, from which this subordinate principle derives its attributes. Now is this highest principle (*ex hypothesi* all-powerful) also intelligent and moral, then it is itself alone the veritable Deity; on the other hand is it, though the author of intelligence and goodness in another, itself unintelligent, — then is a blind Fate constituted the first and universal cause, and atheism is asserted.

Conditions of the proof of the existence of a God. — The peculiar attributes which distinguish a Deity from the original omnipotence or blind fate of the atheist, being thus those of intelligence and holiness of will, — and the assertion of theism being only the assertion that the universe is created by intelligence, and governed not only by physical but by moral laws, we have next to consider how we are warranted in these two affirmations; 1°, That intelligence stands first in the absolute order of existence, — in other words, that final preceded efficient causes; and, 2°, That the universe is governed by moral laws.

The proof of these two propositions is the proof of a God; and it establishes its foundation exclusively on the phænomena of mind. I shall endeavor to show you this, in regard to both these propositions; but, before considering how far the phænomena of mind and of matter do and do not allow us to infer the one position or the other, I must solicit your attention to the characteristic contrasts which these two classes of phænomena in themselves exhibit.

Contrasts of the phænomena of matter and mind. — In the compass of our experience, we distinguish two series of facts, — the facts of the external or material world, and the facts of the internal world or world of intelligence. These concomitant series of phænomena are not like streams which merely run parallel to each other; they do not, like the Alpheus and Arethusa, flow on side by side without a commingling of their waters. They cross, they combine, they are interlaced; but notwithstanding their intimate connection, their mutual action and reaction, we are able to discriminate them without difficulty, because they are marked out by characteristic differences.

The phænomena of the material world are subjected to immutable laws, are produced and reproduced in the same invariable succession, and manifest only the blind force of a mechanical necessity.

The phænomena of man are, in part, subjected to the laws of the external universe. As dependent upon a bodily organization, as actuated by sensual propensities and animal wants, he belongs to matter, and, in this respect, he is the slave of necessity. But what man holds of matter does not make up his personality. They are his, not he; man is not an organism, — he is an intelligence served by organs. For in man there are tendencies, — there is a law, — which continually urge him to prove that he is more powerful than the nature by which he is surrounded and penetrated. He is conscious to himself of faculties not comprised in the chain of physical necessity; his intelligence reveals prescriptive principles of action, absolute and universal, in the Law of Duty, and a liberty capable of carrying that law into effect, in opposition to the solicitations, the impulsions, of his material nature. From the coëxistence of these opposing forces in man, there results a ceaseless struggle between physical necessity and moral liberty, — in the language of Revelation, between the Flesh and the Spirit; and this struggle constitutes at once the distinctive character of humanity, and the essential condition of human development and virtue.

In the facts of intelligence, we thus become aware of an order of existence diametrically in contrast to that displayed to us in the facts of the material universe. There is made known to us an order of things, in which intelligence, by recognizing the unconditional law of duty and an absolute obligation to fulfil it, recognizes its own possession of a liberty incompatible with a dependence upon fate, and of a power capable of resisting and conquering the counteraction of our animal nature.

Consciousness of freedom, and of a law of duty, the conditions of Theology. — Now, it is only as man is a free intelligence, a moral power, that he is created after the image of God, and it is only as a spark of divinity glows as the life of our life in us, that we can rationally believe in an Intelligent Creator and Moral Governor of the universe. For, let us suppose, that in man intelligence is the product of organization, that our consciousness of moral liberty is itself only an illusion; in short, that acts of volition are results of the same iron necessity which determines the phænomena of matter; — on this supposition, I say, the foundations of all religion, natural and revealed, are subverted.

The truth of this will be best seen by applying the supposition of the two positions of theism previously stated — namely, that the notion of God necessarily supposes, 1°, That in the absolute order of existence, intelligence should be first, that is, not itself the product of an unintelligent antecedent; and, 2°, That the universe should be governed not only by physical, but by moral laws.

Analogy between our experience and the absolute order of existence. — Now, in regard to the former, how can we attempt to prove that the universe is the creation of a free original intelligence, against the counter-position of the atheist, that liberty is an illusion, and intelligence, or the adaptation of means to ends, only the product of a blind fate? As we know nothing of the absolute order of existence in itself, we can only attempt to infer its character from that of the particular order within the sphere of our experience; and as we can affirm naught of intelligence and its conditions, except what we may discover from the observation of our own minds, it is evident that we can only analogically carry out into the order of the universe the relation in which we find intelligence to stand in the order of the human constitution. If in man intelligence be a free power,—in so far as its liberty extends, intelligence must be independent of necessity and matter; and a power independent of matter necessarily implies the existence of an immaterial subject,—that is, a spirit. If, then, the original independence of intelligence on matter in the human constitution, in other words, if the spirituality of mind in man, be supposed a datum of observation, in this datum is also given both the condition and the proof of a God. For we have only to infer, what analogy entitles us to do, that intelligence holds the same relative supremacy in the universe which it holds in us, and the first positive condition of a Deity is established, in the establishment of the absolute priority of a free creative intelligence. On the other hand, let us suppose the result of our study of man to be, that intelligence is only a product of matter, only a reflex of organization, such a doctrine would not only afford no basis on which to rest any argument for a God, but, on the contrary, would positively warrant the atheist in denying his existence. For if, as the materialist maintains, the only intelligence of which we have any experience be a consequent of matter,—on this hypothesis, he not only cannot assume this order to be reversed in the relations of an intelligence beyond his observation, but, if he argue logically, he must positively conclude, that, as in man, so in the universe, the phænomena of intelligence or design are only in their last analysis the products of a brute necessity. Psychological materialism, if carried out fully and fairly to its conclusions, thus inevitably results in theological atheism; as it has been well expressed by Dr. Henry More, *nullus in microcosmo spiritus, nullus in macrocosmo Deus.* I do not, of course, mean to assert that all materialists deny, or actually disbelieve, a God. For, in very many cases, this would be at once an unmerited compliment to their reasoning, and an unmerited reproach to their faith.

Second condition of the proof of a Deity. — Such is the manifest dependence of our theology on our psychology in reference to the first condition of a Deity, — the absolute priority of a free intelligence. But this is perhaps even more conspicuous in relation to the second, that the universe is governed not merely by physical but by moral laws; for God is only God inasmuch as he is the Moral Governor of a Moral World.

Our interest, also, in its establishment is incomparably greater; for while a proof that the universe is the work of an omnipotent intelligence, gratifies only our speculative curiosity, — a proof that there is a holy legislator, by whom goodness and felicity will be ultimately brought into accordance, is necessary to satisfy both our intellect and our heart. A God is, indeed, to us, only of practical interest, inasmuch as he is the condition of our immortality.

Now, it is self-evident, in the first place, that, if there be no moral world, there can be no moral governor of such a world; and, in the second, that we have, and can have, no ground on which to believe in the reality of a moral world, except in so far as we ourselves are moral agents. This being undeniable, it is further evident, that, should we ever be convinced that we are not moral agents, we should likewise be convinced that there exists no moral order in the universe, and no supreme intelligence by which that moral order is established, sustained, and regulated.

Theology is thus again wholly dependent on Psychology; for, with the proof of the moral nature of man, stands or falls the proof of the existence of a Deity.*

* [It is chiefly, if not solely, to explain the one phenomenon of *morality*, — of *freewill*, that we are warranted in assuming a second and hyperphysical substance, in an immaterial principle of thought; for it is only on the supposition of a moral liberty in man, that we can attempt to vindicate, as truths, a moral order, and, consequently, a moral governor in the universe;

Wherein the moral agency of man consists. — But in what does the character of man as a moral agent consist? Man is a moral agent only as he is accountable for his actions, — in other words, as he is the object of praise or blame; and this he is, only inasmuch as he has prescribed to him a rule of duty, and as he is able to act, or not to act, in conformity with its precepts. The possibility of morality thus depends on the possibility of liberty; for, if man be not a free agent, he is not the author of his actions, and has, therefore, no responsibility, — no moral personality at all.

How philosophy establishes human liberty. — Now the study of Philosophy, or mental science, operates in three ways to establish that assurance of human liberty, which is necessary for a rational belief in our own moral nature, in a moral world, and in a moral ruler of that world. In the *first* place, an attentive consideration of the phænomena of mind is requisite in order to a luminous and distinct apprehension of liberty as a fact or datum of intelligence. For though, without philosophy, a natural conviction of free agency lives and works in the recesses of every human mind, it requires a process of philosophical thought to bring this conviction to clear consciousness and scientific certainty. In the *second* place, a profound philosophy is necessary

and it is only on the hypothesis of a soul within us, that we can assert the reality of a God above us.

In the hands of the materialist, or physical necessitarian, every argument for the existence of a Deity is either annulled or reversed into a demonstration of atheism. In his hands, with the moral worth of man, the inference to a moral ruler of a moral universe is gone. In his hands, the argument from the adaptations of end and mean, everywhere apparent in existence, to the primary causality of intelligence and liberty, if applied, establishes, in fact, the primary causality of necessity and matter. For, as this argument is only an extension to the universe of the analogy observed in man; if in man, design, intelligence, be only a phenomenon of matter, only a reflex of organization; this consecution of first and second in us, extended to the universal order of things, reverses the absolute priority of intelligence to matter; that is, subverts the fundamental condition of a Deity. Thus it is, that our theology is necessarily founded on our psychology; that we must *recognize a God in our own minds,* before we can *detect a God in the universe of nature.*] — *Discussions.*

to obviate the difficulties which meet us when we attempt to explain the possibility of this fact, and to prove that the datum of liberty is not a mere illusion. For though an unconquerable feeling compels us to recognize ourselves as accountable, and therefore free, agents, still, when we attempt to realize in thought how the fact of our liberty can be, we soon find that this altogether transcends our understanding, and that every effort to bring the fact of liberty within the compass of our conceptions, only results in the substitution in its place of some more or less disguised form of necessity. For, — if I may be allowed to use expressions which many of you cannot be supposed at present to understand, — we are only able to conceive a thing, inasmuch as we conceive it under conditions; while the possibility of a free act supposes it to be an act which is not conditioned or determined. The tendency of a superficial philosophy is, therefore, to deny the fact of liberty, on the principle that what cannot be conceived is impossible. A deeper and more comprehensive study of the facts of mind overturns this conclusion, and disproves its foundation. It shows that, — so far from the principle being true, that what is inconceivable is impossible, — on the contrary, all that is conceivable is a mean between two contradictory extremes, both of which are inconceivable, but of which, as mutually repugnant, one or the other must be true. Thus philosophy, in demonstrating that the limits of thought are not to be assumed as the limits of possibility, while it admits the weakness of our discursive intellect, reëstablishes the authority of consciousness, and vindicates the veracity of our primitive convictions. It proves to us, from the very laws of mind, that while we can never understand *how* any original datum of intelligence is possible, we have no reason from this inability to doubt *that* it is true. A learned ignorance is thus the end of philosophy, as it is the beginning of theology.

In the *third* place, the study of mind is necessary to counterbalance and correct the influence of the study of matter; and this utility of metaphysics rises in proportion to the progress of the natural sciences, and to the greater attention which they engross.

Twofold evil of exclusive physical study. — An exclusive devotion to physical pursuits exerts an evil influence in two ways. In the *first* place, it diverts from all notice of the phænomena of moral liberty, which are revealed to us in the recesses of the human mind alone; and it disqualifies from appreciating the import of these phænomena, even if presented, by leaving uncultivated the finer power of psychological reflection, in the exclusive exercise of the faculties employed in the easier and more amusing observation of the external world. In the *second* place, by exhibiting merely the phænomena of matter and extension, it habituates us only to the contemplation of an order in which every thing is determined by the laws of a blind or mechanical necessity. Now, what is the inevitable tendency of this one-sided and exclusive study? That the student becomes a materialist, if he speculate at all. For, in the first place, he is familiar with the obtrusive facts of necessity, and is unaccustomed to develop into consciousness the more recondite facts of liberty; he is, therefore, disposed to disbelieve in the existence of phænomena whose reality he may deny, and whose possibility he cannot understand. At the same time, the love of unity, and the philosophical presumption against the multiplication of essences, determine him to reject the assumption of a second, and that an hypothetical, substance, — ignorant as he is of the reasons by which that assumption is legitimated.

In the infancy of science, this tendency of physical study was not experienced. When men first turned their attention on the phænomena of nature, every event was viewed as a miracle, for every effect was considered as the operation of an intelligence. God was not exiled from the universe of matter; on the contrary, he was multiplied in proportion to its phænomena. As science advanced, the deities were gradually driven out; and long after the sublunary world had been disenchanted, they were left for a season in possession of the starry heavens. The movement of the celestial bodies, in which Kepler still saw the agency of a free intelligence, was at length by Newton resolved into a few mathematical principles; and at last, even the irregularities which Newton was compelled to leave for the miraculous correction of the Deity, have been proved to require no supernatural interposition; for La Place has shown that all contingencies, past and future, in the heavens, find their explanation in the one fundamental law of gravitation.

But the very contemplation of an order and adaptation so astonishing, joined to the knowledge that this order and adaptation are the necessary results of a brute mechanism, — when acting upon minds which have not looked into themselves for the light of which the world without can only afford them the reflection, — far from elevating them more than any other aspect of external creation to that inscrutable Being who reigns beyond and above the universe of nature, tends, on the contrary, to impress on them, with peculiar force, the conviction, that as the mechanism of nature can explain so much, the mechanism of nature can explain all.

If all existence be but mechanism, philosophical interest extinguished. — "Wonder," says Aristotle, "is the first cause of philosophy:" but in the discovery that all existence is but mechanism, the consummation of science would be an extinction of the very interest from which it originally sprang. "Even the gorgeous majesty of the heavens," says a religious philosopher, "the object of a kneeling adoration to an infant world, subdues no more the mind of him who comprehends the one mechanical law by which the planetary systems move, maintain their motion, and even originally form themselves. He no longer wonders at the object, infinite as it always is, but at the human intellect alone, which, in a Copernicus, Kepler, Gassendi, Newton, and La Place, was able to transcend the object, by science to terminate the miracle, to reave the heaven of its divinities, and to exorcise the universe. But even this, the only admiration of which our intelligent faculties are now capable would vanish, were a future Hartley, Darwin, Condillac, or Bonnet, to succeed in displaying to us a mechanical system of the human mind, as comprehensive, intelligible, and satisfactory as the Newtonian mechanism of the heavens."

To this testimony I may add, that, should Physiology ever succeed in reducing the facts of intelligence to phænomena of matter, Philosophy would be subverted in the subversion of its three great objects, — God, Free-Will, and Immortality. True wisdom would then consist, not in speculation, but in repressing thought during our brief transit from nothingness to nothingness. For why? Philosophy would have become a meditation, not merely of death, but of annihilation; the precept, *Know thyself*, would have been replaced by the terrific oracle to Œdipus —

"May'st thou ne'er know the truth of what thou art;"

and the final recompense of our scientific curiosity would be wailing, deeper than Cassandra's, for the ignorance that saved us from despair.

Coincidence of these views with those of previous philosophers. — The views which I have now taken of the respective influence of the sciences of mind and of matter in relation to our religious belief, are those which have been deliberately adopted by the profoundest thinkers, ancient and modern. Were I to quote to you the testimonies that crowd on my recollection, to the effect that ignorance of Self is ignorance of God, I should make no end, for this is a truth proclaimed by Jew and Gentile, Christian and Mohammedan. "The cause," says Plato, "of all impiety and irreligion among men is, that, reversing in themselves the relative subordination of mind and body, they have, in like manner, in the universe, made that to be first which is second, and that to be second which is first; for while, in the generation of all things, intelligence and final causes precede matter and efficient causes, they, on the contrary, have viewed matter and material things as absolutely prior, in the order of existence, to intelligence and design; and thus, departing from an original error in relation to themselves, they have ended in the subversion of the Godhead."

The pious and profound Jacobi states the truth boldly and without disguise in regard to the relation of Physics and Metaphysics to Religion. "But is it unreasonable to confess, that we believe in God, not by reason of the nature * which con-

* In the philosophy of Germany, *Natur* and its correlatives, whether of Greek or Latin derivation, are, in general, expressive of the world of Matter, in contrast to the world of Intelligence.

ceals him, but by reason of the supernatural in man, which alone reveals and proves him to exist?

"*Nature conceals God:* for through her whole domain, Nature reveals only fate, only an indissoluble chain of mere efficient causes without beginning and without end, excluding, with equal necessity, both providence and chance. An independent agency, a free original commencement within her sphere and proceeding from her powers, is absolutely impossible. Working without will, she takes counsel neither of the good nor of the beautiful; creating nothing, she casts up from her dark abyss only eternal transformations of herself, unconsciously and without an end; furthering, with the same ceaseless industry, decline and increase, death and life, — never producing what alone is of God and what supposes liberty, — the virtuous, the immortal.

"*Man reveals God:* for man, by his intelligence, rises above nature, and, in virtue of this intelligence, is conscious of himself as a power not only independent of, but opposed to, nature, and capable of resisting, conquering, and controlling her. As man has a living faith in this power, superior to nature, which dwells in him; so has he a belief in God, a feeling, an experience of his existence. As he does not believe in this power, so does he not believe in God; he sees, he experiences naught in existence but nature, — necessity, — fate."

These uses of Psychology not superseded by the Christian revelation. — Such is the comparative importance of the sciences of mind and of matter in relation to the interests of religion. But it may be said, how great soever be the value of philosophy in this respect, were man left to rise to the divinity by the unaided exercise of his faculties, this value is superseded under the Christian dispensation, the Gospel now assuring us of all and more than all philosophy could ever warrant us in surmising. It is true, indeed, that in Revelation there is contained a great complement of truths of which natural reason could afford us no knowledge or assurance; but still the importance of mental science to theology has not become superfluous in Christianity; for whereas, anterior to Revelation, religion rises out of psychology as a result, subsequently to revelation, it supposes a genuine philosophy of mind as the condition of its truth. This is at once manifest. Revelation is a revelation to man and concerning man; and man is only the object of revelation, inasmuch as he is a moral, a free, a responsible being. The Scriptures are replete with testimonies to our natural liberty; and it is the doctrine of every Christian church, that man was originally created with a will capable equally of good as of evil, though this will, subsequently to the fall, has lost much of its primitive liberty. Christianity thus, by universal confession, supposes as a condition the moral nature of its object; and if some individual theologians be found who have denied to man a higher liberty than a machine, this is only another example of the truth, that there is no opinion which has been unable to find not only its champions but its martyrs. The differences which divide the Christian churches on this question, regard only the liberty of man in certain particular relations; for fatalism, or a negation of human responsibility in general, is equally hostile to the tenets of the Calvinist and Arminian.

In these circumstances, it is evident, that he who disbelieves the moral agency of man must, in consistency with that opinion, disbelieve Christianity. And therefore, inasmuch as Philosophy, — the Philosophy of Mind, — scientifically establishes the proof of human liberty, philosophy, in this, as in many other relations not now to be considered, is the true preparative and best aid of an enlightened Christian Theology.

CHAPTER II.

THE NATURE AND COMPREHENSION OF PHILOSOPHY.

You are about to commence a course of philosophical discipline; — for Psychology is preëminently a philosophical science. It is therefore proper that you should obtain at least a notion of what philosophy is. But in affording you this information, it is evident that there lie considerable difficulties in the way. For the definition and the divisions of philosophy are the results of a lofty generalization from particulars, of which particulars you are, or must be presumed to be, still ignorant. You cannot, therefore, it is manifest, be made adequately to comprehend, in the commencement of your philosophical studies, notions which these studies themselves are intended to enable you to understand. But although you cannot at once obtain a full knowledge of the nature of philosophy, it is desirable that you should be enabled to form at least some vague conception of the road you are about to travel, and of the point to which it will conduct you. I must, therefore, beg that you will, for the present, hypothetically believe, — believe upon authority, — what you may not now adequately understand; but this only to the end that you may not hereafter be under the necessity of taking any conclusion upon trust. Nor is this temporary exaction of credit peculiar to philosophical education. In the order of nature, belief always precedes knowledge, — it is the condition of instruction. The child (as observed by Aristotle) must believe, in order that he may learn; and even the primary facts of intelligence, — the facts which precede, as they afford the conditions of, all knowledge, — would not be original, were they revealed to us under any other form than that of natural or necessary beliefs.

There are two questions to be answered: — 1st, What is the meaning of the *name?* and 2d, What is the meaning of the *thing?* An answer to the former question is afforded in a nominal definition of the term *philosophy*, and in a history of its employment and application.

Philosophy — the name. — In regard to the etymological signification of the word, Philosophy is a term of Greek origin. It is a compound of φίλος, a *lover* or *friend*, and σοφία,* *wisdom* — speculative wisdom. Philosophy is thus, literally, *a love of wisdom.* But if the grammatical meaning of the word be unambiguous, the history of its application is, I think, involved in considerable doubt. According to the commonly received account, the designation of philosopher (*lover or suitor of wisdom*) was first assumed and applied by Pythagoras; whilst of the occasion and circumstances of its assumption, we have a story by Cicero, on the authority of Heraclides Ponticus. Pythagoras, once upon a time, says the Roman orator, having come to Phlius, a city of Peloponnesus, displayed, in a conversation which he had with Leon, who then governed that city, a range of knowledge so extensive, that the prince, admiring his eloquence and ability, inquired to what art he had principally devoted himself. Pythagoras answered, that he professed no art, and was simply a *philosopher.* Leon, struck by the novelty of the name, again inquired who were the philosophers, and in what they differed from other men. Pythagoras replied, that human life seemed to resemble the great fair, held on occasion of those solemn games which all Greece met to celebrate. For some, exercised in athletic contests, resorted thither in quest of glory and the crown of victory; while a greater number flocked to them in order to buy and sell, attracted by the love of gain. There were a few, however, — and they were those distinguished by their liberality and intelligence, — who came from no motive of glory or of gain, but simply to look about them, and to take note of what was done, and in what manner. So likewise, continued

* Σοφία in Greek, though sometimes used in a wide sense, like the term *wise* applied to skill in handicraft, yet properly denoted speculative, not practical, wisdom or prudence.

Pythagoras, we men all make our entrance into this life on our departure from another. Some are here occupied in the pursuit of honors, others in the search of riches; a few there are who, indifferent to all else, devote themselves to an inquiry into the nature of things. These, then, are they whom I call students of wisdom, for such is meant by philosopher.

The anecdote rests on very slender authority. It is probable, I think, that Socrates was the first who adopted, or, at least, the first who familiarized, the expression. It was natural that he should be anxious to contradistinguish himself from the Sophists (οἱ σοφοὶ, οἱ σοφισταὶ), literally, the *wise* men; and no term could more appropriately ridicule the arrogance of these pretenders, or afford a happier contrast to their haughty designation, than that of philosopher (*i. e.* the *lover* of wisdom); and, at the same time, it is certain that the substantives φιλοσοφία and φιλόσοφος first appear in the writings of the Socratic school. It is true, indeed, that the verb φιλοσοφεῖν is found in Herodotus, in the address by Crœsus to Solon; and that, too, in a participial form, to designate the latter as a man who had travelled abroad for the purpose of acquiring knowledge. It is, therefore, not impossible that, before the time of Socrates, those who devoted themselves to the pursuit of the higher branches of knowledge, were occasionally designated philosophers: but it is far more probable that Socrates and his school first appropriated the term as a distinctive appellation; and that the word *philosophy*, in consequence of this appropriation, came to be employed for the complement of all higher knowledge, and, more especially, to denote *the science conversant about the principles or causes of existence.* The term *philosophy*, I may notice, which was originally assumed in modesty, soon lost its Socratic and etymological signification, and returned to the meaning of σοφία, or wisdom. Quintilian calls it *nomen insolentissimum;* Seneca, *nomen invidiosum;* Epictetus counsels his scholars not to call themselves "Philosophers;" and *proud* is one of the most ordinary epithets with which philosophy is now associated.

Philosophy — the thing — its definitions. — So much for the name signifying; we proceed now to the thing signified. Were I to detail the various definitions of philosophy which philosophers have promulgated — far more, were I to explain the grounds on which the author of each maintains the exclusive adequacy of his peculiar definition — I should, in the present stage of your progress, only perplex and confuse you. All such definitions are (if not positively erroneous), either so vague that they afford no precise knowledge of their object; or they are so partial, that they exclude what they ought to comprehend; or they are of such a nature that they supply no preliminary information, and are only to be understood (if ever), after a knowledge has been acquired of that which they profess to explain. It is, indeed, perhaps impossible adequately to define philosophy. For what is to be defined comprises what cannot be included in a single definition. For *philosophy is not regarded from a single point of view;* — it is sometimes considered as *theoretical,* — that is, in relation to man as a thinking and cognitive intelligence; sometimes as *practical,* — that is, in relation to man as a moral agent; — and sometimes, as *comprehending both theory and practice.* Again, philosophy may either be regarded *objectively,* that is, as a complement of truths known; or *subjectively,* — that is, as a habit or quality of the mind knowing. In these circumstances, I shall not attempt a definition of philosophy, but shall endeavor to accomplish the end which every definition proposes, — make you understand, as precisely as the unprecise nature of the object-matter permits, what is meant by philosophy, and what are the sciences it properly comprehends within its sphere.

Definitions in Greek antiquity. — As a matter of history, I may here, however, parenthetically mention, that in Greek antiquity, there were, in all, six definitions of philosophy which obtained celebrity. The first and second define philosophy from its object matter, — that which it is about; the third and fourth, from its end, — that for the sake of which it is; the fifth, from its relative preëminence; and the sixth, from its etymology.

The first of these definitions of philosophy is, — "the knowledge of things existent as existent." The second is, — "the knowledge of things divine and human." These are both from the object-matter; and both were referred to Pythagoras.

The third and fourth, the two definitions of philosophy from its end, are, again, both taken from Plato. Of these, the third is, — "philosophy is a meditation of death;" the fourth, — "philosophy is a resembling of the Deity in so far as that is competent to man."

The fifth, that from its preëminence, was borrowed from Aristotle, and defined philosophy "the art of arts, and science of sciences."

Finally, the sixth, that from the etymology, was, like the first and second, carried up to Pythagoras; — it defined philosophy "the love of wisdom."

To these a seventh and even an eighth were sometimes added; — but the seventh was that by the physicians, who defined medicine the philosophy of bodies, and philosophy the medicine of souls. This was derided by the philosophers; as, to speak with Homer, being an exchange of brass for gold, and of gold for brass, and as defining the more known by the less known. The eighth is from an expression of Plato, who, in the Theætetus, calls philosophy "the greatest music," meaning thereby the harmony of the rational, irascible, and appetent parts of the soul.

What Philosophy is. — But to return: All philosophy is knowledge, but all knowledge is not philosophy. Philosophy is, therefore, a kind of knowledge.

Philosophical and empirical knowledge. — What, then, is philosophical knowledge, and how is it discriminated from knowledge in general? We are endowed by our Creator with certain faculties of observation, which enable us to become aware of certain appearances or phænomena. These faculties may be stated as two, — Sense, or External Perception, and Self-Consciousness, or Internal Perception; and these faculties severally afford us the knowledge of a different series of phænomena. Through our senses, we apprehend what exists, or what occurs, in the external or material world; by our self-consciousness, we apprehend what is, or what occurs, in the internal world, or world of thought. What is the extent, and what the certainty, of the knowledge acquired through sense and self-consciousness, we do not at present consider. It is now sufficient that the simple fact be admitted, that we do actually thus know; and that fact is so manifest, that it requires, I presume, at my hands, neither proof nor illustration. The information which we thus receive, — that certain phænomena are, or have been, is called Historical or Empirical knowledge. It is called historical, because, in this knowledge, we know only the fact, only that the phænomenon is; for history is properly only the narration of a consecutive series of phænomena in time, or the description of a coëxistent series of phænomena in space. Civil history is an example of the one; natural history, of the other. It is called *empirical* or *experiential*, if we might use that term, because it is given us by experience or observation, and not obtained as the result of inference or reasoning.

By-meaning of the term empirical. — I may notice, by parenthesis, that you must discharge from your minds the by-meaning accidentally associated with the word *empiric*, or *empirical*, in common English. This term is, with us, more familiarly used in reference to medicine, and from its fortuitous employment in that science, in a certain sense, the word empirical has unfortunately acquired, in our language, a one-sided and an unfavorable meaning. Of the origin of this meaning many of you may not be aware. You are aware, however, that ἐμπειρία is the Greek term for experience, and ἐμπειρικὸς an epithet applied to one who uses experience. Now, among the Greek physicians, there arose a sect who, professing to employ experience alone, to the exclusion of generalization, analogy, and reasoning, denominated themselves distinctively οἱ ἐμπειρικοί — the Empirics. The opposite extreme was adopted by another sect, who, rejecting observation, founded their doctrine exclusively on reasoning and theory; — and these called themselves οἱ μεθοδικοί — or Methodists. A third school, of whom Galen was the head, opposed equally to the two extreme sects of the Empirics and of the Methodists, and, availing themselves both of experience and reasoning, were styled *οἱ δογματικοί* — the Dogmatists, or rational physicians. A keen controversy arose; the Empirics were defeated; they gradually died out; and their doctrine, of which nothing is known to us, except through the writings of their adversaries, has probably been painted in blacker colors than it deserved. Be this, however, as it may, the word was first naturalized in English, at a time when the Galenic works were of paramount authority in medicine, as a term of medical import — of medical reproach; and the collateral meaning, which it had accidentally obtained in that science, was associated with an unfavorable signification, so that an Empiric, in common English, has been long a synonyme for a charlatan or quack-doctor, and, by a very natural extension, in general, for any ignorant pretender in science. In philosophical language, the term *empirical* means simply what belongs to, or is the product of, experience or observation, and, in contrast to another term afterwards to be explained, is now technically in general use through every other country of Europe. Were there any other word to be found of a corresponding signification in English, it would perhaps, in consequence of the by-meaning attached to empirical, be expedient not to employ this latter. But there is not. *Experiential* is not in common use, and *experimental* only designates a certain kind of experience — namely, that in which the fact observed has been brought about by a certain intentional prearrangement of its coefficients. But this by the way.

Empirical knowledge. — Returning, then, from our digression: Historical or empirical knowledge is simply the knowledge that something is. Were we to use the expression, *the knowledge that*, it would sound awkward and unusual in our modern languages. In Greek, the most philosophical of all tongues, its parallel, however, was familiarly employed, more especially in the Aristotelic philosophy, in contrast to another knowledge of which we are about to speak. It was called the *τὸ ὅτι, ἡ γνῶσις ὅτι ἔστιν*. I should notice, that with us, *the knowledge that*, is commonly called the knowledge of the *fact*. As examples of empirical knowledge, take the facts, whether known on our own experience or on the testified experience of others, — that a stone falls, — that smoke ascends, — that the leaves bud in spring and fall in autumn, — that such a book contains such a passage, — that such a passage contains such an opinion, — that Cæsar, that Charlemagne, that Napoleon, existed. [Empirical is also used in contrast with Necessary knowledge; the former signifying the knowledge simply of what is, the latter of what must be.]

Philosophical knowledge — what. — But things do not exist, events do not occur, isolated, — apart — by themselves; they exist, they occur, and are by us conceived, only in connection. Our observation affords us no example of a phænomenon which is not an effect; nay, our thought cannot even realize to itself the possibility of a phænomenon without a cause. We do not at present inquire into the nature of the connection of effect and cause, — either in reality, or in thought. It is sufficient for our present purpose to observe that, while, by the constitution of our nature, we are unable to conceive any thing to begin to be, without referring it to some cause, — still the knowledge of its particular cause is not involved in the knowledge of any particular effect. By this necessity which we are under, of thinking some cause for every phænomenon; and by our original ignorance of what particular causes belong to what particular effects, — it is rendered impossible for us to acquiesce in the mere knowledge of the fact of a phænomenon: on the contrary, we are determined, — we are necessitated, to regard each phænomenon as only partially known, until we discover the causes on which it depends for its existence. For example, we are struck with the appearance in the heavens called a rainbow. Think we cannot that this phænomenon has no cause, though we may be wholly ignorant of what that cause is. Now, our knowledge of the phænomenon as a mere fact, — as a mere isolated event, — does not content us; we therefore set about an inquiry into the cause, — which the constitution of our mind compels us to suppose, — and at length, discover that the rainbow is the effect of the refraction of the solar rays by the watery particles of a cloud. Having ascertained the cause, but not till then, we are satisfied that we fully know the effect.

Now, this knowledge of the cause of a phænomenon is different from, is something more than, the knowledge of that phænomenon simply as a fact; and these two cognitions or knowledges have, accordingly, received different names. The latter, we have seen, is called *historical* or *empirical* knowledge; the former is called *philosophical*, or *scientific*, or *rational* knowledge. Historical, is the knowledge that a thing is — philosophical, is the knowledge why or how it is. And as the Greek language, with peculiar felicity, expresses historical knowledge by the *ὅτι* — the *γνῶσις ὅτι ἔστι*: so, it well expresses philosophical knowledge by the *διότι* — the *γνῶσις διότι ἔστι*, though here its relative superiority is not the same. To recapitulate what has now been stated: — There are two kinds or degrees of knowledge. The first is a knowledge that a thing is — *ὅτι χρῆμα ἔστι, rem esse;* — and it is called the knowledge of the fact, historical or empirical knowledge. The second is a knowledge why or how a thing is, *διότι χρῆμα ἔστι, cur res sit;* — and is termed the knowledge of the cause, philosophical, scientific, rational knowledge.

Philosophy implies a search after first causes. — Philosophical knowledge, in the widest acceptation of the term, and as synonymous with science, is thus the knowledge of effects as dependent on their causes. Now, what does this imply? In the first place, as every cause to which we can ascend is itself also an effect, — it follows that it is the scope, that is, the aim of philosophy, to trace up the series of effects and causes, until we arrive at causes which are not also themselves effects. These first causes do not indeed lie within the reach of philosophy, nor even within the sphere of our comprehension; nor, consequently, on the actual reaching them does the existence of philosophy depend. But as philosophy is the knowledge of effects in their causes, the tendency of philosophy is ever upwards; and philosophy can, in thought, in theory, only be viewed as accomplished, — which in reality it never can be, — when the ultimate causes, — the causes on which all other causes depend, — have been attained and understood.

But, in the second place, as every effect is only produced by the concurrence of at least two causes (and by *cause*, be it observed, I mean *every thing without which the effect could not be realized*), and as these concurring or coefficient causes, in fact, constitute the effect, it follows, that the lower we descend in the series of causes, the more complex will be the product; and that the higher we ascend, it will be the more simple. Let us take, for example, a neutral salt. This, as you probably know is the product, the combination, of an alkali and an acid. Now, considering the salt as an effect, what are the concurrent causes, — the co-efficients, — which constitute it what it is? These are, *first*, the acid, with its affinity to the alkali; *secondly*, the alkali, with its affinity to the acid; and *thirdly*, the translating force (perhaps the human hand) which made their affinities available, by bringing the two bodies within the sphere of mutual attraction. Each of these three concurrents must be considered as a partial cause; for, abstract any one, and the effect is not produced. Now, these three partial causes are each of them again effects; but effects evidently less complex than the effect which they, by their concurrence, constituted. But each of these three constituents is an effect; and therefore to be analyzed into its causes; and these causes again into others, until the procedure is checked by our inability to resolve the last constituent into simpler elements. But, though thus unable to carry our analysis beyond a limited extent, we neither conceive, nor are we able to conceive, the constituent in which our analysis is arrested, as itself any thing but an effect. We therefore carry on the analysis in imagination; and as each step in the procedure carries us from the more complex to the more simple, and, consequently, nearer to unity, we at last arrive at that unity itself, — at that ultimate cause which, as ultimate, cannot again be conceived as an effect.*

* I may notice that an ultimate cause, and a first cause, are the same, but viewed in different relations. What is called the ultimate cause in ascending from effects to causes, — that is, in the regressive order, is called the first cause in descending from causes to effects, — that is, in the progressive order.

Philosophy thus, as the knowledge of effects in their causes, necessarily tends, not towards a plurality of ultimate or first causes, but towards one alone. This first cause, — the Creator, — it can indeed never reach, as an object of immediate knowledge; but, as the convergence towards unity in the ascending series is manifest, in so far as that series is within our view, and as it is even impossible for the mind to suppose the convergence not continuous and complete, it follows, — unless all analogy be rejected, — unless our intelligence be declared a lie, — that we must, philosophically, believe in that ultimate or primary unity which, in our present existence, we are not destined in itself to apprehend.

Such is philosophical knowledge in its most extensive signification; and, in this signification, all the sciences, occupied in the research of causes, may be viewed as so many branches of philosophy. There is, however, one section of these sciences which is denominated philosophical by preëminence; — sciences which the term philosophy exclusively denotes, when employed in propriety and rigor. What these sciences are, and why the term philosophy has been specially limited to them, I shall now endeavor to make you understand.

Man's knowledge relative. — "Man," says Protagoras, "is the measure of the universe;" and, in so far as the universe is an object of human knowledge, the paradox is a truth. Whatever we know, or endeavor to know, God or the world, — mind or matter, — the distant or the near, — we know, and can know, only in so far as we possess a faculty of knowing in general; and we can only exercise that faculty under the laws which control and limit its operations. However great, and infinite, and various, therefore, may be the universe and its contents, — these are known to us, not as they exist, but as our mind is capable of knowing them. Hence the brocard — "Quicquid recipitur, recipitur ad modum recipientis."

In the first place, therefore, as philosophy is a knowledge, and as all knowledge is only possible under the conditions to which our faculties are subjected, — the grand, the primary, problem of philosophy must be to investigate and determine these conditions, as the necessary conditions of its own possibility.

The study of mind the first object of philosophy. — In the second place, as philosophy is not merely a knowledge, but a knowledge of causes, and as the mind itself is the universal and principal concurrent cause in every act of knowledge; philosophy is, consequently, bound to make the mind its first and paramount object of consideration. The study of mind is thus the philosophical study by preëminence. There is no branch of philosophy which does not suppose this as its preliminary, which does not borrow from this its light. A considerable number, indeed, are only *the science of mind viewed in particular aspects*, or considered in certain special applications. *Logic*, for example, or the science of the laws of thought, is only a fragment of the general science of mind, and presupposes a certain knowledge of the operations which are regulated by these laws. *Ethics* is the science of the laws which govern our actions as moral agents; and a knowledge of these laws is only possible through a knowledge of the moral agent himself. *Political science*, in like manner, supposes a knowledge of man in his natural constitution, in order to appreciate the modifications which he receives, and of which he is susceptible, in social and civil life. The *Fine Arts* have all their foundation in the theory of the beautiful; and this theory is afforded by that part of the philosophy of mind, which is conversant with the phænomena of feeling. *Religion, Theology*, in fine, is not independent of the same philosophy. For as God only exists for us as we have faculties capable of apprehending his existence, and of fulfilling his behests, nay, as the phænomena from which we are warranted to infer his being are wholly mental, the examination of these faculties and of these phænomena is, consequently, the primary condition of every sound theology. In short, the science of mind, whether considered in itself, or in relation to the other branches of our knowledge, constitutes the principal and most important object of philosophy, — constitutes in propriety, with its suit of dependent sciences, philosophy itself.

Misapplication of the term Philosophy in England.—The limitation of the term Philosophy to the sciences of mind, when not expressly extended to the other branches of science, has been always that generally prevalent;—yet it must be confessed that, in this country, the word is applied to subjects with which, on the continent of Europe, it is rarely, if ever, associated. With us, the word philosophy, taken by itself, does not call up the precise and limited notion which it does to a German, a Hollander, a Dane, an Italian, or a Frenchman; and we are obliged to say the philosophy of mind, if we do not wish it to be vaguely extended to the sciences conversant with the phænomena of matter. We not only call Physics by the name of Natural Philosophy, but every mechanical process has with us its philosophy. We have books on the philosophy of Manufactures, the philosophy of Agriculture, the philosophy of Cookery, etc. In all this we are the ridicule of other nations. Socrates, it is said, brought down philosophy from the clouds,—the English have degraded her to the kitchen; and this, our prostitution of the term, is, by foreigners, alleged as a significant indication of the low state of the mental sciences in Britain.

From what has been said, you will, without a definition, be able to form at least a general notion of what is meant by philosophy. In its more extensive signification, it is equivalent to *a knowledge of things by their causes*,—and this is, in fact, Aristotle's definition; while, in its stricter meaning, it is confined to *the sciences which constitute*, or hold immediately of, *the science of mind.*

CHAPTER III.

THE CAUSES OF PHILOSOPHY, AND THE DISPOSITIONS WITH WHICH IT OUGHT TO BE STUDIED.

The causes of philosophy. — Having thus endeavored to make you vaguely apprehend what cannot be precisely understood, — the Nature and Comprehension of Philosophy, — I now proceed to another question, — What are the Causes of Philosophy? The causes of philosophy lie in the original elements of our constitution. We are created with the faculty of knowledge, and, consequently, created with the tendency to exert it. Man philosophizes as he lives. He may philosophize well or ill, but philosophize he must. Philosophy can, indeed, only be assailed through philosophy itself. "If," says Aristotle, in a passage preserved to us by Olympiodorus, "we must philosophize, we must philosophize; if we must not philosophize, we must philosophize; — in any case, therefore, we must philosophize." "Were philosophy," says Clement of Alexandria, "an evil, still philosophy is to be studied, in order that it may be scientifically contemned." And Averroes, — "Philosophi solum est spernere philosophiam." Of the causes of philosophy some are, therefore, contained in man's very capacity for knowledge; these are *essential and necessary.* But there are others, again, which lie in certain feelings with which he is endowed; these are *complementary and assistant.*

Essential Causes of Philosophy. — Of the former class, — that is, of the essential causes, — there are in all two: the one is, *the necessity we feel to connect Causes with Effects;* the other, *to carry up our knowledge into Unity.* These tendencies, however, if not identical in their origin, coincide in their result; for, as I have previously explained to you, in ascending from cause to cause, we necessarily (could we carry our analysis to its issue), arrive at absolute unity. Indeed, were it not a discussion for which you are not as yet prepared, it might be shown, that both principles originate in the same condition; — that both emanate, not from any original power, but from the same original powerlessness of mind.

1. *The principle of Cause and Effect.* — Of the former, — namely, the tendency, or rather the necessity, which we feel to connect the objects of our experience with others which afford the reasons of their existence, — it is needful to say but little. The nature of this tendency is not a matter on which we can at present enter; and the fact of its existence is too notorious to require either proof or illustration. It is sufficient to say, or rather to repeat what we have already stated, that the mind is unable to realize in thought the possibility of any absolute commencement; it cannot conceive that any thing which begins to be is any thing more than a new modification of preëxistent elements; it is unable to view any individual thing as other than a link in the mighty chain of being; and every isolated object is viewed by it only as a fragment which, to be known, must be known in connection with the whole of which it constitutes a part.* It is thus that we are unable to rest satisfied with a

* [The phenomenon is this: — When aware of a new appearance, we are *unable* to conceive that therein has originated any new existence, and are, therefore, *constrained* to think, that what now appears to us under a new form, had previously an existence under others, — others conceivable by us or not. These others (for they are always plural) are called its cause; for a cause is simply every thing without which the effect would not result, and all such concurring, the effect cannot but result. We are utterly unable to construe it in thought as possible, that the complement of existence has been either increased or diminished. We cannot conceive, either, on the one hand, nothing becoming something, or, on the other, something becoming nothing. When God is said to create the universe out of nothing, we think this, by supposing that he evolves the universe out of nothing but himself; and, in like manner, we conceive annihilation, only by conceiving the Creator to withdraw his creation, by withdrawing his creative energy from actuality into power. . . . . The mind is thus compelled to recognize an absolute identity of existence in the effect and in the complement of its causes, — between the *causatum* and the *causæ*. We think the

mere historical knowledge of existence; and that even our happiness is interested in discovering causes, hypothetical at least, if not real, for the various phænomena of the existence of which our experience informs us.

"Felix qui potuit rerum cognoscere causas."

2. *The love of Unity.*—The second tendency of our nature, of which philosophy is the result, is the desire of Unity. On this, which indeed involves the other, it is necessary to be some what more explicit. This tendency is one of the most prominent characteristics of the human mind. It, in part, originates in the imbecility of our faculties. We are lost in the multitude of the objects presented to our observation, and it is only by assorting them in classes that we can reduce the infinity of nature to the finitude of mind. The conscious Ego, the conscious Self, by its nature one, seems also constrained to require that unity by which it is distinguished, in every thing which it receives, and in every thing which it produces. I regret that I can illustrate this only by examples which cannot, I am aware, as yet be fully intelligible to all. We are conscious of a scene presented to our senses only by uniting its parts into a perceived whole. *Perception* is thus a unifying act. The *Imagination* cannot represent an object without uniting, in a single combination, the various elements of which it is composed. *Generalization* is only the apprehension of the one in the many, and language little else than a registry of the factitious unities of thought. The *Judgment* cannot affirm or deny one notion of another, except by uniting the two in one indivisible act of comparison. *Syllogism* is simply the union of two judgments in a third. *Reason*, *Intellect*, *νοῦς*, in fine, concatenating thoughts and objects into system, and tending always upwards from particular facts to general laws, from general laws to universal principles, is never satisfied in its ascent till it comprehend

causes to contain all that is contained in the effect; the effect to contain nothing but what is contained in the causes. Each is the sum of the other. "Omnia mutantur, nihil interit."] — *Discussions.*

(what, however, it can never do) all laws in a single formula, and consummate all conditional knowledge in the unity of unconditional existence. Nor is it only in science that the mind desiderates the one. We seek it equally in works of art. A work of art is only deserving of the name, inasmuch as an idea of the work has preceded its execution, and inasmuch as it is itself a realization of the ideal model in sensible forms. All languages express the mental operations by words which denote a reduction of the many to the one. *Σύνεσις*, *περίληψις*, *συναίσθησις*, *συνεπιγνῶσις*, etc. in Greek; — in Latin, *cogere*, (*co-agere*), *cogitare*, (*co-agitare*), *concipere*, *cognoscere*, *comprehendere*, *conscire*, with their derivatives, may serve for examples.

Testimonies to the love of Unity. — The history of philosophy is only the history of this tendency; and philosophers have amply testified to its reality. "The mind," says Anaxagoras, "only knows when it subdues its objects, when it reduces the many to the one." "All knowledge," say the Platonists, "is the gathering up into one, and the indivisible apprehension of this unity by the knowing mind." Leibnitz and Kant have, in like manner, defined knowledge by the representation of multitude in unity. "The end of philosophy," says Plato, "is the intuition of unity;" and Plotinus, among many others, observes that our knowledge is perfect as it is one. The love of unity is by Aristotle applied to solve a multitude of psychological phænomena. St. Augustin even analyzes pain into a feeling of the frustration of unity. "Quid est enim aliud dolor, nisi quidam sensus divisionis vel corruptionis impatiens? Unde luce clarius apparet, quam sit illa anima in sui corporis universitate avida unitatis et tenax."

Love of unity a guiding principle in philosophy. — This love of unity, this tendency of mind to generalize its knowledge, leads us to anticipate in nature a corresponding uniformity; and as this anticipation is found in harmony with experience, it not only affords the efficient cause of philosophy, but the guiding principle to its discoveries. "Thus, for instance, when it is observed that solid bodies are compressible, we are inclined to expect that liquids will be found to be so likewise we subject them, consequently, to a series of experiments; nor do we rest satisfied until it be proved that this quality is common to both classes of substances. Compressibility is then proclaimed a physical law, — a law of nature in general; and we experience a vivid gratification in this recognition of unconditioned universality." Another example; Kant, reflecting on the differences among the planets, or rather among the stars revolving round the sun, and having discovered that these differences betrayed a uniform progress and proportion, — a proportion which was no longer to be found between Saturn and the first of the comets, — the law of unity and the analogy of nature, led him to conjecture that, in the intervening space, there existed a star, the discovery of which would vindicate the universality of the law.* This anticipation was verified. Uranus was discovered by Herschel, and our dissatisfaction at the anomaly appeased. Franklin, in like manner, surmised that lightning and the electric spark were identical; and when he succeeded in verifying this conjecture, our love of unity was gratified. From the moment an isolated fact is discovered, we endeavor to refer it to other facts which it resembles. Until this be accomplished, we do not view it as understood. This is the case, for example, with sulphur, which, in a certain degree of temperature melts like other bodies, but at a higher degree of heat, instead of evaporating, again consolidates. When a fact is generalized, our discontent is quieted, and we consider the generality itself as tantamount to an explanation. Why does this apple fall to the ground? Because all bodies gravitate towards each other. Arrived at this general fact, we inquire no more, although ignorant now as previously of the cause of gravitation; for gravitation is nothing more than a name for a general fact, the *why* of which we know not. A mystery, if recognized as universal, would no longer appear mysterious.

* Kant's conjecture was founded on a supposed progressive increase in the eccentricities of the planetary orbits. This progression, however, is only true of Venus, the Earth, Jupiter, and Saturn. The eccentricity diminishes again in Uranus, and still more in Neptune. Subsequent discoveries have thus rather weakened than confirmed the theory. — *English Editors.*

The love of unity also a source of error. — "But this thirst of unity," as Garnier remarks, "this tendency of mind to generalize its knowledge, and our concomitant belief in the uniformity of natural phænomena, is not only an effective mean of discovery, but likewise an abundant source of error. Hardly is there a similarity detected between two or three facts, than men hasten to extend it to all others; and if, perchance, the similarity has been detected by ourselves, self-love closes our eyes to the contradictions which our theory may encounter from experience." "I have heard," says Condillac, "of a philosopher who had the happiness of thinking that he had discovered a principle which was to explain all the wonderful phænomena of chemistry, and who, in the ardor of his self-gratulation, hastened to communicate his discovery to a skilful chemist. The chemist had the kindness to listen to him, and then calmly told him that there was but one unfortunate circumstance for his discovery, — that the chemical facts were precisely the converse of what he had supposed them to be. 'Well, then,' said the philosopher, 'have the goodness to tell me what they are, that I may explain them on my system.'" We are naturally disposed to refer every thing we do not know to principles with which we are familiar. As Aristotle observes, the early Pythagoreans, who first studied arithmetic, were induced, by their scientific predilections, to explain the problem of the universe by the properties of number; and he notices also that a certain musical philosopher was, in like manner, led to suppose that the soul was but a kind of harmony. The musician suggests to my recollection a passage of Dr. Reid. "Mr. Locke," says he, "mentions an eminent musician who believed that God created the world in six days, and rested the seventh, because there are but seven notes in music. I myself," he continues, "knew one of that profession who thought there could be only three parts in harmony — to wit, bass, tenor, and treble; because there are but three persons in the Trinity." The alchemists would see in nature only a single metal, clothed with the different appearances which we denominate gold, silver, copper, iron, mercury, etc., and they confidently explained the mysteries, not only of nature, but of religion, by salt, sulphur, and mercury. Some of our modern zoölogists recoil from the possibility of nature working on two different plans, and rather than renounce the unity which delights them, they insist on recognizing the wings of insects in the gills of fishes, and the sternum of quadrupeds in the antennæ of butterflies; — and all this that they may prove that man is only the evolution of a molluscum! Descartes saw in the physical world only matter and motion; and, more recently, it has been maintained that thought itself is only a movement of matter. Of all the faculties of the mind, Condillac recognized only one, which transformed itself like the Protean metal of the alchemists; and he maintains that our belief in the rising of to-morrow's sun is a sensation. It is this tendency, indeed, which has principally determined philosophers, as we shall hereafter see, to neglect or violate the original duality of consciousness; in which, as an ultimate fact, — a self and not-self, — mind knowing and matter known, — are given in counterpoise and mutual opposition; and hence the three Unitarian schemes of Materialism, Idealism, and Absolute Identity. In fine, Pantheism, or the doctrine which identifies mind and matter, — the Creator and the creature, God and the universe, — how are we to explain the prevalence of this modification of atheism in the most ancient and in the most recent times? Simply because it carries our love of unity to its highest fruition.

Influence of preconceived opinion reducible to love of unity. — To this love of unity — to this desire of reducing the objects of our knowledge to harmony and system — a source of truth and discovery if subservient to observation, but of error and delusion if allowed to dictate to observation what phænomena are to be perceived; to this principle, I say, we may refer the influence which preconceived opinions exercise upon our perceptions and our judgments, by inducing us to see and require only what is in unison with them. What we wish, says Demosthenes, that we believe; what we expect, says Aristotle, that we find; — truths which have been reëchoed by a thousand confessors, and confirmed by ten thousand examples. Opinions once adopted become part of the intellectual system of their holders. If opposed to prevalent doctrines, self-love defends them as a point of honor, exaggerates whatever may confirm, overlooks or extenuates whatever may contradict. Again, if accepted as a general doctrine, they are too often recognized, in consequence of their prevalence, as indisputable truths, and all counter appearances peremptorily overruled as manifest illusions. Thus it is that men will not see in the phænomena what alone is to be seen; in their observations they interpolate and they expunge; and this mutilated and adulterated product they call a fact. And why? Because the real phænomena, if admitted, would spoil the pleasant music of their thoughts, and convert its factitious harmony into discord. "Quæ volunt sapiunt, et nolunt sapere quæ vera sunt." In consequence of this, many a system, professing to be reared exclusively on observation and fact, rests in reality mainly upon hypothesis and fiction. A pretended experience is, indeed, the screen behind which every illusive doctrine regularly retires. "There are more false facts," says Cullen, "current in the world, than false theories;" — and the livery of Lord Bacon has been most ostentatiously paraded by many who were no members of his household. Fact, — observation, — induction, have always been the watchwords of those who have dealt most extensively in fancy. It is now above three centuries since Agrippa, in his *Vanity of the Sciences*, observed of Astrology, Physiognomy, and Metoposcopy (the Phrenology of those days), that experience was professedly their only foundation and their only defence: "Solent omnes illæ divinationum prodigiosæ artes non, nisi experientiæ titulo, se defendere et se objectionum vinculis extricare." It was on this ground, too, that, at a later period, the great Kepler vindicated the first of these arts, Astrology. "For," said he, "how could the principle of a science be false, where experience showed that its predictions were uniformly fulfilled." Now, truth was with Kepler even as a passion; and his, too, was one of the most powerful intellects that ever cultivated and promoted a science. To him, astronomy, indeed, owes perhaps even more than to Newton. And yet, even his great mind, preoccupied with a certain prevalent belief, could observe and judge only in conformity with that belief. This tendency to look at realities only through the spectacles of an hypothesis, is perhaps seen most conspicuously in the fortunes of medicine. The history of that science is, in truth, little else than an incredible narrative of the substitution of fictions for facts; the converts to an hypothesis (and every, the most contradictory, doctrine has had its day), regularly seeing and reporting only in conformity with its dictates. The same is also true of the philosophy of mind; and the variations and alternations in this science, which are perhaps only surpassed by those in medicine, are to be traced to a refusal of the real phænomenon revealed in consciousness, and to the substitution of another, more in unison with preconceived opinions of what it ought to be. Nor, in this commutation of fact with fiction, should we suspect that there is any *mala fides.* Prejudice, imagination, and passion sufficiently explain the illusion. "Fingunt simul creduntque." "When," says Kant, "we have once heard a bad report of this or that individual, we incontinently think that we read the rogue in his countenance; fancy here mingles with observation, which is still further vitiated when affection or passion interferes."

Auxiliary cause of philosophy — Wonder. — Such are the two intellectual necessities which afford the two principal sources of philosophy: — the intellectual necessity of refunding effects into their causes; — and the intellectual necessity of carrying up our knowledge into unity or system. But, besides these intellectual necessities, which are involved in the very existence of our faculties of knowledge, there is another powerful subsidiary to the same effect, — in a certain affection of our capacities of feeling. This feeling, according to circumstances, is denominated *surprise*, *astonishment*, *admiration*, *wonder*, and, when blended with the intellectual tendencies we have considered, it obtains the name of *curiosity*. This feeling, though it cannot, as some have held, be allowed to be the principal, far less the only, cause of philosophy, is, however, a powerful auxiliary to speculation; and, though inadequate to account for the existence of philosophy absolutely, it adequately explains the preference with which certain parts of philosophy have been cultivated, and the order in which philosophy in general has been developed. We may err both in exaggerating, and in extenuating, its influence. Wonder has been contemptuously called the daughter of ignorance; true! but wonder, we should add, is the mother of knowledge. Among others, Plato, Aristotle, Plutarch, and Bacon have all concurred in testifying to the influence of this principle. "Admiration," says the Platonic Socrates in the *Theætetus*, — "admiration is a highly philosophical affec tion; indeed, there is no other principle of philosophy but this." — "That philosophy," says Aristotle, "was not originally studied for any practical end, is manifest from those who first began to philosophize. It was, in fact, wonder, which then, as now, determined men to philosophical researches. Among the phænomena presented to them, their admiration was first directed to those more proximate and more on a level with their powers, and then, rising by degrees, they came at length to demand an explanation of the higher phænomena, — as the different states of the moon, sun, and stars, — and the origin of the universe. Now, to doubt and to be astonished is to recognize our ignorance. Hence it is, that the lover of wisdom is, in a certain sort, a lover of mythi, (φιλόμυθός πως); for the subject of mythi is the astonishing and marvellous. If, then, men philosophize to escape ignorance, it is clear that they pursue knowledge on its own account, and not for the sake of any foreign utility. This is proved by the fact; for it was only after all that pertained to the wants, welfare, and conveniences of life had been discovered, that men commenced their philosophical researches. It is, therefore, manifest that we do not study philosophy for the sake of any thing ulterior; and, as we call him a free man who belongs to himself and not to another so philosophy is, of all sciences, the only free or liberal study, for it alone is unto itself an end." — "It is the business of philosophy," says Plutarch, "to investigate, to admire, and to doubt."

Wonder explains the order in which objects are studied. — We have already remarked, that the principle of wonder affords an explanation of the order in which the different objects of philosophy engaged the attention of mankind. The aim of all philosophy is the discovery of principles, that is, of higher causes; but, in the procedure to this end, men first endeavored to explain those phænomena which attracted their attention by arousing their wonder. The child is wholly absorbed in the observation of the world without; the world within first engages the contemplation of the man. As it is with the individual, so was it with the species. Philosophy, before attempting the problem of intelligence, endeavored to resolve the problem of nature. The spectacle of the external universe was too imposing not first to solicit curiosity, and to direct upon itself the prelusive efforts of philosophy. Thales and Pythagoras, in whom philosophy finds its earliest representatives, endeavored to explain the organization of the universe, and to substitute a scientific for a religious cosmogony. For a season, their successors toiled in the same course; and it was only after philosophy had tried, and tired, its forces on external nature, that the human mind recoiled upon itself, and sought in the study of its own nature the object and end of philosophy. The mind now became to itself its point of departure, and its principal object; and its progress, if less ambitious, was more secure. Socrates was he who first decided this new destination of philosophy. From his epoch, man sought in himself the solution of the great problem of existence; and the history of philosophy was henceforward only a development, more or less successful, more or less complete, of the inscription on the Delphic temple — *Γνῶθι σεαυτόν* — Know thyself.

Having informed you, — 1°, What Philosophy is, and 2°, What are its Causes, I would now say a few words on the Dispositions with which Philosophy ought to be studied; for, without certain practical conditions, a speculative knowledge of the most perfect Method of procedure (our next following question), remains barren and unapplied.

"To attain to a knowledge of ourselves," says Socrates, "we must banish prejudice, passion, and sloth;" and no one who neglects this precept, can hope to make any progress in the philosophy of the human mind, which is only another term for the knowledge of ourselves.

First condition, — renunciation of prejudice. — In the first place, then, all prejudices, — that is, all opinions formed on irrational grounds, — ought to be removed. A preliminary doubt is thus the fundamental condition of philosophy; and the necessity of such a doubt is no less apparent than is its difficulty. We do not approach the study of philosophy ignorant, but perverted. "There is no one," says Gatien-Arnoult, "who has not grown up under a load of beliefs — beliefs which he owes to the accidents of country and family, to the books he has read, to the society he has frequented, to the education he has received, and, in general, to the circumstances which have concurred in the formation of his intellectual and moral habits. These beliefs may be true, or they may be false, or, what is more probable, they may be a medley of truths and errors. It is, however, under their influence that he studies, and through them, as through a prism, that he views and judges the objects of knowledge. Every thing is therefore seen by him in false colors, and in distorted relations. And this is the reason why philosophy, as the science of truth, requires a renunciation of prejudices (*præ-judicia, opiniones præ-judicatæ*), — that is, conclusions formed without a previous examination of their grounds."

In this, Christianity and Philosophy are at one. — In this, if I may without irreverence compare things human with things divine, Christianity and Philosophy coincide, — for truth is equally the end of both. What is the primary condition which our Saviour requires of his disciples? That they throw off their old prejudices, and come with hearts willing to receive knowledge, and understandings open to conviction. "Unless," He says, "ye become as little children, ye shall not enter the kingdom of heaven." Such is true religion; such also is true philosophy. Philosophy requires an emancipation from the yoke of foreign authority, a renunciation of all blind adhesion to the opinions of our age and country, and a purification of the intellect from all assumptive beliefs. Unless we can cast off the prejudices of the man, and become as children, docile and unperverted, we need never hope to enter the temple of philosophy. It is the neglect of this primary condition, which has mainly occasioned men to wander from the unity of truth, and caused the endless variety of religious and philosophical sects. Men would not submit to approach the word of God in order to receive from that alone their doctrine and their faith; but they came, in general, with preconceived opinions, and, accordingly, each found in revelation only what he was predetermined to find. So, in like manner, is it in philosophy. *Consciousness is to the philosopher what the Bible is to the theologian.* Both are revelations of the truth; and both afford the truth to those who are content to receive it, as it ought to be received, with reverence and submission. But as it has, too frequently, fared with the one revelation, so has it with the other. Men turned, indeed, to consciousness, and professed to regard its authority as paramount; but they were not content humbly to accept the facts which consciousness revealed, and to establish these without retrenchment or distortion, as the only principles of their philosophy; on the contrary, they came with opinions already formed, with systems already constructed; and while they eagerly appealed to consciousness when its data supported their conclusions, they made no scruple to overlook, or to misinterpret, its facts, when these were not in harmony with their speculations. Thus, religion and philosophy, as they both terminate in the same end, so they both depart from the same fundamental condition.

But the influence of early prejudice is the more dangerous, inasmuch as this influence is unobtrusive. Few of us are, perhaps, fully aware of how little we owe to ourselves, — how much to the influence of others.

Source of the power of custom. — Man is by nature a social animal. "He is more political," says Aristotle, "than any bee or ant." But the existence of society, from a family to a state, supposes a certain harmony of sentiment among its members; and nature has, accordingly, wisely implanted in us a tendency to assimilate, in opinions and habits of thought, to those with whom we live and act. There is thus, in every society, great or small, a certain gravitation of opinions towards a common centre. As in our natural body, every part has a necessary sympathy with every other, and all together form, by their harmonious conspiration, a healthy whole; so, in the social body, there is always a strong predisposition, in each of its members, to act and think in unison with the rest. This universal sympathy, or fellow-feeling, of our social nature, is the principle of the different spirit dominant in different ages, countries, ranks, sexes, and periods of life. It is the cause why fashions, why political and religious enthusiasm, why moral example, either for good or evil, spread so rapidly, and exert so powerful an influence. As men are naturally prone to imitate others, they consequently regard, as important or insignificant, as honorable or disgraceful, as true or false, as good or bad, what those around them consider in the same light. They love and hate what they see others desire and eschew. This is not to be regretted; it is natural, and, consequently, it is right. Indeed, were it otherwise, society could not subsist, for nothing can be more apparent than that mankind in general, destined as they are to occupations incompatible with intellectual cultivation, are wholly incapable of forming opinions for themselves on many of the most important objects of human consideration. If such, however, be the intentions of nature with respect to the unenlightened classes, it is manifest that a heavier obligation is thereby laid on those who enjoy the advantages of intellectual cultivation, to examine with diligence and impartiality the foundations of those opinions which have any connection with the welfare of mankind. If the multitude must be led, it is of consequence that it be led by enlightened conductors. That the great multitude of mankind are, by natural disposition, only what others are, is a fact at all times so obtrusive, that it could not escape observation from the moment a reflective eye was first turned upon man. "The whole conduct of Cambyses," says Herodotus, the father of history, "towards the Egyptian gods, sanctuaries, and priests, convinces me that this king was in the highest degree insane; for otherwise, he would not have insulted the worship and holy things of the Egyptians. If any one should accord to all men the permission to make free choice of the best among all customs, undoubtedly each would choose his own. That this would certainly happen, can be shown by many examples, and, among others, by the following. The King Darius once asked the Greeks who were resident in his court, at what price they could be induced to devour their dead parents. The Greeks answered, that to this no price could bribe them. Thereupon the king asked some Indians, who were in the habit of eating their dead parents, what they would take, not to eat, but to burn them ; and the Indians answered even as the Greeks had done." Herodotus concludes this narrative with the observation, that "Pindar had justly entitled Custom — the Queen of the World."

Sceptical inference from the influence of custom. — The ancient sceptics, from the conformity of men, in every country, in their habits of thinking, feeling, and acting, and from the diversity of different nations in these habits, inferred that nothing was by nature beautiful or deformed, true or false, good or bad, but that these distinctions originated solely in custom. The modern scepticism of Montaigne terminates in the same assertion ; and the sublime misanthropy of Pascal has almost carried him to a similar exaggeration. "In the just and the unjust," says he, "we find hardly any thing which does not change its character in changing its climate. Three degrees of an elevation of the pole reverses the whole of jurisprudence. A meridian is decisive of truth, and a few years of possession Fundamental laws change. Right has its epochs. A pleasant justice, which a river or a mountain limits ! Truth, on this side the Pyrenees, error on the other ! " This doctrine is exaggerated, but it has a foundation in truth ; and the most zealous champions of the immutability of moral distinctions are unanimous in acknowledging the powerful influence which the opinions, tastes, manners, affections, and actions of the society in which we live, exert upon all and each of its members.

Influence of custom and example in revolutionary times. — Nor is this influence of man on man less unambiguous in times of social tranquillity, than in crises of social convulsion. In seasons of political and religious revolution, there arises a struggle between the resisting force of ancient habits and the contagious sympathy of new modes of feeling and thought. In one portion of society, the inveterate influence of custom prevails over the contagion of example; in others, the contagion of example prevails over the conservative force of antiquity and habit. In either case, however, we think and act always in sympathy with others. "We remain," says an illustrious philosopher, "submissive so long as the world continues to set the example. As we follow the herd in forming our conceptions of what is respectable, so we are ready to follow the multitude also, when such conceptions come to be questioned or rejected; and are no less vehement reformers, when the current of opinion has turned against former establishments, than we were zealous abettors, while that current continued to set in a different direction."

Relation of the individual to social crises.—Thus it is, that no revolution in public opinion is the work of an individual, of a single cause, or of a day. When the crisis has arrived, the catastrophe must ensue; but the agents through whom it is apparently accomplished, though they may accelerate, cannot originate its occurrence. Who believes, that, but for Luther or Zwingli, the Reformation would not have been? Their individual, their personal energy and zeal, perhaps, hastened by a year or two the event; but had the public mind not been already ripe for their revolt, the fate of Luther and Zwingli, in the sixteenth century, would have been that of Huss and Jerome of Prague, in the fifteenth. Woe to the revolutionist who is not himself a creature of the revolution! If he anticipate, he is lost; for it requires, what no individual can supply, a long and powerful counter-sympathy in a nation to untwine the ties of custom which bind a people to the established and the old.

Testimonies to the power of received opinion.—I should have no end, were I to quote to you all that philosophers have said of the prevalence and evil influence of prejudice and opinion. "Opinion," says the great Pascal, "disposes of all things. It constitutes beauty, justice, happiness; and these are the all in all of the world."

"Almost every opinion we have," says the pious Charon, "we have but by authority; we believe, judge, act, live, and die on trust, as common custom teaches us; and rightly! for we are too weak to decide and choose of ourselves. But the wise do not act thus." "Every opinion," says Montaigne, "is strong enough to have had its martyrs;" and Sir W. Raleigh — "It is opinion, not truth, that travelleth the world without passport."

Doubt the first step to philosophy. — Such being the recognized universality and evil effect of prejudice, philosophers have, consequently, been unanimous in making doubt the first step towards philosophy. Aristotle has a fine chapter in his *Metaphysics* on the utility of doubt, and on the things which we ought first to doubt of; and he concludes by establishing that the success of philosophy depends on the art of doubting well. This is even enjoined on us by the Apostle. For in saying "Prove" (which may be more correctly translated *test*) — "Test all things," he implicitly commands us to doubt all things. "He," says Bacon, "who would become a philosopher, must commence by repudiating belief;" and he concludes one of the most remarkable passages of his writings with the observation, that, "were there a single man to be found with a firmness sufficient to efface from his mind the theories and notions vulgarly received, and to apply his intellect free and without prevention, the best hopes might be entertained of his success." "To philosophize," says Descartes, "seriously, and to good effect, it is necessary for a man to renounce all prejudices; in other words, to apply the greatest care to doubt of all his previous opinions, so long as these have not been subjected to a new examination, and been recognized as true." But it is needless to multiply authorities in support of so obvious a truth. The ancient philosophers refused to admit slaves to their instruction. Prejudice makes men slaves; it disqualifies them for the pursuit of truth; and their emancipation from prejudice is what philosophy first inculcates on, what it first requires of, its disciples.

Philosophical doubt distinguished from scepticism. — Let us, however, beware that we act not the part of revolted slaves; that, in asserting our liberty, we do not run into license. Philosophical doubt is not an end, but a mean. We doubt in order that we may believe; we begin, that we may not end with, doubt. We doubt once that we may believe always; we renounce authority that we may follow reason; we surrender opinion that we may obtain knowledge. We must be protestants, not infidels, in philosophy. "There is a great difference," says Malebranche, "between doubting and doubting. — We may doubt through passion and brutality; through blindness and malice, and finally through fancy, and from the very wish to doubt; but we doubt also from prudence and through distrust, from wisdom and through penetration of mind. The former doubt is a doubt of darkness, which never issues to the light, but leads us always further from it; the latter is a doubt which is born of the light, and which aids in a certain sort, to produce light in its turn." Indeed, were the effect of philosophy the establishment of doubt, the remedy would be worse than the disease. Doubt, as a permanent state of mind, would be, in fact little better than an intellectual death. The mind lives as it believes, — it lives in the affirmation of itself, of nature, and of God; a doubt upon any one of these would be a diminution of its life; — a doubt upon the three, were it possible, would be tantamount to a mental annihilation.

It is well observed, by Mr. Stewart, "that it is not merely in order to free the mind from the influence of error, that it is useful to examine the foundation of established opinions. It is such an examination alone, that, in an inquisitive age like the present, can secure a philosopher from the danger of unlimited scepticism. To this extreme, indeed, the complexion of the times is more likely to give him a tendency, than to implicit credulity. In the former ages of ignorance and superstition, the intimate association which had been formed in the prevailing systems of education, between truth and error had given to the latter an ascendant over the minds of men, which it could never have acquired if divested of such an alliance. The case has, of late years, been most remarkably reversed: the common sense of mankind, in consequence of the growth of a more liberal spirit of inquiry, has revolted against many of those absurdities which had so long held human reason in captivity; and it was, perhaps, more than could have been reasonably expected, that, in the first moments of their emancipation, philosophers should have stopped short at the precise boundary which cooler reflection and more moderate views would have prescribed. The fact is, that they have passed far beyond it; and that, in their zeal to destroy prejudices, they have attempted to tear up by the roots many of the best and happiest and most essential principles of our nature. . . . . In the midst of these contrary impulses of fashionable and vulgar prejudices, he alone evinces the superiority and the strength of his mind, who is able to disentangle truth from error; and to oppose the clear conclusions of his own unbiased faculties to the united clamors of superstition and of false philosophy. Such are the men whom nature marks out to be the lights of the world; to fix the wavering opinions of the multitude, and to impress their own characters on that of their age." In a word, philosophy is, as Aristotle has justly expressed, not the art of doubting, but the art of doubting well.

Subjugation of the passions. — In the second place, in obedience to the precept of Socrates, the passions, under which we shall include sloth, ought to be subjugated. These ruffle the tranquillity of the mind, and consequently deprive it of the power of carefully considering all that the solution of a question requires should be examined. A man under the agitation of any lively emotion, is hardly aware of aught but what has immediate relation to the passion which agitates and engrosses him. Among the affections which influence the will, and induce it to adhere to scepticism or error, there is none more dangerous than sloth. The greater proportion of mankind are inclined to spare themselves the trouble of a long and laborious inquiry; or they fancy that a superficial examination is enough; and the slightest agreement between a few objects, in a few petty points, they at once assume as evincing the correspondence of the whole throughout. Others apply themselves exclusively to the matters which it is absolutely necessary for them to know, and take no account of any opinion but that which they have stumbled on, — for no other reason than that they have embraced it, and are unwilling to recommence the labor of learning. They receive their opinion on the authority of those who have had suggested to them their own; and they are always facile scholars, for the slightest probability is, for them, all the evidence that they require.

Pride is a powerful impediment to a progress in knowledge. Under the influence of this passion, men seek honor, but not truth. They do not cultivate what is most valuable in reality, but what is most valuable in opinion. They disdain, perhaps, what can be easily accomplished, and apply themselves to the obscure and recondite; but as the vulgar and easy is the foundation on which the rare and arduous is built, they fail even in attaining the object of their ambition, and remain with only a farrago of confused and ill-assorted notions. In all its phases, self-love is an enemy to philosophical progress; and the history of philosophy is filled with the illusions of which it has been the source. On the one side, it has led men to close their eyes against the most evident truths which were not in harmony with their adopted opinions. It is said that there was not a physician in Europe, above the age of forty, who would admit Harvey's discovery of the circulation of the blood. On the other hand, it is finely observed by Bacon, that "the eye of human intellect is not dry, but receives a suffusion from the will and from the affections, so that it may almost be said to engender any science it pleases. For what a man wishes to be true, that he prefers believing." And, in another place, "if the human intellect hath once taken a liking to any doctrine, either because received and credited, or because otherwise pleasing, — it draws every thing else into harmony with that doctrine, and to its support; and albeit there may be found a more powerful array of contradictory instances, these, however, it either does not observe, or it contemns, or by distinction extenuates and rejects."

CHAPTER IV.

THE METHOD OF PHILOSOPHY.

THERE is only one possible method in philosophy; and what have been called the different methods of different philosophers, vary from each other only as more or less perfect applications of this one Method to the objects of knowledge.

What is Method? — All method is a rational progress, — a progress towards an end; and the method of philosophy is the procedure conducive to the end which philosophy proposes. The ends, — the final causes of philosophy, — as we have seen, are two; first, the discovery of efficient causes; secondly, the generalization of our knowledge into unity; — two ends, however, which fall together into one, inasmuch as the higher we proceed in the discovery of causes, we necessarily approximate more and more to unity. The detection of the one in the many might, therefore, be laid down as the end to which philosophy, though it can never reach it, tends continually to approximate. But, considering philosophy in relation to both these ends, I shall endeavor to show you that it has only one possible method.

But one method in relation to the first end of Philosophy. — Considering philosophy, in the first place, in relation to its first end, — the discovery of causes, — we have seen that causes (taking that term as synonymous for all without which the effect would not be) are only the coefficients of the effect; an effect being nothing more than the sum or complement of all the partial causes, the concurrence of which constitute its existence. This being the case, — and as it is only by experience that we discover what particular causes must conspire in order to produce such or such an effect, — it follows, that nothing can become known to us as a cause except in and through its effect; in other words, that we can only attain to the knowledge of a cause by extracting it out of its effect. To take the example, we formerly employed, of a neutral salt. This, as I observed, was made up by the conjunction of three proximate causes, — namely, an acid, — an alkali, — and the force which brought the alkali and the acid into the requisite approximation. This last, as a transitory condition, and not always the same, we shall throw out of account. Now, though we might know the acid and the alkali in themselves as distinct phænomena, we could never know them as the concurrent causes of the salt, unless we had known the salt as their effect. And though, in this example, it happens that we are able to compose the effect by the union of its causes, and to decompose it by their separation, — this is only an accidental circumstance; for the far greater number of the objects presented to our observation can only be decomposed, but not actually recomposed; and in those which can be recomposed, this possibility is itself only the result of a knowledge of the causes previously obtained by an original decomposition of the effect.

This method is by Analysis and Synthesis. — In so far, therefore, as philosophy is the research of causes, the one necessary condition of its possibility is the decomposition of effects into their constituted causes. This is the fundamental procedure of philosophy, and is called by a Greek term *Analysis.* But though analysis be the fundamental procedure, it is still *only a mean towards an end.* We analyze only that we may comprehend; and we comprehend only inasmuch as we are able to reconstruct, in thought, the complex effects which we have analyzed into their elements. This mental reconstruction is, therefore, the final, the consummative procedure of philosophy, and it is familiarly known by the Greek term *Synthesis.* Analysis and synthesis, though commonly treated as two different methods, are, if properly understood, only the two necessary parts of the same method. Each is the relative and the correlative of the other. Analysis, without a subsequent synthesis, is incomplete; it is a mean cut off from its end. Synthesis, without a previous analysis, is baseless; for synthesis receives from analysis the elements which it recomposes. And, as synthesis supposes analysis as the prerequisite of its possibility, — so it is also dependent on analysis for the qualities of its existence. The value of every synthesis depends upon the value of the foregoing analysis. If the precedent analysis afford false elements, the subsequent synthesis of these elements will necessarily afford a false result. If the elements furnished by analysis are assumed, and not really discovered, — in other words, if they be hypothetical, the synthesis of these hypothetical elements will constitute only a conjectural theory. The legitimacy of every synthesis is thus necessarily dependent on the legitimacy of the analysis which it presupposes, and on which it founds.

These two relative procedures are thus equally necessary to each other. On the one hand, analysis without synthesis affords only a commenced, only an incomplete, knowledge. On the other, synthesis without analysis is a false knowledge, — that is, no knowledge at all. Both, therefore, are absolutely necessary to philosophy, and both are, in philosophy, as much parts of the same method as, in the animal body, inspiration and expiration are of the same vital function. But though these operations are each requisite to the other, yet were we to distinguish and compare what ought only to be considered as conjoined, it is to analysis that the preference must be accorded. An analysis is always valuable; for though now without a synthesis, this synthesis may at any time be added; whereas a synthesis without a previous analysis is radically and *ab initio* null.

So far, therefore, as regards the *first* end of philosophy, or the discovery of causes, it appears that there is only one possible method, — that method of which analysis is the foundation, synthesis the completion. In the *second* place, considering philosophy in relation to its second end, the carrying up our knowledge into unity, — the same is equally apparent.

Only one method in relation to the second end of Philoso-

phy. — Every thing presented to our observation, whether external or internal, whether through sense or self-consciousness, is presented in complexity. Through sense, the objects crowd upon the mind in multitudes, and each separate individual of these multitudes is itself a congeries of many various qualities. The same is the case with the phænomena of self-consciousness. Every modification of mind is a complex state; and the different elements of each state manifest themselves only in and through each other. Thus, nothing but multiplicity is ever presented to our observation; and yet our faculties are so limited that they are able to comprehend at once only the very simplest conjunctions. There seems, therefore, a singular disproportion between our powers of knowledge and the objects to be known. How is the equilibrium to be restored? This is the great problem proposed by nature, and which analysis and synthesis, in combination, enable us to solve. For example, I perceive a tree, among other objects of an extensive landscape, and I wish to obtain a full and distinct conception of that tree. What ought I to do? *Divide et impera:* I must attend to it by itself, that is, to the exclusion of the other constituents of the scene before me. I thus analyze that scene; I separate a petty portion of it from the rest, in order to consider that portion apart. But this is not enough, the tree itself is not a unity, but, on the contrary, a complex assemblage of elements, far beyond what my powers can master at once. I must carry my analysis still further. Accordingly, I consider successively its height, its breadth, its shape; I then proceed to its trunk, rise from that to its branches, and follow out its different ramifications; I now fix my attention on the leaves, and severally examine their form, color, etc. It is only after having thus, by analysis, detached all these parts, in order to deal with them one by one, that I am able, by reversing the process, fully to comprehend them again in a series of synthetic acts. By synthesis, rising from the ultimate analysis, step by step, I view the parts in relation to each other, and, finally, to the whole of which they are the constituents; I reconstruct them; and it is only through these two counter-processes of analysis and synthesis, that I am able to convert the confused perception of the tree, which I obtained at first sight, into a clear, and distinct, and comprehensive knowledge.

How a multitude is reduced to unity.— But if analysis and synthesis be required to afford us a perfect knowledge even of one individual object of sense, still more are they required to enable the mind to reduce an indefinite multitude of objects, — the infinitude, we may say, of nature, — to the limits of its own finite comprehension. To accomplish this, it is requisite to extract the one out of the many, and thus to recall multitude to unity, — confusion to order. And how is this performed? The one in the many being that in which a plurality of objects agree, — or that in which they may be considered as the same; and the agreement of objects in any common quality being discoverable only by an observation and comparison of the objects themselves, it follows that a knowledge of the one can only be evolved out of a foregoing knowledge of the many. But this evolution can only be accomplished by an analysis and a synthesis. By analysis, from the infinity of objects presented to our observation, we select some. These we consider apart, and, further, only in certain points of view, — and we compare these objects with others also considered in the same points of view. So far the procedure is analytic. Having discovered, however, by this observation and comparison, that certain objects agree in certain respects, we generalize the qualities in which they coincide, — that is, from a certain number of individual instances we infer a general law; we perform what is called an act of Induction.

What is Induction?— This induction is erroneously viewed as analytic; it is purely a synthetic process. For example, from our experience, — and all experience, be it that of the individual or of mankind, is only finite, — from our limited experience, I say, that bodies, as observed by us, attract each other, we infer by induction the unlimited conclusion that all bodies gravitate towards each other. Now, here the consequent contains much more than was contained in the antecedent. Experience, the antecedent, only says, and only can say, this, that, and the other body gravitate (that is, *some* bodies gravitate); the consequent educed from that antecedent, says, — *all* bodies gravitate. The antecedent is limited, — the consequent unlimited. Something, therefore, has been added to the antecedent in order to legitimate the inference, if we are not to hold the consequent itself as absurd; for, as you will hereafter learn, no conclusion must contain more than was contained in the premises from which it is drawn. What then is the *something?* If we consider the inductive process, this will be at once apparent.

The affirmation, this, that, and the other body gravitate, is connected with the affirmation, all bodies gravitate, only by inserting between the two a third affirmation, by which the two other affirmations are connected into reason and consequent, — that is, into a logical cause and effect. What that is I shall explain. All scientific induction is founded on the presumption that nature is uniform in her operations. Of the ground and origin of this presumption, I am not now to speak. I shall only say, that, as it is a principle which we suppose in all our inductions, it cannot be itself a product of induction. It is, therefore, interpolated in the inductive reasoning by the mind itself. In our example the reasoning will, accordingly, run as follows: —

This, that, and the other body (some bodies) are observed to gravitate;

But (as nature is uniform in her operations) this, that, and the other body (some bodies) represent all bodies;

Therefore, all bodies gravitate.

Now, in this and other examples of induction, it is the mind which binds up the separate substances observed and collected into a whole, and converts what is only the observation of many particulars into a universal law. This procedure is manifestly synthetic.

Now, you will remark that analysis and synthesis are here absolutely dependent on each other. The previous observation and comparison, — the analytic foundation, — are only instituted for the sake of the subsequent induction, — the synthetic consummation. What boots it to observe and to compare, if the uniformities we discover among objects are never generalized into laws? We have obtained an historical, but not a philosophical knowledge. Here, therefore, analysis without synthesis is incomplete. On the other hand, an induction which does not proceed upon a competent enumeration of particulars, is either doubtful, improbable, or null; for all synthesis is dependent on a foregone analysis for whatever degree of certainty it may pretend to. Thus, considering philosophy in relation to its second end, unity or system, it is manifest that the method by which it accomplishes that end, is a method involving both an analytic and a synthetic process.

Now, as philosophy has only one possible method, so *the history of philosophy* only manifests the conditions of this one method, more or less accurately fulfilled. There are aberrations *in* the method, — no aberrations *from* it.

Earliest problem of philosophy. — "Philosophy," says Geruzez, "commenced with the first act of reflection on the objects of sense or self-consciousness, for the purpose of explaining them. And with that first act of reflection, the method of philosophy began, in its application of an analysis, and in its application of a synthesis, to its object. The first philosophers naturally endeavored to explain the enigma of external nature. The magnificent spectacle of the material universe, and the marvellous demonstrations of power and wisdom which it everywhere exhibited, were the objects which called forth the earliest efforts of speculation. Philosophy was thus, at its commencement, physical, not psychological; it was not the problem of the soul, but the problem of the world, which it first attempted to solve.

"And what was the procedure of philosophy in its solution of this problem? Did it first decompose the whole into its parts, in order again to reconstruct them into a system? This it could not accomplish; but still it attempted this, and nothing else. A complete analysis was not to be expected from the first efforts of intelligence; its decompositions were necessarily partial and imperfect; a partial and imperfect analysis afforded only hypothetical elements; and the synthesis of these elements issued, consequently, only in a one-sided or erroneous theory.

Thales and the Ionic School. — "Thales, the founder of the Ionian philosophy, devoted an especial study to the phænomena of the material universe; and, struck with the appearances of power which water manifested in the formation of bodies, he analyzed all existences into this element, which he viewed as the universal principle, — the universal agent of creation. He proceeded by an incomplete analysis, and generalized, by hypothesis, the law which he drew by induction from the observation of a small series of phænomena.

"The Ionic school continued in the same path. They limited themselves to the study of external nature, and sought in matter the principle of existence. Anaximander of Miletus, the countryman and disciple of Thales, deemed that he had traced the primary cause of creation to an ethereal principle, which occupied space, and whose different combinations constituted the universe of matter. Anaximenes found the original element in air, from which, by rarefaction and condensation, he educed existences. Anaxagoras carried his analysis further, and made a more discreet use of hypothesis; he rose to the conception of an intelligent first cause, distinct from the phænomena of nature; and his notion of the Deity was so far above the gross conceptions of his contemporaries, that he was accused of atheism.

Pythagoras and the Italic School. — "Pythagoras, the founder of the Italic school, analyzed the properties of number; and the relations which this analysis revealed, he elevated into principles of the mental and material universe. Mathematics were his only objects; his analysis was partial, and his synthesis was consequently hypothetical. The Italic school developed the notions of Pythagoras, and, exclusively preoccupied with the relations and harmonies of existence, its disciples did not extend their speculation to the consideration either of substance or of cause.

"Thus, these earlier schools, taking external nature for their point of departure, proceeded by an imperfect analysis, and a presumptuous synthesis, to the construction of exclusive systems, — in which Idealism or Materialism preponderated, according to the kind of data on which they founded.

"The Eleatic school, which is distinguished into two branches, the one of Physical, the other of Metaphysical, speculation, exhibits the same character, the same point of departure, the same tendency, and the same errors.

"These errors led to the scepticism of the Sophists, which was assailed by Socrates, — the sage who determined a new epoch in philosophy by directing observation on man himself; and henceforward the study of mind becomes the prime and central science of philosophy.

"The point of departure was changed, but not the method. The observation or analysis of the human mind, though often profound, remained always incomplete. Fortunately, the first disciples of Socrates, imitating the prudence of their master, and warned by the downfall of the systems of the Ionic, Italic, and Eleatic schools, made a sparing use of synthesis, and hardly a pretension to system.

"Plato and Aristotle directed their observation on the phænomena of intelligence, and we cannot too highly admire the profundity of their analysis, and even the sobriety of their synthesis. Plato devoted himself more particularly to the higher faculties of intelligence; and his disciples were led, by the love of generalization, to regard as the intellectual whole those portions of intelligence which their master had analyzed; and this exclusive spirit gave birth to systems false, not in themselves, but as resting upon a too narrow basis. Aristotle, on the other hand, whose genius was of a more positive character, analyzed with admirable acuteness those operations of mind which stand in more immediate relation to the senses; and this tendency, which among his followers became often exclusive and exaggerated, naturally engendered systems which more or less tended to materialism."

School of Alexandria. — The school of Alexandria, in which the systems resulting from those opposite tendencies were combined, endeavored to reconcile and to fuse them into a still more comprehensive system. Eclecticism, — conciliation, — union, were, in all things, the grand aim of the Alexandrian school. Geographically situated between Greece and Asia, it endeavored to ally Greek with Asiatic genius, religion with philosophy. Hence the Neoplatonic system, of which the last great representative is Proclus. This system is the result of the long labor of the Socratic schools. It is an edifice reared by synthesis out of the materials which analysis had collected, proved, and accumulated, from Socrates down to Plotinus.

But a synthesis is of no greater value than its relative analysis; and as the analysis of the earlier Greek philosophy was not complete, the synthesis of the Alexandrian school was necessarily imperfect.

In the Scholastic philosophy, analysis and observation were too often neglected in some departments of philosophy, and too often carried rashly to excess in others.

Bacon and Descartes. — After the revival of letters, during the fifteenth and sixteenth centuries, the labors of philosophy were principally occupied in restoring and illustrating the Greek systems; and it was not until the seventeenth century, that a new epoch was determined by the genius of Bacon and Descartes. In Bacon and Descartes our modern philosophy may be said to originate, inasmuch as they were the first who made the doctrine of method a principal object of consideration. They both proclaimed, that, for the attainment of scientific knowledge, it is necessary to observe with care, — that is, to analyze; to reject every element as hypothetical, which this analysis does not spontaneously afford; to call in experiment in aid of observation; and to attempt no synthesis or generalization, until the relative analysis has been completely accomplished. They showed that previous philosophers had erred, not by rejecting either analysis or synthesis, but by hurrying on to synthetic induction from a limited or specious analytic observation. They propounded no new method of philosophy, they only expounded the conditions of the old. They showed that these conditions had rarely been fulfilled by philosophers in time past; and exhorted them to their fulfilment in time to come. Thus they explained the petty progress of the past philosophy; — and justly anticipated a gigantic advancement for the future. Such was their precept, but such unfortunately was not their example. There are no philosophers who merit so much in the one respect, none, perhaps, who deserve less in the other.

Of philosophy since Bacon and Descartes, we at present say nothing. Of that we shall hereafter have frequent occasion to speak. But to sum up what this historical sketch was intended to illustrate. There is but one possible method of philosophy, — a combination of analysis and synthesis; and the purity and equilibrium of these two elements constitute its perfection. The aberrations of philosophy have been all so many violations of the laws of this one method. Philosophy has erred, because it built its systems upon incomplete or erroneous analysis, and it can only proceed in safety, if from accurate and unexclusive observation, it rise, by successive generalization, to a comprehensive system.

CHAPTER V.

THE DIVISIONS OF PHILOSOPHY.

Expediency of a division of Philosophy. — As we cannot survey the universe at a glance, neither can we contemplate the whole of philosophy in one act of consciousness. We can only master it gradually and piecemeal; and this is in fact the reason why philosophers have always distributed their science (constituting, though it does, one organic whole) into a plurality of sciences. The expediency, and even necessity, of a division of philosophy, in order that the mind may be enabled to embrace in one general view its various parts, in their relation to each other, and to the whole which they constitute, is admitted by every philosopher. "Res utilis," continues Seneca, "et ad sapientiam properanti utique necessaria, dividi philosophiam, et ingens corpus ejus in membra disponi. Facilius enim per partes in cognitionem totius adducimur."

But, although philosophers agree in regard to the utility of such a distribution, they are almost as little at one in regard to the parts, as they are in respect to the definition, of their science; and, indeed, their differences in reference to the former, mainly arise from their discrepancies in reference to the latter. For they who vary in their comprehension of the whole, cannot agree in their division of the parts.

Division into Theoretical and Practical. — The most ancient and universally recognized distinction of philosophy, is into Theoretical and Practical. These are discriminated by the different nature of their ends. Theoretical, called likewise speculative and contemplative, philosophy has for its highest end mere truth or knowledge. Practical philosophy, on the other hand, has truth or knowledge only as its proximate end,

— this end being subordinate to the ulterior end of some practical action. In theoretical philosophy, we know for the sake of knowing, *scimus ut sciamus:* in practical philosophy, we know for the sake of acting, *scimus ut operemur.* I may here notice the poverty of the English language, in the want of a word to express that practical activity which is contradistinguished from mere intellectual or speculative energy, — what the Greeks express by *πράσσειν*, the Germans by *handeln.* The want of such a word occasions frequent ambiguity; for, to express the species which has no appropriate word, we are compelled to employ the generic term *active.* Thus our philosophers divide the powers of the mind into Intellectual and Active. They do not, however, thereby mean to insinuate that the powers called intellectual are a whit less energetic than those specially denominated active. But, from the want of a better word, they are compelled to employ a term which denotes at once much more and much less than they are desirous of expressing. I ought to observe, that the term *practical* has also obtained with us certain collateral significations, which render it in some respects unfit to supply the want. But to return.

This distinction of Theoretical and Practical philosophy was first explicitly enounced by Aristotle; and the attempts of the later Platonists to carry it up to Plato, and even to Pythagoras, are not worthy of statement, far less of refutation. Once promulgated, the division was, however, soon generally recognized. The Stoics borrowed it, as may be seen, from Seneca: — " Philosophia et contemplativa est et activa; spectat, simulque agit." It was also adopted by the Epicureans; and, in general, by those Greek and Roman philosophers who viewed their science as versant either in the contemplation of nature (φυσική), or in the regulation of human action (ἠθική); for by *nature,* they did not denote the material universe alone, but their Physics included Metaphysics, and their Ethics embraced Politics and Economics. There was thus only a difference of nomenclature; for Physical and Theoretical, — Ethical and Practical Philosophy, — were with them terms absolutely equivalent.

This division unsound. — I regard the division of philosophy into Theoretical and Practical as unsound, and this for two reasons.

The first is, that philosophy, as philosophy, is only cognitive, — only theoretical; whatever lies beyond the sphere of speculation or knowledge, transcends the sphere of philosophy; consequently, to divide philosophy by any quality ulterior to speculation, is to divide it by a difference which does not belong to it. Now, the distinction of practical philosophy from theoretical commits this error. For, while it is admitted that all philosophy, as cognitive, is theoretical, some philosophy is again taken out of this category, on the ground, that, beyond the mere theory, — the mere cognition, — it has an ulterior end in its application to practice.

But, in the second place, this difference, even were it admissible, would not divide philosophy; for, in point of fact, all philosophy must be regarded as practical, inasmuch as mere knowledge, — that is, the mere possession of truth, — is not the highest end of any philosophy; but on the contrary, all truth or knowledge is valuable only inasmuch as it determines the mind to its contemplation, — that is, to practical energy. Speculation, therefore, inasmuch as it is not a negation of thought, but on the contrary, the highest energy of intellect, is, in point of fact, preëminently practical. The practice of one branch of philosophy is, indeed, different from that of another; but all are still practical; for in none is mere knowledge the ultimate, the highest, end.

It is manifest that, in our sense of the term *practical*, Logic, as an instrumental science, would be comprehended under the head of practical philosophy.

The terms Art and Science. — I shall take this opportunity of explaining an anomaly which you will find explained in no work with which I am acquainted. Certain branches of philosophical knowledge are called Arts, — or Arts and Sciences indifferently; others are exclusively denominated Sciences. Were this distinction coincident with the distinction of sciences speculative and sciences practical, — taking the term practical in its ordinary acceptation, — there would be no difficulty; for, as every practical science necessarily involves a theory, nothing could be more natural than to call the same branch of knowledge an art, when viewed as relative to its practical application, and a science when viewed in relation to the theory which that application supposes. But this is not the case. The speculative sciences, indeed, are never denominated arts; we may, therefore, throw them aside. The difficulty is exclusively confined to the practical. Of these, some never receive the name of arts; others are called arts and sciences indifferently. Thus the sciences of Ethics, Economics, Politics, Theology, etc., though all practical, are never denominated arts; whereas this appellation is very usually applied to the practical sciences of Logic, Rhetoric, Grammar, etc.

That the term *art* is with us not coextensive with practical science, is thus manifest; and yet these are frequently confounded. Thus, for example, Dr. Whately, in his definition of Logic, thinks that Logic is a science, in so far as it institutes an analysis of the process of the mind in reasoning, and an art, in so far as it affords practical rules to secure the mind from error in its deductions; and he defines an art, the application of knowledge to practice. Now, if this view were correct, art and practical science would be convertible terms. But that they are not employed as synonymous expressions is, as we have seen, shown by the incongruity we feel in talking of the art of Ethics, the art of Religion, etc., though these are eminently practical sciences.

The question, therefore, still remains, Is this restriction of the term *art* to certain of the practical sciences the result of some accidental and forgotten usage, or is it founded on any rational principle which we are able to trace? The former alternative seems to be the common belief; for no one, in so far as I know, has endeavored to account for the apparently vague and capricious manner in which the terms art and science are applied. The latter alternative, however, is the true; and I shall endeavor to explain to you the reason of the application of the term art to certain practical sciences, and not to others.

Historical origin of this use of language. — You are aware that the Aristotelic philosophy was, for many centuries, not only the prevalent, but during the middle ages, the one exclusive philosophy in Europe. This philosophy of the middle ages, or, as it is commonly called, the Scholastic Philosophy, has exerted the most extensive influence on the languages of modern Europe; and from this common source has been principally derived that community of expression which these languages exhibit. Now, the peculiar application of the term *art* was introduced into the vulgar tongues from the scholastic philosophy; and was borrowed by that philosophy from Aristotle. This is only one of a thousand instances, which might be alleged, of the unfelt influence of a single powerful mind, on the associations and habits of thought of generations to the end of time; and of Aristotle is preëminently true, what has been so beautifully said of the ancients in general: —

> "The great of old!
> The dead but sceptred sovrans who still rule
> Our spirits from their urns."

Now, then, the application of the term *art* in the modern languages being mediately governed by certain distinctions which the capacities of the Greek tongue allowed Aristotle to establish, these distinctions must be explained.

In the Aristotelic philosophy, the terms πρᾶξις and πρακτικός, — that is, *practice* and *practical*, were employed both in a generic or looser, and in a special or stricter signification. In its generic meaning, πρᾶξις, *practice*, was opposed to theory or speculation, and it comprehended under it practice in its special meaning, and another coördinate term to which practice, in this, its stricter signification, was opposed. This term was ποίησις, which we may inadequately translate by *production*. The distinction of πρακτικός and ποιητικός consisted in this: the former denoted that action which terminated in action, — the latter, that action which resulted in some permanent product. For example, dancing and music are practical, as leaving no work after their performance; whereas, painting and statuary are productive, as leaving some product over and above their energy.

Now Aristotle, in formally defining art, defines it as a habit productive, and not as a habit practical, ἕξις ποιητικὴ μετὰ λόγου; — and, though he has not always himself adhered strictly to this limitation, his definition was adopted by his followers, and the term in its application to the practical sciences (the term practical being here used in its generic meaning), came to be exclusively confined to those whose end did not result in mere action or energy. Accordingly, as Ethics, Politics, etc., proposed happiness as their end, — and as happiness was an energy, or at least the concomitant of energy, these sciences terminated in action, and were consequently *practical*, not *productive*. On the other hand, Logic, Rhetoric, etc., did not terminate in a mere, — an evanescent action, but in a permanent, — an enduring product. For the end of Logic was the production of a reasoning, the end of Rhetoric the production of an oration, and so forth. This distinction is not perhaps beyond the reach of criticism, and I am not here to vindicate its correctness. My only aim is to make you aware of the grounds of the distinction, in order that you may comprehend the principle which originally determined the application of the term *art* to some of the practical sciences and not to others, and without a knowledge of which principle, the various employment of the term must appear to you capricious and unintelligible. It is needless, perhaps, to notice that the rule applies only to the philosophical sciences, — to those which received their form and denominations from the learned. The mechanical dexterities were beneath their notice; and these were accordingly left to receive their appellations from those who knew nothing of the Aristotelic proprieties. Accordingly, the term *art* is in them applied, without distinction, to productive and unproductive operations. We speak of the art of rope-dancing, equally as of the art of rope-making. But to return.

Universality of this division of Philosophy. — The division of philosophy into Theoretical and Practical is the most important that has been made; and it is that which has entered into nearly all the distributions attempted by modern philosophers. Bacon was the first, after the revival of letters, who essayed a distribution of the sciences and of philosophy. He divided all human knowledge into History, Poetry, and Philosophy. Philosophy he distinguished into branches conversant about the Deity, about Nature, and about Man; and each of these had their subordinate divisions, which, however, it is not necessary to particularize.

Descartes distributed philosophy into theoretical and practical, with various subdivisions; but his followers adopted the division of Logic, Metaphysics, Physics, and Ethics. Gassendi recognized, like the ancients, three parts of philosophy, Logic, Physics, and Ethics, and this, along with many other of Gassendi's doctrines, was adopted by Locke. Kant distinguished philosophy into theoretical and practical, with various subdivisions; and the distribution into theoretical and practical was also established by Fichte.

I have now concluded the general Introduction to Philosophy, in which, from the general nature of the subjects, I have been compelled to anticipate conclusions, and to depend on your being able to supply a good deal of what it was impossible for me articulately to explain. I now enter upon the consideration of the matters which are hereafter to occupy our attention, with comparatively little apprehension, — for, in these, we shall be able to dwell more upon details, while, at the same time, the subject will open upon us by degrees, so that, every step that we proceed, we shall find the progress easier. But I have to warn you, that you will probably find the very commencement the most arduous, and this not only because you will come less inured to difficulty, but because it will there be necessary to deal with principles, and these of a general and abstract nature; whereas, having once mastered these, every subsequent step will be comparatively easy.

Without entering upon details, I may now summarily state the order which I propose to follow. This requires a preliminary exposition of the different departments of Philosophy, in order that you may obtain a comprehensive view of the proper objects of our consideration, and of the relations in which they stand to others.

Distribution of the Sciences. — Science and philosophy are conversant either about Mind or about Matter. The former of these is Philosophy, properly so called. With the latter we have nothing to do, except in so far as it may enable us to throw light upon the former; for Metaphysics, in whatever latitude the term be taken, is a science, or complement of sciences, exclusively occupied with mind. Now the Philosophy of Mind, — Psychology or Metaphysics, in the widest signification of the terms, — is *threefold;* for the object it immediately proposes for consideration may be either, 1°, PHÆNOMENA in general; or, 2°, LAWS; or, 3°, INFERENCES, — RESULTS. This I will endeavor to explain.

The three grand questions of Philosophy. — The whole of philosophy is the answer to these three questions: 1°, What are the Facts or Phænomena to be observed? 2°, What are the Laws which regulate these facts, or under which these phænomena appear? 3°, What are the real Results, not immediately manifested, which these facts or phænomena warrant us in drawing?

Phenomenology. — If we consider the mind merely with the view of observing and generalizing the various phænomena it reveals, — that is, of analyzing them into capacities or faculties, — we have one mental science, or one department of mental science; and this we may call the PHÆNOMENOLOGY OF MIND. It is commonly called PSYCHOLOGY — EMPIRICAL PSYCHOLOGY, or the INDUCTIVE PHILOSOPHY of MIND; we might call it PHÆNOMENAL PSYCHOLOGY. It is evident that the divisions of this science will be determined by the classes into which the phænomena of mind are distributed.

Nomology and its subdivisions. — If, again, we analyze the mental phænomena with the view of discovering and considering, not contingent appearances, but the *necessary* and *universal* facts, — *i. e.* the laws by which our faculties are governed, to the end that we may obtain a criterion by which to judge or to explain their procedures and manifestations, — we have a science which we may call the NOMOLOGY OF MIND, — NOMOLOGICAL PSYCHOLOGY. Now, there will be as many distinct classes of Nomological Psychology, as there are distinct classes of mental phænomena under the Phænomenological division. I shall, hereafter, show you that there are Three great classes of these phænomena, — namely, 1°, The phænomena of our Cognitive faculties, or faculties of Knowledge; 2°, The phænomena of our Feelings, or the phænomena of Pleasure and Pain; and, 3°, The phænomena of our Conative powers, — in other words, the phænomena of Will and Desire. Each of these classes of phænomena has, accordingly, a science which is conversant about its Laws. For, as each proposes a different end, and, in the accomplishment of that end, is regulated by peculiar laws, each must, consequently, have a different science conversant about these laws, — that is, a different Nomology.

There is no one, no *Nomological, science of the Cognitive faculties*, in general; though we have some older treatises which, though partial in their subject, afford a name not unsuitable for a nomology of the cognitions, — namely, Gnoseologia or Gnostologia. There is no independent science of the laws of Perception; if there were, it might be called Æsthetic, which, however, as we shall see, would be ambiguous. Mnemonic, or the science of the laws of Memory, has been elaborated at least in numerous treatises; but the name Anamnestic, the art of Recollection or Reminiscence, might be equally well applied to it. The laws of the Representative faculty, — that is, the laws of Association, have not yet been elevated into a separate nomological science. Neither have the conditions of the Regulative or Legislative faculty, the faculty itself of Laws, been fully analyzed, far less reduced to system; though we have several deservedly forgotten treatises, of an older date, under the inviting name of *Noologies*. The only one of the cognitive faculties, whose laws constitute the object-matter of a separate science, is the Elaborative, — the Understanding Special, the faculty of relations, the faculty of Thought Proper. This nomology has obtained the name of LOGIC among other appellations, but not from Aristotle. The best name would have been DIANOETIC. Logic is the science of the laws of thought, in relation to the end which our cognitive faculties propose, —

i. e. the TRUE. To this head might be referred Grammar, — Universal Grammar, — Philosophical Grammar, or the science conversant with the laws of Language, as the instrument of thought.

The *Nomology of our Feelings*, or the science of the laws which govern our capacities of enjoyment, in relation to the end which they propose, — *i. e.* the PLEASURABLE, — has obtained no precise name in our language. It has been called the Philosophy of Taste, and, on the Continent especially, it has been denominated Æsthetic. Neither name is unobjectionable. The first is vague, metaphorical, and even delusive. In regard to the second, you are aware that *αἴσθησις* in Greek means feeling in general, as well as sense in particular; as our term *feeling* means either the sense of touch in particular, or sentiment, — and the capacity of the pleasurable and painful in general. Both terms are, therefore, to a certain extent, ambiguous; but this objection can rarely be avoided, and Æsthetic, if not the best expression to be found, has already been long and generally employed. It is now nearly a century since Baumgarten, a celebrated philosopher of the Leibnitzio-Wolfian school, first applied the term Æsthetic to the doctrine which we vaguely and periphrastically denominate the Philosophy of Taste, the theory of the Fine Arts, the science of the Beautiful and Sublime, etc., — and this term is now in general acceptance, not only in Germany, but throughout the other countries of Europe. The term Apolaustic would have been a more appropriate designation.

Finally, the *Nomology of our Conative powers* is Practical Philosophy, properly so called; for practical philosophy is simply the science of the laws regulative of our Will and Desires, in relation to the end which our conative powers propose, — *i. e.* the GOOD. This, as it considers these laws in relation to man as an individual, or in relation to man as a member of society, will be divided into two branches, — Ethics and Politics; and these again admit of various subdivisions.

So much for those parts of the Philosophy of Mind, which are conversant about Phænomena, and about Laws. The

Third great branch of this philosophy is that which is engaged in the deduction of Inferences or Results.

Ontology, or Metaphysics Proper. — In the First branch, — the Phænomenology of mind, — philosophy is properly limited to the facts afforded in consciousness, considered exclusively in themselves. But these facts may be such as not only to be objects of knowledge in themselves, but likewise to furnish us with grounds of inference to something out of themselves. As effects, and effects of a certain character, they may enable us to infer the analogous character of their unknown causes; as phænomena, and phænomena of peculiar qualities, they may warrant us in drawing many conclusions regarding the distinctive character of that unknown principle, of that unknown substance, of which they are the manifestations. Although, therefore, existence be only revealed to us in phænomena, and though we can, therefore, have only a relative knowledge either of mind or of matter; still, by inference and analogy, we may legitimately attempt to rise above the mere appearances which experience and observation afford. Thus, for example, the existence of God and the Immortality of the Soul are not given us as phænomena, as objects of immediate knowledge; yet, if the phænomena actually given do necessarily require, for their rational explanation, the hypotheses of immortality and of God, we are assuredly entitled, from the existence of the former, to infer the reality of the latter. Now, the science conversant about all such inferences of unknown being from its known manifestations, is called ONTOLOGY, or METAPHYSICS PROPER. We might call it INFERENTIAL PSYCHOLOGY.

The following is a tabular view of the distribution of Philosophy as here proposed:

Mind or Consciousness affords	Facts, — Phænomenology, Empirical Psychology.	Cognitions.	
		Feelings.	
		Conative Powers (Will and Desire).	
	Laws, — Nomology, Rational Psychology.	Cognitions, — Logic	
		Feelings, — Æsthetic.	
		Conative Powers.	Moral Philosophy.
			Political Philosophy.
	Results, — Ontology, Inferential Psychology	Being of God.	
		Immortality of the Soul, etc	

In this distribution of the philosophical sciences, you will observe that I take little account of the celebrated division of philosophy into Speculative and Practical, which I have already explained to you, for I call only one minor division of philosophy practical, — namely, the Nomology of the Conative powers, not because that science is not equally theoretical with any other, but simply because these powers are properly called practical, as tending to practice or overt action.

Distribution of Philosophy in the Universities. — The subjects assigned to the various chairs of the Philosophical Faculty, in the different Universities of Europe, were not calculated upon any comprehensive view of the parts of philosophy, and of their natural connection. The universities were founded when the Aristotelic philosophy was the dominant, or rather the exclusive, system, and the parts distributed to the different classes, in the faculty of Arts or Philosophy, were regulated by the contents of certain of the Aristotelic books, and by the order in which they were studied. Of these, there were always Four great divisions. There was first, Logic, in relation to the Organon of Aristotle; secondly, Metaphysics, relative to his books under that title; thirdly, Moral Philosophy, relative to his Ethics, Politics, and Economics; and, fourthly, Physics, relative to his Physics, and the collection of treatises styled in the schools the *Parva Naturalia.* But every university had not a full complement of classes, that is, did not devote a separate year to each of the four subjects of study; and, accordingly, in those seats of learning where three years formed the curriculum of philosophy, two of these branches were combined. In the university of Edinburgh, Logic and Metaphysics were taught in the same year; in others, Metaphysics and Moral Philosophy were conjoined; and, when the old practice was abandoned of the several Regents or Professors carrying on their students through every department, the two branches which had been taught in the same year were assigned to the same chair. What is most curious in the matter is this, — Aristotle's treatise *On the Soul* being (along with his lesser treatises on *Memory and Reminiscence*, on *Sense and its Objects*, etc.) included in the *Parva Naturalia*, and, he having declared that the consideration of the soul was part of the philosophy of nature, the science of Mind was always treated along with Physics. The professors of Natural Philosophy have, however, long abandoned the philosophy of mind, and this branch has been, as more appropriate to their departments, taught both by the Professors of Moral Philosophy and by the Professors of Logic and Metaphysics; — for you are not to suppose that metaphysics and psychology are, though vulgarly used as synonymous expressions, by any means the same.

In this work, we have nothing to do with Practical Philosophy, — that is, Ethics, Politics, Economics. But with this exception, there is no other branch of philosophy which does not fall naturally within our sphere.

CHAPTER VI.

DEFINITION OF PSYCHOLOGY; RELATIVITY OF HUMAN KNOWLEDGE; EXPLICATION OF TERMS.

PSYCHOLOGY, or the Philosophy of the Human Mind, strictly so denominated, is the science conversant about the *phænomena*, or *modifications*, or *states* of the *Mind*, or *Conscious-Subject*, or *Soul*, or *Spirit*, or *Self*, or *Ego*.

In this definition, you will observe that I have purposely accumulated a variety of expressions, in order that I might have the earliest opportunity of making you accurately acquainted with their meaning; for they are terms of vital importance and frequent use in philosophy. — Before, therefore, proceeding further, I shall pause a moment in explanation of the terms in which this definition is expressed. Without restricting myself to the following order, I shall consider the word *Psychology;* the correlative terms *subject* and *substance*, *phænomenon*, *modification*, *state*, etc., and, at the same time, take occasion to explain another correlative, the expression *object;* and, finally, the words *mind*, *soul*, *spirit*, *self*, and *ego*.

Indeed, after considering these terms, it may not be improper to take up, in one series, the philosophical expressions of principal importance and most ordinary occurrence, in order to render less frequent the necessity of interrupting the course of our procedure, to afford the requisite verbal explanations.

The use of the term Psychology vindicated. — The term *Psychology*, is a Greek compound, its elements ψυχή, signifying *soul* or *mind*, and λόγος, signifying *discourse* or *doctrine*. Psychology, therefore, is the *discourse* or *doctrine treating of the human mind.* But, though composed of Greek elements, it is, like the greater number of the compounds of λόγος, of modern combination. I may be asked, — why use an exotic, a technical name? Why not be contented with the more popular terms, *Philosophy of Mind*, or *Mental Philosophy*, — *Science of Mind*, or *Mental Science?* — expressions by which this department of knowledge has been usually designated by those who, in Scotland, have cultivated it with the most distinguished success. To this there are several answers. In the *first* place, philosophy itself, and all, or almost all, its branches, have, in our language, received Greek technical denominations; — why not also the most important of all, the science of mind? In the *second* place, the term *psychology* is now, and has long been, the ordinary expression for the doctrine of mind in the philosophical language of every other European nation. Nay, in point of fact, it is now naturalized in English, *psychology* and *psychological* having of late years come into common use; and their employment is warranted by the authority of the best English writers. But these are reasons in themselves of comparatively little moment: they tend merely to show that, if otherwise expedient, the nomenclature is permissible; and that it is expedient, the following reasons will prove. For, in the *third* place, it is always of consequence, for the sake of precision, to be able to use one word instead of a plurality of words, — especially where the frequent occurrence of a descriptive appellation might occasion tedium, distraction, and disgust; and this must necessarily occur in the treatment of any science, if the science be able to possess no single name vicarious of its definition. In this respect, therefore, *Psychology* is preferable to *Philosophy of Mind*. But, in the *fourth* place, even if the employment of the description for the name could, in this instance, be tolerated when used substantively, what are we to do when we require (which we do unceasingly) to use the denomination of the science adjectively? For example, I have occasion to say a *psychological fact*, a *psychological law*, a *psychological curiosity*, etc. How can we express these by the descriptive appellation? A psychological fact may indeed be styled "a fact considered relatively to the philosophy of the human mind," — a psychological law may be called "a law by which the mental phænomena are governed," —

a psychological curiosity may be rendered — by what, I really do not know. But how miserably weak, awkward, tedious, and affected, is the commutation when it can be made; not only do the vivacity and precision of the original evaporate, the meaning itself is not even adequately conveyed. But this defect is still more manifestly shown, when we wish to place in contrast the matters proper to this science, with the matters proper to others. Thus, for example, to say, — this is a *psychological*, not a *physiological* doctrine — this is a *psychological* observation, not a *logical* inference. How is the contradistinction to be expressed by a periphrasis? It is impossible; — for the intensity of the contrast consists, first, in the two opposite terms being single words, and second, in their being both even technical and precise Greek. This necessity has, accordingly, compelled the adoption of the terms *psychology* and *psychological* into the philosophical nomenclature of every nation, even where the same necessity did not vindicate the employment of a non-vernacular expression. Thus in Germany, though the native language affords a facility of composition only inferior to the Greek, and though it possesses a word (*Seelenlehre*) exactly correspondent to ψυχολογία, yet because this substantive did not easily allow of an adjective flexion, the Greek terms, substantive and adjective, were both adopted, and have been long in as familiar use in the Empire, as the terms geography and geographical, — physiology and physiological, are with us.

Other terms inappropriate. — What I have now said may suffice to show that, to supply necessity, we must introduce these words into our philosophical vocabulary. But the propriety of this is still further shown by the inauspicious attempts that have been recently made on the name of the science. Dr. Brown, in the very title of the abridgment of his lectures on mental philosophy, has styled this philosophy, "*The Physiology of the Human Mind;*" and I have also seen two English publications of modern date, — one entitled the "*Physics of the Soul,*" the other "*Intellectual Physics.*" Now the term *nature* (φύσις, *natura*), though in common language of a more extensive meaning, has, in general, by philosophers, been applied appropriately to denote the laws which govern the appearances of the material universe. And the words Physiology and Physics have been specially limited to denote sciences conversant about these laws as regulating the phænomena of organic and inorganic bodies. The empire of nature is the empire of a mechanical necessity; the necessity of nature, in philosophy, stands opposed to the liberty of intelligence. Those, accordingly, who do not allow that mind is matter, — who hold that there is in man a principle of action superior to the determinations of a physical necessity, a brute or blind fate, — must regard the application of the terms Physiology and Physics to the doctrine of the mind as either singularly inappropriate, or as significant of a false hypothesis in regard to the character of the thinking principle.

Use and derivation of Spirit, Soul. — Mr. Stewart objects to the term *Spirit*, as seeming to imply an hypothesis concerning the nature and essence of the sentient or thinking principle, altogether unconnected with our conclusions in regard to its phænomena, and their general laws; and, for the same reason, he is disposed to object to the words Pneumatology and Psychology, the former of which was introduced by the schoolmen. In regard to *Spirit* and *Pneumatology*, Mr. Stewart's criticism is perfectly just. They are unnecessary; and, besides the etymological metaphor, they are associated with a certain theological limitation, which spoils them as expressions of philosophical generality.* But this is not the case with *Psychology*. For though, in its etymology, it is, like almost all metaphysical terms, originally of physical application, still this had been long forgotten even by the Greeks; and, if we were to reject philosophical expressions on this account, we should be left without any terms for the mental phænomena at all. The term *soul*

* The terms *Psychology* and *Pneumatology*, or *Pneumatic*, are not equivalents. The latter word was used for the doctrine of spirit in general, which was subdivided into three branches, as it treated of the three orders of spiritual substances, — God, — Angels and Devils, — and Man. Thus —

Pneumatologia or Pneumatica,
1. Theologia (Naturalis).
2. Angelographia, Dæmonologia.
3. Psychologia.

(and what I say of the term *soul* is true of the term *spirit*), though in this country less employed than the term *mind*, may be regarded as another synonym for the unknown basis of the mental phænomena. Like nearly all the words significant of the internal world, there is here a metaphor borrowed from the external; and this is the case not merely in one, but, as far as we can trace the analogy, in all languages. You are aware that ψυχή, the Greek term for soul, comes from ψύχω, *I breathe* or *blow*, — as πνεῦμα in Greek, and *spiritus* in Latin, from verbs of the same signification. In like manner, *anima* and *animus* are words which, though in Latin they have lost their primary signification, and are only known in their secondary or metaphorical, yet in their original physical meaning, are preserved in the Greek ἄνεμος, *wind* or *air*. The English *soul*, and the German *Seele*, come from a Gothic root *saivala*, which signifies to *storm*. *Ghost*, the old English word for *spirit* in general, and so used in our English version of the Scriptures, is the same as the German *Geist*, and is derived from *Gas*, or *Gescht*, which signifies *air*. In like manner, the two words in Hebrew for soul or spirit, *nephesh* and *ruach*, are derivatives of a root which means *to breathe;* and in Sanscrit, the word *atmā* (analogous to the Greek ἀτμός, *vapor* or *air*) signifies both *mind* and *wind* or *air*. *Sapientia*, in Latin, originally meant only the power of tasting; as *sagacitas* only the faculty of scenting. In French, *penser* comes from the Latin *pendere*, through *pensare* to weigh, and the terms, *attentio*, *intentio* (*entendement*), *comprehensio*, *apprehensio*, *penetratio*, *understanding*, etc., are just so many bodily actions transferred to the expression of mental energies.

In the second place, I said that Psychology is conversant about the *phænomena* of the thinking *subject*, etc.; and I now proceed to expound the import of the correlative terms *phænomenon*, *subject*, etc.

Correlative terms illustrated by the relativity of human knowledge. — But the meaning of these terms will be best illustrated by now stating and explaining the great axiom, that all human knowledge, consequently that all human philosophy, is only of the relative or phænomenal. In this proposition, the term *relative* is opposed to the term *absolute*; and, therefore, in saying that we know only the relative, I virtually assert that we know nothing absolute, — nothing existing absolutely; that is, in and for itself, and without relation to us and our faculties. I shall illustrate this by its application. Our knowledge is either of matter or of mind. Now, what is matter? What do we know of matter? Matter, or body, is to us the name either of something known, or of something unknown. In so far as matter is a name for something known, it means that which appears to us under the forms of extension, solidity, divisibility, figure, motion, roughness, smoothness, color, heat, cold, etc.; in short, it is a common name for a certain series, or aggregate, or complement of appearances or phænomena manifested in coexistence.

But as the phænomena appear only in conjunction, we are compelled by the constitution of our nature to think them conjoined in and by something; and as they are phænomena, we cannot think them the phænomena of nothing, but must regard them as the properties or qualities of something that is extended, solid, figured, etc. But this something, absolutely and in itself, — *i. e.* considered apart from its phænomena, — is to us as zero. It is only in its qualities, only in its effects, in its relative or phænomenal existence, that it is cognizable or conceivable; and it is only by a law of thought, which compels us to think something, absolute and unknown, as the basis or condition of the relative and known, that this something obtains a kind of incomprehensible reality to us. Now, that which manifests its qualities, — in other words, that in which the appearing causes inhere, that to which they belong, is called their *subject*, or *substance*, or *substratum*. To this subject of the phænomena of extension, solidity, etc., the term *matter* or *material substance* is commonly given; and, therefore, as contradistinguished from these qualities, it is the name of something unknown and inconceivable.

The same is true in regard to the term *mind*. In so far as mind is the common name for the states of knowing, willing, feeling, desiring, etc., of which I am conscious, it is only the

8*

name for a certain series of connected phænomena or qualities, and, consequently, expresses only what is known. But in so far as it denotes that subject or substance in which the phænomena of knowing, willing, etc., inhere, — something behind or under these phænomena, — it expresses what, in itself, or in its absolute existence, is unknown.

Thus, mind and matter, as known or knowable, are only two different series of phænomena or qualities; mind and matter, as unknown and unknowable, are the two substances in which these two different series of phænomena or qualities are supposed to inhere. The existence of an unknown substance is only an inference we are compelled to make, from the existence of known phænomena; and the distinction of two substances is only inferred from the seeming incompatibility of the two series of phænomena to coinhere in one.

Our whole knowledge of mind and matter is thus, as we have said, only relative; of existence, absolutely and in itself, we know nothing; and we may say of man what Virgil says of Æneas, contemplating in the prophetic sculpture of his shield the future glories of Rome —

"Rerumque ignarus, imagine gaudet."

Testimonies to the relativity of human knowledge. — This is, indeed, a truth, in the admission of which philosophers, in general, have been singularly harmonious; and the praise that has been lavished on Dr. Reid for this observation, is wholly unmerited. In fact, I am hardly aware of the philosopher who has not proceeded on the supposition, and there are few who have not explicitly enounced the observation. It is only since Reid's death that certain speculators have arisen, who have obtained celebrity by their attempt to found philosophy on an immediate knowledge of the absolute or unconditioned. I shall quote to you a few examples of this general recognition, as they happen to occur to my recollection; and, in order to manifest the better its universality, I purposely overlook the testimonies of a more modern philosophy.

Aristotle, among many similar observations, remarks in regard to matter, that it is incognizable in itself; while in regard to mind he says, "that the intellect does not know itself directly, but only indirectly, in knowing other things;" and he defines the soul from its phænomena, "the principle by which we live, and move, and perceive, and understand." St. Augustin, the most philosophical of the Christian fathers, admirably says of body, — "Materiam cognoscendo ignorari, et ignorando cognosci;" ["By assuming that we know matter, we betray our ignorance of it; and it is only by admitting this ignorance, that we can be said to know it;"] and of mind, — "Mens se cognoscit cognoscendo se vivere, se meminisse, se intelligere, se velle, cogitare, scire, judicare." ["The mind knows itself only by knowing that it lives, remembers, understands, wills, thinks, knows, and judges."] "Non incurrunt," says Melanchthon, "ipsæ substantiæ in oculos, sed vestitæ et ornatæ accidentibus; hoc est, non possumus, in hac vita, acie oculorum perspicere ipsas substantias: sed utcunque, ex accidentibus quæ in sensus exteriores incurrunt, ratiocinamur, quomodo inter se differant substantiæ." ["The substances themselves are not exposed to sight, but only so far they are covered and adorned with their attributes; that is, we are not able, in this life, to behold the substances themselves; but from the phenomena which are manifest to our external senses, we somehow infer the distinguishing peculiarities of the substances to which the phenomena belong."]

All relative existence is not relative to us. — Thus, our knowledge is of partial and relative existence only, seeing that existence in itself, or absolute existence,* is no object of knowledge. But it does not follow that all relative existence is relative *to us;* that all that can be known, even by a limited intelligence, is actually cognizable by us. We must, therefore, more precisely limit our sphere of knowledge, by adding, that all we know is known only under the special conditions of our faculties. This is a truth likewise generally acknowledged. "Man," says Protagoras, "is the measure of the universe," — a truth

* Absolute in two senses: 1°, As opposed to partial; 2°, As opposed to relative

which Bacon has well expressed: ["All perceptions, as well of the senses as of the mind, are conformed to the nature of the percipient individual, and not to the true nature of the universe; and the human understanding is like a false mirror, which distorts and discolors the nature of things, by mingling its own nature with it."] "In perception," says Kant, "every thing is known according to the constitution of our faculty of sense."

This principle has two branches. — Now this principle, in which philosophers of the most opposite opinions equally concur, divides itself into two branches. In the *first* place, it would be unphilosophical to conclude that the properties of existence necessarily are, *in number*, only as the number of our faculties of apprehending them; or, in the *second*, that the properties known, are known *in their native purity*, and without addition or modification from our organs of sense, or our capaci ties of intelligence. I shall illustrate these in their order.

In regard to the first assertion, it is evident that nothing exists for us, except in so far as it is known to us, and that nothing is known to us, except certain properties or modes of existence, which are relative or analogous to our faculties. Beyond these modes we know, and can assert, the reality of no existence. But if, on the one hand, we are not entitled to assert, as actually existent, except what we know; neither, on the other, are we warranted in denying, as possibly existent, what we do not know. The universe may be conceived as a polygon of a thousand, or a hundred thousand, sides or facets, — and each of these sides or facets may be conceived as representing one special mode of existence. Now, of these thousand sides or modes, all may be equally essential, but three or four only may be turned towards us, or be analogous to our organs. One side or facet of the universe, as holding a relation to the organ of sight, is the mode of luminous or visible existence; another, as proportional to the organ of hearing, is the mode of sonorous or audible existence; and so on. But if every eye to see, if every ear to hear, were annihilated, the mode of existence to which these organs now stand in relation, — that which could be seen, that which could be heard, would still remain; and if the intelligences, reduced to the three senses of touch, smell, and taste, were then to assert the impossibility of any modes of being except those to which these three senses were analogous, the procedure would not be more unwarranted, than if we now ventured to deny the possible reality of other modes of material existence than those to the perception of which our five senses are accommodated. I will illustrate this by an hypothetical parallel. Let us suppose a block of marble, on which there are four different inscriptions, — in Greek, in Latin, in Persic, and in Hebrew; and that four travellers approach, each able to read only the inscription in his native tongue. The Greek is delighted with the information the marble affords him of the siege of Troy. The Roman finds interesting matter regarding the expulsion of the kings. The Persian deciphers an oracle of Zoroaster. And the Jew is surprised by a commemoration of the Exodus. Here, as each inscription exists or is significant only to him who possesses the corresponding language; so the several modes of existence are manifested only to those intelligences who possess the corresponding organs. And as each of the four readers would be rash, if he maintained that the marble could be significant only as significant to him, so should we be rash, were we to hold that the universe had no other phases of being than the few that are turned towards our faculties, and which our five senses enable us to perceive.

Before leaving this subject, it is perhaps proper to observe, that had we faculties equal in number to all the possible modes of existence, whether of mind or matter, still would our knowledge of mind or matter be only relative. If material existence could exhibit ten thousand phænomena, and if we possessed ten thousand senses to apprehend these ten thousand phænomena of material existence, — of existence absolutely and in itself, we should be then as ignorant as we are at present.

The properties of existence not known in their native purity. — But the consideration that our actual faculties of knowledge are probably wholly inadequate in number to the possible modes of being, is of comparatively less importance than the other consideration to which we now proceed, — that whatever we know is *not known as it is, but only as it seems to us to be;* for it is of less importance that our knowledge should be limited, than that our knowledge should be pure. It is, therefore, of the highest moment that we should be aware, that what we know is not a simple relation apprehended between the object known and the subject knowing, — but that every knowledge is a sum made up of several elements, and that the great business of philosophy is to analyze and discriminate these elements, and to determine from whence these contributions have been derived. I shall explain what I mean by an example. In the perception of an external object, the mind does not know it in immediate relation to itself, but mediately, in relation to the material organs of sense. If, therefore, we were to throw these organs out of consideration, and did not take into account what they contribute to, and how they modify our knowledge of that object, it is evident that our conclusion in regard to the nature of external perception would be erroneous. Again, an object of perception may not even stand in immediate relation to the organ of sense, but may make its impression on that organ through an intervening medium. Now, if this medium be thrown out of account, and if it be not considered that the real external object is the sum of all that externally contributes to affect the sense, we shall, in like manner, run into error. For example, I see a book, — I see that book through an external medium (what that medium is, we do not now inquire), — and I see it through my organ of sight, the eye. Now, as the full object presented to the mind (observe that I say *the mind*), in perception, is an object compounded of (1.) the external object emitting or reflecting light, *i. e.* modifying the external medium, of (2.) this external medium, and of (3.) the living organ of sense, in their mutual relation, — let us suppose, in the example I have taken, that the full or adequate object perceived is equal to twelve, and that this amount is made up of three several parts, — of four contributed by the book, — of four contributed by all that intervenes between the book and the organ, and of four contributed by the living organ itself.

I use this illustration to show, that the phænomenon of the external object is not presented immediately to the mind, but is known by it only as modified through certain intermediate agencies; and to show that sense itself may be a source of error, if we do not analyze and distinguish what elements, in an act of perception, belong to the outward reality, what to the outward medium, and what to the action of sense itself. But this source of error is not limited to our perceptions; and we are liable to be deceived, not merely by not distinguishing in an act of knowledge what is contributed by sense, but by not distinguishing what is contributed by the mind itself. This is the most difficult and important function of philosophy; and the greater number of its higher problems arise in the attempt to determine the shares to which the knowing subject, and the object known, may pretend in the total act of cognition. For according as we attribute a larger or a smaller proportion to each, we either run into the extremes of Idealism and Materialism, or maintain an equilibrium between the two.

In what sense human knowledge is relative. — From what has been said, you will be able, I hope, to understand what is meant by the proposition, that all our knowledge is only relative. It is relative, 1°, Because existence is not cognizable absolutely and in itself, but only in special modes; 2°, Because these modes can be known only if they stand in a certain relation to our faculties; and 3°, Because the modes thus relative to our faculties are presented to, and known by, the mind only under modifications determined by these faculties themselves.

Two series of expressions applied to human knowledge. — This general doctrine being premised, it will be proper now to take some special notice of the several terms significant of the relative nature of our knowledge. And here there are two opposite series of expressions, — 1°, Those which denote the relative and the known; 2°, Those which denote the absolute and the unknown. Of the former class, are the words *phænomenon*, *mode*, *modification*, *state*, — words which are employed in the definition of Psychology; and to these may be added the analogous terms, — *quality*, *property*, *attribute*, *accident*. Of the latter class, — that is, the absolute and the unknown, — is the word *subject*, which we have to explain as an element of the definition, and its analogous expressions, *substance* and *substratum*. These opposite classes cannot be explained apart; for, as each is correlative of the other, each can be comprehended only in and through its correlative.

The term *subject* (*subjectum*, *ὑπόστασις*, *ὑποκείμενον*) is used to denote the unknown basis which lies under the various phænomena or properties of which we become aware, whether in our internal or external experience. In the more recent philosophy, especially in that of Germany, it has, however, been principally employed to denote the basis of the various mental phænomena; but of this special signification we are hereafter more particularly to speak.

The word *substance* (*substantia*) may be employed in two, but two kindred, meanings. It may be used either to denote that which exists absolutely and of itself; in this sense, it may be viewed as derived from *subsistendo*, and as meaning *ens per se subsistens;* or it may be viewed as the basis of attributes, in which sense it may be regarded as derived from *substando*, and as meaning *id quod substat accidentibus*, like the Greek *ὑπόστασις*, *ὑποκείμενον*. In either case, it will, however, signify the same thing viewed in a different aspect. In the former meaning, it is considered in contrast to, and independent of, its attributes; in the latter, as conjoined with these, and as affording them the condition of existence. In different relations, a thing may be at once considered as a *substance*, and as an *attribute*, *quality*, or *mode*. This paper is a substance, in relation to the attribute of white; but it is itself a mode in relation to the substance, matter. Substance is thus a term for the substratum we are obliged to think to all that we variously denominate a *mode*, a *state*, a *quality*, an *attribute*, a *property*, an accident, a *phænomenon*, an *appearance*, etc. These, though expressions generically the same, are, however, used with specific distinctions. The terms *mode*, *state*, *quality*, *attribute*, *property*, *accident*, are employed in reference to a substance, as existing; the terms *phænomenon*, *appearance*, etc. in reference to it, as known. But each of these expressions has also its peculiar signification. A *mode* is the manner of the existence of a thing. Take, for example, a piece of wax. The wax may be round, or square, or of any other definite figure; it may also be solid or fluid. Its existence in any of these modes is not essential; it may change from one to the other without any substantial alteration. As the mode cannot exist without a substance, we can afford to it only a secondary or precarious existence in relation to the substance, to which we accord the privilege of existing by itself, *per se existere;* but though the substance be not astricted to any particular mode of existence, we must not suppose that it can exist, or, at least, be conceived by us to exist, in none. All modes are, therefore, variable states; and though some mode is necessary for the existence of a thing, any individual mode is accidental. The word *modification* is properly the bringing a thing into a certain mode of existence, but it is very commonly employed for the mode of existence itself. *State* is a term nearly synonymous with *mode,* but of a meaning more extensive, as not exclusively limited to the mutable and contingent.

Quality is, likewise, a word of a wider signification, for there are essential and accidental qualities.* The *essential qualities* of a thing are those aptitudes, those manners of existence and action, which it cannot lose without ceasing to be. For example, in man, the faculties of sense and intelligence; in body, the dimensions of length, breadth, and thickness; in God, the attributes of eternity, omniscience, omnipotence, etc. By *accidental qualities,* are meant those aptitudes and manners of existence and action, which substances have at one time and not at another; or which they have always, but may lose without ceasing to be. For example, of the transitory class are the whiteness of a wall, the health which we enjoy, the fineness of the weather, etc. Of the permanent class are the gravity of bodies, the periodical movement of the planets, etc.

* The term *quality* should, in strictness, be confined to accidental attributes.

The term *attribute* is a word properly convertible with *quality*, for every quality is an attribute, and every attribute is a quality; but, in our language, custom has introduced a certain distinction in their application. Attribute is considered as a word of loftier significance, and is, therefore, conveniently limited to qualities of a higher application. Thus, for example, it would be felt as indecorous to speak of the qualities of God, and as ridiculous to talk of the attributes of matter.

Property is correctly a synonym for peculiar quality;* but it is frequently used as coextensive with quality in general. *Accident*, on the contrary, is an abbreviated expression for accidental or contingent quality.

Phænomenon is the Greek word for *that which appears*, and may, therefore, be translated by *appearance*. There is, however, a distinction to be noticed. In the first place, the employment of the Greek term shows that it is used in a strict and philosophical application. In the second place, the English name is associated with a certain secondary or implied meaning, which, in some degree, renders it inappropriate as a precise and definite expression. For the term *appearance* is used to denote not only that which reveals itself to our observation, as existent, but also to signify that which only seems to be, in contrast to that which truly is. There is thus not merely a certain vagueness in the word, but it even involves a kind of contradiction to the sense in which it is used when employed for *phænomenon*. In consequence of this, the term *phænomenon* has been naturalized in our language, as a philosophical substitute for the term *appearance*.

* In the older and Aristotelian sense of the term. By the later Logicians, the term *property* was less correctly used to denote a necessary quality, whether peculiar or not. — English Ed.

CHAPTER VII.

EXPLICATION OF TERMS CONTINUED.

Recapitulation. — In the last chapter, I illustrated the principle, that all our knowledge of mind and matter is merely relative. We know, and can know, nothing absolutely and in itself; all that we know is *existence in certain special forms or modes*, and these, likewise, only in so far as they may be analogous to our faculties. We may suppose existence to have a thousand modes; — but these thousand modes are all to us as zero, unless we possess faculties accommodated to their apprehension. But were the number of our faculties coextensive with the modes of being, — had we, for each of these thousand modes, a separate organ competent to make it known to us, — still would our whole knowledge be, as it is at present, only of the relative. Of existence, absolutely and in itself, we should then be as ignorant as we are now. We should still apprehend existence only in certain special modes, — only in certain relations to our faculties of knowledge.

These relative modes, whether belonging to the world without, or to the world within, are, under different points of view, and different limitations, known under various names, as *qualities, properties, essence, accidents, phænomena, manifestations, appearances*, and so forth; — whereas the unknown something of which they are the modes, — the unknown ground, which affords them support, is usually termed their *substance* or *subject*. *Substance* (*substantia*), I noticed, is considered either in contrast to its accidents, as *res per se subsistens*, or in connection with them, as *id quod substat accidentibus*. It, therefore, comprehends both the Greek terms *οὐσία* and *ὑποκείμενον*, — *οὐσία* being equivalent to *substantia* in the meaning of *ens per se sub-*

sistens; — *ὑποκείμενον* to it, as *id quod substat accidentibus.* The term *subject* is used only for substance in its second meaning, and thus corresponds to *ὑποκείμενον;* its literal signification is, as its etymology expresses, that which lies, or is placed, *under* the phænomena.

Three different errors regarding Substance. — I at present avoid entering into the metaphysics of substance and phænomenon. I shall only observe, in general, that philosophers have frequently fallen into one or other of three different errors. *Some* have denied the reality of any unknown ground of the known phænomena; and have maintained that mind and matter have no substantial existence, but are merely the two complements of two series of associated qualities. This doctrine is, however, altogether futile. It belies the veracity of our primary beliefs; it leaves unsatisfied the strongest necessities of our intellectual nature; it admits as a fact that the phænomena are connected, but allows no cause explanatory of the fact of their connection. *Others,* again, have fallen into an opposite error. They have endeavored to speculate concerning the nature of the unknown grounds of the phænomena of mind and matter, apart from the phænomena, and have, accordingly, transcended the legitimate sphere of philosophy. *A third party* have taken some one, or more, of the phænomena themselves as the basis or substratum of the others. Thus Descartes, at least as understood and followed by Malebranche and others of his disciples, made *thought* or consciousness convertible with *the substance of mind;* and Bishops Brown and Law, with Dr. Watts, constituted *solidity* and *extension* into *the substance of body.* This theory is, however, liable to all the objections which may be alleged against the first.

I defined Psychology, the science conversant about the *phænomena* of the *mind,* or *conscious-subject,* or *self,* or *ego.* The former parts of the definition have been explained; the terms *mind, conscious-subject, self,* and *ego,* come now to be considered. These are all only expressions for the unknown basis of the mental phænomena, viewed, however, in different relations.

What we mean by mind. — Of these the word *mind* is the

first. In regard to the etymology of this term, it is obscure and doubtful; perhaps, indeed, none of the attempts to trace it to its origin are successful. It seems to hold an analogy with the Latin *mens*, and both are probably derived from the same common root. This root, which is lost in the European languages of Scytho-Indian origin, is probably preserved in the Sanscrit *mena, to know* or *understand.* The Greek *νοῦς, intelligence*, is, in like manner, derived from a verb of precisely the same meaning (*νοέω*). The word *mind* is of more limited signification than the term *soul.* In the Greek philosophy, the term *ψυχὴ, soul*, comprehends, besides the sensitive and rational principle in man, the principle of organic life, both in the animal and vegetable kingdoms; and, in Christian theology, it is likewise used, in contrast to *πνεῦμα* or *spirit*, in a vaguer and more extensive signification.

Since Descartes limited Psychology to the domain of consciousness, the term *mind* has been rigidly employed for the self-knowing principle alone. Mind, therefore, is to be understood as the subject of the various internal phænomena of which we are conscious, or that subject of which consciousness is the general phænomenon. Consciousness is, in fact, to the mind what extension is to matter or body. Though both are phænomena, yet both are essential qualities; for we can neither conceive mind without consciousness, nor body without extension. Mind can be defined only *a posteriori*, — that is, only from its manifestations. What it is in itself, that is, apart from its manifestations, — we, philosophically, know nothing, and, accordingly, what we mean by mind is simply *that which perceives, thinks, feels, wills, desires*, etc. Mind, with us, is thus nearly coextensive with the Rational and Animal souls of Aristotle; for the faculty of voluntary motion, which is a function of the animal soul in the Peripatetic doctrine, ought not, as is generally done, to be excluded from the phænomena of consciousness and mind.

Consciousness and Conscious-subject. — The next term to be considered is *conscious-subject.* And first, what is it to be conscious? Without anticipating the discussion relative to consciousness, as the fundamental function of intelligence, I may, at present, simply indicate to you what an act of consciousness denotes. This act is of the most elementary character; it is the condition of all knowledge; I cannot, therefore, define it to you; but, as you are all familiar with the thing, it is easy to enable you to connect the thing with the word. I know, — I desire, — I feel. What is it that is common to all these? *Knowing* and *desiring* and *feeling* are not the same, and may be distinguished. But they all agree in one fundamental condition. Can I know, without *knowing* that I know? Can I desire, without *knowing* that I desire? Can I feel, without *knowing* that I feel? This is impossible. Now this knowing that I know or desire or feel, — this common condition of self-knowledge, is precisely what is denominated Consciousness.

[Consciousness is a knowledge *solely of what is now and here present* to the mind. . . . Again, Consciousness is a knowledge of *all* that is now and here present to the mind; every immediate object of cognition is thus an object of consciousness, and every intuitive cognition itself is simply a special form of consciousness.

Consciousness comprehends every cognitive act; in other words, whatever we are not conscious of, that we do not know. . . . The *actual* modifications — the *present acts* and affections of the Ego, are objects of immediate cognition, as themselves objects of Consciousness.] — *Diss. supp. to Reid.*

So much at present for the adjective of *conscious;* now for the substantive, *subject,* — *conscious-subject.* Though consciousness be the condition of all internal phænomena, still it is itself only a phænomenon; and, therefore, supposes a subject in which it inheres; — that is, supposes something that is conscious, — something that manifests itself as conscious. And, since consciousness comprises within its sphere the whole phænomena of mind, the expression *conscious-subject* is a brief, but comprehensive, definition of mind itself.

I have already informed you of the general meaning of the word *subject* in its philosophical application, — namely, the unknown basis of phænomenal or manifested existence. It is thus, in its application, common equally to the external and to the internal worlds. But the philosophers of mind have, in a manner, usurped and appropriated this expression to themselves. Accordingly, in their hands, the phrases *conscious or thinking subject*, and *subject* simply, mean precisely the same thing; and custom has prevailed so far, that, in psychological discussions, *the subject* is a term now currently employed, throughout Europe, for the *mind* or *thinking principle*.

Use of the term Subject vindicated. — The question here occurs, what is the reason of this employment? If *mind* and *subject* are only convertible terms, why multiply synonyms? Why exchange a precise and proximate expression for a vague and abstract generality? The question is pertinent, and merits a reply; for unless it can be shown that the word is necessary, its introduction cannot possibly be vindicated. Now, the utility of this expression is founded on two circumstances. The first, that it affords an adjective; the second, that the terms *subject* and *subjective* have opposing relatives in the terms *object* and *objective*, so that the two pairs of words together enable us to designate the primary and most important analysis and antithesis of philosophy, in a more precise and emphatic manner than can be done by any other technical expressions. This will require some illustration.

Terms Subjective and Objective. — *Subject*, we have seen, is a term for that in which the phænomena revealed to our observation inhere; — what the schoolmen have designated the *materia in qua*. Limited to the mental phænomena, *subject*, therefore, denotes the mind itself; and *subjective*, that which belongs to, or proceeds from, the thinking subject. *Object*, on the other hand, is a term for that about which the knowing subject is conversant, what the schoolmen have styled the *materia circa quam*; while *objective* means that which belongs to, or proceeds from, the object known, and not from the subject knowing; and thus denotes what is real in opposition to what is ideal, — what exists in nature, in contrast to what exists merely in the thought of the individual. All knowledge is a relation — a relation between that which knows (in scholastic language, the *subject* in which knowledge inheres), and that which is known (in scholastic language, the *object* about which knowledge is conversant); and the contents of every act of knowledge are made up of elements, and regulated by laws, proceeding partly from its object and partly from its subject. Now philosophy proper is principally and primarily the *science of knowledge;* its first and most important problem being to determine — *What can we know?* that is, what are the conditions of our knowing, whether these lie in the nature of the object, or in the nature of the subject, of knowledge?

[But Philosophy being the *Science of knowledge;* and the science of knowledge supposing, in its most fundamental and thorough-going analysis, the distinction of the *subject and object of knowledge;* it is evident, that, *to philosophy*, the *subject of knowledge* would be, by preëminence, *The Subject*, and the *object of knowledge*, by preëminence, *The Object.* It was, therefore, natural that the *object* and the *objective*, the *subject* and the *subjective*, should be employed by philosophers as simple terms, compendiously to denote the grand discrimination about which philosophy was constantly employed, and which no others could be found so precisely and promptly to express. In fact, had it not been for the special meaning given to *objective* in the Schools, their employment in this, their natural relation, would probably have been of a much earlier date; not, however, that they are void of ambiguity, and have not been often abusively employed. This arises from the following circumstance: — The *subject* of knowledge is, exclusively, the Ego or conscious mind. *Subject* and *subjective*, considered in themselves, are therefore little liable to equivocation. But, on the other hand, the *object* of knowledge is not necessarily a phænomenon of the Non-ego; for the phænomena of the Ego itself constitute as veritable, though not so various and prominent, objects of cognition, as the phænomena of the Non-ego.

Subjective and *objective* do not, therefore, thoroughly and adequately discriminate that which *belongs to mind*, and that which *belongs to matter;* they do not even competently distinguish what is *dependent*, from what is *independent, on the conditions of the mental self.* But in these significations they are and must be frequently employed. Without, therefore, discarding this nomenclature, which, so far as it goes, expresses, in general, a distinction of the highest importance, in the most apposite terms; these terms may, by qualification, easily be rendered adequate to those subordinate discriminations, which it is often requisite to signalize, but which they cannot simply and of themselves denote.

Subject and *subjective*, without any qualifying attribute, I would therefore employ, as has hitherto been done, to mark out what inheres in, pertains to, or depends on, the knowing mind, whether of man in general, or of this or that individual man in particular; and this in contrast to *object* and *objective*, as expressing what does not so inhere, pertain, and depend. Thus, for example, an art or science is said to be *objective*, when considered simply as a system of speculative truths or practical rules, but without respect of any actual possessor; *subjective*, when considered as a habit of knowledge or dexterity, inherent in the mind, either vaguely of any, or precisely of this or that, possessor.

But, as has been stated, an *object* of knowledge may be a mode of mind, or it may be something different from mind; and it is frequently of importance to indicate precisely under which of these classes that object comes. In this case, by an internal development of the nomenclature itself, we might employ, on the former alternative, the term *subject-object;* on the latter, the term *object-object.*

But the *subject-object* may be either a mode of mind, of which we are conscious as absolute and for itself alone, — as, for example, a pain or pleasure; or a mode of mind, of which we are conscious, as relative to, and representative of something else, — as, for instance, the imagination of something past or possible. Of these we might distinguish, when necessary, the one, as the *absolute* or the *real subject-object*, the other, as the *relative*, or the *ideal*, or the *representative*, *subject-object.*

Finally, it may be required to mark whether the *object-object* and the *subject-object* be immediately known as present, or only as represented. In this case we must resort, on the former alternative, to the epithet *presentative* or *intuitive;* on the latter, to those of *represented*, *mediate*, *remote*, *primary*, *principal*, *etc.*] — *Diss. supp. to Reid.*

Now, the great problem of philosophy is, to analyze the contents of our acts of knowledge or cognitions, — to distinguish what elements are contributed by the knowing subject, what elements by the object known. There must, therefore, be terms adequate to designate these correlative opposites, and to discriminate the share which each has in the total act of cognition. But, if we reject the terms *subject* and *subjective*, *object* and *objective*, there are no others competent to the purpose.

At this stage of your progress, it is not easy to make you aware of the paramount necessity of such a distinction, and of such terms, — or to show you how, from the want of words expressive of this primary antithesis, the mental philosophy of [Great Britain] has been checked in its development, and involved in the utmost perplexity and misconception. It is sufficient to remark at present, that to this defect in the language of his psychological analysis, is, in a great measure, to be attributed the confusion, not to say the errors, of Reid, in the very cardinal point of his philosophy, — a confusion so great that the whole tendency of his doctrine was misconceived by Brown, who, in adopting a modification of the hypothesis of a representative perception, seems not even to have suspected, that he, and Reid, and modern philosophers in general, were not in this at one. The terms *subjective* and *objective* denote the primary distinction in consciousness of *self* and *not-self*, and this distinction involves the whole science of mind; for this science is nothing more than a determination of the subjective and objective, in themselves and in their mutual relations. The distinction is of paramount importance, and of infinite application, not only in Philosophy proper, but in Grammar, Rhetoric, Criticism, Ethics, Politics, Jurisprudence, Theology. I will give you an example, — a philological example. Suppose a lexicographer had to distinguish the two meanings of the word *certainty*. Certainty expresses either the firm conviction which we have of the truth of a thing; or the character of the proof on which its reality rests. The former is the *subjective* meaning; the latter the *objective*. By what other terms can they be distinguished and described?

History of the terms Subject and Object. — The distinction of subject and object, as marking out the fundamental and most thorough-going antithesis in philosophy, we owe, among many other important benefits, to the schoolmen, and from the schoolmen the terms passed, both in their substantive and adjective forms, into the scientific language of modern philosophers. Deprived of these terms, the Critical Philosophy, indeed the whole philosophy of Germany and France, would be a blank. In [Great Britain], though familiarly employed in scientific language, even subsequently to the time of Locke, the adjective forms seem at length to have dropt out of the English tongue. That these words waxed obsolete, was, perhaps, caused by the ambiguity which had gradually crept into the signification of the substantives. *Object*, besides its proper signification, came to be abusively applied to denote *motive, end, final cause* (a meaning, by the way, not recognized by Johnson). This innovation was probably borrowed from the French, in whose language the word had been similarly corrupted, after the commencement of the last century. Subject in English, as *sujet* in French, had not been rightly distinguished from object, taken in its proper meaning, and had thus returned to the original ambiguity of the corresponding term (*ὑποκείμενον*) in Greek. It is probable that the logical application of the word (subject of predication) facilitated or occasioned this confusion. In using the terms, therefore, we think that an explanation, but no apology, is required. The distinction is expressed by no other terms; and if these did not already enjoy a prescriptive right as denizens of the language, it cannot be denied, that, as strictly analogical, they are well entitled to sue out their naturalization. We shall have frequent occasion to recur to this distinction, — and it is eminently worthy of your attention.

Self, Ego — illustrated from Plato. — The last parallel expressions are the terms *self* and *ego*. These we shall take together, as they are absolutely convertible. As the best preparative for the proper understanding of these terms, I shall translate to you a passage from the *First Alcibiades* of Plato. The interlocutors are Socrates and Alcibiades.

" *Socr.* Hold, now, with whom do you at present converse? Is it not with me? — *Alcib.* Yes.

Socr. And I also with you? — *Alcib.* Yes.

Socr. It is Socrates then who speaks? — *Alcib.* Assuredly.

Socr. And Alcibiades who listens? — *Alcib.* Yes.

Socr. Is it not with language that Socrates speaks? — *Alcib.* What now? of course.

Socr. To converse, and to use language, are not these then the same? — *Alcib.* The very same.

Socr. But he who uses a thing, and the thing used, — are these not different? — *Alcib.* What do you mean?

Socr. A currier, — does he not use a cutting knife, and other instruments? — *Alcib.* Yes.

Socr. And the man who uses the cutting knife, is he different from the instrument he uses? — *Alcib.* Most certainly.

Socr. In like manner, the lyrist, is he not different from the lyre he plays on? — *Alcib.* Undoubtedly.

Socr. This, then, was what I asked you just now, — does not he who uses a thing seem to you always different from the thing used? — *Alcib.* Very different.

Socr. But the currier, does he cut with his instruments alone, or also with his hands? — *Alcib.* Also with his hands.

Socr. He then uses his hands? — *Alcib.* Yes.

Socr. And in his work he uses also his eyes? — *Alcib.* Yes.

Socr. We are agreed, then, that he who uses a thing, and the thing used, are different? — *Alcib.* We are.

Socr. The currier and lyrist are, therefore, different from the hands and eyes, with which they work? — *Alcib.* So it seems.

Socr. Now, then, does not a man use his whole body? — *Alcib.* Unquestionably.

Socr. But we are agreed that he who uses, and that which is used, are different? — *Alcib.* Yes.

Socr. A man is, therefore, different from his body? — *Alcib.* So I think

Socr. What then is the man? — *Alcib.* I cannot say.

Socr. You can at least say that the man is that which uses the body? — *Alcib.* True

Socr. Now, does any thing use the body but the mind? — *Alcib.* Nothing.

Socr. The mind is, therefore, the man? — *Alcib.* The mind alone."

To the same effect, Aristotle asserts that the mind contains the man, not the man the mind. "Thou art the soul," says Hierocles, "but the body is thine."

The Self or Ego in relation to bodily organs, and thoughts. — But let us come to a closer determination of the point; let us appeal to our experience. "I turn my attention on my being" [says Gatien-Arnoult], "and find that I have organs, and that I have thoughts. My body is the complement of my organs; am I then my body, or any part of my body? This I cannot be. The matter of my body, in all its points, is in a perpetual flux, in a perpetual process of renewal. I, — *I* do not pass away, I am not renewed. None probably of the molecules which constituted my organs some years ago, form any part of the material system which I now call mine. It has been made up anew; but I am still what I was of old. These organs may be mutilated; one, two, or any number of them may be removed; but not the less do I continue to be what I was, one and entire. It is even not impossible to conceive me existing, deprived of every organ; I, therefore, who have these organs, or this body, *I* am neither an organ nor a body.

"Neither am I identical with my thoughts, for they are manifold and various. I, on the contrary, am one and the same. Each moment they change and succeed each other; this change and succession takes place in me, but I neither change nor succeed myself in myself. Each moment I am aware or am conscious of the existence and change of my thoughts: this change is sometimes determined by me, sometimes by something different from me; but I always can distinguish myself from them: I am a permanent being, an enduring subject, of whose existence these thoughts are only so many modes, appearances, or phænomena ; — I who possess organs and thoughts am, therefore, neither these organs nor these thoughts.

"I can conceive myself to exist apart from every organ. But if I try to conceive myself existent without a thought, — without some form of consciousness, — I am unable. This or that thought may not be perhaps necessary ; but of some thought it is necessary that I should be conscious, otherwise I can no longer conceive myself to be. A suspension of thought is thus a suspension of my intellectual existence ; I am, therefore, essentially a thinking, — a conscious being ; and my true character is that of an intelligence, — an intelligence served by organs."

But this thought, this consciousness, is possible only in, and through, the consciousness of Self. The Self, the I, is recognized in every act of intelligence, as the subject to which that act belongs. It is I that perceive, I that imagine, I that remember, I that attend, I that compare, I that feel, I that desire, I that will, I that am conscious. The I, indeed, is only manifested in one or other of these special modes ; but it is manifested in them all ; they are all only the phænomena of the I, and, therefore, the science conversant about the phænomena of the mind is, most simply and unambiguously, said to be conversant about the phænomena of the *I* or *Ego.*

This expression, as that which, in many relations, best marks and discriminates the conscious mind, has now become familiar in every country, with the exception of our own. Why it has not been naturalized with us is not unapparent. The French have two words for the Ego or I — *Je* and *Moi.* The former of these is less appropriate as an abstract term, being in sound ambiguous ; but *le moi* admirably expresses what the Germans denote, but less felicitously, by their *Das Ich.* In English, *the I* could not be tolerated ; because in sound it could not be distinguished from the word significant of the organ of sight. We must, therefore, renounce the term, or resort to the Latin *Ego ;* and this is perhaps no disadvantage, for, as the word is only employed in a strictly philosophical relation, it is better that this should be distinctly marked, by its being used in that relation alone. The term *Self* is more allowable; yet still the expressions *Ego* and *Non-Ego* are felt to be less awkward than those of *Self* and *Not-Self*.

So much in explanation of the terms involved in the definition which I gave of Psychology. I now proceed, as I proposed, to the consideration of a few other words of frequent occurrence in philosophy, and which it is expedient to explain at once, before entering upon discussions in which they will continually recur. I take them up without order, except in so far as they may be grouped together by their meaning; and the first I shall consider, are the terms *hypothesis* and *theory*.

Hypothesis. — When a phænomenon is presented to us which can be explained by no cause within the sphere of our experience, we feel dissatisfied and uneasy. A desire arises to escape from this unpleasing state; and the consequence of this desire is an effort of the mind to recall the outstanding phænomenon to unity, by assigning it, *ad interim*, to some cause, or class, to which we imagine that it may possibly belong, until we shall be able to refer it, permanently, to that cause, or class, to which we shall have proved it actually to appertain. The judgment by which the phænomenon is thus *provisorily* referred, is called an *hypothesis*, — a *supposition*.

Hypotheses have thus no other end than to satisfy the desire of the mind to reduce the objects of its knowledge to unity and system; and they do this in recalling them, *ad interim*, to some principle, through which the mind is enabled to comprehend them. From this view of their nature it is manifest how far they are permissible, and how far they are even useful and expedient, — throwing altogether out of account the possibility that what is at first assumed as hypothetical, may subsequently be proved true.

Conditions of a legitimate hypothesis. — An hypothesis is allowable only under certain conditions. Of these the *first* is, — that the phænomenon to be explained should be ascertained actually to exist. It would, for example, be absurd to propose an hypothesis to account for the possibility of apparitions, until it be proved that ghosts do actually appear. This precept, to establish your fact before you attempt to conjecture its cause, may, perhaps, seem to you too elementary to be worth the statement. But a longer experience will convince you of the contrary. That the enunciation of the rule is not only not superfluous, but even highly requisite as an admonition, is shown by great and numerous examples of its violation in the history of science; and, as Cullen has truly observed, there are more false facts current in the world than false hypotheses to explain them. There is, in truth, nothing which men seem to admit so lightly as an asserted fact. It would be easy to adduce extensive hypotheses, very generally accredited, even at the present hour, which are, however, nothing better than assumptions founded on, or explanatory of, phænomena which do not really exist in nature.

The *second* condition of a permissible hypothesis is, — that the phænomenon cannot be explained otherwise than by an hypothesis. It would, for example, have been absurd, even before the discoveries of Franklin, to account for the phænomenon of lightning by the hypothesis of supernatural agency. These two conditions, of the reality of the phænomenon, and the necessity of an hypothesis for its explanation, being fulfilled, an hypothesis is allowable.

Criteria of the excellence of an hypothesis. — But the necessity of some hypothesis being conceded, how are we to discriminate between a good and a bad, — a probable and an improbable, hypothesis? The comparative excellence of an hypothesis requires, in the *first* place, that it involve nothing contradictory, either internally or externally, — that is, either between the parts of which it is composed, or between these and any established truths. Thus, the Ptolemaic hypothesis of the heavenly revolutions became worthless, from the moment that it was contradicted by the ascertained phænomena of the planets Venus and Mercury. Thus the Wernerian hypothesis in geology is improbable, inasmuch as it is obliged to maintain that water was originally able to hold in solution substances which it is now incapable of dissolving. The Huttonian hypothesis, on the contrary, is so far preferable, that it assumes no effect to have been produced by any agent, which that agent is not known to be capable of producing. In the *second* place, an hypothesis is probable in proportion as the phænomenon in question can be by it more completely explained. Thus the Copernican hypothesis is more probable than the Tychonic and semi-Tychonic, inasmuch as it enables us to explain a greater number of phænomena. In the *third* place, an hypothesis is probable in proportion as it is independent of all subsidiary hypotheses. In this respect, again, the Copernican hypothesis is more probable than the Tychonic. For, though both save all the phænomena, the Copernican does this by one principal assumption; whereas the Tychonic is obliged to call in the aid of several subordinate suppositions, to render the principal assumption available. So much for *hypothesis*.

Theory; Practice. — I shall be more concise in treating of the cognate expression, — *theory*. This word is employed by English writers in a very loose and improper sense. It is with them usually convertible with *hypothesis*, and hypothesis is commonly used as another term for *conjecture*. Dr. Reid, indeed, expressly does this; he identifies the two words, and explains them as philosophical conjectures, as you may see in his First Essay on the *Intellectual Powers*. This is, however, wrong; wrong, in relation to the original employment of the terms by the ancient philosophers; and wrong, in relation to their employment by the philosophers of the modern nations.

The terms *theory* and *theoretical* are properly used in opposition to the terms *practice* and *practical;* in this sense they were exclusively employed by the ancients; and in this sense they are almost exclusively employed by the continental philosophers. *Practice* is the exercise of an art, or the application of a science, in life, which application is itself an art, for it is not every one who is able to apply all he knows; there being required, over and above knowledge, a certain dexterity and skill *Theory*, on the contrary, is mere knowledge or science. There is a distinction, but no opposition, between theory and practice; each to a certain extent supposes the other. On the one hand theory is dependent on practice; practice must have preceded theory; for theory being only a generalization of the principles on which practice proceeds, these must originally have been taken out of, or abstracted from, practice. On the other hand, this is true only to a certain extent; for there is no practice without a theory. The man of practice must have always known something, however little, of what he did, of what he intended to do, and of the means by which his intention was to be carried into effect. He was, therefore, not wholly ignorant of the principles of his procedure; he was a limited, he was, in some degree, an unconscious, theorist. As he proceeded, however, in his practice, and reflected on his performance, his theory acquired greater clearness and extension, so that he became at last distinctly conscious of what he did, and could give, to himself and others, an account of his procedure.

> "Per varios usus artem experientia fecit,
> Exemplo monstrante viam."

In this view, theory is, therefore, simply a knowledge of the principles by which practice accomplishes its end.

The opposition of Theoretical and Practical philosophy is somewhat different; for these do not stand simply related to each other as theory and practice. Practical philosophy involves likewise a theory, — a theory, however, subordinated to the practical application of its principles; while theoretical philosophy has nothing to do with practice, but terminates in mere speculative or contemplative knowledge.

The next group of associated words to which I would call your attention is composed of the terms, — *power, faculty, capacity, disposition, habit, act, operation, energy, function*, etc.

Power. Reid's criticism of Locke. — Of these the first is *power*, and the explanation of this, in a manner, involves that of all the others.

I have, in the first place, to correct an error of Dr. Reid, in relation to this term, in his criticism of Locke's statement of its import. — You will observe that I do not, at present, enter on the question, *How do we acquire the notion of power?* and I defend the following passage of Locke, only in regard to the meaning and comprehension of the term. "The mind," says Locke, "being every day informed, by the senses, of the alteration of those simple ideas it observes in things without, and taking notice how one comes to an end, and ceases to be, and another begins to exist which was not before; reflecting, also, on what passes within itself, and observing a constant change of its ideas, sometimes by the impression of outward objects on the senses, and sometimes by the determination of its own choice; and concluding from what it has so constantly observed to have been, that the like changes will, for the future, be made in the same things, by like agents, and by the like ways; considers, in one thing, the possibility of having any of its simple ideas changed, and, in another, the possibility of making that change; and so comes by that idea which we call power. Thus we say, fire has a power to melt gold, — that is, to destroy the consistency of its insensible parts, and, consequently, its hardness, and make it fluid, and gold has a power to be melted: that the sun has a power to blanch wax, and wax a power to be blanched by the sun, whereby the yellowness is destroyed, and whiteness made to exist in its room. In which, and the like cases, the power, we consider, is in reference to the change of perceivable ideas; for we cannot observe any alteration to be made in, or operation upon, any thing, but by the observable change of its sensible ideas; nor conceive any alteration to be made, but by conceiving a change of some of its ideas. Power, thus considered, is twofold — namely, as able to make, or able to receive, any change: the one may be called *active*, and the other *passive* power."

Active and Passive Power. — I have here only to call your attention to the distinction of power into two kinds, *active* and *passive* — the former meaning, *id quod potest facere*, that which *can effect* or *can do*, — the latter, *id quod potest fieri*, that which *can be effected* or *can be done*. In both cases, the general notion of power is expressed by the verb *potest* or *can*. Now, on this, Dr. Reid makes the following strictures: "Whereas Locke distinguishes power into *active* and *passive*, I conceive passive power is no power at all. He means by it, the possibility of being changed. To call this, *power*, seems to be a misapplication of the word. I do not remember to have met with the phrase *passive power* in any other good author. Mr. Locke seems to have been unlucky in inventing it; and it deserves not to be retained in our language. Perhaps he was unwarily led into it, as an opposite to *active power*. But I conceive we call certain powers *active*, to distinguish them from other powers that are called *speculative*. As all mankind distinguish action from speculation, it is very proper to distinguish the powers by which those different operations are performed into active and speculative. Mr. Locke, indeed, acknowledges that active power is more properly called power: but I see no propriety at all in passive power; it is a powerless power, and a contradiction in terms."

These observations of Dr. Reid are, I am sorry to say, erroneous from first to last. The latter part, in which he attempts to find a reason for Locke being unwarily betrayed into making this distinction, is, supposing the distinction untenable, and Locke its author, wholly inadequate to account for his hallucination: for, surely, the powers by which we speculate are, in their operations, not more passive than those that have sometimes been styled *active*, but which are properly denominated *practical*. But in the censure itself on Locke, Reid is altogether mistaken. In the *first* place, so far was Locke from being unlucky in inventing the distinction, it was invented some two thousand years before. In the *second* place, to call the *possibility of being changed* a *power*, is no misapplication of the word. In the *third* place, so far is the phrase *passive power* from not being employed by any good author, — there is hardly a metaphysician, previous to Locke, by whom it was not familiarly used. In fact, this was one of the most celebrated distinctions in philosophy. It was first formally enounced by Aristotle, and from him was universally adopted. Active and passive power are in Greek styled *δύναμις ποιητική*, and *δύναμις παθητική*; in Latin, *potentia activa*, and *potentia passiva*.

Power, therefore, is a word which we may use both in an

active, and in a passive, signification; and in psychology, we may apply it both to the active faculties, and to the passive capacities, of mind.

Faculty. — This leads to the meaning of the terms *faculties* and *capacities.* *Faculty* (*facultas*) is derived from the obsolete Latin *facul*, the more ancient form of *facilis*, from which again *facilitas* is formed. It is properly limited to active power, and, therefore, is abusively applied to the mere passive affections of mind.

Capacity (*capacitas*), on the other hand, is more properly limited to these. Its primary signification, which is literally *room for*, as well as its employment, favors this; although it cannot be denied, that there are examples of its usage in an active sense. Leibnitz, as far as I know, was the first who limited its psychological application to the passivities of mind. In his famous *Nouveaux Essais sur l'Entendement Humain*, a work written in refutation of Locke's *Essay* on the same subject, he observes: "We may say that power, in general, is the possibility of change. Now the change, or the act of this possibility, being action in one subject and passion in another, there will be two powers, the one *passive*, the other *active.* The active may be called *faculty*, and perhaps the passive might be called *capacity*, or receptivity. It is true that the active power is sometimes taken in a higher sense, when, over and above the simple faculty, there is also a tendency, a *nisus*; and it is thus that I have used it in my dynamical considerations. We might give it in this meaning the special name of *force.*" I may notice that Reid seems to have attributed no other meaning to the term *power* than that of *force.*

Power, then, is active and passive; faculty is active power, — capacity is passive power.

Disposition, Habit. — The two terms next in order, are *disposition*, in Greek, διάθεσις; and *habit*, in Greek ἕξις. I take these together, as they are similar, yet not the same. Both are tendencies to action; but they differ in this, that disposition properly denotes a natural tendency, habit an acquired tendency. Aristotle distinguishes them by another difference.

"Habit (ἕξις) is discriminated from disposition (διάθεσις) in this, that the latter is easily movable, the former of longer duration, and more difficult to be moved." I may notice that *habit* is formed by the frequent repetition of the same action or passion, and that this repetition is called *consuetude*, or *custom*. The latter terms, which properly signify the cause, are not unfrequently abusively employed for habit, their effect.

I may likewise observe that the terms *power*, *faculty*, *capacity*, are more appropriately applied to natural, than to acquired, capabilities, and are thus inapplicable to mere habits. I say *mere* habits, for where habit is superinduced upon a natural capability, both terms may be used. Thus we can say both the faculty of abstraction, and the habit of abstraction, — the capacity of suffering, and the habit of suffering; but still the meanings are not identical.

The last series of cognate terms are *act*, *operation*, *energy*. They are all mutually convertible, as all denoting the present exertion or exercise of a power, a faculty, or a habit. I must here explain to you the famous distinction of *actual* and *potential* existence; for, by this distinction, act, operation, energy, are contra-discriminated from power, faculty, capacity, disposition, and habit. This distinction, when divested of certain subordinate subtleties of no great consequence, is manifest and simple. Potential existence means merely that the thing *may be* at some time; actual existence, that it now *is*. Thus, the mathematician, when asleep or playing at cards, does not exercise his skill; his geometrical knowledge is all latent, but he is still a mathematician — potentially.

Hermogenes, says Horace, was a singer, even when silent; how? — a singer, not *in actu*, but *in posse*. So Alfenus was a cobbler, even when not at work; that is, he was a cobbler *potential;* whereas, when busy in his booth, he was a cobbler *actual*.

In like manner, my sense of sight potentially exists, though my eyelids are closed; but when I open them, it exists actually. Now, *power*, *faculty*, *capacity*, *disposition*, *habit*, are all different expressions for potential or possible existence; *act*, *opera-*

tion, *energy*, for actual or present existence. Thus the *power* of imagination expresses the unexerted capability of imagining; the *act* of imagination denotes that power elicited into immediate — into present existence. The different synonyms for potential existence, are existence *ἐν δυνάμει*, *in potentia*, *in posse*, *in power*; for actual existence, existence *ἐν ἐνεργείᾳ*, or *ἐν ἐντελεχείᾳ*, *in actu*, *in esse*, *in act*, *in operation*, *in energy*. The term *energy* is precisely the Greek term for act of operation; but it has vulgarly obtained the meaning of forcible activity.

The word *functio*, in Latin, simply expresses performance or operation; *functio muneris* is the exertion of an energy of some determinate kind. But with us, the word *function* has come to be employed in the sense of *munus* alone, and means not the exercise, but the specific character, of a power. Thus the function of a clergyman does not mean with us the performance of his duties, but the peculiarity of those duties themselves. The function of nutrition does not mean the operation of that animal power, but its discriminate character.

CHAPTER VIII.

DISTRIBUTION OF MENTAL PHÆNOMENA: — SPECIAL CONDITIONS OF CONSCIOUSNESS.

Consciousness comprehends all the mental phænomena. — In taking a comprehensive survey of the mental phænomena, these are all seen to comprise one essential element, or to be possible only under one necessary condition. This element or condition is Consciousness, or the knowledge that I, — that the Ego exists, in some determinate state. In this knowledge they appear, or are realized as phænomena, and with this knowledge they likewise disappear, or have no longer a phænomenal existence; so that consciousness may be compared to an internal light, by means of which, and which alone, what passes in the mind is rendered visible. Consciousness is simple, — is not composed of parts, either similar or dissimilar. It always resembles itself, differing only in the degrees of its intensity; thus, there are not various kinds of consciousness, although there are various kinds of mental modes, or states, of which we are conscious. Whatever division, therefore, of the mental phænomena may be adopted, all its members must be within consciousness itself, which must be viewed as comprehensive of the whole phænomena to be divided; far less should we reduce it, as a special phænomenon, to a particular class. Let consciousness, therefore, remain one and indivisible, comprehending all the modifications, — all the phænomena, of the thinking subject.

Three classes of mental phænomena. — But taking, again, a survey of the mental modifications, or phænomena, of which we are conscious, — these are seen to divide themselves into THREE great classes. In the first place, there are the phænomena of *Knowledge;* in the second place, there are the phænomena of *Feeling*, or the phænomena of *Pleasure and Pain;* and, in the third place, there are the phænomena of *Will and Desire.*

Let me illustrate this by an example. I see a picture. Now, first of all, — I am conscious of perceiving a certain complement of colors and figures, — I recognize what the object is. This is the phænomenon of Cognition or Knowledge. But this is not the only phænomenon of which I may be here conscious. I may experience certain affections in the contemplation of this object. If the picture be a masterpiece, the gratification will be unalloyed; but if it be an unequal production, I shall be conscious, perhaps, of enjoyment, but of enjoyment alloyed with dissatisfaction. This is the phænomenon of Feeling, — or of Pleasure and Pain. But these two phænomena do not yet exhaust all of which I may be conscious on the occasion. I may desire to see the picture long, — to see it often, — to make it my own, and, perhaps, I may will, resolve, or determine so to do. This is the complex phænomenon of Will and Desire.

Their nomenclature. — The English language, unfortunately, does not afford us terms competent to express and discriminate, with even tolerable clearness and precision, these classes of phænomena. In regard to the *first*, indeed, we have comparatively little reason to complain; the synonymous terms, *knowledge* and *cognition*, suffice to distinguish the phænomena of this class from those of the other two. In the *second* class, the defect of the language becomes more apparent. The word *feeling* is the only term under which we can possibly collect the phænomena of pleasure and pain, and yet this word is ambiguous. For it is not only employed to denote what we are conscious of as agreeable or disagreeable in our mental states, but it is likewise used as a synonym for the sense of touch. It is, however, principally in relation to the *third* class that the deficiency is manifested. In English, unfortunately, we have no term capable of adequately expressing what is common both to will and desire; that is, the *nisus* or *conatus*, —

the tendency towards the realization of their end. By will is meant a free and deliberate, by desire a blind and fatal, tendency to act. Now, to express, I say, the tendency to overt action, — the quality in which desire and will are equally contained, — we possess no English term to which an exception of more or less cogency may not be taken. Were we to say the phænomena of *tendency*, the phrase would be vague; and the same is true of the phænomena of *doing*. Again, the term phænomena of *appetency* is objectionable, because (to say nothing of the unfamiliarity of the expression) *appetency*, though perhaps etymologically unexceptionable, has, both in Latin and English, a meaning almost synonymous with desire. Like the Latin *appetentia*, the Greek ὄρεξις is equally ill-balanced; for, though used by philosophers to comprehend both will and desire, it more familiarly suggests the latter, and we need not, therefore, be solicitous, with Mr. Harris and Lord Monboddo, to naturalize in English the term *orectic*. Again, the phrase phænomena of *activity* would be even worse; every possible objection can be made to the term *active powers*, by which the philosophers of this country have designated the *orectic faculties* of the Aristotelians. For you will observe, that all faculties are equally active; and it is not the overt performance, but the tendency towards it, for which we are in quest of an expression. The German is the only language I am acquainted with which is able to supply the term of which philosophy is in want. The expression *Bestrebungs Vermögen*, which is most nearly, though awkwardly and inadequately, translated by *striving faculties*, — faculties of effort or endeavor, — is now generally employed, in the philosophy of Germany, as the genus comprehending desire and will. Perhaps the phrase, phænomena of *exertion*, is, upon the whole, the best expression to denote the manifestations, and *exertive* faculties, the best expression to denote the faculties, of will and desire. *Exero*, in Latin, means literally *to put forth*; — and, with us, *exertion* and *exertive* are the only endurable words that I can find which approximate, though distantly, to the strength and precision of the German expression. I shall, however occasionally employ likewise the term *appetency*, in the rigorous signification I have mentioned, — as a genus comprehending under it both desires and volitions.*

This division of mind into the three great classes of the Cognitive faculties, — the Feelings, or capacities of Pleasure and Pain, — and the Exertive or Conative Powers, — I do not propose as original. It was first promulgated by Kant; and the felicity of the distribution was so apparent, that it has now been long all but universally adopted in Germany by the philosophers of every school. To English psychologists it is apparently wholly unknown. They still adhere to the old scholastic division into powers of the Understanding and powers of the Will; or, as it is otherwise expressed, into Intellectual and Active powers.

Objection to the classification obviated. — An objection to the arrangement may, perhaps, be taken on the ground that the three classes are not coördinate. It is evident that every mental phænomenon is either an act of knowledge, or only possible through an act of knowledge, for consciousness is a knowledge, — a phænomenon of cognition; and, on this principle, many philosophers have been led to regard the knowing, or representative faculty, as they called it, — the faculty of cognition, as the fundamental power of mind, from which all others are derivative. To this the answer is easy. These philosophers did not observe that, although pleasure and pain, — although desire and volition, are only as they are known to be yet, in these modifications, a quality, a phænomenon of mind absolutely new, has been superadded, which was never involved in, and could, therefore, never have been evolved out of, the mere faculty of knowledge. The faculty of knowledge is certainly the first in order, inasmuch as it is the *conditio sine qua non* of the others; and we are able to conceive a being possessed of the power of recognizing existence, and yet wholly

* The term *Conative* (from *Conari*) is employed by Cudworth in his *Treatise on Free Will*. The terms *Conation* and *Conative* are those finally adopted by the Author, as the most appropriate expressions for the class of phænomena in question. — English Ed.

void of all feeling of pain and pleasure, and of all powers of desire and volition. On the other hand, we are wholly unable to conceive a being possessed of feeling and desire, and, at the same time, without a knowledge of any object upon which his affections may be employed, and without a consciousness of these affections themselves.

We can further conceive a being possessed of knowledge and feeling alone — a being endowed with a power of recognizing objects, of enjoying the exercise, and of grieving at the restraint, of his activity, — and yet devoid of that faculty of voluntary agency — of that *conation*, which is possessed by man. To such a being would belong feelings of pain and pleasure, but neither desire nor will properly so called. On the other hand, however, we cannot possibly conceive the existence of a voluntary activity independently of all feeling; for voluntary conation is a faculty which can only be determined to energy through a pain or pleasure, — through an estimate of the relative worth of objects.

In distinguishing the cognitions, feelings, and conations, it is not, therefore, to be supposed that these phænomena are possible independently of each other. In our philosophical systems, they may stand separated from each other in books and chapters; — in nature, they are ever interwoven. In every, the simplest, modification of mind, knowledge, feeling, and desire or will go to constitute the mental state; and it is only by a scientific abstraction that we are able to analyze the state into elements, which are never really existent but in mutual combination. These elements are found, indeed, in very various proportions in different states, — sometimes one preponderates, sometimes another; but there is no state in which they are not all coexistent.

Let the mental phænomena, therefore, be distributed under the three heads of phænomena of Cognition, or the faculties of Knowledge; phænomena of Feeling, or the capacities of Pleasure and Pain; and phænomena of Desiring or Willing, or the powers of Conation. The order of these is determined by their relative consecution. Feeling and appetency suppose knowledge. The cognitive faculties, therefore, stand first. But as will, and desire, and aversion suppose a knowledge of the pleasurable and painful, the feelings will stand second as intermediate between the other two.

Consciousness cannot be defined. — Such is the highest or most general classification of the mental phænomena, or of the phænomena of which we are conscious. But as these primary classes are, as we have shown, all included under one universal phænomenon, — the phænomenon of Consciousness, — it follows that Consciousness must form the first object of our consideration.

Nothing has contributed more to spread obscurity over a very transparent matter, than the attempts of philosophers to define consciousness. Consciousness cannot be defined; we may be ourselves fully aware what consciousness is, but we cannot, without confusion, convey to others a definition of what we ourselves clearly apprehend. The reason is plain. Consciousness lies at the root of all knowledge. Consciousness is itself the one highest source of all comprehensibility and illustration; — how, then, can we find aught else by which consciousness may be illustrated or comprehended? To accomplish this, it would be necessary to have a second consciousness, through which we might be conscious of the mode in which the first consciousness was possible. Many philosophers, — and among others Dr. Brown, — have defined consciousness a *feeling*. But how do they define a feeling? They define, and must define it, as something of which we are conscious; for a feeling of which we are not conscious, is no feeling at all. Here, therefore, they are guilty of a logical see-saw or circle. They define consciousness by feeling, and feeling by consciousness, — that is, they explain the same by the same, and thus leave us in the end no wiser than we were in the beginning. Other philosophers say that consciousness is a *knowledge*, — and others again, that it is a *belief* or *conviction of a knowledge*. Here, again, we have the same violation of logical law. Is there any knowledge of which we are not conscious? Is there any belief of which we are not conscious? There is not, — there cannot be; therefore, consciousness is not contained under either knowledge or belief, but on the contrary, knowledge and belief are both contained under consciousness. In short, the notion of consciousness is so elementary, that it cannot possibly be resolved into others more simple. It cannot, therefore, be brought under any genus, — any more general conception; and, consequently, it cannot be defined.

But though consciousness cannot be logically defined, it may, however, be philosophically analyzed. This analysis is effected by observing and holding fast the phænomena or facts of consciousness, comparing these, and, from this comparison, evolving the universal conditions under which alone an act of consciousness is possible.

What the word consciousness denotes, and what it involves. — But before proceeding to show in detail what the act of consciousness comprises, it may be proper, in the first place, to recall in general what kind of act the word is employed to denote. *I know*, *I feel*, *I desire*, etc. What is it that is necessarily involved in all these? It requires only to be stated to be admitted, that when I know, I must *know that I know*, — when I feel, I must *know that I feel*, — when I desire, I must *know that I desire*. The knowledge, the feeling, the desire, are possible only under the condition of being known, and being known by me. For if I did not know that I knew, I would not know, — if I did not know that I felt, I would not feel, — if I did not know that I desired, I would not desire. Now, this knowledge, which I, the subject, have of these modifications of my being, and through which knowledge alone these modifications are possible, is what we call *consciousness*. The expressions, *I know that I know*, — *I know that I feel*, — *I know that I desire*, — are thus translated by, *I am conscious that I know*, — *I am conscious that I feel*, — *I am conscious that I desire*. Consciousness is thus, on the one hand, the recognition by the mind or ego of its acts and affections; — in other words, the self-affirmation, that certain modifications are known by me, and that these modifications are mine. But on the other hand, consciousness is not to be viewed as any thing different from these modifications themselves, but is, in fact, the general condition of their existence, or of their existence within the sphere of intelligence. Though the simplest act of mind, consciousness thus expresses a relation subsisting between two terms. These terms are, on the one hand, an I or Self, as the subject of a certain modification, — and, on the other, some modification, state, quality, affection, or operation belonging to the subject. Consciousness, thus, in its simplicity, necessarily involves three things, — 1°, A recognizing or knowing subject; 2°, A recognized or known modification; and, 3°, A recognition or knowledge by the subject of the modification.

Consciousness and knowledge involve each other. — From this it is apparent, that consciousness and knowledge each involve the other. An act of knowledge may be expressed by the formula, *I know;* an act of consciousness by the formula, *I know that I know:* but as it is impossible for us to know without at the same time knowing that we know, so it is impossible to know that we know without our actually knowing. The one merely explicitly expresses what the other implicitly contains. Consciousness and knowledge are thus not opposed as really different. Why, then, it may be asked, employ two terms to express notions, which, as they severally infer each other, are really identical? To this the answer is easy. Realities may be in themselves inseparable, while, as objects of our knowledge, it may be necessary to consider them apart. Notions, likewise, may severally imply each other, and be inseparable, even in thought; yet, for the purposes of science, it may be requisite to distinguish them by different terms, and to consider them in their relations or correlations to each other. Take a geometrical example, — a triangle. This is a whole composed of certain parts. Here the whole cannot be conceived as separate from its parts, and the parts cannot be conceived as separate from their whole. Yet it is scientifically necessary to have different names for each, and it is necessary now to consider the whole in relation to the parts, and now the parts in correlation to the whole. Again, the constituent parts of a triangle are sides and angles. Here the sides suppose the angles, —

the angles suppose the sides; — and, in fact, the sides and angles are, in themselves, in reality, one and indivisible. But they are not the same to us, — to our knowledge. For though we cannot abstract in thought the sides from the angle, the angle from the sides, we may make one or other the principal object of attention. We may either consider the angles in relation to each other, and to the sides; or the sides in relation to each other, and to the angles. And to express all this, it is necessary to distinguish, in thought and expression, what, in nature, is one and indivisible.

As it is in geometry, so it is in the philosophy of mind. We require different words, not only to express objects and relations different in themselves, but to express the same objects and relations under the different points of view in which they are placed by the mind, when scientifically considering them. Thus, in the present instance, consciousness and knowledge are not distinguished by different words as different things, but only as the same thing considered in different aspects. The verbal distinction is taken for the sake of brevity and precision, and its convenience warrants its establishment. *Knowledge is a relation*, and every relation supposes two terms. Thus, in the relation in question, there is, on the one hand, a *subject of knowledge*, — that is, the knowing mind, — and on the other, there is an *object of knowledge*, — that is, the thing known; and the knowledge itself is the relation between these two terms. Now, though each term of a relation necessarily supposes the other, nevertheless one of these terms may be to us the more interesting, and we may consider that term as the principal, and view the other only as subordinate and correlative. Now, this is the case in the present instance. In an act of knowledge, my attention may be principally attracted either to the object known, or to myself as the subject knowing; and, in the latter case, although no new element be added to the act, the condition involved in it, — *I know that I know*, — becomes the primary and prominent matter of consideration. And when, as in the philosophy of mind, the act of knowledge comes to be specially considered in relation to the knowing subject, it is at last, in the progress of the science, found convenient, if not absolutely necessary, to possess a scientific word in which this point of view should be permanently and distinctively embodied.

History of the term consciousness. — But, as the want of a technical and appropriate expression could be experienced only after psychological abstraction had acquired a certain stability and importance, it is evident that the appropriation of such an expression could not, in any language, be of very early date. And this is shown by the history of the synonymous terms for *consciousness* in the different languages, — a history which, though curious, you will find noticed in no publication whatever. The employment of the word *conscientia*, of which our term consciousness is a translation, is, in its *psychological* signification, not older than the philosophy of Descartes. Previously to him, this word was used almost exclusively in the *ethical* sense, expressed by our term *conscience*; and in the striking and apparently appropriate dictum of St. Augustin, — "certissima scientia et clamante conscientia," — which you may find so frequently paraded by the Continental philosophers, when illustrating the certainty of consciousness, in that quotation, the term is, by its author, applied only in its moral or religious signification. Besides the moral application, the words *conscire* and *conscientia* were frequently employed to denote *participation in a common knowledge.* Thus the members of a conspiracy were said *conscire*; and *conscius* is even used for conspirator; and, metaphorically, this community of knowledge is attributed to inanimate objects, — as wailing to the rocks, a lover says of himself, —

"Et conscia saxa fatigo."

I would not, however, be supposed to deny that these words were sometimes used, in ancient Latinity, in the modern sense of consciousness, or being conscious.

Until Descartes, therefore, the Latin terms *conscire* and *conscientia* were very rarely usurped in their present psychological meaning, — a meaning which, it is needless to add, was not expressed by any term in the vulgar languages; for, besides Tertullian, I am aware of only one or two obscure instances in which, as translations of the Greek terms *συναισθάνομαι* and *συναίσθησις*, of which we are about to speak, the terms *conscio* and *conscientia* were, as the nearest equivalents, contorted from their established signification to the sense in which they were afterwards employed by Descartes. Thus, in the philosophy of the West, we may safely affirm that, prior to Descartes, there was no psychological term in recognized use for what, since his time, is expressed in philosophical Latinity by *conscientia*, in French by *conscience*, in English by *consciousness*, in Italian by *conscienza*, and in German by *Bewusstseyn*. It will be observed that in Latin, French, and Italian (and I might add the Spanish and other Romanic languages), the terms are analogous, the moral and psychological meaning being denoted by the same word.

No term for consciousness in Greek until the decline of philosophy. — In Greek, there was no term for consciousness until the decline of philosophy, and in the later ages of the language. Plato and Aristotle, to say nothing of other philosophers, had no special term to express the knowledge which the mind affords of the operations of its faculties, though this, of course, was necessarily a frequent matter of their consideration. Intellect was supposed by them to be cognizant of its own operations; it was only doubted whether by a direct or by a reflex act. In regard to sense, the matter was more perplexed; and, on this point, both philosophers seem to vacillate in their opinions. In his *Theætetus*, Plato accords to sense the power of perceiving that it perceives; whereas, in his *Charmides*, this power he denies to sense, and attributes to intelligence (*νοῦς*). In like manner, an apparently different doctrine may be found in different works of Aristotle. But what concerns us at present, in all these discussions by the two philosophers, there is no single term employed to denote that special aspect of the phænomenon of knowledge, which is thus by them made a matter of consideration. It is only under the later Platonists and Aristotelians, that peculiar terms, tantamount to our consciousness, were adopted into the language of philosophy.

The special conditions of consciousness. — But to return from our historical digression. We may lay it down as the most general characteristic of *consciousness*, that it *is the recognition by the thinking subject of its own acts or affections.* So far there is no difference and no dispute. In this all philosophers are agreed. The more arduous task remains of determining the special conditions of consciousness. Of these, likewise, some are almost too palpable to admit of controversy. Before proceeding to those in regard to which there is any doubt or difficulty, it will be proper, in the first place, to state and dispose of such determinations as are too palpable to be called in question. Of these admitted limitations, the *first* is, that *consciousness is an actual, and not a potential, knowledge.* Thus, a man is said to know, — *i. e.* is able to know, that 7 + 9 are = 16, though that equation be not, at the moment, the object of his thought; but we cannot say that he is conscious of this truth unless while actually present to his mind.

The *second* limitation is, that *consciousness is an immediate, not a mediate, knowledge.* We are said, for example, to know a past occurrence when we represent it to the mind in an act of memory. We know the mental representation, and this we do immediately and in itself, and are also said to know the past occurrence, as mediately knowing it through the mental modification which represents it. Now, we are conscious of the representation as immediately known, but we cannot be said to be conscious of the thing represented, which, if known, is only known through its representation. If, therefore, mediate knowledge be in propriety a knowledge, consciousness is not coextensive with knowledge. This is, however, a problem we are hereafter specially to consider. I may here also observe, that, while all philosophers agree in making consciousness an immediate knowledge, some, as Reid and Stewart, do not admit that all immediate knowledge is consciousness. They hold that we have an immediate knowledge of external objects, but they hold that these objects are beyond the sphere of consciousness. This is an opinion we are, likewise, soon to canvass.

The *third* condition of consciousness, which may be held as universally admitted, is, that *it supposes a contrast, — a discrimination;* for we can be conscious only inasmuch as we are conscious of something; and we are conscious of something only inasmuch as we are conscious of what that something is, — that is, distinguish it from what it is not. This discrimination is of different kinds and degrees.

This discrimination of various kinds and degrees. — In the *first* place, there is the contrast between the two grand opposites, *self* and *not-self*, — *ego* and *non-ego*, — *mind* and *matter* (the contrast of *subject* and *object* is more general). We are conscious of self only in and by its contradistinction from not-self; and are conscious of not-self only in and by its contradistinction from self. In the *second* place, there is the discrimination of the states or modifications of the internal subject or self from each other. We are conscious of one mental state only as we contradistinguish it from another; where two, three, or more such states are confounded, we are conscious of them as one; and were we to note no difference in our mental modifications, we might be said to be absolutely unconscious. Hobbes has truly said, "Idem semper sentire, et non sentire, ad idem recidunt;" [To have always the same sensation, and not to have any sensation at all, amount to the same thing.] In the *third* place, there is the distinction between the parts and qualities of the outer world. We are conscious of an external object only as we are conscious of it as distinct from others; — where several distinguishable objects are confounded, we are conscious of them as one; where no object is discriminated, we are not conscious of any. Before leaving this condition, I may parenthetically state, that, while all philosophers admit that consciousness involves a discrimination, many do not allow it any cognizance of aught beyond the sphere of self. The great majority of philosophers do this because they absolutely deny the possibility of an immediate knowledge of external things, and, consequently, hold that consciousness in distinguishing the non-ego from the ego, only distinguishes self from self; for they maintain, that what we are conscious of as something different from the perceiving mind is only, in reality, a modification of that mind, which we are condemned to mistake for the material reality. Some philosophers, however, (as Reid and Stewart,) who hold, with mankind at large, that we do possess an immediate knowledge of something different from the knowing self, still limit consciousness to a cognizance of self; and, consequently, not only deprive it of the power of distinguishing external objects from each other, but even of the power of discriminating the ego and non-ego. These opinions we are afterwards to consider. With this qualification, all philosophers may be viewed as admitting that discrimination is an essential condition of consciousness.

The *fourth* condition of consciousness, which may be assumed as very generally acknowledged, is, that *it involves judgment.* A judgment is the mental act by which one thing is affirmed or denied of another. This fourth condition is, in truth, only a necessary consequence of the third; — for it is impossible to discriminate without judging, — discrimination, or contradistinction, being in fact only the denying one thing of another. It may to some seem strange that consciousness, the simple and primary act of intelligence, should be a judgment, — which philosophers, in general, have viewed as a compound and derivative operation. This is, however, altogether a mistake. A judgment is, as I shall hereafter show you, a simple act of mind, for every act of mind implies a judgment. Do we perceive or imagine, without affirming, in the act, the external or internal existence of the object? Now these fundamental affirmations are the affirmations, — in other words, the judgments, of consciousness.

The *fifth* undeniable condition of consciousness is *memory.* This condition, also, is a corollary of the third. For without memory, our mental states could not be held fast, compared, distinguished from each other, and referred to self. Without memory, each indivisible, each infinitesimal, moment in the mental succession would stand isolated from every other, —

would constitute, in fact, a separate existence. The notion of the ego or self arises from the recognized permanence and identity of the thinking subject, in contrast to the recognized succession and variety of its modifications. But this recognition is possible only through memory. The notion of self is, therefore, the result of memory. But the notion of self is involved in consciousness; so, consequently, is memory.

CHAPTER IX.

CONSCIOUSNESS NOT A SPECIAL FACULTY.

So far as we have proceeded, our determination of the contents of consciousness may be viewed as that universally admitted. Let us, therefore, sum up the points we have established. We have shown, in general, that consciousness is the self-recognition that we know, or feel, or desire, etc. We have shown, in particular, 1°, That consciousness is an actual or living, and not a potential or dormant, knowledge; — 2°, That it is an immediate, and not a mediate, knowledge; — 3°, That it supposes a discrimination; — 4°, That it involves a judgment; — and, 5°, That it is possible only through memory.

We are now about to enter on a more disputed territory; and the first thesis I shall attempt to establish, involves several subordinate questions.

Our consciousness coextensive with our knowledge. — I state, then, as the first contested position which I am to maintain, that our *consciousness is coextensive with our knowledge.* But this assertion, that we have no knowledge of which we are not conscious, is tantamount to the other, that *consciousness is coextensive with our cognitive faculties,* — and this, again, is convertible with the assertion, that *consciousness is not a special faculty,* but that our special faculties of knowledge are only modifications of consciousness. The question, therefore, may be thus stated, — Is consciousness the genus under which our several faculties of knowledge are contained as species, — or, is consciousness itself a special faculty coördinate with, and not comprehending, these?

By Hutcheson, Reid, and Stewart, — to say nothing of inferior names, — consciousness has been considered as nothing higher than a special faculty. As I regard this opinion to be erroneous, and as the error is one affecting the very cardinal point of philosophy, — as it stands opposed to the peculiar and most important principles of the philosophy of Reid and Stewart themselves, and has even contributed to throw around their doctrine of perception an obscurity that has caused Dr. Brown absolutely to mistake it for its converse, and as I have never met with any competent refutation of the grounds on which it rests, — I shall endeavor to show you that, notwithstanding the high authority of its supporters, this opinion is altogether untenable.

Reid and Stewart on consciousness. — As I previously stated, neither Dr. Reid nor Mr. Stewart has given us any regular account of consciousness; their doctrine on this subject is to be found scattered in differents parts of their works. The two following brief passages of Reid contain the principal positions of that doctrine. The first is: "Consciousness is a word used by philosophers to signify that immediate knowledge which we have of our present thoughts and purposes, and, in general, of all the present operations of our minds. Whence we may observe, that consciousness is only of things present. To apply consciousness to things past, which sometimes is done in popular discourse, is to confound consciousness with memory; and all such confusion of words ought to be avoided in philosophical discourse. It is likewise to be observed, that consciousness is only of things in the mind, and not of external things. It is improper to say, I am conscious of the table which is before me. I perceive it, I see it; but do not say I am conscious of it. As that consciousness, by which we have a knowledge of the operations of our own minds, is a different power from that by which we perceive external objects, and as these different powers have different names in our language, and, I believe, in all languages, a philosopher ought carefully to preserve this distinction, and never to confound things so different in their nature." The second is: "Consciousness is an operation of the understanding of its own kind, and cannot be logically defined. The objects of it are our present pains, our pleasures, our hopes, our fears, our desires, our doubts, our thoughts of every kind; in a word, all the passions and all the actions and operations of our own minds, while they are present. We may remember them when they are past; but we are conscious of them only while they are present." Besides what is thus said in general of consciousness, in his treatment of the different special faculties, Reid contrasts consciousness with each. Thus, in his essays on Perception, on Conception or Imagination, and on Memory, he specially contradistinguishes consciousness from each of these operations; and it is also incidentally by Reid, but more articulately by Stewart, discriminated from Attention and Reflection.

According to the doctrine of these philosophers, consciousness is thus a special faculty, coördinate with the other intellectual powers, having like them a particular operation and a peculiar object. And what is the peculiar object which is proposed to consciousness? The peculiar objects of consciousness, says Dr. Reid, are all the present passions and operations of our minds. Consciousness thus has for its objects, among the other modifications of the mind, the acts of our cognitive faculties. Now here a doubt arises. If consciousness has for its object the cognitive operations, it must know these operations, and, *as it knows these operations, it must know their objects:* consequently, consciousness is either not a special faculty, but a faculty comprehending every cognitive act;* or it must be held

* [*We know;* and *We know that we know:* — these propositions, *logically* distinct, are *really* identical; each implies the other. The attempt to analyze the cognition *I know*, and the cognition *I know that I know*, into the separate energies of distinct faculties, is therefore vain. But this is the analysis of Reid. Consciousness, which the formula *I know that I know* adequately expresses, he views as a power specifically distinct from the various cognitive faculties comprehended under the formula *I know*, precisely as these faculties are severally contradistinguished from each other. But here the parallel does not hold. I can feel without perceiving, I can perceive without imagining, I can imagine without remembering, I can remember without judging (in the emphatic signification), I can judge without willing. One of these acts does not immediately suppose the other Though modes merely of the same indivisible subject, they are modes in

that *there is a double knowledge of every object*, — *first*, the knowledge of that object *by its particular faculty*, and *second*, a knowledge of it *by consciousness*, as taking cognizance of every mental operation. But the former of these alternatives is a surrender of consciousness as a coördinate and special faculty, and the latter is a supposition not only unphilosophical but absurd. Now, you will attend to the mode in which Reid escapes, or endeavors to escape, from this dilemma. This he does by assigning to consciousness, as its object, the various intellectual operations to the exclusion of their several objects. "I am conscious," he says, "of perception, but not of the object I perceive; I am conscious of memory, but not of the object I remember." By this limitation, if tenable, he certainly escapes the dilemma, for he would thus disprove the truth of the principle on which it proceeds — namely, that to be conscious of the operation of a faculty is, in fact, to be conscious of the object of that operation. The whole question, therefore, turns upon the proof or disproof of this principle; — for if it can be shown that *the knowledge of an operation necessarily involves the knowledge of its object*, it follows that it is impossible to make consciousness conversant about the intellectual operations to the exclusion of their objects. And that this principle must be admitted, is what, I hope, it will require but little argument to demonstrate.

relation to each other, really distinct, and admit, therefore, of psychological discrimination. But can I feel without being conscious that I feel? — can I remember, without being conscious that I remember? or, can I be conscious, without being conscious that I perceive, or imagine, or reason, — that I energize, in short, in some determinate mode, which Reid would view as the act of a faculty specifically different from consciousness? That this is impossible, Reid himself admits. But if, on the one hand, consciousness be only realized under specific modes, and cannot therefore exist apart from the several faculties *in cumulo;* and if, on the other, these faculties can all and each only be exerted under the condition of consciousness; consciousness, consequently, is not one of the special modes into which our mental activity may be resolved, but the fundamental form, — the generic condition of them all. Every intelligent act is thus a modified consciousness; and consciousness a comprehensive term for the complement of our cognitive energies.] — *Discussions.*

No consciousness of a cognitive act without a consciousness of its object. — Some things can be conceived by the mind each separate and alone; others, only in connection with something else. The former are said to be things absolute; the latter, to be things relative. Socrates and Xanthippe may be given as examples of the former; husband and wife, of the latter. Socrates and Xanthippe can each be represented to the mind without the other; and, if they are associated in thought, it is only by an accidental connection. Husband and wife, on the contrary, cannot be conceived apart. As relative and correlative, the conception of husband involves the conception of wife, and the conception of wife involves the conception of husband. Each is thought only in and through the other, and it is impossible to think of Socrates as the husband of Xanthippe, without thinking of Xanthippe as the wife of Socrates. We cannot, therefore, know what a husband is without also knowing what is a wife, as, on the other hand, we cannot know what a wife is without also knowing what is a husband. You will, therefore, understand from this example, the meaning of the logical axiom, that *the knowledge of relatives is one,* — or that the knowledge of relatives is the same.

This being premised, it is evident that, if our intellectual operations exist only in relation, it must be impossible that consciousness can take cognizance of one term of this relation, without also taking cognizance of the other. *Knowledge*, in general, *is a relation between a subject knowing and an object known*, and each operation of our cognitive faculties only exists by relation to a particular object, — this object at once calling it into existence, and specifying the quality of its existence. It is, therefore, palpably impossible that we can be conscious of an act without being conscious of the object to which that act is relative.* This, however, is what Dr. Reid and Mr. Stewart

* [The assertion, that we can be conscious of an act of knowledge, without being conscious of its object, is virtually suicidal. A mental operation is what it is, only by relation to its object; the object at once determining its existence, and specifying the character of its existence. But if a relation cannot be comprehended in one of its terms, so we cannot be conscious of

maintain. They maintain that I can know that I know, without knowing what I know, — or that I can know the knowledge without knowing what the knowledge is about; for example, that I am conscious of perceiving a book without being conscious of the book perceived, — that I am conscious of remembering its contents, without being conscious of these contents remembered, — and so forth. The unsoundness of this opinion must, however, be articulately shown by taking the different faculties in detail, which they have contradistinguished from consciousness, and by showing, in regard to each, that it is altogether impossible to propose the operation of that faculty to the consideration of consciousness, and to withhold from consciousness its object.

Imagination. — I shall commence with the faculty of Imagination, to which Dr. Reid and Mr. Stewart have chosen, under various limitations, to give [erroneously] the name of Conception. This faculty is peculiarly suited to evince the error of holding that consciousness is cognizant of acts, but not of the objects of these acts.

"Conceiving, Imagining, and Apprehending," says Dr. Reid, "are commonly used as synonymous in our language, and signify the same thing which the logicians call Simple Apprehen-

an operation, without being conscious of the object to which it exists only as correlative. For example, — We are conscious of a perception, says Reid, but are not conscious of its object. Yet how can we be conscious of a *perception*, that is, how can we *know* that a perception exists, — that it is a perception, and not another mental state, — and that it is the perception of a rose, and of nothing but a rose; unless this *consciousness* involve a knowledge (or consciousness) of the object, which at once determines the existence of the act, — specifies its kind, — and distinguishes its individuality? Annihilate the object, you annihilate the operation; annihilate the consciousness of the object, you annihilate the consciousness of the operation. In the greater number indeed of our cognitive energies, the two terms of the relation of knowledge exist only as identical; the object admitting only of a logical discrimination from the subject. I imagine a Hippogryph. The Hippogryph is at once the object of the act and the act itself. Abstract the one, the other has no existence: deny me the consciousness of the Hippogryph you deny me the consciousness of the imagination; I am conscious of zero; I am not conscious at all.] — *Discussions.*

sion. This is an operation of the mind different from all those we have mentioned [Perception, Memory, etc.]. Whatever we perceive, whatever we remember, whatever we are conscious of, we have a full persuasion or conviction of its existence. What never had an existence cannot be remembered; what has no existence at present cannot be the object of perception or of consciousness; but what never had, nor has any existence, may be conceived. Every man knows that it is as easy to conceive a winged horse or a centaur, as it is to conceive a horse or a man. Let it be observed, therefore, that to conceive, to imagine, to apprehend, when taken in the proper sense, signify an act of the mind which implies no belief or judgment at all. It is an act of the mind by which nothing is affirmed or denied, and which, therefore, can neither be true nor false." And again: "Consciousness is employed solely about objects that do exist, or have existed. But conception is often employed about objects that neither do, nor did, nor will, exist. This is the very nature of this faculty, that its object, though distinctly conceived, may have no existence. Such an object we call a creature of imagination, but this creature never was created.

"That we may not impose upon ourselves in this matter, we must distinguish between that act or operation of the mind, which we call conceiving an object, and the object which we conceive. When we conceive any thing, there is a real act or operation of the mind; of this we are conscious, and can have no doubt of its existence. But every such act must have an object; for he that conceives must conceive something. Suppose he conceives a centaur, he may have a distinct conception of this object, though no centaur ever existed." And again: "I conceive a centaur. This conception is an operation of the mind of which I am conscious, and to which I can attend. The sole object of it is a centaur, an animal which, I believe, never existed."

Now, here it is admitted by Reid, that imagination has an object, and, in the example adduced, that this object has no existence out of the mind. The object of imagination is, there fore, in the mind, — is a modification of the mind. Now, can it be maintained that there can be a modification of mind, — a modification of which we are aware, but of which we are not conscious? But let us regard the matter in another aspect. We are conscious, says Dr. Reid, of *the imagination of a centaur*, but *not of the centaur imagined.* Now, nothing can be more evident than that the object and the act of imagination are *identical.* Thus, in the example alleged, the centaur imagined, and the act of imagining it, are one and indivisible. What is the act of imagining a centaur but the centaur imaged, or the image of the centaur; what is the image of the centaur but the act of imagining it? The centaur is both the object and the act of imagination: it is the same thing viewed in different relations. It is called the object of imagination, when considered as representing a possible existence; — for every thing that can be construed to the mind, every thing that does not violate the laws of thought, in other words, every thing that does not involve a contradiction, may be conceived by the mind as possible.* I say, therefore, that the centaur is

* [Reid says, "The sole object of conception (imagination) is an animal which I believe never existed." It 'never existed;' that is, never really, never in nature, never externally, existed. But it is 'an object of imagination.' It is not, therefore, a mere non-existence; for if it had no kind of existence, it could not possibly be the positive object of any kind of thought. For were it an absolute nothing, it could have no qualities (*non-entis nulla sunt attributa*); but the object we are conscious of, as a Centaur, has qualities, — qualities which constitute it a determinate something, and distinguish it from every other entity whatsoever. We must, therefore, per force, allow it some sort of imaginary, ideal, representative, or (in the older meaning of the term) *objective*, existence in the mind. Now this existence can only be one or other of two sorts; for such object in the mind either *is*, or *is not, a mode of mind.* Of these alternatives the latter cannot be supposed; for this would be an affirmation of the crudest kind of non-egoistical representation — the very hypothesis against which Reid so strenuously contends. The former alternative remains — that it is a mode of the imagining mind, — that it is, in fact, the plastic act of imagination, considered as representing to itself a certain possible form — a Centaur. But then Reid's assertion — that there is always an object distinct from the operation of the mind conversant about it, the act being one thing, the object of the act another — must be surrendered. For the *object* and the

called the object of imagination, when considered as representing a possible existence; whereas the centaur is called the act of imagination, when considered as the creation, work, or operation, of the mind itself. The centaur imagined and the imagination of the centaur are thus as much the same indivisible modification of mind, as a square is the same figure, whether we consider it as composed of four sides, or as composed of four angles, — or as paternity is the same relation whether we look from the son to the father, or from the father to the son. We cannot, therefore, be conscious of imagining an object, without being conscious of the object imagined; and as regards imagination, Reid's limitation of consciousness is, therefore, futile.

Memory. — I proceed next to Memory: — "It is by Memory," says Dr. Reid, "that we have an immediate knowledge of things past. The senses give us information of things only as they exist in the present moment; and this information, if it were not preserved by memory, would vanish instantly, and leave us as ignorant as if it had never been. Memory must have an object. Every man who remembers must remember something, and that which he remembers is called the object of his remembrance. In this, memory agrees with perception, but differs from sensation, which has no object but the feeling itself. Every man can distinguish the thing remembered from the remembrance of it. We may remember any thing which we have seen, or heard, or known, or done, or suffered; but the remembrance of it is a particular act of the mind which now exists, and of which we are conscious. To confound these two is an absurdity which a thinking man could not be led into, but by some false hypothesis which hinders him from reflecting upon the thing which he would explain by it." "The object of memory, or thing remembered, must be something that is past; as the object of perception and of consciousness must be

act are here only one and the same thing in two several relations. Reid's error consists in mistaking a logical for a metaphysical difference — a distinction of relation for a distinction of entity. Or is the error only from the vagueness and ambiguity of expression?] — *Diss. supp. to Reid.*

something which is present. What now is, cannot be an object of memory; neither can that which is past and gone be an object of perception, or of consciousness." "Sometimes, in popular discourse, a man says he is conscious that he did such a thing, meaning that he distinctly remembers that he did it. It is unnecessary, in common discourse, to fix accurately the limits between consciousness and memory. This was formerly shown to be the case with regard to sense and memory. And, therefore, distinct remembrance is sometimes called sense, sometimes consciousness, without any inconvenience. But this ought to be avoided in philosophy, otherwise we confound the different powers of the mind, and ascribe to one what really belongs to another. If a man be conscious of what he did twenty years or twenty minutes ago, there is no use for memory, nor ought we to allow that there is any such faculty. The faculties of consciousness and memory are chiefly distinguished by this, that the first is an immediate knowledge of the present, the second an immediate knowledge of the past."

From these quotations it appears, that Reid distinguishes memory from consciousness in this, — that memory is an immediate knowledge of the past, consciousness an immediate knowledge of the present. We may, therefore, be conscious of the act of memory as present, but of the object of memory as past, consciousness is impossible. Now if memory and consciousness be, as Reid asserts, the one an immediate knowledge of the past, the other an immediate knowledge of the present, it is evident that memory is a faculty whose object lies beyond the sphere of consciousness; and, consequently, that consciousness cannot be regarded as the general condition of every intellectual act. We have only, therefore, to examine whether this attribution of repugnant qualities to consciousness and memory be correct, — whether there be not assigned to one or other a function which does not really belong to it.

Now, in regard to what Dr. Reid says of consciousness, I admit that no exception can be taken. Consciousness is an immediate knowledge of the present. We have, indeed, already shown that consciousness is an immediate knowledge, and, therefore, only of the actual or now-existent. This being admitted, and professing, as we do, to prove that consciousness is the one generic faculty of knowledge, we consequently must maintain that all knowledge is immediate, and only of the actual or present, — in other words, that what is called mediate knowledge, knowledge of the past, knowledge of the absent, knowledge of the non-actual or possible, is either no knowledge at all, or only a knowledge contained in, and evolved out of, an immediate knowledge of what is now existent and actually present to the mind. This, at first sight, may appear like paradox; I trust you will soon admit that the counter doctrine is self-repugnant.

Conditions of immediate knowledge. — Let us first determine what immediate knowledge is, and then see whether the knowledge we have of the past, through memory, can come under the conditions of immediate knowledge. Now nothing can be more evident than the following positions: 1°, An object to be known immediately must be known in itself, — that is, in those modifications, qualities, or phænomena, through which it manifests its existence, and not in those of something different from itself; for, if we suppose it known not in itself, but in some other thing, then this other thing is what is immediately known, and the object known through it is only an object mediately known.

But 2°, If a thing can be immediately known only if known in itself, it is manifest that it can only be known in itself, if it be itself actually in existence, and actually in immediate relation to our faculties of knowledge.

Memory not an immediate knowledge of the past. — Such are the necessary conditions of immediate knowledge; and they disprove at once Dr. Reid's assertion, that memory is an immediate knowledge of the past. An immediate knowledge is only conceivable of the now existent, as the now existent alone can be known in itself. But the past is only past, inasmuch as it is not now existent; and as it is not now existent, it cannot be known in itself. The immediate knowledge of the past is, therefore, impossible.

We have, hitherto, been considering the conditions of immediate knowledge *in relation to the object;* let us now consider them *in relation to the cognitive act.* Every act, and consequently, every act of knowledge, exists only as it now exists; and as it exists only in the *now*, it can be cognizant only of a now-existent object. Memory is an act, — an act of knowledge; it can, therefore, be cognizant only of a now-existent object. But the object known in memory is, *ex hypothesi*, past; consequently, we are reduced to the dilemma, either of refusing a past object to be known in memory at all, or of admitting it to be only mediately known, in and through a present object. That the latter alternative is the true, it will require a very few explanatory words to convince you. What are the contents of an act of memory? An act of memory is merely a present state of mind, which we are conscious of, not as absolute, but as relative to, and representing, another state of mind, and accompanied with the belief that the state of mind, as now represented, has actually been. I remember an event I saw, — the landing of George IV. at Leith. This remembrance is only a consciousness of certain imaginations, involving the conviction that these imaginations now represent ideally what I formerly really experienced. All that is immediately known in the act of memory, is the present mental modification; that is, the representation and concomitant belief. Beyond this mental modification, we know nothing; and this mental modification is not only known to consciousness, but only exists in and by consciousness. Of any past object, real or ideal, the mind knows and can know nothing, for *ex hypothesi*, no such object now exists; or if it be said to know such an object, it can only be said to know it mediately, as represented in the present mental modification.

Properly speaking, however, we know only the actual and present, and *all real knowledge is an immediate knowledge.* What is said to be mediately known, is, in truth, not known to be, but only *believed* to be; for its existence is only an inference resting on the belief, that the mental modification truly represents what is in itself beyond the sphere of knowledge. What is immediately known must be; for what is immediately known is supposed to be known as existing. The denial of the existence, and of the existence within the sphere of consciousness, involves, therefore, a denial of the immediate knowledge of an object. We may, accordingly, doubt the reality of any object of mediate knowledge, without denying the reality of the immediate knowledge on which the mediate knowledge rests. In memory, for instance, we cannot deny the existence of the present representation and belief, for their existence is the consciousness of their existence itself. To doubt their existence, therefore, is for us to doubt the existence of our consciousness. But as this doubt itself exists only through consciousness, it would, consequently, annihilate itself. But, though in memory we must admit the reality of the representation and belief, as facts of consciousness, we may doubt, we may deny, that the representation and belief are true. We may assert that they represent what never was, and that all beyond their present mental existence is a delusion. This, however, could not be the case if our knowledge of the past were immediate. So far, therefore, is memory from being an immediate knowledge of the past, that it is at best only a mediate knowledge of the past; while, in philosophical propriety, it is not a knowledge of the past at all, but a knowledge of the present and a belief of the past. But in whatever terms we may choose to designate the contents of memory, it is manifest that these contents are all within the sphere of consciousness.*

* [This criticism on Reid's doctrine of memory is hardly fair, for it seems to be founded on a misapprehension of his use of language. The word "immediate" has two meanings: — first, as *present, instant,* or *now existing.* In this sense, we say, "There is a call for *immediate* action," meaning thereby *instant* action. Secondly, it may mean *direct, proximate,* or *without the intervention of any other thing;* thus, "The *immediate* agency of God," signifies his *direct* action, without the intervention of any second cause. In treating of memory, Reid uses the word "immediate" in the former acceptation, Hamilton in the latter. Hence there is no contradiction between them. Either might have accepted the other's doctrine as supplementary to his own, — certainly as not contradicting it.] — *Am. Ed.*

CHAPTER X.

CONSCIOUSNESS NOT A SPECIAL FACULTY CONTINUED; ITS RELATION TO PERCEPTION, ATTENTION, AND REFLECTION.

Reid contradistinguishes consciousness from perception.— We now proceed to consider the third faculty which Dr. Reid specially contradistinguishes from Consciousness, — I mean Perception, or that faculty through which we obtain a knowledge of the external world. Now, you will observe that Reid maintains, against the immense majority of all, and the entire multitude of modern, philosophers, that we have a *direct and immediate knowledge of the external world.* He thus vindicates to mind not only an immediate knowledge of its own modifications, but also an immediate knowledge of what is essentially different from mind or self, — the modifications of matter. He did not, however, allow that these were known by any common faculty, but held that the qualities of mind were exclusively made known to us by Consciousness, the qualities of matter exclusively made known to us by Perception. Consciousness was, thus, the faculty of immediate knowledge purely *subjective;* perception, the faculty of immediate knowledge purely *objective.* The Ego was known by one faculty, the Non-Ego by another. "Consciousness," says Dr. Reid, "is only of things in the mind, and not of external things. It is improper to say, I am conscious of the table which is before me. I perceive it, I see it, but do not say I am conscious of it. As that consciousness by which we have a knowledge of the operations of our own minds, is a different power from that by which we perceive external objects, and as these different powers have different names in our language, and, I believe, in all languages, a philosopher ought carefully to preserve this distinction, and never to confound things so different in their nature." And in another place he observes: — "Consciousness always goes along with perception; but they are different operations of the mind, and they have their different objects. Consciousness is not perception, nor is the object of consciousness the object of perception."

Dr. Reid has many merits as a speculator, but the only merit which he arrogates to himself, — the principal merit accorded to him by others, — is, that he was the first philosopher, in more recent times, who dared, in his doctrine of immediate perception, to vindicate, against the unanimous authority of philosophers, the universal conviction of mankind. But this doctrine he has at best imperfectly developed, and, at the same time, has unfortunately obscured it by errors of so singular a character, that some acute philosophers have never even suspected what his doctrine of perception actually is. One of these errors is the contradistinction of perception from consciousness.

Doctrine of representative perception in two forms. — I may here notice, by anticipation, that philosophers, at least modern philosophers, before Reid, allowed to the mind no immediate knowledge of the external reality. They conceded to it only a representative or mediate knowledge of external things. Of these *some*, however, held that the representative object — the object immediately known — was *different from the mind knowing*, as it was *also different from the reality it represented;* while *others*, on a simpler hypothesis, maintained that there was *no immediate entity, no tertium quid, between the reality and the mind*, but that the immediate or *representative object was itself a mental modification.* The latter thus granting to mind no immediate knowledge of aught beyond its own modification, could, consequently, only recognize a consciousness of self. The former, on the contrary, could, as they actually did, accord to consciousness a cognizance of not-self. Now Reid, after asserting against the philosophers the immediacy of our knowledge of external things, would almost appear to have been startled by his own boldness, and, instead of carrying his principle fairly to its issue, by according to consciousness on his doctrine that knowledge of the external world as existing, which, in the doctrine of the philosophers, it obtained of the external world as represented, he inconsistently stopped short, split immediate knowledge into two parts, and bestowed the knowledge of material qualities on perception alone, allowing that of mental modifications to remain exclusively with consciousness. Be this, however, as it may, the exemption of the objects of perception from the sphere of consciousness can be easily shown to be self-contradictory.

Reid maintains that we are not conscious of matter. — What! say the partisans of Dr. Reid, are we not to distinguish, as the product of different faculties, the knowledge we obtain of objects in themselves the most opposite? Mind and matter are mutually separated by the whole diameter of being. Mind and matter are, in fact, nothing but words to express two series of phænomena known less in themselves than in contradistinction from each other. The difference of the phænomena to be known, surely legitimates a difference of faculty to know them. In answer to this, we admit at once, that — were the question merely whether we should not distinguish, under consciousness, two special faculties, — whether we should not study apart, and bestow distinctive appellations on consciousness considered as more particularly cognizant of the external world, and on consciousness considered as more particularly cognizant of the internal — this would be highly proper and expedient. But this is not the question. Dr. Reid distinguishes consciousness as a special faculty from perception as a special faculty, and he allows to the former the cognizance of the latter in its operation, to the exclusion of its object. He maintains that we are conscious of our perception of a rose, but not of the rose perceived; that we know the ego by one act of knowledge, the non-ego by another. This doctrine I hold to be erroneous, and it is this doctrine I now proceed to refute.

Reid is wrong, because 1°, *the knowledge of opposites is one.* — In the first place, it is not only a logical axiom, but a self-evident truth, that the knowledge of opposites is one. Thus, we cannot know what is tall without knowing what is short, — we know what is virtue only as we know what is vice, — the science of health is but another name for the science of disease. Nor do we know the opposites, the I and Thou, the Ego and the Non-ego, the subject and object, mind and matter, by a different law. The act which affirms that this particular phænomenon is a modification of Me, virtually affirms that the phænomenon is not a modification of any thing different from Me, and, consequently implies a common cognizance of self and not-self; the act which affirms that this other phænomenon is a modification of something different from Me, virtually affirms that the phænomenon is not a modification of Me, and, consequently, implies a common cognizance of not-self and self. But unless we are prepared to maintain that the faculty cognizant of self and not-self is different from the faculty cognizant of not-self and self, we must allow that the ego and non-ego are known and discriminated in the same indivisible act of knowledge. What, then, is the faculty of which this act of knowledge is the energy? It cannot be Reid's consciousness, for that is cognizant only of the ego or mind; — it cannot be Reid's perception, for that is cognizant only of the non-ego or matter. But as the act cannot be denied, so the faculty must be admitted. It is not, however, to be found in Reid's catalogue. But though not recognized by Reid in his system, its necessity may, even on his hypothesis, be proved. For if, with him, we allow only a special faculty immediately cognizant of the ego, and a special faculty immediately cognizant of the non-ego, we are at once met by the question, By what faculty are the ego and non-ego discriminated? We cannot say by consciousness, for that knows nothing but mind; — we cannot say by perception, for that knows nothing but matter. But as mind and matter are never known apart and by themselves, but always in mutual correlation and contrast, this knowledge of them in connection must be the function of some faculty, not like Reid's consciousness and perception, severally limited to mind and to matter as exclusive objects, but cognizant of them as the ego and non-ego, — as the two terms of a relation. It is thus shown that an act and a faculty must, perforce, on Reid's own hypothesis, be admitted, in which these two terms shall be comprehended together in the unity of knowledge, — in short, a higher consciousness, embracing Reid's consciousness and perception, and in which the two acts, severally cognitive of mind and of matter, shall be comprehended and reduced to unity and correlation. But what is this but to admit at last, in an unphilosophical complexity, the common consciousness of subject and object, of mind and matter, which we set out with denying in its philosophical simplicity?

[The immediate knowledge which Reid allows of things different from the mind, and the immediate knowledge of mind itself, cannot therefore be split into two distinct acts. In perception, as in the other faculties, the same indivisible consciousness is conversant about both terms of the relation of knowledge. Distinguish the cognition of the subject from the cognition of the object of perception, and you *either* annihilate the relation of knowledge itself, which exists only in its terms being comprehended together in the unity of consciousness; *or* you must postulate a higher faculty, which shall again reduce to one the two cognitions you have distinguished; — that is, you are at last compelled to admit, in an unphilosophical complexity, that common consciousness of subject and object, which you set out with denying in its philosophical simplicity. *Consciousness* and *immediate knowledge* are thus terms universally convertible; and if there be an immediate knowledge of things external, there is consequently the *consciousness of an outer world.*

(To obviate misapprehension, we may here parenthetically observe, that all we *do* intuitively know of self, — all that we *may* intuitively know of not-self, is only *relative.* Existence, *absolutely and in itself*, is to us as zero; and while nothing *is*, so nothing is *known* to us, except those phases of being which stand in analogy to our faculties of knowledge. These we call *qualities*, *phenomena*, *properties*, etc. When we say, therefore, that a thing is *known in itself*, we mean only that it stands face to face, in direct and immediate relation to the conscious mind; in other words, that, *as existing*, its phenomena form part of the circle of our knowledge, — exist *since* they are known, and are known *because* they exist.) — *Discussions.*

Because, 2°, *he thus contradicts his own doctrine of an immediate knowledge of the external world.* — But in the second place, the attempt of Reid to make consciousness conversant about the various cognitive faculties to the exclusion of their objects, is equally impossible in regard to Perception, as we have shown it to be in relation to Imagination and Memory; nay, the attempt, in the case of perception, would, if allowed, be even suicidal of his great doctrine of our immediate knowledge of the external world.

Reid's assertion, that we are conscious of the act of perception, but not of the object perceived, involves, first of all, a general absurdity. For it virtually asserts that we can know what we are not conscious of knowing. An act of perception is an act of knowledge; what we perceive, that we know. Now, if in perception there be an external reality known, but of which external reality we are, on Reid's hypothesis, not conscious, then is there an object known, of which we are not conscious. But as we know only inasmuch as we know that we know, — in other words, inasmuch as we are conscious that we know, — we cannot know an object without being conscious of that object as known; consequently, we cannot perceive an object without being conscious of that object as perceived.

But, again, how is it possible that we can be conscious of an operation of perception, unless consciousness be coextensive with that act; and how can it be coextensive with the act, and not also conversant with its object? An act of knowledge is only possible in relation to an object, — and it is an act of one kind or another only by special relation to a particular object. Thus the object at once determines the existence, and specifies the character of the existence, of the intellectual energy. An act of knowledge existing, and being what it is, only by relation to its object, it is manifest that the act can be known only through the object to which it is correlative; and Reid's supposition, that an operation can be known in consciousness to the exclusion of its object, is impossible. For example, I see the inkstand. How can I be conscious that my present modification exists, — that it is a perception, and not another mental state, — that it is a perception of sight to the exclusion of every other sense, — and, finally, that it is a perception of the inkstand and of the inkstand only, — unless my consciousness comprehend within its sphere the object, which at once determines the existence of the act, qualifies its kind, and distinguishes its individuality? Annihilate the inkstand, you annihilate the perception; annihilate the consciousness of the object, you annihilate the consciousness of the operation.

The apparent incongruity of the expression explained. — It undoubtedly sounds strange to say, I am conscious of the inkstand, instead of saying, I am conscious of the perception of the inkstand. This I admit; but the admission can avail nothing to Dr. Reid, for *the apparent incongruity of the expression arises only from the prevalence of that doctrine of perception* in the schools of philosophy, *which it is his principal merit to have so vigorously assailed.* So long as it was universally assumed by the learned, that the mind is cognizant of nothing beyond, either, on one theory, its own representative modifications, or, on another, the species, ideas, or representative entities, different from itself, which it contains, and that all it knows of a material world is only an internal representation which, by the necessity of its nature, it mistakes for an external reality, — the supposition of an immediate knowledge of material phænomena was regarded only as a vulgar, an unphilosophical illusion; and the term consciousness, which was exclusively a learned or technical expression for all immediate knowledge, was, consequently, never employed to express an immediate knowledge of aught beyond the mind itself; and thus, when at length, by Reid's own refutation of the prevailing doctrine, it becomes necessary to extend the term to the immediate knowledge of external objects, this extension, so discordant with philosophic usage, is, by the force of association and custom, felt at first as strange and even contradictory. A slight consideration, however, is sufficient to reconcile us to the expression, in showing, if we hold the doctrine of immediate perception, the necessity of not limiting consciousness to our subjective states. In fact, if we look beneath the surface, *consciousness was not, in general, restricted,* even in philosophical usage, *to the modifications of the conscious self.* That great majority of philosophers who held that, in perception, we know nothing of the external reality as existing, but that we are immediately cognizant only of a representative something, different both from the object represented and from the percipient mind, — these philosophers, one and all, admitted that we are conscious of this *tertium quid* present to, but not a modification of, mind; — for, except Reid and his school, I am aware of no philosophers who denied that consciousness was coextensive or identical with immediate knowledge.

How some of the self-contradictions of Reid's doctrine may be avoided. — But, in the third place, we have previously reserved a supposition on which we may possibly avoid some of the self-contradictions which emerge from Reid's proposing as the object of consciousness the act, but excluding from its cognizance the object, of perception; that is, the object of its own object. The supposition is, that Dr. Reid committed the same error in regard to perception, which he did in regard to memory and imagination; and that, in maintaining our immediate knowledge in perception, he meant nothing more than to maintain, that the mind is not, in that act, cognizant of any representative object different from its own modification, of any *tertium quid* ministering between itself and the external reality; but that, in perception, the mind is determined itself to represent the unknown external reality, and that, on this self-representation, he abusively bestowed the name of immediate knowledge, in contrast to that more complex theory of perception, which holds that there intervenes between the percipient mind and the external existence an intermediate something, different from both, by which the former knows, and by which the latter is represented. On the supposition of this mistake, we may believe him guiltless of the others; and we can certainly, on this ground, more easily conceive how he could accord to consciousness a knowledge only of the percipient act, — meaning by that act the representation of the external reality; and how he could deny to consciousness a knowledge of the object of perception,—meaning by that object the unknown reality itself. This is the only opinion which Dr. Brown and others ever suspect him of maintaining; and a strong case might certainly be made out to prove that this view of his doctrine is correct. But if such were, in truth, Reid's opinion, then has he accomplished nothing,—his whole philosophy is one mighty blunder For, as I shall hereafter show, idealism finds in this simpler hypothesis of representation even a more secure foundation than on the other; and, in point of fact, on this hypothesis, the most philosophical scheme of idealism that exists,—the Egoistic or Fichtean,—is established.

Taking, however, the general analogy of Reid's system, and a great number of unambiguous passages into account, I am satisfied that this view of his doctrine is erroneous; and I shall endeavor, when we come to treat of mediate and immediate knowledge, to explain how, from his never having formed to himself an adequate conception of these under all their possible forms, and from his historical ignorance of them as actually held by philosophers,—he often appears to speak in contradiction of the vital doctrine which, in equity, he must be held to have steadily maintained.

Reid and Stewart on Attention and Reflection.—Besides the operations we have already considered,—Imagination or Conception, Memory, and Perception, which Dr. Reid and Mr. Stewart have endeavored to discriminate from Consciousness,—there are further to be considered Attention and Reflection, which, in like manner, they have maintained to be an act or acts, not subordinate to, or contained in, Consciousness. But before proceeding to show that their doctrine on this point is almost equally untenable as on the preceding, it is necessary to clear up some confusion, and to notice certain collateral errors.

Reid either employs these terms as synonymous expressions, or he distinguishes them only by making Attention relative to the consciouness and perception of the present; Reflection to the memory of the past. He says, "In order, however, to our having a distinct notion of any of the operations of our own minds, it is not enough that we be conscious of them, for all men have this consciousness: it is further necessary that we attend to them while they are exerted, and reflect upon them with care while they are recent and fresh in our memory. It is necessary that, by employing ourselves frequently in this way, we get the habit of this attention and reflection," etc. And "Mr. Locke," he says, "has restricted the word *reflection* to that which is employed about the operations of our minds, without any authority, as I think, from custom, the arbiter of language: for surely I may reflect upon what I have seen or heard, as well as upon what I have thought. The word, in its proper and common meaning, is equally applicable to objects of sense, and to objects of consciousness. He has likewise confounded reflection with consciousness, and seems not to have been aware that they are different powers, and appear at very different periods of life." In the first of these quotations, Reid might use *attention* in relation to the consciousness of the present, *reflection*, to the memory of the past; but in the second, in saying that reflection "is equally applicable to objects of sense and to objects of consciousness," he distinctly indicates that the two terms are used by him as convertible. Reid (I may notice by the way) is wholly wrong in his strictures on Locke for his restricted usage of the term *reflection;* for it was not until after his time, that the term came, by Wolf, to be philosophically employed in a more extended signification than that in which Locke correctly applies it. Reid is likewise wrong, if we literally understand his words, in saying that reflection is employed in common language in relation to objects of sense. It is never employed except upon the mind and its contents. We cannot be said to reflect upon any external object, except in so far as that object has been previously perceived, and its image become part and parcel of our intellectual furniture. We may be said to reflect upon it in memory, but not in perception. But to return.

Reid, therefore, you will observe, identifies Attention and

Reflection. Now Mr. Stewart says, "Some important observations on the subject of attention occur in different parts of Dr. Reid's writings. To this ingenious author we are indebted for the remark, that attention to things external is properly called *observation;* and attention to the subjects of our consciousness, *reflection.*

There is, likewise, another oversight of Mr. Stewart which I may notice. "Although," he says, "the connection between attention and memory has been frequently remarked in general terms, I do not recollect that the power of attention has been mentioned by any of the writers on pneumatology in their enumeration of faculties of the mind; nor has it been considered by any one, so far as I know, as of sufficient importance to deserve a particular examination." So far is this from being the case, that there are many previous authors who have considered attention as a separate faculty, and treated of it even at greater length than Mr. Stewart himself. This is true not only of the celebrated Wolf, but of the whole Wolfian school; and to these I may add Condillac, Malebranche, and many others. But this by the way.

Is Attention a faculty distinct from consciousness? — Taking, however, Attention and Reflection for acts of the same faculty, and supposing, with Mr. Stewart, that reflection is properly attention directed to the phænomena of mind; observation, attention directed to the phænomena of matter; the main question comes to be considered, Is Attention a faculty different from Consciousness, as Reid and Stewart maintain? As the latter of these philosophers has not argued the point himself, but merely refers to the arguments of the former in confirmation of their common doctrine, it will be sufficient to adduce the following passage from Reid, in which his doctrine on this head is contained. "I return," he says, "to what I mentioned as the main source of information on this subject, — attentive reflection upon the operations of our own minds.

"All the notions we have of mind and its operations, are, by Mr. Locke, called *ideas of reflection.* A man may have as distinct notions of remembrance, of judgment, of will, of desire, as he has of any object whatever. Such notions, as Mr. Locke justly observes, are got by the power of reflection. But what is this power of reflection? 'It is,' says the same author, 'that power by which the mind turns its view inward, and observes its own actions and operations.' He observes elsewhere, 'That the understanding, like the eye, whilst it makes us see and perceive all other things, takes no notice of itself; and that it requires art and pains to set it at a distance, and make it its own object.'

"This power of the understanding to make its own operations its object, to attend to them, and examine them on all sides, is the power of reflection, by which alone we can have any distinct notions of the powers of our own or of other minds.

"*This reflection ought to be distinguished from consciousness*, with which it is too often confounded, even by Mr. Locke. All men are conscious of the operations of their own minds, at all times while they are awake; but there are few who reflect upon them, or make them objects of thought."

What Attention is.—Dr. Reid has rightly said that Attention is a voluntary act. This remark might have led him to the observation, that *Attention is not a separate faculty*, or a faculty of intelligence at all, *but merely an act of will or desire*, subordinate to a certain law of intelligence. This law is, that the greater number of objects to which our consciousness is simultaneously extended, the smaller is the intensity with which it is able to consider each, and consequently, the less vivid and distinct will be the information it obtains of the several subjects. This law is expressed in the old adage,

"Pluribus intentus minor est ad singula sensus."

Such being the law, it follows that, when our interest in any particular object is excited, and when we wish to obtain all the knowledge concerning it in our power, it behooves us to limit our consideration to that object, to the exclusion of others. This is done by an act of volition or desire, which is called *attention*. But to view attention as a special act of intelligence, and to distinguish it from consciousness, is utterly inept. Consciousness may be compared to a telescope, attention to the pulling out or in of the tubes in accommodating the focus to the object; and we might, with equal justice, distinguish in the eye the adjustment of the pupil from the general organ of vision, as, in the mind, distinguish attention from consciousness, as separate faculties. Not, however, that they are to be accounted the same. Attention is consciousness, and something more. It is consciousness voluntarily applied, under its law of limitations, to some determinate object; it is consciousness concentrated. In this respect, attention is an interesting subject of consideration; and having now finished what I proposed in proof of the position, that consciousness is not a special faculty of knowledge, but coextensive with all our cognitions, I shall proceed to consider it in its various aspects and relations; and having just stated the law of limitation, I shall go on to what I have to say in regard to attention as a general phænomenon of consciousness.

Can we attend to more than one object at once? — And, here, I have first to consider a question in which I am again sorry to find myself opposed to many distinguished philosophers, and in particular, to one whose opinion on this, as on every other point of psychological observation, is justly entitled to the highest consideration. The philosopher I allude to is Mr. Stewart. The question is, Can we attend to more than a single object at once? For if attention be nothing but the concentration of consciousness on a smaller number of objects than constitute its widest compass of simultaneous knowledge, it is evident that, unless this widest compass of consciousness be limited to only two objects, we do attend when we converge consciousness on any smaller number than that total complement of objects which it can embrace at once. For example, if we suppose that the number of objects which consciousness can simultaneously apprehend be six, the limitation of consciousness to five, or four, or three, or two, or one, will all be acts of attention, different in degree, but absolutely identical in kind.

Stewart's doctrine of attention. — Mr. Stewart's doctrine is as follows: — "Before," he says, "we leave the subject of Attention, it is proper to take notice of a question which has been stated with respect to it; whether we have the power of attending to more than one thing at one and the same instant; or, in other words, whether we can attend, at one and the same instant, to objects which we can attend to separately? This question has, if I am not mistaken, been already decided by several philosophers in the negative; and I acknowledge, for my own part, that although their opinion has not only been called in question by others, but even treated with some degree of contempt as altogether hypothetical, it appears to me to be the most reasonable and philosophical that we can form on the subject.

"There is, indeed, a great variety of cases in which the mind apparently exerts different acts of attention at once; but from the instances which have already been mentioned, of the astonishing rapidity of thought, it is obvious that all this may be explained without supposing those acts to be coexistent; and I may even venture to add, it may all be explained in the most satisfactory manner, without ascribing to our intellectual operations a greater degree of rapidity than that with which we know, from the fact, that they are sometimes carried on. The effect of practice in increasing this capacity of apparently attending to different things at once, renders this explanation of the phænomenon in question more probable than any other.

"The case of the equilibrist and rope-dancer is particularly favorable to this explanation, as it affords direct evidence of the possibility of the mind's exerting different successive acts in an interval of time so short, as to produce the same sensible effect as if they had been exerted at one and the same moment. In this case, indeed, the rapidity of thought is so remarkable, that if the different acts of the mind were not all necessarily accompanied with different movements of the eye, there can be no reason for doubting that the philosophers whose doctrine I am now controverting, would have asserted that they are all mathematically coexistent.

"Upon a question, however, of this sort, which does not admit of a perfectly direct appeal to the fact, I would by no means be understood to decide with confidence; and, therefore, I should wish the conclusions I am now to state, to be received as only conditionally established. They are necessary and obvious consequences of the general principle, 'that the mind can only attend to one thing at once;' but must stand or fall with the truth of that supposition.

"It is commonly understood, I believe, that in a concert of music, a good ear can attend to the different parts of the music separately, or can attend to them all at once, and feel the full effect of the harmony. If the doctrine, however, which I have endeavored to establish be admitted, it will follow that, in the latter case, the mind is constantly varying its attention from the one part of the music to the other, and that its operations are so rapid as to give us no perception of an interval of time.

"The same doctrine leads to some curious conclusions with respect to vision. Suppose the eye to be fixed in a particular position, and the picture of an object to be painted on the retina. Does the mind perceive the complete figure of the object at once, or is this perception the result of the various perceptions we have of the different points in the outline? With respect to this question, the principles already stated lead me to conclude, that the mind does, at one and the same time, perceive every point in the outline of the object (provided the whole of it be painted on the retina at the same instant); for perception, like consciousness, is an involuntary operation. As no two points, however, of the outline are in the same direction, every point by itself constitutes just as distinct an object of *attention* to the mind, as if it were separated by an interval of empty space from all the rest. If the doctrine, therefore, formerly stated be just, it is impossible for the mind to attend to more than one of these points at once; and as the perception of the figure of the object implies a knowledge of the relative situation of the different points with respect to each other, we must conclude, that the perception of figure by the eye is the result of a number of different acts of attention. These acts of attention, however, are performed with such rapidity, that the effect, with respect to us, is the same as if the perception were instantaneous.

"In further confirmation of this reasoning, it may be remarked, that if the perception of visible figure were an immediate consequence of the picture on the retina, we should have, at the first glance, as distinct an idea of a figure of a thousand sides as of a triangle or a square. The truth is, that when the figure is very simple, the process of the mind is so rapid that the perception seems to be instantaneous; but when the sides are multipled beyond a certain number, the interval of time necessary for these different acts of attention becomes perceptible.

"It may, perhaps, be asked what I mean by a *point* in the outline of a figure, and what it is that constitutes this point *one* object of attention. The answer, I apprehend, is that this point is the *minimum visibile.* If the point be less, we cannot perceive it; if it be greater, it is not all seen in one direction.

"If these observations be admitted, it will follow that, without the faculty of memory, we could have had no perception of visible figure."

On this point, Dr. Brown not only coincides with Mr. Stewart in regard to the special fact of attention, but asserts in general that the mind cannot exist at the same moment in two different states, that is, in two states in either of which it can exist separately. "If the mind of man," he says, "and all the changes which take place in it, from the first feeling with which life commenced to the last with which it closes, could be made visible to any other thinking being, a certain series of feelings alone, — that is to say, a certain number of successive states of mind, would be distinguishable in it, forming indeed a variety of sensations, and thoughts, and passions, as momentary states of the mind, but all of them existing individually, and successively to each other. To suppose the mind to exist in two different states, in the same moment, is a manifest absurdity."

Criticism of Stewart's doctrine. — I shall consider these statements in detail. Mr. Stewart's first illustration of his doctrine is drawn from a concert of music, in which, he says, "a good ear can attend to the different parts of the music separately, or can attend to them all at once, and feel the full effect of the harmony." This example, however, appears to me to amount to a reduction of his opinion to the impossible. What are the facts in this example? In a musical concert, we have a multitude of different instruments and voices emitting at once an infinity of different sounds. These all reach the ear at the same indivisible moment in which they perish, and, consequently, if heard at all, much more if their mutual relation or harmony be perceived, they must be all heard simultaneously. This is evident. For if the mind can attend to each minimum of sound only successively, it, consequently, requires a minimum of time in which it is exclusively occupied with each minimum of sound. Now, in this minimum of time, there coexist with it, and with it perish, many minima of sound which, *ex hypothesi*, are not perceived, are not heard, as not attended to. In a concert, therefore, on this doctrine, a small number of sounds only could be perceived, and above this petty maximum, all sounds would be to the ear as zero. But what is the fact? No concert, however numerous its instruments, has yet been found to have reached, far less to have surpassed, the capacity of mind and its organ.

But it is even more impossible, on this hypothesis, to understand how we can perceive *the relation of different sounds*, that is, have *any feeling of the harmony* of a concert. In this respect, it is, indeed, *felo de se*. It is maintained that we cannot attend at once to two sounds, we cannot perceive them as coexistent, — consequently, the feeling of harmony of which we are conscious, must proceed from the feeling of the relation of these sounds as successively perceived in different points of time. We must, therefore, compare the past sound, as retained in memory, with the present, as actually perceived. But this is impossible on the hypothesis itself. For we must, in this case, attend to the past sound in memory, and to the present sound in sense at once, or they will not be perceived in mutual relation as harmonic. But one sound in memory and another sound in sense, are as much two different objects as two different sounds in sense. Therefore, one of two conclusions is inevitable, — either we can attend to two different objects at once, and the hypothesis is disproved, or we cannot, and all knowledge of relation and harmony is impossible, which is absurd.

His illustration from the phænomena of vision. — The consequences of this doctrine are equally startling, as taken from Mr. Stewart's second illustration from the phænomena of vision. He holds that the perception of figure by the eye is the result of a number of separate acts of attention, and that each act of attention has for its object a point the least that can be seen, the *minimum visibile*. On this hypothesis, we must suppose that, at every instantaneous opening of the eyelids, the moment sufficient for us to take in the figure of the objects comprehended in the sphere of vision, is subdivided into almost infinitesimal parts, in each of which a separate act of attention is performed. This is, of itself, sufficiently inconceivable. But this being admitted, no difficulty is removed. The separate acts must be laid up in memory, in imagination. But how are they there to form a single whole, unless we can, in imagination, attend to all the *minima visibilia* together, which, in perception, we could only attend to severally? On this subject I shall, however, have a more appropriate occasion of speaking, when I consider Mr. Stewart's doctrine of the relation of color to extension.

Attention possible without an act of free-will. — I think Reid and Stewart incorrect in asserting that attention is only a voluntary act, meaning, by the expression *voluntary*, an act of free-will. I am far from maintaining, as Brown and others do, that all *will* is *desire;* but still I am persuaded that we are frequently determined to an act of attention, as to many other acts, independently of our free and deliberate volition. Nor is it, I conceive, possible to hold that, though immediately determined to an act of attention by desire, it is only by the permission of our will that this is done; consequently, that every act of attention is still under the control of our volition. This I cannot maintain. Let us take an example:— When occupied with other matters, a person may speak to us, or the clock may strike, without our having any consciousness of the sound; but it is wholly impossible for us to remain in this state of unconsciousness intentionally and with will. We cannot determinately refuse to hear by voluntarily withholding our attention; and we can no more open our eyes, and, by an act of will, avert our minds from all perception of sight, than we can, by an act of will, cease to live. We may close our ears or shut our eyes, as we may commit suicide; but we cannot, with our organs unobstructed, wholly refuse our attention at will.

Attention of three degrees or kinds. — It, therefore, appears to me the more correct doctrine to hold that there is no consciousness without attention, — without concentration, — but that attention is of three degrees or kinds. The first, a mere vital and irresistible act; the second, an act determined by desire, which, though involuntary, may be resisted by our will; the third, an act determined by a deliberate volition. An act of attention, — that is, an act of concentration, — seems thus necessary to every exertion of consciousness, as a certain contraction of the pupil is requisite to every exercise of vision. We have formerly noticed, that discrimination is a condition of consciousness; and a discrimination is only possible by a concentrative act, or act of attention. This, however, which corresponds to the lowest degree, — to the mere vital or automatic act of attention, has been refused the name; and *attention*, in contradistinction to this mere automatic contraction, given to the two other degrees, of which, however, Reid only recognizes the third.

Attention, then, is to consciousness, what the contraction of the pupil is to sight; or to the eye of the mind, what the microscope or telescope is to the bodily eye. The faculty of attention is not, therefore, a special faculty, but merely consciousness acting under the law of limitation to which it is subjected. But whatever be its relations to the special faculties, attention doubles all their efficiency, and affords them a power of which they would otherwise be destitute. It is, in fact, as we are at present constituted, the primary condition of their activity.

Brown's doctrine that the mind cannot exist in two different states at once. — I have now only to say a word in answer to Dr. Brown's assertion that the mind cannot exist, at the same moment, in two different states, — that is, in two states in either of which it can exist separately; he affirms that the contrary supposition is a manifest absurdity. I find the same doctrine maintained by Locke; he says: "Different sentiments are different modifications of the mind. The mind or the soul that perceives, is one immaterial, indivisible substance. Now, I see the white and black on this paper, I hear one singing in the next room, I feel the warmth of the fire I sit by, and I taste an apple I am eating, and all this at the same time. Now, I ask, take modification for what you please, can the same unextended, indivisible substance have different, nay, inconsistent and opposite (as these of white and black must be), modifications at the same time? Or must we suppose distinct parts in an indivisible substance, one for black, another for white, and another for red ideas, and so of the rest of those infinite sensations which we have in sorts and degrees; all which we can distinctly perceive, and so are distinct ideas, some whereof are opposite as heat and cold, which yet a man may feel at the same time?"

Opposed by Leibnitz and Aristotle. — In reference to this passage, Leibnitz says: "Mr. Locke asks, 'Can the same unextended, indivisible substance have different, nay, inconsistent and opposite, modifications at the same time?' I reply, it can. What is inconsistent in the same object, is not inconsistent in the representation of different objects which we conceive at the same moment. For this, there is no necessity that there should be different parts in the soul, as it is not necessary that there should be different parts in the point on which, however, different angles rest." The same thing had, however, been even better said by Aristotle, whose doctrine I prefer translating to you, as more perspicuous, in the following passage from Joannes Grammaticus (better known by the surname Philoponus), — a Greek philosopher, who flourished towards the middle of the sixth century. It is taken from the Prologue to his valuable commentary on the *De Anima* of Aristotle; and, what is curious, the very supposition which, on Locke's doctrine, would infer the corporeal nature of mind, is alleged, by the Aristotelians and Condillac, in proof of its immateriality. "Nothing bodily," says Aristotle, "can, at the same time, in the same part, receive contraries. The finger cannot at once be wholly participant of white and of black, nor can it, at once and in the same place, be both hot and cold. But the sense at the same moment apprehends contraries. Wherefore, it knows that this is first, and that second, and that it discriminates the black from the white. In what manner, therefore, does sight simultaneously perceive contraries? Does it do so by the same? or does it by one part apprehend black, by another, white? If it does so by the same, it must apprehend these without parts, and it is incorporeal. But if by one part it apprehends this quality, and by another, that, — this, he says, is the same as if I perceived this, and you that. But it is necessary that that which judges should be one and the same, and that it should even apprehend by the same the objects which are judged. Body cannot, at the same moment and by the same part, apply itself to contraries or things absolutely different. But sense at once applies itself to black and to white; it, therefore, applies itself indivisibly. It is thus shown to be incorporeal. For if by one part it apprehended white, by another part apprehended black, it could not discern the one color from the other; for no one can distinguish that which is perceived by himself as different from that which is perceived by another."

Criticism of Brown's doctrine. — Dr. Brown calls the sensation of sweet one mental state, the sensation of cold another; and as the one of these states may exist without the other, they are consequently different states. But will it be maintained that we cannot, at one and the same moment, feel the sensations of sweet and cold, or that sensations forming apart different states, do, when coexistent in the same subject, form only a single state?

On this view, comparison is impossible. — The doctrine that the mind can attend to, or be conscious of, only a single object at a time, would, in fact, involve the conclusion that all comparison and discrimination are impossible; but comparison and discrimination being possible, this possibility disproves the truth of the counter proposition. An act of comparison or discrimination supposes that we are able to comprehend, in one indivisible consciousness, the different objects to be compared or discriminated. Were I only conscious of one object at one time, I could never possibly bring them into relation; each could be apprehended only separately, and for itself. For in the moment in which I am conscious of the object A, I am, *ex hypothesi*, unconscious of the object B; and in the moment I am conscious of the object B, I am unconscious of the object A. So far, in fact, from consciousness not being competent to the cognizance of two things at once, it is only possible under that cognizance as its condition. For without discrimination there could be no consciousness; and discrimination necessarily supposes two terms to be discriminated.

No judgment could be possible were not the subject and predicate of a proposition thought together by the mind, although expressed in language one after the other. Nay, as Aristotle has observed, a syllogism forms, in thought, one simultaneous act; and it is only the necessity of retailing it piecemeal and by succession, in order to accommodate thought to the imperfection of its vehicle, language, that affords the appearance of a consecutive existence. Some languages, as the Sanscrit, the Latin, and the Greek, express the syntactical relations by flexion, and not by mere juxtaposition. Their sentences are thus bound up in one organic whole, the preceding parts remaining suspended in the mind, till the meaning, like an electric spark, is flashed from the conclusion to the commencement. This is the reason of the greater rhetorical effect of terminating the Latin period by the verb. And to take a more elementary example,—"How could the mind comprehend these words of Horace,

'Bacchum in remotis carmina rupibus
Vidi docentem,'

unless it could seize at once those images in which the adjectives are separated from their substantives?"

How many objects can the mind embrace at once? — Supposing that the mind is not limited to the simultaneous consideration of a single object, a question arises, How many objects can it embrace at once? You will recollect that I formerly stated, that the greater the number of objects among which the attention of the mind is distributed, the feebler and less distinct will be its cognizance of each.

Consciousness will thus be at its maximum of intensity when attention is concentrated on a single object; and the question comes to be, how many several objects can the mind simultaneously survey, not with vivacity, but without absolute confusion? I find this problem stated and differently answered, by different philosophers, and apparently without a knowledge of each other. By Charles Bonnet, the mind is allowed to have a distinct notion of six objects at once; by Abraham Tucker, the number is limited to four; while Destutt-Tracy again amplifies it to six. The opinion of the first and last of these philosophers appears to me correct. You can easily make the experiment for yourselves, but you must beware of grouping the objects into classes. If you throw a handful of marbles on the floor, you will find it difficult to view at once more than six, or seven at most, without confusion; but if you group them into twos, or threes, or fives, you can comprehend as many groups as you can units; because the mind considers these groups only as units; — it views them as wholes, and throws their parts out of consideration. You may perform the experiment also by an act of imagination.

Value of attention considered as an act of will. — Before leaving this subject, I shall make some observations on the value of attention, considered in its highest degree as an act of will, and on the importance of forming betimes the habit of deliberate concentration.

The greater capacity of continuous thinking that a man possesses, the longer and more steadily can he follow out the same train of thought, — the stronger is his power of attention; and in proportion to his power of attention will be the success with which his labor is rewarded. All commencement is difficult; and this is more especially true of intellectual effort. When we turn for the first time our view on any given object, a hundred other things still retain possession of our thoughts. Even when we are able, by an arduous exertion, to break loose from the matters which have previously engrossed us, or which every moment force themselves on our consideration, — even when a resolute determination, or the attraction of the new object, has smoothed the way on which we are to travel; still the mind is continually perplexed by the glimmer of intrusive and distracting thoughts, which prevent it from placing that which should exclusively occupy its view, in the full clearness of an undivided light. How great soever may be the interest which we take in the new object, it will, however, only be fully established as a favorite, when it has been fused into an integral part of the system of our previous knowledge, and of our established associations of thoughts, feelings, and desires. But this can only be accomplished by time and custom. Our imagination and our memory, to which we must resort for materials with which to illustrate and enliven our new study, accord us their aid unwillingly, — indeed, only by compulsion. But if we are vigorous enough to pursue our course in spite of obstacles, every step, as we advance, will be found easier; the mind becomes more animated and energetic; the distractions gradually diminish; the attention is more exclusively concentrated upon its object; the kindred ideas flow with greater freedom and abundance, and afford an easier selection of what is suitable for illustration. At length, our system of thought harmonizes with our pursuit. The whole man, becomes, as it may be, philosopher, or historian, or poet; he lives only in the trains of thought relating to this character. He now energizes freely, and, consequently, with pleasure; for pleasure is the reflex of unforced and unimpeded energy. All that is produced in this state of mind, bears the stamp of excellence and perfection.

Helvetius justly observes, that the very feeblest intellect is capable of comprehending the inference of one mathematical position from another, and even of making such an inference itself. Now, the most difficult and complicate demonstrations in the works of a Newton or a Laplace, are all made up of such immediate inferences. They are like houses composed of single bricks. No greater exertion of intellect is required to make a thousand such inferences than is requisite to make one; as the effort of laying a single brick is the maximum of any individual effort in the construction of such a house. Thus, the difference between an ordinary mind and the mind of a Newton consists principally in this, that the one is capable of the application of a more continuous attention than the other, — that a Newton is able without fatigue to connect inference with inference in one long series towards a determinate end; while the man of inferior capacity is soon obliged to break or let fall the thread which he had begun to spin. This is, in fact, what Sir Isaac, with equal modesty and shrewdness, himself admitted. To one who complimented him on his genius, he replied that if he had made any discoveries, it was owing more tc patient attention than to any other talent. There is but little analogy between mathematics and play-acting; but I heard the great Mrs. Siddons, in nearly the same language, attribute the whole superiority of her unrivalled talent to the more intense study which she bestowed upon her parts.

If what Alcibiades, in the *Symposium* of Plato, narrates of Socrates were true, the father of Greek philosophy must have possessed this faculty of meditation or continuous attention in the highest degree. The story, indeed, has some appearance of exaggeration; but it shows what Alcibiades, or rather Plato through him, deemed the requisite of a great thinker. According to this report, in a military expedition which Socrates made along with Alcibiades, the philosopher was seen by the Athenian army to stand for a whole day and a night, until the breaking of the second morning, motionless, with a fixed gaze, — thus showing that he was uninterruptedly engrossed with the consideration of a single subject: "And thus," says Alcibiades, "Socrates is ever wont to do, when his mind is occupied with inquiries in which there are difficulties to be overcome. He then never interrupts his meditation, and forgets to eat, and drink, and sleep, — everything, in short, until his inquiry has reached its termination, or, at least, until he has seen some light in it." In this history, there may be, as I have said, exaggeration; but still the truth of the principle is undeniable. Like Newton, Descartes arrogated nothing to the force of his intellect. What he had accomplished more than other men, that he attributed to the superiority of his method; and Bacon, in like manner, eulogizes his method, — in that it places all men with equal attention upon a level, and leaves little or nothing to the prerogatives of genius. Nay, genius itself has been analyzed by the shrewdest observers into a higher capacity of attention. "Genius," says Helvetius, whom we have already quoted, "is nothing but a continued attention" (*une attention suivie*).

These examples and authorities concur in establishing the important truth, that he who would, with success, attempt discovery, either by inquiry into the works of nature, or by meditation on the phænomena of mind, must acquire the faculty of abstracting himself, for a season, from the invasion of surrounding objects; must be able even, in a certain degree, to emancipate himself from the dominion of the body, and live, as it were, a pure intelligence, within the circle of his thoughts. This faculty has been manifested, more or less, by all whose names are associated with the progress of the intellectual sciences. In some, indeed, the power of abstraction almost degenerated into a habit akin to disease, and the examples which now occur to me would almost induce me to retract what I have said about the exaggeration of Plato's history of Socrates. Archimedes, it is well known, was so absorbed in a geometrical meditation, that he was first aware of the storming of Syracuse by his own death-wound, and his exclamation on the entrance of Roman soldiers was, — *Noli turbare circulos meos*. In like manner, Joseph Scaliger, the most learned of men, when a Protestant student in Paris, was so engrossed in the study of Homer, that he became aware of the massacre of

St. Bartholomew, and of his own escape, only on the day subsequent to the catastrophe.

I have dwelt at greater length upon the practical bearings of Attention, not only because this principle constitutes the better half of all intellectual power, but because it is of consequence that you should be fully aware of the incalculable importance of acquiring, by early and continued exercise, the habit of attention. There are, however, many points of great moment on which I have not touched, and the dependence of Memory upon Attention might alone form an interesting matter of discussion.

CHAPTER XI.

CONSCIOUSNESS,—ITS EVIDENCE AND AUTHORITY.

HAVING now concluded the discussion in regard to what Consciousness is, and shown you that it constitutes the fundamental form of every act of knowledge;—I now proceed to consider it as the source from whence we must derive every fact in the Philosophy of Mind. And, in prosecution of this purpose, I shall, in the *first* place, endeavor to show that it really is the principal, if not the only source, from which all knowledge of the mental phænomena must be obtained; in the *second* place, I shall consider the character of its evidence, and what, under different relations, are the different degrees of its authority; and, in the *last* place, I shall state what, and of what nature, are the more general phænomena which it reveals. Having terminated these, I shall then descend to the consideration of the special faculties of knowledge, that is, to the particular modifications of which consciousness is susceptible.

Philosophy implies the veracity of consciousness.—We proceed to consider, in the first place, the authority,—the certainty, of this instrument. Now, it is at once evident, that philosophy, as it affirms its own possibility, must affirm the veracity of consciousness; for, as philosophy is only a scientific development of the facts which consciousness reveals, it follows, that philosophy, in denying or doubting the testimony of consciousness, would deny or doubt its own existence. If, therefore, philosophy be not *felo de se*, it must not invalidate the integrity of that which is, as it were, the heart, the *punctum saliens*, of its being; and as it would actively maintain its own credit, it must be able positively to vindicate the truth of consciousness. Leibnitz truly says, — "If our immediate internal experience could possibly deceive us, there could no longer be for us any truth of fact, nay, nor any truth of reason."

So far there is, and can be, no dispute; if philosophy is possible, the evidence of consciousness is authentic. No philosopher denies its authority, and even the Sceptic can only attempt to show, on the hypothesis of the Dogmatist, that consciousness, as at variance with itself, is, therefore, on that hypothesis, mendacious.

But if the testimony of consciousness be in itself confessedly above all suspicion, it follows, that we inquire into the conditions or laws which regulate the legitimacy of its applications. The conscious mind being at once the source from which we must derive our knowledge of its phænomena, and the mean through which that knowledge is obtained, Psychology is only an evolution, by consciousness, of the facts which consciousness itself reveals. As every system of Mental Philosophy is thus only an exposition of these facts, every such system, consequently, is true and complete, as it fairly and fully exhibits what, and what only, consciousness exhibits.

Consciousness naturally clear and unerring. — But it may be objected, — if consciousness be the only revelation we possess of our intellectual nature, and if consciousness be also the sole criterion by which we can interpret the meaning of what this revelation contains, this revelation must be very obscure, — this criterion must be very uncertain, seeing that the various systems of philosophy all equally appeal to this revelation and to this criterion, in support of the most contradictory opinions. As to the fact of the variety and contradiction of philosophical systems, — this cannot be denied; and it is also true that all these systems either openly profess allegiance to consciousness, or silently confess its authority. But admitting all this, I am still bold enough to maintain, that consciousness affords not merely the only revelation, and only criterion of philosophy, but that this revelation is naturally clear, — this criterion, in itself, unerring. The history of philosophy, like the history of theology, is only, it is too true, the history of variations; and we must admit of the book of consciousness what a great Calvinist divine bitterly confessed of the book of Scripture, —

> "Hic liber est in quo quærit sua dogmata quisque;
> Invenit et pariter dogmata quisque sua."

Cause of variation in philosophy. — In regard, however, to either revèlation, it can be shown that the source of this diversity is not in the book, but in the reader. If men will go to the Bible, not to ask of it what they shall believe, but to find in it what they believe already, the standard of unity and truth becomes in human hands only a Lesbian rule.* And if philosophers, in place of evolving their doctrines out of consciousness, resort to consciousness only when they are able to quote its authority in confirmation of their preconceived opinions, philosophical systems, like the sandals of Theramenes,† may fit any feet, but can never pretend to represent the immutability of nature. And that philosophers have been, for the most part, guilty of this, it is not extremely difficult to show. They have seldom or never taken the facts of consciousness, the whole facts of consciousness, and nothing but the facts of consciousness. They have either overlooked, or rejected, or interpolated.

Before we are entitled to accuse consciousness of being a false, or vacillating, or ill-informed witness, — we are bound, first of all, to see whether there be any rules by which, in employing the testimony of consciousness, we must be governed; and whether philosophers have evolved their systems out of consciousness in obedience to these rules. For if there be

* [A Lesbian (carpenter's) rule or level, being made of lead, did not measure correctly the inequalities of the surface to which it was applied, but bent under its own weight so as to adapt itself to those inequalities, instead of gauging their amount. See Aristotle, *Eth. Nic.* v. 10, 7.] — *Am. Ed.*

† [As Theramenes readily attached himself to any party that happened to be uppermost, he was nicknamed ὁ Κόθορνος, the name for a sort of sandal, which, unlike those made as rights and lefts, would fit equally well either foot.] — *Am. Ed.*

rules under which alone the evidence of consciousness can be fairly and fully given, and, consequently, under which alone consciousness can serve as an infallible standard of certainty and truth, and if philosophers have despised or neglected these, — then must we remove the reproach from the instrument, and affix it to those blundering workmen who have not known how to handle and apply it. In attempting to vindicate the veracity and perspicuity of this, the natural, revelation of our mental being, I shall, therefore, first, endeavor to enumerate and explain the general rules by which we must be governed in applying consciousness as a mean of internal observation, and thereafter show how the variations and contradictions of philosophy have all arisen from the violation of one or more of these laws.

Three rules for applying the testimony of consciousness. — There are, in all, if I generalize correctly, three laws which afford the exclusive conditions of psychological legitimacy. These laws, or regulative conditions, are self-evident, and yet they seem never to have been clearly proposed to themselves by philosophers; — in philosophical speculation, they have certainly never been adequately obeyed.

The First of these rules is, — That no fact be assumed as a fact of consciousness but what is ultimate and simple. This I would call the law of Parcimony.

The Second, — that which I would style the law of Integrity, is — That the whole facts of consciousness be taken without reserve or hesitation, whether given as constituent, or as regulative data.

The Third is, — That nothing but the facts of consciousness be taken, or, if inferences of reasoning be admitted, that these at least be recognized as legitimate only as deduced from, and in subordination to, the immediate data of consciousness, and every position rejected as illegitimate, which is contradictory of these. This I would call the law of Harmony.

I shall consider these in their order.

I. The first law, that of Parcimony, is, — That no fact be assumed as a fact of consciousness but what is ultimate and simple. What is a fact of consciousness? This question, of all others, requires a precise and articulate answer; but I have not found it adequately answered in any psychological author.

Every fact of consciousness — 1. *Primary and universal.* — In the first place, — every mental phænomenon may be called a fact of consciousness. But as we distinguish consciousness from the special faculties, though these are all only modifications of consciousness, — only branches of which consciousness is the trunk, so we distinguish the special and derivative phænomena of mind from those that are primary and universal, and give to the latter the name of *facts of consciousness*, as more eminently worthy of that appellation. In an act of Perception, for example, I distinguish the pen I hold in my hand, and my hand itself, from my mind perceiving them. This distinction is a particular fact, — the fact of a particular faculty, Perception. But there is a general fact, a general distinction, of which this is only a special case. This general fact is the distinction of the Ego and non-Ego, and it belongs to consciousness as the general faculty. Whenever, therefore, in our analysis of the intellectual phænomena, we arrive at an element which we cannot reduce to a generalization from experience, but which lies at the root of all experience, and which we cannot, therefore, resolve into any higher principle, — this we properly call a fact of consciousness. Looking to such a fact of consciousness as the last result of an analysis, we call it an *ultimate* principle; looking from it as the first constituent of all intellectual combination, we call it a *primary* principle. A fact of consciousness is, thus, a simple, and, as we regard it, either an ultimate or a primary, datum of intelligence. It obtains also various denominations; sometimes it is called an *a priori principle*, sometimes a *fundamental law* of mind, sometimes a *transcendental condition* of thought, etc.

2. *Necessary.* — But, in the second place, this, its character of ultimate priority supposes its character of necessity. It must be impossible not to think it. In fact, by its necessity alone can we recognize it as an original datum of intelligence, and distinguish it from any mere result of generalization and custom.

3. *Incomprehensible.* — In the third place, this fact, as ultimate, is also given to us with a mere belief of its reality; in other words, consciousness reveals that it is, but not *why* or *how* it is. This is evident. Were this fact given us, not only with a belief, but with a knowledge of how or why it is, in that case it would be a derivative, and not a primary, datum. For that whereby we were thus enabled to comprehend its *how* and *why*, — in other words, the reason of its existence, — this would be relatively prior, and to it or to its antecedent must we ascend, until we arrive at that primary fact, in which we must at last believe, — which we must take upon trust, but which we could not comprehend, that is, think under a higher notion.*

* Elsewhere, in the "Dissertations Supplementary to Reid," the author gives a somewhat different, and more clearly explicated, enumeration of ["the essential notes and characters by which we are enabled to distinguish our original from our derivative convictions. These characters, I think, may be reduced to four; — 1°, their *Incomprehensibility* — 2°, their *Simplicity* — 3°, their *Necessity* and *absolute Universality* — 4°, their *comparative Evidence* and *Certainty*.

"1. In reference to the first; — A conviction is incomprehensible when there is merely given us in consciousness — *That its object is* (ὅτι ἔστι); and when we are unable to comprehend through a higher notion or belief, *Why or How it is* (διότι ἔστι). When we are able to comprehend why or how a thing is, the belief of the existence of that thing is not a primary datum of consciousness, but a subsumption under the cognition or belief which affords its reason.

"2. As to the second; — It is manifest that if a cognition or belief be made up of, and can be explicated into, a plurality of cognitions or beliefs, that, as compound, it cannot be original.

"3. Touching the third; — Necessity and Universality may be regarded as coincident. For when a belief is necessary, it is, *eo ipso*, universal; and that a belief is universal, is a certain index that it must be necessary. To prove the necessity, the universality must, however, be absolute; for a relative universality indicates no more than custom and education, howbeit the subjects themselves may deem that they follow only the dictates of nature. As St. Jerome has it — 'Unaquæque gens hoc legem naturæ putat, quod didicit.'

"4. The fourth and last character of our original beliefs is their comparative Evidence and Certainty. This, along with the third, is well stated by Aristotle — 'What *appears to all*, that we affirm *to be*; and he who rejects this belief will assuredly advance *nothing better deserving of credence*.' And

A fact of consciousness is thus, — that whose existence is given and guaranteed by an original and necessary belief. But there is an important distinction to be here made, which has not only been overlooked by all philosophers, but has led some of the most distinguished into no inconsiderable errors.

The facts of consciousness considered in two points of view. — The facts of consciousness are to be considered in two points of view; either as evidencing their own ideal or phænomenal existence, or as evidencing the objective existence of something else beyond them. A belief in the former is not identical with a belief in the latter. The one cannot, the other may possibly, be refused. In the case of a common witness, we cannot doubt the fact of his personal reality, nor the fact of his testimony as emitted; — but we can always doubt the truth of that which his testimony avers. So it is with consciousness. We cannot possibly refuse the fact of its evidence as given, but we may hesitate to admit that beyond itself of which it assures us. I shall explain by taking an example. In the act of External Perception, consciousness gives, as a conjunct fact, the existence of Me or Self as perceiving, and the existence of something different from Me or Self as perceived. Now the reality of

again: — 'If we know and believe through certain original principles, we must know and believe these with *paramount certainty*, for the very reason that we know and believe all else through them.' And such are the truths in regard to which the Aphrodisian says, — 'though some men may verbally dissent, all men are in their hearts agreed.' This constitutes the first of Buffier's essential qualities of primary truths, which is, as he expresses it, — 'to be so clear, that if we attempt to prove or to disprove them, this can be done only by propositions which are manifestly *neither more evident nor more certain*.'

"A good illustration of this character is afforded by the assurance — to which we have already so frequently referred — that in perception, mind is immediately cognizant of matter. *How* self can be conscious of not-self, *how* mind can be cognizant of matter, we do not know; but we know as little *how* mind can be percipient of itself. In both cases, we only know the fact, on the authority of consciousness; and when the conditions of the problem are rightly understood — when it is established that it is only the *primary* qualities of body which are apprehended in themselves, and this only in so far as they are in immediate relation to the organ of sense, the difficulty in the one case is not more than in the other."]

this, as a subjective datum, — as an ideal phænomenon, it is impossible to doubt without doubting the existence of consciousness, for consciousness is itself this fact; and to doubt the existence of consciousness is absolutely impossible; for as such a doubt could not exist, except in and through consciousness, it would, consequently, annihilate itself. We should doubt that we doubted. As contained, — as given, in an act of consciousness, the contrast of mind knowing and matter known cannot be denied.

But the whole phænomenon as given in consciousness may be admitted, and yet its inference disputed. It may be said, consciousness gives the mental subject as perceiving an external object, contradistinguished from it as perceived; all this we do not, and cannot, deny. But consciousness is only a phænomenon; the contrast between the subject and object may be only apparent, not real; the object given as an external reality may only be a mental representation, which the mind is, by an unknown law, determined unconsciously to produce, and to mistake for something different from itself. All this may be said and believed, without self-contradiction; — nay, all this has, by the immense majority of modern philosophers, been actually said and believed.*

* This distinction is, perhaps, more distinctly stated and illustrated by the author in the "notes to Reid." ["There is no scepticism possible touching the facts of consciousness in themselves. We cannot doubt that the phænomena of consciousness are real, in so far as we are conscious of them. I cannot doubt, for example, that I am actually conscious of a certain feeling of fragrance, and of certain perceptions of color, figure, etc., when I see and smell a rose. Of the reality of these, as experienced, I cannot doubt, because they are facts of consciousness; and of consciousness I cannot doubt, because such doubt being itself an act of consciousness, would contradict, and, consequently, annihilate itself. But of all beyond the mere phænomena of which we are conscious, we may — without fear of self-contradiction, at least — doubt. I may, for instance, doubt whether the rose I see and smell has any existence beyond a phænomenal existence in my consciousness. I cannot doubt that I am conscious of it *as* something different from self; but whether it have indeed any reality beyond my mind — whether the *not-self* be not in truth only *self* — that I may philosophically question. In like manner, I am conscious of the memory of a cer-

The case of Memory. — In like manner, in an act of Memory, consciousness connects a present existence with a past. I cannot deny the actual phænomenon, because my denial would be suicidal, but I can, without self-contradiction, assert that consciousness may be a false witness in regard to any former existence; and I may maintain, if I please, that the memory of the past, in consciousness, is nothing but a phænomenon, which has no reality beyond the present. There are many other facts of consciousness which we cannot but admit as ideal phænomena, but may discredit as guaranteeing aught beyond their phænomenal existence itself. The legality of this doubt I do not at present consider, but only its possibility; all that I have now in view being to show, that we must not confound, as has been done, the double import of the facts, and the two degrees of evidence for their reality. This mistake has, among others, been made by Mr. Stewart. "The belief," he says, "which accompanies consciousness, as to the present existence of its appropriate phænomena, has been commonly considered as much less obnoxious to cavil, than any of the principles which philosophers are accustomed to assume as self-evident, in the formation of their metaphysical systems. No doubts on this head have yet been suggested by any philosopher, how sceptical soever; even by those who have called in question the existence both of mind and of matter. And yet the fact is, that it rests on no foundation more solid than our belief of the existence of external objects; or our belief, that other men possess intellectual powers and faculties similar to those of which we are conscious in ourselves. In all these cases, the only account that can be given of our belief is, that it forms a necessary part of our constitution; against which metaphysicians may easily argue, so as to perplex the judgment, but of which it is impossible for us to divest ourselves for a moment, when we are called on to employ our reason either in the busi-

tain past event. Of the contents of this memory, as a phænomenon given in consciousness, scepticism is impossible. But I may by possibility demur to the reality of all beyond these contents and the sphere of present consciousness."]

ness of life, or in the pursuits of science. While we are under the influence of our appetites, passions, or affections, or even of a strong speculative curiosity, all those difficulties, which bewildered us in the solitude of the closet, vanish before the essential principles of the human frame."

Criticism of Stewart's view. — With all the respect to which the opinion of so distinguished a philosopher as Mr. Stewart is justly entitled, I must be permitted to say, that I cannot but regard his assertion, — that the present existence of the phænomena of consciousness, and the reality of that to which these phænomena bear witness, rest on a foundation equally solid, — as wholly untenable. The second fact, the fact testified to, may be worthy of all credit, — as I agree with Mr. Stewart in thinking that it is; but still it does not rest on a foundation equally solid as the fact of the testimony itself. Mr. Stewart confesses, that, of the former, no doubt had ever been suggested by the boldest sceptic; and the latter, in so far as it assures us of our having an immediate knowledge of the external world, — which is the case alleged by Mr. Stewart, — has been doubted, nay, denied, not merely by sceptics, but by modern philosophers almost to a man. This historical circumstance, therefore, of itself, would create a strong presumption, that the two facts must stand on very different foundations; and this presumption is confirmed when we investigate what these foundations themselves are.

The one fact, — the fact of the testimony, is an act of consciousness itself; it cannot, therefore, be invalidated without self-contradiction. For, as we have frequently observed, to doubt the reality of that of which we are conscious is impossible; for as we can only doubt through consciousness, to doubt of consciousness is to doubt of consciousness by consciousness. If, on the one hand, we affirm the reality of the doubt, we thereby explicitly affirm the reality of consciousness, and contradict our doubt; if, on the other hand, we deny the reality of consciousness, we implicitly deny the reality of our denial itself. Thus, in the act of perception, consciousness gives, as a conjunct fact, an *ego* or mind, and a *non-ego* or matter, known together, and contradistinguished from each other. Now, as a present phænomenon, this double fact cannot possibly be denied. I cannot, therefore, refuse the fact, that, in perception, I am conscious of a phænomenon, which I am compelled to regard as the attribute of something different from my mind or self. This I must perforce admit, or run into self-contradiction. But admitting this, may I not still, without self-contradiction, maintain that what I am compelled to view as the phænomenon of something different from me is, nevertheless (unknown to me), only a modification of my mind? In this I admit the fact of the testimony of consciousness as given, but deny the truth of its report. Whether this denial of the truth of consciousness, as a witness, is or is not legitimate, we are not, at this moment, to consider: all I have in view at present is, as I said, to show that we must distinguish in consciousness two kinds of facts, — the fact of consciousness testifying, and the fact of which consciousness testifies; and that we must not, as Mr. Stewart has done, hold that we can as little doubt of the fact of the existence of an external world, as of the fact that consciousness gives, in mutual contrast, the phænomenon of self in contrast to the phænomenon of not-self.

Results of the Law of Parcimony. — Under this first law, let it, therefore, be laid down, in the first place, that by a fact of consciousness, properly so called, is meant a primary and universal fact of our intellectual being; and, in the second, that such facts are of two kinds, — 1°, The facts given in the act of consciousness itself; and, 2°, The facts which consciousness does not at once give, but to the reality of which it only bears evidence. And as simplification is always a matter of importance, we may throw out of account altogether the former class of these facts; for of such no doubt can be, or has been, entertained. It is only the authority of these facts as evidence of something beyond themselves, — that is, only the second class of facts, — which become matter of discussion; it is not the *reality* of consciousness that we have to prove, but its *veracity*.

II. *The Law of Integrity.* — The second rule is, That the whole facts of consciousness be taken without reserve or hesitation, whether given as constituent, or as regulative, data. This rule is too manifest to require much elucidation. As philosophy is only a development of the phænomena and laws of consciousness, it is evident that philosophy can only be complete, as it comprehends, in one harmonious system, all the constituent, and all the regulative, facts of consciousness. If any phænomenon or constituent fact of consciousness be omitted, the system is not complete; if any law or regulative fact is excluded, the system is not legitimate.

III. *The Law of Harmony.* — The violation of this second rule is, in general, connected with a violation of the third, and we shall accordingly illustrate them together. The third is, — That nothing but the facts of consciousness be taken; or, if inferences of reasoning be admitted, that these at least be recognized as legitimate only as deduced from, and only in subordination to, the immediate data of consciousness, and that every position be rejected as illegitimate which is contradictory to these.

The truth and necessity of this rule are not less evident than the truth and necessity of the preceding. Philosophy is only a systematic evolution of the contents of consciousness, by the instrumentality of consciousness; it, therefore, necessarily supposes, in both respects, the veracity of consciousness.

How Scepticism arises out of partial dogmatic systems. — But, though this be too evident to admit of doubt, and though no philosopher has ever openly thrown off allegiance to the authority of consciousness, we find, nevertheless, that its testimony has been silently overlooked, and systems established upon principles in direct hostility to the primary data of intelligence. It is only such a violation of the integrity of consciousness, by the dogmatist, that affords, to the sceptic, the foundation on which he can establish his proof of the nullity of philosophy. The sceptic cannot assail the truth of the facts of consciousness in themselves. In attempting this, he would run at once into self-contradiction. In the first place, he would enact the part of a dogmatist, — that is, he would positively, dogmatically, establish his doubt. In the second, waiving this, how can he accomplish what he thus proposes? For why? He must attack consciousness either from a higher ground, or from consciousness itself. Higher ground than consciousness there is none; he must, therefore, invalidate the facts of consciousness from the ground of consciousness itself. On this ground, he cannot, as we have seen, deny the facts of consciousness as given; he can only attempt to invalidate their testimony. But this again can be done only by showing that consciousness tells different tales, — that its evidence is contradictory, — that its data are repugnant. But this no sceptic has ever yet been able to do. Neither does the sceptic or negative philosopher himself assume his principles; he only accepts those on which the dogmatist or positive philosopher attempts to establish his doctrine; and this doctrine he reduces to zero, by showing that its principles are either mutually repugnant, or repugnant to facts of consciousness, on which, though it may not expressly found, still, as facts of consciousness, it cannot refuse to recognize without denying the possibility of philosophy in general.

Violations of these laws in Dr. Brown's doctrine of external perception. — I shall illustrate the violation of this rule by examples taken from the writings of the late ingenious Dr. Thomas Brown. — I must, however, premise that this philosopher, so far from being singular in his easy way of appealing to, or overlooking, the facts of consciousness, as he finds them convenient or inconvenient for his purpose, supplies only a specimen of the too ordinary style of philosophizing. Now, you must know, that Dr. Brown maintains the *common doctrine* of the philosophers, that we have *no immediate knowledge of any thing beyond the states or modifications of our own minds,* — that *we are only conscious of the ego,* — the non-ego, as known, being only a modification of self, which mankind at large are illusively determined to view as external and different from self. This doctrine is contradictory to *the fact* to which consciousness testifies, — that *the object of which we are conscious in perception, is the external reality as existing, and not merely its representation in the percipient mind.* That this is the fact testified to by consciousness, and believed by the common sense of mankind, is admitted even by those philosophers who reject the truth of the testimony and the belief. It is of no consequence to us at present what are the grounds on which the principle is founded, that the mind can have no knowledge of aught besides itself; it is sufficient to observe, that, this principle being contradictory to the testimony of consciousness, Dr. Brown, by adopting it, virtually accuses consciousness of falsehood. But if consciousness be false in its testimony to one fact, we can have no confidence in its testimony to any other; and Brown, having himself belied the veracity of consciousness cannot, therefore, again appeal to this veracity as to a credible authority. But he is not thus consistent. Although he does not allow that we have any knowledge of the existence of an outer world, the existence of that world he still maintains. And on what grounds? He admits the reasoning of the idealist, that is, of the philosopher who denies the reality of the material universe, — he admits this to be invincible. How, then, is this conclusion avoided? Simply by appealing to the universal belief of mankind in favor of the existence of external things,* — that is, to the authority of a fact of consciousness. But to him this appeal is incompetent. For, in the first place, having already virtually given up, or rather positively rejected, the testimony of consciousness, when consciousness deposed to our immediate knowledge of external things, — how can he even found upon the veracity of that mendacious principle, when bearing evidence to the unknown existence of external things? *I cannot but believe that the material reality exists; therefore, it does exist, for consciousness does not deceive*

* [Tennemann, speaking of Plato, says: "*The illusion that things in themselves are cognizable, is so natural*, that we need not marvel if even philosophers have not been able to emancipate themselves from the prejudice. The common sense of mankind (gemeine Menschenverstand), which remains steadfast *within the sphere of experience*, recognizes *no distinction* between *things in themselves* [unknown reality existing] and *phenomena* [representation, object known]; and the philosophizing reason, commences therewith its attempt to investigate the foundation of this knowledge, and to recall itself into system."] — *Quoted in Notes to Discussions*, p. 92.

us, — this reasoning Dr. Brown employs when defending his assertion of an outer world. *I cannot but believe that the material reality is the object immediately known in perception; therefore, it is immediately known, for consciousness does not deceive us,* — this reasoning Dr. Brown rejects when establishing the foundation of his system. In the one case, he maintains, — this belief, because irresistible, is true; in the other case, he maintains, — this belief, though irresistible, is false. Consciousness is veracious in the former belief, mendacious in the latter. I approbate the one, I reprobate the other. The inconsistency of this is apparent. It becomes more palpable when we consider, in the second place, that the belief which Dr. Brown assumes as true rests on — is, in fact, only the reflex of — the belief which he repudiates as false. Why do mankind believe in the existence of an outer world? They do not believe in it as in something unknown; but, on the contrary, they believe it to exist, only because they believe that they immediately know it to exist. The former belief is only as it is founded on the latter. Of all absurdities, therefore, the greatest is to assert, — on the one hand, that consciousness deceives us in the belief that we know any material object to exist, and, on the other, that the material object exists, because, though on false grounds, we believe it to exist.

Brown's proof of our Personal Identity. — I may give you another instance, from the same author, of the wild work that the application of this rule makes, among philosophical systems not legitimately established. Dr. Brown, with other philosophers, rests the proof of our Personal Identity, and of our Mental Individuality, on the ground of beliefs, which, as "intuitive, universal, immediate, and irresistible," he, not unjustly, regards as the "internal and never-ceasing voice of our Creator, — revelations from on high, omnipotent [and veracious] as their Author." To him this argument is, however, incompetent, as contradictory.

What we know of *self* or *person*, we know only as a fact of consciousness. In our perceptive consciousness, there is revealed, in contrast to each, a *self* and a *not-self*. This contrast is either true or false. If true, then am I *conscious of an object different from me,* — that is, I have an immediate perception of the external reality. If false, then am I not conscious of any thing different from me, but what I am constrained to regard as not-me is only a modification of me, which, by an illusion of my nature, I mistake, and must mistake, for something different from me.

Now, will it be credited that Dr. Brown — and be it remembered that I adduce him only as the representative of a great majority of philosophers — affirms or denies, just as he finds it convenient or inconvenient, this fact, — this distinction of consciousness? In his doctrine of Perception, he explicitly denies its truth, in denying that mind is conscious of aught beyond itself. But, in other parts of his philosophy, this false fact, this illusive distinction, and the deceitful belief founded thereupon, are appealed to (I quote his expressions), as "revelations from on high, — as the never-ceasing voice of our Creator," etc.

Thus, on the veracity of this mendacious belief, Dr. Brown establishes his proof of our personal identity. Touching the object of perception, when its evidence is inconvenient, this belief is quietly passed over, as incompetent to distinguish not-self from self; in the question regarding our personal identity, where its testimony is convenient, it is clamorously cited as an inspired witness, exclusively competent to distinguish self from not-self. Yet why, if, in the one case, it mistook self for not-self, it may not, in the other, mistake not-self for self, would appear a problem not of the easiest solution.

And of our Individuality. — The same belief, with the same inconsistency, is called in to prove the Individuality of mind. But if we are fallaciously determined, in our perceptive consciousness, to regard mind both as mind and as matter, — for, on Brown's hypothesis, in perception, the object perceived is only a mode of the percipient subject, — if, I say, in this act, I must view what is supposed one and indivisible, as plural, and different, and opposed, — how is it possible to appeal to the authority of a testimony so treacherous as consciousness for an evidence of the real simplicity of the thinking principle?

How, says the materialist to Brown, — how can you appeal against me to the testimony of consciousness, which you yourself reject when against your own opinions, and how can you, on the authority of that testimony, maintain the unity of self to be more than an illusive appearance, when self and not-self, as known to consciousness, are, on your own hypothesis, confessedly only modifications of the same percipient subject? If, on your doctrine, consciousness can split what you hold to be one and indivisible into two, not only different but opposed, existences, — what absurdity is there, on mine, that consciousness should exhibit as phænomenally one, what we both hold to be really manifold? If you give the lie to consciousness in favor of your hypothesis, you can have no reasonable objection that I should give it the lie in favor of mine. If you can maintain that not-self is only an illusive phænomenon, — being, in fact, only self in disguise; I may also maintain, *e contra*, that self is only an illusive phænomenon, — and that the apparent unity of the ego is only the result of an organic harmony of action between the particles of matter.

The absolute and universal veracity of consciousness. — From these examples, the truth of the position I maintain is manifest, — that a fact of consciousness can only be rejected on the supposition of falsity, and that, the falsity of one fact of consciousness being admitted, the truth of no other fact of consciousness can be maintained. The legal brocard, *Falsus in uno, falsus in omnibus*, is a rule not more applicable to other witnesses than to consciousness. Thus, every system of philosophy which implies the negation of any fact of consciousness, is not only necessarily unable, without self-contradiction, to establish its own truth by any appeal to consciousness; it is also unable, without self-contradiction, to appeal to consciousness against the falsehood of any other system. If the absolute and universal veracity of consciousness be once surrendered, every system is equally true, or rather all are equally false; philosophy is impossible, for it has now no instrument by which truth can be discovered, — no standard by which it can be tried; the root of our nature is a lie. But though it is thus manifestly the common interest of every scheme of philosophy to preserve intact the integrity of consciousness, almost every scheme of philosophy is only another mode in which this integrity has been violated. If, therefore, I am able to prove the fact of this various violation, and to show that the facts of consciousness have never, or hardly ever, been fairly evolved, it will follow, as I said, that no reproach can be justly addressed to consciousness as an ill-informed, or vacillating, or perfidious witness, but to those only who were too proud, or too negligent, to accept its testimony, to employ its materials, and to obey its laws. And on this supposition, so far should we be from despairing of the future advance of philosophy from the experience of its past wanderings, that we ought, on the contrary, to anticipate for it a steady progress, the moment that philosophers can be persuaded to look to consciousness, and to consciousness alone, for their materials and their rules.

CHAPTER XII.

VIOLATIONS OF THE AUTHORITY OF CONSCIOUSNESS IN VARIOUS THEORIES OF PERCEPTION.

No retrenchment possible of the facts of consciousness. — As all philosophy is evolved from consciousness, so, on the truth of consciousness, the possibility of all philosophy is dependent. Hence, it is manifest, at once and without further reasoning, that no philosophical theory can pretend to truth except that single theory which comprehends and develops the fact of consciousness on which it founds, without retrenchment, distortion, or addition. Were a philosophical system to pretend that it culls out all that is correct in a fact of consciousness, and rejects only what is erroneous, — what would be the inevitable result? In the first place, this system admits, and must admit, that it is wholly dependent on consciousness for its constituent elements, and for the rules by which these are selected and arranged, — in short, that it is wholly dependent on consciousness for its knowledge of true and false. But, in the second place, it pretends to select a part, and to reject a part, of a fact given and guaranteed by consciousness. Now, by what criterion, by what standard, can it discriminate the true from the false in this fact? This criterion must be either consciousness itself, or an instrument different from consciousness If it be an instrument different from consciousness, what is it? No such instrument has ever yet been named — has ever yet been heard of. If it exist, and if it enable us to criticize the data of consciousness, it must be a higher source of knowledge than consciousness, and thus it will replace consciousness as the first and generative principle of philosophy. But of any principle of this character, different from consciousness, philosophy is yet in ignorance. It remains unenounced and unknown. It may, therefore, be safely assumed not to be.

The standard, therefore, by which any philosophical theory can profess to regulate its choice among the elements of any fact of consciousness, must be *consciousness itself.* Now, mark the dilemma. The theory makes consciousness the discriminator between what is true and what is false in its own testimony. But if consciousness be assumed to be a mendacious witness in certain parts of its evidence, how can it be presumed a veracious witness in others? This it cannot be. It must be held as false in all, if false in any; and the philosophical theory which starts from this hypothesis, starts from a negation of itself in the negation of philosophy in general. Again, on the hypothesis that part of the deliverance of consciousness is true, part false, how can consciousness enable us to distinguish these? This has never yet been shown; it is, in fact, inconceivable. But, further, how is it discovered that any part of a datum of consciousness is false, another true? This can only be done if the datum involve a contradiction. But if the facts of consciousness be contradictory, then is consciousness a principle of falsehood; and the greatest of conceivable follies would be an attempt to employ such a principle in the discovery of truth. And such an act of folly is every philosophical theory, which, departing from an admission that the data of consciousness are false, would still pretend to build out of them a system of truth. But, on the other hand, if the data of consciousness are not contradictory, and consciousness, therefore, not a self-convicted deceiver, how is the unapparent falsehood of its evidence to be evinced? This is manifestly impossible; for such falsehood is not to be presumed; and, we have previously seen, there is no higher principle by which the testimony of consciousness can be canvassed and redargued. Consciousness, therefore, is to be presumed veracious; a philosophical theory which accepts one part of the harmonious data of consciousness, and rejects another, is manifestly a mere caprice, a chimera not worthy of consideration, far less of articulate disproof. It is *ab initio* null.

The Duality of Consciousness. — In order still further to evince to you the importance of the precept (namely, that we must look to consciousness, and to consciousness alone, for the materials and rules of philosophy), and to show articulately how all the variations of philosophy have been determined by its neglect, I will take those facts of consciousness which lie at the very root of philosophy, and with which, consequently, all philosophical systems are necessarily and primarily conversant; and point out how, besides the one true doctrine which accepts and simply states the fact as given, there are always as many various actual theories as there are various possible modes of distorting or mutilating this fact. I shall commence with that great fact to which I have already alluded, — that *we are immediately conscious in perception of an Ego and a Non-ego, known together, and known in contrast to each other.* This is the fact of the Duality of Consciousness. It is clear and manifest. When I concentrate my attention in the simplest act of perception, I return from my observation with the most irresistible conviction of two facts, or rather two branches of the same fact; — that I am, — and that something different from me exists. In this act, I am conscious of myself as the perceiving subject, and of an external reality as the object perceived; and I am conscious of both existences in the same indivisible moment of intuition. The knowledge of the subject does not precede, nor follow, the knowledge of the object; — neither determines, neither is determined by, the other.

The fact of this testimony allowed even by those who deny its truth. — Such is the fact of perception revealed in consciousness, and as it determines mankind in general in their almost equal assurance of the reality of an external world, as of the existence of their own minds. Consciousness declares our knowledge of material qualities to be intuitive or immediate, — not representative or mediate. Nor is the fact, as given, denied even by those who disallow its truth. So clear is the deliverance, that even the philosophers who reject an intuitive perception, find it impossible not to admit, that their doctrine stands decidedly opposed to the voice of consciousness, — to the natural convictions of mankind. I may give you some examples of the admission of this fact, which it is of the utmost importance to place beyond the possibility of doubt. I quote, of course, only from those philosophers whose systems are in contradiction of the testimony of consciousness, which they are forced to admit.

The following is [Reid's quotation] from Berkeley, towards the conclusion of the work, in which his system of Idealism is established: — "When Hylas is at last entirely converted, he observes to Philonous, — 'After all, the controversy about matter, in the strict acceptation of it, lies altogether between you and the philosophers, whose principles, I acknowledge, are not near so natural, or so agreeable to the common sense of mankind and Holy Scripture, as yours.' Philonous observes in the end, — 'That he does not pretend to be a setter-up of new notions; his endeavors tend only to unite, and to place in a clearer light, that truth which was before shared between the vulgar and the philosophers; the former being of opinion, that those things they immediately perceive are the real things; and the latter, that the things immediately perceived are ideas which exist only in the mind; which two things put together do, in effect, constitute the substance of what he advances.' And he concludes by observing, — 'That those principles which at first view lead to scepticism, pursued to a certain point, bring men back to common sense.' "

Here you will notice that Berkeley admits that the common belief of mankind is, that the things immediately perceived are not representative objects in the mind, but the external realities themselves. Hume, in like manner, makes the same confession; and the confession of that sceptical Idealist, or sceptical Nihilist, is of the utmost weight.

"It seems evident that men are carried by a natural instinct or prepossession to repose faith in their senses; and that, without any reasoning, or even almost before the use of reason, we always suppose an external universe, which depends not on our perception, but would exist though we and every sensible creature were absent or annihilated. Even the animal creation are governed by a like opinion, and preserve this belief of external objects in all their thoughts, designs, and actions.

"It seems also evident that, when men follow this blind and powerful instinct of nature, they always suppose the very images presented by the senses to be the external objects, and never entertain any suspicion that the one are nothing but representations of the other. This very table, which we see white, and which we feel hard, is believed to exist, independent of our perception, and to be something external to our mind, which perceives it. Our presence bestows not being on it, — our absence does not annihilate it. It preserves its existence uniform and entire, independent of the situation of intelligent beings, who perceive or contemplate it. . . . .

"Do you follow the instincts and propensities of nature, may they say, in assenting to the veracity of sense? But these lead you to believe that the very perception or sensible image is the external object. Do you disclaim this principle, in order to embrace a more rational opinion, that the perceptions are only representations of something external? You here depart from your natural propensities and more obvious sentiments; and yet are not able to satisfy your reason, which can never find any convincing argument from experience to prove that the perceptions are connected with any external objects."

We are conscious of an immediate knowledge of the not-self. — The fact that consciousness does testify to an immediate knowledge by mind of an object different from any modification of its own, is thus admitted even by those philosophers who still do not hesitate to deny the truth of the testimony; for to say that all men do naturally believe in such a knowledge, is only, in other words, to say that they believe it upon the authority of consciousness. A fact of consciousness, and a fact of the common sense of mankind, are only various expressions of the same import. We may, therefore, lay it down as an undisputed truth, that consciousness gives, as an ultimate fact, a primitive duality; — a knowledge of the Ego in relation and contrast to the Non-ego; and a knowledge of the Non-ego in relation and contrast to the Ego. The Ego and Non-ego are, thus, given in an original synthesis, as conjoined in the unity of knowledge, and, in an original antithesis, as opposed in the contrariety of existence. In other words, we are conscious of them in an indivisible act of knowledge together and at once, — but we are conscious of them as, in themselves, different and exclusive of each other.

Again, consciousness not only gives us a duality, but it gives its elements in equal counterpoise and independence. The Ego and Non-ego — mind and matter — are not only given together, but in absolute coequality. The one does not precede, the other does not follow; and, in their mutual relations, each is equally dependent, equally independent. Such is the fact as given in and by consciousness.

Different philosophical systems which deny this fact. — Philosophers have not, however, been content to accept the fact in its integrity, but have been pleased to accept it only under such qualifications as it suited their systems to devise. In truth, there are just as many different philosophical systems originating in this fact, as it admits of various possible modifications. An enumeration of these modifications, accordingly, affords an enumeration of philosophical theories.

Natural Realists. — In the first place, there is the grand division of philosophers into those who do, and those who do not, accept the fact in its integrity. Of modern philosophers, almost all are comprehended under the latter category; while of the former, — if we do not remount to the Schoolmen and the ancients, — I am only aware of a single philosopher before Reid, who did not reject, at least in part, the fact as consciousness affords it. As it is always expedient to possess a precise name for a precise distinction, I would be inclined to denominate those who implicitly acquiesce in the primitive duality as given in consciousness, the Natural Realists or Natural Dualists; and their doctrine, Natural Realism or Natural Dualism.

In the second place, the philosophers who do not accept the fact, and the whole fact, may be divided and subdivided into various classes by various principles of distribution.

Substantialists and Nihilists. — The first subdivision will be taken from the total, or partial, rejections of the import of the fact. I have previously shown you that to deny any fact of consciousness as an actual phænomenon is utterly impossible. But, though necessarily admitted as a present phænomenon, the import of this phænomenon, — all beyond our actual consciousness of its existence, may be denied. We are able, without self-contradiction, to suppose, and, consequently, to assert, that all to which the phænomenon of which we are conscious refers, is a deception; — that, for example, the past to which an act of memory refers, is only an illusion involved in our consciousness of the present; — that the unknown subject to which every phænomenon of which we are conscious involves a reference, has no reality beyond this reference itself; — in short, that all our knowledge of mind or matter is only a consciousness of various bundles of baseless appearances. This doctrine, as refusing a substantial reality to the phænomenal existence of which we are conscious, is called Nihilism; and, consequently, philosophers, as they affirm or deny the authority of consciousness in guaranteeing a substratum or substance to the manifestations of the Ego and Non-ego, are divided into Realists or Substantialists, and Nihilists or Non-Substantialists. Of positive or dogmatic Nihilism, there is no example in modern philosophy; for Oken's deduction of the universe from the original nothing, — the nothing being equivalent to the Absolute or God, — is only the paradoxical foundation of a system of Realism; and, in ancient philosophy, we know too little of the book of Gorgias the Sophist, entitled Περὶ τοῦ μὴ ὄντος, ἢ περὶ φύσεως, — *Concerning Nature or the Non-existent,* — to be able to affirm whether it were maintained by him as a dogmatic and *bona fide* doctrine. But as a sceptical conclusion from the premises of previous philosophers, we have an illustrious example of Nihilism in Hume; and the celebrated Fichte admits that the speculative principles of his own Idealism would, unless corrected by his practical, terminate in this result.*

* [In the *Notes to Reid,* Hamilton translates the following passage from Fichte's "Destination of Man," to prove that Fichtean idealism terminates in thorough-going Nihilism. "The sum total," says Fichte, "is this: —

Realists divided into Hypothetical Dualists and Monists. — The Realists † or Substantialists are again divided into Dualists,

there is absolutely nothing permanent either without or within me, but only an unceasing change. I know absolutely nothing of any existence, not even of my own. I myself know nothing and am nothing. Images (*Bilder*) there are; they constitute all that apparently exists, and what they know of themselves is after the manner of images; images that pass and vanish without there being aught to witness their transition; that consist in fact of the images of images, without significance and without an aim. I myself am one of these images; nay, I am not even thus much, but only a confused image of images. All reality is converted into a marvellous dream, without a life to dream of, and without a mind to dream; into a dream made up only of a dream of itself. Perception is a dream; thought — the source of all the existence and all the reality which I imagine to myself of my existence, of my power, of my destination — is the dream of that dream."]

† [The term *Real* (realis), though always importing *the existent*, is used in various significations and oppositions. The following occur to me:

1. As denoting *existence*, in contrast to the *nomenclature* of existence, — the *thing*, as contradistinguished from its *name*. Thus we have definitions and divisions *real*, and definitions and divisions *nominal* or *verbal*.

2. As expressing the *existent* opposed to the *non-existent*, — a *something* in contrast to a *nothing*. In this sense, the diminutions of existence, to which reality, in the *following* significations, is counterposed, are *all real*.

3. As denoting *material* or *external*, in contrast to *mental*, *spiritual*, or *internal*, existence. This meaning is improper; so, therefore, is the term *Realism*, as equivalent to *Materialism*, in the nomenclature of some recent philosophers.

4. As synonymous with *actual;* and this (a. as opposed to *potential*, b.) as opposed to *possible* existence.

5. As denoting *absolute* or *irrespective*, in opposition to *phenomenal* or *relative*, existence; in other words, as denoting things in themselves, and out of relation to all else, in contrast to things in relation to, and as known by, intelligences, like men, who know only under the conditions of plurality and difference. In this sense, which is rarely employed and may be neglected, the Real is only another term for the Unconditioned or Absolute, — τὸ ὄντως ὄν.

6. As indicating existence considered as a *subsistence in nature* (*ens extra animam, ens naturæ*), it stands counter to an existence considered as a *representation in thought*. In this sense, *reale*, in the language of the older philosophy (Scholastic, Cartesian, Gassendian), as applied to *esse* or *ens*, is opposed to *intentionale, notionale, conceptibile, imaginarium, rationis, cognitionis, in anima, in intellectu, prout cognitum, ideale, etc.;* and corresponds with *a parte rei*, as opposed to *a parte intellectus*, — with *subjectivum*, as opposed to

and Unitarians or Monists, according as they are, or are not, contented with the testimony of consciousness to the ultimate duplicity of subject and object in perception. The Dualists, of whom we are now first speaking, are distinguished from the Natural Dualists of whom we formerly spoke, in this; — that the latter establish the existence of the two worlds of mind and matter on the immediate knowledge we possess of both series of phænomena, — a knowledge of which consciousness assures us; whereas the former, surrendering the veracity of consciousness to our immediate knowledge of material phænom-

objectivum, — with *proprium, principale,* and *fundamentale,* as opposed to *vicarium*, — with *materiale*, as opposed to *formale*, and with *formale in seipso*, and *entitativum*, as opposed to *representativum, etc.* Under this head, in the vacillating language of our more recent philosophy, *real* approximates to, but is hardly convertible with, *objective*, in contrast to *subjective* in the signification there prevalent.

7. In close connection with the sixth meaning, *real*, in the last place, denotes an identity or difference founded on the conditions of the existence of a thing in itself, in contrast to an identity or difference founded only on the relation or point of view in which the thing may be regarded by the thinking subject. In this sense it is opposed to *logical* or *rational*, the terms being here employed in a peculiar meaning. Thus a thing which, *really* (*re*) or in itself, is one and indivisible, may *logically* (*ratione*), by the mind, be considered as diverse and plural; and vice versa, what are *really* diverse and plural, may *logically* be viewed as one and indivisible. As an example of the former; — the sides and angles of a triangle (or trilateral), as mutually correlative — as together making up the same simple figure — and as, without destruction of that figure, actually inseparable from it, and from each other, are *really* one; but inasmuch as they have peculiar relations which may, in thought, be considered severally and for themselves, they are *logically* twofold. In like manner, take apprehension and judgment. These are *really* one, as each involves the other (for we apprehend only as we judge something to be, and we judge only as we apprehend the existence of the terms compared), and as together they constitute a single indivisible act of cognition; but they are *logically* double, inasmuch as, by mental abstraction, they may be viewed each for itself, and as a distinguishable element of thought. As an example of the latter; individual things, as John, James, Richard, etc., are *really* (numerically) different, as coexisting in nature only under the condition of plurality; but, as resembling objects constituting a single class or notion (man), they are *logically* considered (generically or specifically) identical and one.] — *Diss. supp. to Reid.*

ena, and, consequently, our immediate knowledge of the existence of matter, still endeavor, by various hypotheses and reasonings, to maintain the existence of an unknown external world. As we denominate those who maintain a dualism as involved in the fact of consciousness, Natural Dualists; so we may style those Dualists who deny the evidence of consciousness to our immediate knowledge of aught beyond the sphere of mind, Hypothetical Dualists or Cosmothetic Idealists.

To the class of *Cosmothetic Idealists*, the great majority of modern philosophers are to be referred. Denying an immediate or intuitive knowledge of the external reality, whose existence they maintain, they, of course, hold a doctrine of mediate or representative perception; and, according to the various modifications of that doctrine, they are again subdivided into those who view, in the immediate object of perception, a representative entity present to the mind, but not a mere mental modification, and into those who hold that the immediate object is only a representative modification of the mind itself. It is not always easy to determine to which of these classes some philosophers belong. To the former, or class holding the cruder hypothesis of representation, certainly belong the followers of Democritus and Epicurus, those Aristotelians who held the vulgar doctrine of species (Aristotle himself was probably a Natural Dualist), and in recent times, among many others, Malebranche, Berkeley, Clarke, Newton, Abraham Tucker, etc. To these is also, but problematically, to be referred Locke. To the second, or class holding the finer hypothesis of representation, belong, without any doubt, many of the Platonists, Leibnitz, Arnauld, Crousaz, Condillac, Kant, etc.; and to this class is also, probably, to be referred Descartes.

Monists subdivided. — The philosophical Unitarians or Monists reject the testimony of consciousness to the ultimate duality of the subject and object in perception, but they arrive at the unity of these in different ways. Some admit the testimony of consciousness to the equipoise of the mental and material phænomena, and do not attempt to reduce either mind to matter, or matter to mind. They reject, however, the evidence of consciousness to their antithesis in existence, and maintain that mind and matter are only phænomenal modifications of the same common substance. This is the doctrine of Absolute Identity, — a doctrine of which the most illustrious representatives among recent philosophers are Schelling, Hegel, and Cousin. Others, again, deny the evidence of consciousness to the equipoise of the subject and object as coördinate and coöriginal elements; and as the balance is inclined in favor of the one relative or the other, two opposite schemes of psychology are determined. If the subject be taken as the original and genetic, and the object evolved from it as its product, the theory of Idealism is established. On the other hand, if the object be assumed as the original and genetic, and the subject evolved from it as its product, the theory of Materialism is established.

Opposite errors often counteract each other. — In regard to these two opposites schemes of a one-sided philosophy, I would at present make an observation to which it may be afterwards necessary to recur; — namely, that a philosophical system is often prevented from falling into absolute Idealism or absolute Materialism, and held in a kind of vacillating equilibrium, not in consequence of being based on the fact of consciousness, but from the circumstance, that its Materialistic tendency in one opinion happens to be counteracted by its Idealistic tendency in another; — two opposite errors, in short, coöperating to the same result as one truth. On this ground is to be explained, why the philosophy of Locke and Condillac did not more easily slide into Materialism. Deriving our whole knowledge, mediately or immediately, from the senses, this philosophy seemed destined to be fairly analyzed into a scheme of Materialism; but from this it was for a long time preserved, in consequence of involving a doctrine, which, on the other hand, if not counteracted, would have naturally carried it over into Idealism. This was the doctrine of a Representative Perception. The legitimate issue of such a doctrine is now admitted, on all hands, to be absolute Idealism; and the only ground on which it has been latterly thought possible to avoid this conclusion, —

an appeal to the natural belief of mankind in the existence of an external world, — is, as I showed you, incompetent to the Hypothetical Dualist or Cosmothetic Idealist. In his hands, such an appeal is self-contradictory. For, if this universal belief be fairly applied, it only proves the existence of an outer world by disproving the hypothesis of a Representative Perception.

To recapitulate what I have now said: [When I concentrate my attention in the simplest act of Perception, I return from my observation with the most irresistible conviction of *two* facts, or rather two branches of the *same* fact, — that *I am*, — and that *something different from me exists.* In this act, I am conscious of myself as the perceiving *subject*, and of an external reality as the *object* perceived; and I am conscious of both existences in the same indivisible moment of intuition. The knowledge of the subject does not precede or follow the knowledge of the object; — neither determines, neither is determined by, the other. The two terms of correlation stand in mutual counterpoise and equal independence; they are given as connected in the synthesis of knowledge, but as contrasted in the antithesis of existence.

Such is the fact of Perception revealed in consciousness, and as it determines mankind in general in their equal assurance of the reality of an external world, and of the existence of their own minds. *Consciousness declares our knowledge of material qualities to be intuitive.* Nor is the fact, *as given*, denied even by those who disallow its truth. So clear is the deliverance, that even the philosophers who reject an intuitive perception, find it impossible not to admit, that their doctrine stands decidedly opposed to the voice of consciousness and the natural conviction of mankind.

According as the truth of the fact of consciousness in perception is *entirely* accepted, accepted *in part*, or *wholly* rejected, *six* possible and actual systems of philosophy result. We say explicitly — the *truth* of the fact. For the *fact*, as a phenomenon of consciousness, cannot be doubted; since to doubt that we are conscious of this or that, is impossible. The doubt, as itself a phænomenon of consciousness, would annihilate itself.

1. If the veracity of consciousness be unconditionally admitted, — if the intuitive knowledge of mind and matter, and the consequent reality of their antithesis be taken as truths, to be explained if possible, but in themselves to be held as paramount to all doubt, the doctrine is established which we would call the scheme of *Natural Realism*, or *Natural Dualism*. — 2. If the veracity of consciousness be allowed to the equipoise of the object and subject in the act, but rejected as to the reality of their antithesis, the system of *Absolute Identity* emerges, which reduces both mind and matter to phænomenal modifications of the same common substance. — 3 and 4. If the testimony of consciousness be refused to the co-originality and reciprocal independence of the subject and object, two schemes are determined, according as the one or the other of the terms is placed as the original and genetic. Is the object educed from the subject, *Idealism;* is the subject educed from the object, *Materialism*, is the result. — 5. Again, is the consciousness itself recognized only as a phænomenon, and the substantial reality of both subject and object denied, the issue is *Nihilism*.

6. These systems are all conclusions from an original interpretation of the fact of consciousness in Perception, carried intrepidly forth to its legitimate issue. But there is one scheme, which, violating the integrity of this fact, and, with the complete Idealist, regarding the object of consciousness in Perception as only a modification of the percipient subject, or, at least, a phænomenon numerically different from the object it represents, — endeavors, however, to stop short of the negation of an external world, the reality of which, and the knowledge of whose reality, it seeks by various hypotheses to establish and explain. This scheme, — which we would term *Cosmothetic Idealism*, *Hypothetical Realism*, or *Hypothetical Dualism*, — although the most inconsequent of all systems, has been embraced, under various forms, by the immense majority of philosophers.

Of these systems, Dr. Brown adheres to the last. He holds that the mind *is conscious, or immediately cognizant, of nothing beyond its subjective states;* but he assumes the existence of an external world beyond the sphere of consciousness, exclusively

18

on the ground of our irresistible *belief* in its unknown reality Independent of this belief, there is no reasoning on which the existence of matter can be vindicated; the logic of the Idealist he admits to be unassailable.

It will be proper, first, to generalize the *possible forms under which the hypothesis of a Representative Perception* can be realized; as a confusion of some of these as actually held, on the part both of Reid and Brown, has tended to introduce no small confusion into the discussion.

The Hypothetical Realist contends, that he is wholly ignorant of *things in themselves*, and that these are known to him only through a vicarious phænomenon, of which he is conscious in perception;

'*Rerum*que ignarus, *Imagine* gaudet.'

In other words, that the object immediately known and representing is numerically different from the object really existing and represented. Now this vicarious phænomenon, or immediate object, must *either* be numerically different from the percipient intellect, *or* a modification of that intellect itself. If the latter, it must, again, *either* be a modification of the thinking substance, with a transcendent existence beyond the act of thought, *or* a modification identical with the act of perception itself.

All possible forms of the representative hypothesis are thus reduced to three, and these have all been actually maintained.

1. *The representative object not a modification of mind.*

2. *The representative object a modification of mind, dependent for its apprehension, but not for its existence, on the act of consciousness.*

3. *The representative object a modification of mind, non-existent out of consciousness; — the idea and its perception only different relations of an act really identical.*] — *Discussions.*

It would be turning aside from my present purpose, were I to attempt any articulate refutation of these various systems. What I have now in view is to exhibit to you how, the moment that the fact of consciousness in its absolute integrity is surrendered, philosophy at once falls from unity and truth into variety and error. In reality, by the very act of refusing any one datum of consciousness, philosophy invalidates the whole credibility of consciousness, and consciousness ruined as an instrument, philosophy is extinct. Thus, the refusal of philosophers to accept the fact of the duality of consciousness is virtually an act of philosophical suicide. Their various systems are now only so many empty spectres, — so many enchanted corpses, which the first exorcism of the sceptic reduces to their natural nothingness. The mutual polemic of these systems is like the warfare of shadows; as the heroes in Valhalla, they hew each other into pieces, only in a twinkling to be reunited, and again to amuse themselves in other bloodless and indecisive contests.

Mode of intercourse between Mind and Body. — Having now given a general view of the various systems of philosophy, in their mutual relations, as founded on the great fact of the Duality of Consciousness, I proceed, in subordination to this fact, to give a brief account of certain famous hypotheses which it is necessary for you to know, — hypotheses proposed in solution of the problem of how intercourse of substances so opposite as mind and body could be accomplished. These hypotheses, of course, belong exclusively to the doctrine of Dualism; for in the Unitarian system, the difficulty is resolved by the annihilation of the opposition, and the reduction of the two substances to one. The hypotheses I allude to are known under the names, 1°, Of the system of Assistance or of Occasional Causes; 2°, Of the Preëstablished Harmony; 3°, Of the Plastic Medium; and, 4°, Of Physical Influence. The first belongs to Descartes De la Forge, Malebranche, and the Cartesians in general; th second to Leibnitz and Wolf, though not universally adopted by their school; the third was an ancient opinion revived in mod ern times by Cudworth and Le Clerc; the fourth is the common doctrine of the Schoolmen, and, though not explicitly enounced, that generally prevalent at present; — among modern philosophers, it has been expounded with great perspicuity by Euler We shall take these in their order.

Occasional Causes. — The hypothesis of Divine Assistance or of Occasional Causes, sets out from the apparent impossibility, involved in Dualism, of any actual communication between a spiritual and a material substance, — that is, between extended and non-extended existences; and it terminates in the assertion, that the Deity, on occasion of the affections of matter — of the motions of the bodily organism, excites in the mind correspondent thoughts and representations; and on occasion of thoughts or representations arising in the mind, that He, in like manner, produces the correspondent movements in the body. But more explicitly: — [as Laromiguière remarks,] "God, according to the advocates of this scheme, governs the universe, and its constituent existences, by the laws according to which He has created them; and as the world was originally called into being by a mere fiat of the divine will, so it owes the continuance of its existence from moment to moment only to the unremitted perseverance of the same volition. Let the sustaining energy of the divine will cease, but for an instant, and the universe lapses into nothingness. The existence of created things is thus exclusively maintained by a creation, as it were, incessantly renewed. God is, thus, the necessary cause of every modification of body, and of every modification of mind; and his efficiency is sufficient to afford an explanation of the union and intercourse of extended and unextended substances.

"External objects determine certain movements in our bodily organs of sense, and these movements are, by the nerves and animal spirits, propagated to the brain. The brain does not act immediately and really upon the soul; the soul has no direct cognizance of any modification of the brain; this is impossible. It is God himself, who, by a law which he has established, when movements are determined in the brain, produces analogous modifications in the conscious mind. In like manner, suppose the mind has a volition to move the arm; this volition is, of itself, inefficacious; but God, in virtue of the same law, causes the answering motion in our limb. The body is not, therefore, the real cause of the mental modifications; nor the mind the real cause of the bodily movements. Nevertheless, as the soul would not be modified without the antecedent changes in the body, nor the body moved without the antecedent determination of the soul, — these changes and determinations are in a certain sort necessary. But this necessity is not absolute; it is only hypothetical or conditional. The organic changes, and the mental determinations, are nothing but simple conditions, and not real causes; in short, they are occasions or occasional causes." This doctrine of occasional causes is called, likewise, the hypothesis of Assistance, as supposing the immediate coöperation or intervention of the Deity. It is involved in the Cartesian theory, and, therefore, belongs to Descartes; but it was fully evolved by De la Forge, Malebranche, and other followers of Descartes. It may, however, be traced far higher. Many of the most illustrious philosophers of the middle ages maintained that God is the only real agent in the universe. To this doctrine Dr. Reid inclines, and it is expressly maintained by Mr. Stewart.

Preëstablished Harmony. — This hypothesis did not satisfy Leibnitz. "He reproaches the Cartesians," [says Laromiguière,] "with converting the universe into a perpetual miracle, and of explaining the natural, by a supernatural, order. This would annihilate philosophy; for philosophy consists in the investigation and discovery of the second causes which produce the various phænomena of the universe. You degrade the Divinity," he subjoined; — "you make him act like a watchmaker, who, having constructed a timepiece, would still be obliged himself to turn the hands to make it mark the hours. A skilful mechanist would so frame his clock, that it would go for a certain period without assistance or interposition. So, when God created man, he disposed his organs and faculties in such a manner that they are able, of themselves, to execute their functions and maintain their activity from birth to death."

Leibnitz thought he had devised a more philosophical scheme, in the hypothesis of the preëstablished or predetermined Harmony. This hypothesis denies all real connection, not only between spiritual and material substances, but between substances in general; and explains their apparent communion from a previously decreed coärrangement of the Supreme Being, in the following manner:* — "God, before creating souls and bodies, knew all these souls and bodies; he knew also all possible souls and bodies. Now, in this infinite variety of possible souls and bodies, it was necessary that there should be souls whose series of perceptions and determinations would correspond to the series of movements which some of these possible bodies would execute; for in an infinite number of souls, and in an infinite number of bodies, there would be found all possible combinations. Now, suppose that, out of a soul whose series of modifications corresponded exactly to the series of modifications which a certain body was destined to perform, and of this body whose successive movements were correspondent to the successive modifications of this soul, God should make a man; — it is evident, that between the two substances which constitute this man, there would subsist the most perfect harmony. It is, thus, no longer necessary to devise theories to account for the reciprocal intercourse of the material and the spiritual substances. These have no communication, no mutual influence. The soul passes from one state, from one perception, to another, by virtue of its own nature. The body executes the series of its movements without any participation or interference of the soul in these. The soul and body are like two clocks accurately regulated, which point to the same hour and minute, although the spring which gives motion to the one is not the spring which gives motion to the other. Thus the harmony which appears to combine the soul and body is, however, independent of any reciprocal action. This harmony was established before the creation of man; and hence it is called the Preëstablished or predetermined Harmony."

It is needless to attempt a refutation of this hypothesis, which its author himself probably regarded more as a specimen of ingenuity than as a serious doctrine.

Plastic Medium. — The third hypothesis is that of a Plastic

* [The following expositions of the second, third, and fourth hypotheses are all translated by Hamilton from Laromiguière.] — *Am. Ed.*

Medium between the soul and body. "This medium participates of the two natures; it is partly material, partly spiritual. As material, it can be acted on by the body; and as spiritual, it can act upon the mind. It is the middle term of a continuous proportion. It is a bridge thrown over the abyss which separates matter from spirit. This hypothesis is too absurd for refutation; it annihilates itself. Between an extended and unextended substance, there can be no middle existence; [these being not simply different in degree, but contradictory.] If the medium be neither body nor soul, it is a chimera; if it is at once body and soul, it is contradictory; or if, to avoid the contradiction, it is said to be, like us, the union of soul and body, it is itself in want of a medium."

Physical Influence. — The fourth hypothesis is that of Physical Influence. "On this doctrine, external objects affect our senses, and the organic motion they determine is communicated to the brain. The brain acts upon the soul, and the soul has an idea, — a perception. The mind, thus possessed of a perception or idea, is affected for good or ill. If it suffers, it seeks to be relieved of pain. It acts in its turn upon the brain, in which it causes a movement in the nervous system; the nervous system causes a muscular motion in the limbs, — a motion directed to remove or avoid the object which occasions the sensation of pain.

"The brain is the seat of the soul, and, on this hypothesis, the soul has been compared to a spider seated in the centre of its web. The moment the least agitation is caused at the extremity of this web, the insect is advertised and put upon the watch. In like manner, the mind situated in the brain has a point on which all the nervous filaments converge; it is informed of what passes at the different parts of the body; and forthwith it takes its measures accordingly. The body thus acts with a real efficiency on the mind, and the mind acts with a real efficiency upon the body. This action or influence being real, — physical, in the course of nature, — the body exerts a physical influence upon the soul, the soul a physical influence upon the body.

"This system is simple, but it affords us no help in explaining the mysterious union of an extended and an unextended substance.

'Tangere enim et tangi nisi corpus nulla potest res.'

Nothing can touch and be touched but what is extended; and if the soul be unextended, it can have no connection by touch with the body, and the physical influence is inconceivable or contradictory."

Historical order of these hypotheses. — If we consider these hypotheses in relation to their historical manifestation, — the doctrine of Physical Influence would stand first; for this doctrine, which was only formally developed into system by the later Peripatetics, was that prevalent in the earlier schools of Greece. The Aristotelians, — who held that the soul was the substantial form, the vital principle, of the body, that the soul was all in the whole and all in every part of the body, — naturally allowed a reciprocal influence of these. By *influence* (in Latin, *influxus*), you are to understand the relation of a cause to its effect; and the term, now adopted into every vulgar language of Europe, was brought into use principally by the authority of Suarez, a Spanish Jesuit, who flourished at the close of the sixteenth and beginning of the seventeenth centuries, and one of the most illustrious metaphysicians of modern times. By him a cause is defined, *principium per se influens esse in aliud.* This definition, however, and the use of the metaphysical term *influence,* (for it is nothing more,) are not, as is supposed, original with him. They are to be found in the pseudo-Aristotelic treatise, *De Causis.*

The second hypothesis in chronological order is that of the Plastic Medium. It is to be traced to Plato. That philosopher, in illustrating the relations of the two constituents of man, says that the soul is in the body like a sailor in a ship; that the soul employs the body as its instrument; but that the energy, or life and sense, of the body, is the manifestation of a different substance, — of a substance which holds a kind of intermediate existence between mind and matter. This conjecture, which

Plato only obscurely hinted at, was elaborated with peculiar partiality by his followers of the Alexandrian school; and, in their psychology, the ὄχος, or vehicle of the soul, the medium through which it is united to the body, is a prominent element and distinctive principle. To this opinion St. Austin, among other Christian fathers, was inclined; and, in modern times, it has been revived and modified by Gassendi, Cudworth, and Le Clerc.

Descartes agrees with the Platonists, in opposition to the Aristotelians, that the soul is not the substantial form of the body, but is connected with it only at a single point in the brain, — namely, the pineal gland. The pineal gland, he supposes, is the central point at which the organic movements of the body terminate, when conveying to the mind the determinations to voluntary motion. But Descartes did not allow, like the Platonists, any intermediate or connecting substance. The nature of the connection he himself does not very explicitly state; — but his disciples have evolved the hypothesis, already explained, of Occasional Causes, in which God is the connecting principle, — an hypothesis at least implicitly contained in his philosophy.

Finally, Leibnitz and Wolf agree with the Cartesians, that there is no real, but only an apparent, intercourse between mind and body. To explain this apparent intercourse they do not, however, resort to the continual assistance or interposition of the Deity, but have recourse to the supposition of a harmony between mind and body, established before the creation of either.

These hypotheses unphilosophical. — All these theories are unphilosophical, because they all attempt to establish something beyond the sphere of observation, and, consequently, beyond the sphere of genuine philosophy; and because they are either, like the Cartesian and Leibnitzian theories, contradictions of the fact of consciousness; or, like the two other hypotheses, at variance with the fact which they suppose. What St. Austin so admirably says of the substance, either of mind or of body, — "Materiam spiritumque cognoscendo ignorari, et ignorando cognosci," — I would exhort you to adopt as your opinion in regard to the union of these two existences. In short, in the words of Pascal, "Man is to himself the mightiest prodigy of nature; for he is unable to conceive what is body, still less what is mind, but least of all, is he able to conceive how a body can be united to a mind; yet this is his proper being." A contented ignorance is, indeed, wiser than a presumptuous knowledge; but this is a lesson which seems the last that philosophers are willing to learn. In the words of one of the acutest modern thinkers — "Magna, immo maxima, pars sapientiæ est, quædam æquo animo nescire velle."

CHAPTER XIII.

GENERAL PHÆNOMENA OF CONSCIOUSNESS — ARE WE ALWAYS CONSCIOUSLY ACTIVE?

The second General Fact of Consciousness which we shall consider, and out of which several questions of great interest rise, is the fact, or correlative facts, of the Activity and Passivity of Mind.

Activity and Passivity always conjoined in mind. — There is no pure activity, no pure passivity in creation. All things in the universe of nature are reciprocally in a state of continual action and counter-action; they are always active and passive at once. God alone must be thought of as being active without any mixture of passivity, as his activity is subjected to no limitation. But precisely because it is unlimited, is it for us wholly incomprehensible.

Activity and passivity are not, therefore, in the manifestations of mind, distinct and independent phænomena. This is a great, though a common, error. They are always conjoined. There is no operation of mind which is purely active; no affection which is purely passive. In every mental modification, action and passion are the two necessary elements or factors of which it is composed. But though both are always present, each is not, however, always present in equal quantity. Sometimes the one constituent preponderates, sometimes the other; and it is from the preponderance of the active element in some modifications, of the passive element in others, that we distinguish these modifications by different names, and consider them as activities or passivities according as they approximate to one or other of the two factors. Thus *faculty*, *operation*, *energy*, are words that we employ to designate the manifestations in which activity is predominant. *Faculty* denotes an active power; *action*, *operation*, *energy*, denote its present exertion. On the other hand, *capacity* expresses a passive power; *affection*, *passion*, express a present suffering. The terms, *mode*, *modification*, *state*, may be used indifferently to signify both phænomena; but it must be acknowledged that these, especially the word *state*, are now closely associated with the passivity of mind, which they, therefore, tend rather to suggest. The passivity of mind is expressed by another term, *receptivity;* for passivity is only the condition, the necessary antecedent of activity, only the property possessed by the mind of standing in relation to certain foreign causes, — of receiving from them impressions, determinations to act.

No consciousness of passivity. — It is to be observed, that we are never directly conscious of passivity. Consciousness only commences with, is only cognizant of, the reaction consequent upon the foreign determination to act; and this reaction is not itself passive. In so far, therefore, as we are conscious, we are active; whether there be a mental activity of which we are not conscious, is another question.

There are certain arduous problems connected with the activity of mind, which will be more appropriately considered [hereafter]. At present, I shall only treat of those questions which are conversant about the immediate phænomena of activity. Of these, the first that I shall consider is one of considerable interest, and which, though variously determined by different philosophers, does not seem to lie beyond the sphere of observation. I allude to the question, Whether we are always consciously active?

Are we always consciously active? — It is evident that this question is not convertible with the question, Have we always a memory of our consciousness? — for the latter problem must be at once answered in the negative. It is also evident, that we must exclude the consideration of those states in which the mind is apparently without consciousness, but in regard to which, in reality, we can obtain no information from experiment. Concerning these, we must be contented to remain in ignorance; at least, only to extend to them the analogical conclusions which our observations on those within the sphere of experiment warrant us inferring. Our question, as one of possible solution, must, therefore, be limited to the states of sleep and somnambulism, to the exclusion of those states of insensibility which we cannot terminate suddenly at will. It is hardly necessary to observe, that with the nature of sleep and somnambulism, as psychological phænomena, we have at present nothing to do; our consideration is now strictly limited to the inquiry, Whether the mind, in as far as we can make it matter of observation, is always in a state of conscious activity. The general problem in regard to the ceaseless activity of the mind has been one agitated from very ancient times, but it has also been one on which philosophers have pronounced less on grounds of experience than of theory. Plato and the Platonists were unanimous in maintaining the continual energy of intellect. The opinion of Aristotle appears doubtful, and passages may be quoted from his works in favor of either alternative. The Aristotelians, in general, were opposed, but a considerable number were favorable, to the Platonic doctrine. The question, however, obtained its principal importance in the philosophy of Descartes. That philosopher made the essence, the very existence, of the soul to consist in actual thought, under which he included even the desires and feelings; and *thought* he defined all of which we are conscious. The assertion, therefore, of Descartes, that the mind always thinks, is, in his employment of language, tantamount to the assertion that the mind is always conscious.

Locke's argument for the negative.—That the mind is always conscious, though a fundamental position of the Cartesian doctrine, was rather assumed than proved by an appeal to fact and experience. All is theoretical in Descartes; all is theoretical in his disciples. Even Malebranche assumes our consciousness in sleep, and explains our oblivion only by a mechanical hypothesis. It was, therefore, easy for Locke to deny the truth of the Cartesian opinion, and to give a strong semblance of probability to his own doctrine by its apparent conformity with the phænomena. Omitting a good deal of what is either irrelevant to the general question, or what is now admitted to be false, as founded on his erroneous doctrine of personal identity, the following is the sum of Locke's argument upon the point. "We know certainly by experience," [he says,] "that we *sometimes* think, and thence draw this infallible consequence, that there is something in us that has a power to think: but whether that substance *perpetually* thinks or no, we can be no further assured than experience informs us. For to say that actually thinking is essential to the soul, and inseparable from it, is to beg what is in question, and not to prove it by reason; which is necessary to be done, if it be not a self-evident proposition. But whether this, 'that the soul always thinks,' be a self-evident proposition, that everybody assents to at first hearing, I appeal to mankind. It is doubted whether I thought all last night or no; the question being about a matter of fact, it is begging it to bring as a proof for it an hypothesis which is the very thing in dispute; by which way one may prove any thing." . . . . "It will, perhaps, be said, that 'the soul thinks even in the soundest sleep, but the memory retains it not.' That the soul in a sleeping man should be this moment busy a-thinking, and the next moment in a waking man not remember nor be able to recollect one jot of all those thoughts, is very hard to be conceived, and would need some better proof than bare assertion to make it be believed. For who can, without any more ado but being barely told so, imagine that the greatest part of men do, during all their lives, for several hours every day, think of something which, if they were asked even in the middle of these thoughts, they could remember nothing at all of? Most men, I think, pass a great part of their sleep without dreaming. I once knew a man that was bred a scholar and had no bad memory, who told me he had never dreamed in his life, till he had that fever he was then newly recovered of, which was about the five or six and twentieth year of his age. I suppose the world affords more such instances; at least every one's acquaintance will furnish him with examples enough of such as pass most of their nights without dreaming." . . . . And again, "If they say that a man is always conscious to himself of thinking; I ask how they know it? 'Consciousness is the perception of what passes in a man's own mind. Can another man perceive that I am conscious of any thing, when I perceive it not myself?' No man's knowledge here can go beyond his experience. Wake a man out of a sound sleep, and ask him what he was that moment thinking on. If he himself be conscious of nothing he then thought on, he must be a notable diviner of thoughts that can assure him that he was thinking: may he not with more reason assure him he was not asleep? This is something beyond philosophy; and it cannot be less than revelation that discovers to another thoughts in my mind when I can find none there myself; and they must needs have a penetrating sight who can certainly see what I think when I cannot perceive it myself, and when I declare that I do not. This some may think to be a step beyond the Rosicrucians, it being easier to make one's self invisible to others, than to make another's thoughts visible to one which are not visible to himself. But it is but defining the soul to be 'a substance that always thinks,' and the business is done."

Locke's view opposed by Leibnitz. — This decision of Locke was rejected by Leibnitz. He observes, in reply to the supposition that continual consciousness is an attribute of Him "who neither slumbereth nor sleepeth," 'that this affords no inference that in sleep we are wholly without perception.' To the remark, "that it is difficult to conceive, that a being can think and not be conscious of thought," he replies, 'that in this lies the whole knot and difficulty of the matter. But this is not insoluble.' "We must observe," he says, "that we think of a multitude of things at once, but take heed only of those thoughts that are the more prominent. Nor could it be otherwise. For were we to take heed of every thing, it would be necessary to attend to an infinity of matters at the same moment, all of which make an effectual impression on the senses. Nay, I assert that there remains always something of all our past thoughts, — that none is ever entirely effaced. Now when we sleep without dreaming, and when stunned by a blow or other accident, there are formed in us an infinity of small confused perceptions." And again he remarks: "That even when we sleep without dreaming, there is always some feeble perception. The act of awakening, indeed, shows this: and the more easily we are roused, the clearer is the perception we have of what passes without, although this perception is not always strong enough to cause us to awake."

Now, in all this it will be observed, that Leibnitz does not precisely answer the question we have mooted. He maintains that the mind is never without perceptions, but, as he holds that perceptions exist without consciousness, he cannot, though he opposes Locke, be considered as affirming that the mind is never without consciousness during sleep, — in short, does always dream.

But if Leibnitz cannot be adduced as categorically asserting that there is no sleep without its dream, this cannot be said of Kant. That great thinker distinctly maintains that we always dream when asleep; that to cease to dream would be to cease to live; and that those who fancy they have not dreamt have only forgotten their dream. This is all that the manual of *Anthropology*, published by himself, contains upon the question; but in a manuscript in my possession, which bears to be a work of Kant, but is probably only a compilation from notes taken at his lectures on Anthropology, it is further stated that we can dream more in a minute than we can act during a day, and that the great rapidity of the train of thought in sleep, is one of the principal causes why we do not always recollect what we dream. He elsewhere also observes, that the cessation of a force to act is tantamount to its cessation to be.

The wakefulness of mind proved from somnambulism. — Though the determination of this question is one that seems not extremely difficult, we find it dealt with by philosophers, on the one side and the other, rather by hypothesis than by experiment; at least, we have, with one partial exception, which I am soon to quote to you, no observations sufficiently accurate and detailed to warrant us in establishing more than a very doubtful conclusion. I have myself at different times turned my attention to the point, and, as far as my observations go, they certainly tend to prove that, during sleep, the mind is never either inactive or wholly unconscious of its activity. As to the objection of Locke and others, that, as we have often no recollection of dreaming, we have, therefore, never dreamt, it is sufficient to say that the assumption in this argument — that consciousness, and the recollection of consciousness, are convertible — is disproved in the most emphatic manner by experience. You have all heard of the phænomenon of somnambulism. In this remarkable state, the various mental faculties are usually in a higher degree of power than in the natural. The patient has recollections of what he has wholly forgotten. He speaks languages of which, when awake, he remembers not a word. If he use a vulgar dialect when out of this state, in it he employs only a correct and elegant phraseology. The imagination, the sense of propriety, and the faculty of reasoning, are all in general exalted. The bodily powers are in high activity, and under the complete control of the will; and, it is well known, persons in this state have frequently performed feats, of which, when out of it, they would not even have imagined the possibility. And what is even more remarkable, the difference of the faculties in the two states seems not confined merely to a difference in degree. For it happens, for example, that a person who has no ear for music when awake, shall, in his somnambulic crisis, sing with the utmost correctness and with full enjoyment of his performance. Under this affection persons sometimes live half their lifetime, alternating between the normal and abnormal states, and performing the ordinary functions of life indifferently in both, with this distinction, that if the patient be dull and doltish when he is said to be awake, he is comparatively alert and intelligent when nominally asleep. I am in possession of three works, written during the crisis by three different somnambulists. Now it is evident that consciousness, and an exalted consciousness, must be allowed in somnambulism. This cannot possibly be denied; — but mark what follows. It is the peculiarity of somnambulism, — it is the differential quality by which that state is contradistinguished from the state of dreaming, — that we have no recollection, when we awake, of what has occurred during its continuance. Consciousness is thus cut in two; memory does not connect the train of consciousness in the one state with the train of consciousness in the other. When the patient again relapses into the state of somnambulism, he again remembers all that had occurred during every former alternative of that state; but he not only remembers this, he recalls also the events of his normal existence; so that, whereas the patient in his somnambulic crisis has a memory of his whole life, in his waking intervals he has a memory only of half his life.

Dreaming possible without memory. — At the time of Locke, the phænomena of somnambulism had been very little studied; nay, so great is the ignorance that prevails in regard to its nature even now, that you will find this, its distinctive character, wholly unnoticed in the best works upon the subject. But this distinction, you observe, is incompetent always to discriminate the states of dreaming and somnambulism. It may be true that, if we recollect our visions during sleep, this recollection excludes somnambulism; but the want of memory by no means proves that the visions we are known by others to have had, were not common dreams. The phænomena, indeed, do not always enable us to discriminate the two states. Somnambulism may exist in many different degrees; the sleep-walking from which it takes its name is only one of its higher phænomena, and one comparatively rare. In general, the subject of this affection does not leave his bed, and it is then frequently impossible to say, whether the manifestations exhibited are the phænomena of somnambulism or of dreaming. Talking during sleep, for example, may be a symptom of either; and it is often only from our general knowledge of the habits and predispositions of the sleeper, that we are warranted in referring this effect to the one and not to the other class of phænomena. We have, however, abundant evidence to prove that forgetfulness is not a decisive criterion of somnambulism. Persons whom there is no reason to suspect of this affection often manifest during sleep the strongest indications of dreaming, and yet, when they awaken in the morning, retain no memory of what they may have done or said during the night. Locke's argument, that because we do not always remember our consciousness during sleep, we have not, therefore, been always conscious, is thus, on the ground of fact and analogy, disproved.

Results of personal experience. — But this is not all. We can not only show that the fact of the mind remaining conscious during sleep is possible, is even probable, we can also show, by an articulate experience, that this actually occurs. The following observations are the result of my personal experience, and similar experiments every one of you is competent to institute for himself.

In the first place, when we compose ourselves to rest, we do not always fall at once asleep, but remain for a time in a state of incipient slumber, — in a state intermediate between sleep and waking. Now, if we are gently roused from this transition-state, we find ourselves conscious of being in the commencement of a dream; we find ourselves occupied with a train of thought, and this train we are still able to follow out to a point when it connects itself with certain actual perceptions. We can still trace imagination to sense, and show how, departing from the last sensible impressions of real objects, the fancy proceeds in its work of distorting, falsifying, and perplexing these, in order to construct out of their ruins its own grotesque edifices.

In the second place, I have always observed, that when suddenly awakened during sleep, (and to ascertain the fact I have caused myself to be roused at different seasons of the night,) I have always been able to observe that I was in the middle of a dream. The recollection of this dream was not always equally vivid. On some occasions, I was able to trace it back until the train was gradually lost at a remote distance; on others, I was hardly aware of more than one or two of the latter links of the chain; and, sometimes, was scarcely certain of more than the fact, that I was not awakened from an unconscious state. Why we should not always be able to recollect our dreams, it is not difficult to explain. In our waking and our sleeping states, we are placed in two worlds of thought, not only different but contrasted, and contrasted both in the character and in the intensity of their representations. When snatched suddenly from the twilight of our sleeping imaginations, and placed in the meridian lustre of our waking perceptions, the necessary effect of the transition is at once to eclipse or obliterate the traces of our dreams. The act itself, also, of rousing us from sleep, by abruptly interrupting the current of our thoughts, throws us into confusion, disqualifies us for a time from recollection, and before we have recovered from our consternation, what we could at first have easily discerned is fled or flying.

A sudden and violent is, however, in one respect, more favorable than a gradual and spontaneous, wakening to the observation of the phænomena of sleep. For, in the former case, the images presented are fresh and prominent; while in the latter, before our attention is applied, the objects of observation have withdrawn darkling into the background of the soul. We may, therefore, I think, assert, in general, that whether we recollect our dreams or not, we always dream. Something similar, indeed, to the rapid oblivion of our sleeping consciousness, happens to us occasionally even when awake. When our mind is not intently occupied with any subject, or more frequently when fatigued, a thought suggests itself. We turn it lazily over and fix our eyes in vacancy; interrupted by the question what we are thinking of, we attempt to answer, but the thought is gone; we cannot recall it, and say that we are thinking of nothing.

General conclusion. — The observations I have hitherto made tend only to establish the fact, that the mind is never wholly inactive, and that we are never wholly unconscious of its activity. Of the degree and character of that activity, I at present say nothing. But in confirmation of the opinion I have now hazarded, and in proof of something more even than I have ventured to maintain, I have great pleasure in quoting the substance of a remarkable essay on sleep by one of the most distinguished of the philosophers of France. I refer to M. Jouffroy, who, along with M. Royer Collard, was at the head of the pure school of Scottish Philosophy in France.

The mind often awake when the senses sleep.—"I have never well understood those who admit that in sleep the mind is dormant. When we dream, we are assuredly asleep, and assuredly also our mind is not asleep, because it thinks; it is, therefore, manifest, that the mind *frequently* wakes when the senses are in slumber. But this does not prove that it *never* sleeps along with them. To sleep is for the mind not to dream; and it is impossible to establish the fact, that there are in sleep moments in which the mind does not dream. To have no recollection of our dreams, does not prove that we have not dreamt; for it can be often proved that we have dreamt, although the dream has left no trace on our memory.

"The fact, then, that the mind *sometimes* wakes while the senses are asleep, is thus established; whereas the fact, that it sometimes sleeps along with them is not; *the probability*, therefore, is, that *it wakes always*. It would require contradictory facts to destroy the force of this induction, which, on the contrary, every fact seems to confirm. I shall proceed to analyze some of these which appear to me curious and striking. They manifestly imply this conclusion, that the mind, during sleep, is not in a peculiar state, but that its activity is carried on precisely as when awake.

Facts in support of this conclusion.—"When an inhabitant of the province comes to Paris, his sleep is at first disturbed, and continually broken, by the noise of the carriages passing under his window. He soon, however, becomes accustomed to the turmoil, and ends by sleeping at Paris as he slept in his village.

"The noise, however, remains the same, and makes an equal impression on his senses; how comes it that this noise at first hinders, and then, at length, does not hinder him, from sleeping?

"The state of waking presents analogous facts. Every one knows that it is difficult to fix our attention on a book, when surrounded by persons engaged in conversation; at length however, we acquire this faculty. A man unaccustomed to the tumult of the streets of Paris is unable to think consecutively while walking through them; a Parisian finds no difficulty. He meditates as tranquilly in the midst of the crowd and bustle of men and carriages, as he could in the centre of the forest. The analogy between these facts taken from the state of waking, and the fact which I mentioned at the commencement, taken from the state of sleep, is so close, that the explanation of the former should throw some light upon the latter. We shall attempt this explanation.

Analysis of Attention and Distraction. — "Attention is the voluntary application of the mind to an object. It is established, by experience, that we cannot give our attention to two different objects at the same time. Distraction is the removal of our attention from a matter with which we are engaged, and our bestowal of it on another which crosses us. In distraction, attention is only diverted because it is attracted by a new perception or idea soliciting it more strongly than that with which it is occupied; and this diversion diminishes exactly in proportion as the solicitation is weaker on the part of the intrusive idea. All experience proves this. The more strongly attention is applied to a subject, the less susceptible is it of distraction; thus it is, that a book which awakens a lively curiosity retains the attention captive; a person occupied with a matter affecting his life, his reputation, or his fortune, is not easily distracted; he sees nothing, he understands nothing, of what passes around him; we say that he is deeply preoccupied. In like manner, the greater our curiosity, or the more curious the things that are spoken of around us, the less able are we to rivet our attention on the book we read. In like manner, also, if we are waiting in expectation of any one, the slightest noises occasion distraction, as these noises may be the signal of the approach we anticipate. All these facts tend to prove, that distraction results only when the intrusive idea solicits us more strongly than that with which we are occupied.

"Hence it is, that the stranger in Paris cannot think in the bustle of the streets. The impressions which assail his eyes and ears on every side, being for him the signs of things new or little known, when they reach his mind, interest him more strongly than the matter even to which he would apply his thoughts. Each of these impressions announces a cause which may be beautiful, rare, curious, or terrific; the intellect cannot refrain from turning out to verify the fact. It turns out, however, no longer when experience has made it familiar with all that can strike the senses on the streets of Paris; it remains within, and no longer allows itself to be deranged.

"The other admits of a similar explanation. To read without distraction, in the midst of an unknown company, would be impossible. Curiosity would be too strong. This would also be the case if the subject of conversation were very interesting. But in a familiar circle, whose ordinary topics of conversation are well known, the ideas of the book make an easy conquest of our thoughts.

"The will, likewise, is of some avail in resisting distraction. Not that it is able to retain the attention when disquieted and curious; but it can recall, and not indulge it in protracted absences, and, by constantly remitting it to the object of its volition, the interest of this object becomes at last predominant. Rational considerations, and the necessity of remaining attentive, likewise exert an influence; they come in aid of the idea, and lend it, so to speak, a helping hand in concentrating on it the attention.

Distraction and Non-distraction matters of intelligence.—"But, howsoever it may be with all these petty influences, it remains evident that distraction and non-distraction are neither of them matters of sense, but both matters of intelligence. It is not the senses which become accustomed to hear the noises of the street and the sounds of conversation, and which end in being less affected by them; if we are at first vehemently affected by the noises of the street or drawing-room, and then little or not at all, it is because at first attention occupies itself with these impressions, and afterwards neglects them; when it neglects them, it is not diverted from its object, and distraction does not take place; when, on the contrary, it accords them notice, it abandons its object, and is then distracted.

"We may observe, in support of this conclusion, that the habit of hearing the same sounds renders us sometimes highly sensible to them, as occurs in savages and in the blind; sometimes, again, almost insensible to them, as exemplified in the apathy of the Parisian for the noise of carriages. If the effect were physical, — if it depended on the body and not on the mind, there would be a contradiction, for the habit of hearing the same sounds either blunts the organ or sharpens it; it could not at once have two, and two contrary, effects; — it could have only one. The fact is, it neither blunts nor sharpens; the organ remains the same; the same sensations are determined; but when these sensations interest the mind, it applies itself to them, and becomes accustomed to their discrimination; when they do not interest it, it becomes accustomed to neglect, and does not discriminate them. This is the whole mystery; the phænomenon is psychological, not physiological.

The phænomena of sleep. — "Let us now turn our attention to the state of sleep, and consider whether analogy does not demand a similar explanation of the fact which we stated at the commencement. What takes place when a noise hinders us from sleeping? The body fatigued begins to slumber; then, of a sudden, the senses are struck, and we awake; then fatigue regains the ascendant, we relapse into drowsiness, which is soon again interrupted; and so on for a certain continuance. When, on the contrary, we are accustomed to noise, the impressions it makes no longer disturb our first sleep; the drowsiness is prolonged, and we fall asleep. That the senses are more torpid in sleep than in our waking state, is not a matter of doubt. But when I am once asleep, they are then equally torpid on the first night of my arrival in Paris as on the hundredth. The noise being the same, they receive the same impressions, which they transmit in equal vivacity to the mind. Whence comes it, then, that on the first night I am awakened, and not on the hundredth? The physical facts are identical; the difference can originate only in the mind, as in the case of distraction and of non-distraction in the waking state. Let us suppose that the soul has fallen asleep along with the body; on this hypothesis, the slumber would be equally deep in both cases, for the mind and for the senses; and we should be unable to see why, in the one case, it was aroused more than in the other. It remains, therefore, certain that it does not sleep like the body; and that, in the one case, disquieted by unusual impressions, it awakens the senses to inquire what is the matter; whilst in the other, knowing by experience of what external fact these impressions are the sign, it remains tranquil, and does not disturb the senses to obtain a useless explanation.

"For let us remark, that the mind has need of the senses to obtain a knowledge of external things. In sleep, the senses are some of them closed, as the eyes; the others half torpid, as touch and hearing. If the soul be disquieted by the impressions which reach it, it requires the senses to ascertain the cause, and to relieve its inquietude. This is the cause why we find ourselves in a disquieted state, when aroused by an extraordinary noise; and this could not have occurred had we not been occupied with this noise before we awoke.

"This is also the cause why we sometimes feel, during sleep, the efforts we make to awaken our senses, when an unusual noise or any painful sensation disturbs our rest. If we are in a profound sleep, we are for a long time agitated before we have it in our power to awake; — we say to ourselves, we must awake in order to get out of pain; but the sleep of the senses resists, and it is only by little and little that we are able to rouse them from torpidity. Sometimes, when the noise ceases before the issue of the struggle, the awakening does not take place, and, in the morning, we have a confused recollection of having been disturbed during our sleep, — a recollection which becomes distinct only when we learn from others that such and such an occurrence has taken place while we were asleep.

Illustrated by personal experience. — "I had given orders some time ago, that a parlor adjoining to my bedroom should be swept before I was called in the morning. For the first two days, the noise awoke me; but, thereafter, I was not aware of it. Whence arose the difference? The noises are the same, and at the same hour I am in the same degree of slumber;

the same sensations, consequently, take place. Whence comes it that I awoke, and do no longer awake? For this, it appears to me, there is but one explanation; — namely, that my mind which awakes, and which is now aware of the cause of these sensations, is no longer disquieted, and no longer rouses my senses. It is true that I do not retain the recollection of this reasoning; but this oblivion is not more extraordinary than that of so many others which cross our mind, both when awake and when asleep.

"I add a single observation. The noise of the brush on the carpet of my parlor is as nothing compared with that of the heavy wagons, which pass under my windows at the same hour, and which do not trouble my repose in the least. I was, therefore, awakened by a sensation much feebler than a crowd of others, which I received at the same time. Can that hypothesis afford the reason, which supposes that the awakening is a necessary event; that the sensations rouse the senses, and that the senses rouse the mind? It is evident that my mind alone, and its activity, can explain why the fainter sensation awoke me; as these alone can explain why, when I am reading in my study, the small noise of a mouse playing in a corner can distract my attention, while the thundering noise of a passing wagon does not affect me at all.

"The explanation fully accounts for what occurs with those who sleep in attendance on the sick. All noises foreign to the patient have no effect on them; but let the patient turn him on the bed, let him utter a groan or sigh, or let his breathing become painful or interrupted, forthwith the attendant wakes, however little inured to the vocation, or interested in the welfare of the patient. Whence comes this discrimination between the noises which deserve the attention of the attendant, and those which do not, if, whilst the senses are asleep, the mind does not remain observant, — does not act the sentinel, does not consider the sensations which the senses convey, and does not awaken the senses as it finds these sensations disquieting or not? It is by being strongly impressed, previous to going to sleep, with the duty of attending to the respiration, motions, complaints of the sufferer, that we come to awaken at all such noises, and at no others. The habitual repetition of such an impression gives this faculty to professional sick-nurses; a lively interest in the health of the patient gives it equally to the members of his family.

"It is in precisely the same manner that we waken at the appointed hour, when before going to sleep we have made a firm resolution of so doing. I have this power in perfection, but I notice that I lose it if I depend on any one calling me. In this latter case, my mind does not take the trouble of measuring the time or of listening to the clock. But in the former, it is necessary that it do so, otherwise the phænomenon is inexplicable. Every one has made, or can make, this experiment; when it fails, it will be found, if I mistake not, either that we have not been sufficiently preoccupied with the intention, or were over-fatigued; for when the senses are strongly benumbed, they convey to the mind, on the one hand, more obtuse sensations of the monitory sounds, and, on the other, they resist for a longer time the efforts the mind makes to awaken them, when these sounds have reached it.

"After a night passed in this effort, we have, in general, the recollection, in the morning, of having been constantly occupied during sleep with this thought. The mind, therefore, watched, and, full of its resolution, awaited the moment. It is thus that when we go to bed much interested with any subject, we remember, on awakening, that during sleep we have been continually haunted by it. On these occasions, the slumber is light, for, the mind being untranquil, its agitation is continually disturbing the torpor of the senses. When the mind is calm, it does not sleep more, but it is less restless.

"It would be curious to ascertain, whether persons of a feeble memory, and of a volatile disposition, are not less capable than others of awakening at an appointed hour; for these two circumstances ought to produce this effect, if the notion I have formed of the phænomenon be correct. A volatile disposition is unable strongly to preoccupy itself with the thought, and to form a determined resolution; and, on the other hand, it is the memory which preserves a recollection of the resolution taken before falling asleep. I have not had an opportunity of making the experiment.

General conclusions.—"It appears to me, that, from the previous observations, it inevitably follows:—

1°, That in sleep the senses are torpid, but that the mind wakes.

2°, That certain of our senses continue to transmit to the mind the imperfect sensations they receive.

3°, That the mind judges these sensations, and that it is in virtue of its judgments that it awakens, or does not awaken, the senses.

4°, That the reason why the mind awakens the senses is, that sometimes the sensation disquiets it, being unusual or painful, and that sometimes the sensation warns it to rouse the senses, as being an indication of the moment when it ought to do so.

5°, That the mind possesses the power of awakening the senses, but that it only accomplishes this by its own activity overcoming their torpor; that this torpor is an obstacle,—an obstacle greater or less as it is more or less profound.

"If these inferences are just, it follows that we can waken ourselves at will and at appointed signals; that the instrument called an alarum does not act so much by the noise it makes, as by the associations we have established in going to bed between the noise and the thought of wakening; that, therefore, an instrument much less noisy, and emitting only a feeble sound, would probably produce the same effect. It follows, moreover, that we can inure ourselves to sleep profoundly in the midst of the loudest noises; that to accomplish this, it is perhaps sufficient, on the first night, to impress it on our minds that these sounds do not deserve attention, and ought not to awaken us; and that by this mean, any one may probably sleep as well in the mill as the miller himself. It follows, in fine, that the sleep of the strong and courageous ought to be less easily disturbed, all things equal, than the sleep of the weak and timid. Some historical facts may be quoted in proof of this last conclusion."

I may notice a rather curious case which occurs to my recollection, and which tends to corroborate the theory of the French psychologist. The object of observation was the postman between Halle and a town, I forget which, some eight miles distant. This distance the postman was in the habit of traversing daily. A considerable part of his way lay across a district of unenclosed champaign meadow-land, and in walking over this smooth surface, the postman was generally asleep. But at the termination of this part of his road, there was a narrow footbridge over a stream, and to reach this bridge, it was necessary to ascend some broken steps. Now, it was ascertained as completely as any fact of the kind could be, — the observers were shrewd, and the object of observation was a man of undoubted probity, — I say, it was completely ascertained: — 1°, That the postman was asleep in passing over this level course; 2°, That he held on his way in this state without deflection towards the bridge; and, 3°, That before arriving at the bridge, he awoke. But this case is not only deserving of all credit from the positive testimony by which it is vouched; it is also credible as only one of a class of analogous cases which it may be adduced as representing. This case, besides showing that the mind must be active though the body is asleep, shows also that certain bodily functions may be dormant, while others are alert. The locomotive faculty was here in exercise, while the senses were in slumber.

This suggests to me another example of the same phænomenon. It is found in a story told by Erasmus in one of his letters, concerning his learned friend Oporinus, the celebrated professor and printer of Basle. Oporinus was on a journey with a bookseller; and, on their road, they had fallen in with a manuscript. Tired with their day's travelling, — travelling was then almost exclusively performed on horseback, — they came at nightfall to their inn. They were, however, curious to ascertain the contents of their manuscript, and Oporinus undertook the task of reading it aloud. This he continued for some time, when the bookseller found it necessary to put a question concerning a word which he had not rightly understood. It was now discovered that Oporinus was asleep, and being awakened by his companion, he found that he had no recollection of what for a considerable time he had been reading. This is a case concurring with a thousand others to prove, 1°, That one bodily sense or function may be asleep while another is awake; and, 2°, That the mind may be in a certain state of activity during sleep, and no memory of that activity remain after the sleep has ceased. The first is evident; for Oporinus, while reading, must have had his eyes, and the muscles of his tongue and fauces awake; though his ears and other senses were asleep; and the second is no less so, for the act of reading supposed a very complex series of mental energies. I may notice, by the way, that physiologists have observed, that our bodily senses and powers do not fall asleep simultaneously, but in a certain succession. We all know that the first symptom of slumber is the relaxation of the eyelids; whereas, hearing continues alert for a season after the power of vision has been dormant. In the case last alluded to, this order was, however, violated; and the sight was forcibly kept awake while the hearing had lapsed into torpidity.

In the case of sleep, therefore, so far is it from being proved that the mind is at any moment unconscious, that the result of observation would incline us to the opposite conclusion.

CHAPTER XIV.

GENERAL PHÆNOMENA OF CONSCIOUSNESS,—IS THE MIND EVER UNCONSCIOUSLY MODIFIED?

I PASS now to a question in some respects of still more proximate interest to the psychologist than that discussed in the preceding [chapter]; for it is one which, according as it is decided, will determine the character of our explanation of many of the most important phænomena in the philosophy of mind, and, in particular, the great phænomena of Memory and Association. The question I refer to is, *Whether the mind exerts energies, and is the subject of modifications, of neither of which it is conscious.* This is the most general expression of a problem which has hardly been mentioned, far less mooted, in [Great Britain]; and when it has attracted a passing notice, the supposition of an unconscious action or passion of the mind has been treated as something either unintelligible, or absurd. In Germany, on the contrary, it has not only been canvassed, but the alternative which the philosophers of this country have lightly considered as ridiculous, has been gravely established as a conclusion which the phænomena not only warrant, but enforce. The French philosophers, for a long time, viewed the question in the same light as the British. Condillac, indeed, set the latter the example; but of late, a revolution is apparent, and two recent French psychologists have marvellously propounded the doctrine, long and generally established in Germany, as something new and unheard of before their own assertion of the paradox.

Three degrees of mental latency.—This question is one not only of importance, but of difficulty; I shall endeavor to make you understand its purport, by arguing it upon broader grounds than has hitherto been done, and shall prepare you, by some preliminary information, for its discussion. I shall, first of all, adduce some proof of the fact, that the mind may, and does, contain far more latent furniture than consciousness informs us it possesses. To simplify the discussion, I shall distinguish three degrees of this mental latency.

In the *first* place, it is to be remembered that the riches, the possessions, of our mind are not to be measured by its present momentary activities, but by the amount of its acquired habits. I know a science, or language, not merely while I make a temporary use of it, but inasmuch as I can apply it when and how I will. Thus the infinitely greater part of our spiritual treasures lies beyond the sphere of consciousness, hid in the obscure recesses of the mind. This is the first degree of latency. In regard to this, there is no difficulty or dispute; and I only take it into account in order to obviate misconception, and because it affords a transition towards the other two degrees, which it conduces to illustrate.

The *second* degree of latency exists when the mind contains certain systems of knowledge, or certain habits of action, which it is wholly unconscious of possessing in its ordinary state, but which are revealed to consciousness in certain extraordinary exaltations of its powers. The evidence on this point shows that the mind frequently contains whole systems of knowledge, which, though, in our normal state, they have faded into absolute oblivion, may, in certain abnormal states, as madness, febrile delirium, somnambulism, catalepsy, etc., flash out into luminous consciousness, and even throw into the shade of unconsciousness those other systems by which they had, for a long period, been eclipsed, and even extinguished. For example, there are cases in which the extinct memory of whole languages was suddenly restored, and, what is even still more remarkable, in which the faculty was exhibited of accurately repeating, in known or unknown tongues, passages which were never within the grasp of conscious memory in the normal state. This degree, this phænomenon of latency, is one of the most marvellous in the whole compass of philosophy; and the proof of its reality will prepare us for an enlightened consideration of the third, of which the evidence, though not less certain, is not equally obtrusive. But, however remarkable and important, this phænomenon has been almost wholly neglected by psychologists, and the cases which I adduce in illustration of its reality have never been previously collected and applied. That in madness, in fever, in somnambulism, and other abnormal states, the mind should betray capacities and extensive systems of knowledge, of which it was at other times wholly unconscious, is a fact so remarkable that it may well demand the highest evidence to establish its truth. But of such a character is the evidence which I am now to give. It consists of cases reported by the most intelligent and trustworthy observers, — by observers wholly ignorant of each other's testimony; and the phænomena observed were of so palpable and unambiguous a nature, that they could not possibly have been mistaken or misinterpreted.

Evidence from cases of madness. — The first, and least interesting, evidence I shall adduce, is derived from cases of madness; it is given by a celebrated American physician, Dr. Rush.

"The records of the wit and cunning of madmen," says the Doctor, "are numerous in every country. Talents for eloquence, poetry, music, and painting, and uncommon ingenuity in several of the mechanical arts, are often evolved in this state of madness. A gentleman, whom I attended in an hospital in the year 1810, often delighted as well as astonished the patients and officers of our hospital by his displays of oratory, in preaching from a table in the hospital yard every Sunday. A female patient of mine who became insane after parturition, in the year 1807, sang hymns and songs of her own composition during the latter stage of her illness, with a tone of voice so soft and pleasant that I hung upon it with delight every time I visited her. She had never discovered a talent for poetry or music in any previous part of her life. Two instances of a talent for drawing, evolved by madness, have occurred within my knowledge. And where is the hospital for mad people, in which elegant and completely rigged ships, and curious pieces of machinery, have not been exhibited by persons who never discovered the least turn for a mechanical art, previous to their derangement? Sometimes we observe in mad people an unexpected resuscitation of knowledge; hence we hear them describe past events, and speak in ancient or modern languages, or repeat long and interesting passages from books, none of which, we are sure, they were capable of recollecting in the natural and healthy state of their mind."

From cases of fever. — The second class of cases are those of fever; and the first I shall adduce is given on the authority of the patient himself. This is Mr. Flint, a very intelligent American clergyman. I take it from his *Recollections of the Valley of the Mississippi.* He was travelling in the State of Illinois, and suffered the common lot of visitants from other climates, in being taken down with a bilious fever. "I am aware," he remarks, "that every sufferer in this way is apt to think his own case extraordinary. My physicians agreed with all who saw me that my case was so. As very few live to record the issue of a sickness like mine, and as you have requested me, and as I have promised, to be particular, I will relate some of the circumstances of this disease. And it is in my view desirable, in the bitter agony of such diseases, that more of the symptoms, sensations, and sufferings should have been recorded than have been; that others, in similar predicaments, may know that some before them have had sufferings like theirs, and have survived them. I had had a fever before, and had risen and been dressed every day. But in this, with the first day, I was prostrated to infantine weakness, and felt, with its first attack, that it was a thing very different from what I had yet experienced. Paroxysms of derangement occurred the third day, and this was to me a new state of mind. That state of disease in which partial derangement is mixed with a consciousness generally sound, and a sensibility preternaturally excited, I should suppose the most distressing of all its forms. At the same time that I was unable to recognize my friends, I was informed that my memory was more than ordinarily exact and retentive, and that I repeated whole passages in the different languages which I knew, with entire accuracy. I recited, without losing or misplacing a word, a passage of poetry which I could not so repeat after I recovered my health."

The following more curious case is given by Lord Monboddo, in his *Ancient Metaphysics*.

"'The Comtesse de Laval had been observed, by servants who sate up with her on account of some indisposition, to talk in her sleep a language that none of them understood; nor were they sure, or, indeed, herself able to guess, upon the sounds being repeated to her, whether it was or was not gibberish.

"'Upon her lying in of one of her children, she was attended by a nurse, who was of the province of Brittany, and who immediately knew the meaning of what she said, it being in the idiom of the natives of that country; but she herself, when awake, did not understand a single syllable of what she had uttered in her sleep, upon its being retold her.

"'She was born in that province, and had been nursed in a family where nothing but that language was spoken; so that, in her first infancy, she had known it, and no other; but when she returned to her parents, she had no opportunity of keeping up the use of it; and, as I have before said, she did not understand a word of *Breton* when awake, though she spoke it in her sleep.

"'I need not say that the Comtesse de Laval never said or imagined that she used any words of the Breton idiom, more than were necessary to express those ideas that are within the compass of a child's knowledge of objects,'" etc.

A highly interesting case is given by Mr. Coleridge in his *Biographia Literaria*.

"It occurred," says Mr. Coleridge, "in a Roman Catholic town in Germany, a year or two before my arrival at Göttingen, and had not then ceased to be a frequent subject of conversation. A young woman of four or five and twenty, who could neither read nor write, was seized with a nervous fever; during which, according to the asseverations of all the priests and monks of the neighborhood, she became possessed, and, as it appeared, by a very learned devil. She continued incessantly talking

Latin, Greek, and Hebrew, in very pompous tones, and with most distinct enunciation. . . . . . Sheets full of her ravings were taken down from her own mouth, and were found to consist of sentences, coherent and intelligible each for itself, but with little or no connection with each other. Of the Hebrew, a small portion only could be traced to the Bible; the remainder seemed to be in the Rabbinical dialect. All trick or conspiracy was out of the question. Not only had the young woman ever been a harmless, simple creature; but she was evidently laboring under a nervous fever. In the town, in which she had been resident for many years as servant in different families, no solution presented itself. A young physician, however, determined to trace her past life step by step; for the patient herself was incapable of returning a rational answer. He at length succeeded in discovering the place where her parents had lived: travelled thither, found them dead, but an uncle surviving; and from him learned that the patient had been charitably taken by an old Protestant pastor at nine years old, and had remained with him some years, even till the old man's death. . . . . . Anxious inquiries were then, of course, made concerning the pastor's habits; and the solution of the phænomenon was soon obtained. For it appeared that it had been the old man's custom, for years, to walk up and down a passage of his house into which the kitchen-door opened, and to read to himself, with a loud voice, out of his favorite books. A considerable number of these were still in the niece's possession. She added, that he was a very learned man, and a great Hebraist. Among his books were found a collection of Rabbinical writings, together with several of the Greek and Latin fathers; and the physician succeeded in identifying so many passages with those taken down at the young woman's bedside, that no doubt could remain in any rational mind concerning the true origin of the impressions made on her nervous system."

These cases thus evince the general fact, that a mental modification is not proved not to be, merely because consciousness affords us no evidence of its existence. This general fact being established, I now proceed to consider the question in relation to the third class or degree of latent modifications, — a class in relation to, and on the ground of which alone, it has ever hitherto been argued by philosophers.

The third degree of latency. — The problem, then, in regard to this class is, — Are there, in ordinary, *mental modifications, — i. e. mental activities and passivities, of which we are unconscious, but which manifest their existence by effects of which we are conscious?*

In the question proposed, I am not only strongly inclined to the affirmative; — nay, I do not hesitate to maintain, that what we are conscious of is constructed out of what we are not conscious of, — that our whole knowledge, in fact, is made up of the unknown and the incognizable.

This, at first sight, may appear not only paradoxical, but contradictory. It may be objected, 1°, How can we know that to exist which lies beyond the one condition of all knowledge, — consciousness? And, 2°, How can knowledge arise out of ignorance, — consciousness out of unconsciousness, — the cognizable out of the incognizable, — that is, how can one opposite proceed out of the other?

In answer to the first objection, — how can we know that of which we are unconscious, seeing that consciousness is the condition of knowledge, — it is enough to allege, that there are many things which we neither know nor can know in themselves, — that is, in their direct and immediate relation to our faculties of knowledge, but which manifest their existence indirectly through the medium of their effects. This is the case with the mental modifications in question; they are not in themselves revealed to consciousness, but as certain facts of consciousness necessarily suppose them to exist, and to exert an influence in the mental processes, we are thus constrained to admit, as modifications of mind, what are not in themselves phænomena of consciousness. The truth of this will be apparent, if, before descending to any special illustration, we consider that *consciousness cannot exist independently of some peculiar modification of mind;* we are only conscious as we are conscious of a determinate state. To be conscious, we must be conscious of some particular perception, or remembrance, or imagination, or feeling, etc.; *we have no general consciousness.* But as consciousness supposes a special mental modification as its object, it must be remembered, that this modification or state supposes a change, — a transition from some other state or modification. But as the modification must be present, before we have a consciousness of the modification, it is evident, that we can have no consciousness of its rise or awakening; for its rise or awakening is also the rise or awakening of consciousness.

But the illustration of this is contained in an answer to the second objection, which asks, — How can knowledge come out of ignorance, — consciousness out of unconsciousness, — the known out of the unknown, — how can one opposite be made up of the other?

In the removal of this objection, the proof of the thesis which I support is involved. And without dealing in any general speculation, I shall at once descend to the special evidence, which appears to me not merely to warrant, but to necessitate the conclusion, that the sphere of our conscious modifications is only a small circle in the centre of a far wider sphere of action and passion, of which we are only conscious through its effects.

I. *External Perception.* 1. *The sense of Sight.* — Let us take our first example from Perception, — the perception of external objects, and in that faculty, let us commence with the sense of sight. Now, you either already know, or can be at once informed, what it is that has obtained the name of *Minimum Visibile.* You are of course aware, in general, that vision is the result of the rays of light reflected from the surface of objects to the eye; a greater number of rays is reflected from a larger surface; if the superficial extent of an object, and, consequently, the number of rays which it reflects, be diminished beyond a certain limit, the object becomes invisible; and the *minimum visibile* is the smallest expanse which can be seen, — which can consciously affect us, — which we can be conscious of seeing. This being understood, it is plain that, if we divide this *minimum visibile* into two parts, neither half can, by itself, be an object of vision, or visual consciousness. They are, severally and apart, to consciousness as zero. But it is evident, that each half must, by itself, have produced in us a certain modification, real though unperceived; for as the perceived whole is nothing but the union of the unperceived halves, so the perception — the perceived affection itself of which we are conscious — is only the sum of two modifications, each of which severally eludes our consciousness. When we look at a distant forest, we perceive a certain expanse of green. Of this, as an affection of our organism, we are clearly and distinctly conscious. Now, the expanse, of which we are conscious, is evidently made up of parts of which we are not conscious. No leaf, perhaps no tree, may be separately visible. But the greenness of the forest is made up of the greenness of the leaves; that is, the total impression of which we are conscious, is made up of an infinitude of small impressions of which we are not conscious.

2. *Sense of Hearing.* — Take another example, from the sense of hearing. In this sense, there is, in like manner, a *Minimum Audibile*, that is, a sound the least which can come into perception and consciousness. But this *minimum audibile* is made up of parts which severally affect the sense, but of which affections, separately, we are not conscious, though of their joint result we are. We must, therefore, here likewise, admit the reality of modifications beyond the sphere of consciousness. To take a special example. When we hear the distant murmur of the sea, — what are the constituents of the total perception of which we are conscious? This murmur is a sum made up of parts, and the sum would be as zero if the parts did not count as something. The noise of the sea is the complement of the noise of its several waves; — *ποντίων τε κυμάτων 'Ανήριθμον γέλασμα*· and if the noise of each wave made no impression on our sense, the noise of the sea, as the result of these impressions, could not be realized. But the noise of each several wave, at the distance we suppose, is inaudible; we must, however, admit that they produce a certain modification, beyond consciousness, on the percipient subject;

for this is necessarily involved in the reality of their result. The same is equally the case in the other senses; the taste or smell of a dish, be it agreeable or disagreeable, is composed of a multitude of severally imperceptible effects, which the stimulating particles of the viand cause on different points of the nervous expansion of the gustatory and olfactory organs; and the pleasant or painful feeling of softness or roughness is the result of an infinity of unfelt modifications, which the body handled determines on the countless papillæ of the nerves of touch.

II. *Association of Ideas.* — Let us now take an example from another mental process. We have not yet spoken of what is called the Association of Ideas; and it is enough for our present purpose that you should be aware, that one thought suggests another in conformity to certain determinate laws, — laws to which the successions of our whole mental states are subjected. Now it sometimes happens, that we find one thought rising immediately after another in consciousness, but whose consecution we can reduce to no law of association. Now in these cases we can generally discover, by an attentive observation, that these two thoughts, though not themselves associated, are each associated with certain other thoughts; so that the whole consecution would have been regular, had these intermediate thoughts come into consciousness, between the two which are not immediately associated. Suppose, for instance, that A, B, C, are three thoughts, — that A and C cannot immediately suggest each other, but that each is associated with B, so that A will naturally suggest B, and B naturally suggest C. Now it may happen, that we are conscious of A, and, immediately thereafter, of C. How is the anomaly to be explained? It can only be explained on the principle of latent modifications. A suggests C, not immediately, but through B; but as B, like the half of the *minimum visibile* or *minimum audibile*, does not rise into consciousness, we are apt to consider it as non-existent. You are probably aware of the following fact in mechanics. If a number of billiard balls be placed in a straight row and touching each other, and if a ball be made to strike, in the line of the row, the ball at one end of the series, what will happen? The motion of the impinging ball is not divided among the whole row; this, which we might *a priori* have expected, does not happen; but the impetus is transmitted through the intermediate balls, which remain each in its place, to the ball at the opposite end of the series, and this ball alone is impelled on. Something like this seems often to occur in the train of thought. One idea mediately suggests another into consciousness, — the suggestion passing through one or more ideas which do not themselves rise into consciousness. The awakening and awakened ideas here correspond to the ball striking and the ball struck off; while the intermediate ideas of which we are unconscious, but which carry on the suggestion, resemble the intermediate balls which remain moveless, but communicate the impulse. An instance of this occurs to me with which I was recently struck. Thinking of Ben Lomond, this thought was immediately followed by the thought of the Prussian system of education. Now, conceivable connection between these two ideas in themselves, there was none. A little reflection, however, explained the anomaly. On my last visit to the mountain, I had met upon its summit a German gentleman, and though I had no consciousness of the intermediate and unawakened links between Ben Lomond and the Prussian schools, they were undoubtedly these; — the German, — Germany, — Prussia, — and, these media being admitted, the connection between the extremes was manifest.

Stewart's explanation of the phænomenon. — I should perhaps reserve for a future occasion noticing Mr. Stewart's explanation of this phænomenon. He admits that a perception or idea may pass through the mind without leaving any trace in the memory, and yet serve to introduce other ideas connected with it by the laws of association. Mr. Stewart can hardly be said to have contemplated the possibility of the existence and agency of mental modifications of which we are unconscious. He grants the necessity of interpolating certain intermediate ideas, in order to account for the connection of thought, which could otherwise be explained by no theory of association; and he admits that these intermediate ideas are not known by memory to have actually intervened. So far, there is no difference in the two doctrines. But now comes the separation. Mr. Stewart supposes that the intermediate ideas are, for an instant, awakened into consciousness, but, in the same moment, utterly forgot; whereas the opinion I would prefer, holds that they are efficient without rising into consciousness. Mr. Stewart's doctrine on this point is exposed to all the difficulties, and has none of the proofs in its favor which concur in establishing the other.

Difficulties of Stewart's doctrine. — In the *first* place, to assume the existence of acts of consciousness of which there is no memory beyond the moment of existence, is at least as inconceivable an hypothesis as the other. But, in the *second* place, it violates the whole analogy of consciousness, which the other does not. Consciousness supposes memory; and we are only conscious as we are able to connect and contrast one instance of our intellectual existence with another. Whereas, to suppose the existence and efficiency of modifications beyond consciousness, is not at variance with its conditions; for consciousness, though it assures us of the reality of what is within its sphere, says nothing against the reality of what is without. In the *third* place, it is demonstrated, that, in perception, there are modifications, efficient, though severally imperceptible; why, therefore, in the other faculties, should there not likewise be modifications, efficient, though unapparent? In the *fourth* place, there must be some reason for the assumed fact, that there are perceptions or ideas of which we are conscious, but of which there is no memory. Now, the only reason that can possibly be assigned is, that the consciousness was too faint to afford the condition of memory. But of consciousness, however faint, there must be some memory, however short. But this is at variance with the phænomenon; for the ideas A and C may precede and follow each other without any perceptible interval, and without any, the feeblest, memory of B. If there be no memory, there could have been no consciousness; and, therefore, Mr. Stewart's hypothesis, if strictly interrogated, must, even at last, take refuge in our doctrine; for it can easily be shown, that the degree of memory is directly in proportion to the degree of consciousness, and, consequently, that an absolute negation of memory is an absolute negation of consciousness.

III. *Our Acquired Dexterities and Habits.* — Let us now turn to another class of phænomena, which in like manner are capable of an adequate explanation only on the theory I have advanced; — I mean the operations resulting from our Acquired Dexterities and Habits.

To explain these, three theories have been advanced. The *first* regards them as merely mechanical or automatic, and thus denying to the mind all active or voluntary intervention, consequently removes them beyond the sphere of consciousness. The *second*, again, allows to each several motion a separate act of conscious volition; while the *third*, which I would maintain, holds a medium between these, constitutes the mind the agent, accords to it a conscious volition over the series, but denies to it a consciousness and deliberate volition in regard to each separate movement in the series which it determines.

The first or mechanical theory. — The first of these has been maintained, among others, by two philosophers who in other points are not frequently at one, — by Reid and Hartley. "Habit," says Reid, "differs from instinct, not in its nature, but in its origin; the last being natural, the first acquired. Both operate without will or intention, without thought, and therefore may be called mechanical principles." In another passage, he expresses himself thus: "I conceive it to be a part of our constitution, that what we have been accustomed to do, we acquire not only a facility but a proneness to do on like occasions; so that it requires a particular will or effort to forbear it, but to do it requires very often no will at all."

The same doctrine is laid down still more explicitly by Dr. Hartley. "Suppose," says he, "a person who has a perfectly voluntary command over his fingers, to begin to learn to play on the harpsichord. The first step is to move his fingers, from key to key, with a slow motion, looking at the notes, and exerting an express act of volition in every motion. By degrees, the motions cling to one another, and to the impressions of the notes, in the way of *association*, so often mentioned; the acts of volition growing less and less express all the time, till, at last, they become evanescent and imperceptible. For an expert performer will play from notes, or ideas laid up in the memory, and, at the same time, carry on a quite different train of thoughts in his mind; or even hold a conversation with another. Whence we conclude, that there is no intervention of the idea, or state of mind, called will." Cases of this sort Hartley calls "transitions of voluntary actions into automatic ones."

The second theory by Stewart. — The second theory is maintained against the first by Mr. Stewart; and I think his refutation valid, though not his confirmation. "I cannot help thinking it," he says, "more philosophical to suppose, that those actions which are originally voluntary always continue so, although, in the case of operations which are become habitual in consequence of long practice, we may not be able to recollect every different volition. Thus, in the case of a performer on the harpsichord, I apprehend that there is an act of the will preceding every motion of every finger, although he may not be able to recollect these volitions afterwards, and although he may, during the time of his performance, be employed in carrying on a separate train of thought. For it must be remarked, that the most rapid performer can, when he pleases, play so slowly as to be able to attend to, and to recollect, every separate act of his will in the various movements of his fingers; and he can gradually accelerate the rate of his execution, till he is unable to recollect these acts. Now, in this instance, one of two suppositions must be made. The one is, that the operations in the two cases are carried on precisely in the same manner, and differ only in the degree of rapidity; and that when this rapidity exceeds a certain rate, the acts of the will are too momentary to leave any impression on the memory. The other is, that when the rapidity exceeds a certain rate, the operation is taken entirely out of our hands, and is carried on by some unknown power, of the nature of which we are as ignorant as of the cause of the circulation of the blood, or of the motion of the intestines. The last supposition seems to me to be somewhat similar to that of a man who should maintain, that although a body projected with a moderate velocity is seen to pass through all the intermediate spaces in moving from one place to another, yet we are not entitled to conclude that this happens when the body moves so quickly as to become invisible to the eye. The former supposition is supported by the analogy of many other facts in our constitution. Of some of these I have already taken notice, and it would be easy to add to the number. An expert accountant, for example, can sum up, almost with a single glance of his eye, a long column of figures. He can tell the sum, with unerring certainty, while, at the same time, he is unable to recollect any one of the figures of which that sum is composed; and yet nobody doubts that each of these figures has passed through his mind, or supposes, that, when the rapidity of the process becomes so great that he is unable to recollect the various steps of it, he obtains the result by a sort of inspiration. This last supposition would be perfectly analogous to Dr. Hartley's doctrine concerning the nature of our habitual exertions.

"The only plausible objection which, I think, can be offered to the principles I have endeavored to establish on this subject, is founded on the astonishing and almost incredible rapidity they necessarily suppose in our intellectual operations. When a person, for example, reads aloud, there must, according to this doctrine, be a separate volition preceding the articulation of every letter; and it has been found by actual trial, that it is possible to pronounce about two thousand letters in a minute. Is it reasonable to suppose that the mind is capable of so many different acts, in an interval of time so very inconsiderable?

"With respect to this objection, it may be observed, in the first place, that all arguments against the foregoing doctrine with respect to our habitual exertions, in so far as they are founded on the inconceivable rapidity which they suppose in our intellectual operations, apply equally to the common doctrine concerning our perception of distance by the eye. But this is not all. To what does the supposition amount which is considered as so incredible? Only to this, that the mind is so formed as to be able to carry on certain intellectual processes in intervals of time too short to be estimated by our faculties; a supposition which, so far from being extravagant, is supported by the analogy of many of our most certain conclusions in natural philosophy. The discoveries made by the microscope have laid open to our senses a world of wonders, the existence of which hardly any man would have admitted upon inferior evidence; and have gradually prepared the way for those physical speculations, which explain some of the most extraordinary phænomena of nature by means of modifications of matter far too subtile for the examination of our organs. Why, then, should it be considered as unphilosophical, after having demonstrated the existence of various intellectual processes which escape our attention in consequence of their rapidity, to carry the supposition a little further, in order to bring under the known laws of the human constitution a class of mental operations which must otherwise remain perfectly inexplicable? Surely, our ideas of time are merely relative, as well as our ideas of extension; nor is there any good reason for doubting that, if our powers of attention and memory were more perfect than they are, so as to give us the same advantage in examining rapid events, which the microscope gives for examining minute portions of extension, they would enlarge our views with respect to the intellectual world, no less than that instrument has with respect to the material."

Stewart's theory shown to involve contradictions. — This doctrine of Mr. Stewart, — that our acts of knowledge are made up of an infinite number of acts of attention, that is, of various acts of concentrated consciousness, there being required a separate act of attention for every minimum possible of knowledge, — I have already shown you, by various examples, to involve contradictions. In the present instance, its admission would constrain our assent to the most monstrous conclusions. Take the case of a person reading. Now, all of you must have experienced, if ever under the necessity of reading aloud, that, if the matter be uninteresting, your thoughts, while you are going on in the performance of your task, are wholly abstracted from the book and its subject, and you are perhaps deeply occupied in a train of serious meditation. Here the process of reading is performed without interruption, and with the most punctual accuracy; and, at the same time, the process of meditation is carried on without distraction or fatigue. Now this, on Mr. Stewart's doctrine, would seem impossible; for what does his theory suppose? It supposes that separate acts of concentrated consciousness or attention are bestowed on each least movement in either process. But be the velocity of the mental operations what it may, it is impossible to conceive how transitions between such contrary operations could be kept up for a continuance without fatigue and distraction, even if we throw out of account the fact, that the acts of attention to be effectual must be simultaneous, which on Mr. Stewart's theory is not allowed.

We could easily give examples of far more complex operations; but this, with what has been previously said, I deem sufficient to show, that we must either resort to the first theory, which, as nothing but the assumption of an occult and incomprehensible principle, in fact explains nothing, or adopt the theory that there are acts of mind so rapid and minute as to elude the ken of consciousness.

The doctrine of unconscious mental modifications. — I shall now say something of the history of this opinion. It is a curious fact that Locke attributes this opinion to the Cartesians, and he thinks it was employed by them to support their doctrine of the ceaseless activity of mind. In this, as in many other points of the Cartesian philosophy, he is, however, wholly wrong. On the contrary, the Cartesians made consciousness the essence of thought; and their assertion that the mind always thinks is, in their language, precisely tantamount to the assertion that the mind is always conscious.

But what was not maintained by the Cartesians, and even in opposition to their doctrine, was advanced by Leibnitz. To this great philosopher belongs the honor of having originated this opinion, and of having supplied some of the strongest arguments in its support. He was, however, unfortunate in the terms which he employed to propound his doctrine. The latent modifications, — the unconscious activities of mind, he denominated *obscure ideas*, *obscure representations*, *perceptions without apperception or consciousness*, *insensible perceptions*, etc. In this he violated the universal usage of language. For *perception*, and *idea*, and *representation*, all properly involve the notion of consciousness, — it being, in fact, contradictory to speak of a representation not really represented — a perception not really perceived — an actual idea of whose presence we are not aware.

The close affinity of mental modifications with perceptions, ideas, representations, and the consequent commutation of these terms, have been undoubtedly the reasons why the Leibnitzian doctrine was not more generally adopted, and why, in France and in Britain, succeeding philosophers have almost admitted, as a self-evident truth, that there can be no modification of mind devoid of consciousness. As to any refutation of the Leibnitzian doctrine, I know of none. Condillac is, indeed, the only psychologist who can be said to have formally proposed the question. He, like Mr. Stewart, attempts to explain why it can be supposed, that the mind has modifications of which we are not conscious, by asserting that we are, in truth, conscious of the modification, but that it is immediately forgotten. In Germany, the doctrine of Leibnitz was almost universally adopted. I am not aware of a philosopher of the least note by whom it has been rejected.

This doctrine explains the phænomena. — The third hypothesis, then, — that which employs the single principle of latent agencies to account for so numerous a class of mental phænomena, — how does it explain the phænomenon under consideration? Nothing can be more simple and analogical than its solution. As, to take an example from vision, — in the external perception of a stationary object, a certain space, an expanse of surface, is necessary to the *minimum visibile;* in other words, an object of sight cannot come into consciousness unless it be of a certain size; in like manner, in the internal perception of a series of mental operations, a certain time, a certain duration, is necessary for the smallest section of continuous energy to which consciousness is competent. Some minimum of time must be admitted as the condition of consciousness and as time is divisible *ad infinitum*, whatever minimum be taken, there must be admitted to be, beyond the cognizance of consciousness, intervals of time, in which, if mental agencies be performed, these will be latent to consciousness. If we suppose that the minimum of time, to which consciousness can descend, be an interval called six, and that six different movements be performed in this interval, these, it is evident, will appear to consciousness as a simple indivisible point of modified time; precisely as the *minimum visibile* appears as an indivisible point of modified space. And, as in the extended parts of the *minimum visibile*, each must determine a certain modification on the percipient subject, seeing that the effect of the whole is only the conjoined effect of its parts, in like manner, the protended parts of each conscious instant, — of each distinguishable minimum of time, — though themselves beyond the ken of consciousness, must contribute to give the character to the whole mental state which that instant, that minimum, comprises. This being understood, it is easy to see how we lose the consciousness of the several acts, in the rapid succession of many of our habits and dexterities. At first, and before the habit is acquired, every act is slow, and we are conscious of the effort of deliberation, choice, and volition; by degrees, the mind proceeds with less vacillation and uncertainty; at length, the acts become secure and precise: in proportion as this takes place, the velocity of the procedure is increased, and as this acceleration rises, the individual acts drop one by one from consciousness, as we lose the leaves in retiring further and further from the tree; and, at last, we are only aware of the general state which results from these unconscious operations, as we can at last only perceive the greenness which results from the unperceived leaves.

CHAPTER XV.

GENERAL PHÆNOMENA OF CONSCIOUSNESS. — DIFFICULTIES AND FACILITIES OF PSYCHOLOGICAL STUDY. — CLASSIFICATION OF THE COGNITIVE FACULTIES.

Before terminating the consideration of the general phænomena of consciousness, there are Three Principal Facts, which it would be improper altogether to pass over without notice, but the full discussion of which I reserve for Metaphysics Proper, when we come to establish upon their foundation our conclusions in regard to the Immateriality and Immortality of Mind; — I mean the fact of our Mental Existence or Substantiality, the fact of our Mental Unity or Individuality, and the fact of our Mental Identity or Personality. In regard to these three facts, I shall, at present, only attempt to give a very summary view of what place they naturally occupy in our psychological system.

Self-Existence. — The first of these — the fact of our own Existence — I have already incidentally touched on, in giving a view of the various possible modes in which the fact of the Duality of Consciousness may be conditionally accepted.

The various modifications of which the thinking subject, Ego, is conscious, are accompanied with the feeling, or intuition, or belief, — or by whatever name the conviction may be called, — that I, the thinking subject, exist. This feeling has been called by philosophers the apperception, or consciousness, of our own existence; but, as it is a simple and ultimate fact of consciousness, though it be clearly given, it cannot be defined or described. And for the same reason that it cannot be defined, it cannot be deduced or demonstrated; and the apparent enthymeme of Descartes — *Cogito ergo sum*, [I think, therefore I am,] — if really intended for an inference, — if really intended to be more than a simple enunciation of the proposition, that the fact of our existence is given in the fact of our consciousness, is either tautological or false. Tautological, because nothing is contained in the conclusion which was not explicitly given in the premise, — the premise, *Cogito, I think*, being only a grammatical equation of *Ego sum cogitans, I am*, or *exist, thinking*. False, inasmuch as there would, in the first place, be postulated the reality of thought as a quality or modification, and then, from the fact of this modification, inferred the fact of existence, and of the existence of a subject; whereas it is self-evident, that in the very possibility of a quality or modification, is supposed the reality of existence, and of an existing subject. Philosophers in general, among whom may be particularly mentioned Locke and Leibnitz, have accordingly found the evidence in a clear and immediate belief in the simple datum of consciousness; and that this was likewise the opinion of Descartes himself, it would not be difficult to show.

Mental Unity. — The second fact — our Mental Unity or Individuality — is given with equal evidence as the first. As clearly as I am conscious of existing, so clearly am I conscious at every moment of my existence, (and never more so than when the most heterogeneous mental modifications are in a state of rapid succession,) that the conscious Ego is not itself a mere modification, nor a series of modifications of any other subject, but that it is itself something different from all its modifications, and a self-subsistent entity. This feeling, belief, datum, or fact of our mental individuality or unity, is not more capable of explanation than the feeling or fact of our existence, which it indeed always involves. *The fact* of the deliverance of consciousness to our mental unity has, of course, never been doubted; but philosophers have been found to doubt *its truth*. According to Hume, our thinking Ego is nothing but a bundle of individual impressions and ideas, out of whose union in the imagination, the notion of a whole, as of a subject of that which is felt and thought is formed. According to Kant, it cannot be properly determined whether we exist as substance or as accident, because the datum of individuality is a condition of the possibility of our having thoughts and feelings; in other words, of the possibility of consciousness; and, therefore, although consciousness gives — cannot but give — the phænomenon of individuality, it does not follow that this phænomenon may not be only a necessary illusion. An articulate refutation of these opinions I cannot attempt at present, but their refutation is, in fact, involved in their statement. In regard to Hume, his sceptical conclusion is only an inference from the premises of the dogmatical philosophers, who founded their systems on a violation or distortion of the facts of consciousness. His conclusion is, therefore, refuted in the refutation of their premises, which is accomplished in the simple exposition that they at once found on, and deny, the veracity of consciousness. And by this objection the doctrine of Kant is overset. For if he attempts to philosophize, he must assert the possibility of philosophy. But the possibility of philosophy supposes the veracity of consciousness as to the contents of its testimony; therefore, in disputing the testimony of consciousness to our mental unity and substantiality, Kant disputes the possibility of philosophy, and, consequently, reduces his own attempts at philosophizing to absurdity.

Mental Identity. — The third datum under consideration is the Identity of Mind or Person. This consists in the assurance we have, from consciousness, that our thinking Ego, notwithstanding the ceaseless changes of state or modification, of which it is the subject, is essentially the same thing, — the same person, at every period of its existence. On this subject, laying out of account certain subordinate differences on the mode of stating the fact, philosophers, in general, are agreed. Locke, in the *Essay on the Human Understanding;* Leibnitz, in the *Nouveaux Essais;* Butler and Reid are particularly worthy of attention. In regard to this deliverance of consciousness, the truth of which is of vital importance, affording, as it does, the basis of moral responsibility and hope of immortality, — it is, like the last, denied by Kant to afford a valid ground of scientific certainty. He maintains that there is no cogent proof of the substantial permanence of our thinking self, because the feeling of identity is only the condition under which that thought is possible. Kant's doubt in regard to the present fact is refuted in the same manner as his doubt in regard to the preceding, and there are also a number of special grounds on which it can be shown to be untenable. But of these at another time.

The peculiar difficulties of psychological investigation. — We have now terminated the consideration of Consciousness as the general faculty of thought, and as the only instrument and only source of Philosophy. But before proceeding to treat of the Special Faculties, it may be proper here to premise some observations in relation to the peculiar Difficulties and peculiar Facilities which we may expect in the application of consciousness to the study of its own phænomena. I shall first speak of the difficulties.

The *first* difficulty in psychological observation arises from this, that *the conscious mind is at once the observing subject and the object observed.* What are the consequences of this? In the first place, the mental energy, instead of being concentrated, is divided, and divided in two divergent directions. The state of mind observed, and the act of mind observing, are mutually in an inverse ratio; each tends to annihilate the other. Is the state to be observed intense, all reflex observation is rendered impossible; the mind cannot view as a spectator; it is wholly occupied as an agent or patient. On the other hand, exactly in proportion as the mind concentrates its force in the act of reflective observation, in the same proportion must the direct phænomenon lose in vivacity, and, consequently, in the precision and individuality of its character. This difficulty is manifestly insuperable in those states of mind, which, of their very nature, as suppressing consciousness, exclude all contemporaneous and voluntary observation, as in sleep and fainting. In states like dreaming, which allow at least of a mediate, but, therefore, only of an imperfect, observation, through recollection, it is not altogether exclusive. In all states of strong mental emotion, the passion is itself, to a certain extent, a negation of the tranquillity requisite for observation, so that we are thus impaled on the awkward dilemma, — either we possess the necessary tranquillity for observation, with little or nothing to observe, or there is something to observe, but we have not the necessary tranquillity for observation. All this is completely opposite in our observation of the external world. There the objects lie always ready for our inspection; and we have only to open our eyes, and guard ourselves from the use of hypotheses and green spectacles, to carry our observations to an easy and successful termination.

Want of mutual coöperation. — In the *second* place, in the study of external nature, several observers may associate themselves in the pursuit; and it is well known how coöperation and mutual sympathy preclude tedium and languor, and brace up the faculties to their highest vigor. Hence the old proverb, *unus homo, nullus homo.* "As iron," says Solomon, "sharpeneth iron, so a man sharpeneth the understanding of his friend." "In my opinion," says Plato, "it is well expressed by Homer,

> By mutual confidence and mutual aid,
> Great deeds are done, and great discoveries made;'

for if we labor in company, we are always more prompt and capable for the investigation of any hidden matter. But if a man works out any thing by solitary meditation, he forthwith goes about to find some one with whom he may commune, nor does he think his discovery assured until confirmed by the acquiescence of others." Aristotle, in like manner, referring to the same passage of Homer, gives the same solution. "Social operation," he says, "renders us more energetic both in thought and action." Of this advantage the student of Mind is in a great measure deprived. He who would study the internal world must isolate himself in the solitude of his own thought; and for man, who, as Aristotle observes, is more social by nature than any bee or ant, this isolation is not only painful in itself, but, in place of strengthening his powers, tends to rob them of what maintains their vigor and stimulates their exertion.

No fact of consciousness can be accepted at second hand. — In the *third* place, "In the study of the material universe," [says Cardaillac,] "it is not necessary that each observer should himself make every observation. The phænomena are here so palpable and so easily described, that the experience of one observer suffices to make the facts which he has witnessed intelligible and credible to all. In point of fact, our knowledge of the external world is taken chiefly upon trust. The phænomena of the internal world, on the contrary, are not thus capable of being described; all that the first observer can do is to lead others to repeat his experience: in the science of mind, we can believe nothing upon authority, take nothing upon trust. In the physical sciences, a fact viewed in different aspects and in different circumstances, by one or more observers of acknowledged sagacity and good faith, is not only comprehended as clearly by those who have not seen it for themselves, but is also admitted without hesitation, independently of all personal verification. Instruction thus suffices to make it understood, and the authority of the testimony carries with it a certainty which almost precludes the possibility of doubt.

"But this is not the case in the philosophy of mind. On the contrary, we can here neither understand nor believe at second hand. Testimony can impose nothing on its own authority; and instruction is only instruction when it enables us to teach ourselves. A fact of consciousness, however well observed, however clearly expressed, and however great may be our confidence in its observer, is for us as nothing, until, by an experience of our own, we have observed and recognized it ourselves. Till this be done, we cannot comprehend what it means, far less admit it to be true. Hence it follows that, in philosophy proper, instruction is limited to an indication of the position in which the pupil ought to place himself, in order, by his own observation, to verify for himself the facts which his instructor pronounces true."

Phænomena of consciousness only to be studied through memory. — In the *fourth* place, the phænomena of consciousness are not arrested during observation; — they are in a ceaseless and rapid flow; each state of mind is indivisible but for a moment, and there are not two states or two moments of whose precise identity we can be assured. Thus, before we can observe a modification, it is already altered; nay, the very intention of observing it, suffices for the change. It hence results that the phænomenon can only be studied through its reminiscence; but memory reproduces it often very imperfectly, and always in lower vivacity and precision. The objects of the external world, on the other hand, remain either unaltered during our observation, or can be renewed without change; and we can leave off at will, and recommence our investigation, without detriment to its result.

Presented only in succession. — In the *fifth* place, "The phænomena of the mental world," [says Biunde,] "are not, like those of the material, placed by the side of each other in space. They want that form by which external objects attract and fetter our attention; they appear only in rows on the thread of time, occupying their fleeting moment, and then vanishing into oblivion; whereas, external objects stand before us steadfast, and distinct, and simultaneous, in all the life and emphasis of extension, figure, and color."

Naturally blend with each other. — In the *sixth* place, the perceptions of the different qualities of external objects are decisively discriminated by different corporeal organs, so that color, sound, solidity, odor, flavor, are, in the sensations themselves, contrasted, without the possibility of confusion. In an individual sense, on the contrary, it is not always easy to draw the line of separation between its perceptions, as these are continually running into each other. Thus red and yellow are, in their extreme points, easily distinguished, but the transition point from one to the other is not precisely determined. Now, in our internal observation, the mental phænomena cannot be discriminated like the perceptions of one sense from the perceptions of another, but only like the perceptions of the same. Thus the phænomenon of feeling, of pleasure or pain, and the phænomenon of desire, are, when considered in their remoter divergent aspects, manifestly marked out and contradistinguished as different original modifications; whereas, when viewed on their approximating side, they are seen to slide so insensibly into each other, that it becomes impossible to draw between them any accurate line of demarcation. Thus the various qualities of our internal life can be alone discriminated by a mental process called Abstraction; and abstraction is exposed to many liabilities of error. Nay, the various mental operations do not present themselves distinct and separate; they are all bound up in the same unity of action; and as they are only possible through each other, they cannot, even in thought, be dealt with as isolated and apart. In the perception of an external object, the qualities are, indeed, likewise presented by the different senses in connection, as, for example, vinegar is at once seen as yellow, felt as liquid, tasted as sour, and so on; nevertheless, the qualities easily allow themselves in abstraction to be viewed as really separable, because they are all the properties of an extended and divisible body; whereas in the mind, thoughts, feelings, desires, do not stand separate, though in juxtaposition, but every mental act contains at once all these qualities, as the constituents of its indivisible simplicity.

Self-observation costs painful effort. — In the *seventh* place, the act of reflection on our internal modifications is not accompanied with that frequent and varied sentiment of pleasure, which we experience from the impression of external things. Self-observation costs us a greater effort, and has less excitement than the contemplation of the material world; and the higher and more refined gratification, which it supplies when its habit has been once formed, cannot be conceived by those who have not as yet been trained to its enjoyment. "The first part of our life," [says Cardaillac,] "is fled before we possess the capacity of reflective observation; while the impressions which, from earliest infancy, we receive from material objects, the wants of our animal nature, and the prior development of our external senses, all contribute to concentrate, even from the first breath of life, our attention on the world without. The second passes without our caring to observe ourselves. The outer life is too agreeable to allow the soul to tear itself from its gratifications, and return frequently upon itself. And at the period when the material world has at length palled upon the senses, when the taste and the desire of reflection gradually become predominant, we then find ourselves, in a certain sort, already made up, and it is impossible for us to resume our life from its commencement, and to discover how we have become what we now are." "Hitherto," [says Ancillon,] "external objects have exclusively riveted our attention; our organs have acquired the flexibility requisite for this peculiar kind of observation; we have learned the method, acquired the habit, and feel the pleasure which results from performing what we perform with ease. But let us recoil upon ourselves; the scene changes; the charm is gone; difficulties accumulate; all that is done, is done irksomely and with effort; in a word, every thing within repels, every thing without attracts; we reach the age of manhood without being taught another lesson than reading what takes place without and around us, whilst we possess neither the habit nor the method of studying the volume of our own thoughts." "For a long time, we are too absorbed in life to be able to detach ourselves from it in thought; and when the desires and the feelings are at length weakened or tranquillized, — when we are at length restored to ourselves, we can no longer judge of the preceding state, because we can no longer reproduce or replace it. Thus it is that our life, in a philosophical sense, runs like water through our fingers. We are carried along lost, whelmed in our life; we live, but rarely see ourselves to live.

"The reflective Ego, which distinguishes self from its transitory modifications, and which separates the spectator from the spectacle of life, which it is continually representing to itself, is never developed in the majority of mankind at all; and even in the thoughtful and reflective few, it is formed only at a mature period, and is even then only in activity by starts and at intervals."

The facilities of philosophical study. — But Philosophy has not only peculiar difficulties, it has also peculiar facilities. There is, indeed, only one external condition on which it is dependent, and that is language; and when, in the progress of civilization, a language is once formed of a copiousness and pliability capable of embodying its abstractions without figurative ambiguity, then a genuine philosophy may commence. With this one condition, all is given; the Philosopher requires for his discoveries no preliminary preparations, — no apparatus of instruments and materials. He has no new events to seek, as the Historian; no new combinations to form, as the Mathematician. The Botanist, the Zoölogist, the Mineralogist, can accumulate only by care, and trouble, and expense, an inadequate assortment of the objects necessary for their labors and observations. But that most important and interesting of all studies of which man himself is the object, has no need of any thing external; it is only necessary that the observer enter into his inner self, in order to find there all he stands in need of, or rather it is only by doing this, that he can hope to find any thing at all. If he only effectively pursue the method of observation and analysis, he may even dispense with the study of philosophical systems. This is at best only useful as a mean towards a deeper and more varied study of himself, and is often only a tribute paid by philosophy to erudition.

We have now concluded the consideration of Consciousness, viewed in its more general relations, and shall proceed to analyze its more particular modifications, that is, to consider the various Special Faculties of Knowledge.

It is here proper to recall to your attention the division I gave of the Mental Phænomena into three great classes, — namely, the phænomena of Knowledge, the phænomena of Feeling, and the phænomena of Conation. But as these various phænomena all suppose Consciousness as their condition, — those of the first class, the phænomena of Knowledge, being, indeed, nothing but consciousness in various relations, — it was necessary, before descending to the consideration of the subordinate, first to exhaust the principal; and in doing this, the discussion has been protracted to a greater length than I anticipated.

I now proceed to the particular investigation of the first class of the mental phænomena, — those of Knowledge or Cognition, — and shall commence by delineating to you the distribution of the cognitive faculties which I shall adopt; — a distribution different from any other with which I am acquainted. But I would first premise an observation in regard to psychological powers, and to psychological divisions.

Mental powers not distinguishable from the thinking principle, nor from each other. — As to mental powers, — under which term are included mental faculties and capacities, — you are not to suppose entities really distinguishable from the thinking principle, or really different from each other. Mental powers are not like bodily organs. It is the same simple substance which exerts every energy of every faculty, however various, and which is affected in every mode of every capacity, however opposite. This has frequently been wilfully or ignorantly misunderstood; and, among others, Dr. Brown has made it a matter of reproach to philosophers in general, that they regarded the faculties into which they analyzed the mind as so many distinct and independent existences. No reproach, however, can be more unjust, no mistake more flagrant; and it can easily be shown that this is perhaps the charge, of all others, to which the very smallest number of psychologists need plead guilty. On this point, Dr. Brown does not, however, stand alone as an accuser; and, both before and since his time, the same charge has been once and again preferred, and this, in particular, with singular infelicity, against Reid and Stewart. To speak only of the latter, — he sufficiently declares his opinion on the subject in a foot-note of the *Dissertation:* — "I quote," he says, "the following passage from Addison, *not* as a specimen of his metaphysical acumen, but as a proof of his good sense in divining and obviating a difficulty, which, I believe, most persons will acknowledge occurred to themselves when they first entered on metaphysical studies: — 'Although we divide the soul into several powers and faculties, there is no such division in the soul itself, since it is the *whole soul* that remembers, understands, wills, or imagines. Our manner of considering the memory, understanding, will, imagination, and the like faculties, is for the better enabling us to express ourselves in such abstracted subjects of speculations, not that there is any such division in the soul itself.' In another part of the same paper, Addison observes, 'that what we call the faculties of the soul are only the different ways or modes in which the soul can exert herself.'"

What is a mental power? — I shall first state to you what is intended by the terms *mental power*, *faculty*, or *capacity;* and then show you that no other opinion has been generally held by philosophers.

It is a fact too notorious to be denied, that the mind is capable of different modifications, — that is, can exert different actions, and can be affected by different passions. This is admitted. But these actions and passions are not all dissimilar; every action and passion is not different from every other. On the contrary, they are like, and they are unlike. Those, therefore, that are like, we group or assort together in thought, and bestow on them a common name; nor are these groups or assortments manifold, — they are in fact few and simple. Again, every action is an effect; every action and passion a modification. But every effect supposes a cause; every modification supposes a subject. When we say that the mind exerts an energy, we virtually say that the mind is the cause of the energy; when we say that the mind acts or suffers, we say in other words, that the mind is the subject of a modification. But the modifications, that is, the actions and passions, of the mind, as we stated, all fall into a few resembling groups, which we designate by a peculiar name; and as the mind is the common cause and subject of all these, we are surely entitled to say in general that the mind has the faculty of exerting such and such a class of energies, or has the capacity of being modified by such and such an order of affections. We here excogitate no new, no occult principle. We only generalize certain effects, and then infer that common effects must have a common cause; we only classify certain modes, and conclude that similar modes indicate the same capacity of being modified. There is nothing in all this contrary to the most rigid rules of philosophizing; nay, it is the purest specimen of the inductive philosophy.

On this doctrine, a *faculty* is nothing more than a general term for the causality the mind has of originating a certain class of energies; a *capacity*, only a general term for the susceptibility the mind has of being affected by a particular kind of emotions. All mental powers are thus, in short, nothing more than names determined by various orders of mental phænomena. But as these phænomena differ from, and resemble, each other in various respects, various modes of classification may, therefore, be adopted, and consequently, various faculties and capacities, in different views, may be the result.

Value of Philosophical System. — And this is what we actually see to be the case in the different systems of philosophy; for each system of philosophy is a different view of the phænomena of mind. Now, here I would observe that we might fall into one or other of two errors, either by attributing too great or too small importance to a systematic arrangement of the mental phænomena. It must be conceded to those who affect to undervalue psychological system, that system is neither the end first in the order of time, nor that paramount in the scale of importance. To attempt a definitive system or synthesis, before we have fully analyzed and accumulated the facts to be arranged, would be preposterous, and necessarily futile; and system is only valuable when it is not arbitrarily devised, but arises naturally out of an observation of the facts, and of the whole facts themselves; *τῆς πολλῆς πείρας τελευταῖον ἐπιγέννημα.*

On the other hand, to despise system is to despise philosophy; for the end of philosophy is the detection of unity. Even in the progress of a science, and long prior to its consummation, it is indeed better to assort the materials we have accumulated, even though the arrangement be only temporary, only provisional, than to leave them in confusion. For without such arrangement, we are unable to overlook our possessions; and as experiment results from the experiment it supersedes, so system is destined to generate system in a progress never attaining, but ever approximating to, perfection.

Having stated what a psychological power in propriety is, I may add that this, and not the other, opinion, has been the one prevalent in the various schools and ages of philosophy. I could adduce to you passages in which the doctrine that the faculties and capacities are more than mere possible modes, in which the simple indivisible principle of thought may act and exist, is explicitly denied by [many of] the fathers of the Church, by [many of] the Platonists, the Aristotelians, and by the whole host of recent philosophers. During the middle ages, the question was indeed one which divided the schools. St. Thomas, at the head of one party, held that the faculties were distinguished not only from each other, but from the essence of the mind; and this, as they phrased it, really and not formally. Henry of Ghent, at the head of another party, maintained a modified opinion, — that the faculties were really distinguished from each other, but not from the essence of the soul. Scotus, again, followed by Occam and the whole sect of Nominalists, denied all real difference either between the several faculties, or between the faculties and the mind; allowing between them only a formal or logical distinction. This last is the doctrine that has subsequently prevailed in the latter ages of philosophy; and it is a proof of its universality, that few modern psychologists have ever thought it necessary to make an explicit profession of their faith in what they silently assumed. No accusation can, therefore, be more ungrounded than that which has been directed against philosophers, — that they have generally harbored the opinion that faculties are, like organs in the body, distinct constituents of mind. The Aristotelic principle, that in relation to the body, "the soul is all in the whole and all in every part," — that it is the same indivisible mind that operates in sense, in imagination, in memory, in reasoning, etc., differently indeed, but differently only because operating in different relations, — this opinion is the one dominant among psychologists, and the one which, though not always formally proclaimed, must, if not positively disclaimed, be in justice presumptively attributed to every philosopher of mind. Those who employed the old and familiar language of philosophy meant, in truth, exactly the same as those who would establish a new doctrine on a newfangled nomenclature.

What is Psychological Division? — From what I have now said, you will be better prepared for what I am about to state in regard to the classification of the first great order of mental phænomena, and the distribution of the faculties of Knowledge founded thereon. I formerly told you that the mental qualities — the mental phænomena — are never presented to us separately; they are always in conjunction, and it is only by an ideal analysis and abstraction that, for the purposes of science, they can be discriminated and considered apart. The problem proposed in such an analysis is to find the primary threads which, in their composition, form the complex tissue of thought. In what ought to be accomplished by such an analysis, all philosophers are agreed, however different may have been the result of their attempts. I shall not state and criticize the various classifications propounded of the cognitive faculties, as I did not state and criticize the classifications propounded of the mental phænomena in general. The reasons are the same. You would be confused, not edified. I shall only delineate the distribution of the faculties of knowledge, which I have adopted, and endeavor to afford you some general insight into its principles. At present, I limit my consideration to the phænomena of Knowledge; with the two other classes — the phænomena of Feeling and the phænomena of Conation — we have at present no concern.

I again repeat that consciousness constitutes, or is coextensive with, all our faculties of knowledge, — these faculties being only special modifications under which consciousness is manifested. It being, therefore, understood that consciousness is not a special faculty of knowledge, but the general faculty out of which the special faculties of knowledge are evolved, I proceed to this evolution.

I. *The Presentative Faculty.* — In the first place, as we are endowed with a faculty of Cognition, or Consciousness in general, and since it cannot be maintained that we have always possessed the knowledge which we now possess, it will be admitted, that we must have a faculty of acquiring knowledge. But this acquisition of knowledge can only be accomplished by the immediate presentation of a new object to consciousness, in other words, by the reception of a new object within the sphere of our cognition. We have thus a faculty which may be called the Acquisitive, or the Presentative, or the Receptive. The term *Presentative* I use, as you will see, in contrast and correlation to a *Representative* Faculty, of which I am immediately to speak.

Subdivided into Perception and Self-Consciousness. — Now, new or adventitious knowledge may be either of things external, or of things internal; in other words, either of the phænomena of the Non-ego, or of the phænomena of the Ego; and this distinction of object will determine a subdivision of this, the Acquisitive Faculty. If the object of knowledge be external, the faculty receptive or presentative of the qualities of such object will be a consciousness of the Non-ego. This has obtained the name of External Perception, or of Perception simply. If, on the other hand, the object be internal, the faculty receptive or presentative of the qualities of such subject-object will be a consciousness of the Ego. This faculty obtains the name of Internal or Reflex Perception, or of Self-Consciousness. By the foreign psychologists, this faculty is termed also the Internal Sense.

Under the general faculty of cognition is thus, in the first place, distinguished an Acquisitive, or Presentative, or Receptive Faculty; and this acquisitive faculty is subdivided into the consciousness of the Non-ego, or External Perception simply, and into the consciousness of the Ego, or Self-Consciousness, or Internal Perception.

This acquisitive faculty is the faculty of Experience. It affords us exclusively all the knowledge we possess *a posteriori*: that is, our whole contingent knowledge, — our whole knowledge of fact. External perception is the faculty of external, self-consciousness is the faculty of internal, experience. If we limit the term Reflection in conformity to its original employment and proper signification, — an attention to the internal phænomena, — *reflection* will be an expression for self-consciousness concentrated.

II. *The Conservative Faculty.* — In the second place, inasmuch as we are capable of knowledge, we must be endowed not only with a faculty of acquiring, but with a faculty of retaining or conserving it when acquired. By this faculty, I mean merely, and in the most limited sense, the power of mental retention. If our knowledge of any object terminated when the object ceased to exist, or to exist within the sphere of consciousness, our knowledge would hardly deserve the name; for what we actually perceive by the faculties of external and of internal perception is but an infinitesimal part of the knowledge which we actually possess. We have thus, as a second necessary faculty, one that may be called the Conservative or Retentive. This is Memory strictly so denominated, — that is, the power of retaining knowledge in the mind, but out of consciousness; I say retaining knowledge in the mind, but out of consciousness, for to bring the *retentum* out of memory into consciousness is the function of a totally different faculty, of which we are immediately to speak. Under the general faculty of cognition is thus, in the second place, distinguished the Conservative or Retentive Faculty, or Memory Proper. Whether there be subdivisions of this faculty, we shall not here inquire.

III. *The Reproductive Faculty.* — But, in the third place, if we are capable of knowledge, it is not enough that we possess a faculty of acquiring, and a faculty of retaining it in the mind, but out of consciousness; we must further be endowed with a faculty of recalling it out of unconsciousness into consciousness, in short, a reproductive power. This Reproductive Faculty is governed by the laws which regulate the succession of our thoughts, — the laws, as they are called, of Mental Association. If these laws are allowed to operate without the intervention of the will, this faculty may be called *Suggestion*, or Spontaneous Suggestion; whereas, if applied under the influence of the will, it will properly obtain the name of *Reminiscence*, or Recollection. By *reproduction*, it should be observed, that I strictly mean the process of recovering the absent thought from unconsciousness, and not its representation in consciousness. This reproductive faculty is commonly confounded with the conservative, under the name of Memory; but most erroneously. These qualities of mind are totally unlike, and are possessed by different individuals in the most different degrees. Some have a strong faculty of conservation, and a feeble faculty of reproduction; others, again, a prompt and active reminiscence, but an evanescent retention. Under the general faculty of cognition, there is thus discriminated, in the third place, the Reproductive Faculty.

IV. *The Representative Faculty.* — In the fourth place, as capable of knowledge, we must not only be endowed with a presentative, a conservative, and a reproductive faculty; there is required for their consummation — for the keystone of the arch — a faculty of representing in consciousness, and of keeping before the mind the knowledge presented, retained, and reproduced. We have thus a Representative Faculty; and this obtains the name of Imagination or Phantasy. The word Fancy is an abbreviation of the latter; but with its change of form, its meaning has been somewhat modified. *Phantasy*, which latterly has been little used, was employed in the language of the older English philosophers, as, like its Greek original, strictly synonymous with Imagination.

The element of imagination is not to be confounded with the element of reproduction, though this is frequently, nay commonly, done; and this either by comprehending these two qualities under imagination, or by conjoining them with the quality of retention under memory. The distinction I make is valid. For the two faculties are possessed by different individuals in very different degrees. It is not, indeed, easy to see how, without a representative act, an object can be reproduced. But the fact is certain, that the two powers have no necessary proportion to each other. The representative faculty has, by philosophers, been distinguished into the Productive or Creative, and the Reproductive, Imagination. I shall hereafter show you that this distinction is untenable.

V. *The Elaborative Faculty.* — In the fifth place, all the faculties we have considered are only subsidiary. They acquire, preserve, call out, and hold up the materials, for the use of a higher faculty which operates upon these materials, and which we may call the Elaborative or Discursive Faculty. This faculty has only one operation, it only compares; — it is *Comparison*, — the faculty of Relations. It may startle you to hear that the highest function of mind is nothing higher than comparison, but in the end, I am confident of convincing you of the paradox. Under Comparison, I include the conditions, and the results, of Comparison. In order to compare, the mind must divide or separate, and conjoin or compose. *Analysis* and *synthesis* are, therefore, the conditions of comparison. Again, the result of comparison is either the affirmation of one thing of another, or the negation of one thing of another. If the mind affirm one thing of another, it conjoins them, and is thus again synthesis. If it deny one thing of another, it disjoins them, and is thus again analysis. *Generalization*, which is the result of synthesis and analysis, is thus an act of comparison, and is properly denominated *Conception*. *Judgment* is only the comparison of two terms or notions directly together; *Reasoning*, only the comparison of two terms or notions with each other through a third. Conception or Generalization, Judgment and Reasoning, are thus only various applications of Comparison, and not even entitled to the distinction of separate faculties.

Under the general cognitive faculty, there is thus discriminated a fifth special faculty in the Elaborative Faculty, or Comparison. This is Thought, strictly so called; it corresponds to the *Διάνοια* of the Greek, to the *Discursus* of the Latin, to the *Verstand* of the German philosophy; and its laws are the object of Logic.

VI. *The Regulative Faculty.* — But, in the sixth and last place, the mind is not altogether indebted to experience for the whole apparatus of its knowledge; — its knowledge is not all adventitious, not all *a posteriori*. What we know by experience, without experience we should not have known; and as all our experience is contingent, all the knowledge derived from experience is contingent also. But there are cognitions in the mind which are not contingent, — which are necessary, — which we cannot but think, — which thought supposes as its fundamental condition. These *a priori* cognitions are the laws or conditions of thought in general; consequently, the laws and conditions under which our knowledge *a posteriori* is possible. These cognitions, therefore, are not mere generalizations from experience. But if not derived from experience, they must be native to the mind; unless, on an alternative that we need not at present contemplate, we suppose with Plato, St. Austin, Cousin, and other philosophers, that Reason, or more properly Intellect, is impersonal, and that we are conscious of these necessary cognitions in the divine mind. These native, these necessary cognitions, are the laws by which the mind is governed in its operations, and which afford the conditions of its capacity of knowledge. These necessary laws, or primary conditions, of intelligence, are phænomena of a similar character; and we must, therefore, generalize or collect them into a class; and on the power possessed by the mind of manifesting these phænomena, we may bestow the name of the Regulative Faculty. This faculty corresponds in some measure to what, in the Aristotelic philosophy, was called *Νοῦς*, — *νοῦς* (*intellectus, mens*), when strictly employed, being a term, in that philosophy, for the place of principles, — the *locus principiorum*. It is analogous, likewise, to the term *Reason*, as occasionally used by some of the older English philosophers, and to the *Vernunft* (*reason*) in the philosophy of Kant, Jacobi, and others of the recent German metaphysicians, and from them adopted into France and England. It is also nearly convertible with what I conceive to be Reid's, and certainly Stewart's, notion of Common Sense. This, the last general faculty which I would distinguish under the Cognitive Faculty, is thus what I would call the Regulative or Legislative, — its synonyms being *Νοῦς*, Intellect, or Common Sense.

You will observe that the term *faculty* can be applied to the class of phænomena here collected under one name, only in a very different signification from what it bears when applied to the preceding powers. For *νοῦς*, intelligence or common sense, meaning merely the complement of the fundamental principles or laws of thought, is not properly a faculty; that is, it is not an active power at all. As it is, however, not a capacity, it is not easy to see by what other word it can be denoted.

Knowledge a priori *and* a posteriori *explained.* — By the way, you will please to recollect these two relative expressions. As used in a psychological sense, a knowledge *a posteriori* is a synonym for knowledge empirical, or from experience; and, consequently, is adventitious to the mind, as subsequent to, and in consequence of, the exercise of its faculties of observation. Knowledge *a priori*, on the contrary, called likewise native, pure, or transcendental knowledge, embraces those principles which, as the conditions of the exercise of its faculties of observation and thought, are, consequently, not the result of that exercise. True it is that, chronologically considered, our *a priori* is not antecedent to our *a posteriori* knowledge; for the internal conditions of experience can only operate when an object of experience has been presented. In the order of time, our knowledge, therefore, may be said to commence with experience, but to have its principle antecedently in the mind. Much as has been written on this matter by the greatest philosophers, this all-important doctrine has never been so well stated as in an unknown sentence of an old and now forgotten thinker: "Cognitio omnis a mente primam originem, a sensibus exordium habet primum" — [All knowledge has its primitive source in the mind, its beginning in the senses.] These few words are worth many a modern volume of philosophy. You will observe the felicity of the expression. The whole sentence has not a superfluous word, and yet is absolute and complete. *Mens*, the Latin term for *νοῦς*, is the best possible word to express the intellectual source of our *a priori* principles, and is well opposed to *sensus*. But the happiest contrast is in the terms *origo* and *exordium;* the former denoting priority in the order of existence, the latter priority in the order of time.

The following is a tabular view of the distribution of the Special Faculties of Knowledge:

Cognitive Faculties.		
	I. Presentative	External = Perception. Internal = Self-consciousness.
	II. Conservative	= Memory.
	III. Reproductive	Without will = Suggestion. With will = Reminiscence.
	IV. Representative	= Imagination.
	V. Elaborative	= Comparison, — Faculty of Relations.
	VI. Regulative	= Reason, — Common Sense.

Besides these faculties, there are, I conceive, no others; and, in the sequel, I shall endeavor to show you, that while these are attributes of mind not to be confounded, — not to be analyzed into each other, — the other faculties which have been devised by philosophers are either factitious and imaginary, or easily reducible to these.

CHAPTER XVI.

THE PRESENTATIVE FACULTY.—REID'S HISTORICAL VIEW OF THE THEORIES OF PERCEPTION.

Use of the term Cognition vindicated.—I may here notice, parenthetically, the reason why I frequently employ *cognition* as a synonym of knowledge. This is not done merely for the sake of varying the expression. In the first place, it is necessary to have a word of this signification, which we can use in the plural. Now the term *knowledges* has waxed obsolete, though I think it ought to be revived. It is frequently employed by Bacon. We must, therefore, have recourse to the term *cognition*, of which the plural is in common usage. But in the second place, we must likewise have a term for knowledge which we can employ adjectively. The word *knowledge* itself has no adjective, for the participle *knowing* is too vague and unemphatic to be employed, at least, alone. But the substantive *cognition* has the adjective *cognitive*. Thus, in consequence of having a plural and an adjective, *cognition* is a word we cannot possibly dispense with in psychological discussion. It would also be convenient, in the third place, for psychological precision and emphasis, to use the word *to cognize* in connection with its noun *cognition*, as we use the decompound *to recognize* in connection with its noun *recognition*. But in this instance, the necessity is not strong enough to warrant our doing what custom has not done. You will notice, such an innovation is always a question of circumstances; and though I would not subject Philosophy to Rhetoric more than Gregory the Great would Theology to Grammar, still, without an adequate necessity, I should always recommend you, in your English compositions, to prefer a word of Saxon to a word of Greek or Latin derivation. It would be absurd to sacrifice meaning to its mode of utterance, — to make thought subordinate to its expression; but still where no higher authority, no imperious necessity, dispenses with philological precepts, these, as themselves the dictates of reason and philosophy, ought to be punctiliously obeyed. "It is not in language," says Leibnitz, "that we ought to play the puritan;" but it is not either for the philosopher or the theologian to throw off all deference to the laws of language, — to proclaim of their doctrines,

> "Mysteria tanta
> Turpe est grammaticis submittere colla capistris"

The general right must certainly be asserted to the philosopher of usurping a peculiar language, if requisite to express his peculiar analyses; but he ought to remember that the exercise of this right, as odious and suspected, is *strictissimi juris*, and that, to avoid the pains and penalties of grammatical recusancy, he must always be able to plead a manifest reason of philosophical necessity. But to return from this digression.

Mental phænomena distinguished only by abstraction. — The phænomena of mind are never presented to us undecomposed and simple; that is, we are never conscious of any modification of mind which is not made up of many elementary modes; but these simple modes we are able to distinguish, by abstraction, as separate forms or qualities of our internal life, since, in different states of mind, they are given in different proportions and combinations. We are thus able to distinguish as simple, by an ideal abstraction and analysis, what is never actually given except in composition; precisely as we distinguish color from extension, though color is never presented to us apart, nay, cannot even be conceived as actually separable, from extension. The aim of the psychologist is thus to analyze, by abstraction, the mental phænomena into those ultimate or primary qualities, which, in their combination, constitute the concrete complexities of actual thought. If the simple constituent phænomenon be a mental activity, we give to the active power thus possessed by the mind of eliciting such elementary energy the name of *faculty;* whereas, if the simple or constituent phænomenon be a mental passivity, we give to the passive power thus possessed by the mind of receiving such an elementary affection, the name of *capacity.* Thus it is that there are just as many simple faculties as there are ultimate activities of mind; as many simple capacities as there are ultimate passivities of mind; and it is consequently manifest that a system of the mental powers can never be final and complete, until we have accomplished a full and accurate analysis of the various fundamental phænomena of our internal life. And what does such an analysis suppose? Manifestly three conditions: — 1°, That no phænomenon be assumed as elementary which can be resolved into simpler principles; 2°, That no elementary phænomenon be overlooked; and 3°, That no imaginary element be interpolated.

These are the rules which ought evidently to govern our psychological analyses. I could show, however, that these have been more or less violated in every attempt that has been made at a determination of the constituent elements of thought; for philosophers have either stopped short of the primary phænomenon, or they have neglected it, or they have substituted another in its room. I declined, however, at present, an articulate criticism of the various systems of the human powers proposed by philosophers, and passed on to the summary distribution of the cognitive faculties given in the last chapter. It is evident that such a distribution, as the result of an analysis, cannot be appreciated until the analysis itself be understood; and this can only be understood after the discussion of the several faculties and elementary phænomena has been carried through. You are, therefore, at present to look upon this scheme as little more than a table of contents to the various chapters, under which the phænomena of knowledge will be considered. I now only make a statement of what I shall subsequently attempt to prove. The principle of the distribution is, however, of such a nature that I flatter myself it can, in some measure, be comprehended even on its first enunciation: for the various elementary phænomena, and the relative faculties which it assumes, are of so notorious and necessary a character, that they cannot possibly be refused; and, at the same time, they are discriminated from each other both by obvious contrast, and by the fact that they are manifested in different individuals each in very various proportions to each other.

The general faculty of knowledge is thus, according to this distribution, divided into six special faculties: first, the Acquisitive, Presentative, or Receptive; second, the Conservative; third, the Reproductive; fourth, the Representative; fifth, the Elaborative; and sixth, the Regulative. The first of these, the Acquisitive, is again subdivided into two faculties, — Perception and Self-Consciousness; the third into Suggestion and Reminiscence; and the fifth may likewise admit of subdivisions, into Conception, Judgment, and Reasoning, which, however, as merely applications of the same act in different degrees, hardly warrant a distinction into separate faculties. I now proceed to consider these faculties in detail.

The Presentative Faculty — Perception. — Perception, or the consciousness of external objects, is the first power in order. And, in treating of this faculty, — the faculty on which turns the whole question of Idealism and Realism, — it is perhaps proper, in the first place, to take an historical survey of the hypotheses of philosophers in regard to Perception. In doing this, I shall particularly consider the views which Reid has given of these hypotheses: his authority on this the most important part of his philosophy is entitled to high respect; and it is requisite to point out to you, both in what respects he has misrepresented others, and in what been misrepresented him self.

Before commencing this survey, it is proper to state, in a few words, the one, the principal, point in regard to which opinions vary. The grand distinction of philosophers is determined by the alternative they adopt on the question, — *Is our perception or our consciousness of external objects, mediate or immediate?*

As we have seen, those who maintain our knowledge of external objects to be immediate, accept implicitly the datum of consciousness, which gives as an ultimate fact, in this act, an ego immediately known, and a non-ego immediately known. Those again who deny that an external object can be immediately known, do not accept one-half of the fact of consciousness, but substitute some hypothesis in its place, — not, however, always the same. Consciousness declares that we have an immediate knowledge of a non-ego, and of an *external* non-ego.

Two hypotheses of Mediate Perception. — Now, of the philosophers who reject this fact, some admit our immediate knowledge of a non-ego, but not of an *external* non-ego. They do not limit the consciousness or immediate knowledge of the mind to its own modes, but conceiving it impossible for the external reality to be brought within the sphere of consciousness, they hold that it is represented by a vicarious image, numerically different from mind, but situated somewhere, either in the brain or mind, within the sphere of consciousness. Others, again, deny to the mind not only any consciousness of an external non-ego, but of a non-ego at all, and hold that what the mind immediately perceives, and mistakes for an external object, is only the ego itself peculiarly modified. These two are the only generic varieties possible of the representative hypothesis. And they have each their respective advantages and disadvantages. They both equally afford a basis for Idealism. On the former, Berkeley established his Theological, on the latter, Fichte his Anthropological, Idealism. Both violate the testimony of consciousness, the one the more complex and the clumsier, in denying that we are conscious of an external non-ego, though admitting that we are conscious of a non-ego within the sphere of consciousness, either in the mind or brain. The other, the simpler and more philosophical, outrages, however, still more flagrantly, the veracity of consciousness, in denying not only that we are conscious of an external non-ego, but that we are conscious of a non-ego at all.*

* [Nothing is easier than to show that, so far from refuting Idealism, this doctrine affords it the best of all possible foundations. . . . . An Egoistical Idealism is established on the doctrine that all our knowledge is merely subjective, or of the mind itself; that the Ego has no immediate cognizance of a Non-Ego as existing, but that the Non-Ego is only represented to us

Each of these hypotheses of a representative perception admits of various subordinate hypotheses. Thus the former, which holds that the representative or immediate object is a *tertium quid*, different both from the mind and from the external reality, is subdivided, according as the immediate object is viewed as material, as immaterial, or as neither, or as both, as something physical or as something hyperphysical, as propagated from the external object, as generated in the medium, or as fabricated in the soul itself; and this latter, either in the intelligent mind or in the animal life, as infused by God or by angels, or as identical with the divine substance, and so forth. In the latter, the representative modification has been regarded either as factitious, that is, a mere product of mind; or as innate, that is, as independent of any mental energy.

Reid's error. — Reid, who, as I shall hereafter endeavor to show you, probably holds the doctrine of an Intuitive or Immediate Perception, never generalized, never articulately understood, the distinction of the two forms of the Representative Hypothesis. This was the cause of the most important errors on his part. In the *first* place, it prevented him from drawing the obtrusive and vital distinction between Perception, to him a

in a modification of the self-conscious Ego. This doctrine being admitted, the Idealist has only to show, that the supposition of a Non-Ego, or an external world really existent, is a groundless and unnecessary assumption; for, while the Law of Parcimony prohibits the multiplication of substances or causes beyond what the phænomena require, we have manifestly no right to postulate for the Non-Ego the dignity of an independent substance beyond the Ego, seeing that this Non-Ego is, *ex hypothesi*, known to us, consequently exists for us, only as a phænomenon of the Ego. . . . . All our knowledge of the Non-Ego is thus merely ideal and mediate; we have no knowledge of any really objective reality, except through a subjective representation or notion; in other words, we are only immediately cognizant of certain modes of our own minds, and, in and through them, mediately warned of the phænomena of the material universe. . . . . The common sense of mankind only assures us of the existence of an external and extended world, in assuring us that we are conscious, not merely of the phænomena of mind in relation to matter, but of the phænomena of matter in relation to mind; — in other words, that we are immediately percipient of extended things.] — *Notes to Reid.*

faculty immediately cognitive, or presentative of external objects, and the faculties of Imagination and Memory, in which external objects can only be known to the mind mediately, or in a representation. In the *second* place, this, as we shall see, causes him the greatest perplexity, and sometimes leads him into errors in his history of the opinions of previous philosophers, in regard to which he has, independently of this, been guilty of various mistakes.

Brown's error. — As to Brown, he holds the simple doctrine of a representative perception, — a doctrine which Reid does not seem to have understood; and this opinion he not only holds himself, but attributes, with one or two exceptions, to all modern philosophers, nay, even to Reid himself, whose philosophy he thus maintains to be one great blunder, both in regard to the new truths it professes to establish, and to the old errors it professes to refute. It turns out, however, that Brown in relation to Reid is curiously wrong from first to last, — not one of Reid's numerous mistakes, historical and philosophical, does he touch, far less redargue; whereas, in every point on which he assails Reid, he himself is historically or philosophically in error.

Reid's historical review. — *The Platonic theory.* — This being premised, I now proceed to follow Reid through his historical view and scientific criticism of the various theories of Perception; and I accordingly commence with the Platonic. In this, however, he is unfortunate, for the simile of the cave, which is applied by Plato in the seventh book of the Republic, was not intended by him as an illustration of the mode of our sensible perception at all. "Plato," says Reid, "illustrates our manner of perceiving the objects of sense in this manner. He supposes a dark subterraneous cave, in which men lie bound in such a manner that they can direct their eyes only to one part of the cave: far behind, there is a light, some rays of which come over a wall to that part of the cave which is before the eyes of our prisoners. A number of persons, variously employed, pass between them and the light, whose shadows are seen by the prisoners, but not the persons themselves. In this manner, that philosopher conceived that, by our senses, we perceive the shadows of things only, and not things themselves. He seems to have borrowed his notions on this subject from the Pythagoreans, and they very probably from Pythagoras himself. If we make allowance for Plato's allegorical genius, his sentiments on this subject correspond very well with those of his scholar Aristotle, and of the Peripatetics. The shadows of Plato may very well represent the species and phantasms of the Peripatetic school, and the ideas and impressions of modern philosophers."

Reid's account of the Platonic theory of perception is utterly wrong. Plato's simile of the cave he completely misapprehends. By his cave, images, and shadows, this philosopher intended only to illustrate the great principle of his philosophy, that the sensible or ectypal world, — the world phænomenal, transitory, ever becoming but never being (*ἀεὶ γιγνόμενον, μηδέποτε ὂν*), stands to the noetic or archetypal world, — the world substantial, permanent (*ὄντως ὂν*), in the same relation of comparative unreality, in which the shadows or the images of sensible existences themselves stand to the objects of which they are the dim and distant adumbrations.

But not only is Reid wrong in regard to the meaning of the cave, he is curiously wrong in regard to Plato's doctrine, — at least, of vision. For so far was Plato from holding that we only perceive in consequence of the representations of objects being thrown upon the percipient mind, — he, on the contrary, maintained, in the *Timæus*, that, in vision, a percipient power of the sensible soul sallies out towards the object, the images of which it carries back into the eye; — an opinion, by the way, held likewise by Empedocles, Alexander of Aphrodisias, [and many others].

The Aristotelic doctrine. — The account which Reid gives of the Aristotelic doctrine is, likewise, very erroneous. "Aristotle seems to have thought that the soul consists of two parts, or rather, that we have two souls, — the animal and the rational; or, as he calls them, the soul and the intellect. To the *first*, belong the senses, memory and imagination; to the *last*, judgment, opinion, belief, and reasoning. The first we have in common with brute animals; the last is peculiar to man. The animal soul he held to be a certain form of the body, which is inseparable from it, and perishes at death. To this soul the senses belong; and he defines a sense to be that which is capable of receiving the sensible forms or species of objects, without any of the matter of them; as wax receives the form of the seal without any of the matter of it. The forms of sound, of color, of taste, and of other sensible qualities, are, in a manner, received by the senses. It seems to be a necessary consequence of Aristotle's doctrine, that bodies are constantly sending forth, in all directions, as many different kinds of forms without matter as they have different sensible qualities; for the forms of color must enter by the eye, the forms of sound by the ear, — and so of the other senses. This, accordingly, was maintained by the followers of Aristotle, though not, as far as I know, expressly mentioned by himself. They disputed concerning the nature of those forms of species, whether they were real beings or nonentities; and some held them to be of an intermediate nature between the two. The whole doctrine of the Peripatetics and schoolmen concerning forms, substantial and accidental, and concerning the transmission of sensible species from objects of sense to the mind, if it be at all intelligible, is so far above my comprehension that I should perhaps do it injustice by entering into it more minutely."

In regard to the statement of the Peripatetic doctrine of species, I must observe, that it is correct only as applied to the doctrine taught as the Aristotelic in the Schools of the middle ages; and even in these Schools, there was a large party who not only themselves disavowed the whole doctrine of species, but maintained that it received no countenance from the authority of Aristotle. This opinion is correct; and I could easily prove to you, had we time, that there is nothing in the metaphorical expressions of εἶδος and τύπος, which, on one or two occasions, he cursorily uses, to warrant the attribution to him of the doctrine of his disciples. This is even expressly maintained by several of his Greek commentators, — as the Aphrodisian,

Michael Ephesius, and Philoponus. In fact, Aristotle appears to have held the same doctrine in regard to perception as Reid himself. He was a Natural Realist.

Reid gives no account of the famous doctrine of Perception held by Epicurus, and which that philosopher had borrowed from Democritus, — namely, that the εἴδωλα, ἀπόῤῥοιαι, *imagines, simulacra rerum*, etc., are like pellicles continually flying off from objects; and that these material likenesses, diffusing themselves everywhere in the air, are propagated to the perceptive organs. In the words of Lucretius, —

> "Quæ, quasi membranæ, summo de cortice rerum
> Dereptæ, volitant ultro citroque per auras."

The Cartesian doctrine. — Reid's statement of the Cartesian doctrine of perception is not exempt from serious error. After giving a long, and not very accurate, account of the philosophy of Descartes in general, he proceeds: —

"There are two points, in particular, wherein I cannot reconcile him to himself: the *first*, regarding the place of the ideas or images of external objects, which are the immediate objects of perception; the *second*, with regard to the veracity of our external senses.

"As to the *first*, he sometimes places the ideas of material objects in the brain, not only when they are perceived, but when they are remembered or imagined; and this has always been held to be the Cartesian doctrine; yet he sometimes says, that we are not to conceive the images or traces in the brain to be perceived, as if there were eyes in the brain; these traces are only occasions on which, by the laws of the union of soul and body, ideas are excited in the mind; and, therefore, it is not necessary that there should be an exact resemblance between the traces and the things represented by them, any more than that words or signs should be exactly like the things signified by them.

"These two opinions, I think, cannot be reconciled. For, if the images or traces in the brain are perceived, they must be the objects of perception, and not the occasions of it only. On the other hand, if they are only the occasions of our perceiving, they are not perceived at all. Descartes seems to have hesitated between the two opinions, or to have passed from the one to the other."

Reid's principal error consists in charging Descartes with vacillation and inconsistency, and in possibly attributing to him the opinion that the representative object, of which the mind is conscious in perception, is something material, — something in the brain. This arose from his ignorance of the fundamental principle of the Cartesian doctrine. By those not possessed of the key to the Cartesian theory, there are many passages in the writings of its author which, taken by themselves, might naturally be construed to import, that Descartes supposed the mind to be conscious of certain motions in the brain, to which, as well as to the modifications of the intellect itself, he applies the terms *image* and *idea*. Reid, who did not understand the Cartesian philosophy as a system, was puzzled by these superficial ambiguities. Not aware that the cardinal point of that system is, that mind and body, as essentially opposed, are naturally to each other as zero; and that their mutual intercourse can, therefore, only be supernaturally maintained by the concourse of the Deity, Reid was led into the error of attributing, by possibility, to Descartes, the opinion that the soul was immediately cognizant of material images in the brain. But in the Cartesian theory, mind is only conscious of itself; the affections of body may, by the law of union, be proximately the occasions, but can never constitute the immediate objects, of knowledge. Reid, however, supposing that nothing could obtain the name of *image*, which did not represent a prototype, or the name of *idea*, which was not an object of thought, wholly misinterpreted Descartes, who applies, abusively indeed, these terms to the occasion of perception, that is, the motion in the sensorium, unknown in itself and representing nothing; as well as to the object of thought, that is, the representation of which we are conscious in the mind itself. In the Leibnitzo-Wolfian system, two elements, both also denominated *ideas*, are in like manner accurately to be contradistinguished in the process of perception.

The idea in the brain, and the idea in the mind, are, to Descartes, precisely what the "*material idea*" and the "*sensual idea*" are to the Wolfians. In both philosophies, the two ideas are harmonic modifications, correlative and coexistent; but in neither is the organic affection or sensorial idea an object of consciousness. It is merely the unknown and arbitrary condition of the mental representation; and in the hypothesis, both of Assistance and of Preëstablished Harmony, the presence of the one idea implies the concomitance of the other, only by virtue of the hyperphysical determination.

Reid confused in his account of Arnauld. — In treating of Arnauld's opinion, we see the confusion arising from Reid's not distinctly apprehending the two forms of the representative hypothesis. Arnauld held, and was the first of the philosophers noticed by Reid or Brown who clearly held, the simpler of these forms. Now, in his statement of Arnauld's doctrine, Reid was perplexed, — was puzzled. As opposing the philosophers who maintained the more complex doctrine of representation, Arnauld seemed to Reid to coincide in opinion with himself; but yet, though he never rightly understood the simpler doctrine of representation, he still feels that Arnauld did not hold with him an intuitive perception. Dr. Brown is, therefore, wrong in asserting that Reid admits Arnauld's opinion on perception and his own to be identical.

It cannot be maintained, that Reid admits a philosopher to hold an opinion convertible with his own, whom he states to "profess the doctrine, universally received, that we perceive not material things immediately, — that it is their ideas that are the immediate objects of our thoughts, — and that it is in the idea of every thing that we perceive its properties." This fundamental contrast being established, we may safely allow that the original misconception, which caused Reid to overlook the difference of our intuitive and representative faculties, caused him, likewise, to believe that Arnauld had attempted to unite two contradictory theories of perception. Not aware that it was possible to maintain a doctrine of perception in which the idea was not really distinguished from its cognition, and yet to hold that the mind had no immediate knowledge of external things. Reid supposes, in the first place, that Arnauld, in rejecting the hypothesis of ideas, as representative existences really distinct from the contemplative act of perception, coincided with him in viewing the material reality as the immediate object of that act; and, in the second, that Arnauld again deserted this opinion, when, with the philosophers, he maintained that the idea, or act of the mind representing the external reality, and not the external reality itself, was the immediate object of perception. Arnauld's theory is one and indivisible; and, as such, no part of it is identical with Reid's. Reid's confusion, here as elsewhere, is explained by the circumstance, that he had never speculatively conceived the possibility of the simplest modification of the representative hypothesis. He saw no medium between rejecting ideas as something different from thought, and his own doctrine of an immediate knowledge of the material object. Neither does Arnauld, as Reid supposes, ever assert against Malebranche, "that we perceive external things immediately," that is, in themselves: maintaining that all our perceptions are modifications essentially representative, he everywhere avows, that he denies ideas only as existences distinct from the act itself of perception.

Reid was, therefore, wrong, and did Arnauld less than justice, in viewing his theory "as a weak attempt to reconcile two inconsistent doctrines:" he was wrong, and did Arnauld more than justice, in supposing that one of these doctrines was not incompatible with his own. The detection, however, of this error only tends to manifest more clearly, how just, even when under its influence, was Reid's appreciation of the contrast subsisting between his own and Arnauld's opinion, considered as a whole; and exposes more glaringly Brown's general misconception of Reid's philosophy, and his present gross misrepresentation, in affirming that the doctrines of the two philosophers were identical, and by Reid admitted to be the same.

Reid on Locke. — Locke is the philosopher next in order, and it is principally against Reid's statement of the Lockian doctrine of ideas, that the most vociferous clamor has been raised, by those who deny that the cruder form of the representative hypothesis was the one prevalent among philosophers, after the decline of the Scholastic theory of species; and who do not see that, though Reid's refutation, from the cause I have already noticed, was ostensibly directed only against that cruder form, it was virtually and in effect levelled against the doctrine of a representative perception altogether. Even supposing that Reid was wrong in attributing this particular modification of the representative hypothesis to Locke, and the philosophers in general, — this would be a trivial error, provided it can be shown that he was opposed to every doctrine of perception, except that founded on the fact of the duality of consciousness. But let us consider whether Reid be really in error when he attributes to Locke the opinion in question. Both Priestley and Brown strenuously contend against Reid's interpretation of the doctrine of Locke, who states it as that philosopher's opinion, "that images of external objects were conveyed to the brain; but whether he thought with [Dr. Clarke] and Newton, that the images in the brain are perceived by the mind, there present, or that they are imprinted on the mind itself, is not so evident."

This, Brown, Priestley, and others pronounce a flagrant misrepresentation. Not only does Brown maintain that Locke never conceived the idea to be substantially different from the mind, as a material image of the brain; but that he never supposed it to have an existence apart from the mental energy of which it is the object. Locke, he asserts, like Arnauld, considered the idea perceived and the percipient act to constitute the same indivisible modification of the conscious mind. This we shall consider.

In his language, Locke is, of all philosophers, the most figurative, ambiguous, vacillating, various, and even contradictory; as has been noticed by Reid and Stewart, and Brown himself, — indeed, we believe, by every philosopher who has had occasion to animadvert on Locke. The opinions of such a writer are not, therefore, to be assumed from isolated and casual expressions, which themselves require to be interpreted on the general analogy of the system; and yet this is the only ground on which Dr. Brown attempts to establish his conclusions. Thus, on the matter under discussion, though really distinguishing, Locke verbally confounds, the objects of sense and of pure intellect, the operation and its object, the objects immediate and mediate, the object and its relations, the images of fancy and the notions of the understanding. Consciousness is converted with Perception; Perception with Idea; Idea with the object of Perception, and with Notion, Conception, Phantasm, Representation, Sense, Meaning, etc. Now, his language identifying ideas and perceptions, appears conformable to a disciple of Arnauld; and now it proclaims him a follower of Democritus and Digby, — explaining ideas by mechanical impulse and the propagation of material particles from the external reality to the brain. In one passage, the idea would seem an organic affection, — the mere occasion of a spiritual representation; in another, a representative image, in the brain itself. In employing thus indifferently the language of every hypothesis, may we not suspect that he was anxious to be made responsible for none? One, however, he has formally rejected, and that is the very opinion attributed to him by Dr. Brown, — that the idea, or object of consciousness in perception, is only a modification of the mind itself.

I do not deny that Locke occasionally employs expressions, which, in a writer of more considerate language, would imply the identity of ideas with the act of knowledge; and, under the circumstances, I should have considered suspense more rational than a dogmatic confidence in any conclusion, did not the following passage, which has never, I believe, been noticed, afford a positive and explicit contradiction of Dr. Brown's interpretation. It is from Locke's *Examination of Malebranche's Opinion*, which, as subsequent to the publication of the *Essay*, must be held decisive in relation to the doctrines of that work. At the same time, the statement is articulate and precise, and possesses all the authority of one cautiously emitted in the course of a polemical discussion. Malebranche coincided with Arnauld, Reid, and recent philosophers in general, and consequently with

Locke, as interpreted by Brown, to the extent of supposing that *sensation proper* is nothing but a state or modification of the mind itself; and Locke had thus the opportunity of expressing, in regard to this opinion, his agreement or dissent. An acquiescence in the doctrine, that the secondary qualities, of which we are conscious in sensation, are merely mental states, by no means involves an admission that the primary qualities, of which we are conscious in perception, are nothing more. Malebranche, for example, affirms the one and denies the other. But if Locke be found to ridicule, as he does, even the opinion which merely reduces the secondary qualities to mental states, *a fortiori*, and this on the principle of his own philosophy, he must be held to reject the doctrine, which would reduce not only the non-resembling sensations of the secondary, but even the resembling, and consequently extended, ideas of the primary, qualities of matter to modifications of the immaterial unextended mind. In these circumstances, the following passage is superfluously conclusive against Brown; and equally so whether we coincide or not in all the doctrines it involves. "But to examine their doctrine of *modification* a little further. — Different sentiments (sensations) are different modifications of the mind. The mind, or soul, that perceives, is one immaterial indivisible substance. Now I see the white and black on this paper; I hear one singing in the next room; I feel the warmth of the fire I sit by; and I taste an apple I am eating, and all this at the same time. Now, I ask, take modification for what you please, can the same unextended indivisible substance have different, nay, inconsistent and opposite (as these of white and black must be) modifications at the same time? Or must we suppose distinct parts in an indivisible substance, one for black, another for white, and another for red ideas, and so of the rest of those infinite sensations, which we have in sorts and degrees; all which we can distinctly perceive, and so are distinct ideas, some whereof are opposite, as heat and cold, which yet a man may feel at the same time? I was ignorant before, how sensation was performed in us: this they call an explanation of it! Must I say now I understand it better? If this be to cure one's ignorance, it is a very slight disease, and the charm of two or three insignificant words will at any time remove it; *probatum est.*"

But if it be thus evident that Locke held neither the third form of representation, that lent to him by Brown, nor even the second; it follows that Reid did him any thing but injustice, in supposing him to maintain that ideas are objects, either in the brain, or in the mind itself. Even the more material of these alternatives has been the one generally attributed to him by his critics, and the one adopted from him by his disciples. Nor is this to be deemed an opinion too monstrous to be entertained by so enlightened a philosopher. It was the common opinion of the age; the opinion, in particular, held by the most illustrious philosophers, his countrymen and contemporaries, — by Newton, Clarke, Willis, Hook, etc.

Reid and Brown on Hobbes. — To adduce Hobbes as an instance of Reid's misrepresentation of the "common doctrine of ideas," betrays, on the part of Brown, a total misapprehension of the conditions of the question; or he forgets that Hobbes was a materialist. The doctrine of representation, under all its modifications, is properly subordinate to the doctrine of a spiritual principle of thought; and on the supposition, all but universally admitted among philosophers, that the relation of knowledge implied the analogy of existence, it was mainly devised to explain the possibility of a knowledge by an immaterial subject, of an existence so disproportioned to its nature, as the qualities of a material object. Contending, that an immediate cognition of the accidents of matter, infers an essential identity of matter and mind, Brown himself admits, that the hypothesis of representation belongs exclusively to the doctrine of dualism; whilst Reid, assailing the hypothesis of ideas only as subverting the reality of matter, could hardly regard it as parcel of that scheme, which acknowledges the reality of nothing else. But though Hobbes cannot be adduced as a competent witness against Reid, he is, however, valid evidence against Brown. Hobbes, though a materialist, admitted no knowledge of an external world. Like his friend Sorbiere, he was a kind of Material Idealist. According to him, we know nothing of the qualities or existence of any outward reality. All that we know is the "seeming," the "apparition," the "aspect," the "phænomenon," the "phantasm," within ourselves; and this subjective object, of which we are conscious, and which is consciousness itself, is nothing more than the "agitation" of our internal organism, determined by the unknown "motions," which are supposed, in like manner, to constitute the world without. Perception he reduces to Sensation. Memory and Imagination are faculties specifically identical with Sense, differing from it simply in the degree of their vivacity: and this difference of intensity, with Hobbes as with Hume, is the only discrimination between our dreaming and our waking thoughts. — A doctrine of perception identical with Reid's!

Le Clerc and Crousaz. — Dr. Brown at length proceeds to consummate his victory, by "that most decisive evidence, found not in treatises read only by a few, but in the popular elementary works of science of the time, the general text-books of schools and colleges." He quotes however, only two, — the *Pneumatology* of Le Clerc, and the *Logic* of Crousaz.

"Le Clerc," says Dr. Brown, "in his chapter on the nature of ideas, gives the history of the opinions of philosophers on this subject, and states among them the very doctrine which is most forcibly and accurately opposed to the ideal system of perception. ["Others suppose," says Le Clerc, "that an idea and the perception of an idea are the same thing, though they differ in their relations. The idea, as they think, is properly referred to *the object* which the mind considers, while the perception is referred to *the mind itself* which perceives; but this twofold relation belongs to one and the same modification of mind. Therefore, according to these philosophers, there are not, properly speaking, any ideas distinct from the mind."] What is it, I may ask, which Dr. Reid considers himself as having added to this very philosophical view of perception? and if he added nothing, it is surely too much to ascribe to him the merit of detecting errors, the counter-statement of which had long formed a part of the elementary works of the schools."

In the first place, Dr. Reid certainly "added" nothing "to

this very philosophical view of perception," but he exploded it altogether. In the second, it is false either that this doctrine of perception "had long formed part of the elementary works of the schools," or that Le Clerc affords any countenance to this assertion. On the contrary, it is virtually stated by him to be the novel paradox of a single philosopher; nay, it is already, as such a singular opinion, discussed and referred to its author by Reid himself. Had Dr. Brown proceeded from the tenth paragraph, which he quotes, to the fourteenth, which he could not have read, he would have found that the passage extracted, so far from containing the statement of an old and familiar dogma in the schools, was neither more nor less than a statement of the contemporary hypothesis of Antony Arnauld, and of Antony Arnauld alone. In the third place, from the mode in which he cites Le Clerc, his silence to the contrary, and the general tenor of his statement, Dr. Brown would lead us to believe that Le Clerc himself coincides in "this very philosophical view of perception." So far, however, from coinciding with Arnauld, he pronounces his opinion to be false; controverts it upon very solid grounds; and in delivering his own doctrine touching ideas, though sufficiently cautious in telling us what they are, he has no hesitation in assuring us, among other things which they cannot be, that they are not modifications or essential states of mind. ["The idea," says Le Clerc, "is not a modification, nor is it the essence, of the mind; for, besides the fact that there is a great difference between the *perception of an idea* and a *sensation*, what is there in the mind which is like a mountain, or many other ideas of this sort?"] Such is the judgment of that authority to which Dr. Brown appealed as the most decisive.

In Crousaz, Dr. Brown has actually succeeded in finding one example (he might have found twenty) of a philosopher, before Reid, holding the same theory of ideas with Arnauld and himself.

CHAPTER XVII.

THE PRESENTATIVE FACULTY.—PERCEPTION.—WAS REID A NATURAL REALIST?

In the last chapter, I concluded the review of Reid's Historical Account of the previous Opinions on Perception. In entering upon this review, I proposed the following ends. In the first place, to afford you, not certainly a complete, but a competent insight into the various theories on this subject; and this was sufficiently accomplished by limiting myself to the opinions touched upon by Reid. My aim, in the second place, was to correct some errors of Reid arising from, and illustrative of, those fundamental misconceptions which have infected his whole doctrine of the cognitive faculties with confusion and error; and, in the third place, I had in view to vindicate Reid from the attack made on him by Brown. Perception, as matter of psychological consideration, is of the very highest importance in philosophy; as the doctrine in regard to the object and operation of this faculty affords the immediate data for determining the great question touching the existence or non-existence of an external world; and there is hardly a problem of any moment in the whole compass of philosophy, of which it does not mediately affect the solution. The doctrine of perception may thus be viewed as a cardinal point of philosophy It is also exclusively in relation to this faculty, that Reid must claim his great, his distinguishing glory, as a philosopher; and of this no one was more conscious than himself. "The merit," he says, in a letter to Dr. James Gregory, "of what you are pleased to call my philosophy, lies, I think, chiefly in having called in question the common theory of ideas or images of things in the mind being the only objects of thought — a theory founded on natural prejudices, and so universally received, as to be interwoven with the structure of language." "I think," he adds, "there is hardly any thing that can be called science in the philosophy of the mind, which does not follow with ease from the detection of this prejudice."

To enable you provisionally to understand Reid's errors, I showed you how, holding himself the doctrine of an intuitive or immediate perception of external things, he did not see that the counter doctrine of a mediate or representative perception admitted of a subdivision into two forms, — a simpler and a more complex. The simpler, that the immediate or representative object is a mere modification of the percipient mind, — the more complex, that this representative object is something different both from the reality and from the mind. His ignorance of these two forms has caused him great confusion, and introduced much subordinate error into his system, as he has often confounded the simpler form of the representative hypothesis with the doctrine of an intuitive perception; but if he be allowed to have held the essential doctrine of an immediate perception, his errors in regard to the various forms of the representative hypothesis must be viewed as accidental, and comparatively unimportant.

Brown's errors, on the contrary, are vital. In the first place, he is fundamentally wrong in holding, in the teeth of consciousness, that the mind is incapable of an immediate knowledge of aught but its own modes. He adopts the simpler form of a representative perception. In the second place, he is wrong in reversing Reid's whole doctrine, by attributing to him the same opinion, on this point, which he himself maintains. In the third place, he is wrong in thinking that Reid only attacked the more complex, and not the more dangerous, form of the representative hypothesis, and did not attack the hypothesis of representation altogether. In the fourth place, he is wrong in supposing that modern philosophers, in general, held the simpler form of the representative hypothesis, and that Reid was, therefore, mistaken in supposing them to maintain the more complex, —

mistaken, in fact, in supposing them to maintain a doctrine different from his own.

Was Reid himself a Natural Realist? — But a more important historical question remains, and one which even more affects the reputations of Reid and Brown. It is this: — Did Reid, as Brown supposes, hold, not the doctrine of Natural Realism, but the finer hypothesis of a Representative Perception?

If Reid did hold this doctrine, I admit at once that Brown is right. Reid accomplished nothing; his philosophy is a blunder, and his whole polemic against the philosophers, too insignificant for refutation or comment. The one form of representation may be somewhat simpler and more philosophical than the other; but the substitution of the former for the latter is hardly deserving of notice; and of all conceivable hallucinations, the very greatest would be that of Reid, in arrogating to himself the merit of thus subverting the foundation of Idealism and Scepticism, and of philosophers at large in acknowledging the pretension. The idealist and sceptic can establish their conclusions indifferently on either form of a representative perception; nay, the simpler form affords a securer, as the more philosophical, foundation. The idealism of Fichte is accordingly a system far more firmly founded than the idealism of Berkeley; and as the simpler involves a contradiction of consciousness more extensive and direct, so it furnishes to the sceptic a longer and more powerful lever.

The distinction of Intuitive and Representative Knowledge. — Before, however, discussing this question, it may be proper here to consider more particularly a matter of which we have hitherto treated only by the way, — I mean the distinction of Immediate or Intuitive, in contrast to Mediate or Representative, Knowledge. This is a distinction of the most important kind, and it is one which has, however, been almost wholly overlooked by philosophers. This oversight is less to be wondered at in those who allowed no immediate knowledge to the mind, except of its proper modes; in their systems the distinction, though it still subsisted, had little relevancy or effect, as it did not discriminate the faculty by which we are aware of the presence of external objects, from that by which, when absent, these are imaged to the mind. In neither case, on this doctrine, are we conscious or immediately cognizant of the external reality, but only of the mental mode through which it is represented. But it is more astonishing that those who maintain that the mind is immediately percipient of external things, should not have signalized this distinction; as on it is established the essential difference of Perception as a faculty of Intuitive, Imagination as a faculty of Representative, knowledge. But the marvel is still more enhanced when we find that Reid and Stewart — (if to them this opinion really belongs), so far from distinguishing Perception as an immediate and intuitive, from Imagination (and under Imagination, be it observed, I include both the Conception and the Memory of these philosophers) as a mediate or representative, faculty, — in language make them both equally immediate. You will recollect the refutation I formerly gave you of Reid's self-contradictory assertion, that in Memory we are immediately cognizant of that which, as past, is not now existent, and cannot, therefore, be known in itself; and that, in Imagination, we are immediately cognizant of that which is distant, or of that which is not, and probably never was, in being. Here the term *immediate* is either absurd, as contradictory; or it is applied only, in a certain special meaning, to designate the simpler form of representation, in which nothing is supposed to intervene between the mental cognition and the external reality; in contrast to the more complex, in which the representative or vicarious image is supposed to be something different from both. Thus, in consequence of this distinction not only not having been traced by Reid as the discriminative principle of his doctrine, but having been even overlaid, obscured, and perplexed, his whole philosophy has been involved in haze and confusion; insomuch that a philosopher of Brown's acuteness could (as we have seen and shall see) actually so far misconceive, as even to reverse its import. The distinction is, therefore, one which, on every account, merits your most sedulous attention; but though of primary importance, it is fortunately not of any considerable difficulty.

This distinction stated and illustrated. — As every cognitive act which, in one relation, is a mediate or representative, is, in another, an immediate or intuitive, knowledge, let us take a particular instance of such an act; as hereby we shall at once obtain an example of the one kind of knowledge, and of the other, and these also in proximate contrast to each other. I call up an image of the *High Church* [a Cathedral edifice in Edinburgh]. Now, in this act, what do I know immediately or intuitively; what mediately or by representation? It is manifest that I am conscious, or immediately cognizant, of all that is known as an act or modification of my mind, and, consequently, of the modification or act which constitutes the mental image of the Cathedral. But as, in this operation, it is evident, that I am conscious, or immediately cognizant, of *the Cathedral as imaged in my mind;* so it is equally manifest, that I am not conscious or immediately cognizant of *the Cathedral as existing.* But still I am said to know it; it is even called the object of my thought. I can, however, only know it *mediately, — only through the mental image which represents it* to consciousness; and it can only be styled the object of thought, inasmuch as a reference to it is necessarily involved in the act of representation. From this example is manifest, what in general is meant by immediate or intuitive, — what, by mediate or representative knowledge. All philosophers are at one in regard to *the immediate knowledge of our present mental modifications;* and all are equally agreed, if we remove some verbal ambiguities, that we are only mediately cognizant of all past thoughts, objects, and events, and of every external reality not at the moment within the sphere of sense. There is but one point on which they are now at variance, — namely, whether the thinking subject is competent to an intuitive knowledge of aught but the modifications of the mental self; in other words, whether we can have any *immediate perception of external things.* Waiving, however, this question for the moment, let us articulately state what are the different conditions involved in the two kinds of knowledge

In the *first* place, considered *as acts.* — An act of immediate knowledge is simple; there is nothing beyond the mere consciousness, by that which knows, of that which is known. Here consciousness is simply contemplative. On the contrary, an act of mediate knowledge is complex; for the mind is not only conscious of the act as its own modification, but of this modification as an object representative of, or relative to, an object beyond the sphere of consciousness. In this act, consciousness is both representative and contemplative of the representation.

In the *second* place, *in relation to their objects.* — In an immediate cognition, the object is single, and the term unequivocal. Here, the object in consciousness and the object in existence are the same; in the language of the Schools, the *esse intentionale* or *representativum* coincides with the *esse entitativum.* In a mediate cognition, on the other hand, the object is twofold, and the term equivocal; the object known and representing being different from the object unknown, except as represented. The immediate object, or object known in this act, should be called the *subjective object,* or *subject-object,* in contradistinction to the mediate or unknown object, which might be discriminated as the *object-object.* A slight acquaintance with philosophical writings will show you how necessary such a distinction is; the want of it has caused Reid to puzzle himself, and Kant to perplex his readers.

In the *third* place, considered *as judgments* (for you will recollect that every act of Consciousness involves an affirmation). — In an intuitive act, the object known is known as actually existing; the cognition, therefore, is assertory, inasmuch as the reality of that, its object, is given unconditionally as a fact. In a representative act, on the contrary, the represented object is unknown as actually existing; the cognition, therefore, is problematical, the reality of the object represented being only given as a possibility, on the hypothesis of the object representing.

In the *fourth* place, *in relation to their sphere.* — Representative knowledge is exclusively subjective, for its immediate object is a mere mental modification, and its mediate object is unknown, except in so far as that modification represents it. Intuitive knowledge, on the other hand, if consciousness is to be credited, is either subjective or objective, for its single object may be either a phænomenon of the ego or of the non-ego, — either mental or material.

In the *fifth* place, considered *in reference to their perfection.* — An intuitive cognition, as an act, is complete and absolute, as irrespective of aught beyond the dominion of consciousness; whereas, a representative cognition, as an act, is incomplete, being relative to, and vicarious of, an existence beyond the sphere of actual knowledge. The object likewise of the former is complete, being at once known and real; whereas, in the latter, the object known is ideal, the real object unknown. In their relations to each other, immediate knowledge is complete, as self-sufficient; mediate knowledge, on the contrary, is incomplete, as dependent on the other for its realization.

[For the sake of distinctness, I shall state [over again and more fully] the different momenta of the distinction in separate *Propositions;* and these for more convenient reference I shall number.

1. — A thing is known *immediately* or *proximately*, when we cognize it *in itself; mediately* or *remotely*, when we cognize it *in or through something numerically different from itself.* Immediate cognition, thus the knowledge of a thing in itself, involves the *fact* of its existence; mediate cognition, thus the knowledge of a thing in or through something not itself, involves only the *possibility* of its existence.

2. — An immediate cognition, inasmuch as the thing known is *itself presented* to observation, may be called a *presentative;* and inasmuch as the thing presented is, as it were, *viewed by the mind face to face*, may be called an *intuitive* cognition. — A mediate cognition, inasmuch as the thing known is *held up or mirrored to the mind in a vicarious representation*, may be called a *representative* cognition.

3. — A *thing known* is called an *object* of knowledge.

4. — In a presentative or immediate cognition there is *one sole object;* the thing (immediately) known and the thing existing being one and the same. — In a representative or mediate cog

nition there may be discriminated *two objects;* the thing (immediately) known and the thing existing being numerically different.

5.—A thing known *in itself* is the (sole) *presentative* or *intuitive object* of knowledge, or the (sole) object of a *presentative* or *intuitive knowledge.*—A thing known *in and through something else* is the *primary, mediate, remote,** *real, existent,* or *represented, object* of (mediate) knowledge, *objectum quod;* and a thing *through which something else is known* is the *secondary, immediate, proximate, ideal, vicarious,* or *representative, object* of (mediate) knowledge,—*objectum quo* or *per quod.* The former may likewise be styled *objectum entitativum.*

6.—If the representative object be supposed (according to one theory) a mode of the conscious mind or self, it may be distinguished as *Egoistical;* if it be supposed (according to another) something numerically different from the conscious mind or self, it may be distinguished as *Non-Egoistical.* The former theory supposes *two* things numerically different: 1°, the object represented,—2°, the representing and cognizant mind:—the latter, *three;* 1°, the object represented,—2°, the object representing,—3°, the cognizant mind. Compared merely with each other, the former, as simpler, may, *by contrast* to the latter, be considered, but still inaccurately, as an immediate cognition. The latter of these, as limited in its application to certain faculties, and now in fact wholly exploded, may be thrown out of account.

7.—*External Perception,* or *Perception* simply, is the faculty *presentative* or *intuitive* of the phenomena of the Non-Ego or

* The distinction of *proximate* and *remote* object is sometimes applied to perception in a different manner. Thus Color (the white of the wall for instance) is said to be the *proximate* object of vision, because it is seen immediately; the colored thing (the wall itself for instance) is said to be the *remote* object of vision, because it is seen only through the mediation of the color. This however is inaccurate. For the wall, that in which the color inheres, however mediately *known,* is never mediately *seen.* It is not indeed an *object* of *perception* at all; it is only the *subject* of such an *object,* and is reached by a cognitive process, different from the merely perceptive.

matter — if there be any *intuitive* apprehension allowed of the Non-Ego at all. *Internal Perception* or *Self-consciousness* is the faculty *presentative* or *intuitive* of the phenomena of the Ego or mind.

8. — *Imagination* or *Phantasy*, in its most extensive meaning, is the faculty *representative* of the phenomena both of the external and internal worlds.

9. — A representation considered as an *object* is logically, not really, different from a representation considered as an *act*. Here, object and act are merely the same indivisible mode of mind viewed in two different relations. Considered by reference to a (mediate) object represented, it is a representative object; considered by reference to the mind representing and contemplating the representation, it is a representative act. A representative *object* being viewed as posterior in the order of nature, but not of time, to the representative *act*, is viewed as a *product;* and the representative act being viewed as prior in the order of nature, though not of time, to the representative object, is viewed as a *producing process*. The same may be said of Image and Imagination.

10. — A thing to be known *in itself* must be known as *actually existing*, and it cannot be known as actually existing unless it be known as existing in its *When* and its *Where*. But the When and Where of an object are *immediately* cognizable by the subject, only if the When be *now* (*i. e.* at the same moment with the cognitive act), and the Where be *here* (*i. e.* within the sphere of the cognitive faculty); therefore a presentative or intuitive knowledge is only competent of an object *present* to the mind, both in *time* and in *space*.

11. — E converso — whatever is known, but not as *actually* existing *now* and *here*, is known not in itself, as the presentative object of an intuitive, but only as the remote object of a representative, cognition.

12. — A representative object, considered irrespectively of what it represents, and simply as a mode of the conscious subject, is an intuitive or presentative object. For it is known in itself, as a mental mode, actually existing now and here.

13. — The *actual* modifications — the *present acts* and affections of the *Ego*, are objects of immediate cognition, as themselves objects of consciousness. The *past* and *possible* modifications of the Ego are objects of mediate cognition, as represented to consciousness in a present or actual modification.

14. — As not *now present in time*, an immediate knowledge of the *past* is impossible. The past is only immediately cognizable in and through a present modification relative to, and representative of, it as having been. To speak of an immediate knowledge of the past involves a contradiction *in adjecto*. For to know the past immediately, it must be known *in itself*; — and to be known in itself, it must be known as *now existing*. But the past is just a negation of the now existent: its very notion, therefore, excludes the possibility of its being immediately known. So much for Memory, or Recollective Imagination.

15. — In like manner, supposing that a knowledge of the *future* were competent, this can only be conceived possible in and through a now present representation; that is, only as a mediate cognition. For, as *not yet existent*, the future cannot be known in itself, or as *actually* existent. As *not here present*, an immediate knowledge of an object *distant in space* is likewise impossible. For, as beyond the sphere of our organs and faculties, it cannot be known by them in itself; it can only, therefore, if known at all, be known through something different from itself, — that is mediately, in a reproductive or a constructive act of imagination.

16. — A *possible* object — an *ens rationis* — is a mere fabrication of the mind itself; it exists only ideally in and through an act of imagination, and has only a logical existence, apart from that act with which it is really identical. It is therefore an intuitive object in itself; but in so far as, not involving a contradiction, it is conceived as prefiguring something which may possibly exist some-where and some-when — this something, too, being constructed out of elements which had been previously given in Presentation — it is Representative.] — *Diss. supp. to Reid.*

Such are the two kinds of knowledge which it is necessary to distinguish, and such are the principal contrasts they present. I said a little ago that this distinction, so far from being signalized, had been almost abolished by philosophers. I ought, however, to have excepted certain of the Schoolmen, by whom this discrimination was not only taken, but admirably applied; and though I did not originally borrow it from them, I was happy to find that what I had thought out for myself, was confirmed by the authority of these subtle spirits. The names given in the Schools to the immediate and mediate cognitions were *intuitive* and *abstractive*, meaning by the latter term not merely what we, with them, call abstract knowledge, but also the representations of concrete objects in the imagination or memory.

Order of the discussion. — Having now prepared you for the question concerning Reid, I shall proceed to its consideration; and shall, in the first place, state the arguments that may be adduced in favor of the opinion, that Reid did not assert a doctrine of Natural Realism, — did not accept the fact of the duality of consciousness in its genuine integrity, but only deluded himself with the belief that he was originating a new or an important opinion, by the adoption of the simpler form of Representation; and, in the second place, state the arguments that may be alleged in support of the opposite conclusion, that his doctrine is in truth the simple doctrine of Natural Realism.

Brown's interpretation of Reid's doctrine refuted. — But before proceeding to state the grounds on which alone I conceive any presumption can be founded, that Reid is not a Natural Realist, but, like Brown, a Cosmothetic Idealist, I shall state and refute the only attempt made by Brown to support this, his interpretation of Reid's fundamental doctrine. Brown's interpretation of Reid seems, in fact, not grounded on any thing which he found in Reid, but simply on his own assumption of what Reid's opinion must be. For, marvellous as it may sound, Brown hardly seems to have contemplated the possibility of an immediate knowledge of any thing beyond the sphere of self; and I should say, without qualification, that he had never at all imagined this possibility, were it not for the single attempt he makes at a proof of the impossibility of Reid holding such an opinion, when on one occasion Reid's language seems for a moment to have actually suggested to him the question: Might that philosopher not perhaps regard the external object as identical with the immediate object in perception?

Now the sum and substance of [Brown's] reasoning is, as far as I can comprehend it, to the following effect:—To assert an immediate perception of material qualities, is to assert an identity of matter and mind; for that which is immediately known must be the same in nature as that which immediately knows.

But Reid was not a materialist, was a sturdy spiritualist; therefore he could not really maintain an immediate perception of the qualities of matter.

The whole validity of this argument consists in the truth of the major proposition (for the minor proposition, that Reid was not a materialist, is certain),—To assert an immediate perception of material qualities, is to assert an identity of matter and mind; for that which is immediately known must be the same in essence as that which immediately knows.

Now, in support of the proposition which constitutes the foundation of his argument, Brown offers no proof. He assumes it as an axiom. But so far from his being entitled to do so, by its being too evident to fear denial, it is, on the contrary, not only not obtrusively true, but, when examined, precisely the reverse of truth.

In the *first* place, if we appeal to the only possible arbiter in the case,—the authority of consciousness,—we find that consciousness gives as an ultimate fact, in the unity of knowledge, the duality of existence; that is, it assures us that, in the act of perception, the percipient subject is at once conscious of something which it distinguishes as a modification of self, and of something which it distinguishes as a modification of not-self Reid, therefore, as a dualist, and a dualist founding not on the hypotheses of philosophers, but on the data of consciousness, might safely maintain the fact of our immediate perception of external objects, without fear of involving himself in an assertion of the identity of mind and matter.

But, in the *second* place, if Reid did not maintain this immediacy of perception, and assert the veracity of consciousness, he would at once be forced to admit one or other of the unitarian conclusions of materialism or idealism. Our knowledge of mind and matter, as substances, is merely relative; they are known to us only in their qualities; and we can justify the postulation of two different substances, exclusively on the supposition of the incompatibility of the double series of phænomena to coinhere in one. Is this supposition disproved? — The presumption against dualism is again decisive. Entities are not to be multiplied without necessity; a plurality of principles is not to be assumed, where the phænomena can be explained by one. In Brown's theory of perception, he abolishes the incompatibility of the two series; and yet his argument, as a dualist, for an immaterial principle of thought, proceeds on the ground that this incompatibility subsists. This philosopher denies us an immediate knowledge of aught beyond the accidents of mind. The accidents which we refer to body, as known to us, are only states or modifications of the percipient subject itself; in other words, the qualities we call *material*, are known by us to exist, only as they are known by us to inhere in the same substance as the qualities we denominate *mental*. There is an apparent antithesis, but a real identity. On this doctrine, the hypothesis of a double principle, losing its necessity, becomes philosophically absurd; on the law of parcimony, a psychological unitarianism is established. To the argument, that the qualities of the object, are so repugnant to the qualities of the subject, of perception, that they cannot be supposed the accidents of the same substance, the unitarian — whether materialist, idealist, or absolutist — has only to reply: — that so far from the attributes of the object being exclusive of the attributes of the subject, in this act, the hypothetical dualist himself establishes, as the fundamental axiom of his philosophy of mind, that the object known is universally identical with the subject knowing. The materialist may now derive the subject from the object, the idealist derive the object from the subject, the absolutist sublimate both into indifference, nay, the nihilist subvert the substantial reality of either; — the hypothetical realist, so far from being able to resist the conclusion of any, in fact accords their assumptive premises to all.

So far, therefore, is Brown's argument from inferring the conclusion, that Reid could not have maintained our immediate perception of external objects, that not only is its inference expressly denied by Reid, but if properly applied, it would prove the very converse of what Brown employs it to establish.

Second reason for supposing that Reid was not a Natural Realist. — But there is a ground considerably stronger than that on which Brown has attempted to evince the identity of Reid's opinion on perception with his own. This ground is *his equalizing Perception and Imagination.* (Under Imagination, you will again observe that I include Reid's Conception and Memory.) Other philosophers brought perception into unison with imagination, by making perception a faculty of mediate knowledge. Reid, on the contrary, has brought imagination into unison with perception, by calling imagination a faculty of immediate knowledge. Now, as it is manifest that, in an act of imagination, the object-object is and can possibly be known only, mediately, through a representation, it follows that we must perforce adopt one of two alternatives; — we may either suppose that Reid means by immediate knowledge only that simpler form of representation from which the idea or *tertium quid*, intermediate between the external reality and the conscious mind, is thrown out, or that, in his extreme horror of the hypothesis of ideas, he has altogether overlooked the fundamental distinction of mediate and immediate cognition, by which the faculties of perception and imagination are discriminated; and that thus his very anxiety to separate more widely his own doctrine of intuition from the representative hypothesis of the philosophers, has, in fact, caused him almost inextricably to confound the two opinions.

Positive evidence that Reid held Natural Realism. — That this latter alternative is greatly the more probable, I shall now proceed to show you; and in doing this, I beg you to keep in mind the necessary contrasts by which an immediate or intuitive is opposed to a mediate or representative cognition. The question to be solved is, — Does Reid hold that in perception we immediately know the external reality, in its own qualities, as existing; or only mediately know them, through a representative modification of the mind itself? In the following proof, I select only a few out of a great number of passages which might be adduced from the writings of Reid, in support of the same conclusions. I am, however, confident that they are sufficient; and quotations longer or more numerous would tend rather to obscure than to illustrate.

The conditions of Immediate Knowledge, applied to Reid's statements. — In the *first* place, *knowledge and existence are then only convertible when the reality is known in itself;* for then only can we say, that it is known because it exists, and exists since it is known. And this constitutes an immediate or intuitive cognition, rigorously so called. Nor did Reid contemplate any other. "It seems admitted," he says, "as a first principle, by the learned and the unlearned, that what is really perceived must exist, and that to perceive what does not exist is impossible. So far the unlearned man and the philosopher agree."

In the *second* place, philosophers agree, that *the idea or representative object, in their theory, is,* in the strictest sense, *immediately perceived.* And so Reid understands them. "I perceive not, says the Cartesian, the external object itself (so far he agrees with the Peripatetic, and differs from the unlearned man); but I perceive an image, or form, or idea, in my own mind, or in my brain. I am certain of the existence of the idea, because I immediately perceive it."

In the *third* place, philosophers concur in acknowledging that *mankind at large believe that the external reality itself constitutes the immediate and only object of perception.* So also Reid: "On the same principle, the unlearned man says, I perceive the external object, and I perceive it to exist." — "The vulgar, undoubtedly, believe that it is the external object which we immediately perceive, and not a representative image of it only. It is for this reason that they look upon it as perfect lunacy to call in question the existence of external objects." — "The vulgar are firmly persuaded that the very identical objects which they perceive, continue to exist when they do not perceive them: and are no less firmly persuaded, that when ten men look at the sun or the moon they all see the same individual object." Speaking of Berkeley, — "The vulgar opinion he reduces to this, that the very things which we perceive by our senses do really exist. This he grants." — "It is, therefore, acknowledged by this philosopher to be a natural instinct or prepossession, a universal and primary opinion of all men, that the objects which we immediately perceive by our senses are not images in our minds, but external objects, and that their existence is independent of us and our perception."

In the *fourth* place, all philosophers agree that *consciousness has an immediate knowledge, and affords an absolute certainty of the reality, of its object.* Reid, as we have seen, limits the name of consciousness to self-consciousness, that is, to the immediate knowledge we possess of the modifications of self; whereas, he makes perception the faculty by which we are immediately cognizant of the qualities of the not-self.

In these circumstances, if Reid either, 1°, Maintain, that his immediate perception of external things is convertible with their reality; or, 2°, Assert, that, in his doctrine of perception, the external reality stands to the percipient mind face to face, in the same immediacy of relation which the idea holds in the representative theory of the philosophers; or, 3°, Declare the identity of his own opinion with the vulgar belief, as thus expounded by himself and the philosophers; or, 4°, Declare, that his Perception affords us equal evidence of the existence of external phænomena, as his Consciousness affords us of the existence of internal; — in all and each of these suppositions, he would unambiguously declare himself a Natural Realist, and evince that his doctrine of perception is one not of a mediate or representative, but of an immediate or intuitive knowledge. And he does all four.

The first and second. — "We have before examined the reasons given by philosophers to prove that ideas, and not external objects, are the immediate objects of perception We shall only here observe, that if external objects be perceived immediately" [and he had just before asserted for the hundredth time that they were so perceived], "we have the same reason to believe their existence, as philosophers have to believe the existence of ideas, while they hold them to be the immediate objects of perception."

The third. — Speaking of the perception of the external world, — "We have here a remarkable conflict between two contradictory opinions, wherein all mankind are engaged. On the one side, stand all the vulgar, who are unpractised in philosophical researches, and guided by the uncorrupted primary instincts of nature. On the other side, stand all the philosophers, ancient and modern; every man, without exception, who reflects. In this division, to my great humiliation, I find myself classed with the vulgar."

The fourth. — "Philosophers sometimes say that we perceive ideas, — sometimes that we are conscious of them. I can have no doubt of the existence of any thing which I either perceive, or of which I am conscious; but I cannot find that I either perceive ideas or am conscious of them."

General conclusion and caution. — On these grounds, therefore, I am confident that Reid's doctrine of Perception must be pronounced a doctrine of Intuition, and not of Representation; and though, as I have shown you, there are certainly some plausible arguments which might be alleged in support of the opposite conclusion; still, these are greatly overbalanced by stronger positive proofs, and by the general analogy of his philosophy. And here I would impress upon you an important lesson. That Reid, a distinguished philosopher, and even the founder of an illustrious school, could be so greatly misconceived, as that an eminent disciple of that school itself should actually reverse the fundamental principle of his doctrine, — this may excite your wonder, but it ought not to move you to disparage either the talent of the philosopher misconceived, or of the philosopher misconceiving. It ought, however, to prove to you the permanent importance, not only in speculation, but in practice, of precise thinking. You ought never to rest content, so long as there is aught vague or indefinite in your reasonings, — so long as you have not analyzed every notion into its elements, and excluded the possibility of all lurking ambiguity in your expressions. One great, perhaps the one greatest advantage, resulting from the cultivation of Philosophy, is the habit it induces of vigorous thought; that is, of allowing nothing to pass without a searching examination, either in your own speculations, or in those of others. We may never, perhaps arrive at truth, but we can always avoid self-contradiction.

CHAPTER XVIII.

THE PRESENTATIVE FACULTY.—THE DISTINCTION OF PERCEPTION PROPER FROM SENSATION PROPER.—PRIMARY AND SECONDARY QUALITIES.

Of the doctrine of an intuitive perception of external objects,—which, as a fact of consciousness, ought to be unconditionally admitted,—Reid has the merit, in these latter times, of being the first champion. I have already noticed that, among the Scholastic philosophers, there were some who maintained the same doctrine, and with far greater clearness and comprehension than Reid. These opinions are, however, even at this moment, I may say, wholly unknown; and it would be ridiculous to suppose that their speculations had exerted any influence, direct or indirect, upon a thinker so imperfectly acquainted with what had been done by previous philosophers, as Reid. Since the Revival of Letters, I have met with only two, anterior to Reid, whose doctrine on the present question coincided with his. One of these [John Sergeant] may, indeed, be discounted; for he has stated his opinions in so paradoxical a manner, that his authority is hardly worthy of notice. The other, [Peter Poiret,] who flourished about a century before Reid, has, on the contrary, stated the doctrine of an intuitive, and refuted the counter hypothesis of a representative, perception, with a brevity, perspicuity, and precision far superior to the Scottish philosopher. Both of these authors, I may say, are at present wholly unknown.

Having concluded the argument by which I endeavored to satisfy you that Reid's doctrine is Natural Realism, I should now proceed to show that Natural Realism is a more philosophical doctrine than Hypothetical Realism. Before, however, taking up the subject, I think it better to dispose of certain subordinate matters, with which it is proper to have some preparatory acquaintance.

Of these the first is the distinction of Perception Proper from Sensation Proper.

Use of the term Perception previously to Reid. — I have had occasion to mention, that the word *Perception* is, in the language of philosophers previous to Reid, used in a very extensive signification. By Descartes, Malebranche, Locke, Leibnitz, and others, it is employed in a sense almost as unexclusive as Consciousness in its widest signification. By Reid, this word was limited to our faculty acquisitive of knowledge, and to that branch of this faculty whereby, through the senses, we obtain a knowledge of the external world. But his limitation did not stop here. In the act of external perception, he distinguished two elements, to which he gave the names of Perception and Sensation. He ought, perhaps, to have called these *perception proper* and *sensation proper*, when employed in his special meaning; for, in the language of other philosophers, *sensation* was a term which included his Perception, and *perception* a term comprehensive of what he called Sensation.

Reid's account of Perception. — There is a great want of precision in Reid's account of Perception and Sensation. Of Perception he says: "If, therefore, we attend to that act of our mind, which we call the perception of an external object of sense, we shall find in it these three things. *First*, Some conception or notion of the object perceived. *Secondly*, A strong and irresistible conviction and belief of its present existence; and, *Thirdly*, That this conviction and belief are immediate, and not the effect of reasoning.

"*First*, it is impossible to perceive an object without having some notion or conception of what we perceive. We may indeed *conceive* an object which we do not *perceive;* but when we perceive the object, we must have some conception of it at the same time; and we have commonly a more clear and steady notion of the object while we perceive it, than we have from memory or imagination, when it is not perceived. Yet, even in perception, the notion which our senses give of the object may be more or less clear, more or less distinct in all possible degrees."

Now here you will observe that the "having a notion or conception," by which he explains the act of perception, might at first lead us to conclude that he held, as Brown supposes, the doctrine of a representative perception; for notion and conception are generally used by philosophers for a representation or mediate knowledge of a thing. But though Reid cannot escape censure for ambiguity and vagueness, it appears, from the analogy of his writings, that by *notion* or *conception* he meant nothing more than knowledge or cognition.

Reid's account of Sensation. — Sensation he thus describes: "Almost all our perceptions have corresponding sensations, which constantly accompany them, and, on that account, are very apt to be confounded with them. Neither ought we to expect that the sensation, and its corresponding perception, should be distinguished in common language, because the purposes of common life do not require it. Language is made to serve the purposes of ordinary conversation; and we have no reason to expect that it should make distinctions that are not of common use. Hence it happens that a quality perceived, and the sensation corresponding to that perception, often go under the same name.

"This makes the names of most of our sensations ambiguous, and this ambiguity hath very much perplexed the philosophers. It will be necessary to give some instances, to illustrate the distinction between our sensations and the objects of perception.

"When I smell a rose, there is in this operation both sensation and perception. The agreeable odor I feel, considered by itself, without relation to any external object, is merely a sensation. It affects the mind in a certain way; and this affection of the mind may be conceived, without a thought of the rose or any other object. This sensation can be nothing else than it is felt to be. Its very essence consists in being felt; and when it is not felt, it is not. There is no difference between the sensation and the feeling of it; they are one and the same thing. It is for this reason, that we before observed, that in sensation, there is no object distinct from that act of mind by which it is felt; and this holds true with regard to all sensations.

"Let us next attend to the perception which we have in smelling a rose. Perception has always an external object; and the object of my perception, in this case, is that quality in the rose which I discern by the sense of smell. Observing that the agreeable sensation is raised when the rose is near, and ceases when it is removed, I am led, by my nature, to conclude some quality to be in the rose which is the cause of this sensation. This quality in the rose is the object perceived; and that act of the mind, by which I have the conviction and belief of this quality, is what in this case I call perception."

By *perception*, Reid, therefore, means *the objective knowledge* we have of an external reality, through the senses; by *sensation*, *the subjective feeling* of pleasure or pain, with which the organic operation of sense is accompanied. This distinction of the objective from the subjective element in the act is important. Reid is not, however, the author of this distinction. He himself notices of Malebranche, that "he distinguished more accurately than any philosopher had done before, the objects which we perceive from the sensations in our own minds, which, by the laws of nature, always accompany the perception of the object. As in many things, so particularly in this, he has great merit; for this, I apprehend, is a key that opens the way to a right understanding both of our external senses, and of other powers of the mind." I may notice that Malebranche's distinction is into *Idée*, corresponding to Reid's Perception, and *Sentiment*, corresponding to his Sensation; and this distinction is as precisely marked in Malebranche as in Reid. Subsequently to Malebranche, the distinction became even common; and there is no reason for Mr. Stewart being struck when he found it in Crousaz and Hutcheson.

The nature of Perception and Sensation illustrated. — Before proceeding to state to you the great law which regulates the mutual relation of these phænomena, — a law which has been wholly overlooked by our psychologists, — it is proper to say a few words illustrative of the nature of the phænomena themselves.

The opposition of Perception and Sensation is true, but it is not a statement adequate to the generality of the contrast. Perception is only a special kind of Knowledge, and Sensation only a special kind of Feeling; and *Knowledge* and *Feeling*, you will recollect, are two out of the three great classes, into which we primarily divided the phænomena of mind. *Conation* was the third. Now, as Perception is only a special mode of Knowledge, and Sensation only a special mode of Feeling, so the contrast of Perception and Sensation is only the special manifestation of a contrast, which universally divides the generic phænomena themselves. It ought, therefore, in the first place, to have been noticed, that the generic phænomena of Knowledge and Feeling are always found coexistent, and yet always distinct; and the opposition of Perception and Sensation should have been stated as an obtrusive, but still only a particular example of the general law. But not only is the distinction of Perception and Sensation not generalized, — not referred to its category, by our psychologists; it is not concisely and precisely stated. A Cognition is *objective*, that is, our consciousness is then relative to something different from the present state of the mind itself; a Feeling, on the contrary, is *subjective*, that is, our consciousness is exclusively limited to the pleasure or pain experienced by the thinking subject. Cognition and feeling are always coexistent. The purest act of knowledge is always colored by some feeling of pleasure or pain; for no energy is absolutely indifferent, and the grossest feeling exists only as it is known in consciousness. This being the case of cognition and feeling in general, the same is true of perception and sensation in particular. Perception proper is the consciousness, through the senses, of the qualities of an object known as different from self; Sensation proper is the consciousness of the subjective affection of pleasure or pain, which accompanies that act of knowledge. Perception is thus the objective element in the complex state, — the element of cognition; Sensation is the subjective element, — the element of feeling.*

* [A word as to the various meanings of the terms here prominent — *Perception, Sensation, Sense.*

i. — *Perception* (Perceptio, Wahrnehmung) has different significations; but under all and each of these, the term has a common ambiguity, denoting as it may, either 1° the perceiving Faculty, or 2° the Perceiving Act, or 3° the Object perceived. Of these, the only ambiguity of importance is the last; and to relieve it, I would propose the employment, in this relation, of *Percept,* leaving *Perception* to designate both the Faculty and its Act; for these it is rarely necessary to distinguish, as what is applicable to the one is usually applicable to the other.

But to the significations of the term, as applied to *different* faculties, acts, and objects; of which there are in all four: —

1. *Perception,* in its primary philosophical signification, as in the mouths of Cicero and Quintilian, is vaguely equivalent to *Comprehension, Notion,* or *Cognition* in general.

2. From this first meaning it was easily deflected to a second, in which it corresponds to an *apprehension,* a *becoming aware of,* in a word, a *consciousness.* In this meaning, though long thus previously employed in the Schools, it was brought more prominently and distinctively forward in the writings of Descartes.

Under this second meaning, it is proper to say a word in regard to a special employment of the term. The Leibnitzio-Wolfians distinguish three acts in the process of representative cognition: — 1° *the act of representing* a (mediate) object to the mind; 2° *the representation,* or, to speak more properly, *representamen,* itself as an (immediate or vicarious) object exhibited to the mind; 3° *the act by which the mind is conscious,* immediately *of the representative object,* and, through it, mediately *of the remote object* represented. They called the first *Perception;* the last *Apperception;* the second *Idea — sensual,* to wit; for what they styled the *material* Idea was only an organic motion propagated to the brain, which, on the doctrine of the Preëstablished Harmony, is, in sensitive cognition, the arbitrary concomitant of the former, and, of course, beyond the sphere of consciousness or apperception.

3. In its third signification, Perception is limited to the apprehensions of Sense alone. This limitation was first formally imposed upon the word by Reid, for no very cogent reason besides convenience; and thereafter by Kant. Kant, again, was not altogether consistent; for he employs '*Perception*' in the second meaning, for the consciousness of any mental presentation, and thus in a sense corresponding to the *Apperception* of the Leibnitzians; while its vernacular, synonym, '*Wahrnehmung*' he defines in conformity with the third, as *the consciousness of an empirical intuition.*

Perception and Sensation in their reciprocal relation. — The most remarkable defect, however, in the present doctrine upon this point, is the ignorance of our psychologists in regard to the law by which the phænomena of Cognition and Feeling, — of Perception and Sensation, are governed, in their reciprocal relation. This law is simple and universal; and, once enounced,

Imposed by such authorities, this is now the accredited signification of these terms, in the recent philosophies of Germany, Britain, France, &c.

4. But under this third meaning, it is again, since the time and through the authority of Reid, frequently employed in a still more restricted acceptation, namely, as Perception (proper) in contrast to Sensation (proper). The import of these terms, as used by Reid and other philosophers on the one hand, and by myself on the other, is explained in the text.

ii. — *Sensation* (Sensatio; Sentiment; Empfindung) has various significations; and in all of these, like Perception, Conception, Imagination, and other analogous terms in the philosophy of mind, it is ambiguously applied; — 1°, for a Faculty — 2°, for its Act — 3°, for its Object. Here there is no available term, like Percept, Concept, etc., whereby to discriminate the last.

There are two principal meanings in which this term has been employed.

1. Like the Greek *æsthesis*, it was long and generally used to comprehend *the process of sensitive apprehension, both in its subjective and its objective relations.*

2. As opposed to Idea, Perception, etc., it was limited, first in the Cartesian school, and thereafter in that of Reid, to *the subjective phasis* of our sensitive cognitions; that is, to our *consciousness of the affections of our animated organism,* — or on the Neo-Platonic, Cartesian, and Leibnitzian hypotheses, to the *affections of the mind corresponding to, but not caused by, the unknown mutations of the body.* Under this restriction, *Sensation* may, both in French and English, be employed to designate our *corporeal or lower feelings,* in opposition to *Sentiment,* as a term for our *higher,* that is, our *intellectual and moral, feelings.*

iii. — *Sense* (Sensus; Sens; Sinn) is employed in a looser and in a stricter application.

Under the former head, it has two applications; — 1°, a psychological, as a popular term for *Intelligence:* 2°, a logical, as a synonym for *Meaning.*

Under the latter head, Sense is employed ambiguously; — 1°, for the Faculty of sensitive apprehension; 2°, for its Act; 3°, for its Organ.

In this relation, Sense has been distinguished into External and Internal; but under the second term, in so many vague and various meanings, that I cannot here either explain or enumerate them.] — *Diss. supp. to Reid.*

its proof is found in every mental manifestation. It is this: *Knowledge and Feeling, — Perception and Sensation, though always coexistent, are always in the inverse ratio of each other.* That these two elements are always found in coexistence, as it is an old and a notorious truth, it is not requisite for me to prove. But that these elements are always found to coexist in an inverse proportion, — in support of this universal fact, it will be requisite to adduce proof and illustration.

In doing this I shall, however, confine myself to the relation of Perception and Sensation. These afford the best examples of the generic relation of Knowledge and Feeling; and we must not now turn aside from the special faculty with which we are engaged.

The first proof I shall take from a comparison of the several senses; and it will be found that, *precisely as a sense has more of the one element, it has less of the other.* Laying Touch aside for the moment, as this requires a special explanation, the other four Senses divide themselves into two classes, according as Perception, the objective element, or Sensation, the subjective element, predominates. The two in which the former element prevails, are Sight and Hearing; the two in which the latter, are Taste and Smell.

Now, here, it will be at once admitted, that Sight, at the same instant, presents to us a greater number and a greater variety of objects and qualities, than any other of the senses. In this sense, therefore, Perception, — the objective element, is at its maximum. But Sensation, — the subjective element, is here at its minimum; for, in the eye, we experience less organic pleasure or pain from the impressions of its appropriate objects (colors), than we do in any other sense.

Next to Sight, Hearing affords us, in the shortest interval, the greatest variety and multitude of cognitions; and as sight divides space almost to infinity, through color, so hearing does the same to time, through sound. Hearing is, however, much less extensive in its sphere of Knowledge or Perception than sight; but in the same proportion is its capacity of Feeling or Sensation more intensive. We have greater pleasure and greater pain from single sounds than from single colors; and, in like manner, concords and discords, in the one sense, affect us more agreeably or disagreeably, than any modifications of light in the other.*

In Taste and Smell, the degree of Sensation, that is, of pleasure or pain, is great in proportion as the Perception, that is, the information they afford, is small. In all these senses, therefore, — Sight, Hearing, Taste, Smell, it will be admitted that the principle holds good.

The sense of Touch, or Feeling, strictly so called, I have reserved, as this requires a word of comment. Some philosophers include under this name all our sensitive perceptions, not obtained through some of the four special organs of sense, that is, sight, hearing, taste, smell; others, again, divide the sense into several. To us, at present, this difference is of no interest: for it is sufficient for us to know, that in those parts of the body where Sensation predominates, Perception is feeble; and in those where Perception is lively, Sensation is obtuse. In the finger points, tactile perception is at its height; but there is hardly another part of the body in which sensation is not more acute. Touch, or Feeling strictly so called, if viewed as a single sense, belongs, therefore, to both classes, — the objective and subjective. But it is more correct, as we shall see, to regard it as a plurality of senses, in which case Touch, properly so called, having a principal organ in the finger points, will belong to the first class, — the class of objective senses, — the perceptions, — that class in which Perception proper predominates.

This law governs also the several impressions of the same sense. — The analogy, then, which we have thus seen to hold good in the several senses in relation to each other, prevails likewise among the several impressions of the same sense. Impressions

* [In regard to the subjective and objective nature of the sensations of the several senses, or rather the perceptions we have through them, it may be observed, that what is more objective is more easily remembered; whereas, what is more subjective affords a much less distinct remembrance. Thus, what we perceive by the eye is better remembered than what we hear.]

in the same sense, differ both in degree and in quality or kind. By *impression* you will observe that I mean no explanation of the mode by which the external reality acts upon the sense (the metaphor you must disregard), but simply the fact of the agency itself. Taking, then, their *difference in degree*, and supposing that the degree of the impression determines the degree of the sensation, it cannot certainly be said, that the minimum of Sensation infers the maximum of Perception; for Perception always supposes a certain quantum of Sensation: but this is undeniable, that, above a certain limit, Perception declines, in proportion as Sensation rises. Thus, in the sense of sight, if the impression be strong we are dazzled, blinded, and consciousness is limited to the pain or pleasure of the Sensation, in the intensity of which, Perception has been lost.

Take now the *difference, in kind*, of impressions in the same sense. Of the senses, take again that of Sight. Sight, as will hereafter be shown, is cognizant of color, and, through color, of figure. But though figure is known only through color, a very imperfect cognizance of color is necessary, as is shown in the case (and it is not a rare one) of those individuals who have not the faculty of discriminating colors. These persons, who probably perceive only a certain difference of light and shade, have as clear and distinct a cognizance of figure, as others who enjoy the sense of sight in absolute perfection. This being understood, you will observe, that, in the vision of color, there is more of Sensation; in that of figure, more of Perception. Color affords our faculties of knowledge a far smaller number of differences and relations than figure; but, at the same time, yields our capacity of feeling a far more sensual enjoyment. But if the pleasure we derive from color be more gross and vivid, that from figure is more refined and permanent. It is a law of our nature, that the more intense a pleasure, the shorter is its duration. The pleasures of sense are grosser and more intense than those of intellect; but, while the former alternate speedily with disgust, with the latter we are never satiated. The same analogy holds among the senses themselves. Those in which Sensation predominates, in which pleasure is most intense, soon pall upon us; whereas those in which Perception predominates, and which hold more immediately of intelligence, afford us a less exclusive but a more enduring gratification. How soon are we cloyed with the pleasures of the palate, compared with those of the eye; and, among the objects of the former, the meats that please the most are soonest objects of disgust. This is too notorious in regard to taste to stand in need of proof. But it is no less certain in the case of vision. In painting, there is a pleasure derived from a vivid and harmonious coloring, and a pleasure from the drawing and grouping of the figures. The two pleasures are distinct, and even, to a certain extent, incompatible. For if we attempt to combine them, the grosser and more obstrusive gratification, which we find in the coloring, distracts us from the more refined and intellectual enjoyment we derived from the relation of figure; while, at the same time, the disgust we soon experience from the one tends to render us insensible to the other. This is finely expressed by a modern Latin poet of high genius [Johannes Secundus]: —

> "Mensura rebus est sua dulcibus;
> Ut quodque mentes suavius afficit,
> Fastidium sic triste secum
> Limite proximiore ducit."

His learned commentator, Bosscha, has not, however, noticed that these are only paraphrases of a remarkable passage of Cicero. Cicero and Secundus have not, however, expressed the principle more explicitly than Shakspeare:

> "These violent delights have violent ends,
> And in their triumph die. The sweetest honey
> Is loathsome in its own deliciousness,
> And in the taste confounds the appetite.
> Therefore, love moderately; long love doth so.
> Too swift arrives as tardy as too slow."

The result of what I have now stated, therefore, is, in the first place, that, as philosophers have observed, there is a distinction between Knowledge and Feeling, — Perception and Sensation, as between the objective and the subjective element;

and, in the second, that this distinction is, moreover, governed by the law, — That the two elements, though each necessarily supposes the other, are still always in a certain inverse proportion to each other.

Why this distinction is important. — Before leaving this subject, I may notice that the distinction of Perception proper and Sensation proper, though recognized as phænomenal by philosophers who hold the doctrine of a representative perception, rises into reality and importance *only in the doctrine of an intuitive perception.* In the former doctrine, Perception is supposed to be only apparently objective; being, in reality, no less subjective than Sensation proper, — the subjective element itself. Both are nothing more than mere modes of the ego. The philosophers who hold the hypothesis of a representative perception, make the difference of the two to consist only in this; — that in Perception proper, there is reference to an unknown object, different from me; in Sensation, there is no reference to aught beyond myself. Brown, on the supposition that Reid held that doctrine in common with himself and philosophers at large, states Sensation, as understood by Reid, to be "the simple feeling that immediately follows the action of an external body on any of our organs of sense, considered merely as a feeling of the mind; the corresponding Perception being the reference of this feeling to the external body as its cause." The distinction he allows to be a convenient one, if the nature of the complex process which it expresses be rightly understood. "The only question," he says, "that seems, philosophically, of importance, with respect to it, is whether the Perception in this sense, — the reference of the Sensation to its external corporeal cause, — implies, as Dr. Reid contends, a peculiar mental power, coextensive with Sensation, to be distinguished by a peculiar name in the catalogue of our faculties; or be not merely one of the results of a more general power, which is afterwards to be considered by us, — the power of Association, — by which one feeling suggests, or induces, other feelings that have formerly coexisted with it."

If Brown be correct in his interpretation of Reid's general

doctrine of perception, his criticism is not only true but trite. In the hands of a Cosmothetic Idealist, the distinction is only superficial, and manifestly of no import; and the very fact, that Reid laid so great stress on it, would tend to prove, independently of what we have already alleged, that Brown's interpretation of his doctrine is erroneous. You will remark, likewise, that Brown (and Brown only speaks the language of all philosophers who do not allow the mind a consciousness of aught beyond its own states) misstates the phænomenon, when he asserts that, in perception, there is a reference from the internal to the external, from the known to the unknown. That this is not the fact, an observation of this phænomenon will at once convince you. In an act of perception, I am conscious of something as self, and of something as not-self: — this is the simple fact. The philosophers, on the contrary, who will not accept this fact, misstate it. They say that we are there conscious of nothing but a certain modification of mind; but this modification involves a reference to, — in other words, a representation of, — something external, as its object. Now this is untrue. We are conscious of no reference, — of no representation; we believe that the object of which we are conscious is the object which exists. Nor could there possibly be such reference or representation; for reference or representation supposes a knowledge already possessed of the object referred to or represented; but perception is the faculty by which our first knowledge is acquired, and, therefore, cannot suppose a previous knowledge as its condition. But this I notice only by the way; this matter will be regularly considered in the sequel.

Perception a primary, not a compound and derivative faculty. — I may here notice the false analysis, which has endeavored to take perception out of the list of our faculties, as being only a compound and derivative power. Perception, say Brown and others, supposes memory and comparison and judgment; therefore, it is not a primary faculty of mind. Nothing can be more erroneous than this reasoning. In the first place, I have formerly shown you that consciousness supposes memory, and discrimination, and judgment; and, as perception does not pretend to be simpler than consciousness, but in fact only a modification of consciousness, that, therefore, the objection does not apply. But, in the second place, the objection is founded on a misapprehension of what a faculty properly is. It may be very true, that an act of perception cannot be realized simply and alone. I have often told you that the mental phænomena are never simple, and that, as tissues are woven out of many threads, so a mental phænomenon is made up of many acts and affections, which we can only consider separately by abstraction, but can never even conceive as separately existing. In mathematics, we consider a triangle or a square, the sides and the angles apart from each other, though we are unable to conceive them existing independently of each other. But because the angles and sides exist only through each other, would it be correct to deny their reality as distinct mathematical elements? As in geometry, so is it in psychology. We admit that no faculty can exist itself alone; and that it is only by viewing the actual manifestations of mind in their different relations, that we are able by abstraction to analyze them into elements, which we refer to different faculties. Thus, for example, every judgment, every comparison, supposes two terms to be compared, and, therefore, supposes an act of representative, or an act of acquisitive, cognition. But go back to one or other of these acts, and you will find that each of them supposes a judgment and a memory. If I represent in imagination the terms of comparison, there is involved a judgment; for the fact of their representation supposes the affirmation or judgment that they are called up, that they now ideally exist; and this judgment is only possible, as a result of a comparison of the present consciousness of their existence with a past consciousness of their non-existence, which comparison, again, is only possible through an act of memory.

The Primary and Secondary Qualities of matter. — Connected with the preceding distinction of Perception and Sensation, is the distinction of the Primary and Secondary Qualities of matter.

It would only confuse you were I to attempt to determine

how far this distinction was known to the Atomic physiologists, prior to Aristotle, and how far Aristotle himself was aware of the principle on which it proceeds. — It is enough to notice, as the most remarkable opinion of antiquity, that of Democritus, who, except the common qualities of body which are known by Touch, denied that the senses afforded us any information concerning the real properties of matter. Among modern philosophers, Descartes was the first who recalled attention to the distinction. According to him, the Primary qualities differ from the Secondary in this, — that our knowledge of the former is more clear and distinct than of the latter.

"The qualities of external objects," says Locke, "are of two sorts; first, Original or Primary; such are solidity, extension, motion or rest, number, and figure. These are inseparable from body, and such as it constantly keeps in all its changes and alterations. Thus, take a grain of wheat, divide it into two parts; each part has still solidity, extension, figure, mobility; divide it again, and it still retains the same qualities; and will do so still, though you divide it on till the parts become insensible.

"Secondly, Secondary qualities, such as colors, smells, tastes, sounds, etc., which, whatever reality we by mistake may attribute to them, are, in truth, nothing in the objects themselves, but *powers to produce various sensations in us;* and depend on the qualities before mentioned.

"The ideas of Primary qualities of bodies are resemblances of them; and their patterns really exist in bodies themselves: but the ideas produced in us by Secondary qualities have no resemblance of them at all: and what is sweet, blue, or warm in the idea, is but the certain bulk, figure, and motion of the insensible parts in the bodies themselves, which we call so."

Reid adopted the distinction of Descartes: he holds that our knowledge of the Primary qualities is clear and distinct, whereas our knowledge of the Secondary qualities is obscure. "Every man," he says, "capable of reflection, may easily satisfy himself, that he has a perfectly clear and distinct notion of extension, divisibility, figure, and motion. The solidity of a body means no more, but that it excludes other bodies from occupying the same place at the same time. Hardness, softness, and fluidity are different degrees of cohesion in the parts of a body. It is fluid, when it has no sensible cohesion; soft, when the cohesion is weak; and hard, when it is strong: of the cause of this cohesion we are ignorant, but the thing itself we understand perfectly, being immediately informed of it by the sense of touch. It is evident, therefore, that of the Primary qualities we have a clear and distinct notion; we know what they are, though we may be ignorant of the causes." But he did more; he endeavored to show that this difference arises from the circumstance, that the perception, in the case of the Primary qualities, is direct; in the case of the Secondary, only relative. This he explains: "I observe, further, that the notion we have of Primary qualities is direct, and not relative only. A relative notion of a thing is, strictly speaking, no notion of the thing at all, but only of some relation which it bears to something else.

"Thus, *gravity* sometimes signifies the tendency of bodies towards the earth; sometimes, it signifies the cause of that tendency; when it means the first, I have a direct and distinct notion of gravity; I see it, and feel it, and know perfectly what it is; but this tendency must have a cause; we give the same name to the cause; and that cause has been an object of thought and of speculation. Now, what notion have we of this cause, when we think and reason about it? It is evident we think of it as *an unknown cause of a known effect.* This is a relative notion, and it must be obscure, because it gives us no conception of what the thing is, but of what relation it bears to something else. Every relation which a thing unknown bears to something that is known, may give a relative notion of it; and there are many objects of thought, and of discourse, of which our faculties can give no better than a relative notion.

"Having premised these things to explain what is meant by a relative notion, it is evident, that our notion of Primary Qualities is not of this kind; we know what they are, and not barely what relation they bear to something else.

"It is otherwise with Secondary Qualities. If you ask me, what is that quality or modification in a rose which I call its smell, I am at a loss what to answer directly. Upon reflection, I find, that I have a distinct notion of the sensation which it produces in my mind. But there can be nothing like to this sensation in the rose, because it is insentient. The quality in the rose is something which occasions the sensation in me; but what that something is, I know not. My senses give me no information upon this point. The only notion, therefore, my senses give is this, that smell in the rose is *an unknown quality or modification, which is the cause or occasion of a sensation which I know well.* The relation which this unknown quality bears to the sensation with which nature hath connected it, is all I learn from the sense of smelling; but this is evidently a relative notion. The same reasoning will apply to every Secondary quality."

[The Primary Qualities of Matter or Body, *now* and *here*, — that is, in proximate relation to our organs, — are objects of *immediate* cognition to the Natural Realists, of *mediate*, to the Cosmothetic Idealists; the former, on the testimony of consciousness, asserting to mind the capability of intuitively perceiving what is not itself; the latter denying this capability, but asserting to the mind the power of representing, and truly representing, what it does not know. — To the Absolute Idealists, matter has no existence as an object of cognition, either immediate or mediate.

The Secondary Qualities of Body, *now* and *here*, — as only present affections of the conscious subject, determined by an unknown external cause, — are, on every theory, now allowed to be objects of immediate cognition.] — *Diss. supp. to Reid.*

You will observe that the lists of the primary qualities given by Locke and Reid do not coincide. According to Locke, these are Solidity, Extension, Motion, Hardness, Softness, Roughness, Smoothness, and Fluidity.

Stewart's classification of qualities. — Mr. Stewart proposes another line of demarcation. "I distinguish," he says, "Extension and Figure by the title of the *Mathematical Affections of* matter; restricting the phrase, *Primary Qualities*, to Hardness and Softness, Roughness and Smoothness, and other properties of the same description. The line which I would draw between *Primary* and *Secondary Qualities* is this, that the former necessarily involve the notion of *Extension*, and consequently of *externality* or *outness;* whereas the latter are only conceived as the unknown causes of known sensations; and *when first apprehended by the mind*, do not imply the existence of any thing locally distinct from the subjects of its consciousness."

The Primary Qualities reducible to two. — All these Primary Qualities, including Mr. Stewart's Mathematical Affections of matter, may easily be reduced to two, — *Extension and Solidity.* Thus: Figure is a mere limitation of extension; Hardness, Softness, Fluidity, are only Solidity variously modified, — only its different degrees; while Roughness and Smoothness denote only the sensations connected with certain perceptions of Solidity.* On the other hand, in regard to Divisibility, (which

* [The term *Solidity* (τὸ στερεόν, solidum), as denoting an attribute of body, is a word of various significations; and the non-determination and non-distinction of these have given rise to manifold error and confusion.

First Meaning. — In its most unexclusive signification, the Solid is that which *fills or occupies space.* In this meaning, it is simply convertible with Body; and is opposed, 1°, to the unextended in all or in any of the three dimensions of space; and 2°, to mere extension or empty space itself. This we may call *Solidity* simply.

The occupation of space supposes two necessary conditions; — and each of these has obtained the common name of Solidity, thus constituting a second and a third meaning.

Second Meaning. — What is conceived as occupying space, is necessarily conceived *as extended in the three dimensions of space.* This is the phasis of Solidity which the Geometer exclusively contemplates. Trinal extension has, accordingly, by mathematicians, been emphatically called the Solid; and this first partial Solidity we may therefore distinguish as the *Mathematical*, or rather the *Geometrical.*

Third Meaning. — On the other hand, what is conceived as occupying space, is necessarily conceived as *what cannot be eliminated from space.* But this supposes a power of resisting such elimination. This is the phasis of Solidity considered exclusively from the physical point of view. Accordingly, by the men of natural science, the impossibility of compressing a body from an extended to an unextended has been emphatically styled

is proper to Reid,) and to Motion, — these can hardly be mere data of sense. Divisibility supposes division, and a body

Solidity; and this second partial solidity we may therefore distinguish as the *Physical.* The resisting force here involved has been called the *Impenetrability* of matter; but most improperly and most ambiguously. It might more appropriately be termed its *Ultimate* or *Absolute Incompressibility.*

In a psychological point of view — and this is that of Locke and metaphysicians in general — no attribute of body is Primary which is not necessary in thought; that is, which is not necessarily evolved out of, as necessarily implied in, the very notion of body. And such is Solidity, in the one total and the two partial significations heretofore enumerated. But in its *physical* application, this term is not always limited to denote the ultimate incompressibility of matter. Besides that necessary attribute, it is extended, in common language, to express other powers of resistance in bodies, of a character merely contingent in reference to thought. These may be reduced to the five following.

Fourth Meaning. — The term Solid is very commonly employed to denote not merely the absolutely, but also the relatively, incompressible, the Dense, in contrast to the relatively compressible, the Rare, or Hollow. (In Latin, moreover, *Solidus* was not only employed, in this sense, to denote that a thing fully occupied the space comprehended within its circumference; but likewise to indicate, 1°, its *entireness in quantity* — that it was whole or complete; and, 2°, its *entireness in quality* — that it was pure, uniform, homogeneous. This arose from the original identity of the Latin *Solidum* with the Oscan *sollum* or *solum,* and the Greek *ὅλον.*

Fifth Meaning. — Under the *Vis Inertiæ,* a body is said to be Solid, *i. e.* Inert, Stable, Immovable, in proportion as it, whether in motion or at rest, resists, in general, a removal from the place it would otherwise occupy in space.

Sixth Meaning. — Under *Gravity,* a body is said to be Solid, *i. e.* Heavy, in proportion as it resists, in particular, a displacement by being lifted up.

The two following meanings fall under *Cohesion,* the force with which matter resists the distraction of its parts; for a body is said in a

Seventh Meaning, to be Solid, *i. e.* Hard, in contrast to Soft; and in an

Eighth Meaning, to be Solid, *i. e.* Concrete, in opposition to Fluid.

The term Solidity thus denotes, besides the absolute and necessary property of occupying space, simply and in its two phases of Extension and Impenetrability, also the relative and contingent qualities of the Dense, the Inert, the Heavy, the Hard, the Concrete; and the introduction of these latter, with their correlative opposites, into the list of Primary Qualities was facilitated by Locke's vacillating employment of the vague expression Solid, in partial designation of the former.] — *Diss. supp. to Reid.*

divided supposes memory; for if we did not remember that it had been one, we should not know that it is now two; we could not compare its present with its former state; and it is by this comparison alone that we learn the fact of division. As to Motion, this supposes the exercise of memory, and the notion of time, and, therefore, we do not owe it exclusively to sense. Finally, as to Number, which is peculiar to Locke, it is evident that this, far from being a quality of matter, is only an abstract notion, — the fabrication of the intellect, and not a datum of sense.

Space known a priori; *Extension* a posteriori. — Thus, then, we have reduced all primary qualities to Extension and Solidity; and we are, moreover, it would seem, beginning to see light, inasmuch as the *Primary qualities* are those in which *perception is dominant*, the *Secondary* those in which *sensation prevails.* But here we are again thrown back: for extension is only another name for space, and our notion of space is not one which we derive exclusively from sense, — not one which is generalized only from experience; for it is one of our necessary notions, — in fact, a fundamental condition of thought itself. The analysis of Kant, independently of all that has been done by other philosophers, has placed this truth beyond the possibility of doubt, to all those who understand the meaning and conditions of the problem. For us, however, this is not the time to discuss the subject. But, taking it for granted that the notion of space is native or *a priori*, and not adventitious or *a posteriori*, are we not at once thrown back into Idealism? For if extension itself be only a necessary mental mode, how can we make it a quality of external objects, known to us by sense; or how can we contrast the outer world, as the extended, with the inner, as the unextended world? To this difficulty, I see only one possible answer. It is this: — It cannot be denied that *space*, as a necessary notion, is *native to the mind;* but does it follow, that, because there is an *a priori* space, as a form of thought, we may not also have an *empirical knowledge of extension,* as an element of existence? The former, indeed, may be only the condition through which the latter is possible. It is true that, if we did not possess the general and necessary notion of space anterior to, or as the condition of, experience, from experience we should never obtain more than a generalized and contingent notion of space. But there seems to me no reason to deny, that because we have the one, we may not also have the other. If this be admitted, the whole difficulty is solved; and we may designate by the name of *extension* our empirical knowledge of space, and reserve the term *space* for space considered as a form or fundamental law of thought.* This matter will, however, come appropriately to be considered, in treating of the Regulative Faculty.

General result. — The following is the result of what I think an accurate analysis would afford, though there are no doubt many difficulties to be explained. — That *our knowledge of all the qualities of matter is merely relative.* But though the qualities of matter are all known only in relation to our faculties, and the total or absolute cognition in perception is only matter in a certain relation to mind, and mind in a certain relation to matter; still, in different perceptions, one term of the relation may predominate, or the other. *Where the objective element predominates,* — where matter is known as principal in its relation to mind, and mind only known as subordinate in its correlation to matter, — we have *Perception Proper*, rising superior to Sensation; this is seen in the *Primary Qualities. Where,* on the contrary, *the subjective element predominates,* — where mind is known as principal in its relation to matter, and matter is only known as subordinate in its relation to mind, — we have *Sensation Proper* rising superior to Perception; and this is seen in the *Secondary Qualities.*

The adequate illustration of this will, however, require both a longer, and a more abstruse, discussion, [which is here subjoined from the *Dissertations supplementary to Reid.*]

[The Qualities of Body I divide into *three* classes.

Adopting and adapting, as far as possible, the previous no-

* [So Causality. Causality depends, first, on the *a priori* necessity in the mind to think some cause; and, second, on experience, as revealing to us the particular cause of any effect.]

menclature — the first of these I would denominate the class of *Primary*, or *Objective*, Qualities; the second, the class of *Secundo-Primary*, or *Subjectivo-Objective*, Qualities; the third, the class of *Secondary*, or *Subjective*, Qualities.

The general point of view from which the Qualities of Matter are here considered is not the *Physical*, but the *Psychological*. But, under this, the ground of principle on which these qualities are divided and designated is, again, two-fold. There are, in fact, within the psychological, two special points of view; that of *Sense*, and that of *Understanding*.

The point of view chronologically prior, or first to us, is that of *Sense*. The principle of division is here the different circumstances under which the qualities are originally and immediately *apprehended*. On this ground, as apprehensions or immediate cognitions through Sense, the *Primary* are distinguished as *objective*, not subjective,* as *percepts proper*, not sensations proper; the *Secundo-primary*, as *objective and subjective*, as *percepts proper and sensations proper;* the *Secondary*, as *subjective*, not objective, cognitions, as *sensations proper*, not percepts proper.

The other point of view, chronologically posterior, but first in nature, is that of *Understanding*. The principle of division is here the different character under which the qualities, already apprehended, are *conceived* or construed to the mind in thought. On this ground, the *Primary*, being thought as *essential* to the notion of Body, are distinguished from the *Secundo-primary* and *Secondary*, as *accidental;* while the *Primary* and *Secundo-primary*, being thought as *manifest or conceivable in their own nature*, are distinguished from the *Secondary*, as *in their own nature occult and inconceivable*. For the notion of Matter

* *All* knowledge, in one respect, is *subjective;* for all knowledge is an energy of the Ego. But when I perceive a quality of the Non-ego, of the object-object, as in immediate relation to my mind, I am said to have of it an *objective* knowledge; in contrast to the *subjective* knowledge I am said to have of it when supposing it only as the hypothetical or occult cause of an affection of which I am conscious, or thinking it only mediately through a subject-object or representation in, and of, the mind.

having been once acquired, by reference to that notion, the Primary Qualities are recognized as its *a priori* or necessary constituents; and we clearly conceive how they must exist in bodies in knowing what they are objectively in themselves; the Secundo-primary Qualities, again, are recognized as *a posteriori* or contingent modifications of the Primary, and we clearly conceive how they do exist in bodies in knowing what they are objectively in their conditions; finally, the Secondary Qualities are recognized as *a posteriori* or contingent accidents of matter, but we obscurely surmise how they may exist in bodies only as knowing what they are subjectively in their effects.

It is thus apparent that the Primary Qualities may be *deduced a priori*, the bare notion of matter being given; they being, in fact, only evolutions of the conditions which that notion necessarily implies: whereas the Secundo-primary and Secondary must be *induced a posteriori;* both being attributes contingently superadded to the naked notion of matter. The Primary Qualities thus fall more under the point of view of Understanding, the Secundo-primary and Secondary more under the point of view of Sense.

Deduction of the Primary Qualities. — Space or extension is a necessary form of thought. We cannot think it as non-existent; we cannot but think it as existent. But we are not so necessitated to imagine the reality of aught occupying space; for while unable to conceive as null the space in which the material universe exists, the material universe itself we can, without difficulty, annihilate in thought. All that exists in, all that occupies, space, becomes, therefore, known to us by experience: we acquire, we construct, its notion. The notion of space is thus native or *a priori;* the notion of what space contains, adventitious, or *a posteriori*. Of this latter class is that of Body or Matter.

Now we ask, what are the necessary or essential, in contrast to the contingent or accidental, properties of Body, as apprehended and conceived by us? The answer to this question affords the class of Primary, as contradistinguished from the two classes of Secundo-primary and Secondary Qualities.

It will be admitted, that we are only able to conceive Body as that which (I.) *occupies space*, and (II.) *is contained in space.* But these catholic conditions of body, though really simple, are logically complex. We may view them in different aspects or relations.

I. — The property of *filling space* (Solidity in its unexclusive signification, *Solidity Simple*) implies two correlative conditions: (A) the *necessity of trinal extension, in length, breadth, and thickness* (*Solidity geometrical*); and (B) the corresponding *impossibility of being reduced from what is to what is not thus extended* (*Solidity Physical, Impenetrability*).

A. — Out of the absolute attribute of Trinal Extension may be again explicated three attributes, under the form of necessary relations: — (i.) *Number* or *Divisibility;* (ii.) *Size, Bulk,* or *Magnitude ;* (iii.) *Shape* or *Figure.*

i. — Body necessarily exists, and is necessarily known, either as one body or as many bodies. *Number*, i. e. the alternative attribution of unity or plurality, is, thus, in a first respect, a primary attribute of matter. But again, every single body is also, in different points of view, at the same time one and many. Considered as a *whole*, it is, and is apprehended, as actually one; considered as an *extended* whole, it is, and is conceived, potentially many. Body being thus necessarily known, if not as already divided, still as always capable of division, *Divisibility* or *Number* is thus likewise, in a second respect, a Primary attribute of matter.

ii. — Body (*multo majus* this or that body) is not infinitely extended. Each body must therefore have a certain finite extension, which, by comparison with that of other bodies, must be less, or greater, or equal; in other words, it must by relation have a certain Size, Bulk, or Magnitude; and this, again, as estimated both (a) by the quantity of space occupied, and (b) by the quantity of matter occupying, affords likewise the relative attributes of *Dense* and *Rare.*

iii. — Finally, bodies, as not infinitely extended, have, consequently, their extension bounded. But bounded extension is necessarily of a certain *Shape or Figure.*

B. — The negative notion — the impossibility of conceiving the compression of body from an extended to an unextended, its elimination out of space — affords the positive notion of an insuperable power in body of resisting such compression or elimination. This force, which, as absolute, is a conception of the Understanding, not an apprehension through Sense, has received no precise and unambiguous name. We might call it *Ultimate* or *Absolute Incompressibility*.

II. — The other most general attribute of matter — that of *being contained in space* — in like manner affords, by explication, an absolute and a relative attribute: viz. (A) the *Mobility*, that is, the possible motion, and, consequently, the possible rest, of a body; and (B) the *Situation, Position, Ubication*, that is, the local correlation of bodies in space. For

A. — Space being conceived as infinite (or rather being inconceivable as not infinite), and the place occupied by body as finite, body in general, and, of course, each body in particular, is conceived capable either of remaining in the place it now holds, or of being translated from that to any then unoccupied part of space. And

B. — As every part of space, i. e. every potential *place*, holds a certain position relative to every other, so, consequently, must bodies, in so far as they are all contained in space, and as each occupies, at one time, one determinate space.

The Primary Qualities of matter thus develop themselves with rigid necessity out of the simple datum of — *substance occupying space*. In a certain sort, and by contrast to the others, they are, therefore, notions *a priori*, and to be viewed, *pro tanto*, as products of the Understanding. The others, on the contrary, it is manifestly impossible to *deduce*, i. e. to evolve out of such a given notion. They must be *induced*, i. e. generalized from experience; are, therefore, in strict propriety, notions *a posteriori*, and, in the last resort, mere products of Sense.

Induction of the class of Secundo-Primary Qualities. — This terminates in the following conclusions. — These qualities are modifications, but contingent modifications, of the Primary. They suppose the Primary; the Primary do not suppose them.

They have all relation to space, and motion in space; and are all contained under the category of Resistance or Pressure. For they are all only various forms of a relative or superable resistance to displacement, which, we learn by experience, bodies oppose to other bodies, and, among these, to our organism moving through space; — a resistance similar in kind (and therefore clearly conceived) to that absolute or insuperable resistance, which we are compelled, independently of experience, to think that every part of matter would oppose to any attempt to deprive it of its space, by compressing it into an inextended.

In so far, therefore, as they suppose the Primary, which are necessary, while they themselves are only accidental, they exhibit, on the one side, what may be called a quasi-Primary quality; and, in this respect they are to be recognized as percepts, not sensations, as objective affections of things, and not as subjective affections of us. But, on the other side, this objective element is always found accompanied by a Secondary quality or sensorial passion. The Secundo-primary qualities have thus always two phases, both immediately apprehended. On their Primary or objective phasis, they manifest themselves as *degrees* of resistance opposed to our locomotive energy; on their Secondary or subjective phasis, as *modes* of resistance or pressure affecting our sentient organism. Thus standing between, and, in a certain sort, made up of, the two classes of Primary and Secondary qualities, to neither of which, however, can they be reduced; this their partly common, partly peculiar nature, vindicates to them the dignity of a class apart from both the others, and this under the appropriate appellation of the Secundo-primary qualities.

They admit of a classification from two different points of view. They may be *physically*, they may be *psychologically*, distributed. — Considered *physically*, or in an objective relation, they are to be reduced to classes corresponding to the different sources in external nature from which the resistance or pressure springs. And these sources are, in all, three: — (I.) that of *Co-attraction;* (II.) that of *Repulsion;* (III.) that of *Inertia.*

I. — Of the resistance of *Co-attraction* there may be distinguished, on the same objective principle, two subaltern genera; to wit (A) that of *Gravity*, or the co-attraction of the particles of body in general; and (B) that of *Cohesion*, or the co-attraction of the particles of this and that body in particular.

A. — The resistance of Gravity or Weight according to its degree (which, again, is in proportion to the Bulk and Density of ponderable matter), affords, under it, the relative qualities of *Heavy* and *Light* (absolute and specific).

B. — The resistance of Cohesion (using that term in its most unexclusive universality) contains many species and counter-species. Without proposing an exhaustive, or accurately subordinated, list; — of these there may be enumerated (i.) the *Hard* and *Soft;* (ii.) the *Firm* (Fixed, Stable, Concrete, Solid) and *Fluid* (Liquid), the Fluid being again subdivided into the *Thick* and *Thin;* (iii.) the *Viscid* and *Friable;* with (iv.) the *Tough* and *Brittle* (Irruptile and Ruptile); (v.) the *Rigid* and *Flexible;* (vi.) the *Fissile* and *Infissile;* (vii.) the *Ductile* and *Inductile* (Extensible and Inextensible); (viii.) the *Retractile* and *Irretractile* (Elastic and Inelastic); (ix.) (combined with Figure) the *Rough* and *Smooth;* (x.) the *Slippery* and *Tenacious.*

II. — The resistance from *Repulsion* is divided into the counter qualities of (A) the (relatively) *Compressible* and *Incompressible;* (B) the *Resilient* and *Irresilient* (Elastic and Inelastic).

III. — The resistance from *Inertia* (combined with Bulk and Cohesion) comprises the counter qualities of the (relatively) *Movable* and *Immovable.*

There are thus, at least, fifteen pairs of counter attributes which we may refer to the Secundo-primary Qualities of Body; — all obtained by the division and subdivision of the resisting forces of matter, considered in an objective or physical point of view.

Considered *psychologically*, or in a subjective relation, they are to be discriminated, under the genus of the *Relatively resisting*, [I.] according to the *degree* in which the resisting force might counteract our locomotive faculty or muscular force; and, [II.] according to the *mode* in which it might affect our capacity of feeling or sentient organism. Of these species, the former would contain under it the gradations of the quasi-Primary quality, the latter the varieties of the Secondary quality — these constituting the two elements of which, in combination, every Secundo-primary quality is made up. So much for the induction of the Secundo-primary qualities.

Induction of the Secondary Qualities. — Its results are the following. — The Secondary, as manifested to us, are not, in propriety, qualities of Body at all. As apprehended, they are only subjective affections, and belong only to bodies in so far as these are supposed furnished with the powers capable of specifically determining the various parts of our nervous apparatus to the peculiar action, or rather passion, of which they are susceptible; which determined action or passion is the quality of which alone we are immediately cognizant, the external concause of that internal effect remaining to perception altogether unknown. Thus, the Secondary qualities (and the same is to be said, *mutatis mutandis*, of the Secundo-primary) are, considered subjectively, and considered objectively, affections or qualities of things diametrically opposed in nature — of the organic and inorganic, of the sentient and insentient, of mind and matter; and though, as mutually correlative, and their several pairs rarely obtaining in common language more than a single name, they cannot well be considered, except in conjunction, under the same category or general class; still their essential contrast of character must be ever carefully borne in mind. And in speaking of these qualities, as we are here chiefly concerned with them on their subjective side, I request it may be observed, that I shall employ the expression *Secondary qualities* to denote those phenomenal affections determined in our sentient organism by the agency of external bodies, and not, unless when otherwise stated, the occult powers themselves from which that agency proceeds.

Of the Secondary qualities, in this relation, there are various kinds; the variety principally depending on the differences of the different parts of our nervous apparatus. Such are the proper sensibles, the idiopathic affections of our several organs of sense, as Color, Sound, Flavor, Savor, and Tactual sensation; such are the feelings from Heat, Electricity, Galvanism, etc.; nor need it be added, such are the muscular and cutaneous sensations which accompany the perception of the Secundo-primary qualities. Such, though less directly the result of foreign causes, are Titillation, Sneezing, Horripilation, Shuddering, the feeling of what is called Setting-the-teeth-on-edge, etc., etc.; such, in fine, are all the various sensations of bodily pleasure and pain determined by the action of external stimuli.

What they are in general. — 1. The Primary are less properly denominated Qualities (Suchnesses), and deserve the name only as we conceive them to distinguish body from not-body, — corporeal from incorporeal substance. They are thus merely the attributes of *body as body*, — *corporis ut corpus.* The Secundo-primary and Secondary, on the contrary, are in strict propriety denominated Qualities, for they discriminate body from body. They are the attributes of *body as this or that kind of body*, — *corporis ut tale corpus.*

2. The Primary determine the possibility of matter absolutely; the Secundo-primary, the possibility of the material universe as actually constituted; the Secondary, the possibility of our relation as sentient existences to that universe.

3. Under the Primary, we apprehend modes of the Non-ego; under the Secundo-primary, we apprehend modes both of the Ego and of the Non-ego; under the Secondary, we apprehend modes of the Ego, and infer modes of the Non-ego.

4. The Primary are apprehended as they are in bodies; the Secondary as they are in us; the Secundo-primary as they are in bodies, and as they are in us.

5. The Primary are conceived as necessary and perceived as actual; the Secundo-primary are perceived and conceived as actual; the Secondary are inferred and conceived as possible.

6. The Primary may be roundly characterized as mathematical; the Secundo-primary, as mechanical; the Secondary, as physiological.

CHAPTER XIX.

THE PRESENTATIVE FACULTY. — OBJECTIONS TO THE DOCTRINE OF NATURAL REALISM CONSIDERED. — THE REPRESENTATIVE HYPOTHESIS REFUTED.

From our previous discussions, you are now, in some measure, prepared for a consideration of the grounds on which philosophers have so generally asserted the scientific necessity of repressing the testimony of consciousness to the fact of our immediate perception of external objects, and of allowing us only a mediate knowledge of the material world: a procedure by which they either admit, or cannot rationally deny, that Consciousness is a mendacious witness; that Philosophy and the Common Sense of mankind are placed in contradiction; nay, that the only legitimate philosophy is an absolute and universal scepticism. That consciousness, in perception, affords us, as I have stated, an assurance of an intuitive cognition of the Non-ego, is not only notorious to every one who will interrogate consciousness as to the fact, but is, as I have already shown you, acknowledged not only by Cosmothetic Idealists, but even by absolute Idealists and Sceptics.

Order of the discussion. — In considering this subject, it is manifest that, before rejecting the testimony of consciousness to our immediate knowledge of the Non-ego, the philosophers were bound, in the first place, to evince the absolute necessity of their rejection; and, in the second place, in substituting an hypothesis in the room of the rejected fact, they are bound to substitute a legitimate hypothesis, — that is, one which does not violate the laws under which an hypothesis can be rationally proposed. I shall, therefore, divide the discussion into two sections. In the former, I shall state the reasons, as far as I have been able to discover them, on which philosophers have attempted to manifest the impossibility of acquiescing in the testimony of consciousness and the general belief of mankind; and, at the same time, endeavor to refute these reasons, by showing that they do not establish the necessity required. In the latter, I shall attempt to prove that the hypothesis proposed by the philosophers, in place of the fact of consciousness, does not fulfil the conditions of a legitimate hypothesis, — in fact, violates them almost all. In the first place, then, in regard to the reasons assigned by philosophers for their refusal of the fact of our immediate perception of external things, — of these, I have been able to collect in all five.

The first ground of rejection. — The first, and highest, ground on which it may be held, that the object immediately known in perception is a modification of the mind itself, is the following: Perception is a cognition or act of knowledge; a cognition is an *immanent* act of mind; but to suppose the cognition of any thing external to the mind, would be to suppose an act of the mind going out of itself, in other words, a *transeunt* act; but action supposes existence, and nothing can act where it is not; therefore, to act out of self is to exist out of self, which is absurd.

This argument, though I have never met with it explicitly announced, is still implicitly supposed in the arguments of those philosophers who hold, that the mind cannot be conscious of aught beyond its own modifications. It will not stand examination. It is very true that we can neither prove, nor even conceive, how the Ego can be conscious or immediately cognitive of the Non-ego; but this, our ignorance, is no sufficient reason on which to deny the possibility of the fact. As a fact, and a primary fact, of consciousness, we must be ignorant of the why and the how of its reality, for we have no higher notion through which to comprehend it, and, if it involve no contradiction, we are, philosophically, bound to accept it. But if we examine the argument a little closer, we shall find that it proves too much; for, on the same principle, we should establish the impossibility of any overt act of volition, — nay, even the impossibility of all agency and mutual causation. For if, on the ground that nothing can act out of itself, because nothing exists out of itself, we deny to mind the immediate knowledge of things external; on the same principle, we must deny to mind the power of determining any muscular movement of the body. And if the action of every existence were limited to the sphere of that existence itself, then, no one thing could act upon any other thing, and all action and reaction, in the universe, would be impossible. This is a general absurdity, which follows from the principle in question.

But there is a peculiar and proximate absurdity, into which this theory runs, in the attempt it makes to escape the inexplicable. It is this: — The Cosmothetic Idealists, who found their doctrine on the impossibility of mind acting out of itself, in relation to matter, are obliged to admit the still less conceivable possibility of matter acting out of itself, in relation to mind. They deny that mind is immediately conscious of matter; and, to save the phænomenon of perception, they assert that the Non-ego, as given in that act, is only an illusive representation of the Non-ego, in, and by, the Ego. Well, admitting this, and allowing them to belie the testimony of consciousness to the reality of the Non-ego as perceived, what do they gain by this? They surrender the simple datum of consciousness, — that the external object is immediately known; and, in lieu of that real object, they substitute a representative object. But still they hold (at least those who do not fly to some hyperphysical hypothesis) that the mind is determined to this representation by the material reality, to which material reality they must, therefore, accord the very transeunt efficiency which they deny to the immaterial principle. This first and highest ground, therefore, on which it is attempted to establish the necessity of a representative perception, is not only insufficient, but self-contradictory.

The second ground of rejection. — The second ground on which it has been attempted to establish the necessity of this hypothesis, is one which has been more generally and more openly founded on than the preceding. Mind and matter, it is said, are substances, not only of different, but of the most opposite, natures; separated, as some philosophers express it, by the whole diameter of being: but what immediately knows, must be of a nature correspondent, analogous, to that which is known; mind cannot, therefore, be conscious or immediately cognizant of what is so disproportioned to its essence as matter.

This principle is one whose influence is seen pervading the whole history of philosophy, and the tracing of this influence would form the subject of a curious treatise. To it we principally owe the doctrine of a *representative perception*, in one or other of its forms; and in a higher or lower potence, according as the representative object was held to be, in relation to mind, of a nature either *the same* or *similar*. Derivative from the principle in its lower potence or degree, (that is, the immediate object being supposed to be only something *similar* to the mind,) we have, among other less celebrated and less definite theories, the *intentional species* of the Schoolmen (at least as generally held), and the *ideas* of Malebranche and Berkeley. In its higher potence, (that is, where the representative object is supposed to be of a nature not merely similar to, but *identical with*, mind, though it may be numerically different from individual minds,) it affords us, among other modifications, the *gnostic reasons* of the Platonists, the *preëxisting species* of Avicenna and other Arabian Aristotelians, the *ideas* of Descartes, Arnauld, Leibnitz, Buffier, and Condillac, the *phænomena* of Kant, and the *external states* of Dr. Brown. It is doubtful to which head we should refer Locke, and Newton, and Clarke, — nay, whether we should not refer them to the class of those who, like Democritus, Epicurus, and Digby, viewed the representative or immediate object as a material efflux or propagation from the external reality to the brain. To the influence of the same principle, through the refusal of the testimony of consciousness to the duality of our knowledge, are also mediately to be traced the unitarian systems of *absolute identity*, *materialism*, and *idealism*.

Refutation of this principle. — But, if no principle was ever more universal in its effects, none was ever more arbitrarily assumed. It not only can pretend to no necessity; it has absolutely no probability in its favor. Some philosophers, as Anaxagoras, Heraclitus, Alcmæon, have even held that the relation of knowledge supposes, not a similarity or sameness between subject and object, but, in fact, a contrariety or opposition; and Aristotle himself is sometimes in favor of this opinion, though, sometimes, it would appear, in favor of the other. But, however this may be, each assertion is just as likely, and just as unphilosophical, as its converse. We know, and can know, nothing *a priori* of what is possible or impossible to mind, and it is only by observation and by generalization *a posteriori*, that we can ever hope to attain any insight into the question. But the very first fact of our experience contradicts the assertion, that mind, as of an opposite nature, can have no immediate cognizance of matter; for the primary datum of consciousness is, that in perception, we have an intuitive knowledge of the Ego and of the Non-ego, equally and at once. This second ground, therefore, affords us no stronger necessity than the first, for denying the possibility of the fact of which consciousness assures us.

The third ground of rejection. — The third ground on which the representative hypothesis of perception is founded, and that apparently alone contemplated by Reid and Stewart, is, that the mind can only know immediately that to which it is immediately present; but as external objects can neither themselves come into the mind, nor the mind go out to them, such presence is impossible; therefore, external objects can only be mediately known, through some representative object, whether that object be a modification of mind, or something in immediate relation to the mind. It was this difficulty of bringing the subject and object into proximate relation, that, in part, determined all the various schemes of a representative perception; but it seems to have been the one which solely determined the peculiar form of that doctrine in the philosophy of Democritus, Epicurus, Digby, and others, under which it is held, that the immediate or internal object is a representative emanation, propagated from the external reality to the sensorium.

Now this objection to the immediate cognition of external

objects, has, as far as I know, been redargued in three different ways. In the *first* place, it has been denied, that the external reality cannot itself come into the mind. In the *second*, it has been asserted, that a faculty of the mind itself does actually go out to the external reality; and, in the *third* place, it has been maintained that, though the mind neither goes out, nor the reality comes in, and though subject and object are, therefore, not present to each other, still that the mind, through the agency of God, has an immediate perception of the external object.

The *first mode of obviating the present objection* to the possibility of an immediate perception, might be thought too absurd to have been ever attempted. But the observation of Varro, that there is nothing so absurd which has not been asserted by some philosopher, is not destined to be negatived in the present instance. In opposition to Locke's thesis, "that the mind knows not things immediately, but only by the intervention of the ideas it has of them," and in opposition to the whole doctrine of representation, it is maintained, in terms, by Sergeant, that "I know the very thing; therefore, the very thing is in my act of knowledge; but my act of knowledge is in my understanding; therefore, the thing which is in my knowledge, is also in my understanding." We may suspect that this is only a paradoxical way of stating his opinion; but though this author, the earliest and one of the most eloquent of Locke's antagonists, be destitute neither of learning nor of acuteness, I must confess, that Locke and Molyneux cannot be blamed in pronouncing his doctrine unintelligible.

The *second mode of obviating the objection*, — by allowing to the mind a power of sallying out to the external reality, has higher authority in its favor. That vision is effected by a perceptive emanation from the eye, was held by Empedocles, the Platonists, and Stoics, and was adopted also by Alexander the Aphrodisian, by Euclid, Ptolemy, Galen, and Alchindus. This opinion, as held by these philosophers, was limited; and, though erroneous, is not to be viewed as irrational. But in the hands of Lord Monboddo, it is carried to an absurdity which leaves even Sergeant far behind. "The mind," says the learned author of *Ancient Metaphysics*, "is not where the body is, when it perceives what is distant from the body, either in time or place, because nothing can act but when and where it is. Now the mind acts when it perceives. The mind, therefore, of every animal who has memory or imagination, acts, and, by consequence, exists, when and where the body is not; for it perceives objects distant from the body, both in time and place."

The *third mode* is apparently that adopted by Reid and Stewart, who hold, that the mind has an immediate knowledge of the external reality, though the subject and object may not be present to each other; and, though this be not explicitly or obtrusively stated, that the mind obtains this immediate knowledge through the agency of God. Dr. Reid's doctrine of perception is thus summed up by Mr. Stewart: "To what, then, it may be asked, does this statement amount? Merely to this: that the mind is so formed that certain impressions produced on our organs of sense by external objects are followed by correspondent sensations, and that these sensations, (which have no more resemblance to the qualities of matter than the words of a language have to the things they denote,) are followed by a perception of the existence and qualities of the bodies by which the impressions are made; *that all the steps of this process are equally incomprehensible;* and that, for any thing we can prove to the contrary, the connection between the sensation and the perception, as well as that between the impression and the sensation, may be both arbitrary; that it is, therefore, by no means impossible, that our sensations may be merely the occasions on which the correspondent perceptions are excited; and that, at any rate, the consideration of these sensations, which are attributes of mind, can throw no light on the manner in which we acquire our knowledge of the existence and qualities of body. From this view of the subject it follows, that it is the external objects themselves, and not any species or images of the objects, that the mind perceives; and that, although, by the constitution of our nature, certain sensations are rendered the constant antecedents of our perceptions, yet it is just as difficult to explain how our perceptions are obtained by their means, as it would be upon the supposition that the mind were all at once inspired with them, without any concomitant sensations whatever." *

The doctrine of Occasional Causes. — This statement, when illustrated by the doctrine of these philosophers in regard to the distinctions of Efficient and Physical Causes, might be almost identified with the Cartesian doctrine of Occasional Causes According to Reid and Stewart, — and the opinion has been more explicitly asserted by the latter, — there is no really efficient cause in nature but one, namely, the Deity. What are called Physical causes and effects being antecedents and consequents, but not in virtue of any mutual and necessary dependence; — the only Efficient being God, who, on occasion of the antecedent, which is called the physical cause, produces the consequent, which is called the physical effect. So in the case of perception; the cognition of the external object is not, or may not be, a consequence of the immediate and natural relation of that object to the mind, but of the agency of God, who, as it were, reveals the outer existence to our perception. A similar doctrine is held by a great German philosopher, Frederic Henry Jacobi.

To this opinion many objections occur. In the *first* place, so

* [If an immediate knowledge of external things — that is, a consciousness of the qualities of the *Non-ego* — be admitted, the belief of their existence follows of course. On this supposition, therefore, such a belief would not be unaccountable; for it would be accounted for by the fact of the knowledge, in which it would necessarily be contained. Our belief, in this case, of the existence of external objects would not be more inexplicable than our belief that 2 + 2 = 4. In both cases, it would be sufficient to say, *we believe because we know;* for belief is only unaccountable when it is not the consequent or concomitant of knowledge. By this, however, I do not, of course, mean to say, that knowledge is not in itself marvellous and unaccountable.

Mr. Stewart proposes a supplement to this doctrine of Reid, in order to explain why we believe in the existence of the qualities of external objects when they are not the objects of our perception, — [that is, why we believe that they *continue* to exist *after* we have ceased to perceive them]. This belief he holds to be the result of *experience,* in combination with an original principle of our constitution, whereby we are determined to believe in the permanence of the laws of nature.] — *Notes to Reid.*

far is it from being, as Mr. Stewart affirms, a plain statement of the facts, apart from all hypothesis, it is manifestly *hypothetical.* In the *second* place, the hypothesis assumes an occult principle; — it is *mystical.* In the *third* place, the hypothesis is *hyperphysical,* — calling in the proximate assistance of the Deity, while the necessity of such intervention is not established. In the *fourth* place, it goes even far to frustrate the whole doctrine of the two philosophers in regard to perception, as a doctrine of intuition. For if God has bestowed on me the faculty of immediately perceiving the external object, there is no need to suppose the necessity of an immediate intervention of the Deity to make that act effectual; and if, on the contrary, the perception I have of the reality is only excited by the agency of God, then I can hardly be held to know that reality, immediately and in itself, but only mediately, through the notion of it determined in my mind.

The doctrine of immediate perception not unintelligible. — Let us try, then, whether it be impossible, not to explain (for that it would be ridiculous to dream of attempting), but to render intelligible, the possibility of an immediate perception of external objects, without assuming any of the three preceding hypotheses, and without postulating aught that can fairly be refused.

Where the mind is situated. — Now, in the first place, there is no good ground to suppose, that the mind is situate solely in the brain, or exclusively in any one part of the body. On the contrary, the supposition that *it is really present wherever we are conscious that it acts,* — in a word, the Peripatetic aphorism, *the soul is all in the whole and all in every part,* — is more philosophical, and, consequently, more probable, than any other opinion. It has not been always noticed, even by those who deem themselves the chosen champions of the immateriality of mind, that *we materialize mind, when we attribute to it the relations of matter.* Thus, we cannot attribute a local seat to the soul, without clothing it with the properties of extension and place, and those who suppose this seat to be but a point, only aggravate the difficulty. Admitting the spirituality of mind, all that we know of the relation of soul and body is, that the former is connected with the latter in a way of which we are wholly ignorant; and that it holds relations, different both in degree and kind, with different parts of the organism. We have no right, however, to say that it is limited to any one part of the organism; for even if we admit that the nervous system is the part to which it is proximately united, still the nervous system is itself universally ramified throughout the body; and we have no more right to deny that the mind feels at the finger-points, as consciousness assures us, than to assert that it thinks exclusively in the brain.

The sum of our knowledge of the connection of mind and body is, therefore, this, — that the mental modifications are dependent on certain corporeal conditions; but of the nature of these conditions, we know nothing. For example, we know, by experience, that the mind perceives only through certain organs of sense, and that, through these different organs, it perceives in a different manner. But whether the senses be instruments, whether they be media, or whether they be only partial outlets to the mind incarcerated in the body, — on all this, we can only theorize and conjecture. We have no reason whatever to believe, contrary to the testimony of consciousness, that there is an action or affection of the bodily sense previous to the mental perception; or that the mind only perceives in the head, in consequence of the impression on the organ. On the other hand, we have no reason whatever to doubt the report of consciousness, that we actually perceive at the external point of sensation, and that we perceive the material reality. *But what is meant by perceiving the material reality?*

What is the total and real object of perception? — In the *first* place, it does not mean that we perceive the material reality absolutely and in itself, that is, out of relation to our organs and faculties; on the contrary, the total and real object of perception is *the external object under relation to our sense and faculty of cognition.* But though thus relative to us, the object is still no representation, — no modification of the Ego. It is the Non-ego,

— the Non-ego modified, and relative, it may be, but still the Non-ego. I formerly illustrated this to you by a supposition. Suppose that the total object of consciousness in perception is $= 12$; and suppose that the external reality contributes 6, the material sense 3, and the mind 3; — this may enable you to form some rude conjecture of the nature of the object of perception.

What is the external object perceived? — But, in the second place, what is meant by the external object perceived? Nothing can be conceived more ridiculous than the opinion of philosophers in regard to this. For example, it has been curiously held (and Reid is no exception), that in looking at the sun, moon, or any other object of sight, we are, on the one doctrine, actually conscious of these distant objects; or, on the other, that these distant objects are those really represented in the mind. Nothing can be more absurd: *we perceive, through no sense, aught external but what is in immediate relation and in immediate contact with its organ;* and that is true which Democritus of old asserted, that *all our senses are only modifications of touch.* Through the eye, we perceive nothing but the rays of light in relation to, and in contact with, the retina; what we add to this perception must not be taken into account. The same is true of the other senses.*

* [It is incorrect to say that "we see the object," (meaning the thing from which the rays come by emanation or reflection, but which is unknown or incognizable by sight,) and so forth. It would be more correct to describe vision as a perception by which we take immediate cognizance of light in relation to our organ — that is, as diffused and figured upon the retina, under various modifications of degree and kind (brightness and color) — and likewise as falling upon it in a particular direction. The image on the retina is not itself an object of visual perception. It is only to be regarded as the complement of those points, or of that sensitive surface, on which the rays impinge, and with which they enter into relation. The total object of visual perception is thus, neither the rays in themselves, nor the organ in itself, but the rays and the living organ in reciprocity; this organ is not, however, to be viewed as merely the retina, but as the whole tract of nervous fibre pertaining to the sense. In an act of vision, as also in the other sensitive acts, I am thus *conscious* (the word should not be restricted to *self-consciousness*), or immediately cognizant, not only of the affections of

Now what is there monstrous or inconceivable in this doctrine of an immediate perception? The objects are neither carried into the mind, nor the mind made to sally out to them; nor do we require a miracle to justify its possibility. In fact, the consciousness of external objects, on this doctrine, is not more inconceivable than the consciousness of species or ideas on the doctrine of the Schoolmen, Malebranche, or Berkeley. In either case, there is a consciousness of the Non-ego, and, in either case, the Ego and Non-ego are in intimate relation. There is, in fact, on this hypothesis, no greater marvel, that the mind should be cognizant of the external reality, than that it should be connected with a body at all. The latter being the case, the former is not even improbable; all inexplicable as both equally remain. "We are unable," says Pascal, "to conceive what is mind; we are unable to conceive what is matter; still less are we able to conceive how these are united; — yet this is our proper nature." So much in refutation of the third ground of difficulty to the doctrine of an immediate perception.

The *fourth ground of objection* is that of Hume. It is alleged by him in the sequel of the paragraph of which I have already quoted to you [see page 197] the commencement: "This universal and primary opinion of all men is soon destroyed by the slightest philosophy, which teaches us, that nothing can ever be present to the mind but an image or perception, and that the senses are only the inlets, through which these images are conveyed, without being ever able to produce any immediate intercourse between the mind and the object. The table which we see, seems to diminish, as we remove further from it: but the

self, but of the phenomena of something different from itself, — both, however, always in relation to each other. According as, in different senses, the *subjective* or the *objective* element preponderates, we have *sensation* or *perception*, the *secondary* or the *primary* qualities of matter; — distinctions which are thus identified and carried up into a general law.

It is wrong to say that "*a body is smelled by means of effluvia.*" Nothing is smelt but the effluvia themselves. They constitute the total object of *perception* in smell; and, in all the senses, the only object perceived is that in immediate contact with the organ. There is, in reality, no medium in any sense.] — *Notes to Reid.*

real table, which exists independent of us, suffers no alteration: it was, therefore, nothing but its image, which was present to the mind. These are the obvious dictates of reason; and no man, who reflects, ever doubted that the existences, which we consider, when we say *this house,* and *that tree,* are nothing but perceptions in the mind, and fleeting copies or representations of other existences, which remain uniform and independent."

This objection to the veracity of consciousness will not occasion us much trouble. Its refutation is, in fact, contained in the very statement of the real external object of perception. The whole argument consists in a mistake of what that object is. That a thing, viewed close to the eye, should appear larger and differently figured, than when seen at a distance, and that, at too great a distance, it should even become for us invisible altogether; — this only shows that what changes the real object of sight, — the reflected rays in contact with the eye, — also changes, as it ought to change, our perception of such object. This ground of difficulty could be refuted through the whole senses; but its weight is not sufficient to entitle it to any further consideration.

The *fifth ground,* on which the necessity of substituting a representative for an intuitive perception has been maintained, is that of Fichte. It asserts that the nature of the Ego, as an intelligence endowed with will, makes it absolutely necessary, that, of all external objects of perception, there should be representative modifications in the mind. For as the Ego itself is that which wills; therefore, in so far as the will tends towards objects, these must lie within the Ego. An external reality cannot lie within the Ego; there must, therefore, be supposed, within the mind, a representation of this reality different from the reality itself.

This fifth argument involves sundry vices, and is not of greater value than the four preceding. In the *first* place, it proceeds on the assertion, that the objects on which the will is directed, must lie within the willing Ego itself. But how is this assertion proved? That the will can only tend toward those things of which the Ego has itself a knowledge, is undoubtedly true. But from this it does not follow, that the object to which the knowledge is relative, must, at the same time, be present with it in the Ego; but if there be a perceptive cognition, that is, a consciousness of some object external to the Ego, this perception is competent to excite, and to direct, the will, notwithstanding that its object lies without the Ego. That, therefore, no immediate knowledge of external objects is possible, and that consciousness is exclusively limited to the Ego, is not evinced by this argument of Fichte, but simply assumed.

In the *second* place, this argument is faulty, in that it takes no account of the difference between those cognitions which lie at the root of the energies of will, and the other kinds of knowledge. Thus, our will never tends to what is present, — to what we possess, and immediately cognize; but is always directed on the future, and is concerned either with the continuance of those states of the Ego which are already in existence, or with the production of wholly novel states. But the future cannot be intuitively, immediately, perceived, but only represented and mediately conceived. That a mediate cognition is necessary, as the condition of an act of will, — this does not prove that every cognition must be mediate.

We have thus found by an examination of the various grounds on which it has been attempted to establish the necessity of rejecting the testimony of consciousness to the intuitive perception of the external world, that these grounds are, one and all, incompetent. I shall [now] proceed to the second section of the discussion, — to consider the nature of the hypothesis of Representation or Cosmothetic Idealism, by which it is proposed to replace the fact of consciousness and the doctrine of Natural Realism; and shall show you that this hypothesis, though, under various modifications, adopted in almost every system of philosophy, fulfils none of the conditions of a legitimate hypothesis.

The hypothesis unnecessary. — In the *first* place, from the grounds on which the Cosmothetic Idealist would vindicate the necessity of his rejection of the datum of consciousness, the hypothesis itself is unnecessary. The examination of these grounds proves, that the fact of consciousness is not shown to be impossible. So far, therefore, there is no necessity made out for its rejection. But it is said the fact of consciousness is inexplicable; we cannot understand *how* the immediate perception of an external object is possible: whereas the hypothesis of representation enables us to comprehend and explain the phænomenon, and is, therefore, if not absolutely necessary, at least entitled to favor and preference. But even on this lower, — this precarious ground, the hypothesis is absolutely unnecessary. That, on the incomprehensibility of the fact of consciousness, it is allowable to displace the fact by an hypothesis, is of all absurdities the greatest. As a fact, — an ultimate fact of consciousness, it *must be* incomprehensible; and were it comprehensible, that is, did we know it in its causes, — did we know it as contained in some higher notion, — it would not be a primary fact of consciousness, — it would not be an ultimate datum of intelligence. Every *how* (*διότι*) rests ultimately on a *that* (*ὅτι*); every demonstration is deduced from something given and indemonstrable; all that is comprehensible hangs from some revealed* fact, which we must believe as actual, but cannot construe to the reflective intellect in its possibility. In consciousness, in the original spontaneity of intelligence (*νοῦς*, *locus principiorum*), are revealed the primordial facts of our intelligent nature.

But the Cosmothetic Idealist has no right to ask the Natural Realist for an explanation of the fact of consciousness; supposing even that his own hypothesis were, in itself, both clear and probable, — supposing that the consciousness of self were intelligible, and the consciousness of the not-self the reverse. For, on this supposition, the intelligible consciousness of self could not be an ultimate fact, but must be comprehended through a higher cognition, — a higher consciousness, which would again be itself either comprehensible or not. If comprehensible, this would, of course, require a still higher cognition, and so on, till we arrive at some datum of intelligence, which, as highest, we

* This expression is not meant to imply any thing hyperphysical. It is used to denote the ultimate and incomprehensible nature of the fact, — of the fact which must be believed, though it cannot be understood, — cannot be explained.

could not understand through a higher; so that, at best, the hypothesis of representation, proposed in place of the fact of consciousness, only removes the difficulty by one or two steps. The end to be gained is thus of no value; and, for this end, as we have seen and shall see, there would be sacrificed the possibility of philosophy as a rational knowledge altogether; and, in the possibility of philosophy, of course, the possibility of the very hypothesis itself.

The hypothesis not more intelligible than the fact. — But is the hypothesis really, in itself, a whit more intelligible than the fact which it displaces? The reverse is true. What does the hypothesis suppose? It supposes that the mind can represent that of which it knows nothing, — that of which it is ignorant. Is this more comprehensible than the simple fact, that the mind immediately knows what is different from itself, and what is really an affection of the bodily organism? It seems, in truth, not only incomprehensible, but contradictory. The hypothesis of a representative perception thus violates the first condition of a legitimate hypothesis, — it is unnecessary; — nay, not only unnecessary, it cannot do what it professes, — it explains nothing, it renders nothing comprehensible.

The *second* condition of a legitimate hypothesis is, that *it shall not subvert that which it is devised to explain;* — that it shall not explode the system of which it forms a part. But this, the hypothesis in question does; it annihilates itself in the destruction of the whole edifice of knowledge. Belying the testimony of consciousness to our immediate perception of an outer world, it belies the veracity of consciousness altogether; and the truth of consciousness is the condition of the possibility of all knowledge.

The *third* condition of a legitimate hypothesis is, that *the fact or facts*, in explanation of which it is devised, *be ascertained really to exist*, and be not themselves hypothetical. But so far is the principal fact, which the hypothesis of a representative perception is proposed to explain, from being certain, that its reality is even rendered problematical by the proposed explanation itself. The facts which this hypothesis supposes to be ascertained and established are two — *first*, the fact of *an external world existing; second,* the fact of *an internal world knowing.* These the hypothesis takes for granted. For it is asked, How are these connected? — How can the internal world know the external world existing? And, in answer to this problem, the hypothesis of representation is advanced as explaining the mode of their correlation. This hypothesis denies the immediate connection of the two facts; it denies that the mind, the internal world, can be immediately cognizant of matter, the external; and between the two worlds it interpolates a representation, which is at once the object known by mind, and as known, an image vicarious or representative of matter, *ex hypothesi,* in itself unknown.

The procedure vicious. — But mark the vice of the procedure. We can only, 1°, Assert the existence of an external world, inasmuch as we know it to exist; and we can only, 2°, Assert that one thing is representative of another, inasmuch as the thing represented is known independently of the representation. But how does the hypothesis of a representative perception proceed? It actually converts the fact into an hypothesis; actually converts the hypothesis into a fact. On this theory, we do not know the existence of an external world, except on the supposition that that which we do know, truly represents it as existing. The Hypothetical Realist cannot, therefore, establish the fact of the external world, except upon the fact of its representation. This is manifest. We have, therefore, next to ask him, how he knows the fact, that the external world is actually represented. A representation supposes something represented, and the representation of the external world supposes the existence of that world. Now, the Hypothetical Realist, when asked how he proves the reality of the outer world, which, *ex hypothesi,* he does not know, can only say that he infers its existence from the fact of its representation. But the fact of the representation of an external world supposes the existence of that world; therefore, he is again at the point from which he started. He has been arguing in a circle. There is thus a see-saw between the hypothesis and the fact; the fact is assumed as an hypothesis; the hypothesis explained as a fact; each is established, each is expounded, by the other. To account for the possibility of an unknown external world, the hypothesis of representation is devised; and to account for the possibility of representation, we imagine the hypothesis of an external world.

The Cosmothetic Idealist thus begs the fact which he would explain. And, on the hypothesis of a representative perception, it is admitted by the philosophers themselves who hold it, that the descent to absolute Idealism is a logical precipice, from which they can alone attempt to save themselves by appealing to the natural beliefs, to the common sense, of mankind, — that is, to the testimony of that very consciousness to which their own hypothesis gives the lie.

The hypothesis subverts the phænomenon to be explained. — In the *fourth* place, a legitimate hypothesis must save the phænomena which it is invented to explain; that is, it must account for them adequately and without exclusion, distortion, or mutilation. But the hypothesis of a representative perception proposes to accomplish its end only by first destroying, and then attempting to recreate, the phænomena, for the fact of which it should, as a legitimate hypothesis, only afford a reason. The total, the entire phænomenon to be explained, is the phænomenon given in consciousness of the immediate knowledge by me, or mind, of an existence different from me, or mind. This phænomenon, however, the hypothesis in question does not preserve entire. On the contrary, it hews it into two; — into the immediate knowledge by me, and into the existence of something different from me; — or more briefly, into the intuition and the existence. It separates, in its explanation, what is given it to explain as united. This procedure is, at best, monstrous; but this is not the worst. The entire phænomenon being cut in two, you will observe how the fragments are treated. The existence of the Non-ego, — the one fragment, it admits; its intuition, its immediate cognition by the Ego, — the other fragment, it disallows. Now mark what is the character of this proceeding. The former fragment of the phænomenon, — the fragment admitted, to us exists only through the other fragment which is rejected. The existence of an external world is only given us through its intuition; — we only believe it to exist because we believe that we immediately know it to exist, or are conscious of it as existing. The intuition is the *ratio cognoscendi*, and, therefore, to us the *ratio essendi*, of a material universe. Prove to me that I am wrong in regard to my intuition of an outer world, and I will grant at once, that I have no ground for supposing I am right in regard to the existence of that world. To annihilate the intuition, is to annihilate what is prior and constitutive in the phænomenon; and to annihilate what is prior and constitutive in the phænomenon, is to annihilate the phænomenon altogether. The existence of a material world is no longer, therefore, even a truncated, even a fractional, fact of consciousness; for the fact of the existence of a material world, given in consciousness, necessarily vanished with the fact of the intuition on which it rested. The absurdity is about the same as if we should attempt to explain the existence of color, on an hypothesis which denied the existence of extension. A representative perception is thus an hypothetical explanation of a supposititious fact; it creates the nature it interprets.*

In the *fifth* place, *the fact* which a legitimate hypothesis explains, *must be within the sphere of experience;* but the fact of an external world, for which the Cosmothetic Idealist would account, transcends, *ex hypothesi*, all experience, being unknown in itself, and a mere hyperphysical assumption.

The hypothesis must be single. — In the *sixth* place, an hypothesis is probable in proportion as it works simply and naturally; that is, in proportion as it is dependent on no subsidiary hypothe-

* [With the Hypothetical Realist or Cosmothetic Idealist, it has been a puzzling problem to resolve how, on their doctrine of a representative perception, the mind can attain the notion of externality, or outness, — far more, be impressed with the invincible belief of the reality, and known reality, of an external world. Their attempts at this solution are as unsatisfactory as they are operose. On the doctrine of an intuitive perception, all this is given in the fact of an immediate knowledge of the Non-ego. To us, therefore, the problem does not exist.]

sis, — as it involves nothing petitory, occult, supernatural, as part and parcel of its explanation. In this respect, the doctrine of a representative perception is not less vicious than in others; to explain at all, it must not only postulate subsidiary hypotheses, but subsidiary miracles. The doctrine in question attempts to explain the knowledge of an unknown world, by the ratio of a representative perception: but it is impossible, by any conceivable relation, to apply the ratio to the facts. The mental modification, of which, on the doctrine of representation, we are exclusively conscious in perception, either represents a real external world, or it does not. The latter is a confession of absolute Idealism; we have, therefore, only to consider the former.

The hypothesis of a representative perception supposes, that the mind does not know the external world, which it represents; for this hypothesis is expressly devised only on the supposed impossibility of an immediate knowledge of aught different from, and external to, the mind. The percipient mind must, therefore, be, somehow or other, determined to represent the reality of which it is ignorant. Now, here one of two alternatives is necessary; — either the mind blindly determines itself to this representation, or it is determined to it by some intelligent and knowing cause different from itself. The former alternative would be preferable, inasmuch as it is the more simple, and assumes nothing hyperphysical, were it not irrational, as wholly incompetent to account for the phænomenon. On this alternative, we should suppose, that the mind represented, and truly represented, that of whose existence and qualities it knew nothing. A great effect is here assumed, absolutely without a cause; for we could as easily conceive the external world springing into existence without a Creator, as mind representing that external world to itself without a knowledge of that which it represented. The manifest absurdity of this first alternative has accordingly constrained the profoundest Cosmothetic Idealists to call in supernatural aid by embracing the second. To say nothing of less illustrious schemes, the systems of Divine Assistance, of a Preëstablished Harmony, and of the Vision of all things in the Deity, are only so many subsidiary hypotheses; — so many attempts to bridge, by supernatural machinery, the chasm between the representation and the reality, which all human ingenuity had found, by natural means, to be insuperable. The hypothesis of a representative perception thus presupposes a miracle to let it work. Dr. Brown and others, indeed, reject, as unphilosophical, these hyperphysical subsidiaries; but they only saw less clearly the necessity for their admission. The rejection, indeed, is another inconsequence added to their doctrine. It is undoubtedly true that, without necessity, it is unphilosophical to assume a miracle; but it is doubly unphilosophical first to originate this necessity, and then not to submit to it. It is a contemptible philosophy that eschews the *Deus ex machina*, and yet ties the knot which can only be loosed by his interposition. Nor will it here do for the Cosmothetic Idealist to pretend that the difficulty is of nature's, not of his, creation. In fact, it only arises, because he has closed his eyes upon the light of nature, and refused the guidance of consciousness: but having swamped himself in following the *ignis fatuus* of a theory, he has no right to refer its private absurdities to the imbecility of human reason, or to excuse his self-contracted ignorance by the narrow limits of our present knowledge.

So much for the merits of the hypothesis of a Representative Perception, — an hypothesis which begins by denying the veracity of consciousness, and ends, when carried to its legitimate issue, in absolute Idealism, in utter Scepticism. This hypothesis has been, and is, one more universally prevalent among philosophers than any other; and I have given to its consideration a larger share of attention than I should otherwise have done, in consequence of its being one great source of the dissensions in philosophy, and of the opprobrium thrown on consciousness as the instrument of philosophical observation and the standard of philosophical certainty and truth.

CHAPTER XX.

THE PRESENTATIVE FACULTY. — GENERAL QUESTIONS RELATING TO THE SENSES. — PERCEPTIONS BY SIGHT AND TOUCH.

WITH this terminates the most important of the discussions to which the Faculty of Perception gives rise: the other questions are not, however, without interest, though their determination does not affect the vital interests of philosophy.

Whether we first obtain a knowledge of the whole, or of the parts. — Of these the first that I shall touch upon is the problem, — Whether, in Perception, do we first obtain a general knowledge of the complex wholes presented to us by sense, and then, by analysis and limited attention, obtain a special knowledge of their several parts; or do we not first obtain a particular knowledge of the smallest parts to which sense is competent, and then, by synthesis, collect them into greater and greater wholes?

The second alternative in this question is adopted by Mr Stewart; it is, indeed, involved in his doctrine in regard to Attention, — in holding that we recollect nothing without attention, that we can attend only to a single object at once, which one object is the very smallest that is discernible through sense. He says [see pp. 162, 163], that, in a concert of music, "the mind is constantly varying its attention from the one part of the music to the other, and that its operations are so rapid as to give us no perception of an interval of time."

"The same doctrine leads to some curious conclusions with respect to vision. It is impossible for the mind to attend to more than one of the points [in the outline of an object] at once: and as the perception of the figure of the object implies a knowledge of the relative situation of the different points with respect to each other, we must conclude, that the perception of figure by the eye is the result of a number of different acts of attention. These acts of attention, however, are performed with such rapidity, that the effect with respect to us, is the same as if the perception were instantaneous. If these observations be admitted, it will follow, that, without the faculty of memory, we could have had no perception of visible figure."

Mill's doctrine of Association. — The same conclusion is attained, through a somewhat different process, by Mr. James Mill. This author, following Hartley and Priestley, has pushed the principle of Association to an extreme which refutes its own exaggeration, — analyzing not only our belief in the relation of effect and cause into that principle, but even the primary logical laws. According to Mr. Mill, the necessity under which we lie of thinking that one contradictory excludes another, — that a thing cannot at once be and not be, is only the result of association and custom. It is not, therefore, to be marvelled at, that he should account for our knowledge of complex wholes in perception by the same universal principle; and this he accordingly does. "Where two or more ideas have been often repeated together, and the association has become very strong, they sometimes spring up in such close combination as not to be distinguishable. Some cases of sensation are analogous. For example; when a wheel, on the seven parts of which the seven prismatic colors are respectively painted, is made to revolve rapidly, it appears not of seven colors, but of one uniform color, white. By the rapidity of the succession, the several sensations cease to be distinguishable; they run, as it were, together, and a new sensation, compounded of all the seven, but apparently a simple one, is the result. Ideas, also, which have been so often conjoined, that whenever one exists in the mind, the others immediately exist along with it, seem to run into one another, to coalesce, as it were, and out of many to form one idea; which idea, however in reality complex, appears to be no less simple than any one of those of which it is compounded."

"It is to this great law of Association that we trace the formation of our ideas of what we call external objects; that is, the ideas of a certain number of sensations, received together so frequently that they coalesce as it were, and are spoken of under the idea of unity. Hence, what we call the idea of a tree, the idea of a stone, the idea of a horse, the idea of a man.

"In using the names, tree, horse, man, the names of what I call objects, I am referring, and can be referring, only to my own sensations; in fact, therefore, only naming a certain number of sensations, regarded as in a particular state of combination; that is, concomitance. Particular sensations of sight, of touch, of the muscles, are the sensations, to the ideas of which color, extension, roughness, hardness, smoothness, taste, smell, so coalescing as to appear one idea, I give the name, idea of a tree."

"Some ideas are, by frequency and strength of association, so closely combined, that they cannot be separated. If one exists, the other exists along with it, in spite of whatever effort we make to disjoin them.

"For example; it is not in our power to think of color, without thinking of extension; or of solidity, without figure. We have seen color constantly in combination with extension, — spread, as it were, upon a surface. We have never seen it except in this connection. Color and extension have been invariably conjoined. The idea of color, therefore, uniformly comes into the mind, bringing that of extension along with it; and so close is the association, that it is not in our power to dissolve it. We cannot, if we will, think of color, but in combination with extension. The one idea calls up the other, and retains it, so long as the other is retained."

This doctrine implies that we know the parts better than the whole. — Now, in opposition to this doctrine, nothing appears to me clearer than the first alternative, — and that, in place of ascending upwards from the minimum of perception to its maxima, we descend from masses to details. If the opposite doctrine were correct, what would it involve? It would involve, as a primary inference, that, as we know the whole through the parts, we should know the parts better than the whole. Thus, for example, it is supposed that we know the face of a friend through the multitude of perceptions which we have of the different points of which it is made up; in other words, that we should know the whole countenance less vividly than we know the forehead and eyes, the nose and mouth, etc., and that we should know each of these more feebly than we know the various ultimate points, in fact, unconscious minima, of perceptions, which go to constitute them. According to the doctrine in question, we perceive only one of these ultimate points at the same instant, the others by memory incessantly renewed. Now let us take the face out of perception into memory altogether. Let us close our eyes, and let us represent in imagination the countenance of our friend. This we can do with the utmost vivacity; or, if we see a picture of it, we can determine, with a consciousness of the most perfect accuracy, that the portrait is like or unlike. It cannot, therefore, be denied that we have the fullest knowledge of the face as a whole, — that we are familiar with its expression, with the general result of its parts. On the hypothesis, then, of Stewart and Mill, how accurate should be our knowledge of these parts themselves. But make the experiment. You will find that, unless you have analyzed, — unless you have descended from a conspectus of the whole face to a detailed examination of its parts, — with a most vivid impression of the constituted whole, you are almost totally ignorant of the constituent parts. You may probably be unable to say what is the color of the eyes, and if you attempt to delineate the mouth or nose, you will inevitably fail. Or look at the portrait. You may find it unlike, but unless, as I said, you have analyzed the countenance, unless you have looked at it with the analytic scrutiny of a painter's eye, you will assuredly be unable to say in what respect the artist has failed; — you will be unable to specify what constituent he has altered, though you are fully conscious of the fact and effect of the alteration. What we have shown from this example may equally be done from any other, — a house, a tree, a landscape, a concert of music, etc. But it is needless to multiply illustrations. In fact, on the doctrine of these philosophers, if the mind, as they maintain, were unable to comprehend more than one perceptible minimum at a time, the greatest of all inconceivable marvels would be, how it has contrived to realize the knowledge of wholes and masses which it has. Another refutation of this opinion might be drawn from the doctrine of latent modifications, — the obscure perceptions of Leibnitz, — of which we have recently treated. But this argument I think unnecessary.

Resuming consideration of the more important psychological questions that have been agitated concerning the Senses, I proceed to take up those connected with the sense of Touch. The problems which arise under this sense may be reduced to two opposite questions. The first asks, May not all the Senses be analyzed into Touch? The second asks, Is not Touch or Feeling, considered as one of the five senses, itself only a bundle of various senses?

May all the Senses be analyzed into Touch? — In regard to the first of these questions, — it is an opinion as old at least as Democritus, and one held by many of the ancient physiologists, that the four senses of Sight, Hearing, Taste, and Smell are only modifications of Touch. This opinion Aristotle records in the fourth chapter of his book *On Sense and the Object of Sense*, and contents himself with refuting it by the assertion that its impossibility is manifest. So far, however, from being manifestly impossible, and, therefore, manifestly absurd, it can now easily be shown to be correct, *if by Touch is understood the contact of the external object of perception with the organ of sense.* The opinion of Democritus was revived, in modern times, by Telesius, an Italian philosopher of the sixteenth century, and who preceded Bacon and Descartes, as a reformer of philosophical methods. I say the opinion of Democritus can easily be shown to be correct; for it is only a confusion of ideas, or of words, or of both together, to talk of the perception of a distant object, that is, of an object not in relation to our senses. An external object is only perceived inasmuch as it is in relation to our sense, and it is only in relation to our sense inasmuch as it is present to it. To say, for example, that we perceive by sight the sun or moon, is a false or an elliptical expression. We perceive nothing but certain modifications of light in immediate relation to our organ of vision; and so far from Dr. Reid being philosophically correct, when he says that "when ten men look at the sun or moon, they all see the same individual object," the truth is, that each of these persons sees a different object, because each person sees a different complement of rays, in relation to his individual organ. In fact, if we look alternately with each, we have a different object in our right, and a different object in our left, eye. It is not by perception, but by a process of reasoning, that we connect the objects of sense with existences beyond the sphere of immediate knowledge. It is enough that perception affords us the knowledge of the Non-ego at the point of sense. To arrogate to it the power of immediately informing us of external things, which are only the causes of the object we immediately perceive, is either positively erroneous, or a confusion of language, arising from an inadequate discrimination of the phænomena. Such assumptions tend only to throw discredit on the doctrine of an intuitive perception; and such assumptions you will find scattered over the works both of Reid and Stewart. I would, therefore, establish as a fundamental position of the doctrine of an immediate perception, the opinion of Democritus, that all our senses are only modifications of touch; in other words, that the external object of perception is always in contact with the organ of sense.

Does Touch comprehend a plurality of senses? — This determination of the first problem does not interfere with the consideration of the second; for, in the second, it is only asked, Whether, considering Touch or Feeling as a special sense, there are not comprehended under it varieties of perception and sensation so different, that these varieties ought to be viewed as constituting so many special senses. This question, I think, ought to be answered in the affirmative; for, though I hold that the other senses are not to be discriminated from Touch, in so far as Touch signifies merely the contact of the organ and the object of perception, yet, considering Touch as a special sense distinguished from the other four by other and peculiar characters, it may easily, I think, be shown, that if Sight and

Hearing, if Smell and Taste, are to be divided from each other and from Touch Proper, under Touch there must, on the same analogy, be distinguished a plurality of special senses. This problem, like the other, is of ancient date. It is mooted by Aristotle in the eleventh chapter of the second book *De Anima*, but his opinion is left doubtful. Among modern philosophers, Cardan distinguishes four senses of touch or feeling; one, of the four primary tactile qualities of Aristotle (that is, of cold and hot, and wet and dry); a second, of the light and heavy; a third, of pleasure and pain; and a fourth, of titillation. His antagonist, the elder Scaliger, distinguished as a sixth special sense the sexual appetite, in which he has been followed by Bacon, Voltaire, and others. From these historical notices, you will see how marvellously incorrect is the statement that Locke was the first philosopher who originated this question, in allowing hunger and thirst to be the sensations of a sense different from tactile feeling. Hutcheson, in his work on the *Passions*, says, "the division of our external senses into five common classes is ridiculously imperfect. Some sensations, such as hunger and thirst, weariness and sickness, can be reduced to none of them; or if they are reduced to feelings, they are perceptions as different from the other ideas of touch, such as cold, heat, hardness, softness, as the ideas of taste or smell." Adam Smith, in his posthumous *Essays*, observes that hunger and thirst are objects of feeling, not of touch; and that heat and cold are felt not as pressing on the organ, but as *in* the organ. Kant divides the whole bodily senses into two, — into a Vital Sense and an Organic Sense. To the former class belong the sensations of heat and cold, shuddering, quaking, etc. The latter is divided into the five senses, of Touch Proper, Sight, Hearing, Taste, and Smell.

This division has now become general in Germany, the Vital Sense receiving from various authors various synonyms, as *cœnæsthesis*, *common feeling*, *vital feeling*, and *sense of feeling*, *sensu latiori*, etc.; and the sensations attributed to it are heat and cold, shuddering, feeling of health, hunger and thirst, visceral sensations, etc. This division is, likewise, adopted by Dr.

Brown. He divides our sensations into those which are less definite, and into those which are more definite; and these, his two classes, correspond precisely to the *sensus vagus* and *sensus fixus* of the German philosophers.

Touch distinguished from sensible feeling. — The propriety of throwing out of the sense of Touch those sensations which afford us indications only of the subjective condition of the body, in other words, of dividing touch from sensible feeling, is apparent. In the *first* place, this is manifest on the analogy of the other special senses. These, as we have seen, are divided into two classes, according as Perception proper or Sensation proper predominates; the senses of Sight and Hearing pertaining to the first, those of Smell and Taste to the second. Here each is decidedly either perceptive or sensitive. But in Touch, under the vulgar attribution of qualities, Perception and Sensation both find their maximum. At the finger-points, this sense would give us objective knowledge of the outer world, with the least possible alloy of subjective feeling; in hunger and thirst, etc., on the contrary, it would afford us a subjective feeling of our own state, with the least possible addition of objective knowledge. On this ground, therefore, we ought to attribute to different senses perceptions and sensations so different in degree.

But, in the *second* place, it is not merely in the opposite degree of these two counter elements that this distinction is to be founded, but likewise on the different quality of the groups of the perceptions and sensations themselves. There is nothing similar between these different groups, except the negative circumstance that there is no special organ to which positively to refer them; and, therefore, they are exclusively slumped together under that sense which is not obtrusively marked out and isolated by the mechanism of a peculiar instrument.

Touch, — its sphere and organic seat. — Limiting, therefore, the special sense of Touch to that of objective information, it is sufficient to say that this sense has its seat at the extremity of the nerves which terminate in the skin; its principal organs are the finger-points, the toes, the lips, and the tongue. Of these, the first is the most perfect. At the tips of the fingers, a tender skin covers the nervous papillæ; and here the nail serves not only as a protecting shield to the organ, but, likewise, by affording an opposition to the body which makes an impression on the finger-ends, it renders more distinct our perception of the nature of its surface. Through the great mobility of the fingers, of the wrist, and of the shoulder-joint, we are able with one, and still more effectually, with both hands, to manipulate an object on all sides, and thereby to attain a knowledge of its figure. We likewise owe to the sense of Touch a perception of those conformations of a body, according to which we call it rough or smooth, hard or soft, sharp or blunt. The repose or motion of a body is also perceived through the touch.

To obviate misunderstanding, I should, however, notice that the proper organ of Touch — the nervous papillæ — requires, as the condition of its exercise, *the movement of the voluntary muscles.* This condition, however, ought not to be viewed as a part of the organ itself. This being understood, the perception of the weight of a body will not fall under this sense, as the nerves lying under the epidermis or scurf skin have little or no share in this knowledge. We owe it, almost exclusively, to the consciousness we have of the exertion of the muscles, requisite to lift with the hand a heavy body from the ground, or when it is laid on the shoulders or head, to keep our own body erect, and to carry the burden from one place to another.

I next proceed to consider two counter-questions, which are still agitated by philosophers. The first is, — Does Sight afford us an original knowledge of extension, or do we not owe this exclusively to Touch? The second is, — Does Touch afford us an original knowledge of extension, or do we not owe this exclusively to Sight? Both questions are still undetermined; and, consequently, the vulgar belief is also unestablished, that we obtain a knowledge of extension originally both from sight and touch.

I commence, then, with the first, — *Does Vision afford us a primary knowledge of extension*, or do we not owe this knowledge exclusively to Touch? But, before entering on its discussion, it is proper to state to you, by preamble, what kind of extension it is that those would vindicate to sight, who answer this question in the affirmative. The whole primary objects of sight, then, are colors, and extensions, and forms or figures of extension. And here you will observe, it is not all kind of extension and form that is attributed to sight. It is not figured extension in all the three dimensions, but only extension as involved in plane figures; that is, only length and breadth.

It has generally been admitted by philosophers, after Aristotle, that *color is the proper object of sight*, and that extension and figure, common to sight and touch, are only accidentally its objects, because supposed in the perception of color. The first philosopher, with whom I am acquainted, who doubted or denied that vision is conversant with extension, was Berkeley. [Condillac also, at one time,] maintained the same opinion. This, however, he did not do either very explicitly or without change.* Mr. Stewart maintains that extension is not an object of sight. "I formerly," he says, "had occasion to mention several instances of very intimate associations formed between two ideas which have no necessary connection with each other. One of the most remarkable is, that which exists in every person's mind between the notions of *color* and *extension*. The former of these words expresses (at least in the sense in which we commonly employ it) a sensation in the mind, the latter denotes a quality of an external object; so that there is, in fact, no more connection between the two notions than between those of pain and of solidity; and yet, in consequence of our always perceiving extension at the same time at which the sensation of color is excited in the mind, we find it impossible to think of

* Neither Condillac nor Berkeley goes so far as to say, that color, regarded as an affection of the visual organism, is apprehended as absolutely unextended, as a mathematical point. Nor is this the question in dispute. But granting, as Condillac in his later view expressly asserts, that color, as a visual sensation, necessarily occupies space, do we, by means of that sensation, acquire also the proper idea of extension, as composed of parts exterior to each other? In other words, does the sensation of different colors, which is necessary to the distinction of parts at all, necessarily suggest different and contiguous localities? This question is explicitly answered in the negative by Condillac, and in the affirmative by Sir W. Hamilton. — ENGLISH ED.

that sensation without conceiving extension along with it." But before and after Stewart, a doctrine, virtually the same, is maintained by the Hartleian school; who assert, as a consequence of their universal principle of association, that the perception of color suggests the notion of extension.

Then comes Dr. Brown, who, after having repeatedly asserted, that it is, and always has been, the universal opinion of philosophers, that the superficial extension of length and breadth becomes known to us by sight originally, proceeds, as he says, for the first time, to controvert this opinion; though it is wholly impossible that he could have been ignorant that the same had been done, at least by Condillac and Stewart. He says, "The universal opinion of philosophers is, that it is not color merely which it [the simple original sensation of vision] involves, but extension also, — that there is a visible figure, as well as a tangible figure, — and that the visible figure involves, in our instant original perception, superficial length and breadth, as the tangible figure, which we learn to see, involves length, breadth, and thickness.

"That it is impossible for us, at present, to separate, in the sensation of vision, the color from the extension, I admit; though not more completely impossible than it is for us to look on the thousand feet of a meadow, and to perceive only the small inch of greenness on our retina; and the one impossibility, as much as the other, I conceive to arise only from intimate association, subsequent to the original sensations of sight. Nor do I deny, that a certain part of the retina — which, being limited, must therefore have figure — is affected by the rays of light that fall on it, as a certain breadth of nervous expanse is affected in all the other organs. I contend only, that the perception of this limited figure of the portion of the retina affected does not enter into the sensation itself, more than, in our sensations of any other species, there is a perception of the nervous breadth affected.

"The immediate perception of visible figure has been assumed as indisputable, rather than attempted to be proved; — as before the time of Berkeley, the immediate visual perception of dis-

32

tance, and of the three dimensions of matter, was supposed, in like manner, to be without any need of proof;—and it is, therefore, impossible to refer to arguments on the subject. I presume, however, that the reasons which have led to this belief, of the immediate perception of a figure termed visible, as distinguished from that tangible figure which we learn to see, are the following two,—the only reasons which I can even imagine; —that it is absolutely impossible, in our present sensations of sight, to separate color from extension,—and that there are, in fact, a certain length and breadth of the retina, on which the light falls."

Summary of Brown's argument.—He then goes on to argue, at a far greater length than can be quoted, that the mere circumstance of a certain definite space, namely, the extended retina, being affected by certain sensations, does not necessarily involve the notion of extension. Indeed, in all those cases in which it is supposed, that a certain diffusion of sensations excites the notion of extension, it seems to be taken for granted that the being knows already, that he has an extended body, over which these sensations are thus diffused. Nothing but the sense of touch, however, and nothing but those kinds of touch which imply the idea of continued resistance, can give us any notion of body at all. All mental affections which are regarded merely as feelings of the mind, and which do not give us a conception of their external causes, can never be known to arise from any thing which is extended or solid. So far, however, is the mere sensation of color from being able to produce this, that touch itself, as felt in many of its modifications, could give us no idea of it. That the sensation of color is quite unfit to give us any idea of extension, merely by its being diffused over a certain expanse of the retina, seems to be corroborated by what we experience in the other senses, even after we are perfectly acquainted with the notion of extension. In hearing, for instance, a certain quantity of the tympanum of the ear must be affected by the pulsations of the air; yet it gives us no idea of the dimensions of the part affected. The same may, in general, be said of taste and smell.

Proof that sight takes cognizance of extension.—Now, in all their elaborate argumentation on this subject, these philosophers seem never yet to have seen the real difficulty of their doctrine. It can easily be shown that the perception of color involves the perception of extension. All parties are, of course, at one in regard to the fact that we see color. Those who hold that we see extension, admit that we see it only as colored; and those who deny us any vision of extension, make color the exclusive object of sight. In regard to this first position, all are, therefore, agreed. Nor are they less harmonious in regard to the second; — that the power of perceiving color involves the power of perceiving the differences of colors. By sight we, therefore, perceive color, and discriminate one color, that is, one colored body, — one sensation of color, from another. This is admitted. A third position will also be denied by none, that the colors discriminated in vision are, or may be, placed side by side in immediate juxtaposition; or, one may limit another by being superinduced partially over it. A fourth position is equally indisputable, — that the contrasted colors, thus bounding each other, will form by their meeting a visible line, and that, if the superinduced color be surrounded by the other, this line will return upon itself, and thus constitute the outline of a visible figure.

These four positions command a peremptory assent: they are all self-evident. But their admission at once explodes the paradox under discussion. And thus: a line is extension in one dimension, — length; a figure is extension in two, — length and breadth. Therefore, the vision of a line is a vision of extension in length; the vision of a figure, the vision of extension in length and breadth. This is an immediate demonstration of the impossibility of the opinion in question; and it is curious that the in genuity, which suggested to its supporters the petty and recon dite objections they have so operosely combated, should not have shown them this gigantic difficulty, which lay obtrusively before them.

Extension cannot be imagined except as colored and shaped. — So far, in fact, is the doctrine which divorces the perceptions of color and extension from being true, that we cannot even represent extension to the mind except as colored. When we come to the consideration of the Representative Faculty, — Imagination, — I shall endeavor to show you (what has not been observed by psychologists), that in the representation, — in the imagination of sensible objects, we always represent them in the organ of Sense through which we originally perceived them Thus, we cannot imagine any particular odor but in the nose; nor any sound but in the ear; nor any taste but in the mouth; and if we would represent any pain we have ever felt, this can only be done through the local nerves. In like manner, when we imagine any modification of light we do so in the eye; and it is a curious confirmation of this, as is well known to physiologists, that when not only the external apparatus of the eye, which is a mere mechanical instrument, but the real organ of sight, — the optic nerves and their thalami, have become diseased, the patient loses, in proportion to the extent of the morbid affection, either wholly or in part, the faculty of recalling visible phænomena to his mind. I mention this at present in order to show, that Vision is not only a sense competent to the perception of extension, but the sense *κατ' ἐξοχήν*, if not exclusively, so competent, — and this in the following manner: You either now know, or will hereafter learn, that no notion, whether native and general, or adventitious and generalized, can be represented in imagination, except in a concrete or singular example. For instance, you cannot imagine a triangle which is not either an equilateral, or an isosceles, or a scalene, — in short, some individual form of a triangle; nay, more, you cannot imagine it, except either large or small, on paper, or on a board, of wood or of iron, white or black or green; in short, except under all the special determinations which give it, in thought, as in existence, singularity and individuality. The same happens, too, with extension. Space I admit to be a native form of thought, — not an adventitious notion. We cannot but think it. Yet I cannot actually represent space in imagination, stript of all individualizing attributes. In this act, I can easily annihilate all corporeal existence, — I can imagine empty space. But there are two attributes of which I cannot divest it, that is, shape and color. This may sound almost ridiculous at first statement; but if you attend to the phænomenon, you will soon be satisfied of its truth. And first as to shape. Your minds are not infinite, and cannot, therefore, positively conceive infinite space. Infinite space is only conceived negatively, — only by conceiving it inconceivable; in other words, it cannot be conceived at all. But if we do our utmost to realize this notion of infinite extension by a positive act of imagination, how do we proceed? Why, we think out from a centre, and endeavor to carry the circumference of the sphere to infinity. But by no one effort of imagination can we accomplish this; and as we cannot do it at once by one infinite act, it would require an eternity of successive finite efforts, — an endless series of imaginings beyond imaginings, to equalize the thought with its object. The very attempt is contradictory. But when we leave off, has the imagined space a shape? It has: for it is finite; and a finite, that is, a bounded, space, constitutes a figure. What, then, is this figure? It is spherical, — necessarily spherical; for as the effort of imagining space is an effort outwards from a centre, the space represented in imagination is necessarily circular. If there be no shape, there has been no positive imagination; and for any other shape than the orbicular, no reason can be assigned. Such is the figure of space in a free act of phantasy.

This, however, will be admitted without scruple; for if real space, as it is well described by St. Augustin, be a sphere whose centre is everywhere, and whose circumference is nowhere, imagined space may be allowed to be a sphere whose circumference is represented at any distance from its centre. But will its color be as easily allowed? In explanation of this, you will observe, that under color, I of course include black as well as white; the transparent as well as the opaque, — in short, any modification of light or darkness. This being understood, I maintain that it is impossible to imagine figure, extension, space, except as colored in some determinate mode. You may represent it under any, but you must represent it under some, modification of light, — color. Make the experiment, and you will find I am correct. But I anticipate an objection. The non-perception of color, or the inability of discriminating colors, is a case of not unfrequent occurrence, though the subjects of this deficiency are, at the same time, not otherwise defective in vision. In cases of this description, there is, however, necessarily a discrimination of light and shade; and the colors that to us appear in all "the sevenfold radiance of effulgent light," to them appear only as different gradations of clare-obscure. Were this not the case, there could be no vision. Such persons, therefore, have still two great contrasts of color, — black and white, and an indefinite number of intermediate gradations, in which to represent space to their imaginations. Nor is there any difficulty in the case of the blind, the absolutely blind, — the blind from birth. Blindness is the non-perception of color; the non-perception of color is simple darkness. The space, therefore, represented by the blind, if represented at all, will be represented black. Some modification of ideal light or darkness is thus the condition of the imagination of space. This of itself powerfully supports the doctrine, that vision is conversant with extension as its object. But if the opinion I have stated be correct, that an act of imagination is only realized through some organ of sense, the impossibility of representing space out of all relation to light and color at once establishes the eye as the appropriate sense of extension and figure.

D'Alembert on seeing extension. — In corroboration of the general view I have taken of the relation of Sight to extension, I may translate to you a passage by a distinguished mathematician and philosopher, who, in writing it, probably had in his eye the paradoxical speculation of Condillac. "It is certain," says D' Alembert, "that sight alone, and independently of touch, affords us the idea of extension; for extension is the necessary object of vision, and we should see nothing if we did not see it extended. I even believe that sight must give us the notion of extension more readily than touch, because sight makes us remark more promptly and perfectly than touch, that contiguity, and, at the same time, that distinction, of parts in which extension consists. Moreover, vision alone gives us the idea of the color of objects. Let us suppose now parts of space differently colored, and presented to our eyes; the difference of colors will necessarily cause us to observe the boundaries or limits which separate two neighboring colors, and, consequently, will give us an idea of figure; for we conceive a figure when we conceive a limitation or boundary on all sides."

I am confident, therefore, that we may safely establish the conclusion, that Sight is a sense principally conversant with extension; whether it be the only sense thus conversant, remains to be considered.

Does Touch afford us an original knowledge of extension. — I proceed, therefore, to the second of the counter-problems, — to inquire whether Sight be exclusively the sense which affords us a knowledge of extension, or whether it does this only conjunctly with Touch. As some philosophers have denied to vision all perception of extension and figure, and given this solely to touch, so others have equally refused this perception to touch, and accorded it exclusively to vision.

This doctrine is maintained among others by Platner, — a man no less celebrated as an acute philosopher, than as a learned physician, and an elegant scholar. I shall endeavor to render his philosophical German into intelligible English, and translate some of the preliminary sentences with which he introduces a curious observation by him on a blind subject. "It is very true, as my acute antagonist observes, that the gloomy extension which imagination presents to us as an actual object, is by no means the pure *a priori* representation of space. It is very true, that this is only an empirical or adventitious image, which itself supposes the pure or *a priori* notion of space (or of extension), in other words, the necessity to think every thing as extended. But I did not wish to explain the origin of this mental condition or form of thought objectively, through the sense of sight, but only to say this much: — that empirical space, empirical extension, is dependent on the sense of sight, — that, allowing space or extension, as a form of thought, to be in us, were there even nothing correspondent to it out of us, still the unknown external things must operate upon us, and, in fact, through the sense of sight, do operate upon us, if this unconscious form is to be brought into consciousness."

And after some other observations he goes on: "In regard to the visionless representation of space or extension, — the attentive observation of a person born blind, which I formerly instituted, in the year 1785, and, again, in relation to the point in question, have continued for three whole weeks, — this observation, I say, has convinced me, that the sense of touch, by itself, is altogether incompetent to afford us the representation of extension and space, and is not even cognizant of local exteriority; in a word, that a man deprived of sight has absolutely no perception of an outer world, beyond the existence of something effective, different from his own feeling of passivity, and in general only of the numerical diversity, — shall I say, of impressions, or of things? In fact, to those born blind, time serves instead of space. Vicinity and distance means in their mouths nothing more than the shorter or longer time, the smaller or greater number of feelings, which they find necessary to attain from some one feeling to some other. That a person blind from birth employs the language of vision, — that may occasion considerable error, and did, indeed, at the commencement of my observations, lead me wrong; but, in point of fact, he knows nothing of things as existing out of each other; and (this in particular I have very clearly remarked), if objects, and the parts of his body touched by them, did not make different kinds of impression on his nerves of sensation, he would take every thing external for one and the same. In his own body, he absolutely did not discriminate head and foot at all by their distance, but merely by the difference of the feelings (and his perception of such difference was incredibly fine), which he experienced from the one and from the other; and, moreover, through time. In like manner, in external bodies, he distinguished their figure merely by the varieties of impressed feelings; inasmuch, for example, as the cube, by its angles, affected his feeling differently from the sphere. No one can conceive how deceptive is the use of language accommodated to vision. When my acute antagonist appeals to Cheselden's case, which proves directly the reverse of what it is adduced to refute, he does not consider that the first visual impressions which one born blind receives after couching, do not constitute vision. For the very reason, that space and extension are empirically only possible through a perception of sight, — for that very reason, must such a patient, after his eyes are freed from the cataract, first learn to live in space; if he could do this previously, then would not the distant seem to him near, — the separate would not appear to him as one. These are the grounds which make it impossible for me to believe empirical space in a blind person; and from these I infer, that this form of sensibility, as Mr. Kant calls it, and which, in a certain signification, may very properly be styled a pure representation, cannot come into consciousness otherwise than through the medium of our visual perception; without, however, denying that it is something merely subjective, or affirming that sight affords any thing similar to this kind of representation. The example of blind geometers would likewise argue nothing against me, even if the geometers had been born blind; and this they were not, if, even in their early infancy, they had seen a single extended object."

Phænomena that support Platner's doctrine. — To what Platner has here stated I would add, from personal experiment and observation upon others, that if any one who is not blind will go into a room of an unusual shape, wholly unknown to him, and into which no ray of light is allowed to penetrate, he may grope about for hours, — he may touch and manipulate every side and corner of it; still, notwithstanding every endeavor, — notwithstanding all the previous subsidiary notions he brings to the task, he will be unable to form any correct idea of the room. In like manner, a blindfolded person will make the most curious mistakes in regard to the figure of objects presented to him, if these are of any considerable circumference. But if the sense of touch in such favorable circumstances can effect so little, how much less could it afford us any knowledge of forms, if the assistance which it here brings with it from our visual conceptions were wholly wanting?

This view is, I think, strongly confirmed by the famous case of a young gentleman, blind from birth, couched by Cheselden: — a case remarkable for being perhaps, of those cured, that in which the cataract was most perfect (it only allowed of a distinction of light and darkness); and, at the same time, in which the phænomena have been most distinctly described. In this latter respect, it is, however, very deficient; and it is saying but little in favor of the philosophical acumen of medical men, that the narrative of this case, with all its faults, is, to the present moment, the one most to be relied on.

Now I contend (though I am aware I have high authority against me), that if a blind man had been able to form a conception of a square or globe by mere touch, he would, on first perceiving them by sight, be able to discriminate them from each other; for this supposes only that he had acquired the primary notions of a straight and of a curved line. Again, if touch afforded us the notion of space or extension in general, the patient, on obtaining sight, would certainly be able to conceive the possibility of space or extension beyond the actual boundary of his vision. But of both of these Cheselden's patient was found incapable.

"Though we say of this gentleman, that he was blind," observes Mr. Cheselden, "as we do of all people who have ripe cataracts; yet they are never so blind from that cause but that they can discern day from night; and for the most part, in a strong light, distinguish black, white, and scarlet; but they cannot perceive the shape of any thing; for the light by which these perceptions are made, being let in obliquely through the aqueous humor, or the anterior surface of the crystalline (by which the rays cannot be brought into a focus upon the retina), they can discern in no other manner than a sound eye can through a glass of broken jelly, where a great variety of surfaces so differently refract the light, that the several distinct pencils of rays cannot be collected by the eye into their proper foci; wherefore the shape of an object in such a case cannot be at all discerned, though the color may; and thus it was with this young gentleman, who, though he knew those colors asunder in a good light, yet when he saw them after he was couched, the faint ideas he had of them before were not sufficient for him to know them by afterwards; and therefore he did not think them the same which he had before known by those names. . . . . When he first saw, he was so far from making any judgment about distances, that he thought all objects whatever touched his eyes (as he expressed it), as what he felt did his skin; and thought no objects so agreeable as those which were smooth and regular, though he could form no judgment of their shape, or guess what it was in any object that was pleasing to him. He knew not the shape of any thing, nor any one thing from another, however different in shape or magnitude:* but upon being told what things were, whose form he before knew from feeling, he would carefully observe, that he might know them again; but having too many objects to learn at once, he forgot many of them; and (as he said), at first learned to know, and again forgot a thousand things in a day. One particular only (though it may appear trifling), I will relate: Having often forgot which was the cat, and which the dog, he was ashamed to ask; but catching the cat (which he knew by feeling), he was observed to look at her steadfastly, and then setting her down, said, 'So, puss! I shall know you another time.' . . . . . We thought he soon knew what pictures represented which were showed to him, but we found afterwards we were mistaken; for about two months after he was couched, he discovered at once they represented

* [This cannot mean that he saw no difference between objects of different shapes and sizes; for if this interpretation were adopted, the rest of the statement becomes nonsense. If he had been altogether incapable of apprehending differences, it could not be said that, "being told what things were whose form he before knew from feeling, he would carefully observe that he might know them again;" for observation supposes the power of discrimination, and, in particular, the anecdote of the dog and cat would be inconceivable on that hypothesis. It is plain that Cheselden only meant to say, that the things which the patient could previously distinguish and denominate by touch, he could not now identify and refer to their appellations by sight. And this is what we might, *a priori*, be assured of. A sphere and a cube would certainly make different impressions on him; but it is probable that he could not assign to each its name, though, in this particular case, there is good ground for holding, that the slightest consideration would enable a person, previously acquainted with these figures, and aware that the one was a cube and the other a sphere, to connect them with his anterior experience, and to discriminate them by name.] —*Notes to Reid*.

solid bodies, when, to that time, he considered them only as parti-colored planes, or surfaces diversified with variety of paints; but even then he was no less surprised, expecting the pictures would feel like the things they represented, and was amazed when he found those parts, which by their light and shadow appeared now round and uneven, felt only flat like the rest; and asked which was the lying sense, feeling or seeing."

The whole of this matter is still enveloped in great uncertainty, and I should be sorry either to dogmatize myself, or to advise you to form any decided opinion. Without, however, going the length of Platner, in denying the possibility of a geometer blind from birth, we may allow this, and yet vindicate exclusively to sight the power of affording us our empirical notions of space. The explanation of this supposes, however, an acquaintance with the doctrine of pure or *a priori* space as a form of thought; it must, therefore, for the present be deferred.

How do we perceive visual distance. — The last question on which I shall touch, and with which I shall conclude the consideration of Perception in general, is, — How do we obtain our knowledge of Visual Distance? Is this original, or acquired? With regard to the method by which we judge of distance, it was formerly supposed to depend upon an original law of the constitution, and to be independent of any knowledge gained through the medium of the external senses. This opinion was attacked by Berkeley in his *New Theory of Vision,* one of the finest examples, as Dr. Smith justly observes, of philosophical analysis to be found in our own or in any other language; and in which it appears most clearly demonstrated, that our whole information on this subject is acquired by experience and association. This conclusion is supported by many circumstances of frequent occurrence, in which we fall into the greatest mistakes with respect to the distance of objects, when we form our judgment solely from the visible impression made upon the retina, without attending to the other circumstances which ordinarily direct us in forming our conclusions. It also obtains confirmation from the case of Cheselden, which I have already quoted. It clearly appears that, in the first instance, the patient had no correct ideas of distance; and we are expressly told that he supposed all objects to touch the eye, until he learned to correct his visible, by means of his tangible, impressions, and thus gradnally to acquire more correct notions of the situation of surrounding bodies with respect to his own person.

What enables us to estimate distance. — On the hypothesis that our ideas of distance are acquired, it remains for us to investigate the circumstances which assist us in forming our judgment respecting them. We shall find that they may be arranged under two heads, some of them depending upon certain states of the eye itself, and others upon various accidents that occur in the appearance of the objects. With respect to distances that are so short as to require the adjustment of the eye in order to obtain distinct vision, it appears that a certain voluntary effort is necessary to produce the desired effect: this effort, whatever may be its nature, causes a corresponding sensation, the amount of which we learn by experience to appreciate; and thus, through the medium of association, we acquire the power of estimating the distance with sufficient accuracy.

When objects are placed at only a moderate distance, but not such as to require the adjustment of the eye, in directing the two eyes to the object we incline them inwards; as is the case likewise with very short distances: so that what are termed the axes of the eyes, if produced, would make an angle at the object, the angle varying inversely as the distance. Here, as in the former case, we have certain perceptions excited by the muscular efforts necessary to produce a proper inclination of the axes, and these we learn to associate with certain distances. As a proof that this is the mode by which we judge of those distances where the optic axes form an appreciable angle, when the eyes are both directed to the same object, while the effort of adjustment is not perceptible, — it has been remarked, that persons who are deprived of the sight of one eye, are incapable of forming a correct judgment in this case.

When we are required to judge of still greater distances, where the object is so remote as that the axes of the two eyes are parallel, we are no longer able to form our opinion from any sensation in the eye itself. In this case, we have recourse to a variety of circumstances connected with the appearance of the object; for example, its apparent size, the distinctness with which it is seen, the vividness of its colors, the number of intervening objects, and other similar accidents, all of which obviously depend upon previous experience, and which we are in the habit of associating with different distances, without, in each particular case, investigating the cause on which our judgment is founded.*

But animals have an instinctive perception of distance.— The conclusions of science seem in this case to be decisive; and yet the whole question is thrown into doubt by the analogy of the lower animals. If, in man, the perception of distance be not original but acquired, the perception of distance must be also acquired by them. But as this is not the case in regard to animals, this confirms the reasoning of those who would explain the perception of distance in man as an original, not as an acquired, knowledge. That the Berkeleian doctrine is opposed

* [We must be careful not, like Reid and philosophers in general, to confound the perceptions of mere *externality* or *outness*, and the knowledge we may have of *distance*, through the eye. The former may be, and probably is, natural; while the latter, in a great but unappreciable measure, is acquired. In the case of Cheselden — that in which the blindness previous to the recovery of sight was most perfect, and therefore the most instructive upon record — the patient, though he had little or no perception of *distance*, i. e. of the *degree of externality*, had still a perception of that externality absolutely. The objects, he said, seemed to "touch his eyes, as what he felt did his skin;" but they did not appear to him as if *in* his eyes, far less as a mere affection of the organ. This natural perception of outness, which is the foundation of our acquired knowledge of distance, seems given us in the natural perception we have of the direction of the rays of light.

In like manner, we must not confound, as is commonly done, the fact of the eye affording us a perception of *extension* and *plane figure*, or outline, in the perception of colors, and the fact of its being the vehicle of intimations in regard to the comparative magnitude and cubical forms of the objects from which these rays proceed. The one is a knowledge by sense — natural, immediate, and infallible; the other, like that of distance, is by inference — acquired, mediate, and at best, always insecure]. — *Notes to Reid.*

by the analogy of the lower animals, is admitted by one of its most intelligent supporters, — Dr. Adam Smith.

"That, antecedent to all experience," says Smith, "the young of at least the greater part of animals possess some instinctive perception of this kind, seems abundantly evident. The hen never feeds her young by dropping the food into their bills, as the linnet and the thrush feed theirs. Almost as soon as her chickens are hatched, she does not feed them, but carries them to the field to feed, where they walk about at their ease, it would seem, and appear to have the most distinct perception of all the tangible objects which surround them. We may often see them, accordingly, by the straightest road, run to and pick up any little grains which she shows them, even at the distance of several yards; and they no sooner come into the light than they seem to understand this language of Vision as well as they ever do afterwards. The young of the partridge and the grouse seem to have, at the same early period, the most distinct perceptions of the same kind. The young partridge, almost as soon as it comes from the shell, runs about among long grass and corn, the young grouse among long heath; and both would most essentially hurt themselves, if they had not the most acute as well as distinct perception of the tangible objects, which not only surround them, but press upon them on all sides. This is the case, too, with the young of the goose, of the duck, and, so far as I have been able to observe, with those of at least the greater part of the birds which make their nests upon the ground, with the greater part of those which are ranked by Linnæus in the orders of the hen and the goose, and of many of those long-shanked and wading birds which he places in the order that he distinguishes by the name of Grallæ. . . . . .

"It seems difficult to suppose that man is the only animal of which the young are not endowed with some instinctive perception of this kind. The young of the human species, however, continue so long in a state of entire dependency, they must be so long carried about in the arms of their mothers or of their nurses, that such an instinctive perception may seem less necessary to them than to any other race of animals. Before it could be of any use to them, observation and experience may, by the known principle of the association of ideas, have sufficiently connected in their young minds each visible object with the corresponding tangible one which it is fitted to represent. Nature, it may be said, never bestows upon any animal any faculty which is not either necessary or useful; and an instinct of this kind would be altogether useless to an animal which must necessarily acquire the knowledge which the instinct is given to supply, long before that instinct could be of any use to it.

Children, however, appear at so very early a period to know the distance, the shape, and magnitude of the different tangible objects which are presented to them, that I am disposed to believe that even they may have some instinctive perception of this kind; though possibly in a much weaker degree than the greater part of other animals. A child that is scarcely a month old, stretches out its hands to feel any little plaything that is presented to it. It distinguishes its nurse, and the other people who are much about it, from strangers. It clings to the former, and turns away from the latter. Hold a small looking-glass before a child of not more than two or three months old, and it will stretch out its little arms behind the glass, in order to feel the child which it sees, and which it imagines is at the back of the glass. It is deceived, no doubt; but even this sort of deception sufficiently demonstrates, that it has a tolerably distinct apprehension of the ordinary perspective of Vision, which it cannot well have learnt from observation and experience." *

* [That animals should be enabled *by instinct* to see as soon as they are born, while man, gifted with reason, is obliged to learn slowly, *through experience*, how to see, — is no more remarkable than that birds and spiders should be taught by instinct, without experience or instruction, how to construct their habitations and nets, while man can build neither except he has had opportunities to learn from others, or from his own unsuccessful efforts. It is the distinguishing peculiarity of instinct to learn nothing from experience, and of reason to learn every thing from experience]. — *Am. Ed.*

CHAPTER XXI.

THE PRESENTATIVE FACULTY. — RECAPITULATION. — II. SELF-CONSCIOUSNESS.

HAVING concluded the consideration of External Perception, I may now briefly recapitulate certain results of the discussion, and state in what principal respects the doctrine I would maintain, differs from that of Reid and Stewart, whom I suppose always to hold, in reality, the system of an Intuitive Perception.

[*Author's doctrine of Perception, in contrast to that of Reid, Stewart, Royer-Collard, and other philosophers of the Scottish School.** — 1. [They hold that] Perception (proper) is the *Notion* or *Conception* of an object *instinctively suggested, excited, inspired*, or, as it were, *conjured up, on occasion*, or *at the sign*, of a Sensation (proper).

On the contrary, I hold, in general, that as Perception, in either form, is an immediate or presentative, not a mediate or representative, cognition, that a Perception proper is not, and ought not to be called, a Notion or Conception. And I hold in par-

* I here contrast my own doctrine of perception with that of the philosophers in question, not because their views and mine are those at farthest variance on the point, but on the contrary, precisely because they thereon approximate the nearest. I have already shown that the doctrine touching Perception held by Reid (and, in the present relation, he and his two illustrious followers are in almost all respects at one) is ambiguous. For while some of its statements seem to harmonize exclusively with the conditions of Natural Presentationism, others, again, appear only compatible with those of an Egoistical Representationism. Maintaining, as I do, the former doctrine, it is, of course, only the positions conformable to the latter, which it is, at present, necessary to adduce.

ticular, that, on the one hand, in the consciousness of sensations, out of each other, contrasted, limited, and variously arranged, we have a Perception proper of the Primary qualities, in an externality to the mind, though not to the nervous organism, as an immediate cognition, and not merely as a notion or concept of something extended, figured, etc.; and on the other, as a correlative contained in the consciousness of our voluntary motive energy resisted, and not resisted by aught within the limits of mind and its subservient organs, we have a Perception proper of the Secundo-primary quality of resistance, in an extra-organic force, as an immediate cognition, and not merely as a notion or concept, of a resisting something external to our body; — though certainly in either case, there may be, and probably is, a concomitant act of imagination, by which the whole complex consciousness on the occasion is filled up.

2. [They hold that,] on occasion of the Sensation (proper) along with the notion or conception which constitutes the Perception (proper) of the external object, there is *blindly created* in us, or *instinctively determined*, an invincible *belief* in its existence.

On the contrary, I hold, that we only believe in the existence of what we perceive, as extended, figured, resisting, etc., inasmuch as we believe that we are *conscious of these qualities as existing;* consequently, that a belief in the existence of an extended world, external to the mind, and even external to the organism, is not a faith blindly created or instinctively determined, in supplement of a representative or mediate cognition, but exists in, as an integral constituent of, Perception proper, as an act of intuitive or immediate knowledge.

3. [They hold that] the object of Perception (proper) is a *conclusion*, or *inference*, or *result* (instinctive, indeed, not ratiocinative), from a Sensation proper.

On the contrary, I hold, that the object of Perception proper is given immediately, in and along with the object of Sensation proper.

4. [They hold that] Sensation (proper) *precedes*, Perception (proper) *follows*.

On the contrary, I hold, that though Sensation proper be the condition of, and therefore anterior to, Perception proper in the order of nature, that, in the order of time, both are necessarily coexistent, — the latter being only realized in and through the present existence of the former. Thus, visual extension cannot be perceived, or even imagined, except under the sensation of color; while color, again, cannot be apprehended or imagined, without, respectively, a concomitant apprehension or phantasm of extension.

5. [They hold that] Sensation (proper) is not only an antecedent, but an *arbitrary antecedent*, of Perception (proper). The former is only a sign on occasion of which the latter follows; they have no necessary or even natural connection; and it is only by the will of God, that we do not perceive the qualities of external objects independently of any sensitive affection. This last, indeed, seems to be actually the case in the perception of visible extension and figure.

On the contrary, I hold that Sensation proper is the universal condition of Perception proper. We are never aware even of the existence of our organism except as it is somehow affected; and are only conscious of extension, figure, and the other objects of Perception proper, as realized in the relations of the affections of our sentient organism, as a body extended, figured, etc. As to color and visible extension, neither can be apprehended, neither can be even imagined, apart from the other.

6. [They hold that,] in a Sensation (proper) of the Secondary qualities, as affections in us, we have a *Perception (proper) of them as properties in objects* and causes of the affections in us.

On the contrary, I hold, that as Perception proper is an immediate cognition; and as the Secondary qualities, in bodies, are only inferred, and therefore only mediately known to exist, as occult causes of manifest effects; that these, at best only objects of a mediate knowledge, are not objects of Perception.

7. [They hold that,] in like manner, in the case of various other bodily affections, as the toothache, gout, etc., we have not only a Sensation proper of the painful feeling, but a conception and belief, i. e. a *Perception (proper), of its cause.*

On the contrary, and for the same reason, I hold, that there is in this case no such Perception.

8. [They hold that] Sensation (proper) is an affection *purely of the mind*, and not in any way an affection of the body.

On the contrary, I hold with Aristotle, indeed, with philosophers in general, that Sensation is an affection neither of the body alone, nor of the mind alone, but of the composite of which each is a constituent; and that the subject of Sensation may be indifferently said to be our organism (as animated), or our soul (as united with an organism). For instance, hunger or color are, as apprehended, neither modes of mind apart from body, nor modes of body apart from mind.

9. [They hold that] Sensations (proper), as merely affections of the mind, have *no locality* in the body, no locality at all. From this the inference is necessary, that, though conscious of the relative place and reciprocal outness of sensations, we do not, in this consciousness, apprehend any real externality and extension.

On the contrary, I hold, that Sensation proper, being the consciousness of an affection, not of the mind alone, but of the mind as it is united with the body, that in the consciousness of sensations, relatively localized and reciprocally external, we have a veritable apprehension, and consequently, an immediate perception, of the affected organism, as extended, divided, figured, etc. This alone is the doctrine of Natural Realism, of Common Sense.

10. [They hold that,] in the case of Sensation (proper) and the Secondary qualities, there is a *determinate quality in certain bodies*, exclusively competent to cause a determinate sensation in us, as color, odor, savor, etc.; consequently, that from the fact of a similar internal effect, we are warranted to infer the existence of a similar external concause.

On the contrary, I hold, that a similar sensation only implies a similar idiopathic affection of the nervous organism; but such affection requires only the excitation of an appropriate stimulus; while such stimulus may be supplied by manifold agents of the most opposite nature, both from within the body and from without.

11. [They hold that] Perception excludes *memory;* Perception (proper) cannot therefore be apprehensive of *motion.*

On the contrary, I hold, that as memory, or a certain continuous representation, is a condition of consciousness, it is a condition of Perception; and that motion, therefore, cannot, on this ground, be denied as an object apprehended through sense.

12. [They hold that] an *apprehension of relations* is not an act of Perception (proper).

On the contrary, I hold, in general, that as all consciousness is realized only in the apprehension of the relations of plurality and contrast; and as perception is a consciousness; that the apprehension of relation cannot, *simpliciter*, be denied to perception: and, in particular, that unless we annihilate Perception proper, by denying to it the recognition of its peculiar objects, Extension, Figure, and the other Primary qualities, we cannot deny to it the recognition of relations; for, to say nothing of the others, Extension is perceived only in apprehending sensations out of sensations — a relation; and Figure is only perceived in apprehending one perceived extension as limited, and limited in a certain manner by another — a complexus of relations.

13. [They hold that] *distant* realities are objects of Perception (proper).

On the contrary, I hold, that the mind perceives nothing external to itself, except the affections of the organism as animated, the reciprocal relations of these affections, and the correlative involved in the consciousness of its locomotive energy being resisted.

14. [They hold that] objects not in contact with the organs of sense are perceived by a *medium.*

On the contrary, I hold, that the only object perceived is the organ itself, as modified, or what is in contact with the organ, as resisting.

15. [They hold that] *Extension* and *Figure* are first perceived through the sensations of *Touch.*

On the contrary, I hold, that, (unless by Extension be understood only extension in the three dimensions, as Reid in fact seems to do, but not Stewart,) this is erroneous; for an extension is apprehended in the apprehension of the reciprocal externality of all sensations. Moreover, to allow even the statement as thus restricted to pass, it would be necessary to suppose, that under Touch, it is meant to comprehend the consciousness of the Locomotive energy and of the Muscular feelings.

16. [They hold that] *Externality* is exclusively perceived on occasion of the sensations of *Touch*.

On the contrary, I hold, that it is, primarily, in the consciousness of our locomotive energy being resisted, and, secondarily, through the sensations of muscular feeling, that the perception of Externality is realized. All this, however, might be confusedly involved in the Touch of the philosophers in question.

17. [They hold that] *real* (or absolute) *magnitude* is an object of perception (proper) through *Touch*, but through Touch only.

On the contrary, I hold, that the magnitude perceived through touch is as purely relative as that perceived through vision or any other sense; for the same magnitude does not appear the same to touch at one part of the body and to touch at another.

18. [They hold that] *Color*, though a Secondary quality, is an object, not of Sensation (proper), but of Perception (proper); in other words, we perceive Color, not as an affection of our own minds, but as a quality of external things.

On the contrary, I hold, that Color, in itself, as apprehended or immediately known by us, is a mere affection of the sentient organism; and therefore, like the other Secondary qualities, an object not of Perception, but of Sensation, proper. The only distinguishing peculiarity in this case lies in the three following circumstances: — a) That the organic affection of Color, though not altogether indifferent, still, being accompanied by comparatively little pleasure, comparatively little pain, the apprehension of this affection, *qua* affection, i. e. its Sensation proper, is, consequently, always at a minimum. — b) That the passion of Color first rising into consciousness, not from the amount of the intensive quantity of the affection, but from the amount of the extensive quantity of the organism affected, is necessarily apprehended under the condition of extension. — c) That the isolation, tenuity, and delicacy of the ultimate filaments of the optic nerve afford us sensations minutely and precisely distinguished, sensations realized in consciousness only as we are conscious of them as out of each other in space. — These circumstances show, that while, in vision, Perception proper is at its maximum, and Sensation proper at its minimum, the sensation of Color cannot be realized apart from the perception of extension: but they do not warrant the assertions, that Color is not, like the other Secondary qualities, apprehended by us as a mere sensorial affection, and, therefore, an object, not of Sensation proper, but of Perception proper.] — *Diss. supp. to Reid.*

Sensation and Perception do not always coexist in the same degree of intensity, but they are equally original; and it is only by an act not of the easiest abstraction, that we are able to discriminate them scientifically from each other. So much for the first of the two faculties by which we acquire knowledge, — the faculty of External Perception.

The faculty of Self-consciousness. — The second of these faculties is Self-consciousness, which has likewise received, among others, the name of Internal or Reflex Perception. This faculty will not occupy us long, as the principal questions regarding its nature and operation have been already considered, in treating of Consciousness in general.

I formerly showed that it is impossible to distinguish Perception, or the other Special Faculties, from Consciousness, — in other words, to reduce Consciousness itself to a special faculty; and that the attempt to do so by the Scottish philosophers is self-contradictory. I stated, however, that though it be incompetent to establish a faculty for the immediate knowledge of the external world, and a faculty for the immediate knowledge of the internal, as two ultimate powers, exclusive of each other, and not merely subordinate forms of a higher immediate knowledge, under which they are comprehended or carried up into one, — I stated, I say, that though the immediate knowledges of matter and of mind are still only modifications of Consciousness, yet that their discrimination, as subaltern faculties, is both allowable and convenient. Accordingly, in the scheme which I gave you of the distribution of Consciousness into its special modes, — I distinguished a faculty of External, and a faculty of Internal, Apprehension, constituting together a more general modification of Consciousness, which I called the Acquisitive, or Presentative, or Receptive Faculty.

In regard to Self-consciousness, — the faculty of Internal Experience, — philosophers have been far more harmonious than in regard to External Perception. In fact, their differences touching this faculty originate rather in the ambiguities of language, and the different meanings attached to the same form of expression, than in any fundamental opposition of opinion in regard to its reality and nature. It is admitted equally by all to exist, and to exist as a source of knowledge; and the supposed differences of philosophers in this respect are, as I shall show you, mere errors in the historical statement of their opinions.

Self-consciousness contrasted with Perception. — The sphere and character of this faculty of acquisition will be best illustrated by contrasting it with the other. Perception is the power by which we are made aware of the phænomena of the External world; Self-consciousness, the power by which we apprehend the phænomena of the Internal. The objects of the former are all presented to us in Space and Time; space and time are thus the two conditions, — the two fundamental *forms*, of External Perception.* The objects of the latter are all apprehended by

* [Kant, first, made our actual world one merely of illusion. Time and Space, under which we must perceive and think, he reduced to mere subjective spectral forms, which have no real archetype in the noumenal or real universe. We can infer nothing from this, [the actual, world,] to that, [the noumenal or real universe. The law of] Cause and Effect governs thing and thought in the world of Space and Time; [this law does] not subsist where Time and Space have no reality. Kant, secondly, made Reason, Intelligence, contradict itself in its legitimate exercise. Antinomy [contradiction] is part and parcel of its nature. Thus, scepticism — the conviction that we live in a world of unreality and illusion, and that our very faculty of knowledge is only given us to mislead, is the result of [Kant's philosophy].

On the contrary, my doctrine holds, first, that Space and Time, as given,

us in Time and in Self; time and self are thus the two conditions, — the two fundamental forms, of Internal Perception or Self-consciousness. Time is thus a form or condition common to both faculties; while Space is a form peculiar to the one, Self a form peculiar to the other. What I mean by the *form* or *condition* of a faculty, is that frame, — that setting (if I may so speak), out of which no object can be known. Thus, we only know, through Self-consciousness, the phænomena of the Internal world, as modifications of the indivisible Ego or conscious unit;

are real forms of thought and conditions of things; and, secondly, that Intelligence, Reason, within its legitimate limits, is legitimate; within this sphere, it never deceives; and it is only when transcending this sphere, when founding on its illegitimate as on its legitimate exercise, that it affords a contradictory result.

Kant holds the subjectivity of Space (and Time), and, if he does not deny, will not affirm the existence of a real space, external to our minds; because it is a mere form of our perceptive faculty. He holds that we have no knowledge of any external thing as really existing, and that all our perceptions are merely appearances, *i. e.* subjective representations, — subjective modifications, — which the mind is determined to exhibit, as an apparently objective opposition to itself, — its pure and real subjective modifications. Yet, while he gives up the external existence of space, as beyond the sphere of consciousness, he holds the reality of external material existences (things in themselves), which are equally beyond the sphere of consciousness. It was incumbent on him to render a reason for this seeming inconsistency, and to explain how his system was not, in its legitimate conclusions, an universal Idealism; and he has accordingly attempted to establish, by necessary inference, what his philosophy could not accept as an immediate fact of consciousness.

Kant endeavored to evince that pure Reason, that Intelligence, is naturally, is necessarily, repugnant with itself, and that speculation ends in a series of insoluble antilogies. In its highest potence, in its very essence, thought is thus infected with contradiction; and the worst and most pervading scepticism is the melancholy result. If I have done any thing meritorious in philosophy, it is in the attempt to explain the phænomena of these contradictions; in showing that they arise only when intelligence transcends the limits to which its legitimate exercise is restricted; and that, within these bounds (the Conditioned), natural thought is neither fallible nor mendacious — "Neque decipitur, nec decipit umquam." If this view be correct, Kant's antinomies, with their consequent scepticism, are solved; and the human mind, however weak, is shown not to be the work of a treacherous Creator.] — *Appendix.*

we only know, through Perception, the phænomena of the External world, under Space, or as modifications of the extended and divisible Non-ego or known plurality. That the forms are native, not adventitious, to the mind, is involved in their necessity. What I cannot but think, must be *a priori*, or original to thought; it cannot be engendered by experience upon custom. But this is not a subject the discussion of which concerns us at present.

It may be asked, if self, or Ego, be the form of Self-consciousness, why is the not-self, the Non-ego, not in like manner called the form of Perception? To this I reply, that the not-self is only a negation, and, though it discriminates the objects of the external cognition from those of the internal, it does not afford to the former any positive bond of union among themselves. This, on the contrary, is supplied to them by the form of Space, out of which they can neither be perceived, nor imagined by the mind; — Space, therefore, as the positive condition under which the Non-ego is necessarily known and imagined, and through which it receives its unity in consciousness, is properly said to afford the condition, or *form*, of External Perception.

The mind itself is not extended. — But a more important question may be started. If Space, — if extension, be a necessary form of thought, this, it may be argued, proves that the mind itself is extended. The reasoning here proceeds upon the assumption, that the qualities of the subject knowing must be similar to the qualities of the object known. This, as I have already stated, is a mere philosophical crotchet, — an assumption without a shadow even of probability in its favor. That the mind has the power of perceiving extended objects, is no ground for holding that it is itself extended. Still less can it be maintained, that because it has ideally a native or necessary conception of space, it must really occupy space. Nothing can be more absurd. On this doctrine, to exist as extended is supposed necessary in order to think extension. But if this analogy hold good, the sphere of *ideal* space, which the mind can imagine, ought to be limited to the sphere, of *real* space which the mind actually fills. This is not, however, the case; for though the mind be not absolutely unlimited in its power of conceiving space, still the compass of thought may be viewed as infinite in this respect, as contrasted with the petty point of extension, which the advocates of the doctrine in question allow it to occupy in its corporeal domicil.

Two modes of treating the phænomena of Self-consciousness. — The faculty of self-consciousness affords us a knowledge of the phænomena of our minds. It is the source of internal experience. You will, therefore, observe, that, like External Perception, it only furnishes us with facts; and that the use we make of these facts, — that is, what we find in them, what we deduce from them, — belongs to a different process of intelligence. Self-consciousness affords the materials equally to all systems of philosophy; all equally admit it, and all elaborate the materials which this faculty supplies, according to their fashion. And here I may merely notice, by the way, what, in treating of the Regulative Faculty, will fall to be regularly discussed, that these facts, these materials, may be considered in two ways. We may employ *either Induction alone, or also Analysis.* If we merely consider the phænomena which Self-consciousness reveals, in relation to each other, — merely compare them together, and generalize the qualities which they display in common, and thus arrange them into classes or groups governed by the same laws, we perform the process of Induction. By this process, we obtain *what is general, but not what is necessary.* For example, having observed that external objects presented in perception are extended, we generalize the notion of extension or space. We have thus explained the possibility of a conception of space, but only of space as a general and contingent notion; for if we hold that this notion exists in the mind only as the result of such a process, we must hold it to be *a posteriori* or adventitious, and, therefore, contingent. Such is the process of Induction, or of Simple Observation. The other process, that of Analysis or Criticism, does not rest satisfied with this comparison and generalization, which it, however, supposes. It proposes, not merely to find what is general in the phænomena, but *what is necessary and universal.* It, accordingly, takes mental phænomena, and, by abstraction, throws aside all that it is able to detach, without annihilating the phænomena altogether; — in short, it analyzes thought into its essential or necessary, and its accidental or contingent, elements.

All necessity to us is subjective. — Thus, from Observation and Induction, we discover what experience *affords* as its general result; from Analysis and Criticism, we discover what experience *supposes* as its necessary condition. You will notice, that the critical analysis of which I now speak, is limited to the objects of our internal observation; for in the phænomena of mind alone can we be conscious of absolute necessity. All necessity is, in fact, to us subjective; for a thing is conceived impossible, only as we are unable to construe it in thought. Whatever does not violate the laws of thought is, therefore, not to us impossible, however firmly we may believe that it will not occur. For example, we hold it absolutely impossible, that a thing can begin to be without a cause. Why? Simply because the mind cannot realize to itself the conception of absolute commencement. That a stone should ascend into the air, we firmly believe will never happen; but we find no difficulty in conceiving it possible. Why? Merely because gravitation is only a fact generalized by induction and observation; and its negation, therefore, violates no law of thought. When we talk, therefore, of the *necessity* of any *external* phænomenon, the expression is improper, if the necessity be only an inference of induction, and not involved in any canon of intelligence. For Induction proves to us *only what is, not what must be,* — the actual, not the necessary.

Use of the Inductive and Critical Methods in philosophy. — The two processes of Induction or Observation, and of Analysis or Criticism, have been variously employed by different philosophers. Locke, for instance, limited himself to the former, overlooking altogether the latter. He, accordingly, discovered nothing necessary, or *a priori*, in the phænomena of our internal experience. To him, all axioms are only generalizations of experience. In this respect, he was greatly excelled by Descartes and Leibnitz. The latter, indeed, was the philosopher who clearly enunciated the principle, that the phænomenon of necessity, in our cognitions, could not be explained on the ground of experience. "All the examples," he says, "which confirm a general truth, how numerous soever, would not suffice to establish the universal necessity of this same truth; for it does not follow, that what has hitherto occurred will always occur in future." "If Locke," he adds, "had sufficiently considered the difference between truths which are necessary or demonstrative, and those which we infer from induction alone, he would have perceived that necessary truths could only be proved from principles which command our assent by their intuitive evidence; inasmuch as our senses can inform us only of what is, not of what must necessarily be." Leibnitz, however, was not himself fully aware of the import of the principle; — at least, he failed in carrying it out to its most important applications; and though he triumphantly demonstrated, in opposition to Locke, the *a priori* character of many of those cognitions which Locke had derived from experience, yet he left to Kant the honor of having been the first who fully applied the Critical analysis in the philosophy of mind.

Has Locke been misrepresented by his French disciples? — The faculty of Self-consciousness corresponds with the Reflection of Locke. Now, there is an interesting question concerning this faculty; — whether the philosophy of Locke has been misapprehended and misrepresented by Condillac, and other of his French disciples, as Mr. Stewart maintains; or, whether Mr. Stewart has not himself attempted to vindicate the tendency of Locke's philosophy on grounds which will not bear out his conclusions. Mr. Stewart has canvassed this point at considerable length, [and by him] the point at issue is thus briefly stated: "the objections to which Locke's doctrine concerning the origin of our ideas, or, in other words, concerning the sources of our knowledge, are, in my judgment, liable, I have stated so fully in a former work, that I shall not touch on them here. It is quite sufficient, on the present occasion, to remark, how very unjustly this doctrine (imperfect, on the most favorable construction, as it undoubtedly is) has been confounded with those of Gassendi, of Condillac, of Diderot, and of Horne Tooke. The substance of all that is common in the conclusions of these last writers, cannot be better expressed than in the words of their master, Gassendi. 'All our knowledge,' he observes in a letter to Descartes, 'appears plainly to derive its origin from the senses; and although you deny the maxim, "Quicquid est intellectu præesse debere in sensu," [Whatever is in the intellect must have previously been in the faculty of sense,] yet this maxim appears, nevertheless, to be true; since our knowledge is all ultimately obtained by an *influx* or *incursion* from things external; which knowledge afterwards undergoes various modifications, by means of analogy, composition, division, amplification, extenuation, and other similar processes, which it is unnecessary to enumerate.' This doctrine of Gassendi's coincides exactly with that ascribed to Locke by Diderot and by Horne Tooke; and it differs only verbally from the more concise statement of Condillac, that '*our ideas are nothing more than transformed sensations.*' 'Every idea,' says the first of these writers, 'must necessarily, when brought to its state of ultimate decomposition, resolve itself into a sensible representation or picture; and since every thing in our understanding has been introduced there by the channel of sensation, whatever proceeds out of the understanding is either chimerical, or must be able, in returning by the same road, to reattach itself to its sensible archetype. Hence an important rule in philosophy,—that every expression which cannot find an external and a sensible object, to which it can thus establish its affinity, is destitute of signification.' Such is the exposition given by Diderot, of what is regarded in France as Locke's great and capital discovery; and precisely to the same purpose we are told by Condorcet, that 'Locke was the first who proved that all our ideas are compounded of sensations.' If this were to be admitted as a fair account of Locke's opinion, it would follow that he has not advanced a single step beyond Gassendi and Hobbes; both of whom have repeatedly expressed themselves in nearly the same words with Diderot and Condorcet. But although it must be granted, in favor of their interpretation of his language, that various detached passages may be quoted from his work, which seem, on a superficial view, to justify their comments; yet of what weight, it may be asked, are these passages, when compared with the stress laid by the author on *Reflection*, as an original source of our ideas, altogether different from *Sensation?* 'The other fountain,' says Locke, 'from which experience furnisheth the understanding with ideas, is the perception of the operations of our own minds within us, as it is employed about the ideas it has got; which operations, when the soul comes to reflect on and consider, do furnish the understanding with another set of ideas, which could not be had from things without; and such are Perception, Thinking, Doubting, Believing, Reasoning, Knowing, Willing, and all the different actings of our own minds, which, we being conscious of, and observing in ourselves, do from these receive into our understandings ideas as distinct as we do from bodies affecting our senses. This source of ideas every man has wholly in himself; and though it be not sense, as having nothing to do with external objects, yet it is very like it, and might properly enough be called *Internal Sense.* But as I call the other Sensation, so I call this Reflection; the ideas it affords being such only as the mind gets by reflecting on its own operations within itself.' Again, 'The understanding seems to me not to have the least glimmering of any ideas which it does not receive from one of these two. External objects furnish the mind with the ideas of sensible qualities; and the mind furnishes the understanding with ideas of its own operations.' "

Stewart's vindication unsatisfactory. — On these observations I must remark, that they do not at all satisfy me; and I cannot but regard Locke and Gassendi as exactly upon a par, and both as deriving all our knowledge from experience.* The French philosophers are, therefore, in my opinion, fully justified in their interpretation of Locke's philosophy; and Condillac must, I think, be viewed as having simplified the doctrine of his master, without doing the smallest violence to its spirit. In the first place,

* [True; but from experience *by way both of sensation and reflection;* and not from experience *by way of sensation alone.*] — *Am. Ed.*

I cannot concur with Mr. Stewart in allowing any weight to Locke's distinction of Reflection, or Self-consciousness, as a second source of our knowledge. Such a source of experience no sensualist ever denied, because no sensualist ever denied that sense was cognizant of itself. It makes no difference that Locke distinguished Reflection from Sense, "as having nothing to do with external objects," admitting, however, that "they are very like," and that Reflection "might properly enough be called Internal Sense," while Condillac makes it only a modification of sense. It is a matter of no importance that we do not call Self-consciousness by the name of *Sense*, if we allow that it is only conversant about the contingent. Now, no interpretation of Locke can ever pretend to find in his Reflection a revelation to him of aught native or necessary to the mind, beyond the capability to act and suffer in certain manners, — a capability which no philosophy ever dreamt of denying. And if this be the case, it follows, that the formal reduction, by Condillac, of Reflection to Sensation, is only a consequent following out of the principles of the doctrine itself.

The philosophy of Gassendi. — Of how little import is the distinction of Reflection from Sensation, in the philosophy of Locke, is equally shown in the philosophy of Gassendi; in regard to which I must correct a fundamental error of Mr. Stewart. I had formerly occasion to point out to you the unaccountable mistake of this very learned philosopher, in relation to Locke's use of the term Reflection, which, both in his *Essays* and his *Dissertation*, he states was a word first employed by Locke in its psychological signification. Nothing, I stated, could be more incorrect. When adopted by Locke, it was a word of universal currency, in a similar sense, in every contemporary system of philosophy, and had been so employed for at least a thousand years previously. This being understood, Mr. Stewart's mistake in regard to Gassendi is less surprising. "The word *Reflection*," says Mr. Stewart, "expresses the peculiar and characteristical doctrine, by which Locke's system is distinguished from that of the Gassendists and Hobbists. All this, however, serves only to prove still more clearly, how widely remote his real opinion on this subject was from that commonly ascribed to him by the French and German commentators. For my own part, I do not think, notwithstanding some casual expressions which may seem to favor the contrary supposition, that Locke would have hesitated for a moment to admit, with Cudworth and Price, that the *Understanding* is itself a source of new ideas. That it is by *Reflection*, (which, according to its own definition, means merely the exercise of the *Understanding* on the internal phenomena,) that we get our ideas of Memory, Imagination, Reasoning, and of all other intellectual powers, Mr. Locke has again and again told us; and from this principle it is so obvious an inference, that all the simple ideas, which are necessarily implied in our intellectual operations, are ultimately to be referred to the same source, that we cannot reasonably suppose a philosopher of Locke's sagacity to admit the former proposition, and to withhold his assent to the latter."

The inference which, in the latter part of this quotation, Mr. Stewart speaks of, is not so obvious as he supposes, seeing that it was not till Leibnitz that the character of necessity was enounced, and clearly enounced, as the criterion by which to discriminate the native from the adventitious cognitions of the mind. This is, indeed, shown by the example of Gassendi himself, who is justly represented by Mr. Stewart as a Sensationalist of the purest water; but wholly misrepresented by him, as distinguished from Locke by his negation of any faculty corresponding to Locke's Reflection. So far is this from being correct, — Gassendi not only allowed a faculty of Self-consciousness analogous to the Reflection of Locke, he actually held such a faculty, and even attributed to it far higher functions than did the English philosopher; nay, what is more, held it under the very name of Reflection. In fact, from the French philosopher Locke borrowed this, as he did the principal part of his whole philosophy; and it is saying but little either for the patriotism or intelligence of their countrymen, that the works of Gassendi and Descartes should have been so long eclipsed in France by those of Locke, who was in truth only a follower of the one, and a mistaken refuter of the other. In respect to Gassendi, there are reasons that explain this neglect apart from any want of merit in himself; for he is a thinker fully equal to Locke in independence and vigor of intellect, and, with the exception of Leibnitz, he is, of all the great philosophers of modern times, the most varied and profound in learning.

Gassendi's division of the phænomena of mind. — Now, in regard to the point at issue, so far is Gassendi from assimilating Reflection to Sense, as Locke virtually, if not expressly, does, and for which assimilation he has been principally lauded by those of his followers who analyzed every mental process into Sensation, — so far, I say, is Gassendi from doing this, that he places Sense and Reflection at the opposite mental poles, making the former a mental function wholly dependent upon the bodily organism; the latter, an energy of intellect wholly inorganic and abstract from matter. The cognitive phænomena of mind Gassendi reduces to three general classes of faculties: — 1°. Sense, 2°. Phantasy (or Imagination), and 3°. Intellect. The two former are, however, virtually one, inasmuch as Phantasy, on his doctrine, is only cognizant about the forms which it receives from Sense, and is, equally with Sense, dependent on a corporeal organ. Intellect, on the contrary, he holds, is not so dependent, and that its functions are, therefore, of a kind superior to those of an organic faculty. These functions or faculties of Intellect he reduces to three. "The first," he says, "is Intellectual Apprehension, — that is, the apprehension of things which are beyond the reach of Sense, and which, consequently, leaving no trace in the brain, are also beyond the ken of Imagination. Such, especially, is spiritual or incorporeal nature, as, for example, the Deity. For although in speaking of God, we say that He is incorporeal, yet in attempting to realize Him to Phantasy, we only imagine something with the attributes of body. It must not, however, be supposed that this is all; for besides and above the corporeal form which we thus imagine, there is, at the same time, another conception, which that form contributes, as it were, to veil and obscure. This conception is not confined to the narrow limits of Phantasy; it is proper to Intellect; and, therefore, such an apprehension ought not to be called an *imagination*, but an *intelligence* or *intellection*." In his doctrine of Intellect, Gassendi takes, indeed, far higher ground than Locke; and it is a total reversal of his doctrine, when it is stated, that he allowed to the mind no different, no higher, apprehensions than the derivative images of Sense. He says, indeed, and he says truly, that if we attempt to figure out the Deity in imagination, we cannot depict Him in that faculty, except under sensible forms — as, for example, under the form of a venerable old man. But does he not condemn this attempt as derogatory? and does he not allow us an intellectual conception of the Divinity, superior to the grovelling conditions of Phantasy? The Cartesians, however, were too well disposed to overlook the limits under which Gassendi had advanced his doctrine, — that the senses are the source of all our knowledge; and Mr. Stewart has adopted, from the Port Royal *Logic*, a statement of Gassendi's opinion, which is, to say the least of it, partial and incomplete.

The second function which Gassendi assigns to Intellect is Reflection, and the third is Reasoning. It is with the former of these that we are at present concerned. Mr. Stewart, you have seen, distinguishes the philosophy of Locke from that of his predecessor in this, — that the former introduced Reflection or Self-consciousness as a source of knowledge, which was overlooked or disallowed by the latter. Mr. Stewart is thus wrong in the fact of Gassendi's rejection of any source of knowledge of the name and nature of Locke's Reflection. So far is this from being the case, that Gassendi attributes far more to this faculty than Locke; for he not only makes it an original source of knowledge, but founds upon the nature of its action a proof of the immateriality of mind. "To the second operation," he says, "belongs the Attention or Reflection of the intellect upon its proper acts, — an operation by which it understands that it understands, and thinks that it thinks (qua se intelligere intelligit, cogitatve se cogitare). "We have formerly," he adds, "shown that it is above the power of Phantasy to imagine that it imagines, because, being of a corporeal nature, it cannot act upon itself; in fact, it is as absurd to say that I imagine myself to imagine, as that I see myself to see." He then goes on to show, that the knowledge we obtain of all our mental operations and affections is by this reflection of Intellect; that it is necessarily of an inorganic or purely spiritual character; that it is peculiar to man, and distinguishes him from the brutes; and that it aids us in the recognition of disembodied substances, in the confession of a God, and in according to Him the veneration which we owe Him.

From what I have now said, you will see, that the mere admission of a faculty of Self-consciousness, as a source of knowledge, is of no import in determining the rational, the anti-sensual, character of a philosophy; and that even those philosophers who discriminated it the most strongly from Sense might still maintain that experience is not only the occasion, but the source, of all our knowledge. Such philosophers were Gassendi and Locke.

CHAPTER XXII.

THE CONSERVATIVE FACULTY. — MEMORY PROPER.

THROUGH the powers of External and Internal Perception we are enabled to acquire information, — experience: but this acquisition is not of itself independent and complete; it supposes that we are also able to retain knowledge acquired, for we cannot be said to get what we are unable to keep. The faculty of Acquisition is, therefore, only realized through another faculty, — the faculty of Retention or Conservation. Here we have another example of what I have already frequently had occasion to suggest to your observation; — we have two faculties, two elementary phænomena, evidently distinct, and yet each depending on the other for its realization. Without a power of Acquisition, a power of Conservation could not be exerted; and without the latter, the former would be frustrated, for we should lose as fast as we acquired. But as the faculty of Acquisition would be useless without the faculty of Retention, so the faculty of Retention would be useless without the faculties of Reproduction and Representation. That the mind retained, beyond the sphere of consciousness, a treasury of knowledge, would be of no avail, did it not possess the power of bringing out, and of displaying, — in other words, of reproducing, and representing, this knowledge in consciousness. But because the faculty of Conservation would be fruitless without the ulterior faculties of Reproduction and Representation, we are not to confound these faculties, or to view the act of mind, which is their joint result, as a simple and elementary phænomenon. Though mutually dependent on each other, the faculties of Conservation, Reproduction, and Representation are governed by different laws, and, in different individuals, are found greatly varying in their comparative vigor.

Use of the terms Memory and Recollection. — The intimate connection of these three faculties, or elementary activities, is the cause, however, why they have not been distinguished in the analysis of philosophers; and why their distinction is not precisely marked in ordinary language. In ordinary language, we have, indeed, words which, without excluding the other faculties, denote one of these more emphatically. Thus, in the term *Memory*, the Conservative Faculty, the phænomenon of Retention, is the central notion, with which, however, those of Reproduction and Representation are associated. In the term *Recollection*, again, the phænomenon of Reproduction is the principal notion, accompanied, however, by those of Retention and Representation as its subordinates. This being the case, it is evident what must be our course in regard to the employment of common language. We must either abandon it altogether, or take the term that more proximately expresses our analysis, and, by definition, limit and specify its signification. Thus, in the Conservative Faculty, we may either content ourselves with the scientific terms of *Conservation* and *Retention* alone, or we may moreover use as a synonym the vulgar term *Memory*, determining its application, in our mouths, by a preliminary definition. And that the word *Memory* principally and properly denotes the power the mind possesses of retaining hold of the knowledge it has acquired, is generally admitted by philologists, and is not denied by philosophers. Of the latter, some have expressly avowed this. Of these, I shall quote to you only two or three, which happen to occur the first to my recollection. Plato considers Memory simply as the faculty of Conservation. Aristotle distinguishes Memory (μνήμη), as the faculty of Conservation, from Reminiscence (ἀνάμνησις), the faculty of Reproduction. St. Augustin, who is not only the most illustrious of the Christian fathers, but one of the profoundest thinkers of antiquity, finely contrasts Memory with Recollection or Reminiscence, in one of the most eloquent and philosophical chapters of his *Confessions*. Joseph Scaliger, also, speaking of himself, is made to say: "I have not a good memory, but a good reminiscence; proper names do not easily recur to me, but when I think on them, I find them out." It is sufficient for our purpose that the distinction is here taken between the Retentive Power, — Memory, and the Reproductive Power, — Reminiscence. Scaliger's memory could hardly be called bad, though his reminiscence might be better; and these elements in conjunction go to constitute a good memory, in the comprehensive sense of the expression. I say the retentive faculty of that man is surely not to be despised, who was able to commit to memory Homer in twenty-one days, and the whole Greek poets in three months, and who, taking him all in all, was the most learned man the world has ever seen. I might adduce many other authorities to the same effect; but this, I think, is sufficient to warrant me in using the term *Memory* exclusively to denote the faculty possessed by the mind of preserving what has once been present to consciousness, so that it may again be recalled and represented in consciousness. So much for the verbal consideration.

What is Memory? — By Memory or Retention, you will see, is only meant the condition of Reproduction; and it is, therefore, evident that it is only by an extension of the term that it can be called a faculty, that is, an active power. It is more a passive resistance than an energy, and ought, therefore, perhaps to receive rather the appellation of a capacity. But the nature of this capacity or faculty we must now proceed to consider.

In the first place, then, I presume that the fact of retention is admitted. We are conscious of certain cognitions as acquired, and we are conscious of these cognitions as resuscitated. That, in the interval, when out of consciousness, these cognitions do continue to subsist in the mind, is certainly an hypothesis, because whatever is out of consciousness can only be assumed; but it is an hypothesis which we are not only warranted, but necessitated, by the phænomena, to establish. I recollect, indeed, that one philosopher has proposed another hypothesis. Avicenna, the celebrated Arabian philosopher and physician, denies to the human mind the conservation of its acquired knowledge; and he explains the process of recollection by an irradiation of divine light, through which the recovered cognition is infused into the intellect. Assuming, however, that the knowledge we have acquired is retained in and by the human mind, we must, of course, attribute to the mind a power of thus retaining it. The fact of memory is thus established.

Retention admits of explanation. — But if it cannot be denied that the knowledge we have acquired by Perception and Self-consciousness does actually continue, though out of consciousness, to endure; can we, in the second place, find any ground on which to explain the possibility of this endurance? I think we can, and shall adduce such an explanation, founded on the general analogies of our mental nature. Before, however, commencing this, I may notice some of the similitudes which have been suggested by philosophers, as illustrative of this faculty. It has been compared to a storehouse, — Cicero calls it "*thesaurus omnium rerum*," — provided with cells or pigeon-holes, in which its furniture is laid up and arranged. It has been likened to a tablet, on which characters were written or impressed. But of all these sensible resemblances, none is so ingenious as that of Gassendi, to the folds in a piece of paper or cloth; though I do not recollect to have seen it ever noticed. A sheet of paper, or cloth, is capable of receiving innumerable folds, and the folds in which it has been oftenest laid, it takes afterwards of itself.

All these resemblances, if intended as more than metaphors, are unphilosophical. We do not even obtain any insight into the nature of Memory from any of the physiological hypotheses which have been stated; indeed, all of them are too contemptible even for serious criticism. "The mind," [says Schmid,] "affords us, however, in itself, the very explanation which we vainly seek in any collateral influences. The phænomenon of retention is, indeed, so natural, on the ground of the self-energy of mind, that we have no need to suppose any special faculty for memory; the conservation of the action of the mind being involved in the very conception of its power of self-activity.

The real difficulty of the problem. — "Let us consider how knowledge is acquired by the mind. Knowledge is not acquired by a mere passive affection, but through the exertion of spontaneous activity on the part of the knowing subject; for though this activity be not exerted without some external excitation, still this excitation is only the occasion on which the mind develops its self-energy. But this energy being once determined, it is natural that it should persist, until again annihilated by other causes. This would, in fact, be the case, were the mind merely passive in the impression it receives; for it is a universal law of nature, that every effect endures as long as it is not modified or opposed by any other effect. But the mental activity, the act of knowledge, of which I now speak, is more than this; it is an energy of the self-active power of a subject one and indivisible: consequently, a part of the Ego must be detached or annihilated, if a cognition once existent be again extinguished. Hence it is, that *the problem most difficult of solution is not, how a mental activity endures, but how it ever vanishes.* For as we must here maintain, not merely the possible continuance of certain energies, but the impossibility of the non-continuance of any one, we, consequently, stand in apparent contradiction to what experience shows us; showing us, as it does, our internal activities in a ceaseless vicissitude of manifestation and disappearance. This apparent contradiction, therefore, demands solution. If it be impossible that an energy of mind which has once been should be abolished, without a laceration of the vital unity of the mind as a subject one and indivisible; — on this supposition, the question arises, How can the facts of our self-consciousness be brought to harmonize with this statement, seeing that consciousness proves to us, that cognitions once clear and vivid are forgotten; that feelings, wishes, desires, in a word, every act or modification, of which we are at one time aware, are at another vanished; and that our internal existence seems daily to assume a new and different aspect.

The distribution of the mental force explains forgetfulness. — "The solution of this problem is to be sought for in the theory of obscure or latent modifications, [that is, mental activities, real, but beyond the sphere of consciousness, which I formerly explained.] The disappearance of internal energies from the view of internal perception does not warrant the conclusion, that they no longer exist; for we are not always conscious of all the mental energies whose existence cannot be disallowed. Only the more vivid changes sufficiently affect our consciousness to become objects of its apprehension: we, consequently, are only conscious of the more prominent series of changes in our internal state; the others remain for the most part latent. Thus we take note of our memory only in its influence on our consciousness; and, in general, do not consider that the immense proportion of our intellectual possessions consists of our delitescent cognitions. All the cognitions which we possess, or have possessed, still remain to us, — the whole complement of all our knowledge still lies in our memory; but as new acquisitions are continually pressing in upon the old, and continually taking place along with them among the modifications of the Ego, the old cognitions, unless from time to time refreshed and brought forward, are driven back, and become gradually fainter and more obscure. This obscuration is not, however, to be conceived as an obliteration, or as a total annihilation. The obscuration, the delitescence of mental activities, is explained by the weakening of the degree in which they affect our self-consciousness or internal sense. An activity becomes obscure, because it is no longer able adequately to affect this. To explain, therefore, the disappearance of our mental activities, it is only requisite to explain their weakening or enfeeblement, — which may be attempted in the following way: — Every mental activity belongs to the one vital activity of mind in general; it is, therefore, indivisibly bound up with it, and can neither be torn from, nor abolished in, it. But the mind is only capable, at any one moment, of exerting a certain quantity or degree of force. This quantity must, therefore, be divided among the different activities, so that each has only a part; and the sum of force belonging to all the several activities taken together, is equal to the quantity or degree of force belonging to the vital activity of mind in general. Thus, in proportion to the greater number of activities in the mind, the less will be the proportion of force which will accrue to each; the feebler, therefore, each will be, and the fainter the vivacity with which it can affect self-consciousness. This weakening of vivacity can, in consequence of the indefinite increase in the number of our mental activities, caused by the ceaseless excitation of the mind to new knowledge, be carried to an indefinite tenuity, without the activities, therefore, ceasing altogether to be. Thus it is quite natural, that the great proportion of our mental cognitions should have waxed too feeble to affect our internal perception with the competent intensity; it is quite natural that they should have become obscure or delitescent. In these circumstances, it is to be supposed, that every new cognition, every newly-excited activity, should be in the greatest vivacity, and should draw to itself the greatest amount of force: this force will, in the same proportion, be withdrawn from the other earlier cognitions; and it is they, consequently, which must undergo the fate of obscuration. Thus is explained the phænomenon of Forgetfulness or Oblivion. And here, by the way, it should perhaps be noticed, that forgetfulness is not to be limited merely to our cognitions: it applies equally to the feelings and desires.

"The same principle illustrates, and is illustrated by, the phænomenon of *Distraction* and *Attention.* If a great number of activities are equally excited at once, the disposable amount of mental force is equally distributed among this multitude, so that each activity only attains a low degree of vivacity; the state of mind which results from this is Distraction. Attention is the state the converse of this; that is, the state in which the vital activity of mind is, voluntarily or involuntarily, concentrated, say, in a single activity; in consequence of which concentration, this activity waxes stronger, and, therefore, clearer. On this theory, the proposition with which I started, — that all mental activities, all acts of knowledge, which have been once excited, persist, — becomes intelligible; we never wholly lose them, but they become obscure. This obscuration can be conceived in every infinite degree, between incipient latescence and irrecoverable latency. The obscure cognition may exist simply out of consciousness, so that it can be recalled by a common act of reminiscence. Again, it may be impossible to recover it by an act of voluntary recollection; but some association may revivify it, enough to make it flash after a long oblivion into consciousness. Further, it may be obscured so far that it can only be resuscitated by some morbid affection of the system; or, finally, it may be absolutely lost for us in this life, and destined only for our reminiscence in the life to come.

Conservation of all the mental phænomena. — "That this doctrine admits of an immediate application to the faculty of Retention, or Memory Proper, has been already signified. And in further explanation of this faculty, I would annex two observations, which arise out of the preceding theory. The first is, that retention, that memory, does not belong alone to the cognitive faculties, but that the same law extends, in like manner, over all the three primary classes of the mental phænomena. It is not ideas, notions, cognitions only, but feelings and conations, which are held fast, and which can, therefore, be again awakened. This fact, of the conservation of our practical modifications, is not indeed denied; but psychologists usually so represent the matter, as if, when feelings or conations are retained in the mind, that this takes place only through the medium of the memory; meaning by this, that we must, first of all, have had notions of these affections, which notions being preserved, they, when recalled to mind, do again awaken the modification they represent. From the theory I have detailed to you, it must be seen, that there is no need of this intermediation of notions, but that we immediately retain feelings, volitions, and desires, no less than notions and cognitions; inasmuch as all the three classes of fundamental phænomena arise equally out of the vital manifestations of the same one and indivisible subject.

Memory dependent on corporeal conditions. — "The second result of this theory is, that the various attempts to explain memory by physiological hypotheses are as unnecessary as they are untenable. This is not the place to discuss the general problem touching the relation of mind and body. But in proximate reference to memory, it may be satisfactory to show, that this faculty does not stand in need of such crude modes of explanation. It must be allowed, that no faculty affords a more tempting subject for materialistic conjecture. No other mental power betrays a greater dependence on corporeal conditions than memory. Not only, in general, does its vigorous or feeble activity essentially depend on the health and indisposition of the body, more especially of the nervous systems; but there is manifested a connection between certain functions of memory and certain parts of the cerebral apparatus." This connection, however, is such as affords no countenance to any particular hypotheses at present in vogue. For example, after certain diseases, or certain affections of the brain, some partial loss of memory takes place. Perhaps the patient loses the whole of his stock of knowledge previous to the disease, the faculty of acquiring and retaining new information remaining entire. Perhaps he loses the memory of words, and preserves that of things. Perhaps he may retain the memory of nouns, and lose that of verbs, or *vice versa;* nay, what is still more marvellous, though it is not a very unfrequent occurrence, one language may be taken neatly out of his retention, without affecting his memory of others. "By such observations, the older psychologists were led to the various physiological hypotheses by which they hoped to account for the phænomena of retention, — as, for example, the hypothesis of permanent material impressions on the brain, — or of permanent dispositions in the nervous fibres to repeat the same oscillatory movements, — of particular organs for the different functions of memory, — of particular parts of the brain as the repositories of the various classes of ideas, — or even of a particular fibre, as the instrument of every several notion. But all these hypotheses betray only an ignorance of the proper object of philosophy, and of the true nature of the thinking principle. They are at best but useless; for if the unity and self-activity of mind be not denied, it is manifest, that the mental activities, which have been once determined, must persist, and these corporeal explanations are superfluous. Nor can it be argued, that the limitations to which the Retentive, or rather the Reproductive, Faculty is subjected in its energies, in consequence of its bodily relations, prove the absolute dependence of memory on organization, and legitimate the explanation of this faculty by corporeal agencies; for the incompetency of this inference can be shown from the contradiction in which it stands to the general laws of mind, which, howbeit conditioned by bodily relations, still ever preserves its self-activity and independence."

Two qualities requisite to a good memory. — There is perhaps no mental power in which such extreme differences appear, in different individuals, as in memory. To a good memory there are certainly two qualities requisite, — 1°, The capacity of Retention, and 2°, The faculty of Reproduction. But the former quality appears to be that by which these marvellous contrasts are principally determined. I should only fatigue you, were I to enumerate the prodigious feats of retention, which are proved to have been actually performed. Of these, I shall only select the one which, upon the whole, appears to me the most extraordinary.

The sum of the statement is, that at Padua there dwelt, [near Muretus,] a young man, a Corsican by birth, and of a good family in that island, who had come thither for the cultivation of Civil law, in which he was a diligent and distinguished student. He was a frequent visitor at the house and gardens of Muretus, who, having heard that he possessed a remarkable art, or faculty of memory, took occasion, though incredulous in regard to reports, of requesting from him a specimen of his power. He at once agreed; and having adjourned with a considerable party of distinguished auditors into a saloon, Muretus began to dictate words, Latin, Greek, barbarous, significant and non-significant, disjointed and connected, until he wearied himself, the young man who wrote them down, and the audience who were present; — "we were all," he says, "marvellously tired." The Corsican alone was the one of the whole company alert and fresh, and continually desired Muretus for more words; who declared he would be more than satisfied, if he could repeat the half of what had been taken down, and at length he ceased. The young man, with his gaze fixed upon the ground, stood silent for a brief season, and then, says Muretus, "vidi facinus mirificissimum." Having begun to speak, he absolutely repeated the whole words, in the same order in which they had been delivered, without the slightest hesitation; then, commencing from the last, he repeated them backwards till he came to the first. Then again, so that he spoke the first, the third, the fifth, and so on; did this in any order that was asked, and all without the smallest error. Having subsequently become familiarly acquainted with him, I have had other and frequent experience of his power. He assured me (and he had nothing of the boaster in him) that he could recite, in the manner I have mentioned, to the amount of thirty-six thousand words. And what is more wonderful, they all so adhered to the mind that, after a year's interval, he could repeat them without trouble. I know, from having tried him, he could do so after a considerable time.

Before passing from the faculty of Memory, considered simply as the power of conservation, I may notice two opposite doctrines, that have been maintained, in regard to the relation of this faculty to the higher powers of mind. One of these doctrines holds, that a great development of memory is incompatible with a high degree of intelligence; the other, that a high degree of intelligence supposes such a development of memory as its condition.

Great memory and sound judgment not incompatible. — The former of these opinions is one very extensively prevalent, not only among philosophers, but among mankind in general; and the words — *beati memoria, expectantes judicium* — have been applied to express the supposed incompatibility of great memory and sound judgment. There seems, however, no valid ground for this belief. If an extraordinary power of retention is frequently not accompanied with a corresponding power of intelligence, it is a natural, but not a very logical procedure, to jump to the conclusion, that a great memory is inconsistent with a sound judgment. The opinion is refuted by the slightest induction; for we immediately find, that many of the individuals who towered above their fellows in intellectual superiority, were almost equally distinguished for the capacity of their memory. I recently quoted to you a passage, in which Joseph Scaliger is made to say that he had not a good memory, but a good reminiscence; and he immediately adds, "never, or rarely, are judgment and a great memory found in conjunction." Of this opinion Scaliger himself affords the most illustrious refutation. During his lifetime, he was hailed as the Dictator of the Republic of Letters, and posterity has ratified the decision of his contemporaries, in crowning him as the prince of philologers and critics. But to elevate a man to such an eminence, it is evident, that the most consummate genius and ability were conditions.

For intellectual power of the highest order, none were distinguished above Grotius and Pascal; and Grotius and Pascal forgot nothing they had ever read or thought. Leibnitz and Euler were not less celebrated for their intelligence than for their memory, and both could repeat the whole of the *Æneid*. Donellus knew the *Corpus Juris* by heart, and yet he was one of the profoundest and most original speculators in jurisprudence. Muratori, though not a genius of the very highest order, was still a man of great ability and judgment; and so powerful was his retention, that in making quotations, he had only to read his passages, put the books in their place, and then to write out from memory the words.

But if there be no ground for the vulgar opinion, that a strong faculty of retention is incompatible with intellectual capacity in general, the converse opinion is not better founded, which has been maintained, among others, by Hoffbauer. This doctrine does not, however, deserve an articulate refutation; for the common experience of every one sufficiently proves, that intelligence and memory hold no necessary proportion to each other.

CHAPTER XXIII.

THE REPRODUCTIVE FACULTY.—LAWS OF ASSOCIATION.—SUGGESTION AND REMINISCENCE.

I NOW pass to the next faculty in order,—the faculty which I have called the Reproductive. I am not satisfied with this name; for it does not precisely, of itself, mark what I wish to be expressed,—namely, the process by which what is lying dormant in memory is awakened, as contradistinguished from the representation in consciousness of it as awakened. The two processes certainly suppose each other; for we cannot awaken a cognition without its being represented,—the representation being, in fact, only its state of waking; nor can a latent thought or affection be represented, unless certain conditions be fulfilled, by which it is called out of obscurity into the light of consciousness. The two processes are relative and correlative, but not more identical than hill and valley. I am not satisfied, I say, with the term *reproduction* for the process by which the dormant thought or affection is aroused; for it does not clearly denote what it is intended to express. Perhaps the *Resuscitative Faculty* would have been better; and the term *reproduction* might have been employed to comprehend the whole process, made up of the correlative acts of Retention, Resuscitation, and Representation. Be this, however, as it may, I shall at present continue to employ the term, in the limited meaning I have already assigned.

The phænomenon of Reproduction is one of the most wonderful in the whole compass of psychology; and it is one in the explanation of which philosophy has been more successful than in almost any other. The Scholastic psychologists seem to have regarded the succession in the train of thought, or, as they called it, the excitation of the species, with peculiar wonder, as one of the most inscrutable mysteries of nature; and yet, what is curious, Aristotle has left almost as complete an analysis of the laws by which this phænomenon is regulated, as has yet been accomplished. It required, however, a considerable progress in the inductive philosophy of mind, before this analysis of Aristotle could be appreciated at its proper value; and in fact, it was only after modern philosophers had rediscovered the principal laws of Association, that it was found that these laws had been more completely given two thousand years before.

The faculty of Reproduction is governed by the laws which regulate the Association of the mental train; or, to speak more correctly, Reproduction is nothing but the result of these laws. Every one is conscious of a ceaseless succession or train of thoughts, one thought suggesting another, which again is the cause of exciting a third, and so on. In what manner, it may be asked, does the presence of any thought determine the introduction of another? Is the train subject to laws, and if so, by what laws is it regulated?

The train of thought subject to laws. — That the elements of the mental train are not isolated, but that each thought forms a link of a continuous and uninterrupted chain, is well illustrated by Hobbes. "In a company," he says, "in which the conversation turned upon the late civil war, what could be conceived more impertinent than for a person to ask abruptly, what was the value of a Roman denarius? On a little reflection, however, I was easily able to trace the train of thought which suggested the question; for the original subject of discourse naturally introduced the history of the king, and of the treachery of those who surrendered his person to his enemies; this again introduced the treachery of Judas Iscariot, and the sum of money which he received for his reward."

But if thoughts, and feelings, and conations (for you must observe, that the train is not limited to the phænomena of cognition only), do not arise of themselves, but only in casual connection with preceding and subsequent modifications of mind, it remains to be asked and answered, — Do the links of this chain follow each other under any other condition than that of simple connection? — in other words, *may any thought, feeling, or desire be connected with any other? Or, is the succession regulated by other and special laws*, according to which certain kinds of modification exclusively precede, and exclusively follow, each other? The slightest observation of the phænomenon shows, that the latter alternative is the case; and on this all philosophers are agreed. Nor do philosophers differ in regard to what kind of thoughts are associated together. They differ almost exclusively in regard to the subordinate question, of how these thoughts ought to be classified, and carried up into system. This, therefore, is the question to which I shall address myself.

The laws of Association — how classified. — I have explained to you how thoughts, once experienced, remain, though out of consciousness, still in possession of the mind; and I have now to show, how these thoughts retained in memory may, without any excitation from without, be again retrieved by an excitation or awakening from other thoughts within. Philosophers having observed, that one thought determined another to arise, and that this determination only took place between thoughts which stood in certain relations to each other, set themselves to ascertain and classify the kinds of correlation under which this occurred, in order to generalize the laws by which the phænomenon of Reproduction was governed. Accordingly it has been established, that thoughts are *associated*, that is, are able to excite each other; — 1°, If coexistent, or immediately successive, in time; 2°, If their objects are conterminous or adjoining in space; 3°, If they hold the dependence to each other of cause and effect, or of mean and end, or of whole and part; 4°, If they stand in a relation either of contrast or of similarity; 5°, If they are the operations of the same power, or of different powers conversant about the same object; 6°, If their objects are the sign and the signified; or, 7°, Even if their objects are accidentally denoted by the same sound.

These, as far as I recollect, are all the classes to which philosophers have attempted to reduce the principles of Mental Association. Aristotle recalled the laws of this connection to four, or rather to three, — Contiguity in time and space, Resemblance, and Contrariety. He even seems to have thought they might all be carried up into the one law of Coexistence. St. Augustin explicitly reduces association to a single canon, — namely, Thoughts that have once coexisted in the mind are afterwards associated. This law, which I would call the law of Redintegration, was afterwards enounced by Malebranche, Wolf, and Bilfinger; but without any reference to St. Austin. Hume, who thinks himself the first philosopher who had ever attempted to generalize the laws of association, makes them three, — Resemblance, Contiguity in time and place, and Cause and Effect. Stewart, after disclaiming any attempt at a complete enumeration, mentions two classes of circumstances as useful to be observed. "The relations," he says, "upon which some of them are founded, are perfectly obvious to the mind; those which are the foundation of others, are discovered only in consequence of particular efforts of attention. Of the former kind are the relations of Resemblance and Analogy, of Contrariety, of Vicinity in time and place, and those which arise from accidental coincidences in the sound of different words. These, in general, connect our thoughts together, when they are suffered to take their natural course, and when we are conscious of little or no active exertion. Of the latter kind are the relations of Cause and Effect, of Means and End, of Premises and Conclusion; and those others which regulate the train of thought in the mind of the philosopher, when he is engaged in a particular investigation."

Brown divides the circumstances affecting association into primary and secondary. Under the primary laws of Suggestion, he includes Resemblance, Contrast, Contiguity in time and place, — a classification identical with Aristotle's. By the secondary, he means the vivacity, the recentness, and the frequent repetition of our thoughts; circumstances which, though they exert an influence on the recurrence of our thoughts, belong to a different order of causes from those we are at present considering.

These laws reduced to two, and even to one. — Now all the

laws which I have hitherto enumerated may be easily reduced to two, — the law of the *Simultaneity*, and the law of the *Resemblance* or *Affinity*, of Thought. Under *Simultaneity* I include Immediate Consecution in time; to the other category of *Affinity* every other circumstance may be reduced. I shall take the several cases I have above enumerated, and having exemplified their influence as associating principles, I shall show how they are all only special modifications of the two laws of Simultaneity and Affinity; which two laws, I shall finally prove to you, are themselves only modifications of one supreme law, — the law of *Redintegration*.

The law of Simultaneity. — The first law, — that of Simultaneity, or of Coexistence and Immediate Succession in time, — is too evident to require any illustration. "In passing along a road," as Mr. Stewart observes, "which we have formerly travelled in the company of a friend, the particulars of the conversation in which we were then engaged, are frequently suggested to us by the objects we meet with. In such a scene, we recollect that a particular subject was started; and in passing the different houses, and plantations, and rivers, the arguments we were discussing when we last saw them recur spontaneously to the memory. The connection which is formed in the mind between the words of a language and the ideas they denote; the connection which is formed between the different words of a discourse we have committed to memory; the connection between the different notes of a piece of music in the mind of the musician, are all obvious instances of the same general law of our nature."

The law of Affinity. — The second law, — that of the Affinity of thoughts, — will be best illustrated by the cases of which it is the more general expression. In the *first* place, in the case of *resembling*, or *analogous*, or *partially identical* objects, it will not be denied that these virtually suggest each other. The imagination of Alexander carries me to the imagination of Cæsar, Cæsar to Charlemagne, Charlemagne to Napoleon. The vision of a portrait suggests the image of the person portrayed. In a company one anecdote suggests another analogous. That resembling, analogous, or partially identical objects stand in reciprocal Affinity, is apparent; they are its strongest exemplifications. So far there is no difficulty.

In the *second* place, thoughts standing to each other in the relation of *contrariety* or *contrast* are mutually suggestive. Thus the thought of vice suggests the thought of virtue; and, in the mental world, the prince and the peasant, kings and beggars, are inseparable concomitants. On this principle are dependent those associations which constitute the charms of antithesis and wit. Thus the whole pathos of Milton's apostrophe to light lies in the contrast of his own darkness to the resplendent object he addresses. And in what else does the beauty of the following line consist, but in the contrast and connection of life and death; life being represented as but a wayfaring from grave to grave?

Τίς βίος; — ἐκ τύμβοιο θορὼν, ἐπὶ τύμβον ὁδεύω.

Who can think of Marius sitting amid the ruins of Carthage, without thinking of the resemblance of the consul and the city, — without thinking of the difference between their past and present fortunes? And in the incomparable epigram of Molsa on the great Pompey, the effect is produced by the contrast of the life and death of the hero, and in the conversion of the very fact of his posthumous dishonor into a theme of the noblest panegyric.

"Dux, Pharia quamvis jaceas inhumatus arena,
Non ideo fati est sævior ira tui:
Indignum fuerat tellus tibi victa sepulcrum;
Non decuit cœlo, te, nisi, Magne, tegi."

Thus that objects, though contrasted, are still akin, — still stand to each other in a relation of Affinity, depends on their logical analogy. The axiom, that the knowledge of contraries is one, proves that the thought of the one involves the thought of the other.

In the *third* place, objects *contiguous in place* are associated. You recollect the famous passage of Cicero in the first chapter of the fifth book *De Finibus*, of which the following is the conclusion: — "Tanta vis admonitionis est in locis, ut, non sine causa, ex his memoriæ deducta sit disciplina. . . . . Id quidem infinitum in hac urbe; quocumque enim ingredimur, in aliquam historiam vestigium ponimus." But how do objects adjacent in place stand in Affinity to each other? Simply because local contiguity binds up objects, otherwise unconnected, into a single object of perceptive thought.

In the *fourth* place, thoughts of the *whole* and the *parts*, of the *thing* and its *properties*, of the *sign* and the *thing signified*, — of these it is superfluous to illustrate either the reality of the influence, or to show that they are only so many forms of Affinity; both are equally manifest. But in this case Affinity is not the only principle of association; here Simultaneity also occurs. One observation I may make to show, that what Mr. Stewart promulgates as a distinct principle of association, is only a subordinate modification of the two great laws I have laid down; — I mean his association of objects arising from accidental coincidences in the sound of the words by which they are denoted. Here the association between the objects or ideas is not immediate. One object or idea signified suggests its term signifying. But a complete or partial identity in sound suggests another word, and that word suggests the thing or thought it signifies. The two things or thoughts are thus associated, only mediately, through the association of their signs, and the several immediate associations are very simple examples of the general laws.

In the *fifth* place, thoughts of *causes and effects* reciprocally suggest each other. Thus the falling snow excites the imagination of an inundation; a shower of hail, a thought of the destruction of the fruit; the sight of wine carries us back to the grapes, or the sight of the grapes carries us forward to the wine; and so forth. But cause and effect not only naturally, but necessarily, suggest each other; they stand in the closest Affinity; and, therefore, whatever phænomena are subsumed under this relation, as indeed under all relations, are, consequently, also in Affinity.

One grand law of Redintegration. — I have now, I think,

gone through all the circumstances which philosophers have constituted into separate laws of Association; and shown that they easily resolve themselves into the two laws of Simultaneity and Affinity. I now proceed to show you, that these two laws themselves are reducible to that one law, which I would call the law of Redintegration or Totality, which, as I already stated, I have found incidentally expressed by St. Augustin. This law may be thus enounced, — *Those thoughts suggest each other which had previously constituted parts of the same entire or total act of cognition.* Now to the same entire or total act belong, as integral or constituent parts, in the first place, those thoughts which arose at the same time, or in immediate consecution; and in the second, those thoughts which are bound up into one by their mutual affinity. Thus, therefore, the two laws of Simultaneity and Affinity are carried up into unity, in the higher law of Redintegration or Totality; and by this one law the whole phænomena of Association may be easily explained.

The law of Redintegration explained. — But this law being established by induction and generalization, and affording an explanation of the various phænomena of Association, it may be asked, How is this law itself explained? On what principle of our intellectual nature is it founded? To this no answer can be legitimately demanded. It is enough for the natural philosopher, to reduce the special laws of the attraction of distant bodies to the one principle of gravitation; and his theory is not invalidated, because he can give no account of how gravitation is itself determined. In all our explanations of the phænomena of mind and matter, we must always arrive at an ultimate fact or law, of which we are wholly unable to afford an ulterior explanation. We are, therefore, entitled to decline attempting any illustration of the ground on which the supreme fact or law of Association reposes; and if we do attempt such illustration, and fail in the endeavor, no presumption is, therefore, justly to be raised against the truth of the fact or principle itself.

But an illustration of this great law is involved in the principle of the unity of the mental energies, as the activities of the subject one and indivisible, to which I have had occasion to refer. "The various acts of mind," [says Schmid,] "must not be viewed as single,—as isolated, manifestations; they all belong to the one activity of the Ego: and, consequently, if our various mental energies are only partial modifications of the same general activity, they must all be associated among themselves. Every mental energy,—every thought, feeling, desire that is excited, excites at the same time all other previously existent activities, in a certain degree; it spreads its excitation over the whole activities of the mind, as the agitation of one place of a sheet of water expands itself, in wider and wider circles, over the whole surface of the fluid, although, in proportion to its eccentricity, it is always becoming fainter, until it is at last not to be perceived. The force of every internal activity exists only in a certain limited degree; consequently, the excitation it determines has only likewise a certain limited power of expansion, and is continually losing in vigor in proportion to its eccentricity. Thus there are formed particular centres, particular spheres, of internal unity, within which the activities stand to each other in a closer relation of action and reaction; and this, in proportion as they more or less belong already to a single energy,—in proportion as they gravitate more or less proximately to the same centre of action. A plurality, a complement, of several activities forms, in a stricter sense, one whole activity for itself; an invigoration of any of its several activities is, therefore, an invigoration of the part of a whole activity; and as a part cannot be active for itself alone, there, consequently, results an invigoration of the whole, that is, of all the other parts of which it is composed. Thus the supreme law of association,—that activities excite each other in proportion as they have previously belonged, as parts, to one whole activity,—is explained from the still more universal principle of the unity of all our mental energies in general.

"But *on the same principle, we can also explain the two subaltern laws of Simultaneity and Affinity.* The phænomena of mind are manifested under a twofold condition or form; for they are only revealed, 1°, As occurrences in time; and, 2°, As the energies or modifications of the Ego as their cause and subject.

Time and Self are thus the two forms of the internal world. By these two forms, therefore, every particular, every limited, unity of operation, must be controlled; — on them it must depend. And it is precisely these two forms that lie at the root of the two laws of Simultaneity and Affinity. Thus acts which are exerted at the same time belong, by that very circumstance, to the same particular unity, — to the same definite sphere of mental energy; in other words, constitute through their simultaneity a single activity. Thus energies, however heterogeneous in themselves, if developed at once, belong to the same activity, — constitute a particular unity; and they will operate with a greater suggestive influence on each other, in proportion as they are more closely connected by the bond of time. On the other hand, the affinity of mental acts or modifications will be determined by their particular relations to the Ego, as their cause or subject. As all the activities of mind obtain a unity in being all the energies of the same soul or active principle in general, so they are bound up into particular unities, inasmuch as they belong to some particular faculty, — resemble each other in the common ground of their manifestation. Thus cognitions, feelings, and volitions severally awaken cognitions, feelings, and volitions; for they severally belong to the same faculty, and, through that identity, are themselves constituted into distinct unities: or again, a thought of the cause suggests a thought of the effect, a thought of the mean suggests a thought of the end, a thought of the part suggests a thought of the whole; for cause and effect, end and mean, whole and parts, have subjectively an indissoluble affinity, as they are all so many forms or organizations of thought. In like manner, the notions of all resembling objects suggest each other, for they possess some common quality, through which they are in thought bound up in a single act of thought. Even the notions of opposite and contrasted objects mutually excite each other upon the same principle; for these are logically associated, inasmuch as, by the laws of thought, the notion of one opposite necessarily involves the notions of the other; and it is also a psychological law, that contrasted objects relieve each other. *Opposita, juxta posita, se invicem collustrant.*

When the operations of different faculties are mutually suggestive, they are, likewise, internally connected by the nature of their action; for they are either conversant with the same object, and have thus been originally determined by the same affection from without, or they have originally been associated through some form of the mind itself; thus moral cognitions, moral feelings, and moral volitions, may suggest each other, through the common bond of morality; the moral principle in this case uniting the operations of the three fundamental powers into one general activity."

How thoughts apparently unassociated succeed each other. — It sometimes happens, that thoughts seem to follow each other immediately, between which it is impossible to detect any bond of association. If this anomaly be insoluble, the whole theory of association is overthrown. Philosophers have accordingly set themselves to account for this phænomenon. To deny the fact of the phænomenon is impossible; it must, therefore, be explained on the hypothesis of association. Now, in their attempts at such an explanation, all philosophers agree in regard to the first step of the solution, but they differ in regard to the second. They agree in this, — that, admitting the apparent, the phænomenal, immediacy of the consecution of the two unassociated thoughts, they deny its reality. They all affirm, that there have actually intervened one or more thoughts, through the mediation of which, the suggestion in question has been affected, and on the assumption of which intermediation, the theory of association remains intact. For example, let us suppose that A and C are thoughts, not on any law of association suggestive of each other, and that A and C appear to our consciousness as following each other immediately. In this case, I say, philosophers agree in supposing, that a thought B, associated with A and with C, and which consequently could be awakened by A, and could awaken C, has intervened. So far they are at one. But now comes their separation. It is asked, how can a thought be supposed to intervene, of which consciousness gives us no indication? In reply to this, two answers have been made. By one set of philosophers, among whom I may particularly specify Mr. Stewart, it is said, that the immediate thought B, having been awakened by A, did rise into consciousness, suggested C, and was instantly forgotten. This solution is apparently that exclusively known in Britain. Other philosophers, following the indication of Leibnitz, by whom the theory of obscure or latent activities was first explicitly promulgated, maintain that the intermediate thought never did rise into consciousness. They hold that A excited B, but that the excitement was not strong enough to rouse B from its state of latency, though strong enough to enable it obscurely to excite C, whose latency was less, and to afford it vivacity sufficient to rise into consciousness.

Explained through the latent modifications of mind. — Of these opinions, I have no hesitation in declaring for the latter. I formerly showed you an analysis of some of the most palpable and familiar phænomena of mind, which made the supposition of mental modifications latent, but not inert, one of absolute necessity. In particular, I proved this in regard to the phænomena of Perception. But the fact of such latencies being established in one faculty, they afford an easy and philosophical explanation of the phænomena in all. In the present instance, if we admit, as admit we must, that activities can endure, and consequently can operate, out of consciousness, the question is at once solved. On this doctrine, the whole theory of association obtains an easy and natural completion; as no definite line can be drawn between clear and obscure activities, which melt insensibly into each; and both, being of the same nature, must be supposed to operate under the same laws. In illustration of the mediatory agency of latent thoughts in the process of suggestion, I formerly alluded to an analogous phænomenon under the laws of physical motion, which I may again call to your remembrance. If a series of elastic balls, say of ivory, are placed in a straight line, and in mutual contact, and if the first be sharply struck, what happens? The intermediate balls remain at rest; the last alone is moved.

The other doctrine, which proceeds upon the hypothesis that we can be conscious of a thought and that thought be instantly forgotten, has every thing against it, and nothing in its favor. In the first place, it does not, like the counter hypothesis of latent agencies, only apply a principle which is already proved to exist; it, on the contrary, lays its foundation in a fact which is not shown to be real. But in the second place, this fact is not only not shown to be real: it is improbable, — nay, impossible; for it contradicts the whole analogy of the intellectual phænomena. The memory or retention of a thought is in proportion to its vivacity in consciousness; but that all trace of its existence so completely perished with its presence, that reproduction became impossible, even the instant after, — this assumption violates every probability, in gratuitously disallowing the established law of the proportion between consciousness and memory. But on this subject, having formerly spoken, it is needless now again to dwell.

So much for the Laws of Association, — the laws to which the faculty of Reproduction is subjected.

Spontaneous Suggestion and Reminiscence. — This faculty, I formerly mentioned, might be considered as operating, either spontaneously, without any interference of the will, or as modified in its action by the intervention of volition. In the one case, as in the other, the Reproductive Faculty acts in subservience to its own laws. In the former case, one thought is allowed to suggest another according to the greater general connection subsisting between them; in the latter, the act of volition, by concentrating attention upon a certain determinate class of associating circumstances, bestows on these circumstances an extraordinary vivacity, and, consequently, enables them to obtain the preponderance, and exclusively to determine the succession of the intellectual train. The former of these cases, where the Reproductive Faculty is left wholly to itself, may not improperly be called Spontaneous Suggestion, or Suggestion simply; the latter ought to obtain the name of Reminiscence or Recollection, (in Greek ἀνάμνησις). The employment of these terms in these significations corresponds with the meaning they obtain in common usage. Philosophers have not, however, always so applied them. But as I have not entered on a criticism of the analyses attempted by philosophers of the faculties, so I shall say nothing in illustration of their perversion of the terms by which they have denoted them.

Recollection or Reminiscence supposes two things. "*First*, it is necessary that the mind recognize the identity of two representations, and *then*, it is necessary that the mind be conscious of something different from the first impression, in consequence of which it affirms to itself that it had formerly experienced this modification. It is passing marvellous, this conviction that we have of the identity of two representations; for they are only similar, not the same. Were they the same, it would be impossible to discriminate the thought reproduced from the thought originally experienced." This circumstance justly excited the admiration of St. Augustin, and he asks how, if we had actually forgotten a thing, we could so categorically affirm, — it is not that, when some one named to us another; or, it is that, when it is itself presented. The question was worthy of his subtlety, and the answer does honor to his penetration. His principle is, that we cannot seek in our own memory for that of which we have no sort of recollection. We do not seek what has been our first reflective thought in infancy, the first reasoning we have performed, the first free act which raised us above the rank of automata. We are conscious that the attempt would be fruitless; and even if modifications thus lost should chance to recur to our mind, we should not be able to say with truth that we had recollected them, for we should have no criterion by which to recognize them. And what is the consequence he deduces? It is worthy of your attention.

From the moment, then, that we seek aught in our memory, we declare, by that very act, that we have not altogether forgotten it; we still hold of it, as it were, a part, and by this part, which we hold, we seek that which we do not hold. And what is the secret motive which determines us to this research? It is that our memory feels, that it does not see together all that it was accustomed to see together. It feels with regret that it still only discovers a part of itself, and hence its disquietude to seek out what is missing, in order to reannex it to the whole; like to those reptiles, if the comparison may be permitted, whose members, when cut asunder, seek again to reunite. But when this detached portion of our memory at length presents itself, — the name, for example, of a person, which had escaped us, — how shall we proceed to reannex it to the other? We have only to allow nature to do her work. For if the name, being pronounced, goes of itself to reunite itself to the thought of the person, and to place itself, so to speak, upon his face, as upon its ordinary seat, we will say, without hesitation, — there it is. And if, on the contrary, it obstinately refuses to go there to place itself, in order to rejoin the thought to which we had else attached it, we will say peremptorily and at once, — no, it does not suit. But when it suits, where do we discover this luminous accordance which consummates our research? And where can we discover it, except in our memory itself, — in some back chamber, I mean, of that labyrinth where what we considered as lost had only gone astray. And the proof of this is manifest. When the name presents itself to our mind, it appears neither novel nor strange, but old and familiar, like an ancient property of which we have recovered the title-deeds.

Such is the doctrine of one of the profoundest thinkers of antiquity, and whose philosophical opinions, were they collected, arranged, and illustrated, would raise him to as high a rank among metaphysicians, as he already holds among theologians.

The consecutive order of association not the only one. — "Among psychologists," [says Cardaillac,] "those who have written on Memory and Reproduction with the greatest detail and precision, have still failed in giving more than a meagre outline of these operations. They have taken account only of the notions which suggest each other with a distinct and palpable notoriety. They have viewed the associations only in the order in which language is competent to express them; and *as language*, which renders them still more palpable and distinct, *can only express them in a consecutive order*, — can only express them one after another, they have been led *to suppose that thoughts only awaken in succession.* Thus, a series of ideas mutually associated resembles, on the doctrine of philosophers, a chain, in which every link draws up that which follows; and it is by means of these links that intelligence labors through, in the act of reminiscence, to the end which it proposes to attain.

"There are some, indeed, among them, who are ready to acknowledge, that every actual circumstance is associated to several fundamental notions, and, consequently, to several chains, between which the mind may choose; they admit even, that every link is attached to several others, so that *the whole forms a kind of trellis,—a kind of net-work, which the mind may traverse in every direction*, but still always in a single direction at once,—always in a succession similar to that of speech. This manner of explaining reminiscence is founded solely on this,—that, content to have observed all that is distinctly manifest in the phænomenon, they have paid no attention to the under play of the latescent activities,—paid no attention to all that custom conceals, and conceals the more effectually in proportion as it is more completely blended with the natural agencies of mind.

The movement of thought from one order of subjects to another.—"Thus their theory, true in itself, and departing from a well-established principle, the Association of Ideas, explains in a satisfactory manner a portion of the phænomena of Reminiscence; but it is incomplete, for it is unable to account for the prompt, easy, and varied operation of this faculty, or for all the marvels it performs. On the doctrine of the philosophers, we can explain how a scholar repeats, without hesitation, a lesson he has learned, for all the words are associated in his mind *according to the order in which he has studied them;* how he demonstrates a geometrical theorem, the parts of which are connected together in the same manner; these and similar reminiscences of simple successions present no difficulties which the common doctrine cannot resolve. But it is impossible, on this doctrine, to explain the rapid and certain movement of thought, which, with a marvellous facility, *passes from one order of subjects to another*, only to return again to the first; which advances, retrogrades, deviates, and reverts, sometimes marking all the points on its route, again clearing, as if in play, immense intervals; which runs over, now in a manifest order, now in a seeming irregularity, all the notions relative to an object, often relative to several, between which no connection could be suspected; and this without hesitation, without uncertainty, without error, as the hand of a skilful musician expatiates over the keys of the most complex organ. All this is inexplicable on the meagre and contracted theory on which the phænomena of Reproduction have been thought explained.

Two conditions of Reminiscence. — "To form a correct notion of the phænomena of Reminiscence, it is requisite, that we consider under what conditions it is determined to exertion. In the first place, it is to be noted that, at every crisis of our existence, momentary circumstances are the causes which awaken our activity, and set our recollection at work to supply the necessaries of thought. In the second place, it is as constituting a want (and by *want*, I mean the result either of an act of desire or of volition), that the determining circumstance tends principally to awaken the thoughts with which it is associated. This being the case, we should expect that each circumstance which constitutes a want should suggest, likewise, the notion of an object, or objects, proper to satisfy it; and this is what actually happens. It is, however, further to be observed, that it is not enough that the want suggests the idea of the object; for if that idea were alone, it would remain without effect, since it could not guide me in the procedure I should follow. It is necessary, at the same time, that, to the idea of this object there should be associated the notion of the relation of this object to the want, of the place where I may find it, of the means by which I may procure it, and turn it to account, etc. For instance, I wish to make a quotation: — this want awakens in me the idea of the author in whom the passage is to be found, which I am desirous of citing; but this idea would be fruitless, unless there were conjoined, at the same time, the representation of the volume, of the place where I may obtain it, of the means I must employ, etc.

Accessory notions awakened. — "Hence I infer, in the first place, that a want does not awaken an idea of its object alone, but that it awakens it accompanied with a number, more or less considerable, of accessory notions, which form, as it were, its train or attendance. This train may vary according to the nature of the want which suggests the notion of an object; but the train can never fall wholly off, and it becomes more indissolubly attached to the object, in proportion as it has been more frequently called up in attendance.

"I infer, in the second place, that this accompaniment of accessory notions, simultaneously suggested with the principal idea, is far from being as vividly and distinctly represented in consciousness as that idea itself; and when these accessories have once been completely blended with the habits of the mind, and its reproductive agency, they at length finally disappear, becoming fused, as it were, in the consciousness of the idea to which they are attached. Experience proves this double effect of the habits of Reminiscence. If we observe our operations relative to the gratification of a want, we shall perceive that we are far from having a clear consciousness of the accessory notions; the consciousness of them is, as it were, obscured, and yet we cannot doubt that they are present to the mind, for it is they that direct our procedure in all its details.

These accessory notions unknown to consciousness. — "We must, therefore, I think, admit that the thought of an object immediately suggested by a desire, is always accompanied by an escort, more or less numerous, of accessory thoughts, equally present to the mind, though, in general, unknown in themselves to consciousness; that these accessories are not without their influence in guiding the operations elicited by the principal notion; and, it may even be added, that they are so much the more calculated to exert an effect in the conduct of our procedure, in proportion as, having become more part and parcel of our habits of Reproduction, the influences they exert are further withdrawn, in ordinary, from the ken of consciousness." The same thing may be illustrated by what happens to us in the case of reading. Originally, each word, each letter, was a separate object of consciousness. At length, the knowledge of letters and words and lines being, as it were, fused into our habits, we no longer have any distinct consciousness of them, as severally concurring to the result, of which alone we are conscious. But that each word and letter has its effect, — an effect which can, at any moment, become an object of consciousness, is shown by the following experiment. If we look over a book for the occurrence of a particular name or word, we glance our eye över a page from top to bottom, and ascertain, almost in a moment, that it is or is not to be found therein. Here the mind is hardly conscious of a single word, but that of which it is in quest; but yet it is evident, that each other word and letter must have produced an obscure effect, and which effect the mind was ready to discriminate and strengthen, so as to call it into clear consciousness, whenever the effect was found to be that which the letters of the word sought for could determine. But, if the mind be not unaffected by the multitude of letters and words which it surveys, if it be able to ascertain whether the combination of letters constituting the word it seeks, be or be not actually among them, and all this without any distinct consciousness of all it tries and finds defective, — why may we not suppose, — why are we not bound to suppose, that the mind may, in like manner, overlook its book of memory, and search among its magazines of latescent cognitions for the notions of which it is in want, awakening these into consciousness, and allowing the others to remain in their obscurity?

Each accessory thought calls up other thoughts. — "A more attentive consideration of the subject," [continues Cardaillac,] "will show, that we have not yet divined the faculty of Reminiscence in its whole extent. Let us make a single reflection. Continually struck by relations of every kind, continually assailed by a crowd of perceptions and sensations of every variety, and, at the same time, occupied with a complement of thoughts; we experience at once, and we are more or less distinctly conscious of, a considerable number of wants, — wants sometimes real, sometimes factitious or imaginary, — phænomena, however, all stamped with the same characters, and all stimulating us to act with more or less of energy. And as we choose among the different wants which we would satisfy, as well as among the different means of satisfying that want which we determine to prefer; and as the motives of this preference are taken either from among the principal ideas relative to each of these several wants, or from among the accessory ideas which habit has established into their necessary escorts; — in all these cases, it is requisite that all the circumstances should at once, and from the moment they have taken the character of wants, produce an effect correspondent to that which, we have seen, is caused by each in particular. Hence we are compelled to conclude, that the complement of the circumstances by which we are thus affected, has the effect of rendering always present to us, and, consequently, of placing at our disposal, an immense number of thoughts; some of which certainly are distinctly recognized, being accompanied by a vivid consciousness, but the greater number of which, although remaining latent, are not the less effective in continually exercising their peculiar influence on our modes of judging and acting.

"We might say, that each of these momentary circumstances is a kind of electric shock which is communicated to a certain portion, — to a certain limited sphere, of intelligence; and the sum of all these circumstances is equal to so many shocks, which, given at once at so many different points, produce a general agitation. We may form some rude conception of this phænomenon by an analogy. We may compare it, in the former case, to those concentric circles which are presented to our observation on a smooth sheet of water, when its surface is agitated by throwing in a pebble; and, in the latter case, to the same surface when agitated by a number of pebbles thrown simultaneously at different points.

"To obtain a clearer notion of this phænomenon, I may add some observations on *the relations of our thoughts among themselves*, and with *the determining circumstances of the moment.*

"1°, Among the thoughts, notions, or ideas which belong to the different groups, attached to the principal representations simultaneously awakened, there are some reciprocally connected by relations proper to themselves; so that, in this whole complement of coëxistent activities, these tend to excite each other to higher vigor, and, consequently, to obtain for themselves a kind of preëminence in the group or particular circle of activity to which they belong.

"2°, There are thoughts associated, whether as principals or accessories, to a greater number of determining circumstances, or to circumstances which recur more frequently. Hence they present themselves oftener than the others, they enter more completely into our habits, and take, in a more absolute manner, the character of customary or habitual notions. It hence results, that they are less obtrusive, though more energetic, in their influence, enacting, as they do, a principal part in almost all our deliberations; and exercising a stronger influence on our determinations.

"3°, Among this great crowd of thoughts, simultaneously excited, those which are connected with circumstances which more vividly affect us, assume not only the ascendant over others of the same description with themselves, but likewise predominate over all those which are dependent on circumstances of a feebler determining influence.

"From these three considerations, we ought, therefore, to infer, that the thoughts connected with circumstances on which our attention is more specially concentrated, are those which prevail over the others; for the effect of attention is to render dominant and exclusive the object on which it is directed, and during the moment of attention, it is the circumstance to which we attend that necessarily obtains the ascendant.

"Thus if we appreciate correctly the phænomena of Reproduction or Reminiscence, we shall recognize, as an incontestable fact, that our thoughts suggest each other, not one by one successively, as the order to which language is astricted might lead us to infer; but that the complement of circumstances under which we at every moment exist, awakens simultaneously a great number of thoughts; these it calls into the presence of the mind, either to place them at our disposal, if we find it requisite to employ them, or to make them coöperate in our deliberations, by giving them, according to their nature and our habits, an influence, more or less active, on our judgments and consequent acts

"It is also to be observed, that in this great crowd of thoughts always present to the mind, there is only a small number of which we are distinctly conscious: and that in this small number, we ought to distinguish those which, being clothed in language oral or mental, become the objects of a more fixed attention; those which hold a closer relation to circumstances more impressive than others; or which receive a predominant character by the more vigorous attention we bestow on them. As to the others, although not the objects of clear consciousness, they are nevertheless present to the mind, there to perform a very important part as motive principles of determination; and the influence which they exert in this capacity is even the more powerful in proportion as it is less apparent, being more disguised by habit

CHAPTER XXIV.

THE REPRESENTATIVE FACULTY. — IMAGINATION.

HAVING terminated the separate consideration of the two first of the three correlative processes of Retention, Reproduction, and Representation, I proceed to the special discussion of the last, — the Representative Faculty.

By the faculty of Representation, as I formerly mentioned, I mean strictly the power the mind has of holding up vividly before itself the thoughts which, by the act of Reproduction, it has recalled into consciousness. Though the processes of Representation and Reproduction cannot exist independently of each other, they are nevertheless not more to be confounded into one than those of Reproduction and Conservation. They are, indeed, discriminated by differences sufficiently decisive. Reproduction, as we have seen, operates, in part at least, out of consciousness. Representation, on the contrary, is only realized as it is realized in consciousness; the degree or vivacity of the representation being always in proportion to the degree or vivacity of our consciousness of its reality. Nor are the energies of Representation and Reproduction always exerted by the same individual in equal intensity, any more than the energies of Reproduction and Retention. Some minds are distinguished for a higher power of manifesting one of these phænomena; others, for manifesting another; and as it is not always the person who forgets nothing, who can most promptly recall what he retains, so neither is it always the person who recollects most easily and correctly, who can exhibit what he remembers in the most vivid colors. It is to be recollected, however, that Retention, Reproduction, and Representation, though not in different persons of the same relative vigor, are, however, in the same individuals, all strong or weak in reference to the same classes of objects. For example, if a man's memory be more peculiarly retentive of words, his verbal reminiscence and imagination will, in like manner, be more particularly energetic.

In common language, it is not of course to be expected that there should be found terms to express the result of an analysis, which had not even been performed by philosophers; and, accordingly, the term *Imagination*, or *Phantasy*, which denotes most nearly the Representative process, does this, however, not without an admixture of other processes, which it is of consequence for scientific precision that we should consider apart.

Improper division of Imagination.—Philosophers have divided Imagination into two,—what they call the Reproductive and the Productive. By the former, they mean Imagination considered as simply reëxhibiting, representing, the objects presented by perception, that is, exhibiting them without addition or retrenchment, or any change in the relations which they reciprocally held when first made known to us through sense. This operation Mr. Stewart has discriminated as a separate faculty, and bestowed on it the name of Conception. This discrimination and nomenclature I think unfortunate. The discrimination is unfortunate, because it is unphilosophical to distinguish, as a separate faculty, what is evidently only a special application of a common power. The nomenclature is unfortunate, for the term *Conception*, which means a taking up in bundles, or grasping into unity,—this term, I say, ought to have been left to denote, what it previously was, and only properly could be, applied to express,—the notions we have of classes of objects, in other words, what have been called our *general ideas*. Be this, however, as it may, it is evident, that the Reproductive Imagination (or Conception, in the abusive language of the Scottish philosophers) is *not a simple faculty*. It comprises two processes:—*first*, an act of representation strictly so called; and, *secondly*, an act of reproduction arbitrarily limited by certain contingent circumstances; and it is from the arbitrary limitation of this second constituent, that the faculty obtains the only title it can exhibit to an independent existence. Nor can the Productive Imagination establish a better claim to the distinction of a separate faculty than the Reproductive. The Productive or Creative Imagination is that which is usually signified by the term *Imagination* or *Fancy*, in ordinary language. Now, in the first place, it is to be observed, that the terms *productive* or *creative* are very improperly applied to Imagination, or the Representative Faculty of mind. It is admitted on all hands, that Imagination creates nothing, that is, produces nothing new; and the terms in question are, therefore, by the acknowledgment of those who employ them, only abusively applied to denote the operations of Fancy, in the new arrangement it makes of the old objects furnished to it by the senses. We have now, therefore, only to consider, whether, in this corrected meaning, Imagination, as a plastic energy, be a simple or a complex operation. And that it is a complex operation, I do not think it will be at all difficult to prove.

What is Representation? — In the view I take of the fundamental processes, the act of Representation is merely the energy of the mind in holding up to its own contemplation what it is determined to represent. I distinguish, as essentially different, the Representation, and the determination to represent. I exclude from the Faculty of Representation all power of preference among the objects it holds up to view. This is the function of faculties wholly different from that of Representation, which, though active in representing, is wholly passive as to what it represents.

Two conditions of Representation. — What, then, it may be asked, are the powers by which the Representative Faculty is determined to represent, and to represent this particular object, or this particular complement of objects, and not any other? These are two. The *first* of these is the Reproductive Faculty. This faculty is the great immediate source from which the Representative receives both the materials and the determination to represent; and the laws by which the Reproductive

Faculty is governed, govern also the Representative. Accordingly, if there were no other laws in the arrangement and combination of thought than those of association, the Representative Faculty would be determined in its manifestations, and in the character of its manifestations, by the Reproductive Faculty alone; and, on this supposition, Representation could no more be distinguished from Reproduction than Reproduction from Association.

The Faculty of Relations. — But there is *another* elementary process which we have not yet considered, — Comparison, or the Faculty of relations, to which the representative act is likewise subject, and which plays a conspicuous part in determining in what combinations objects are represented. By the process of Comparison, the complex objects, — the congeries of phænomena called up by the Reproductive Faculty, undergo various operations. They are separated into parts, they are analyzed into elements; and these parts and elements are again compounded in every various fashion. In all this the Representative Faculty coöperates. It, first of all, exhibits the phænomena so called up by the laws of ordinary association. In this it acts as handmaid to the Reproductive Faculty. It then exhibits the phænomena as variously elaborated by the analysis and synthesis of the Comparative Faculty, to which, in like manner, it performs the part of a subsidiary.

Imagination a complex process. — This being understood, you will easily perceive, that the Imagination of common language, — the Productive Imagination of philosophers, — is nothing but the Representative process, *plus* the process to which I would give the name of the *Comparative.* In this compound operation, it is true that the representative act is the most conspicuous, perhaps the most essential, element. For, in the *first* place, it is a condition of the possibility of the act of comparison, — of the act of analytic synthesis, that the material on which it operates (that is, the objects reproduced in their natural connections) should be held up to its observation in a clear light, in order that it may take note of their various circumstances of relation; and, in the *second*, that the result of its own elaboration, that is, the new arrangements which it proposes, should be realized in a vivid act of Representation. Thus it is, that, in the view both of the vulgar and of philosophers, the more obtrusive, though really the more subordinate, element in this compound process has been elevated into the principal constituent; whereas, the act of Comparison, — the act of separation and reconstruction, has been regarded as identical with the act of Representation.

Thus Imagination, in the common acceptation of the term, is not a simple but a compound faculty, — a faculty, however, in which Representation, — the vivid exhibition of an object, — forms the principal constituent. If, therefore, we were obliged to find a common word for every elementary process of our analysis, — *Imagination* would be the term, which, with the least violence to its meaning, could be accommodated to express the Representative Faculty.

Imagination not limited to objects of sense. — By Imagination, thus limited, you are not to suppose that the faculty of representing mere objects of sense alone is meant. On the contrary, a vigorous power of Representation is as indispensable a condition of success in the abstract sciences, as in the poetical and plastic arts; and it may, accordingly, be reasonably doubted whether Aristotle or Homer were possessed of the more powerful Imagination. "We may, indeed, affirm, that there are as many different kinds of imagination as there are different kinds of intellectual activity. There is the imagination of abstraction, which represents to us certain phases of an object to the exclusion of others, and, at the same time, the sign by which the phases are united; the imagination of wit, which represents differences and contrasts, and the resemblances by which these are again combined; the imagination of judgment, which represents the various qualities of an object, and binds them together under the relations of substance, of attribute, of mode; the imagination of reason, which represents a principle in connection with its consequences, the effect in dependence on its cause; the imagination of feeling, which represents the accessory images, kindred to some particular, and which therefore confer on it greater compass, depth, and intensity; the imagination of volition, which represents all the circumstances which concur to persuade or dissuade from a certain act of will; the imagination of the passions, which, according to the nature of the affection, represents all that is homogeneous or analogous; finally, the imagination of the poet, which represents whatever is new, or beautiful, or sublime, — whatever, in a word, it is determined to represent by any interest of art." * The term *Imagination*, however, is less generally applied to the representations of the Comparative Faculty considered in the abstract, than to the representations of sensible objects concretely modified by comparison. The two kinds of imagination are, in fact, not frequently combined. Accordingly, using the term in this its ordinary extent, that is, in its limitation to objects of sense, it is finely said by Mr. Hume: "Nothing is more dangerous to reason than the flights of imagination, and nothing has been the occasion of more mistakes among philosophers. Men of bright fancies may, in this respect, be compared to those angels whom the Scriptures represent as covering their eyes with their wings."

Considering the Representative Faculty in subordination to its two determinants, the faculty of Reproduction and the faculty of Comparison or Elaboration, we may distinguish *three principal orders in which Imagination represents ideas:* — "1°, The Natural order; 2°, The Logical order; 3°, The Poetical order. The Natural order is that in which we receive the impression of external objects, or the order according to which our thoughts spontaneously group themselves. The Logical order consists in presenting what is universal, prior to what is contained under it as particular, or in presenting the particulars first, and then ascending to the universal which they constitute. The former is the order of Deduction, the latter that of Induction. These two orders have this in common, that they deliver to us notions in the dependence in which the antecedent explains the subsequent. The Poetical order consists in seizing

* [Translated by Hamilton, together with the other citations in this chapter, unless otherwise credited, from Ancillon's *Essais Philosophiques*.]

individual circumstances, and in grouping them in such a manner that the Imagination shall represent them so as they might be offered by the sense. The Natural order is *involuntary;* it is established independently of our concurrence. The Logical order is *a child of art,* it is the result of our will; but it is conformed to the laws of intelligence, which tend always to recall the particular to the general, or the general to the particular. The Poetical order is exclusively *calculated on effect.* Pindar would not be a lyric poet, if his thoughts and images followed each other in the common order, or in the logical order. The state of mind in which thought and feeling clothe themselves in lyric forms, is a state in which thoughts and feelings are associated in an extraordinary manner, — in which they have, in fact, no other relation than that which groups and moves them around the dominant thought or feeling which forms the subject of the ode."

Imagination as affected by different trains of association. — "Thoughts which follow each other only in the natural order, or as they are associated in the minds of men in general, form tedious conversations and tiresome books. Thoughts, on the other hand, whose connection is singular, capricious, extraordinary, are unpleasing; whether it be that they strike us as improbable, or that the effort which has been required to produce, supposes a corresponding effort to comprehend. Thoughts whose association is at once simple and new, and which, though not previously witnessed in conjunction, are yet approximated without a violent exertion, — such thoughts please universally, by affording the mind the pleasures of novelty and exercise at once."

"A peculiar kind of Imagination, determined by a peculiar order of association, is usually found in every period of life, in every sex, in every country, in every religion. A knowledge of men principally consists in a knowledge of the principles by which their thoughts are linked and represented. The study of this is of importance to the instructor, in order to direct the character and intellect of his pupils; to the statesman, that he may exert his influence on the public opinion and manners of a people; to the poet, that he may give truth and reality to his dramatic situations; to the orator, in order to convince and persuade; to the man of the world, if he would give interest to his conversation.

"Authors who have made a successful study of this subject skim over a multitude of circumstances under which an occurrence has taken place, because they are aware that it is proper to reject what is only accessory to the object which they would present in prominence. A vulgar mind forgets and spares nothing; he is ignorant that conversation is always but a selection; that every story is subject to the laws of dramatic poetry,—*festinat ad eventum;* and that all which does not concur to the effect, destroys or weakens it. The involuntary associations of their thoughts are imperative on minds of this description; they are held in thraldom to the order and circumstances in which their perceptions were originally obtained." This has not, of course, escaped the notice of the greatest observer of human nature. Mrs. Quickly, in reminding Falstaff of his promise of marriage, supplies a good example of this peculiarity. 'Thou didst swear to me upon a parcel-gilt goblet, sitting in my Dolphin chamber, at the round table, by a sea-coal fire, upon Wednesday in Whitsun week, when the prince broke thy head for likening his father to a singing man of Windsor,'—and so forth.

"Dreaming, Somnambulism, Reverie, are so many effects of imagination determined by association,—at least, states of mind in which these have a decisive influence. If an impression on the sense often commences a dream, it is by imagination and suggestion that it is developed and accomplished. Dreams have frequently a degree of vivacity which enables them to compete with the reality; and if the events which they represent to us were in accordance with the circumstances of time and place in which we stand, it would be almost impossible to distinguish a vivid dream from a sensible perception." "If," says Pascal, "we dreamt every night the same thing, it would perhaps affect us as powerfully as the objects which we perceive every day. And if an artisan were certain of dreaming every night for twelve hours that he was king, I am convinced that he would be almost as happy as a king, who dreamt for twelve hours that he was an artisan. If we dreamt every night that we were pursued by enemies and harassed by horrible phantoms, we should suffer almost as much as if that were true, and we should stand in as great dread of sleep, as we should of waking, had we real cause to apprehend these misfortunes. . . . . It is only because dreams are different and inconsistent, that we can say, when we awake, that we have dreamt; for life is a dream a little less inconstant." Now the case which Pascal here hypothetically supposes, has actually happened. In a very curious German work, by Abel, I find the following case, which I abridge: — A young man had a cataleptic attack, in consequence of which a singular effect was operated in his mental constitution. Some six minutes after falling asleep, he began to speak distinctly, and almost always of the same objects and concatenated events, so that he carried on from night to night the same history, or rather continued to play the same part. On wakening, he had no reminiscence whatever of his dreaming thoughts, — a circumstance, by the way, which distinguishes this as rather a case of somnambulism than of common dreaming. Be this, however, as it may, he played a double part in his existence. By day, he was the poor apprentice of a merchant; by night, he was a married man, the father of a family, a senator, and in affluent circumstances. If, during his vision, any thing was said in regard to his waking state, he declared it unreal and a dream. This case, which is established on the best evidence, is, as far as I am aware, unique.

The influence of dreams upon our character is not without its interest. A particular tendency may be strengthened in a man solely by the repeated action of dreams. Dreams do not, however, as is commonly supposed, afford any appreciable indication of the character of individuals. It is not always the subjects that occupy us most, when awake, that form the matter of our dreams; and it is curious that the persons the dearest to us are precisely those about whom we dream most rarely.

Somnambulism is a phænomenon still more astonishing. In

this singular state, a person performs a regular series of rational actions, and those frequently of the most difficult and delicate nature, and what is still more marvellous, with a talent to which he could make no pretension when awake. His memory and reminiscence supply him with recollections of words and things, which perhaps were never at his disposal in the ordinary state; he speaks more fluently a more refined language; and, if we are to credit what the evidence on which it rests hardly allows us to disbelieve, he has not only perceptions through other channels than the common organs of sense, but the sphere of his cognitions is amplified to an extent far beyond the limits to which sensible perception is confined. This subject is one of the most perplexing in the whole compass of philosophy; for, on the one hand, the phænomena are so marvellous that they cannot be believed, and yet, on the other, they are of so unambiguous and palpable a character, and the witnesses to their reality are so numerous, so intelligent, and so high above every suspicion of deceit, that it is equally impossible to deny credit to what is attested by such ample and unexceptionable evidence.

"The third state, that of Reverie or Castle-building, is a kind of waking dream, and does not differ from dreaming, except by the consciousness which accompanies it. In this state, the mind abandons itself without a choice of subject, without control over the mental train, to the involuntary associations of imagination. The mind is thus occupied without being properly active; it is active, at least, without effort. Young persons, women, the old, the unemployed, and the idle, are all disposed to reverie. There is a pleasure attached to its illusions, which render it as seductive as it is dangerous. The mind, by indulgence in this dissipation, becomes enervated; it acquires the habit of a pleasing idleness, loses its activity, and at length even the power and the desire of action."

Influence of imagination on human life. — "The happiness and misery of every individual of mankind depends almost exclusively on the particular character of his habitual associations, and the relative kind and intensity of his imagination. It is much less what we actually are, and what we actually possess, than what we imagine ourselves to be and have, that is decisive of our existence and fortune." Apicius committed suicide to avoid starvation, when his fortune was reduced to somewhere, in English money, about £100,000. The Roman epicure imagined that he could not subsist on what, to men in general, would seem more than affluence.

"Imagination, by the attractive or repulsive pictures with which, according to our habits and associations, it fills the frame of our life, lends to reality a magical charm, or despoils it of all its pleasantness. The imaginary happy and the imaginary miserable are common in the world, but their happiness and misery are not the less real; every thing depends on the mode in which they feel and estimate their condition. Fear, hope, the recollection of past pleasures, the torments of absence and of desire, the secret and almost resistless tendency of the mind towards certain objects, are the effects of association and imagination. At a distance, things seem to us radiant with a celestial beauty, or in the lurid aspect of deformity. Of a truth, in either case, we are equally wrong. When the event which we dread, or which we desire, takes place, when we obtain, or when there is forced upon us, an object environed with a thousand hopes, or with a thousand fears, we soon discover that we have expected too much or too little; we thought it by anticipation infinite in good or evil, and we find it in reality not only finite, but contracted. 'With the exception,' says Rousseau, 'of the self-existent Being, there is nothing beautiful, but that which is not.' In the crisis, whether of enjoyment or suffering, happiness is not so much happiness, nor misery so much misery, as we had anticipated. In the past, thanks to a beneficent Creator, our joys reappear as purer and more brilliant than they had been actually experienced; and sorrow loses not only its bitterness, but is changed even into a source of pleasing recollection. In early youth, the present and the future are displayed in a factitious magnificence; for at this period of life, imagination is in its spring and freshness, and a cruel experience has not yet exorcised its brilliant enchantments. Hence the fair picture of a golden age, which all nations concur in placing in the past; it is the dream of the youth of mankind." In old age, again, where the future is dark and short, imagination carries us back to the reënjoyment of a past existence. "The young," says Aristotle, "live forwards in hope, the old live backwards in memory."

From all this, however, it appears, that the present is the only time in which we never actually live; we live either in the future, or in the past. So long as we have a future to anticipate, we contemn the present; and when we can no longer look forward to a future, we revert and spend our existence in the past.

Organs of Imagination. — I shall terminate the consideration of Imagination Proper by a speculation concerning the organ which it employs in the representations of sensible objects. The organ which it thus employs seems to be no other than the organs themselves of Sense, on which the original impressions were made, and through which they were originally perceived. Experience has shown, that Imagination depends on no one part of the cerebral apparatus exclusively. There is no portion of the brain which has not been destroyed by mollification, or induration, or external lesion, without the general faculty of Representation being injured. But experience equally proves, that the intracranial portion of any external organ of sense cannot be destroyed, without a certain partial abolition of the Imagination Proper. For example, there are many cases recorded by medical observers, of persons losing their sight, who have also lost the faculty of representing the images of visible objects. They no longer call up such objects by reminiscence, they no longer dream of them. Now in these cases, it is found that not merely the external instrument of sight, — the eye, — has been disorganized, but that the disorganization has extended to those parts of the brain which constitute the internal instrument of this sense, that is, the optic nerves and thalami. If the latter, — the real organ of vision, — remain sound, the eye alone being destroyed, the imagination of colors and forms remains as vigorous as when vision was entire. Similar cases are recorded in regard to the deaf. These facts, added to the observation of the internal phænomena which take place during our acts of representation, make it, I think, more than probable that there are as many organs of Imagination as there are organs of Sense. Thus I have a distinct consciousness, that, in the internal representation of visible objects, the same organs are at work which operate in the external perception of these; and the same holds good in an imagination of the objects of Hearing, Touch, Taste, and Smell.

But not only sensible perceptions, voluntary motions likewise are imitated in and by the imagination. I can, in imagination represent the action of speech, the play of the muscles of the countenance, the movement of the limbs; and when I do this, I feel clearly that I awaken a kind of tension in the same nerves through which, by an act of will, I can determine an overt and voluntary motion of the muscles; nay, when the play of imagination is very lively, this external movement is actually determined. Thus we frequently see the countenances of persons under the influence of imagination undergo various changes; they gesticulate with their hands, they talk to themselves, and all this is in consequence only of the imagined activity going out into real activity. I should, therefore, be disposed to conclude, that, as in Perception the living organs of sense are from without determined to energy, so in Imagination they are determined to a similar energy by an influence from within.

CHAPTER XXV.

THE ELABORATIVE FACULTY. — CLASSIFICATION. – ABSTRACTION AND GENERALIZATION. — NOMINALISM AND CONCEPTUALISM.

The faculties with which we have been hitherto engaged may be regarded as subsidiary to that which we are now about to consider. This, to which I gave the name of the Elaborative Faculty, — the Faculty of Relations, — or Comparison, — constitutes what is properly denominated Thought. It supposes always at least two terms, and its act results in a judgment, that is, an affirmation or negation of one of these terms of the other. You will recollect that, when treating of Consciousness in general, I stated to you, that *consciousness necessarily involves a judgment;* and as every act of mind is an act of consciousness, *every act of mind, consequently, involves a judgment.* A consciousness is necessarily the consciousness of a determinate something; and we cannot be conscious of any thing without virtually affirming its existence, that is, judging it to be. *Consciousness is thus primarily a judgment or affirmation of existence.*

Again, consciousness is not merely the affirmation of naked existence, but *the affirmation of a certain qualified or determinate existence.* We are conscious that we exist, only in and through our consciousness that we exist in this or that particular state, — that we are so or so affected, — so or so active; and we are only conscious of this or that particular state of existence, inasmuch as we discriminate it as different from some other state of existence, of which we have been previously conscious and are now reminiscent; but such a discrimination supposes, in consciousness, the affirmation of the existence of one state of a specific character, and the negation of another. On this ground it was that I maintained, that consciousness necessarily involves, besides recollection, or rather a certain continuity of representation, also judgment or comparison; and, consequently, that, so far from comparison or judgment being a process always subsequent to the acquisition of knowledge, through perception and self-consciousness, it is involved as a condition of the acquisitive process itself. In point of fact, the various processes of Acquisition (Apprehension), Representation, and Comparison, are all *mutually dependent.* Comparison cannot judge without something to compare; we cannot originally acquire, — apprehend, we cannot subsequently represent our knowledge, without in either act attributing existence, and a certain kind of existence, both to the object known and to the subject knowing, — that is, without enouncing certain judgments and performing certain acts of comparison; I say, without performing certain acts of comparison, for taking the mere affirmation that a thing is, — this is tantamount to a negation that it is not, and necessarily supposes a comparison, — a collation, between existence and non-existence.

Comparison supposed in every act of Thought. — What I have now said may perhaps contribute to prepare you for what I am hereafter to say of the faculty or elementary process of Comparison, — a faculty which, in the analysis of philosophers, is exhibited only in part; and even that part is not preserved in its integrity. They take into account only a fragment of the process, and that fragment they again break down into a plurality of faculties. In opposition to the views hitherto promulgated in regard to Comparison, I will show, that this faculty is at work in every, the simplest, act of mind; and that, from the primary affirmation of existence in an original act of consciousness, to the judgment contained in the conclusion of an act of reasoning, every operation is only an evolution of the same elementary process, — that there is a difference in the complexity, none in the nature, of the act; in short, that the various products of Analysis and Synthesis, of Abstraction and Generalization, are all merely the results of Comparison, and that the operations of Conception or Simple Apprehension, of Judgment, and of Reasoning, are all only acts of Comparison in various applications and degrees.

What I have, therefore, to prove is, in the *first* place, that Comparison is supposed in every, the simplest, act of knowledge; in the *second*, that our factitiously simple, our factitiously complex, our abstract, and our generalized notions are all merely so many products of Comparison; in the *third*, that Judgment, and, in the *fourth*, that Reasoning, is identical with Comparison. In doing this, I shall not formally distribute the discussion into these heads, but shall include the proof of what I have now advanced, while tracing Comparison from its simplest to its most complex operations.

Primary acts of Comparison. — The *first* or most elementary act of Comparison, or of that mental process in which the relation of two terms is recognized and affirmed, is the judgment virtually pronounced, in an act of Perception, of the Non-ego, or, in an act of Self-consciousness, of the Ego. This is the primary affirmation of existence. The notion of existence is one native to the mind. It is the primary condition of thought. The first act of experience awoke it, and the first act of consciousness was a subsumption of that of which we were conscious under this notion; in other words, the first act of consciousness was an affirmation of the existence of something. The first or simplest act of Comparison is thus the discrimination of existence from non-existence; and the first or simplest judgment is the affirmation of existence, in other words, the denial of non-existence.

But the something of which we are conscious, and of which we predicate existence, in the primary judgment, is twofold, — the Ego and the Non-ego. We are conscious of both, and affirm existence of both. But we do more; we do not merely affirm the existence of each out of relation to the other, but, in affirming their existence, we affirm their existence in duality, in difference, in mutual contrast; that is, we not only affirm the Ego to exist, but deny it existing as the Non-ego; we not only affirm the Non-ego to exist, but deny it existing as the Ego. The second act of Comparison is thus the discrimination of the Ego and the Non-ego; and the second judgment is the affirmation, that each is not the other.

The *third* gradation in the act of Comparison, is in the recognition of the multiplicity of the coexistent or successive phænomena, presented either to Perception or Self-consciousness, and the judgment in regard to their resemblance or dissimilarity.

The *fourth* is the Comparison of the phænomena with the native notion of Substance, and the judgment is the grouping of these phænomena into different bundles, as the attributes of different subjects. In the external world, this relation constitutes the distinction of things; in the internal, the distinction of powers.

The *fifth* act of Comparison is the collation of successive phænomena under the native notion of Causality, and the affirmation or negation of their mutual relation as cause and effect.

Classification an act of Comparison. — So far, the process of Comparison is determined merely by objective conditions hitherto, it has followed only in the footsteps of nature. In those, again, we are now to consider, the procedure is, in a certain sort, artificial, and determined by the necessities of the thinking subject itself. The mind is finite in its powers of comprehension; the objects, on the contrary, which are presented to it, are, in proportion to its limited capacities, infinite in number. How then is this disproportion to be equalized? How can the infinity of nature be brought down to the finitude of man? This is done by means of Classification. Objects, though infinite in number, are not infinite in variety; they are all, in a certain sort, repetitions of the same common qualities, and the mind, though lost in the multitude of particulars, — individuals, — can easily grasp the classes into which their resembling attributes enable us to assort these. This whole process of Classification is a mere act of Comparison, as the following deduction will show.

In the first place, this may be shown in regard to the formation of Complex notions, with which, as the simplest species of classification, we may commence. By Complex or Collective notions, I mean merely the notion of a class formed by the repetition of the same constituent notion. Such are the notions of *an army*, *a forest*, *a town*, *a number*. These are names of classes, formed by the repetition of the notion of *a soldier*, of *a tree*, of *a house*, of *a unit*. You are not to confound, as has sometimes been done, the notion of *an army*, *a forest*, *a town*, *a number*, with the notions of *army*, *forest*, *town*, and *number*; the former, as I have said, are complex or collective, the latter are general or universal notions.

It is evident that a Collective notion is the result of Comparison. The repetition of the same constituent notion supposes that these notions were compared, their identity or absolute similarity affirmed.

How language aids Classification.—In the whole process of classification, the mind is in a great measure dependent upon language for its success; and in this, the simplest of the acts of classification, it may be proper to show how language affords to mind the assistance it requires. Our complex notions being formed by the repetition of the same notion, it is evident that the difficulty we can experience in forming an adequate conception of a class of identical constituents, will be determined by the difficulty we have in conceiving a multitude. "But the comprehension of the mind," [says Degerando,] "is feeble and limited; it can embrace at once but a small number of objects. It would thus seem that an obstacle is raised to the extension of our complex ideas at the very outset of our combinations. But here language interposes, and supplies the mind with the force of which it is naturally destitute." We have formerly seen that the mind cannot, in one act, embrace more than five or six, at the utmost seven, several units. How then does it proceed? "When, by a first combination, we have obtained a complement of notions as complex as the mind can embrace, we give this complement a name. This being done, we regard the assemblage of units thus bound up under a collective name as itself a unit, and proceed, by a second combination, to accumulate these into a new complement of the same extent. To this new complement we give another name; and then again proceed to perform, on this more complex unit, the same operation we had performed on the first; and so we may go on rising from complement to complement to an indefinite extent. Thus, a merchant, having received a large unknown sum of money in crowns, counts out the pieces by fives, and having done this till he has reached twenty, he lays them together in a heap; around these, he assembles similar piles of coin, till they amount, let us say, to twenty; and he then puts the whole four hundred into a bag. In this manner he proceeds, until he fills a number of bags, and placing the whole in his coffers, he will have a complex or collective notion of the quantity of crowns which he has received." It is on this principle that arithmetic proceeds, — tens, hundreds, thousands, myriads, hundreds of thousands, millions, etc., are all so many factitious units, which enable us to form notions, vague indeed, of what otherwise we could have obtained no conception at all. So much for complex or collective notions, formed without decomposition, — a process which I now go on to consider.

Two modes of decomposing thought. — Our thought, — that is, the sum total of the perceptions and representations which occupy us at any given moment, is always, as I have frequently observed, compound. The composite objects of thoughts may be decomposed in two ways, and for the sake of two different interests. In the first place, we may decompose in order that we may recombine, influenced by the mere pleasure which this plastic operation affords us. This is poetical analysis and synthesis. On this process it is needless to dwell. It is evidently the work of comparison. For example, the minotaur, or chimæra, or centaur, or gryphon (hippogryph), or any other poetical combination of different animals, could only have been effected by an act in which the representations of these animals were compared, and in which certain parts of one were affirmed, compatible with certain parts of another. How, again, is the imagination of all ideal beauty or perfection formed? Simply by comparing the various beauties or excellences of which we have had actual experience, and thus being enabled to pronounce in regard to their common and essential quality.

In the second place, we may decompose in the interest of science; and as the poetical decomposition was principally accomplished by a separation of integral parts, so this is principally accomplished by an abstraction of constituent qualities. On this process it is necessary to be more particular.

Abstraction through the senses. — Suppose an unknown body is presented to my senses, and that it is capable of affecting each of these in a certain manner. "As furnished with five different organs," [says Laromiguière,] "each of which serves to introduce a certain class of perceptions and representations into the mind, we naturally distribute all sensible objects into five species of qualities. The human body, if we may so speak, is thus itself a kind of abstractive machine. The senses cannot but abstract. If the eye did not abstract colors, it would see them confounded with odors and with tastes, and odors and tastes would necessarily become objects of sight."

"The abstraction of the senses is thus an operation the most natural; it is even impossible for us not to perform it. Let us now see whether abstraction by the mind be more arduous than that of the senses." We have formerly found that the comprehension of the mind is extremely limited; that it can only take cognizance of one object at a time, if that be known with full intensity; and that it can accord a simultaneous attention to a very small plurality of objects, and even that imperfectly. Thus it is that attention fixed on one object is tantamount to a withdrawal, — to an abstraction, of consciousness from every other. *Abstraction is thus not a positive act of mind,* as it is often erroneously described in philosophical treatises; — it is merely a negation to one or more objects, in consequence of its concentration on another.

This being the case, Abstraction is not only an easy and natural, but a necessary result. "In studying an object," [continues Laromiguière,] "we neither exert all our faculties at once, nor at once apply them to all the qualities of an object. We know from experience, that the effect of such a mode of procedure is confusion. On the contrary, we converge our attention on one alone of its qualities, — nay, contemplate this quality only in a single point of view, and retain it in that aspect until we have obtained a full and accurate conception of it. The human mind proceeds from the confused and complex to the distinct and constituent, always separating, always dividing, always simplifying; and this is the only mode in which, from the weakness of our faculties, we are able to apprehend and to represent with correctness."

"It is true, indeed, that after having decomposed every thing, we must, as it were, return on our steps by recomposing every thing anew; for unless we do so, our knowledge would not be conformable to the reality and relations of nature. The simple qualities of body have not each a proper and independent existence; the ultimate faculties of mind are not so many distinct and independent existences. On either side, there is a being one and the same; on that side, at once extended, solid, colored, etc.; on this, at once capable of thought, feeling, desire, etc."

"But although all, or the greater number of, our cognitions comprehend different fasciculi of notions, it is necessary to commence by the acquisition of these notions one by one, through a successive application of our attention to the different attributes of objects. The abstraction of the intellect is thus as natural as that of the senses. It is even imposed upon us by the very constitution of our mind."

"I am aware that the expression, *abstraction of the senses*, is incorrect; for it is the mind always which acts, be it through the medium of the senses. The impropriety of the expression is not, however, one which is in danger of leading into error; and it serves to point out the important fact, that Abstraction is not always performed in the same manner. In Perception, — in the presence of physical objects, the intellect abstracts colors by the eyes, sounds by the ear, etc. In Representation, and when the external object is absent, the mind operates on its reproduced cognitions, and looks at them successively in their different points of view."

"However abstraction be performed, the result is notions

which are simple, or which approximate to simplicity; and if we apply it with consistency and order to the different qualities of objects, we shall attain at length to a knowledge of these qualities and of their mutual dependencies; that is, to a knowledge of objects as they really are. In this case, abstraction becomes analysis, which is the method to which we owe all our cognitions."

The process of abstraction is familiar to the most uncultivated minds; and its uses are shown equally in the mechanical arts as in the philosophical sciences. "A carpenter," says Kames, speaking of the great utility of abstraction, "considers a log of wood with regard to hardness, firmness, color, and texture; a philosopher, neglecting these properties, makes the log undergo a chemical analysis, and examines its taste, its smell, and component principles; the geometrician confines his reasoning to the figure, the length, breadth, and thickness; in general, every artist, abstracting from all other properties, confines his observations to those which have a more immediate connection with his profession."

But is Abstraction, or rather, is exclusive attention, the work of Comparison? This is evident. The application of attention to a particular object, or quality of an object, supposes an act of will, — a choice or preference, and this again supposes Comparison and Judgment. But this may be made more manifest from a view of the act of Generalization, on which we are about to enter.

Generalization. Abstract individual ideas. — The notion of the figure of the desk before me is an abstract idea, — an idea that makes part of the total notion of that body, and on which I have concentrated my attention, in order to consider it exclusively. This idea is abstract, but it is at the same time individual; it represents the figure of this particular desk, and not the figure of any other body. But had we only individual abstract notions, what would be our knowledge? We should be cognizant only of qualities viewed apart from their subjects (and of separate phænomena there exists none in nature); and as these qualities are also separate from each other, we should have no knowledge of their mutual relations. We should also be overwhelmed with their number.

Abstract General notions. — It is necessary, therefore, that we should form Abstract General notions. This is done when, comparing a number of objects, we seize on their resemblances; when we concentrate our attention on these points of similarity, thus abstracting the mind from a consideration of their differences; and when we give a name to our notion of that circumstance in which they all agree. The General Notion is thus one which makes us know a quality, property, power, action, relation; in short, any point of view, under which we recognize a plurality of objects as a unity. It makes us aware of a quality, a point of view, common to many things. It is a notion of resemblance; hence the reason why general names or terms, the signs of general notions, have been called *terms of resemblance* (*termini similitudinis*). In this process of generalization, we do not stop short at a first generalization. By a first generalization, we have obtained a number of classes of resembling individuals. But these classes we can compare together, observe their similarities, abstract from their differences, and bestow on their common circumstance a common name. On these second classes we can again perform the same operation, and thus ascending the scale of general notions, throwing out of view always a greater number of differences, and seizing always on fewer similarities in the formation of our classes, we arrive at length at the limit of our ascent in the notion of *being* or *existence*. Thus placed on the summit of the scale of classes, we descend by a process the reverse of that by which we have ascended; we divide and subdivide the classes, by introducing always more and more characters, and laying always fewer differences aside; the notions become more and more composite, until we at length arrive at the individual.

Twofold quantity in notions. — I may here notice, that there is a twofold kind of quantity to be considered in notions. It is evident, that, in proportion as the class is high, it will, in the first place, contain under it a greater number of classes, and, in the second, will include the smallest complement of attributes.

Thus, *being* or *existence* contains under it every class; and yet, when we say that a thing exists, we say the very least of it that is possible. On the other hand, an individual, though it contain nothing but itself, involves the largest amount of predication. For example, when I say, — this is Richard, I not only affirm of the subject every class from existence down to man, but likewise a number of circumstances proper to Richard as an individual. Now, the former of these quantities, the external, is called the *Extension* of a notion; the latter, the internal quantity, is called its *Comprehension* or *Intension.* The extension of a notion is, likewise, styled its *circuit*, *region*, *domain*, or *sphere*, also its *breadth.* On the other hand, the comprehension of a notion is likewise called its *depth.* These names we owe to the Greek logicians. The internal and external quantities are in the inverse ratio of each other. The greater the Extension, the less the Comprehension; the greater the Comprehension, the less the Extension.

I have noticed the improper use of the term *abstraction* by many philosophers, in applying it to that on which attention is converged. This we may indeed be said to *prescind*, but not to *abstract.* Thus, let A, B, C, be three qualities of an object. We prescind A, in abstracting it from B and C; but we cannot, without impropriety, simply say that we abstract A. Thus, by attending to one object to the abstraction from all others, we, in a certain sort, decompose or analyze the complex materials presented to us by Perception and Self-consciousness. This analysis or decomposition is of two kinds. In the first place, by concentrating attention on one integrant part of an object, we, as it were, withdraw or abstract it from the others. For example, we can consider the head of an animal to the exclusion of the other members. This may be called Partial or Concrete Abstraction. The process here noticed has, however, been overlooked by philosophers, insomuch that they have opposed the terms *concrete* and *abstract* as exclusive contraries. In the second place, we can rivet our attention on some particular mode of a thing, as its smell, its color, its figure, its motion, its size, etc., and abstract it from the others. This may be called Modal Abstraction.

The Abstraction we have been now speaking of is performed on individual objects, and is consequently particular. There is nothing necessarily connected with Generalization in Abstraction. Generalization is indeed dependent on Abstraction, which it supposes; but Abstraction does not involve Generalization. I remark this, because you will frequently find the terms *abstract* and *general* applied to notions, used as convertible. Nothing, however, can be more incorrect. "A person," says Mr. Stewart, "who had never seen but one rose, might yet have been able to consider its *color* apart from its other qualities; and, therefore, there may be such a thing as an idea which is at once abstract and particular. After having perceived this quality as belonging to a variety of individuals, we can consider it without reference to any of them, and thus form the notion of redness or whiteness in general, which may be called a *general abstract idea*. The words *abstract* and *general*, therefore, when applied to ideas, are as completely distinct from each other as any two words to be found in the language."

Generalization is the process through which we obtain what are called *general* or *universal* notions. A general notion is nothing but the abstract notion of a circumstance in which a number of individual objects are found to agree, that is, to resemble each other. In so far as two objects resemble each other, the notion we have of them is identical, and, therefore, to us the objects may be considered as the same. Accordingly, having discovered the circumstance in which objects agree, we arrange them by this common circumstance into classes, to which we also usually give a common name.

I have explained how, in the prosecution of this operation, commencing with individual objects, we generalized these into a lowest class. Having found a number of such lowest classes, we then compare these again together, as we had originally compared individuals; we abstract their points of resemblance, and by these points generalize them into a higher class. The same process we perform upon these higher classes; and thus proceed, generalizing class from classes, until we are at last arrested in the one highest class, that of *being*. Thus we find

Peter, Paul, Timothy, etc., all agree in certain common attributes, which distinguish them from other animated beings. We accordingly collect them into a class, which we call *man.* In like manner, out of the other animated beings which we exclude from *man,* we form the classes, *horse, dog, ox,* etc. These and *man* form so many lowest classes or species. But these species, though differing in certain respects, all agree in others. Abstracting from their diversities, we attend only to their resemblances; and as all manifest life, sense, feeling, etc., — this resemblance gives us a class, on which we bestow the name *animal.* Animal, or living sentient existences, we then compare with lifeless existences, and thus going on abstracting from differences, and attending to resemblances, we arrive at naked or undifferenced existence. Having reached the pinnacle of generalization, we may redescend the ladder; and this is done by reversing the process through which we ascended. Instead of attending to the similarities, and abstracting from the differences, we now attend to the differences, and abstract from the similarities. And as the ascending process is called Generalization, this is called Division or Determination; — Division, because the higher or wider classes are cut down into lower or narrower; — Determination, because every quality added on to a class limits or determines its extent, that is, approximates it more to some individual, real, or determinate existence.

Question between the Nominalists and the Conceptualists. — Having given you this necessary information in regard to the nature of Generalization, I proceed to consider one of the most simple, and, at the same time, one of the most perplexed, problems in philosophy, — in regard to the object of the mind, — the object of consciousness, when we employ a general term. In the explanation of the process of generalization, all philosophers are at one; the only differences that arise among them relate to the point, — whether we can form an adequate idea of that which is denoted by an abstract, or abstract and general term. In the discussion of this question, I shall pursue the following order: *first* of all, I shall state the arguments of the Nominalists, — of those who hold, that we are unable to form an idea corresponding to the abstract and general term; in the *second* place, I shall state the arguments of the Conceptualists, — of those who maintain that we are so competent; and, in the *last*, I shall show that the opposing parties are really at one, and that the whole controversy has originated in the imperfection and ambiguity of our philosophical nomenclature. In this discussion, I avoid all mention of the ancient doctrine of Realism. This is curious only in an historical point of view; and is wholly irrelevant to the question at issue among modern philosophers.

This controversy has been principally agitated in [Great Britain] and in France, for a reason that I shall hereafter explain; and, to limit ourselves to Great Britain, the doctrine of Nominalism has, among others, been embraced by Hobbes, Berkeley, Hume, Principal Campbell, and Mr. Stewart; while Conceptualism has found favor with Locke, Reid, and Brown.

Throwing out of view the antiquities of the question, (and this question is perhaps more memorable than any other in the history of philosophy), — laying, I say, out of account opinions which have been long exploded, there are two which still divide philosophers. Some maintain, that *every act and every object of mind is necessarily singular, and that the name is that alone which can pretend to generality.* Others again hold, that *the mind is capable of forming notions, representations, correspondent in universality to the classes contained under, or expressed by, the general term.*

Nominalism. — The former of these opinions, — the doctrine, as it is called, of Nominalism, — maintains that every notion, considered in itself, is singular, but becomes, as it were, general, through the intention of the mind to make it represent every resembling notion, or notion of the same class. Take, for example, the term *man.* Here we can call up no notion, no idea, corresponding to the universality of the class or term. This is manifestly impossible. For as *man* involves contradictory attributes, and as contradictions cannot coexist in one representation, an idea or notion adequate to *man* cannot be realized in thought. The class *man* includes individuals, male and female, white and black and copper-colored, tall and short, fat and thin, straight and crooked, whole and mutilated, etc., etc.; and the notion of the class must, therefore, at once represent all and none of these. It is, therefore, evident, though the absurdity was maintained by Locke, that we cannot accomplish this; and, this being impossible, we cannot represent to ourselves the class *man* by any equivalent notion or idea. All that we can do is to call up some individual image, and consider it as representing, though inadequately representing, the generality. This we easily do, for as we can call into imagination any individual, so we can make that individual image stand for any or for every other which it resembles in those essential points which constitute the identity of the class. This opinion, which, after Hobbes, has been maintained, among others, by Berkeley, Hume, Adam Smith, Campbell, and Stewart, appears to me not only true, but self-evident.

No one has stated the case of the Nominalists more clearly than Bishop Berkeley, and his whole argument is, as far as it goes, irrefragable. "It is agreed," [he says,] "on all hands, that the qualities or modes of things do never really exist each of them apart by itself, and separated from all others, but are mixed, as it were, and blended together, several in the same object. But we are told, the mind, being able to consider each quality singly, or abstracted from those other qualities with which it is united, does by that means frame to itself abstract ideas. For example, there is perceived by sight an object extended, colored, and moved: this mixed or compound idea the mind resolving into its simple, constituent parts, and viewing each by itself, exclusive of the rest, does frame the abstract ideas of extension, color, and motion. Not that it is possible for color or motion to exist without extension; but only that the mind can frame to itself, by *abstraction*, the idea of color exclusive of extension, and of motion exclusive of both color and extension.

"Again, the mind having observed that, in the particular extensions perceived by sense, there is something common and alike in all, and some other things peculiar, as this or that figure or magnitude, which distinguish them one from another; it con siders apart or singles out by itself that which is common, making thereof a most abstract idea of extension, which is neither line, surface, nor solid, nor has any figure or magnitude, but is an idea entirely prescinded from all these. So, likewise, the mind, by leaving out of the particular colors perceived by sense that which distinguishes them one from another, and retaining that only which is common to all, makes an idea of color in abstract which is neither red, nor blue, nor white, nor any other determinate color. And in like manner, by considering motion abstractedly not only from the body moved, but likewise from the figure it describes, and all particular directions and velocities, the abstract idea of motion is framed; which equally corresponds to all particular motions whatsoever that may be perceived by sense.

"Whether others have this wonderful faculty of *abstracting their ideas*, they best can tell: for myself I find, indeed, I have a faculty of imagining, or representing to myself the ideas of those particular things I have perceived, and of variously compounding and dividing them. I can imagine a man with two heads, or the upper parts of a man joined to the body of a horse. I can consider the hand, the eye, the nose, each by itself abstracted or separated from the rest of the body. But then whatever hand or eye I imagine, it must have some particular shape and color. Likewise, the idea of man that I frame to myself must be either of a white, or a black, or a tawny, a straight or a crooked, a tall or a low, or a middle-sized man. I cannot by any effort of thought conceive the abstract idea above described. And it is equally impossible for me to form the abstract idea of motion distinct from the body moving, and which is neither swift nor slow, curvilinear nor rectilinear; and the like may be said of all other abstract general ideas whatsoever. To be plain, I own myself able to abstract in one sense, as when I consider some particular parts or qualities separated from others, with which, though they are united in some object, yet it is possible they may really exist without them. But I deny that I can abstract one from another, or conceive separately, those qualities which it is impossible should exist so separated: or that I can frame a general notion by abstracting from particulars in the manner aforesaid. Which two last are the proper acceptations of *abstraction.* And there are grounds to think most men will acknowledge themselves to be in my case. The generality of men, which are simple and illiterate, never pretend to *abstract notions.* It is said they are difficult, and not to be attained without pains and study. We may therefore reasonably conclude, that, if such there be, they are confined only to the learned."

Such is the doctrine of Nominalism, as asserted by Berkeley, and as subsequently acquiesced in by the principal philosophers of [Great Britain]. Reid himself is, indeed, hardly an exception, for his opinion on this point is, to say the least of it, extremely vague.

Conceptualism. — The counter-opinion, that of Conceptualism, as it is called, has, however, been supported by several philosophers of distinguished ability. Locke maintains the doctrine in its most revolting absurdity, boldly admitting that the general notion must be realized, in spite of the principle of Contradiction. "Does it not require," he says, "some pains and skill to form the *general idea* of a triangle (which is yet none of the most abstract, comprehensive, and difficult), for it must be neither oblique or rectangle, neither equilateral, equicrural, nor scalenon; but all and none of these at once. In effect, it is something imperfect, that cannot exist; an idea wherein some parts of several different and inconsistent ideas are put together."

This doctrine was, however, too palpably absurd to obtain any advocates; and Conceptualism, could it not find a firmer basis, behoved to be abandoned. Passing over Dr. Reid's speculations on the question, which are, as I have said, wavering and ambiguous, I solicit your attention to the principal statement and defence of Conceptualism by Dr. Brown, in whom the doctrine has obtained a strenuous advocate. The following is the seventh, out of nine recapitulations, he has given us of it in his Lectures. "If then the generalizing process be, first, the perception or conception of two or more objects; secondly, the relative feeling of their resemblance in certain respects; thirdly, the designation of these circumstances of resemblance by an appropriate name, the doctrine of the Nominalists, which includes only two of these stages, — the perception of particular objects, and the invention of general terms, — must be false, as excluding that relative suggestion of resemblance in certain respects, which is the second and most important step of the process; since it is this intermediate feeling alone that leads to the use of the term, which, otherwise, it would be impossible to limit to any set of objects."

This contains, in fact, both the whole of his own doctrine, and the whole ground of his rejection of that of the Nominalists. Now, upon this, I would, first of all, say, in general, that what in it is true is not new. But I hold it idle to prove, that his doctrine is old and common, and to trace it to authors with whom Brown has shown his acquaintance, by repeatedly quoting them in his Lectures; it is enough to show that it is erroneous.

The first point I shall consider is his confutation of the Nominalists. In the passage I have just adduced, and in ten others, he charges the Nominalists with excluding "the relative suggestion of resemblance in certain respects, which is the second and most important step in the process." This, I admit, is a weighty accusation, and I admit at once that if it do not prove that his own doctrine is right, it would at least demonstrate theirs to be sublimely wrong. But is the charge well founded? Let us see whether the Nominalists, as he assures us, do really exclude the apprehension of resemblance in certain respects, as one step in their doctrine of generalization. I turn first to Hobbes as the real father of this opinion, — to him, as Leibnitz truly says, "*nominalibus ipsis nominaliorem.*" The classical place of this philosopher on the subject is the fourth chapter of the *Leviathan;* and there we have the following passage — "One universal name is imposed on many things for their *similitude in some quality or other accident;* and whereas a proper name bringeth to mind one thing only, universals recall *any one* of those many." There are other passages to the same effect in Hobbes, but I look no further.

The second great Nominalist is Berkeley; [from whom,] out of many similar passages, I select the two following. In both, he is stating his own doctrine of Nominalism. In the Introduction, sect. 22: "To discern *the agreements or disagreements* that are between my ideas, to see what ideas are included in any compound idea, etc." In the *Minute Philosopher*, sect. 7: "But may not words become general by being made to stand indiscriminately for all particular ideas, which, from a *mutual resemblance*, belong to the same kind, without the intervention of any abstract general idea?"

I next take down Hume. In glancing over [his] exposition of the doctrine, I see the following:—"When we have found a *resemblance* among several objects, we apply the same name to all of them," etc. Again:—"As individuals are collected together and placed under a general term, with a view to that *resemblance* which they bear to each other," etc. In the last page and a half of the section, it is stated, no less than four times, that *perceived resemblance* is the foundation of classification.

Adam Smith's doctrine is to the same effect as his predecessor's. [He says], "It is this application of the name of an individual to a great number of objects, whose *resemblance* naturally recalls the idea of that individual, and of the name which expresses it, that seems originally to have given occasion to the formation of these classes and assortments, which in the Schools are called *genera* and *species*, and of which the ingenious and eloquent Rousseau finds himself so much at a loss to account for the origin. What constitutes a species is merely a number of objects bearing *a certain degree of resemblance* to one another, and on that account denominated by a single appellation, which may be applied to express any one of them."

From the evidence I have already quoted, you will see how marvellously wrong is Brown's assertion. I assure you, that not only no Nominalist ever overlooked, ever excluded, the manifested resemblance of objects to each other, but that every Nominalist explicitly founded his doctrine of classification on this resemblance, and on this resemblance alone. No Nominalist ever dreamt of disallowing the notion of relativity, — the conception of similarity between things; — this they maintain not less strenuously than the Conceptionalist; they only deny that this could ever constitute a general notion.

Brown is wrong in holding that the notion of similitude is general, and constitutes the general notion. But perhaps it may be admitted, that Brown is wrong in asserting that the Nominalist excludes resemblance as an element of generalization, and yet maintained, that he is right in holding, against the Nominalists, that the notion, or, as he has it, the feeling, of the similitude of objects in certain respects, is general, and constitutes what is called the general notion. I am afraid, however, that the misconception in regard to this point will be found not inferior to that in regard to the other.

Resemblance is often an individual, not a general, relation. — In the *first* place, then, resemblance is a relation; and a relation necessarily supposes certain objects as related terms. There can thus be no relation of resemblance conceived, apart from certain resembling objects. This is so manifest, that a formal enumeration of the principle seems almost puerile. Let it, however, be laid down as a first axiom, that the notion of similarity supposes the notion of certain similar objects.

In the *second* place, objects cannot be similar without being similar in some particular mode or accident, — say in color, in figure, in size, in weight, in smell, in fluidity, in life, etc., etc. This is equally evident, and this I lay down as a second axiom.

In the *third* place, I assume, as a third axiom, that a resem blance is not necessarily and of itself universal. On the contrary, a resemblance between two individual objects, in a determinate quality, is as individual and determinate as the objects and their resembling qualities themselves. Who, for example, will maintain that my actual notion of the likeness of a particular snowball and a particular egg, is more general than the representations of the several objects and their resembling accidents of color?

Now let us try Dr. Brown's theory on these grounds. In reference to the first, he does not pretend that what he calls the general feeling of resemblance can exist except between individual objects and individual representations. The universality, which he arrogates to this feeling, cannot accrue to it from any universality in the relative or resembling ideas. This neither he nor any other philosopher ever did or could pretend. They are supposed, *ex hypothesi*, to be individual, — singular.

Neither, in reference to the second axiom, does he pretend to derive the universality which he asserts to his feeling of resemblance from the universality of the notion of the common quality, in which this resemblance is realized. He does not, with Locke and others, maintain this; on the contrary, it is on the admitted absurdity of such a foundation that he attempts to establish the doctrine of Conceptualism on another ground.

But if the universality, assumed by Dr. Brown for his "feeling of resemblance," be found neither in the resembling objects, nor in the qualities through which they are similar, we must look for it in the feeling of resemblance itself, apart from its actual realization; and this, in opposition to the third axiom which we laid down as self-evident. In these circumstances, we have certainly a right to expect that Dr. Brown should have brought cogent proof for an assertion so contrary to all apparent evidence, that although this be the question which perhaps has been more ably, keenly, and universally agitated than any other, still no philosopher before himself was found even to imagine such a possibility. But in proof of this new paradox, Dr. Brown has not only brought no evidence; he does not even attempt to bring any. He assumes and he asserts, but he hazards no argument. In this state of matters, it is perhaps superfluous to do more than to rebut assertion by assertion; and as Dr. Brown is not *in possessorio*, and as his opinion is even opposed to the universal consent of philosophers, the counter assertion, if not overturned by reasoning, must prevail.

But let us endeavor to conceive on what grounds it could possibly be supposed by Dr. Brown, that the feeling of resemblance between certain objects, through certain resembling qualities. has in it any thing of universal, or can, as he says, constitute the general notion. This to me is, indeed, not easy; and every hypothesis I can make is so absurd, that it appears almost a libel to attribute it, even by conjecture, to so ingenious and acute a thinker.

In the *first* place, can it be supposed that Dr. Brown believed that a feeling of resemblance between objects in a certain quality or respect was general, because it was a relation? Then must every notion of a relation be a general notion; which neither he nor any other philosopher ever asserts.

In the *second* place, does he suppose that there is any thing in the feeling or notion of the particular relation called *similarity*, which is more general than the feeling or notion of any other relation? This can hardly be conceived. What is a feeling or notion of resemblance? Merely this; two objects affect us in a certain manner, and we are conscious they affect us in the same way that a single object does, when presented at different times to our perception. In either case, we judge that the affections of which we are conscious are similar or the same. There is nothing general in this consciousness, or in this judgment. At all events, the relation recognized between the consciousness of similarity produced on us by two different eggs, is not more general than the feeling of similarity produced on us by two successive presentations of the same egg. If the one is to be called general, so is the other. Again, if the feeling or notion of resemblance be made general, so must the feeling or notion of difference. They are absolutely the same notion, only in different applications. You know the logical axiom,—the science of contraries is one. We know the like only as we know the unlike. Every affirmation of similarity is virtually an affirmation that difference does not exist; every affirmation of difference is virtually an affirmation that similarity is not to be found. But neither Brown nor any other philosopher has pretended, that the apprehension of difference is either general, or a ground of generalization. On the contrary, the apprehension of difference is the negation of generalization, and a descent from the universal to the particular. But if the notion or feeling of the dissimilarity is not general, neither is the feeling or notion of the similarity.

In the *third* place, can it be that Dr. Brown supposes the particular feeling or consciousness of similarity between certain objects in certain respects to be general, because we have, in general, a capacity of feeling or being conscious of similarity? This conjecture is equally improbable. On this ground, every act of every power would be general; and we should not be obliged to leave Imagination, in order to seek for the universality, which we cannot discover in the light or definitude of tha faculty, in the obscurity and vagueness of another.

Conceptions distinguished from imaginations, or concepts from images. — In the *fourth* place, only one other supposition remains; and this may perhaps enable us to explain the possibility of Dr. Brown's hallucination. A *relation* cannot be represented in Imagination. The two *terms,* the two relative objects, can be severally imaged in the sensible phantasy, but not the relation itself. This is the object of the Comparative Faculty, or of Intelligence Proper. To objects so different as the images of sense and the unpicturable notions of intelligence, different names ought to be given; and, accordingly, this has been done wherever a philosophical nomenclature of the slightest pretensions to perfection has been formed. In the German language, which is now the richest in metaphysical expressions of any living tongue, the two kinds of objects are carefully distinguished. In our language, on the contrary, the *idea, conception, notion,* are used almost as convertible for either; and the vagueness and confusion which is thus produced, even within the narrow sphere of speculation to which the want of the distinction also confines us, can be best appreciated by those who are conversant with the philosophy of the different countries.

Dr. Brown seems to have had some faint perception of the difference between intellectual notions and sensible representations; and if he had endeavored to signalize their contrast by a distinction of terms, he would have deserved well of English philosophy. But he mistook the nature of the intellectual notion, which connects two particular qualities by the bond of similarity, and imagined that there lurked under this intangible relation the universality which, he clearly saw, could not be found in a representation of the related objects, or of their resembling qualities. At least, if this do not assist us in accounting for his misconception, I do not know in what way we otherwise can.

What I have now said is, I think, sufficient in regard to the nature of Generalization. It is notoriously a mere act of Comparison. We compare objects; we find them similar in certain respects, — that is, in certain respects they affect us in the same manner; we consider the qualities in them, that thus affect us in the same manner, as the same; and to this common quality we give a name; and as we can predicate this name of all and each of the resembling objects, it constitutes them into a class. Aristotle has truly said that general names are only abbreviated definitions, and definitions, you know, are judgments. For example, *animal* is only a compendious expression for *organized and animated body; man*, only a summary of *rational animal*, etc.

CHAPTER XXVI.

THE ELABORATIVE FACULTY. — THE PRIMUM COGNITUM. — JUDGMENT AND REASONING.

What does Language originate in? — I proceed now to a very curious question, which has likewise divided philosophers. It is this, — *Does Language originate in General Appellatives, or by Proper Names?* Did mankind in the formation of language, and do children in their first applications of it, commence with the one kind of words or with the other? The determination of this question, — the question of the *Primum Cognitum*, as it was called in the Schools, is not involved in the doctrine of Nominalism. Many illustrious philosophers have maintained that all terms, as at first employed, are expressive of individual objects, and that these only subsequently obtain a general acceptation.

1. *That our first ideas and names are of particulars.* — This opinion I find maintained by Vives, Locke, Rousseau, Condillac, Adam Smith, and others. "The order of learning" (I translate from Vives) "is from the senses to the imagination, and from this to the intellect; — such is the order of life and of nature. We thus proceed from the simple to the complex, from the singular to the universal. This is to be observed in children, who first of all express the several parts of different things, and then conjoin them. Things general they call by a singular name; for instance, they call all smiths by the name of that individual *smith* whom they have first known, and all meats, *beef* or *pork*, as they have happened to have heard the one or the other first, when they begin to speak. Thereafter the mind collects universals from particulars, and then again reverts to partic-

ulars from universals." The same doctrine, without probably any knowledge of Vives, is maintained by Locke. "There is nothing more evident," he says, "than that the ideas of the persons children converse with, (to instance in them alone), are, like the persons themselves, only particular. The ideas of the nurse and the mother are well framed in their minds; and, like pictures of them there, represent only those individuals. The names they first gave to them are confined to these individuals; and the names of *nurse* and *mamma*, the child uses, determine themselves to those persons. Afterwards, when time and a larger acquaintance have made them observe that there are a great many other things in the world, that, in some common agreements of shape, and several other qualities, resemble their father and mother, and those persons they have been used to, they frame an idea which they find those many particulars do partake in; and to that they give, with others, the name *man*, for example. And thus they come to have a general name, and a general idea."

Adam Smith has, however, the merit of having applied this theory to the formation of language; and his doctrine is too important not to be fully stated, and in his own powerful language. "The assignation," says Smith, "of particular names, to denote particular objects, — that is, the institution of nouns substantive, would probably be one of the first steps towards the formation of language. Two savages, who had never been taught to speak, but had been bred up remote from the societies of men, would naturally begin to form that language by which they would endeavor to make their mutual wants intelligible to each other, by uttering certain sounds whenever they meant to denote certain objects. Those objects only which were most familiar to them, and which they had most frequent occasion to mention, would have particular names assigned to them. The particular cave whose covering sheltered them from the weather, the particular tree whose fruit relieved their hunger, the particular fountain whose water allayed their thirst, would first be denominated by the words, *cave*, *tree*, *fountain*, or by whatever appellations they might think proper, in that primitive jargon, to mark them. Afterwards, when the more enlarged experience of these savages had led them to observe, and their necessary occasions obliged them to make mention of other caves, and other trees, and other fountains, they would naturally bestow upon each of those new objects the same name by which they had been accustomed to express the similar object they were first acquainted with. The new objects had none of them any name of its own, but each of them exactly resembled another object, which had such an appellation. It was impossible that those savages could behold the new objects, without recollecting the old ones, and the name of the old ones, to which the new bore so close a resemblance. When they had occasion, therefore, to mention or to point out to each other any of the new objects, they would naturally utter the name of the correspondent old one, of which the idea could not fail, at that instant, to present itself to their memory in the strongest and liveliest manner. And thus those words, which were originally the proper names of individuals, would each of them insensibly become the common name of a multitude. A child that is just learning to speak, calls every person who comes to the house its papa, or its mamma; and thus bestows upon the whole species those names which it had been taught to apply to two individuals. I have known a clown who did not know the proper name of the river which ran by his own door. It was *the river*, he said, and he never heard any other name for it. His experience, it seems, had not led him to observe any other river. The general word *river*, therefore, was, it is evident, in his acceptance of it, a proper name signifying an individual object. If this person had been carried to another river, would he not readily have called it a river? Could we suppose a person living on the banks of the Thames so ignorant as not to know the general word *river*, but to be acquainted only with the particular word *Thames*, if he was brought to any other river, would he not readily call it *a Thames?* This, in reality, is no more than what they who are well acquainted with the general word are very apt to do. An Englishman, describing any great river which he may have seen in some foreign country, naturally says, that it is another Thames. The Spaniards, when they first arrived upon the coast of Mexico, and observed the wealth, populousness, and habitations of that fine country, so much superior to the savage nations which they had been visiting for some time before, cried out that it was another Spain. Hence it was called New Spain; and this name has stuck to that unfortunate country ever since. We say, in the same manner, of a hero, that he is an Alexander; of an orator, that he is a Cicero; of a philosopher that he is a Newton. This way of speaking, which the grammarians call an Antonomasia, and which is still extremely common, though now not at all necessary, demonstrates how much mankind are naturally disposed to give to one object the name of any other which nearly resembles it; and thus, to denominate a multitude by what originally was intended to express an individual.

"It is this application of the name of an individual to a great multitude of objects, whose resemblance naturally recalls the idea of that individual, and of the name which expresses it, that seems originally to have given occasion to the formation of those classes and assortments which, in the Schools, are called *genera* and *species*."

2. *That we first use general terms.* — On the other hand, an opposite doctrine is maintained by many profound philosophers. A large section of the Schoolmen embraced it; and, among more modern thinkers, it is adopted by Leibnitz, who says, that "general terms serve not only for the perfection of languages, but are even necessary for their essential constitution. For if by *particulars* be understood things individual, it would be impossible to speak, if there were only proper names, and no appellatives, that is to say, if there were only names for things individual, since, at every moment, we are met by new ones, when we treat of persons, of accidents, and especially of actions, which are those that we describe the most; but if by particulars be meant the lowest species (*species infimas*), besides that it is frequently very difficult to determine them, it is manifest that these are already universals, founded on similarity. Now, as

the only difference of *species* and *genera* lies in a similarity of greater or less extent, it is natural to note every kind of similarity or agreement, and, consequently, to employ general terms of every degree; nay, the most general being less complex with regard to the essences which they comprehend, although more extensive in relation to the things individual to which they apply, are frequently the easiest to form, and are the most useful. It is likewise seen that children, and those who know but little of the language which they attempt to speak, or little of the subject on which they would employ it, make use of general terms, as *thing*, *plant*, *animal*, instead of using proper names, of which they are destitute. And it is certain that all *proper* or individual names have been originally *appellative* or general." In illustration of this latter most important doctrine, he, in a subsequent part of the work, says: "I would add, in conformity to what I have previously observed, that proper names have been originally appellative, that is to say, general in their origin, as Brutus, Cæsar, Augustus, Capito, Lentulus, Piso, Cicero, Elbe, Rhine, Rhur, Leine, Ocker, Bucephalus, Alps, Pyrenees, etc.," and, after illustrating this in detail, he concludes: — "Thus I would make bold to affirm that almost all words have been originally general terms, because it would happen very rarely that men would invent a name, expressly and without a reason, to denote this or that individual. We may, therefore, assert that the names of individual things were names of species, which were given *par excellence*, or otherwise, to some individual, as the name *Great Head* to him of the whole town who had the largest, or who was the man of most consideration, of the Great Heads known. It is thus, likewise, that men give the names of genera to species, that is to say, that they content themselves with a term more general or vague to denote more particular classes, when they do not care about the differences. As, for example, we content ourselves with the general name *absinthium* (wormwood), although there are so many species of the plant that one of the Bauhins has filled a whole book with them."

That this was likewise the opinion of the great Turgot, we learn from his biographer. "M. Turgot," says Condorcet, "believed that the opinion was wrong, which held that, in general, the mind only acquired general or abstract ideas by the comparison of more particular ideas. On the contrary, our first ideas are very general; for, seeing at first only a small number of qualities, our idea includes all the existences to which these qualities are common. As we acquire knowledge, our ideas become more particular, without ever reaching the last limit; and, what might have deceived the metaphysicians, it is precisely by this process that we learn that these ideas are more general than we had at first supposed."

Here are two opposite opinions, each having nearly equal authority in its favor, maintained on both sides with equal ability and apparent evidence. Either doctrine would be held established were we unacquainted with the arguments in favor of the other.

3. *That our first ideas and terms are only vague and confused.* — But I have now to state to you a third opinion, intermediate between these, which conciliates both, and seems, moreover, to carry a superior probability in its statement. This opinion maintains, that as our knowledge proceeds from the confused to the distinct, — from the vague to the determinate, — so, in the mouths of children, *language at first expresses neither the precisely general nor the determinately individual, but the vague and confused;* and that, out of this, the universal is elaborated by generification, the particular and singular by specification and individualization.

I formerly explained why I view the doctrine held by Mr. Stewart and others in regard to perception in general and vision in particular, as erroneous; inasmuch as they conceive that our sensible cognitions are formed by the addition of an almost infinite number of separate and consecutive acts of attentive perception, each act being cognizant of a certain *minimum sensibile.* On the contrary, I showed that, instead of commencing with minima, perception commences with masses; that, though our capacity of attention be very limited in regard to the number of objects on which a faculty can be simultaneously directed, yet these objects may be large or small. We may make, for example, a single object of attention either of a whole man, or of his face, or of his eye, or of the pupil of his eye, or of a speck upon the pupil. To each of these objects there can only be a certain amount of attentive perception applied, and we can concentrate it all on any one. In proportion as the object is larger and more complex, our attention can of course be less applied to any part of it, and consequently, our knowledge of it in detail will be vaguer and more imperfect. But having first acquired a comprehensive knowledge of it as a whole, we can descend to its several parts, consider these both in themselves, and in relation to each other, and to the whole of which they are constituents, and thus attain to a complete and articulate knowledge of the object. We decompose, and then we recompose.

The mind proceeds by analysis, from the whole to the parts. — But in this we always proceed first by decomposition or analysis. All analysis indeed supposes a foregone composition or synthesis, because we cannot decompose what is not already composite. But in our acquisition of knowledge, the objects are presented to us compounded; and they obtain a unity only in the unity of our consciousness. The unity of consciousness is, as it were, the frame in which objects are seen. I say, then, that the first procedure of mind in the elaboration of its knowledge is always analytical. It descends from the whole to the parts, — from the vague to the definite. Definitude, that is, a knowledge of minute differences, is not, as the opposite theory supposes, the first, but the last, term of our cognitions. Between two sheep an ordinary spectator can probably apprehend no difference, and if they were twice presented to him, he would be unable to discriminate the one from the other. But a shepherd can distinguish every individual sheep; and why? Because he has descended from the vague knowledge which we all have of sheep, — from the vague knowledge which makes every sheep, as it were, only a repetition of the same undifferenced unit, — to a definite knowledge of qualities by which each is contrasted from its neighbor. Now, in this example, we apprehend the sheep by marks not less individual than those by which the shepherd discriminates them; but the whole of each sheep being made an object, the marks by which we know it are the same in each and all, and cannot, therefore, afford the principle by which we can discriminate them from each other. Now this is what appears to me to take place with children. They first know, — they first cognize, the things and persons presented to them as wholes. But wholes of the same kind, if we do not descend to their parts, afford us no difference, — no mark by which we can discriminate the one from the other. Children, thus, originally perceiving similar objects, — persons, for example, — only as wholes, do at first hardly distinguish them. They apprehend first the more obtrusive marks that separate species from species and, in consequence of the notorious contrast of dress, men from women; but they do not as yet recognize the finer traits that discriminate individual from individual. But, though thus apprehending individuals only by what we now call their specific or their generic qualities, it is not to be supposed that children know them by any abstract general attributes, that is, by attributes formed by comparison and attention. On the other hand, because their knowledge is not general, it is not to be supposed to be particular or individual, if by particular be meant a separation of species from species, and by individual, the separation of individual from individual; for children are at first apt to confound individuals together, not only in name but in reality. "A child" [says Degerando] "who has been taught to say *papa*, in pointing to his father, will give at first, as Locke [and Aristotle before him] had remarked, the name of *papa* to all the men whom he sees. As he only at first seizes on the more striking appearances of objects, they would appear to him all similar, and he denotes them by the same names. But when it has been pointed out to him that he is mistaken, or when he has discovered this by the consequences of his language, he studies to discriminate the objects which he had confounded, and he takes hold of their differences. The child commences, like the savage, by employing only isolated words in place of phrases; he commences by taking verbs and nouns only in their absolute state. But as these imperfect attempts at speech express at once many and very different things, and produce, in consequence, manifold ambiguities, he soon discovers the necessity of determining them with greater exactitude; he endeavors to make it understood in what respects the thing which he wishes to denote, is distinguished from those with which it is confounded; and, to succeed in this endeavor, he tries to distinguish them himself. Thus when, at this age, the child seems to us as yet unoccupied, he is in reality very busy; he is devoted to a study which differs not in its nature from that to which the philosopher applies himself; the child, like the philosopher, observes, compares, and analyses."

In support of this doctrine I can appeal to high authority; it is that maintained by Aristotle. Speaking of the order of procedure in physical science, he says, "We ought to proceed from the better known to the less known, and from what is clearer to us to that which is clearer in nature. But those things are first known and clearer, which are more complex and confused; for it is only by subsequent analysis that we attain to a knowledge of the parts and elements of which they are composed. We ought, therefore, to proceed from universals to singulars; for the whole is better known to sense than its parts; and the universal is a kind of whole, as the universal comprehends many things as its parts. Thus it is that names are at first better known to us than definitions; for the name denotes a whole, and that indeterminately; whereas the definition divides and explicates its parts. Children, likewise, at first call all men fathers and all women mothers; but thereafter they learn to discriminate each individual from another."

I have terminated the consideration of the faculty of Comparison in its process of Generalization. I am now to consider it in those of its operations, which have obtained the special names of Judgment and Reasoning.

In these processes, the act of Comparison is a judgment of something more than a mere affirmation of the existence of a phænomenon, — something more than a mere discrimination of one phænomenon from another; and, accordingly, while it has happened, that the intervention of judgment in every, even the simplest, act of primary cognition, as monotonous and rapid, has been overlooked, the name has been exclusively limited to the more varied and elaborate comparison of one notion with another, and the enouncement of their agreement or disagreement. It is in the discharge of this, its more obtrusive, function, that we are now about to consider the Elaborative Faculty.

Why Judgment and Reasoning are necessary. — Considering the Elaborative Faculty as a mean of discovering truth, by a comparison of the notions we have obtained from the Acquisitive Powers, it is evident that, though this faculty be the attribute by which a man is distinguished as a creation higher than the animals, it is equally the quality which marks his inferiority to superior intelligences. *Judgment and Reasoning are rendered necessary by the imperfection of our nature.* Were we capable of a knowledge of things and their relations at a single view, by an intuitive glance, discursive thought would be a superfluous act. It is by such an intuition that we must suppose that the Supreme Intelligence knows all things at once.

I have already noticed that our knowledge does not commence with the individual and the most particular objects of knowledge, — that we do not rise in any regular progress from the less to the more general, first considering the qualities which characterize individuals, then those which belong to species and genera, in regular ascent. On the contrary, our knowledge commences with the vague and confused, in the way which Aristotle has so well illustrated. This I may further explain by another analogy. We perceive an object approaching from a distance. At first, we do not know whether it be a living or an inanimate thing. By degrees, we become aware that it is an animal; but of what kind, — whether man or beast, — we are not as yet able to determine. It continues to advance, we discover it to be a quadruped, but of what species we cannot yet say. At length, we perceive that it is a horse, and again, after a season, we find that it is Bucephalus. Thus, as I formerly observed, children, first of all, take note of the generic differences, and they can distinguish species long before they are able to discriminate individuals. In all this, however, I must again remark, that our knowledge does not properly commence with the general, but with the vague and confused. Out of this the general and the individual are both equally evolved.

What is an act of judgment. — "In consequence of this genealogy of our knowledge," [says Crousaz,] "we usually commence by bestowing a name upon a whole object, or congeries of objects, of which, however, we possess only a partial and indefinite conception. In the sequel, this vague notion becomes somewhat more determinate; the partial idea which we had, becomes enlarged by new accessions; by degrees, our conception waxes fuller, and represents a greater number of attributes. With this conception, thus amplified and improved, we compare the last notion which has been acquired, that is to say, we compare a part with its whole, or with the other parts of this whole, and finding that it is harmonious, — that it dovetails and naturally assorts with other parts, we acquiesce in this union; and this we denominate an act of judgment.

"In learning arithmetic, I form the notion of the number *six*, as surpassing *five* by a single unit, and as surpassed in the same proportion by *seven*. Then I find that it can be divided into two equal halves, of which each contains three units. By this procedure, the notion of the number six becomes more complex; the notion of an even number is one of its parts. Comparing this new notion with that of the number, six becomes fuller by its addition. I recognize that the two notions suit, — in other words I judge that six is an even number.

"I have the conception of a triangle, and this conception is composed in my mind of several others. Among these partial notions, I select that of two sides greater than the third, and this notion, which I had at first, as it were, taken apart, I reunite with the others from which it had been separated, saying the triangle contains always two sides, which together are greater than the third.

"When I say, body is divisible among the notions which concur in forming my conception of body, I particularly attend to that of divisible, and finding that it really agrees with the others, I judge accordingly that body is divisible.

Subject. Predicate. Copula. — "Every time we judge, we compare a total conception with a partial, and we recognize that the latter really constitutes a part of the former. One of these conceptions has received the name of *subject*, the other, that of *attribute* or *predicate*." The verb which connects these two parts is called the *copula*. *The quadrangle is a double triangle; nine is an odd number; body is divisible.* Here *quadrangle, nine, body*, are subjects; *a double triangle, an odd number, divisible*, are predicates. The whole mental judgment, formed by the subject, predicate, and copula, is called, when enounced in words, *proposition.*

"In discourse, the parts of a proposition are not always found placed in logical order; but to discover and discriminate them, it is only requisite to ask, — *What is the thing of which something else is affirmed or denied?* The answer to this question will point out *the subject;* and we shall find *the predicate* if we inquire, — *What is affirmed or denied of the matter of which we speak?*

"A proposition is sometimes so enounced that each of its terms may be considered as subject and as predicate. Thus, when we say, — *Death is the wages of sin;* we may regard *sin* as the subject of which we predicate *death*, as one of its consequences, and we may likewise view *death* as the subject of which we predicate *sin*, as the origin. In these cases, we must consider the general tenor of the discourse, and determine from the context what is the matter of which it principally treats."

"In fine, when we judge, we must have, in the first place, at least two notions; in the second place, we compare these; in the third, we recognize that one contains or excludes the other; and, in the fourth, we acquiesce in this recognition."

Reasoning is complex and mediate judgment. — Simple Comparison or Judgment is conversant with two notions, the one of which is contained in the other. But it often happens, that one notion is contained in another not immediately, but mediately, and we may be able to recognize the relation of these to each other only through a third, which, as it immediately contains the one, is immediately contained in the other. Take the notions, A, B, C. — A contains B; B contains C; — A, there fore, also contains C. But as, *ex hypothesi*, we do not at once and directly know C as contained in A, we cannot immediately compare them together, and judge of their relation. We, therefore, perform a double or complex process of comparison; we compare B with A, and C with B, and then C with A, through B. We say B is a part of A; C is a part of B; therefore, C is a part of A. This double act of comparison has obtained the name of *Reasoning;* the term *Judgment* being left to express the simple act of comparison, or rather its result.

If this distinction between Judgment and Reasoning were merely a verbal difference, to discriminate the simpler and more complex act of comparison, no objection could be raised to it on the score of propriety, and its convenience would fully warrant its establishment. But this distinction has not always been meant to express nothing more. It has, in fact, been generally supposed to mark out two distinct faculties.

Two kinds of Reasoning. — Reasoning is either from the whole to its parts; or from all the parts, discretively, to the whole they constitute, collectively. The former of these is Deductive, the latter is Inductive, Reasoning. The statement you will find, in all logical books, of reasonings from certain parts to the whole, or from certain parts to certain parts, is erroneous. I shall first speak of the reasoning from the whole to its parts, — or of the Deductive Inference.

Axiom of Deductive Reasoning. — 1°, It is self-evident, that *whatever is the part of a part, is a part of the whole.* This one axiom is the foundation of all reasoning from the whole to the parts. There are, however, two kinds of whole and parts; and these constitute two varieties, or rather two phases, of deductive reasoning. This distinction, which is of the most important kind, has nevertheless been wholly overlooked by logicians, in consequence of which the utmost perplexity and confusion have been introduced into the science.

I have formerly stated that a proposition consists of two terms, — the one called subject, the other predicate, the subject being that of which some attribute is said, the predicate being the attribute so said. Now, in different relations, we may regard the subject as the whole, and the predicate as its part, or the predicate as the whole and the subject as its part.

Let us take the proposition, — *milk is white.* Now, here we may either consider the predicate *white* as one of a number of attributes, the whole complement of which constitutes the subject *milk.* In this point of view, the predicate is a part of the subject. Or, again, we may consider the predicate *white* as the name of a class of objects, of which the subject is one. In this point of view, the subject is a part of the predicate.

Comprehension and Extension applied to Reasoning. — You will remember the distinction, which I formerly stated, of the twofold quantity of notions or terms. The Breadth or Extension of a notion or term corresponds to the greater number of subjects contained under a predicate; the Depth, Intension, or Comprehension of a notion or term, to the greater number of predicates contained in a subject. These quantities or wholes are always in the inverse ratio of each other. Now, it is singular, that logicians should have taken this distinction between notions, and yet not have thought of applying it to reasoning. But so it is, and this is not the only oversight they have committed in the application of the very primary principles of their science. The great distinction we have established between the subject and predicate considered severally, as, in different relations, whole and as part, constitutes the primary and principal division of Syllogisms, both Deductive and Inductive; and its introduction wipes off a complex mass of rules and qualifications, which the want of it rendered necessary. I can, of course, at present, only explain in general the nature of this distinction; its details belong to the science of the Laws of Thought, or Logic, of which we are not here to treat.

Essential and Integral wholes. — I shall first consider the process of that Deductive Inference in which the subject is viewed as the whole, the predicate as the part. In this reasoning, the whole is determined by the Comprehension, and is, again, either a Physical or Essential whole, or an Integral or Mathematical whole. A Physical or Essential whole is that

42

which consists of not really separable parts, of or pertaining tc its substance. Thus, man is made up of two substantial parts, — a mind and a body; and each of these has again various qualities, which, though separable only by mental abstraction, are considered as so many parts of an essential whole. Thus, the attributes of respiration, of digestion, of locomotion, of color, are so many parts of the whole notion we have of the human body; cognition, feeling, desire, virtue, vice, etc., so many parts of the whole notion we have of man. A Mathematical, or Integral, or Quantitative whole is that which has part out of part, and which, therefore, can be really partitioned. The Integral or, as it ought to be called, Integrate whole, is composed of integrant parts which are either homogeneous or heterogeneous. An example of the former is given in the division of a square into two triangles; of the latter, of the animal body into head, trunk, extremities, etc.

These wholes (and there are others of less importance which I omit), are varieties of that whole which we may call a Comprehensive, or Metaphysical; it might be called a Natural, whole.

Reasoning in the whole of Comprehension. — This being understood, let us consider how we proceed when we reason from the relation between a Comprehensive whole and its parts. Here, as I have said, the subject is the whole, the predicate its part; in other words, the predicate belongs to the subject. Now here it is evident, that all the parts of the predicate must also be parts of the subject; in other terms, all that belongs to the predicate must also belong to the subject. In the words of the scholastic adage, — *Nota notæ est nota rei ipsius; Predicatum predicati est predicatum subjecti.* An example of this reasoning:

Europe contains England;
England contains Middlesex;
Therefore, Europe contains Middlesex.

In other words, England is an integrant part of Europe, Middlesex is an integrant part of England; therefore, Middlesex is an integrant part of Europe. This is an example from a mathematical whole and parts. Again:

Socrates is just (that is, Socrates contains justice as a quality);

Justice is a virtue (that is, justice contains virtue as a constituent part);

Therefore, Socrates is virtuous.

In other words;—justice is an attribute or essential part of Socrates; virtue is an attribute or essential part of justice; therefore, virtue is an attribute or essential part of Socrates. This is an example from a physical or essential whole and parts.

What I have now said will be enough to show, in general, what I mean by a deductive reasoning, in which the subject is the whole, the predicate the part.

Reasoning in the whole of Extension.—I proceed, in the second place, to the other kind of Deductive Reasoning,—that in which the subject is the part, the predicate is the whole. This reasoning proceeds under that species of whole which has been called the Logical, or Potential, or Universal. This whole is determined by the Extension of a notion; the genera having species, and the species individuals, as their parts. Thus, *animal* is a universal whole, of which *bird* and *beast* are immediate, *eagle* and *sparrow*, *dog* and *horse*, mediate, parts; while *man*, which, in relation to animal, is a part, is a whole in relation to Peter, Paul, Socrates, etc. The parts of a logical or universal whole, I should notice, are called the *subject parts.*

From what you now know of the nature of generalization, you are aware, that general terms are terms expressive of attributes which may be predicated of many different objects; and inasmuch as these objects resemble each other in the common attribute, they are considered by us as constituting a class. Thus, when I say, that a horse is a quadruped; Bucephalus is a horse; therefore, Bucephalus is a quadruped;—I virtually say,—*horse*, the subject, is a part of the predicate *quadruped; Bucephalus*, the subject, is part of the predicate *horse ;* therefore, *Bucephalus,* the subject, is part of the predicate *quadruped.* In the reasoning under this whole, you will observe that the same word, as it is whole or part, changes from predicate to subject; *horse*, when viewed as a part of *quadruped*, being the subject of the proposition; whereas when viewed as a whole, containing *Bucephalus*, it becomes the predicate.

Axiom of Inductive Reasoning. — Such is a general view of the process of Deductive Reasoning under the two great varieties determined by the two different kinds of whole and parts. I now proceed to the counter process, — that of Inductive Reasoning. The Deductive is founded on the axiom, that what is part of the part, is also part of the containing whole; the Inductive on the principle, that what is true of every constituent part belongs, or does not belong, to the constituted whole.

Induction proceeds in the two wholes. — Induction, like Deduction, may be divided into two kinds, according as the whole and parts about which it is conversant, are a Comprehensive or Physical or Natural, or an Extensive or Logical whole. Thus, in the former:

Gold is a metal, yellow, ductile, fusible in *aqua regia*, of a certain specific gravity, and so on;

These qualities constitute this body (are all its parts);

Therefore this body is gold.

In the latter; — Ox, horse, dog, etc., are animals, — that is, are contained under the class animal;

Ox, horse, dog, etc., constitute (are all the constituents of) the class quadruped;

Therefore, quadruped is contained under animal.

Both in the Deductive and Inductive processes, the inference must be of an absolute necessity, in so far as the mental illation is concerned; that is, every consequent proposition must be evolved out of every antecedent proposition with intuitive evidence. I do not mean by this, that the antecedent should be necessarily true, or that the consequent be really contained in it; it is sufficient that the antecedent be assumed as true, and that the consequent be, in conformity to the laws of thought, evolved out of it as its part or its equation. This last is called Logical or Formal or Subjective truth; and an inference may be subjectively or formally true, which is objectively or really false.

The account given of Induction in all works of Logic is utterly erroneous. Sometimes we find this inference described as a precarious, not a necessary reasoning. It is called an illation from some to all. But here *the some*, as it neither contains nor constitutes *the all*, determines no necessary movement, and a conclusion drawn under these circumstances is logically vicious. Others again describe the Inductive process thus:

What belongs to some objects of a class belongs to the whole class;

This property belongs to some objects of the class;

Therefore, it belongs to the whole class.

This account of Induction, which is the one you will find in all the English works on Logic, is not an inductive reasoning at all. It is, logically considered, a deductive syllogism; and, logically considered, a syllogism radically vicious. It is logically vicious to say, that, because some individuals of a class have certain common qualities apart from that property which constitutes the class itself, therefore the whole individuals of the class should partake in these qualities. For this there is no logical reason, — no necessity of thought. The probability of this inference, and it is only probable, is founded on the observation of the analogy of nature, and, therefore, not upon the laws of thought by which alone reasoning, considered as a logical process, is exclusively governed. To become a formally legitimate induction, the objective probability must be clothed with a subjective necessity, and *the some* must be translated into *the all* which it is supposed to represent.

In the deductive syllogism we proceed by analysis, — that is, by decomposing a whole into its parts; but *as the two wholes with which reasoning is conversant are in the inverse ratio of each other, so our analysis in the one will correspond to our synthesis in the other.* For example, when I divide a whole of extension into its parts, — when I divide a genus into the species, a species into the individuals it contains, — I do so by adding new differences, and thus go on accumulating in the parts a complement of qualities which did not belong to the wholes. This, therefore, which, in point of extension, is an analysis, is, in point of comprehension, a synthesis. In like manner, when I decompose a whole of comprehension, that is, decompose a complex predicate into its constituent attributes, I obtain by this process a simpler and more general quality, and thus this, which, in relation to a comprehensive whole, is an analysis, is, in relation to an extensive whole, a synthesis. As the deductive inference is Analytic, the inductive is Synthetic. But as induction, equally as deduction, is conversant with both wholes, so the Synthesis of induction on the comprehensive whole is a reversed process to its synthesis on the extensive whole.

From what I have now stated, you will, therefore, be aware, that the terms *analysis* and *synthesis*, when used without qualification, may be employed at cross purposes, to denote operations precisely the converse of each other. And so it has happened. Analysis, in the mouth of one set of philosophers, means precisely what synthesis denotes in the mouth of another; nay, what is even still more frequent, these words are perpetually converted with each other by the same philosopher. I may notice, what has rarely, if ever, been remarked, that *synthesis* in the writings of the Greek logicians is equivalent to the *analysis* of modern philosophers: the former, regarding the extensive whole as the principal, applied analysis, *κατ' ἐξοχὴν*, to its division; the latter, viewing the comprehensive whole as the principal, in general limit analysis to its decomposition. This, however, has been overlooked, and a confusion the most inextricable prevails in regard to the use of these words, if the thread to the labyrinth is not obtained.

CHAPTER XXVII.

THE REGULATIVE FACULTY.—THE PHILOSOPHY OF THE CONDITIONED.

I NOW enter upon the last of the Cognitive Faculties,—the faculty which I denominated the Regulative. Here the term *faculty*, you will observe, is employed in a somewhat peculiar signification, for it is employed not to denote the proximate cause of any definite energy, but the power the mind has of being the native source of certain necessary or *a priori* cognitions; which cognitions, as they are the conditions, the forms, under which our knowledge in general is possible, constitute so many fundamental laws of intellectual nature. It is in this sense that I call the power which the mind possesses of modifying the knowledge it receives, in conformity to its proper nature, its Regulative Faculty. The Regulative Faculty is, however, in fact, nothing more than the complement of such laws;—it is the *locus principiorum*. It thus corresponds to what was known in the Greek philosophy under the name of *νοῦς*, when that term was rigorously used. To this faculty has been latterly applied the name *Reason;* but this term is so vague and ambiguous, that it is almost unfitted to convey any definite meaning.

Proper use of the term Common Sense.—The term *Common Sense* has likewise been applied to designate the place of principles. This word is also ambiguous. In the *first* place, it was the expression used in the Aristotelic philosophy to denote the *Central or Common Sensory, in which the different external senses met and were united.* In the *second* place, it was employed to signify *a sound understanding applied to vulgar ob-*

jects, in contrast to a scientific or speculative intelligence; and it is in this signification that it has been taken by those who have derided the principle on which the philosophy, which has been distinctively denominated the Scottish, professes to be established. This is not, however, the meaning which has always, or even principally, been attached to it; and an incomparably stronger case might be made out in defence of this expression than has been done by Reid, or even by Mr. Stewart. It is, in fact, a term of high antiquity and very general acceptation. We find it in Cicero, in several passages not hitherto observed. It is found in the meaning in question in Phædrus, and not in the signification of community of sentiment, which it expresses in Horace and Juvenal. And in the same meaning the term *Sensus Communis* is employed by St. Augustin. In modern times, it is to be found in the philosophical writings of every country of Europe. In fact, so far as use and wont may be allowed to weigh, there is perhaps no philosophical expression in support of which a more numerous array of authorities may be alleged. The expression, however, is certainly exceptionable, and it can only claim toleration in the absence of a better.

I may notice that Pascal and Hemsterhuis have applied *Intuition* and *Sentiment* in this sense; and Jacobi originally employed *Belief* or *Faith* in the same way, though he latterly superseded this expression by that of *Reason.*

[Our cognitions, it is evident, are not all at second hand. Consequents cannot, by an infinite regress, be evolved out of antecedents, which are themselves only consequents. Demonstration, if proof be possible, behooves us to repose at last on propositions, which, carrying their own evidence, necessitate their own admission; and which being, as primary, inexplicable, as inexplicable, incomprehensible, must consequently manifest themselves less in the character of cognitions than of *facts,* of which consciousness assures us under the simple form of *feeling* or *belief.*

Without at present attempting to determine the character, number, and relations — waiving, in short, all attempt at an articulate analysis and classification, of the primary elements of cognition, as carrying us into a discussion beyond our limits, and not of indispensable importance for the end we have in view; it is sufficient to have it conceded, in general, *that such elements there are;* and this concession of their existence being supposed, I shall proceed to hazard some observations, principally in regard to their authority as warrants and criteria of truth. Nor can this assumption, of the existence of some original basis of knowledge in the mind itself, be refused by any. For even those philosophers who profess to derive all our knowledge from experience, and who admit no universal truths of intelligence but such as are generalized from individual truths of fact — even these philosophers are forced virtually to acknowledge, at the root of the several acts of observation from which their generalization starts, some law or principle to which they can appeal as guaranteeing the procedure, should the validity of these primordial acts themselves be called in question. This acknowledgment is, among others, made even by Locke; and on such fundamental guarantee of induction he even bestows the name of Common Sense.

Limiting, therefore, our consideration to the question of authority; how, it is asked, do these primary propositions — these cognitions at first hand — these fundamental facts, feelings, beliefs, certify us of their own veracity? To this the only possible answer is — that as elements of our mental constitution — as the essential conditions of our knowledge — they *must* by us be accepted as true. To suppose their falsehood, is to suppose that we are created capable of intelligence, in order to be made the victims of delusion; that God is a deceiver, and the root of our nature a lie. But such a supposition, if gratuitous, is manifestly illegitimate. For, on the contrary, the data of our original consciousness must, it is evident, *in the first instance*, be presumed true. It is only, if proved false, that their authority can, *in consequence of that proof*, be, in the second instance, disallowed. Speaking, therefore, generally, *to argue from Common Sense is simply to show, that the denial of a given proposition would involve the denial of some original datum of consciousness; but as every original datum of consciousness is to be presumed true.*

that the proposition in question, as dependent on such a principle, must be admitted. . . . . .

Though the argument from Common Sense be an appeal to the natural convictions of mankind, it is not an appeal from philosophy to blind feeling. It is only an appeal, from the heretical conclusions of particular philosophies, to the catholic principles of all philosophy. The prejudice which, on this supposition, has sometimes been excited against the argument, is groundless.

Nor is it true, that the argument from Common Sense denies the decision to the judgment of philosophers, and accords it to the verdict of the vulgar. Nothing can be more erroneous. We admit — nay we maintain, as D'Alembert well expresses it, "that the truth in metaphysic, like the truth in matters of taste, is a truth of which all minds have the germ within themselves; to which, indeed, the greater number pay no attention, but which they recognize the moment it is pointed out to them. . . . But if, in this sort, all are able to understand, all are not able to instruct. The merit of conveying easily to others true and simple notions, is much greater than is commonly supposed; for experience proves how rarely this is to be met with. Sound metaphysical ideas are common truths, which every one apprehends, but which few have the talent to develop. So difficult is it on any subject to make our own what belongs to every one." Or, to employ the words of the ingenious Lichtenberg, "Philosophy, twist the matter as we may, is always a sort of chemistry. The peasant employs all the principles of abstract philosophy, only *inveloped*, *latent*, *engaged*, as the men of physical science express it; the Philosopher exhibits the *pure* principle."

The first problem of Philosophy — and it is one of no easy accomplishment — being thus to seek out, purify, and establish, by intellectual analysis and criticism, the elementary feelings or beliefs, in which are given the elementary truths of which all are in possession; and the argument from Common Sense being the allegation of these feelings or beliefs as explicated and ascertained, in proof of the relative truths and their necessary consequences; — this argument is manifestly dependent on philosophy, as an art, as an acquired dexterity, and cannot, notwithstanding the errors which they have so frequently committed, be taken out of the hands of the philosophers. Common Sense is like Common Law. Each may be laid down as the general rule of decision; but in the one case, it must be left to the jurist, in the other, to the philosopher, to ascertain what are the contents of the rule; and though, in both instances, the common man may be cited as a witness for the custom or the fact, in neither can he be allowed to officiate as advocate or as judge.

It must be recollected, also, that in appealing to the consciousness of mankind in general, we only appeal to the consciousness of those not disqualified to pronounce a decision. "In saying," (to use the words of Aristotle), "simply and without qualification, that this or that *is a known truth*, we do not mean that it is in fact recognized by all, but only by such as are of sound understanding; just as in saying absolutely that a thing is wholesome, we must be held to mean, to such as are of a hale constitution." We may, in short, say of the true philosopher what Erasmus, in an epistle to Hutten, said of Sir Thomas More: — "Nemo minus ducitur *vulgi judicio;* sed rursus nemo minus abest a *sensu communi*."] — *Diss. supp. to Reid.*

Nomenclature of the Regulative Faculty. — Were it allowed in metaphysical philosophy, as in physical, to discriminate scientific differences by scientific terms, I would employ the word *noetic*, as derived from νοῦς, to express all those cognitions that originate in the mind itself, *dianoetic* to denote the operations of the Discursive, Elaborative, or Comparative Faculty. So much for the nomenclature of the faculty itself.

On the other hand, the cognitions themselves, of which it is the source, have obtained various appellations. They have been denominated *first principles*,* *common anticipations*, *prin-*

* [Without entering on the various meanings of the term Principle, which Aristotle defines, in general, *that from whence any thing exists, is produced, or is known*, it is sufficient to say that it is always used for that on which something else depends; and thus both for an original *law* and for an original *element*. In the former case it is *regulative*, in the latter a *constitutive*, principle; and in either signification, it may be very properly applied to our original cognitions.] — *Diss. supp. to Reid.*

ciples of common sense, self-evident or *intuitive** *truths, primitive notions, native notions, innate cognitions, natural knowledges* (*cognitions*), *fundamental reasons, metaphysical* or *transcendental truths, ultimate* or *elemental laws of thought, primary* or *fundamental laws of human belief*, or *primary laws of human reason*,†

* [The term Intuition is not unambiguous. Besides its original and proper meaning (as a visual perception), it has been employed to denote a kind of *apprehension* and a kind of *judgment*.

Under the former head, Intuition, or intuitive knowledge, has been used in the following significations:

a. — To denote a perception of the actual and present, in opposition to the "abstractive" knowledge which we have of the possible in imagination, and of the past in memory.

b. — To denote an immediate apprehension of a thing in itself, in contrast to a representative, vicarious, or mediate, apprehension of it, in or through something else.

c. — To denote the knowledge which we can adequately represent in imagination, in contradistinction to the "symbolical" knowledge which we cannot image, but only think or conceive, through and under a sign or word.

Under the latter head, it has only a single signification; namely:

To denote the immediate affirmation by the intellect, that the predicate does or does not pertain to the subject, in what are called self-evident propositions.

All these meanings, however, have this in common, that they express the condition of an immediate, in opposition to a mediate knowledge.] — *Diss. supp. to Reid.*

† [Reason is a very vague, vacillating, and equivocal word. Throwing aside various accidental significations which it has obtained in particular languages, as in Greek denoting not only the *ratio*, but the *oratio*, of the Latins; throwing aside its employment, in most languages, for *cause, motive, argument, principle of probation*, or *middle term of a syllogism*, and considering it only as a philosophical word denoting a faculty or complement of faculties; in this relation, it is found employed in the following meaning:

It has, both in ancient and modern times, been very commonly employed, like *understanding* and *intellect*, to denote our intelligent nature in general; and this usually as distinguished from the lower cognitive faculties, as Sense, Imagination, Memory — but always, and emphatically, as in contrast to the Feelings and Desires. In this signification, to follow the Aristotelic division, it comprehends — 1°, *Conception* or *Simple Apprehension;* 2°, the *Compositive* and *Divisive process, Affirmation and Negation, Judgment;*

pure or *transcendental** or *a priori cognitions, categories of thought, natural beliefs, rational instincts,*† etc.

3°, *Reasoning* or the *Discursive faculty;* 4°, *Intellect* or *Intelligence* proper, either as the intuition, or as the place, of principles or self-evident truths.

In modern times, though we frequently meet with Reason, as a general faculty, distinguished from Reasoning, as a particular; yet until Kant, I am not aware that Reason (Vernunft) was ever exclusively, or even emphatically, used in a signification corresponding to the noetic faculty, in its strict and special meaning, and opposed to understanding (Verstand), viewed as comprehending the other functions of thought.

Though Common Sense be not therefore opposed to Reason, still the term Reason is of so general and ambiguous an import, that its employment in so determinate a meaning as a synonym of Common Sense ought to be avoided. It is only, we have seen, as an expression for the noetic faculty, or Intellect proper, that Reason can be substituted for Common Sense.] — *Diss. supp. to Reid.*

* [In the Schools, *transcendentalis* and *transcendens* were convertible expressions, employed to mark a term or notion which *transcended,* that is, which rose above, and thus contained under it, the Categories, or summa genera, of Aristotle. Such, for example, is Being, of which the ten categories are only subdivisions. Kant, according to his wont, twisted these old terms into a new signification. First of all, he distinguished them from each other. *Transcendent* he employed to denote what is wholly beyond experience, being given neither as an *a posteriori* nor *a priori* element of cognition — what therefore transcends every category of thought. *Transcendental* he applied to signify the *a priori* or necessary cognitions which, though manifested in, as affording the conditions of, experience, transcend the sphere of that contingent or adventitious knowledge which we acquire by experience. Transcendental is not therefore what transcends, but what in fact constitutes, a category of thought.] — *Diss. supp. to Reid.*

† [*Instincts, rational* or *intellectual.*

These terms are intended to express not so much the light, as the dark, side which the elementary facts of consciousness exhibit. They therefore stand opposed to the conceivable, the understood, the known.

As to the impropriety, though, like most other psychological terms, these are not unexceptionable, they are however less so than many, nay than most, others. An Instinct is an agent which performs blindly and ignorantly a work of intelligence and knowledge. The terms, *instinctive belief — judgment — cognition* are therefore expressions not ill adapted to characterize a belief, judgment, cognition, which, as the result of no anterior consciousness, is, like the products of animal instinct, the intelligent effect of (as far as we are concerned) an unknowing cause. In like manner, we can hardly find more suitable expressions to indicate those incomprehensi-

Criterion for distinguishing Native from Adventitious Knowledge. — The history of opinions touching the acceptation, or rejection, of such native notions, is, in a manner, the history of philosophy: for as the one alternative, or the other, is adopted in this question, the character of a system is determined. At present, I content myself with stating, that, though from the earliest period of philosophy, the doctrine was always common, if not always predominant, that our knowledge originated, in part at least, in the mind, yet it was only at a very recent date that the criterion was explicitly enounced, by which the native may be discriminated from the adventitious elements of knowledge. Without touching on some ambiguous expressions in more ancient philosophers, it is sufficient to say, that the character of universality and necessity, as the quality by which the two classes of knowledge are distinguished, was first explicitly proclaimed by Leibnitz. I have already frequently had occasion incidentally to notice, that we should carefully distinguish between those notions or cognitions which are primitive facts, and those notions or cognitions which are generalized or derivative facts. The former are given us; they are not, indeed, obtrusive, — they are not even cognizable of themselves. They lie hid in the profundities of the mind, until drawn from their obscurity by the mental activity itself employed upon the materials of experience. Hence it is, that our knowledge has its commencement in sense, external or internal, but its origin in intellect. The latter, the derivative cognitions, are of our own fabrication; we form them after certain rules; they are the tardy result of Perception and Memory, of Attention, Reflection, Abstraction. The primitive cognitions, on the contrary, seem to leap ready armed from the womb of reason, like Pallas from the head of Jupiter; sometimes the mind places them at the commencement of its operations, in order to have a point of support

ble spontaneities themselves, of which the primary facts of consciousness are the manifestations, than *rational* or *intellectual Instincts*. In fact, if Reason can justly be called a developed Feeling, it may with no less propriety be called an illuminated Instinct.] — *Diss. supp. to Reid.*

Et quod nunc Ratio, Impetus ante fuit.

and a fixed basis, without which the operations would be impossible; sometimes they form, in a certain sort, the crowning, the consummation of all the intellectual operations. The derivative or generalized notions are an artifice of intellect, — an ingenious mean of giving order and compactness to the materials of our knowledge. The primitive and general notions are the root of all principles, — the foundation of the whole edifice of human science. But how different soever be the two classes of our cognitions, and however distinctly separated they may be by the circumstance, — that we cannot but think the one, and can easily annihilate the other in thought, — this discriminative quality was not explicitly signalized till done by Leibnitz. The older philosophers are at best undeveloped. Descartes made the first step towards a more perspicuous discrimination. He frequently enounces that our primitive notions (besides being clear and distinct) are universal. But this universality is only a derived circumstance; — a notion is *universal* (meaning thereby that a notion is common to all mankind), because it is *necessary* to the thinking mind, — because the mind cannot but think it.

The enouncement of this criterion was, in fact, a great discovery in the science of mind; and the fact that a truth so manifest, when once proclaimed, could have lain so long unnoticed by philosophers, may warrant us in hoping that other discoveries of equal importance may still be awaiting the advent of another Leibnitz. Leibnitz has, in several parts of his works, laid down the distinction in question; and, what is curious, almost always in relation to Locke. "In Locke," [he says,] "there are some particulars not ill expounded, but upon the whole he has wandered far from the gate, nor has he understood the nature of the intellect. Had he sufficiently considered the difference between necessary truths or those apprehended by demonstration, and those which become known to us by induction alone, — he would have seen, that those which are necessary could only be approved to us by principles native to the mind; seeing that the senses indeed inform us what *may* take place, but not what *necessarily* takes place. Locke has not observed, that the notions of being, of substance, of one and the same, of the true, of the good, and many others, are innate to our mind, because our mind is innate to itself, and finds all these in its own furniture. It is true, indeed, that there is nothing in the intellect which was not previously in the sense, — except the intellect itself." In [another]. place he says, — "Hence arises another question, namely: Are all truths dependent on experience, that is to say, on induction and examples? Or are there some which have another foundation? For if some events can be foreseen before all trial has been made, it is manifest that we contribute something on our part. The senses, although necessary for all our actual cognitions, are not, however, competent to afford us all that cognitions involve; for the senses never give us more than examples, that is to say, particular or individual truths. Now all the examples, which confirm a general truth, how numerous soever they may be, are insufficient to establish the universal necessity of this same truth; for it does not follow, that what has happened will happen always in like manner. For example: the Greeks and Romans and other nations have always observed, that, during the course of twenty-four hours, day is changed into night, and night into day. But we should be wrong, were we to believe that the same rule holds everywhere, as the contrary has been observed during a residence in Nova Zembla. And he again would deceive himself, who should believe that, in our latitudes at least, this was a truth necessary and eternal; for we ought to consider, that the earth and the sun themselves have no necessary existence, and that there will perhaps a time arrive when this fair star will, with its whole system, have no longer a place in creation, — at least under its present form. Hence it appears, that the necessary truths, such as we find them in Pure Mathematics, and particularly in Arithmetic and Geometry, behoove to have principles the proof of which does not depend upon examples, and, consequently, not on the evidence of sense; howbeit, that without the senses, we should never have found occasion to call them into consciousness. This is what it is necessary to distinguish accurately, and it is what Euclid has so well understood, in demonstrating by reason what is sufficiently apparent by experience and sensible images. Logic, likewise, with Metaphyics and Morals, the one of which constitutes Natural Theology, the other Natural Jurisprudence, are full of such truths; and, consequently, their proof can only be derived from internal principles, which we call innate. It is true, that we ought not to imagine that we can read in the soul these eternal laws of reason *ad aperturam libri*, as we can read the edict of the Prætor, without trouble or research: but it is enough, that we can discover them in ourselves by dint of attention, when the occasions are presented to us by the senses. The success of the observation serves to confirm reason, in the same way as proofs serve in Arithmetic to obviate erroneous calculations, when the computation is long. It is hereby, also, that the cognitions of men differ from those of beasts. The beasts are purely empirical, and only regulate themselves by examples; for as far as we can judge, they never attain to the formation of necessary judgments, whereas, men are capable of demonstrative sciences, and herein the faculty which brutes possess of drawing inferences is inferior to the reason which is in men." And, after some other observations, he proceeds: "In illustration of this, let me make use likewise of the simile of a block of marble which has veins, rather than of a block of marble wholly uniform, or of blank tablets, that is to say, what is called a *tabula rasa* by philosophers; for if the mind resembled these blank tablets, truths would be in us, as the figure of Hercules is in a piece of marble, when the marble is altogether indifferent to the reception of this figure or of any other. But if we suppose that there are veins in the stone which would mark out the figure of Hercules by preference to other figures, this stone would be more determined thereunto, and Hercules would exist there, innately in a certain sort; although it would require labor to discover the veins, and to clear them by polishing and the removal of all that prevents their manifestation. It is thus that ideas and truths are innate in us; like our inclinations, dispositions, natural habitudes or virtualities, and not as actions; although these virtualities be always accompanied by some corresponding actions, frequently however unperceived"

And in another remarkable passage, Leibnitz says, "The mind is not only capable of knowing pure and necessary truths, but likewise of discovering them in itself; and if it possessed only the simple capacity of receiving cognitions, or the passive power of knowledge, as indetermined as that of the wax to receive figures, or a blank tablet to receive letters, it would not be the source of necessary truths, as I am about to demonstrate that it is: for it is incontestable, that the senses could not suffice to make their necessity apparent, and that the intellect has, therefore, a disposition, as well active as passive, to draw them from its own bosom, although the senses be requisite to furnish the occasion, and the attention to determine it upon some in preference to others. You see, therefore, these very able philosophers, who are of a different opinion, have not sufficiently reflected on the consequence of the difference that subsists between necessary or eternal truths and the truths of experience, as I have already observed, and as all our contestation shows. The original proof of necessary truths comes from the intellect alone, while other truths are derived from experience or the observations of sense. Our mind is competent to both kinds of knowledge, but it is itself the source of the former; and how great soever may be the number of particular experiences in support of a universal truth, we should never be able to assure ourselves forever of its universality by induction, unless we knew its necessity by reason. The senses may register, justify, and confirm these truths, but not demonstrate their infallibility and eternal certainty."

And in speaking of the faculty of such truths, he says: "It is not a naked faculty, which consists in the mere possibility of understanding them; it is a disposition, an aptitude, a preformation, which determines our mind to elicit, and which causes that they can be elicited; precisely as there is a difference between the figures which are bestowed indifferently on stone or marble, and those which veins mark out or are disposed to mark out, if the sculptor avail himself of the indications."

Reid made the same discrimination. — We have thus seen that Leibnitz was the first philosopher who explicitly established the quality of necessity as the criterion of distinction between empirical and *a priori* cognitions. I may, however, remark, what is creditable to Dr. Reid's sagacity, that he founded the same discrimination on the same difference: and I am disposed to think that he did this without being aware of his coincidence with Leibnitz; for he does not seem to have studied the system of that philosopher in his own works; and it was not till Kant had shown the importance of the criterion, by its application in his hands, that the attention of the learned was called to the scattered notices of it in the writings of Leibnitz. In speaking of the principle of causality, Dr. Reid says: "We are next to consider whether we may not learn this truth from experience, — That effects which have all the marks and tokens of design, must proceed from a designing cause."

"I apprehend that we cannot learn this truth from experience, for two reasons.

"*First.* Because it is a necessary truth, not a contingent one. It agrees with the experience of mankind since the beginning of the world, that the area of a triangle is equal to half the rectangle under its base and perpendicular. It agrees no less with experience, that the sun rises in the east and sets in the west. So far as experience goes, these truths are upon an equal footing. But every man perceives this distinction between them, — that the first is a necessary truth, and that it is impossible that it should not be true; but the last is not necessary, but contingent, depending upon the will of Him who made the world. As we cannot learn from experience that twice three must necessarily make six, so neither can we learn from experience that certain effects must proceed from a designing and intelligent cause. Experience informs us only of what has been, but never of what must be."

And in speaking of our belief in the principle that an effect manifesting design must have had an intelligent cause, he says, — "It has been thought, that, although this principle does not admit of proof from abstract reasoning, it may be proved from experience, and may be justly drawn by induction from instances that fall within our observation.

"I conceive this method of proof will leave us in great uncertainty, for these three reasons:

"1*st*. Because the proposition to be proved is not a contingent but a *necessary* proposition. It is not that things which begin to exist *commonly* have a cause, or even that they *always* in fact have a cause; but that they *must* have a cause, and cannot begin to exist without a cause.

"Propositions of this kind, from their nature, are incapable of proof by induction. Experience informs us only of what *is* or *has been*, not of what *must be;* and the conclusion must be of the same nature with the premises.

"For this reason, no mathematical proposition can be proved by induction. Though it should be found by experience in a thousand cases, that the area of a plain triangle is equal to the rectangle under the altitude and half the base, this would not prove that it must be so in all cases, and cannot be otherwise; which is what the mathematician affirms.

"In like manner, though we had the most ample experimental proof, that things which had begun to exist had a cause, this would not prove that they must have a cause. Experience may show us what is the established course of nature, but can never show what connection of things are in their nature necessary.

"2*dly*. General maxims, grounded on experience, have only a degree of probability proportioned to the extent of our experience; and ought always to be understood so as to leave room for exceptions, if future experience should discover any such.

"The law of gravitation has as full proof from experience and induction as any principle can be supposed to have. Yet, if any philosopher should, by clear experiment, show that there is a kind of matter in some bodies which does not gravitate, the law of gravitation ought to be limited by that exception.

"Now it is evident that men have never considered the principle of the necessity of causes as a truth of this kind, which may admit of limitation or exception; and therefore it has not been received upon this kind of evidence.

"3*dly*. I do not see that experience could satisfy us that every change in nature actually has a cause.

"In the far greatest part of the changes in nature that fall within our observation, the causes are unknown; and, therefore, from experience, we cannot know whether they have causes or not.

"Causation is not an object of sense. The only experience we can have of it, is in the consciousness we have of exerting some power in ordering our thoughts and actions. But this experience is surely too narrow a foundation for a general conclusion, that all things that have had or shall have a beginning, must have a cause."

How many cognitions should be ranked as ultimate. — But though it be now generally acknowledged, by the profoundest thinkers, that it is impossible to analyze all our knowledge into the produce of experience, external or internal, and that a certain complement of cognitions must be allowed as having their origin in the nature of the thinking principle itself; they are not at one in regard to those which ought to be recognized as ultimate and elemental, and those which ought to be regarded as modifications or combinations of these. Reid and Stewart, (the former in particular), have been considered as too easy in their admission of primary laws; and it must be allowed that the censure, in some instances, is not altogether unmerited. But it ought to be recollected, that those who thus agree in reprehension are not in unison in regard to the grounds of censure; and they wholly forget that our Scottish philosophers made no pretension to a *final* analysis of the primary laws of human reason, — that they thought it enough to classify a certain number of cognitions as native to the mind, leaving it to their successors to resolve these into simpler elements. "The labyrinth," [says Dr. Reid,] "may be too intricate, and the thread too fine, to be traced through all its windings; but, if we stop where we can trace it no further, and secure the ground we have gained, there is no harm done; a quicker eye may in time trace it further." The same view has been likewise well stated by Mr. Stewart. "In all the other sciences, the progress of discovery has been gradual, from the less general to the more general laws of nature; and it would be singular indeed, if, in this science, which but a few years ago was confessedly in its infancy, and which certainly labors under many disadvantages peculiar to itself, a step should all at once be made to a single principle, comprehending all the particular phenomena which we know. As the order established in the intellectual world seems to be regulated by laws analogous to those which we trace among the phenomena of the material system; and as in all our philosophical inquiries (to whatever subject they may relate), the progress of the mind is liable to be affected by the same tendency to a premature generalization, the following extract from an eminent chemical writer may contribute to illustrate the scope and to confirm the justness of some of the foregoing reflections. 'Within the last fifteen or twenty years, several new metals and new earths have been made known to the world. The names that support these discoveries are respectable, and the experiments decisive. If we do not give our assent to them, no single proposition in chemistry can for a moment stand. But whether all these are really simple substances, or compounds not yet resolved into their elements, is what the authors themselves cannot possibly assert; nor would it, in the least, diminish the merit of their observations, if future experiments should prove them to have been mistaken, as to the simplicity of these substances. This remark should not be confined to later discoveries; it may as justly be applied to those earths and metals with which we have been long acquainted.' 'In the dark ages of chemistry, the object was to rival Nature; and the substance which the adepts of those days were busied to create, was universally allowed to be simple. In a more enlightened period, we have extended our inquiries and multiplied the number of the elements. The last task will be to simplify; and by a closer observation of Nature, to learn from what a small store of primitive materials, all that we behold and wonder at was created.'"

That the list of the primary elements of human reason, which our two philosophers have given, has no pretence to order; and that the principles which it contains are not systematically deduced by any ambitious process of metaphysical ingenuity, is no valid ground of disparagement. In fact, which of the vaunted classifications of these primitive truths can stand the test of criticism? The most celebrated, and by far the most ingenious, of these, — the scheme of Kant, — though the truth of its details may be admitted, is no longer regarded as affording either a necessary deduction or a natural arrangement of our native cognitions; and the reduction of these to system still remains a problem to be resolved.

Distinction between Positive and Negative Necessity. — In point of fact, philosophers have not yet purified the antecedent conditions of the problem, — have not yet established the principles on which its solution ought to be undertaken. And here I would solicit your attention to a circumstance, which shows how far philosophers are still removed from the prospect of an ultimate decision. It is agreed, that the quality of necessity is that which discriminates a native from an adventitious element of knowledge. When we find, therefore, a cognition which contains this discriminative quality, we are entitled to lay it down as one which could not have been obtained as a generalization from experience. This I admit. But when philosophers lay it down not only as native to the mind, but as a positive and immediate datum of an intellectual power, I demur. It is evident that the quality of necessity in a cognition may depend on two different and opposite principles, inasmuch as *it may either be the result of a power, or of a powerlessness of the thinking principle.* In the one case, it will be a Positive, in the other a Negative, necessity. Let us take examples of these opposite cases. In an act of perceptive consciousness, I think, and cannot but think, that I and that something different from me exist, — in other words, that my perception, as a modification of the Ego, exists, and that the object of my perception, as a modification of the Non-ego, exists. In these circumstances, I pronounce Existence to be a native cognition, because I find that I cannot think except under the condition of thinking all that I am conscious of to exist. Existence is thus a form, a category, of thought. But here, though I cannot but think existence, I am conscious of this thought as an act of power, — an act of intellectual force. It is the result of strength, and not of weakness.

In like manner, when I think $2 \times 2 = 4$, the thought, though inevitable, is not felt as an imbecility; we know it as true, and, in the perception of the truth, though the act be necessary, the mind is conscious that the necessity does not arise from impotence. On the contrary, we attribute the same necessity to God. Here, therefore, there is a class of natural cognitions, which we may properly view as so many positive exertions of the mental vigor, and the cognitions of this class we consider as Positive. To this class will belong the notion of Existence and its modifications, the principles of Identity, and Contradiction, and Excluded Middle, the intuitions of Space and Time, etc.

The Negative sort of Necessity illustrated. — But besides these, there are other necessary forms of thought, which, by all philosophers, have been regarded as standing precisely on the same footing, which to me seem to be of a totally different kind. In place of being the result of a power, the necessity which belongs to them is merely a consequence of the impotence of our faculties. But if this be the case, nothing could be more unphilosophical than to arrogate to these negative inabilities the dignity of positive energies. Every rule of philosophizing would be violated. The law of Parcimony prescribes, that principles are not to be multiplied without necessity, and that an hypothetical force be not postulated to explain a phænomenon which can be better accounted for by an admitted impotence. The phænomenon of a heavy body rising from the earth, may warrant us in the assumption of a special power; but it would surely be absurd to devise a special power (that is, a power besides gravitation) to explain the phænomenon of its descent.

Now, that the imbecility of the human mind constitutes a great negative principle, to which sundry of the most important phænomena of intelligence may be referred, appears to me incontestable; and though the discussion is one somewhat abstract, I shall endeavor to give you an insight into the nature and application of this principle.

I begin by the statement of certain principles, to which it is necessary in the sequel to refer.

The highest of all logical laws, in other words the supreme law of thought, is what is called the principle of Contradiction, or more correctly the principle of Non-Contradiction.* It is

* [The doctrines of Contradiction, or of Contradictories, that Affirmation or Negation is a necessity of thought, whilst Affirmation and Negation are incompatible, is developed into three sides or phases, each of which implies both the others, — phases which may obtain, and actually have received, severally, the name of *Law*, *Principle*, or *Axiom*. Neglecting the historical order in which these were scientifically named and articulately developed, they are:

1°, The Law, Principle, or Axiom, of *Identity*, which, in regard to the same thing, immediately or directly enjoins the affirmation of it with itself, and mediately or indirectly prohibits its negation: (*A is A*).

2°, The Law, etc., of *Contradiction* (properly *Non-contradiction*), which, in regard to contradictories, explicitly enjoining their reciprocal negation, implicitly prohibits their reciprocal affirmation: (*A is not Not-A*). In other words, contradictories are thought as existences incompatible at the same time, — as at once mutually exclusive.

3°, The Law, etc., of *Excluded Middle* or *Third*, which declares that, whilst contradictories are only two, every thing, if explicitly thought, must be thought as of these either the one or the other: (*A is either B or Not-B*). In different terms: — Affirmation and negation of the same thing, in the same respect, have no conceivable medium; whilst any thing actually may and virtually must, be either affirmed or denied of any thing. In other words: — Every predicate is true or false of every subject; or, contradictories are thought as incompossible, but, at the same time, the one or the other as necessary. The argument from Contradiction is omnipotent within its sphere, but that sphere is narrow. It has the following limitations:

1°, It is negative, not positive; it may refute, but it is incompetent to establish. It may show what is not, but never of itself what is. It is exclusively Logical or Formal, not Metaphysical or Real; it proceeds on a necessity of thought, but never issues in an Ontology or knowledge of existence.

2°, It is dependent; to act it presupposes a counter-proposition to act from.

3°, It is explicative, not ampliative; it analyzes what is given, but does not originate information, or add any thing, through itself, to our stock of knowledge.

4°, But, what is its principal defect, it is partial, not thorough-going. It leaves many of the most important problems of our knowledge out of its determination; and is, therefore, all too narrow in its application as a universal criterion or instrument of judgment. For were we left, in our rea-

this: A thing cannot be and not be at the same time, — *Alpha est, Alpha non est,* are propositions which cannot both be true at once. A second fundamental law of thought, or rather the principle of Contradiction viewed in a certain aspect, is called the principle of Excluded Middle, or, more fully, the principle of Excluded Middle between two Contradictories. A thing either is or is not, — *Aut est Alpha, aut non est;* there is no medium; one must be true, both cannot. These principles require, indeed admit of, no proof. They prove every thing, but are proved by nothing. When I therefore have occasion to speak of these laws by name, you will know to what principle I refer.

Hamilton's one grand law of thought illustrated. — Now, then, I lay it down as a law, which, though not generalized by philosophers, can be easily proved to be true by its application to the phænomena: *That all that is conceivable in thought, lies between two extremes, which, as contradictory of each other, cannot both be true, but of which, as mutual contradictories, one must.* For example, we conceive Space, — we cannot but conceive Space. I admit, therefore, that Space indefinitely is a positive and necessary form of thought. But when philosophers convert the fact, that we cannot but think space, or, to express it differently, that we are unable to imagine any thing out of space, — when philosophers, I say, convert this fact with the assertion, that we have a notion, — a positive notion, of absolute or of infinite space, they assume, not only what is not contained in the phænomenon, nay, they assume what is the very reverse of what the phænomenon manifests. It is plain, that *space must either be bounded or not bounded.* These are contradictory alterna-

sonings, to a dependence on the principle of Contradiction, we should be unable competently to attempt any argument with regard to some of the most interesting and important questions. For there are many problems in the philosophy of mind where the solution necessarily lies between wha are, to us, the one or the other of two counter, and, therefore, incompatible alternatives, neither of which are we able to conceive as possible, but of which, by the very conditions of thought, we are compelled to acknowledge that the one or the other cannot but be; and it is as supplying this deficiency, that what has been called the argument from Common Sense becomes principally useful.] — *Appendix.*

tives; on the principle of Contradiction, they cannot both be true; and, on the principle of Excluded Middle, one must be true. This cannot be denied, without denying the primary laws of intelligence. *But though space must be admitted to be necessarily either finite or infinite, we are able to conceive the possibility neither of its finitude nor of its infinity.*

We are altogether unable to perceive space as bounded, — as finite; that is, as a whole beyond which there is no further space. Every one is conscious that this is impossible. It contradicts also the supposition of space as a necessary notion; for if we could imagine space as a terminated sphere, and that sphere not itself enclosed in a surrounding space, we should not be obliged to think every thing in space; and, on the contrary, if we did imagine this terminated sphere as itself in space, in that case, we should not have actually conceived all space as a bounded whole. The one contradictory is thus found inconceivable; we cannot conceive space as positively limited.

This law applied to space as a maximum. — On the other hand, we are equally powerless to realize in thought the possibility of the opposite contradictory; we cannot conceive space as infinite, as without limits. You may launch out in thought beyond the solar walk, you may transcend in fancy even the universe of matter, and rise from sphere to sphere in the region of empty space, until imagination sinks exhausted; — with all this, what have you done? You have never gone beyond the finite, you have attained at best only to the indefinite, and the indefinite, however expanded, is still always the finite. As Pascal energetically says, "Inflate our conceptions as we may, with all the finite possible, we cannot make one atom of the infinite." "The infinite is infinitely incomprehensible." Now, then, both contradictories are equally inconceivable; and could we limit our attention to one alone, we should deem it at once impossible and absurd, and suppose its unknown opposite as necessarily true. But as we not only can, but are constrained to consider both, we find that both are equally incomprehensible; and yet, though unable to view either as possible, we are forced by a higher law to admit that one, but one only, is necessary.

Space as a minimum also inconceivable. — That the conceivable lies also between two inconceivable extremes, is illustrated by every other relation of thought. We have found the maximum of space incomprehensible; can we comprehend its minimum? This is equally impossible. Here, likewise, we recoil from one inconceivable contradictory only to infringe upon another. Let us take a portion of space, however small; we can never conceive it as the smallest. It is necessarily extended, and may, consequently, be divided into a half or quarters, and each of these halves or quarters may again be divided into other halves or quarters, and this *ad infinitum.* But if we are unable to construe to our mind the possibility of an absolute minimum of space, we can as little present to ourselves the possibility of an infinite divisibility of any extended entity.

Time also inconceivable, either as a maximum or a minimum. — In like manner, Time; — this is a notion even more universal than space, for while we exempt from occupying space the energies of mind, we are unable to conceive these as not occupying time. Thus, we think every thing, mental and material, as in time, and out of time we can think nothing. But, if we attempt to comprehend time, either in whole or in part, we find that thought is hedged in between two incomprehensibles. Let us try the whole. And here let us look back, — let us consider time *a parte ante.* And here, we may surely flatter ourselves, that we shall be able to conceive time as a whole, for here we have the past period bounded by the present; the past cannot, therefore, be infinite or eternal, for a bounded infinite is a contradiction. But we shall deceive ourselves. We are altogether unable to conceive time as commencing; we can easily represent to ourselves time under any relative limitation of commencement and termination; but we are conscious to ourselves of nothing more clearly, than that it would be equally possible to think without thought, as to construe to the mind an absolute commencement, or an absolute termination, of time; that is, a beginning and an end beyond which time is conceived as non-existent. Goad imagination to the utmost, it still sinks paralyzed within the bounds of time, and time survives as the condition of the thought itself in which we annihilate the universe. On the other hand, the concept of past time as without limit, — without commencement, is equally impossible. We cannot conceive the infinite regress of time; for such a notion could only be realized by the infinite addition in thought of finite times, and such an addition would itself require an eternity for its accomplishment. If we dream of effecting this, we only deceive ourselves by substituting the indefinite for the infinite, than which no two notions can be more opposed. The negation of a commencement of time involves, likewise, the affirmation, that an infinite time has, at every moment, already run; that is, it implies the contradiction, that an infinite has been completed. For the same reasons, we are unable to conceive an infinite progress of time; while the infinite regress and the infinite progress, taken together, involve the triple contradiction of an infinite concluded, of an infinite commencing, and of two infinities, not exclusive of each other.

Now take the parts of time, — a moment, for instance; this we must conceive, as either divisible to infinity, or that it is made up of certain absolutely smallest parts. One or the other of these contradictories must be the case. But each is, to us, equally inconceivable. Time is a protensive quantity, and, consequently, any part of it, however small, cannot, without a contradiction, be imagined as not divisible into parts, and these parts into others *ad infinitum*. But the opposite alternative is equally impossible; we cannot think this infinite division. One is necessarily true; but neither can be conceived possible. It is on the inability of the mind to conceive either the ultimate indivisibility, or the infinite divisibility of space and time, that the arguments of the Eleatic Zeno against the possibility of motion are founded, — arguments which at least show, that motion, however certain as a fact, cannot be conceived possible, as it involves a contradiction.*

* [*Contradictions proving the Psychological Theory of the Conditioned.*

1. Finite cannot comprehend, contain the Infinite. — Yet an inch or minute, say, are finites, and are divisible *ad infinitum*, that is, their terminated division incogitable.

This grand principle called the Law of the Conditioned.— The same principle could be shown in various other relations, but what I have now said is, I presume, sufficient to make you understand its import. Now, the law of mind, *that the conceivable is in every relation bounded by the inconceivable*, I call

2. Infinite cannot be terminated or begun.—Yet eternity *ab ante* ends *now;* and eternity *à post* begins *now.*—So apply to Space.

3. There cannot be two infinite maxima.—Yet eternity *ab ante* and *a post* are two infinite maxima of time.

4. If an infinite maximum be cut into two, the halves cannot be each infinite, for nothing can be greater than infinite, and thus they could not be parts; nor finite, for thus two finite halves would make an infinite whole.

5. What contains infinite extensions, protensions, intensions, [three modes of quantity,] cannot be passed through,—come to an end. An inch, a minute, a degree contains these; *ergo*, etc. Take a minute. This contains an infinitude of protended quantities, which must follow one after another; but an infinite series of successive protensions can, *ex termino*, never be ended; *ergo*, etc.

6. An infinite maximum cannot but be all inclusive. Time *ab ante* and *a post* [are] infinite and exclusive of each other; *ergo.*

7. An infinite number of quantities must make up either an infinite or a finite whole. I. The former.—But an inch, a minute, a degree, contain each an infinite number of quantities; therefore, an inch, a minute, a degree, are each infinite wholes; which is absurd. II. The latter.—An infinite number of quantities would thus make up a finite quantity; which is equally absurd.

8. If we take a finite quantity (as an inch, a minute, a degree), it would appear equally that there are, and that there are not, an equal number of quantities between these and a greatest, and between these and a least.

9. An absolutely quickest motion is that which passes from one point to another in space in a minimum of time. But a quickest motion from one point to another, say a mile distance, and from one to another, say a million million of miles, is thought the same; which is absurd.

10. A wheel turned with quickest motion; if a spoke be prolonged, it will therefore be moved by a motion quicker than the quickest. The same may be shown using the rim and the nave.

11. Contradictory are Boscovich Points, which occupy space, and are inextended. Dynamism, therefore, inconceivable. *E contra,*

12. Atomism also inconceivable; for this supposes atoms,—minima extended but indivisible.

13. A quantity, say a foot, has an infinity of parts. Any part of this quantity, say an inch, has also an infinity. But one infinity is not larger than another. Therefore, an inch is equal to a foot.]—*Appendix.*

the Law of the Conditioned. You will find many philosophers who hold an opinion the reverse of this, — maintaining that "the Absolute" is a native or necessary notion of intelligence. This, I conceive, is an opinion founded on vagueness and confusion. They tell us we have a notion of absolute or infinite space, of absolute or infinite time. But they do not tell us in which of the opposite contradictories this notion is realized. Though these are exclusive of each other, and though both are only negations of the conceivable on its opposite poles, they confound together these exclusive inconceivables into a single notion; suppose it positive, and baptize it with the name of Absolute. The sum, therefore, of what I have now stated is, that *the Conditioned is that which is alone conceivable or cogitable; the Unconditioned, that which is inconceivable or incogitable.* The Conditioned or the thinkable lies between two extremes or poles; and these extremes or poles are each of them Unconditioned, each of them inconceivable, each of them exclusive or contradictory of the other. Of these two repugnant opposites, the one is that of Unconditional or Absolute Limitation; the other, that of Unconditional or Infinite Illimitation. The one we may, therefore, in general call the Absolutely Unconditioned, the other the Infinitely Unconditioned; or, more simply, the Absolute and the Infinite; the term *Absolute* expressing that which is finished or complete, the term *Infinite*, that which cannot be terminated or concluded. These terms, which, like the Absolute and Infinite themselves, philosophers have confounded, ought not only to be distinguished, but opposed as contradictory. The notion of either unconditioned is negative:— the Absolute and the Infinite can each only be conceived as a negation of the thinkable. In other words, of the Absolute and Infinite we have no conception at all.

[To recapitulate:— In our opinion, the mind can conceive, and, consequently, can know, only the *limited, and the conditionally limited.* The unconditionally unlimited, or the *Infinite*, — the unconditionally limited, or the *Absolute*, — cannot positively be construed to the mind; they can be conceived, only by a thinking away from, or abstraction of, those very conditions under which thought itself is realized; consequently, the notion of the Unconditioned is only *negative* — negative of the conceivable itself. For example, on the one hand we can positively conceive, neither an absolute whole, that is, a whole so great, that we cannot also conceive it as a relative part of a still greater whole; nor an absolute part, that is, a part so small, that we cannot also conceive it as a relative whole, divisible into smaller parts. On the other hand, we cannot positively represent, or realize, or construe to the mind (as here Understanding and Imagination coincide),* an infinite whole; for this could only be done by the infinite synthesis in thought of finite wholes, which would itself require an infinite time for its accomplishment; nor, for the same reason, can we follow out in thought an infinite divisibility of parts. The result is the same, whether we apply the process to limitation in *space*, in *time*, or in *degree*. The unconditional negation, and the unconditional affirmation of limitation, — in other words, the *Infinite* and the *Absolute*, — *properly so called*,† are thus inconceivable to us.

* [The Understanding, thought proper, notion, concept, etc., may coincide or not with Imagination, representation proper, image, etc. The two faculties do not coincide in a general notion; for we cannot represent Man or Horse in an actual image without individualizing the universal; and thus contradiction emerges. But in the individual, say Socrates or Bucephalus, they do coincide; for I see no valid ground why we should not *think*, in the strict sense of the word, or *conceive*, the individuals which we *represent*. In like manner, there is no mutual contradiction between the image and the concept of the Infinite or Absolute, if these be otherwise possible; for there is not necessarily involved the incompatibility of the one act of cognition with the other.]

† [The terms *Infinite*, and *Absolute*, and *Unconditioned*, ought not to be confounded. The Unconditioned, in our use of language, denotes the genus of which the Infinite and Absolute are the species.

The term Absolute is of twofold (if not threefold) ambiguity, corresponding to the double (or treble) signification of the word in Latin.

1. *Absolutum* means what is *freed* or *loosed*; in which sense, the Absolute will be what is aloof from relation, comparison, limitation, condition, dependence, etc., and thus is tantamount to τὸ ἀπόλυτον of the lower Greeks In this meaning, the Absolute is not opposed to the Infinite.

2. *Absolutum* means *finished*, *perfected*, *completed*; in which sense, the Absolute will be what is out of relation, etc., as finished, perfect, complete,

As the conditionally limited (which we may briefly call the *Conditioned*) is thus the only possible object of knowledge and of positive thought — thought necessarily supposes conditions. *To think* is *to condition;* and conditional limitation is the fundamental law of the possibility of thought. For, as the greyhound cannot outstrip his shadow, nor (by a more appropriate simile) the eagle outsoar the atmosphere in which he floats, and by which alone he is supported; so the mind cannot transcend that sphere of limitation, within and through which exclusively the possibility of thought is realized. Thought is only of the Conditioned; because, as we have said, to think is simply to condition. The *Absolute* is conceived merely by a negation of conceivability; and all that we know, is only known as

——— "won from the void and formless *Infinite.*"

How, indeed, it could ever be doubted that thought is only of the Conditioned, may well be deemed a matter of the profoundest admiration. Thought cannot transcend consciousness; consciousness is only possible under the antithesis of a subject and object of thought, known only in correlation, and mutually limiting each other; while, independently of all this, all that we know either of subject or object, either of mind or matter, is

total, and this corresponds to *τὸ ὅλον* and *τὸ τέλειον* of Aristotle. In this acceptation — and it is that in which for myself I exclusively use it — the Absolute as diametrically opposed to, is contradictory of, the Infinite.

Besides these two meanings, there is to be noticed the use of the word, for the most part in its adverbial form; — *absolutely* (*absolute*) in the sense of *simply, simpliciter* (ἁπλῶς), that is, considered in and for itself — considered not in relation. This holds a similar analogy to the two former meanings of absolute, which the Indefinite (*τὸ ἀόριστον*) does to the Infinite (*τὸ ἄπειρον*). It is subjective as they are objective; it is in our thought as they are in their own existence. This application is to be discounted, as here irrelevant.]

[The Infinite and Absolute are only the names of two counter imbecilities of the human mind, transmuted into properties of the nature of things — of two subjective negations, converted into objective affirmations. We tire ourselves, either in adding to, or in taking from. Some, more reasonably, call the thing unfinishable — *infinite;* others, less rationally, call it finished — *absolute.* But in both cases, the metastasis is in itself irrational.]

only a knowledge in each of the particular, of the plural, of the different, of the modified, of the phænomenal. We admit that the consequence of this doctrine is — that philosophy, if viewed as more than a science of the Conditioned, — is impossible. Departing from the particular, we admit that we can never, in our highest generalizations; rise above the Finite; that our knowledge, whether of mind or matter, can be nothing more than a knowledge of the relative manifestations of an existence, which, in itself, it is our highest wisdom to recognize as beyond the reach of philosophy; — in the language of St. Austin — "*cognoscendo ignorari, et ignorando cognosci.*"

The Conditioned is the mean between two extremes — two inconditionates, exclusive of each other, *neither of which can be conceived as possible,* but of which, on the principles of Contradiction and Excluded Middle, one *must be admitted as necessary.* On this opinion, therefore, our faculties are shown to be weak, but not deceitful. The mind is not represented as conceiving two propositions subversive of each other, as equally possible; but only, as unable to understand as possible either of two extremes; one of which, however, on the ground of their mutual repugnance, it is compelled to recognize as true. We are thus taught the salutary lesson, that the capacity of thought is not to be constituted into the measure of existence; and are warned from recognizing the domain of our knowledge as necessarily coextensive with the horizon of our faith. And by a wonderful revelation, we are thus, in the very consciousness of our inability to conceive aught above the relative and finite, inspired with a belief in the existence of something unconditioned beyond the sphere of all comprehensible reality.*] — *Discussions.*

* [True, therefore, are the declarations of a pious philosophy: "A God understood would be no God at all;" — "To think that God is, as we can think him to be, is blasphemy." — The Divinity, in a certain sense, is revealed; in a certain sense, is concealed: He is at once known and unknown. But the last and highest consecration of all true religion must be an altar — Ἀγνώστῳ Θεῷ — "*To the unknown and unknowable God.*" In this consummation, nature and revelation, paganism and Christianity, are at one: and from either source the testimonies are so numerous that I must refrain from quoting any.]

[In his criticism of Cousin's philosophy, Hamilton argues further:] [Our author maintains that the idea of the infinite, or absolute, and the idea of the finite or relative, are equally real, because the notion of the one necessarily suggests the notion of the other.

Correlatives certainly suggest each other, but correlatives may, or may not, be equally real and positive. In thought, contradictories necessarily imply each other, for the knowledge of contradictories is one. But the reality of one contradictory, so far from guaranteeing the reality of the other, is nothing else than its negation. Thus every positive notion (the concept of a thing by what it is) suggests a negative notion (the concept of a thing by what it is not); and the highest positive notion, the notion of the conceivable, is not without its corresponding negative in the notion of the inconceivable. But though these mutually suggest each other, the positive alone is real; the negative is only an abstraction of the other, and in the highest generality, even an abstraction of thought itself.]

[The philosophy of the Conditioned, even from the preceding outline, is, it will be seen, the express converse of the philosophy of the Absolute — at least, as this system has been latterly evolved in Germany. For this asserts to man a knowledge of the Unconditioned — of the Absolute and Infinite; while that denies to him a knowledge of either, and maintains, all which we immediately know, or can know, to be only the Conditioned, the Relative, the Phænomenal, the Finite. The one, supposing knowledge to be only of existence in itself, and existence in itself to be apprehended, and even understood, proclaims — "Understand that you may believe," ("Intellige ut credas"); the other, supposing that existence, in itself, is unknown, that apprehension is only of phænomena, and that these are received only upon trust, as incomprehensibly revealed facts, proclaims with the Prophet — "Believe that ye may understand," "Crede ut intelligas."] — *Discussions.*

This is the only orthodox inference. — I shall only add in conclusion, that, as this is the one true, it is the only orthodox, inference. We must believe in the infinity of God; but the infinite God cannot by us, in the present limitation of our faculties, be comprehended or conceived. A Deity understood, would be no Deity at all; and it is blasphemy to say that God only is as we are able to think Him to be. We know God according to the finitude of our faculties; but we believe much that we are incompetent properly to know. The Infinite, the infinite God, is what, to use the words of Pascal, is infinitely inconceivable. Faith, — Belief, — is the organ by which we apprehend what is beyond our knowledge. In this all Divines and Philosophers, worthy of the name, are found to coincide; and the few who assert to man a knowledge of the infinite, do this on the daring, the extravagant, the paradoxical supposition, either that Human Reason is identical with the Divine, or that Man and the Absolute are one.

The assertion has, however, sometimes been hazarded, through a mere mistake of the object of knowledge or conception: as if that could be an object of knowledge, which was not known; as if that could be an object of conception, which was not conceived.

It has been held, that the Infinite is known or conceived, though only a part of it (and every part, be it observed, is *ipso facto* finite) can be apprehended; and Aristotle's definition of the infinite has been adopted by those who disregard his declaration, that the infinite, *qua* infinite, is beyond the reach of human understanding. *To say that the infinite can be thought, but only inadequately thought, is a contradiction in adjecto;* it is the same as saying, that the infinite can be known, but only known as finite.

The Scriptures explicitly declare that the infinite is for us now incognizable; — they declare that the finite, and the finite alone, is within our reach. It is said (to cite one text out of many), that "*now* I know *in part*" (*i. e.* the finite); "but *then*" (*i. e.* in the life to come) "shall I know even as I am known" (*i. e.* without limitation).*

* [In a private letter, Hamilton replied as follows to some objections which Mr. H. Calderwood had made to his doctrine of "The Infinite."]

[The Infinite which I contemplate is considered only as *in thought;* the

Infinite beyond thought being, it may be, an object of belief, but not of knowledge. This consideration obviates many of your objections.

The sphere of our belief is much more extensive than the sphere of our knowledge; and, therefore, when I deny that the Infinite can by us be *known*, I am far from denying that by us it is, must, and ought to be, *believed*. This I have indeed anxiously evinced, both by reasoning and authority. When, therefore, you maintain, that in denying to man any positive cognizance of the Infinite, I virtually extenuate his belief in the infinitude of Deity, I must hold you to be wholly wrong, in respect both of my opinion, and of the theological dogma itself.

Assuredly, I maintain that an infinite God cannot be by us (positively comprehended. But the Scriptures, and all theologians worthy of the name, assert the same. Some indeed of the latter, and among them some of the most illustrious Fathers, go the length of asserting, that "an understood God is no God at all," and that, "if we maintain God to be as we think he is, we blaspheme." Hence the assertion of Augustine: "Deum potius ignorantia quam scientia attingi."

There is a fundamental difference between *The Infinite* (τὸ Ἓν καὶ Πᾶν), and a relation to which we may apply the term *infinite*. Thus, Time and Space must be excluded from the supposed notion of *The Infinite;* for The Infinite, if positively thought it could be, must be thought as under neither Space nor Time.

You maintain (*passim*) that thought, conception, knowledge, is and must be finite, whilst the *object of thought*, etc., may be infinite. This appears to me to be erroneous, and even contradictory. An existence can only be an object of thought, conception, knowledge, inasmuch as it is an object thought, conceived, known; as such only does it form a constituent of the circle of thought, conception, knowledge. A thing may be partly known, conceived, thought, — partly unknown, etc. But that part of it only which is thought, can be an object of thought, etc.; whereas the part of it not thought, etc., is, as far as thought, etc., is concerned, only tantamount to zero. The infinite, therefore, in this point of view, can be *no object* of thought, etc.; for nothing can be more self-repugnant than the assertion, that we know the infinite through a finite notion, or have a finite knowledge of an infinite object of knowledge.

But you assert (*passim*) that we have a knowledge, a notion, of the infinite; at the same time, asserting (*passim*) that this knowledge or notion is "inadequate," — "partial," — "imperfect," — "limited," — "not in all its extent," — "incomplete," — "only to some extent," — "in a certain sense," — "indistinct," etc., etc.

Now, in the first place, this assertion is in contradiction of what you also maintain, that "the infinite is one and indivisible;" that is, that having *no parts*, it cannot be *partially* known. But, in the second place, this also subverts the possibility of conceiving, of knowing, the Infinite; for as partial, inadequate, not in all its extent, etc., our conception includes *some part* only of the object supposed infinite, and *does not include* the rest. Our knowledge is, therefore, by your own account, limited and finite; consequently, you implicitly admit that we have no knowledge, at least no positive knowledge, of the infinite.

Again, as stated, you describe the infinite to be "one and indivisible." But to conceive as inseparable into *parts* an entity which, not excluding, in fact includes, the worlds of mind and matter, is for the human intellect utterly improbable. And does not the infinite contain the finite? If it does, then it contains what has parts, and is divisible; if it does not, then it is exclusive: the finite is out of the infinite: and the infinite is conditioned, limited, restricted, — *finite.*

You controvert my assertion, that, to conceive a thing *in relation* is, *ipso facto,* to conceive it as finite; and you maintain that the relative is not incompatible with infinity, unless it be also restrictive. But restrictive, I hold the relative always to be, and therefore, incompatible with *The Infinite* in the more proper signification of the term, though infinity, in a looser signification, may be applied to it. My reasons for this are the following: A relation is always a *particular* point of view; consequently, the things thought as relative and correlative are always thought restrictively, in so far as the thought of the one discriminates and excludes the other, and likewise all things not conceived in the same special or relative point of view. Thus, if we think of Socrates and Xanthippe under the matrimonial relation, not only do the thoughts of Socrates and Xanthippe exclude each other as separate existences, and, *pro tanto,* therefore are restrictive; but thinking of Socrates *as husband,* this excludes our conception of him as citizen, etc., etc. Or, to take an example from higher relatives: what is thought, as the *object,* excludes what is viewed as the *subject,* of thought; and hence the necessity which compelled Schelling and other absolutists to place *The Absolute* in the indifference of subject and object, of knowledge and existence. Again: we conceive God in the relation of Creator, and in so far as we merely conceive Him as Creator, we do not conceive him as unconditioned, as infinite; for there are many other relations of the Deity under which we may conceive Him, but which are not included in the relation of Creator. In so far, therefore, as we conceive God only in this relation, our conception of Him is manifestly restrictive. Further, the created universe is, and you assert it to be, finite. The creation is, therefore, an act, of however great, of finite power; and the Creator is thus thought only in a finite capacity. God, in his own nature, is infinite; but we do not positively think Him as infinite, in thinking Him under the relation of the Creator of a finite creation. Finally, let us suppose the created universe (which you do not) to be infinite; in that case, we should be reduced to the dilemma of asserting *two* infinities, which is contradictory, or of asserting the supernal absurdity, that God the Creator is finite, and the universe created by Him is infinite.] — *Appendix.*

CHAPTER XXVIII.

THE REGULATIVE FACULTY.—LAW OF THE CONDITIONED IN ITS APPLICATION TO THE DOCTRINE OF CAUSALITY.

I HAVE been desirous to explain the principle of the Conditioned, as out of it we are able not only to explain the hallucination of the Absolute, but to solve some of the most momentous, and hitherto most puzzling, problems of mind. In particular, this principle affords us, I think, a solution of the two great intellectual principles of Cause and Effect, and of Substance and Phænomenon or Accident. Both are only applications of the principle of the Conditioned, in different relations.

Of all questions in the history of Philosophy, that concerning the nature and genealogy of the notion of Causality, is, perhaps, the most famous; and I shall endeavor to give a comprehensive, though necessarily a very summary, view of the problem, and of the attempts which have been made at its solution.

What is the phenomenon of Causality. — But before proceeding to consider the different attempts to explain the phænomenon, it is proper to state and to determine what the phænomenon to be explained really is. Nor is this superfluous, for we shall find that some philosophers, instead of accommodating their solutions to the problem, have accommodated the problem to their solutions.

When we are aware of something which begins to be, we are, by the necessity of our intelligence, constrained to believe that it has a Cause. But what does the expression, *that it has a cause*, signify? If we analyze our thought, we shall find that it simply means, that as we cannot conceive any new existence to commence, therefore, all that is now seen to arise under a new appearance had previously an existence under a prior **form.** [We are constrained to think that what now appears to us under a new form, had previously an existence under others — others conceivable by us or not. These others (for they are always plural) are called its *cause;* and a cause, or more properly causes, we cannot but suppose; for a cause is simply every thing without which the effect would not result, and all such concurring, the effect cannot but result.] — *Discussions.* We are utterly unable to realize in thought the possibility of the complement of existence being either increased or diminished. We are unable, on the one hand, to conceive nothing becoming something, — or, on the other, something becoming nothing. When God is said to create out of nothing, we construe this to thought by supposing that He evolves existence out of himself; we view the Creator as the cause of the universe. "Ex nihilo nihil, in nihilum nil posse reverti" expresses, in its purest form, the whole intellectual phænomenon of causality.

There is thus conceived an absolute tautology between the effect and its causes. We think the causes to contain all that is contained in the effect; the effect to contain nothing which was not contained in the causes. Take an example. A neutral salt is an effect of the conjunction of an acid and alkali. Here we do not, and here we cannot, conceive that, in effect, any new existence has been added, nor can we conceive that any has been taken away. But another example: — Gunpowder is the effect of a mixture of sulphur, charcoal, and nitre, and these three substances are again the effect, — result, of simpler constituents, and these constituents again of simpler elements, either known or conceived to exist. Now, in all this series of compositions, we cannot conceive that aught begins to exist. The gunpowder, the last compound, we are compelled to think, contains precisely the same quantum of existence that its ultimate elements contained, prior to their combination. Well; we explode the powder. Can we conceive that existence has been diminished by the annihilation of a single element previously in being, or increased by the addition of a single element which was not heretofore in nature? "Omnia mutantur; nihil interit." —

is what we think, what we must think. This, then, is the mental phænomenon of causality, — that we necessarily deny in thought that the object which appears to begin to be, really so begins; and that we necessarily identify its present with its past existence. Here it is not requisite that we should know under what form, under what combinations, this existence was previously realized; in other words, it is not requisite that we should know what are *the particular causes of the particular effect.* The discovery of the connection of determinate causes and determinate effects is merely contingent and individual, — merely the datum of experience; but the principle that every event should have its causes, is necessary and universal, and is imposed on us as a condition of our human intelligence itself. This *necessity of so thinking is the only phænomenon to be explained.* [The question of philosophy is not concerning *the* cause, but concerning *a* cause.]

Nor are philosophers, in general, really at variance in their statement of the problem. However divergent in their mode of explanation, they are at one in regard to the matter to be explained. But there is one exception. Dr. Brown has given a very different account of the phænomenon in question. To a statement of it, I solicit your attention; for as his theory is solely accommodated to his view of the phænomenon, so his theory is refuted by showing that his view of the phænomenon is erroneous.

Now, in explaining to you the doctrine of Dr. Brown, I am happy to avail myself of the assistance of [Prof. John Wilson] Dr. Brown's successor, whose metaphysical acuteness was not the least remarkable of his many brilliant qualities.

Wilson's confutation of Brown's doctrine. — "The distinct and full purport of Dr. Brown's doctrine, it will be observed, is this, — that when we apply in this way the words *cause* and *power*, we attach no other meaning to the terms than what he has explained. By the word *cause*, we mean no more than that, in this instance, the spark falling is the event immediately prior to the explosion: including the belief that in all cases hitherto, when a spark has fallen on gunpowder (of course, supposing other circumstances the same), the gunpowder has kindled; and that whenever a spark shall again so fall, the grains will again take fire. The present immediate priority, and the past and future invariable sequence of the one event upon the other, are all the ideas that the mind can have in view in speaking of the event in that instance as a cause; and in speaking of the power in the spark to produce this effect, we mean merely to express the invariableness with which this has happened and will happen.

"This is the doctrine; and the author submits it to this test:— 'Let any one,' he says, 'ask himself what it is which he means by the term "power,"' and without contenting himself with a few phrases that signify nothing, reflect before he give his answer,—and he will find that he means nothing more than in that, all similar circumstances, the explosion of gunpowder will be the immediate and uniform consequence of the application of a spark.

"This test, indeed, is the only one to which the question can be brought. For the question does not regard causes themselves, but solely the ideas of cause, in the human mind. If, therefore, every one to whom this analysis of the idea, that is in his mind when he speaks of a cause, is proposed, finds, on comparing it with what passed in his mind, that this is a complete and full account of his conception, there is nothing more to be said, and the point is made good. By that sole possible test the analysis is, in such a case, established. If, on the contrary, when this analysis is proposed, as containing all the ideas which we annex to the words cause and power, the minds of most men cannot satisfy themselves that it is complete, but are still possessed with a strong suspicion that there is something more which is not here accounted for,—then the analysis is not yet established, and it becomes necessary to inquire by additional examination of the subject, what that more may be.

"Let us then apply the test by which Dr. Brown proposes that the truth of his views shall be tried. Let us ask ourselves what we mean when we say, that the spark has power to kindle the gunpowder,—that the powder is susceptible of being kindled by the spark. Do we mean only that whenever they come together this will happen? Do we merely predict this simple and certain futurity?

"We do not fear to say, that when we speak of a power in one substance to produce a change in another, and of a susceptibility of such change in that other, we express more than our belief that the change has taken and will take place. There is more in our mind than a conviction of the past and a foresight of the future. There is, besides this, the conception included of a fixed constitution of their nature, which determines the event, — a constitution, which, while it lasts, makes he event a necessary consequence of the situation in which the objects are placed. We should say then, that there are included in these terms, 'power,' and 'susceptibility of change,' *two ideas which are not expressed in Dr. Brown's analysis, — one of necessity, and the other of a constitution of things, in which that necessity is established.* That these two ideas are not expressed in the terms of Dr. Brown's analysis, is seen by quoting again his words: — 'He will find that he means nothing more than that, in all similar circumstances, the explosion of gunpowder will be the immediate and uniform consequence of the application of a spark.'

"It is certain, from the whole tenor of his work, that Dr. Brown has designed to exclude the idea of necessity from his analysis."

Now this admirably expresses what I have always felt is the grand and fundamental defect in Dr. Brown's theory, — a defect which renders that theory *ab initio* worthless. Brown professes to explain the phænomenon of causality, but, previously to explanation, he evacuates the phænomenon of all that desiderates explanation. What remains in the phænomenon, after the quality of necessity is thrown, or rather silently allowed to drop out, is only accidental, — only a consequence of the essential circumstance.

Classification of opinions respecting the Principle of Causality. — The opinions in regard to the nature and origin of the principle of Causality, in so far as that principle is viewed as a subjective phænomenon, — as a judgment of the human mind, — fall into two great categories. The first category (A) comprehends those theories which consider this principle as Empirical, or *a posteriori*, that is, as *derived from experience;* the other (B) comprehends those which view it as Pure, or *a priori*, that is, as *a condition of intelligence itself.* These two primary genera are, however, severally subdivided into various subordinate classes.

The former category (A), under which this principle is regarded as *the result of experience*, contains *two classes*, inasmuch as the causal judgment may be supposed founded either (a) on an *Original*, or (b) on a *Derivative*, cognition. Each of these again is divided into two, according as the principle is supposed to have an *objective*, or a *subjective*, origin. In the former case, that is, where the cognition is supposed to be original and underived, it is Objective, or rather Objectivo-Objective, when held to consist in *an immediate perception of the power or efficacy of causes in the external and internal worlds* (1); and Subjective, or rather Objectivo-Subjective, when viewed as given in *a self-consciousness alone of the power or efficacy of our own volitions* (2). In the latter case, that is, where the cognition is supposed to be derivative, if *objective*, it is viewed as *a product of Induction and Generalization* (3); if *subjective*, *of Association and Custom* (4).

In like manner, the latter category (B), under which the causal principle is considered *not as a result, but as a condition, of experience*, is variously divided and subdivided. In the first place, the opinions under this category fall into *two classes*, inasmuch as some regard the causal judgment (c) as an *Ultimate* or *Primary* law of mind, while others regard it (d) as a *Secondary* or *Derived*. Those who hold the former doctrine, in viewing it as a simple original principle, hold likewise that it is a positive act, — an affirmative datum of intelligence. This class is finally subdivided into *two opinions*. For some hold that the causal judgment, as necessary, is given in what they call "*the principle of Causality*," that is, *the principle which declares that every thing which begins to be, must have its cause* (5);

A TABULAR VIEW

OF THE

THEORIES IN REGARD TO THE PRINCIPLE OF CAUSALITY.

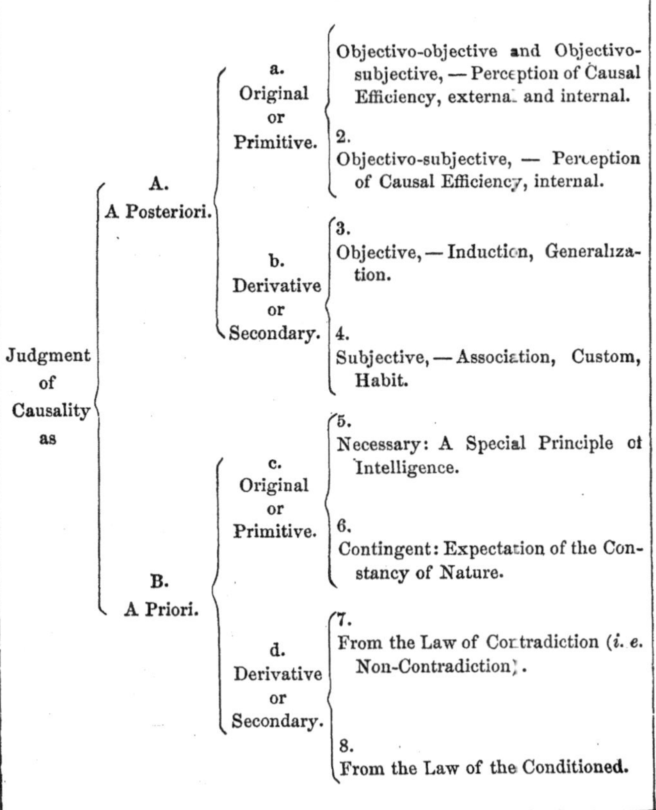

Judgment of Causality as

- A. A Posteriori.
  - a. Original or Primitive.
    - Objectivo-objective and Objectivo-subjective, — Perception of Causal Efficiency, external and internal.
    - 2. Objectivo-subjective, — Perception of Causal Efficiency, internal.
  - b. Derivative or Secondary.
    - 3. Objective, — Induction, Generalization.
    - 4. Subjective, — Association, Custom, Habit.
- B. A Priori.
  - c. Original or Primitive.
    - 5. Necessary: A Special Principle of Intelligence.
    - 6. Contingent: Expectation of the Constancy of Nature.
  - d. Derivative or Secondary.
    - 7. From the Law of Contradiction (*i. e.* Non-Contradiction).
    - 8. From the Law of the Conditioned.

whilst at least one philosopher, without explicitly denying that the causal judgment is necessary, would identify it with the principle of our "*Expectation of the Constancy of nature*" (6).

Those who hold that it can be analyzed into a higher principle, also hold that it is not of a positive, but of a negative, character. These, however, are divided into two classes. By some it has been maintained, that *the principle of Causality can be resolved into the principle of Contradiction* (7), which, as I formerly stated to you, ought in propriety to be called the principle of Non-Contradiction. On the other hand, it may be (though it never has been) argued, that *the judgment of Causality can be analyzed into what I called the principle of the Conditioned,—the principle of relativity* (8). To one or the other of these eight heads, all the doctrines that have been actually maintained in regard to the origin of the principle in question, may be referred; and the classification is the better worthy of your attention, as in no work will you find any attempt at even an enumeration of the various theories, actual and possible, on this subject.

An adequate discussion of these several heads, and a special consideration of the differences of the individual opinions which they comprehend, would far exceed our limits. I shall, therefore, confine myself to a few observations on the value of these eight doctrines in general, without descending to the particular modifications under which they have been maintained by particular philosophers.

1. *External Perception of causal efficiency.*—Of these, the first,—that which asserts that we have a perception of the causal agency, as we have a perception of the existence of external objects,—this opinion has been always held in combination with the second,—that which maintains that we are self-conscious of efficiency; though the second has been frequently held by philosophers who have abandoned the first as untenable. Considering them together, that is, as forming the opinion that we directly and immediately apprehend the efficiency of causes both external and internal,—this opinion is refuted by two objections.

The first is, that we have no such apprehension, — no such knowledge; the second, that if we had, this being merely empirical, — merely conversant with individual instances, could never account for the quality of necessity and universality which accompanies the judgment of causality. In regard to the first of these objections, *it is now universally admitted, that we have no perception of the connection of cause and effect in the external world.* For example; when one billiard-ball is seen to strike another, we perceive only that the impulse of the one is followed by the motion of the other, but have no perception of any force or efficiency in the first, by which it is connected with the second, in the relation of causality. Hume was the philosopher who decided the opinion of the world on this point. He was not, however, the first who stated the fact, or even the reasoner who stated it most clearly. He, however, believed himself, or would induce us to believe, that in this he was original. Speaking of this point, "I am sensible," he says, "that of all the paradoxes, which I have had, or shall hereafter have, occasion to advance, in the course of this treatise, the present one is the most violent, and that it is merely by dint of solid proof and reasoning I can ever hope it will have admission, and overcome the inveterate prejudices of mankind. Before we are reconciled to this doctrine, how often must we repeat to ourselves, that the simple view of any two objects or actions, however related, can never give us any idea of power, or of a connection betwixt them; that this idea arises from the repetition of their union; that the repetition neither discovers nor causes any thing in the objects, but has an influence only on the mind, by that customary transition it produces; that this customary transition is, therefore, the same with the power and necessity; which are consequently qualities of perceptions, not of objects, and are internally felt by the soul, and not perceived externally in bodies?"

I could adduce to you a whole army of philosophers previous to Hume, who had announced and illustrated the fact. As far as I have been able to trace it, this doctrine was first promulgated towards the commencement of the twelfth century, at

Bagdad, by Algazel, a pious Mohammedan philosopher, who not undeservedly obtained the title of Imaum of the World. Algazel did not deny the reality of causation, but he maintained that God was the only efficient cause in nature; and that second causes were not properly causes, but only occasions, of the effect. That we have no perception of any real agency of one body on another, is a truth which has not more clearly been stated or illustrated by any subsequent philosopher than by him who first proclaimed it. The doctrine of Algazel was adopted by that great sect among the Mussulman doctors, who were styled *those speaking in the law*, that is, the law of Mohammed. From the Eastern Schools, the opinion passed to those of the West; and we find it a problem which divided the Scholastic philosophers, whether God were the only efficient, or whether causation could be attributed to created existences. After the Revival of Letters, the opinion of Algazel was maintained by many individual thinkers, though it no longer retained the same prominence in the Schools. It was held, for example, by Malebranche, and his illustration from the collision of two billiard-balls is likewise that of Hume, who probably borrowed from Malebranche both the opinion and the example.

2. *Internal perception of causal efficiency.*— But there are many philosophers who surrender the external perception, and maintain our internal consciousness, of causation or power. This opinion was, in one chapter of his *Essay*, advanced by Locke, and, at a very recent date, it has been amplified and enforced with distinguished ability by the late M. Maine de Biran,— one of the acutest metaphysicians of France. On this doctrine, the notion of cause is not given to us by the observations of external phænomena, which, as considered only by the senses, manifest no causal efficiency, and appear to us only as successive; it is given to us within, in reflection, in the consciousness of our operations and of the power which exerts them,— namely, the will. I make an effort to move my arm, and I move it. When we analyze attentively the phænomenon of *effort*, which M. de Biran considers as the type of the phænomena of volition, the following are the results:— 1°, The consciousness of an act

of will; 2°, The consciousness of a motion produced; 3°, A relation of the motion to the volition. And what is this relation? Not a simple relation of succession. The will is not for us a pure act without efficiency, — it is a productive energy; so that, in a volition there is given to us the notion of cause; and this notion we subsequently transport, — project out from our internal activities, into the changes of the external world.

This doctrine shown to be untenable. — This reasoning, in so far as regards the mere empirical fact of our consciousness of causality, in the relation of our will as moving, and of our limbs as moved, is refuted by the consideration, that between the overt fact of corporeal movement of which we are cognizant, and the internal act of mental determination of which we are also cognizant, there intervenes a numerous series of intermediate agencies of which we have no knowledge; and, consequently, that we can have no consciousness of any causal connection between the extreme links of this chain, — the volition to move and the limb moving, as this hypothesis asserts. No one is immediately conscious, for example, of moving his arm through his volition. Previously to this ultimate movement, muscles, nerves, a multitude of solid and fluid parts, must be set in motion by the will; but of this motion we know, from consciousness, absolutely nothing. A person struck with paralysis is conscious of no inability in his limb to fulfil the determinations of his will; and it is only after having willed, and finding that his limbs do not obey his volition, that he learns by his experience, that the external movement does not follow the internal act. But as the paralytic learns after the volition, that his limbs do not obey his mind; so it is only after volition that the man in health learns, that his limbs do obey the mandates of his will.*

* [Elsewhere, in the *Dissertations supplementary to Reid*, this argument is stated by Hamilton as follows.]

"Volition to move a limb, and the actual moving of it, are the first and last in a series of more than two successive events; and cannot, therefore, stand to each other, immediately, in the relation of cause and effect. They may, however, stand to each other in the relation of cause and effect, mediately. But, then, if they can be known in consciousness

But, independently of all this, the second objection above mentioned is fatal to the theory which would found the judgment

as thus mediately related, it is a necessary condition of such knowledge, that the intervening series of causes and effects, through which the final movement of the limb is supposed to be mediately dependent on the primary volition to move, should be known to consciousness immediately under that relation. But this intermediate, this connecting series is, confessedly, unknown to consciousness at all, far less as a series of causes and effects. It follows, therefore, *a fortiori*, that the dependency of the last on the first of these events, as of an effect upon its cause, must be to consciousness unknown. In other words, — having no consciousness that the volition to move is the efficacious force (power) by which even the event immediately consequent on it (say the transmission of the nervous influence from brain to muscle) is produced, such event being in fact itself to consciousness occult; *multo minus* can we have a consciousness of that volition being the efficacious force by which the ultimate movement of the limb is mediately determined."

[In the same *Dissertation*, Hamilton gives the following analysis of the action of the will in determining motion.]

"We have here to distinguish three things: —

"1°. The still immanent or purely mental act of will: what, for distinction's sake, I would call the *hyperorganic* volition to move; — the *actio elicita* of the Schools. Of this volition we are conscious, even though it do not go out into overt action.

"2°. If this volition become transeunt, be carried into effect, it passes into the mental effort or *nisus* to move. This I would call the *enorganic volition*, or, by an extension of the Scholastic language, the *actio imperans. Of this we are immediately conscious. For we are conscious of it, though, by a narcosis or stupor of the sensitive nerves, we lose all feeling of the movement of the limb;* — though by a paralysis of the motive nerves, no movement in the limb follows the mental effort to move; — though by an abnormal stimulus of the muscular fibres, a contraction in them is caused even in opposition to our will.

"3°. Determined by the enorganic volition, the cerebral influence is transmitted by the motive nerves; the muscles contract, or endeavor to contract, so that the limb moves or endeavors to move. This motion or effort to move I would call the *organic movement*, the *organic nisus;* by a limitation of the scholastic term, it might be denominated the *actio imperata.*"

[It is in this *third* element — the *organic* nisus and the *organic* movement — that Sir William seeks for evidence of the efficiency of the will, and rightly declares that it cannot be found. We agree with him. "Between the extreme links of *this* chain, — that is, between the volition to move, and the

of causality on any empirical cognition, whether of the phænomena of mind or of the phænomena of matter. Admitting that causation were cognizable, and that perception and self-consciousness were competent to its apprehension, still as these faculties could only take note of individual causations, we should be wholly unable, out of such empirical acts, to evolve the quality of necessity and universality, by which this notion is

arm moving," he says, "there intervenes a series of intermediate agencies, of which we are wholly unaware." How mind operates upon matter, — even upon the matter of our own bodies, with which we are so intimately connected, — we do not know. How the action of the will is communicated to the muscles, — whether by one, two, or three intermediate steps, — we do not know.

But we find proof of the efficiency of volition in the *second* of our author's three elements, where his language, which we have italicized, is so explicit that it seems strange the conclusion could have escaped him. By the "*enorganic volition*," we understand neither "the still immanent or purely mental act," nor yet the organic *nisus* or movement which is wholly exterior to the mind, but the transeunt act from one to the other, *the command*, whether it is obeyed or not; — and of this enorganic movement, "we are immediately conscious," though the limb may be paralyzed. It is *action*, of which we are here conscious; otherwise, the "purely mental act of will" could not have "become transeunt." We are conscious of an *effort* in this act — conscious of *putting forth power* — conscious of *attempting* to move the muscles, whether they obey or not. The laborer is not more clearly conscious that he has *tried* to raise the rock. It is certain, also, that power in action is necessarily causative; it forms our only idea of causation. It *must* produce an effect, though perhaps not the whole effect which we desire. The pressure is not lost, though the rock does not move. We have, then, the direct evidence of consciousness, — of that faculty not one of whose dictates can be impeached, — that the will is a true cause — an efficient cause, not a mere antecedent — a *limited* cause, indeed, but supreme within its proper domain — not always *suf*ficient for the end proposed, but always *ef*ficient, or expending force, which is real, though often inadequate. We have here all the marks or tests, by which efficient causation is distinguished from mere antecedence. In the case of material phænomena, the result can be ascertained only *by experience;* we learn only by trial, that one substance is soluble, and another not, — that iron expands, and clay contracts, in the fire. But in the case of mental exertion, the result to be accomplished is *preconsidered*, or meditated, and is therefore known *a priori*, or before experience; the volition succeeds, which is a true effort, or power in action; and this is necessarily followed by an effect, partial or complete.] — *Am Ed.*

distinguished. Admitting that we had really observed the agency of any number of causes, still this would not explain to us, how we are unable to think a manifestation of existence without thinking it as an effect. Our internal experience, especially in the relation of our volitions to their effects, may be useful in giving us a clearer notion of causality; but it is altogether incompetent to account for what in it there is of the quality of necessity. So much for the two theories at the head of the Table.

As the first and second opinions have been usually associated, so also have the third and fourth; — that is, the doctrine that our notion of causality is the offspring of the objective principle of Induction or Generalization, and the doctrine that it is the offspring of the subjective principle of Association or Custom.

3. *Judgment of Causality obtained from Induction and Generalization.* — In regard to the former, — the third, it is plain that the observation, that certain phænomena are found to succeed certain other phænomena, and the generalization consequent thereon, that these are reciprocally causes and effects, could never of itself have engendered, not only the strong, but the irresistible belief, that every event must have its cause. Each of these observations is contingent; and any number of observed contingencies will never impose upon us the feeling of necessity, — of our inability to think the opposite. Nay more, this theory evolves the absolute notion of causality out of the observation of a certain number of uniform consecutions among phænomena; [that is, it would collect that *all must be*, because *some are*.] But we find no difficulty whatever in conceiving the reverse of all or any of the consecutions we have observed; and yet the general notion of causality, which, *ex hypothesi*, is their result, we cannot possibly think as possibly unreal. We have always seen a stone fall to the ground, when thrown into the air; but we find no difficulty in representing to ourselves the possibility of one or all stones gravitating from the earth; only we cannot conceive the possibility of this, or any other event, happening without a cause.

4. *From Association and Custom.* — Nor does the latter, —

the fourth theory, — that of Custom or Association, — afford a better solution. The *necessity* of so thinking cannot be derived from a *custom* of so thinking. Allow the force of custom to be great as may be, still it is always limited to the customary; and the *customary* has nothing whatever in it of the *necessary*. But we have here to account not for a strong, but *for an absolutely irresistible belief*. On this theory, also, the causal judgment, when association is recent, should be weak, and should only gradually acquire its full force in proportion as custom becomes inveterate. But do we find that the causal judgment is weaker in the young, stronger in the old? There is no difference. In either case, there is no less and no more; the necessity in both is absolute. Mr. Hume patronized the opinion, that the notion of causality is the offspring of experience engendered upon custom. But those have a sorry insight into the philosophy of that great thinker, who suppose that this was a dogmatic theory of his own. On the contrary, in his hands, it was a mere reduction of dogmatism to absurdity, by showing the inconsistency of its results. To the Lockian sensualism, Hume proposed the problem, — *to account for the phænomenon of necessity in our notion of the causal nexus*. That philosophy afforded no other principle through which even the attempt at a solution could be made; — and the principle of custom, Hume shows, could not furnish a *real* necessity. The alternative was plain. Either the doctrine of sensualism is false, or our nature is a delusion. Shallow thinkers adopted the latter alternative, and were lost; profound thinkers, on the contrary, were determined to lay a deeper foundation of philosophy than that of the superficial edifice of Locke; and thus it is that Hume became the cause, or the occasion, of all that is of principal value in our more recent metaphysics. Hume is the parent of the philosophy of Kant, and, through Kant, of the whole philosophy of Germany; he is the parent of the philosophy of Reid and Stewart in Scotland, and of all that is of preëminent note in the metaphysics of France and Italy. — But to return.

5. *Causality a special principle of intelligence.* — I now come to the second category (B), and to the first of the four particu-

lar heads which it likewise contains, — the opinion, namely, that the judgment, that every thing that begins to be must have a cause, is a simple primary datum, *a positive revelation of intelligence.* To this head are to be referred the theories on causality of Descartes, Leibnitz, Reid, Stewart, Kant, Fichte, Cousin, and the majority of recent philosophers. This is the fifth theory in order.

Now it is manifest, that, against the assumption of a special principle, which this doctrine makes, there exists a primary presumption of philosophy. This is the law of Parcimony, which forbids, without necessity, the multiplication of entities, powers, principles, or causes; above all, the postulation of an *unknown force,* where a *known impotence* can account for the effect. We are, therefore, entitled to apply Occam's razor * to this theory of causality, unless it be proved impossible to explain the causal judgment at a cheaper rate, by deriving it from a higher, and that a negative, origin. On a doctrine like the present is thrown the onus of vindicating its necessity, by showing that, unless a special and positive principle be assumed, there exists no competent mode to save the phænomena. It can only, therefore, be admitted provisorily; and it falls of course, if the phænomenon it would explain can be explained on less onerous conditions. Leaving, therefore, the theory to stand or fall according as the two remaining opinions are or are not found insufficient, I proceed to the consideration of these.

6. *Expectation of the constancy of nature.* — Dr. Brown has promulgated a doctrine of Causality, which may be numbered as the sixth; though perhaps it is hardly deserving of distinct enumeration. He actually identifies the causal judgment, which to us is *necessary,* with the principle by which we are

* [The dictum, *entia non multiplicanda sunt præter necessitatem,* first explicitly applied by Occam as a summary means of refuting arbitrary and unnecessary hypotheses, has been called "Occam's razor." Hamilton usually calls it the "Law of Parcimony," and elsewhere says that "it has never perhaps been adequately enounced. It should be thus expressed: — *Neither* MORE, *nor* MORE ONEROUS, *causes are to be assumed than are necessary to account for the phænomena.*"] — *Am. Ed.*

merely inclined to believe in the uniformity of nature's operations. [But apart from all subordinate objections, it is sufficient to say, that the phænomenon to be explained is the *necessity* of thinking — the absolute *impossibility* of not thinking — a cause; whilst all that the latter principle pretends to, is, to *incline us to expect* that like antecedents will be followed by like consequents. This *necessity* to suppose a cause for every phænomenon, Dr. Brown, if he does not expressly deny, keeps cautiously out of view, — virtually, in fact, eliminating all that requires explanation in the problem.] — *Discussions.*

7. *The Judgment of Causality demonstrable by abstract reasoning,* — i. e. *by the Principle of Contradiction.* — The seventh is a doctrine that has long been exploded. It attempts to establish the principle of Causality upon the principle of Contradiction. Leibnitz was too acute a metaphysician to attempt to prove the principle of Sufficient Reason or Causality, which is an ampliative or synthetic principle, by the principle of Contradiction, which is merely explicative or analytic. But his followers were not so wise. Wolf, Baumgarten, and many other Leibnitzians, paraded demonstrations of the law of the Sufficient Reason, on the ground of the law of Contradiction; but the reasoning always proceeds on the covert assumption of the very point in question. The same argument is, however, at an earlier date, to be found in Locke, and modifications of it in Hobbes and Clarke. Hume, who was only aware of the argument as in the hands of the English metaphysicians, has given it a refutation, which has earned the approbation of Reid; and by foreign philosophers, its emptiness in the hands of the Wolfian metaphysicians has frequently been exposed. Listen to the pretended demonstration: — *Whatever is produced without a cause, is produced by nothing,* — *in other words, has nothing for its cause. But nothing can no more be a cause, than it can be something. The same intuition that makes us aware, that nothing is not something, shows us that every thing must have a real cause of its existence.* To this it is sufficient to say, that the existence of causes being the point in question, the existence of causes must not be taken for granted in the very reasoning

which attempts to prove their reality. In excluding causes, we exclude *all* causes; and consequently exclude "*nothing*" considered as a cause; it is not, therefore, allowable, contrary to that exclusion, *to suppose "nothing" as a cause*, and then from the absurdity of that supposition to infer the absurdity of the exclusion itself. If every thing must have a cause, it follows that, upon the exclusion of other causes, we must accept of nothing as a cause. But it is the very point at issue, whether every thing must have a cause or not; and, therefore, it violates the first principles of reasoning to take this quæsitum itself as granted. This opinion is now universally abandoned.

8. *A result of the Law of the Conditioned.* — The eighth and last opinion is that which regards the judgment of causality as derived; and derives it not from a power, but from an impotence, of mind; in a word, from the principle of the Conditioned. I do not think it possible, without a detailed exposition of the various categories of thought, to make you fully understand the grounds and bearings of this opinion. In attempting to explain, you must, therefore, allow me to take for granted certain laws of thought, to which I have only been able incidentally to allude. Those, however, which I postulate, are such as are now generally admitted by all philosophers who allow the mind itself to be a source of cognitions; and the only one which has not been recognized by them, but which, as I endeavored briefly to prove, must likewise be taken into account, is the Law of the Conditioned, — *the law that the conceivable has always two opposite extremes, and that the extremes are equally inconceivable.* That the Conditioned is to be viewed, not as a power, but as a powerlessness of mind, is evinced by this, — that *the two extremes are contradictories, and, as contradictories, though neither alternative can be conceived, — thought as possible, one or other must be admitted to be necessary.*

Causality deduced from this law through the three Categories of thought. — Philosophers who allow a native principle to the mind at all, allow that Existence is such a principle. I shall, therefore, take for granted Existence as the highest category or condition of thought. As I noticed in the last chapter, no thought is possible except under this category. All that we perceive or imagine as different from us, we perceive or imagine as objectively existent. All that we are conscious of as an act or modification of self, we are conscious of only as subjectively existent. *All thought*, therefore, *implies the thought of existence;* and this is the veritable exposition of the enthymeme of Descartes, — *Cogito ergo sum.* I cannot think that I think, without thinking that I exist, — I cannot be conscious, without being conscious that I am. Let *existence*, then, be laid down as a necessary form of thought. As a second category or subjective condition of thought, I postulate that of *Time.* This, likewise, cannot be denied me. It is the necessary condition of every conscious act; thought is only realized to us as in succession, and succession is only conceived by us under the concept of time. Existence and Existence in Time is thus an elementary form of our intelligence. But we do not conceive existence in time absolutely or infinitely, — we conceive it only as *conditioned in time;* and *Existence Conditioned in Time* expresses, at once and in relation, the three categories of thought which afford us in combination the principle of Causality. This requires some explanation.

When we perceive or imagine an object, we perceive or imagine it — 1°, As existent, and, 2°, As in Time; Existence and Time being categories of all thought. But what is meant by saying, I perceive, or imagine, or, in general, think an object only as I perceive, or imagine, or, in general, think it to exist? Simply this; — that, as thinking it, I cannot but think it to exist, in other words, that *I cannot annihilate it in thought.* I may think away from it, I may turn to other things; and I can thus exclude it from my consciousness; but, actually thinking it, I cannot think it as non-existent, for as it is thought, so it is thought existent.

But a thing is thought to exist, only as it is thought to exist in time. Time is present, past, and future. We cannot think an object of thought as non-existent *de presenti*, — as actually an object of thought. But can we think that quantum of existence of which an object, real or ideal, is the complement, as non-existent, either in time past, or in time future? Make the experiment. Try to think the object of your thought as non-existent in the moment before the present. — You cannot. Try it in the moment before that. — You cannot. Nor can you annihilate it by carrying it back to any moment, however distant in the past. You may conceive the parts of which this complement of existence is composed, as separated; if a material object, you can think it as shivered to atoms, sublimated into æther; but not one iota of existence can you conceive as annihilated, which subsequently you thought to exist. In like manner, try the future, — try to conceive the prospective annihilation of any present object, — of any atom of any present object. — You cannot. All this may be possible, but of it we cannot think the possibility. But if you can thus conceive neither the absolute commencement nor the absolute termination of any thing that is once thought to exist, try, on the other hand, if you can conceive the opposite alternative of infinite non-commencement, of infinite non-termination. To this you are equally impotent. This is the category of the Conditioned, as applied to the category of Existence under the category of Time.

But in this application is the principle of Causality not given? Why, what is the law of Causality? Simply this, — that when an object is presented phænomenally as commencing, we cannot but suppose that the complement of existence, which it now contains, has previously been; in other words, that all that we at present come to know as an effect must previously have existed in its causes; though what these causes are we may perhaps be altogether unable even to surmise.

The law of the Conditioned. — This theory, which has not hitherto been proposed, is recommended by its extreme simplicity. It postulates no new, no special, no positive principle. It only supposes that the mind is limited; and the law of limitation, the law of the Conditioned, in one of its applications, constitutes the law of Causality. The mind is necessitated to think certain forms; and, under these forms, *thought is only possible in the interval between two contradictory extremes, both of which are absolutely inconceivable, but one of which, on the principle of Excluded Middle, is necessarily true.* In reference to the present subject, it is only requisite to specify two of these forms, — Existence and Time. I showed you that thought is only possible under the native conceptions, — the *a priori* forms, — of existence and time; in other words, the notions of existence and time are essential elements of every act of intelligence. But while the mind is thus astricted to certain necessary modes or forms of thought, in these forms it can only think under certain conditions. Thus, while obliged to think under the thought of time, it cannot conceive, on the one hand, the absolute commencement of time, and it cannot conceive, on the other, the infinite non-commencement of time; in like manner, on the one hand, it cannot conceive an absolute minimum of time, nor yet, on the other, can it conceive the infinite divisibility of time. Yet these form two pairs of contradictories, that is, of counter-propositions, which, if our intelligence be not all a lie, cannot both be true, but of which, on the same authority, one necessarily must be true. This proves: 1°, *That it is not competent to argue, that what cannot be comprehended as possible by us, is impossible in reality;* and 2°, *That the necessities of thought are not always positive powers of cognition, but often negative inabilities to know.* The law of mind, that all that is positively conceivable, lies in the interval between two inconceivable extremes, and which, however palpable when stated, has never been generalized, as far as I know, by any philosopher, I call the Law or Principle of the Conditioned.

This law in its application affords the phænomenon of Causality. — Thus, the whole phænomenon of causality seems to me to be nothing more than the law of the Conditioned, in its application to a thing thought under the form or mental category of Existence, and under the form or mental category of Time. We cannot know, we cannot think a thing, except as existing, that is, under the category of existence; and we cannot know or think of a thing as existing, except in time. Now the application of the law of the conditioned to any object, thought as existent, and thought as in time, will give us at once the phænomenon of causality. And thus:—An object is given us, either by sense or suggestion,—imagination. As known, we cannot but think it existent, and in time. But to say that we cannot but think it to exist, is to say, that we are unable to think it non-existent; that is, that we are unable to annihilate it in thought. And this we cannot do. We may turn aside from it; we may occupy our attention with other objects; and we may thus exclude it from our thoughts. This is certain: we need not think it; but it is equally certain, that thinking it, we cannot think it not to exist. This will be at once admitted of the present; but it may possibly be denied of the past and future. But if we make the experiment, we shall find the mental annihilation of an object equally impossible under time past, present, or future.

Annihilation and Creation,—as conceived by us.—To obviate misapprehension, however, I must make a very simple observation. When I say that it is impossible to annihilate an object in thought—in other words, to conceive it as non-existent,—it is of course not meant that it is impossible to imagine the object wholly changed in form. We can figure to ourselves the elements of which it is composed, distributed and arranged and modified in ten thousand forms,—we can imagine any thing of it, short of annihilation. But the complement, the quantum, of existence, which is realized in any object,—that we can [not] represent to ourselves, either as increased, without abstraction from other bodies, or as diminished, without addition to them. In short, we are unable to construe it in thought, that there can be an atom absolutely added to, or an atom absolutely taken away from, existence in general. Make the experiment. Form to yourselves a notion of the universe; now can you conceive that the quantity of existence, of which the universe is the sum, is either amplified or diminished? You can conceive the creation of a world as lightly as you conceive the creation of an atom. But what is a creation? It is not the springing of nothing into something. Far from it:—it is conceived, and is by us conceivable, merely as the evolution of a new form of existence, by the fiat of the Deity. Let us suppose the very crisis of creation.

Can we realize it to ourselves, in thought, that, the moment after the universe came into manifested being, there was a larger complement of existence in the universe and its Author together, than there was the moment before, in the Deity himself alone? This we cannot imagine. What I have now said of our conceptions of creation, holds true of our conceptions of annihilation. We can conceive no real annihilation, — no absolute sinking of something into nothing. But, as creation is cogitable by us only as an exertion of divine power, so annihilation is only to be conceived by us as a withdrawal of the divine support. All that there is now actually of existence in the universe, we conceive as having virtually existed, prior to creation, in the Creator; and in imagining the universe to be annihilated by its Author, we can only imagine this, as the retractation of an outward energy into power. All this shows how impossible it is for the human mind to think aught that it thinks, as non-existent either in time past or in time future.

[Our inability to think what we have once conceived existent in Time, as in time becoming non-existent, corresponds with our inability to think, what we have conceived existent in Space, as in space becoming non-existent. We cannot realize it to thought, that a thing should be extruded, either from the one quantity or the other. Hence, under extension, the law of Ultimate Incompressibility; under protension, the law of Cause and Effect.] — *Discussions.*

Infinite regress, or non-commencement, equally inconceivable. — We have been hitherto speaking only of one inconceivable extreme of the conditioned, in its application to the category of existence in the category of time, — the extreme of absolute commencement; the other is equally incomprehensible, that is, the extreme of infinite regress or non-commencement. With this latter we have, however, at present nothing to do. [Indeed, as not obtrusive, the Infinite figures far less in the theatre of mind, and exerts a far inferior influence in the modification of thought, than the Absolute. It is, in fact, both distant and delitescent; and in place of meeting us at every turn, it requires some exertion on our part to seek it out.] It is the former alone, — it is the inability we experience of annihilating in thought an existence in time past, in other words, our utter impotence of conceiving its absolute commencement, that constitutes and explains the whole phænomenon of causality. An object is presented to our observation which has phænomenally begun to be. Well, we cannot realize it in thought that the object, that is, this determinate complement of existence, had really no being at any past moment; because this supposes that, once thinking it as existent, we could again think it as non-existent, which is for us impossible. What, then, can we do? That the phænomenon presented to us began, as a phænomenon, to be, — this we know by experience; but that the elements of its existence only began, when the phænomenon they constitute came into being, — this we are wholly unable to represent in thought. In these circumstances, how do we proceed? — How must we proceed? There is only one possible mode. We are compelled to believe that the object (that is, a certain *quale* and *quantum* of being) whose phænomenal rise into existence we have witnessed, did really exist, prior to this rise, under other forms; [and by *form*, be it observed, I mean any mode of existence, conceivable by us or not]. But to say that a thing previously existed under different forms, is only in other words to say, that a thing had causes. I have already noticed to you the error of philosophers in supposing, that any thing can have a single cause. Of course, I speak only of Second Causes. Of the causation of the Deity we can form no possible conception. Of Second Causes, I say, there must almost always be at least a concurrence of two to constitute an effect. Take the example of vapor. Here, to say that heat is the cause of evaporation, is a very inaccurate, — at least a very inadequate, expression. Water is as much the cause of evaporation as heat. But heat and water together are the causes of the phænomenon. Nay, there is a third concause which we have forgot, — the atmosphere. Now, a cloud is the result of these three concurrent causes or constituents; and, knowing this, we find no difficulty in carrying back the complement of existence, which it contains prior to its appearance. But on the hypothesis, that we are not aware what are the real constituents or causes of the cloud, the human mind must still perforce suppose some unknown, some hypothetical, antecedents, into which it mentally refunds all the existence which the cloud is thought to contain.*

Uniform succession not a necessary prerequisite for the causal

* [My doctrine of Causality is accused of neglecting the phænomenon of *change*, and of ignoring the attribute of *power*. This objection precisely reverses the fact. Causation is by me proclaimed to be identical with change, — change of power into act ("omnia mutantur"); change, however, only of appearance, — we being unable to realize in thought either existence (substance) apart from phænomena, or existence absolutely commencing, or absolutely terminating. And specially as to power; power is the property of an existent something (for it is thought only as the essential attribute of what is so or so to exist); power is, consequently, the correlative of existence, and a necessary supposition, in this theory, of causation. Here the cause, or rather the complement of causes, is nothing but powers capable of producing the effect; and the effect is only that now existing actually, which previously existed potentially, or in the causes. We must, in truth, define — a cause, the power of effectuating a change; and an effect, a change actually caused.

Mutation, Causation, Effectuation, are only the same thought in different respects; they may, therefore, be regarded as virtually terms convertible. Every change is an effect; every effect is a change. An effect is, in truth, just a change of power into act; every effect being an actualization of the potential.

But what is now considered as the cause may at another time be viewed as the effect; and *vice versâ*. Thus, we can extract the acid or the alkali, as effect, out of the salt, as principal concause; and the square which, as effect, is made up of two triangles in conjunction, may be viewed as cause when cut into these figures. In opposite views, Addition and Multiplication, Subtraction and Division, may be regarded as causes, or as effects.

Power is an attribute or property of existence, but not coextensive with it; for we may suppose (negatively think) things to exist which have no capacity of change, no capacity of appearing.

Creation is the existing subsequently *in act* of what previously existed *in power;* annihilation, on the contrary, is the subsequent existence *in power* of what previously existed *in act.*

Except the first and last causal agencies (and these, as Divine operations, are by us incomprehensible), every other is conceived also as an effect; therefore, every event is, in different relations, a power and an act. Considered as a cause, it is a power, — a power to coöperate an effect. Considered as an effect, it is an act, — an act coöperated by causes.] — *Appendix.*

judgment. — Nothing can be a greater error in itself, or a more fertile cause of delusion, than the common doctrine, that the causal judgment is elicited only when we apprehend objects in consecution, and uniform consecution. Of course, the observation of such succession prompts and enables us to assign particular causes to particular effects. But this consideration ought to be carefully distinguished from the law of Causality, absolutely, which consists not in the empirical attribution of this phænomenon, as cause, to that phænomenon as effect, but in the universal necessity, of which we are conscious, to think causes for every event, whether that event stand isolated by itself, and be by us referable to no other, or whether it be one in a series of successive phænomena, which, as it were, spontaneously arrange themselves under the relation of effect and cause. [Of no phænomenon, as observed, need we think *the* cause; but of every phænomenon, must we think *a* cause. The former we may learn through a process of induction and generalization; the latter we must always and at once admit, constrained by the condition of Relativity. On this, not sunken rock, Dr. Brown and others have been shipwrecked.] — *Discussions.*

Reasons for preferring this doctrine. — In the *first* place, to explain the phænomenon of the Causal Judgment, *it postulates no new, no extraordinary, no express principle.* It does not even found upon a positive power; for, while it shows that the phænomenon in question is only one of a class, it assigns, as their common cause, only a negative impotence. In this, it stands advantageously contrasted with the one other theory which saves the phænomenon, but which saves it only by the hypothesis of a special principle, expressly devised to account for this phænomenon alone. Nature never works by more, and more complex, instruments than are necessary; — *μηδὲν περιττῶς*; and to assume a particular force, to perform what can be better explained by a general imbecility, is contrary to every rule of philosophizing.

It averts scepticism. — But, in the *second* place, if there be postulated an express and positive affirmation of intelligence to account for the fact, that existence cannot absolutely commence, we must equally postulate a counter affirmation of intelligence, positive and express, to explain the counter fact, that existence cannot infinitely not-commence. The one necessity of mind is equally strong as the other; and if the one be a positive doctrine, an express testimony of intelligence, so also must be the other. But they are contradictories; and, as contradictories, they cannot both be true. On this theory, therefore, the root of our nature is a lie! By the doctrine, on the contrary, which I propose, these contradictory phænomena are carried up into the common principle of a limitation of our faculties. Intelligence is shown to be feeble, but not false; our nature is, thus, not a lie, nor the Author of our nature a deceiver.

It avoids fatalism or inconsistency. — In the *third* place, this simpler and easier doctrine avoids a serious inconvenience, which attaches to the more difficult and complex. It is this: — To suppose a positive and special principle of causality, is to suppose, that there is expressly revealed to us, through intelligence, the fact that there is no free causation, — that is, that there is no cause which is not itself merely an effect; existence being only a series of determined antecedents and determined consequents. But this is an assertion of Fatalism. Such, however, most of the patrons of that doctrine will not admit. The assertion of absolute necessity, they are aware, is virtually the negation of a moral universe, consequently of the Moral Governor of a moral universe; in a word, Atheism. Fatalism and Atheism are, indeed, convertible terms. The only valid arguments for the existence of a God, and for the immortality of the soul, rest on the ground of man's moral nature; consequently, if that moral nature be annihilated, which in any scheme of necessity it is, every conclusion established on such a nature, is annihilated also. Aware of this, some of those who make the judgment of causality a special principle, — a positive dictate of intelligence, — find themselves compelled, in order to escape from the consequences of their doctrine, to deny that this dictate, though universal in its deliverance, should be allowed to hold universally true; and, accordingly, they would exempt from it the facts of volition. Will, they hold to be a *free* cause, that is, a cause *which is not an effect;* in other words, they attribute to will the power of absolute origination.* But here their own principle of causality is too strong for them. They say, that it is unconditionally given, as a special and positive law of intelligence, that every origination is only an apparent, not a real, commencement. Now to exempt certain phænomena from this law, for the sake of our moral consciousness, cannot be validly done. For, in the first place, this would be to admit that the mind is a complement of contradictory revelations. If mendacity be admitted of some of our mental dictates, we cannot vindicate veracity to any. "Falsus in uno, falsus in omnibus." Absolute scepticism is hence the legitimate conclusion. But, in the second place, waiving this conclusion, what right have we, on this doctrine, to subordinate the positive affirmation of causality to our consciousness of moral liberty, — what right have we, for the interest of the latter, to derogate from the universality of the former? We have none. If both are equally positive, we have no right to sacrifice to the other the alternative, which our wishes prompt us to abandon.

But the doctrine which I propose is not exposed to these difficulties. It does not suppose that the judgment of Causality is founded on a power of the mind to recognize as necessary in thought what is necessary in the universe of existence; it, on the contrary, founds this judgment merely on the impotence of the mind to conceive either of two contradictories, and, as one or the other of two contradictories must be true, though both cannot, it shows that there is no ground for inferring from the inability of the mind to conceive an alternative as possible, that such alternative is really impossible. At the same time, if the causal judgment be not an affirmation of mind, but merely an incapacity of positively thinking the contrary, it follows that such a negative judgment cannot stand in opposition to the positive consciousness, — the affirmative deliverance, that we are truly the authors, — the responsible originators, of our actions,

* [To conceive *a free act,* is to conceive an act, which, being *a cause,* is not itself *an effect;* in other words, to conceive an absolute commencement. But is such by us conceivable?] — *Notes to Reid*

and not merely links in the adamantine series of effects and causes. It appears to me that it is only on this doctrine that we can philosophically vindicate the liberty of the will, — that we can rationally assert to a man "fatis avolsa voluntas." How the will can possibly be free must remain to us, under the present limitation of our faculties, wholly incomprehensible. We cannot conceive absolute commencement; we cannot, therefore, conceive a free volition. But as little can we conceive the alternative on which liberty is denied, on which necessity is affirmed. And in favor of our moral nature, the fact that we are free, is given us in the consciousness of an uncompromising law of Duty, in the consciousness of our moral accountability; and this fact of liberty cannot be redargued on the ground, that it is incomprehensible; for the doctrine of the Conditioned proves, against the necessitarian, that something may, nay must, be true, of which the mind is wholly unable to construe to itself the possibility; whilst it shows that the objection of incomprehensibility applies no less to the doctrine of fatalism than to the doctrine of moral freedom. If the deduction, therefore, of the Causal Judgment, which I have attempted, should speculatively prove correct, it will, I think, afford a securer and more satisfactory foundation for our practical interests, than any other which has ever yet been promulgated.

[The question of Liberty and Necessity may be dealt with in two ways.

I. The opposing parties may endeavor to show each that his thesis is distinct, intelligible, and consistent, whereas that the anti-thesis of his opponent is indistinct, unintelligible, and contradictory.

II. An opposing party may endeavor to show that the thesis of either side is unthinkable, and thus abolish logically the whole problem, as, on both alternatives, beyond the limits of human thought; it being, however, open to him to argue that, though unthinkable, his thesis is not annihilated, there being contradictory opposites, one of which must consequently be held as true, though we be unable to think the possibility of either opposite; whilst he may be able to appeal to a direct or indi rect declaration of our conscious nature in favor of the alternative which he maintains.] — *Appendix.*

Reid says that, according to one meaning of the word *Liberty*, "it is opposed to confinement of the body by superior force; so we say a prisoner is set at liberty, when his fetters are knocked off and he is discharged from confinement;" and he grants that "this liberty extends not to the will." [This is called the *liberty from Coaction or Violence* — *the liberty of Spontaneity* — *Spontaneity*. In the present question, this species of liberty ought to be thrown altogether out of account; it is admitted by all parties; it is common equally to brutes and men; is not a peculiar quality of the will; and is, in fact, essential to it, for the will cannot possibly be forced. *The greatest spontaneity is, in fact, the greatest necessity.* Thus, a hungry horse, who turns of necessity to food, is said, on this definition of liberty, to do so with freedom, because he does so spontaneously; and, in general, the desire of happiness, which is the most necessary tendency, will, on this application of the term, be the most free.

Again, "liberty is opposed to obligation by law, or lawful authority." With this description of liberty, also, the present question has no concern.

Moral liberty does not merely consist in the power of *doing what we will*, but in the power of *willing what we will.* This is variously denominated the *Liberty from Necessity* — *Moral Liberty* — *Philosophical Liberty* — *Essential Liberty* — *Liberty from Indifference*, etc. A Power over the determinations of our Will supposes an act of Will that our Will should determine so and so; for we can only freely exert power through a rational determination or Volition. This definition of Liberty is right. But then question upon question remains — and this *ad infinitum.* Have we a power (a will) over such anterior will? And until this question be definitively answered, which it never can, we must be *unable to conceive the possibility of the fact of Liberty.* But though inconceivable, this fact is not therefore false. For there are many contradictories (and of contradictories, *one must* and *one only can*, be true), of which we are equally unable to conceive the possibility of either.

The philosophy, therefore, which I profess, annihilates the theoretical problem — How is the scheme of Liberty, or the scheme of Necessity, to be rendered comprehensible? — by showing that both schemes are equally inconceivable; but it establishes Liberty practically as a fact, by showing that it is either itself an immediate *datum*, or is involved in an immediate *datum*, of consciousness. Reid has done nothing to render the scheme of Liberty *conceivable*. But if our intellectual nature be not a lie, if our consciousness and conscience do not deceive us in the immediate datum of an *Absolute Law of Duty*, we are *free*, as we are *moral*, agents; for Morality involves Liberty as its essential condition, its *ratio essendi*.

Is the person an *original undetermined* cause of the determination of his will? If he be not, then he is not a *free* agent, and the scheme of Necessity is admitted. If he be, in the first place, it is impossible to conceive the possibility of this; and, in the second, if the fact, though inconceivable, be allowed, it is impossible to see how a *cause undetermined by any motive** can be a *rational, moral, and accountable cause.* There is no conceivable medium between *Fatalism* and *Casuism*; and the contradictory schemes of Liberty and Necessity themselves are inconceivable. For, as we cannot compass in thought an *undetermined cause — an absolute commencement* — the fundamental hypothesis of the one; so we can as little think *an infinite series of determined causes* — of *relative commencements* — the fundamental hypothesis of the other. The champions of the

* [A motive, abstractly considered, is called *an end* or *final cause*. It is well denominated in the Greek philosophy, τὸ ἕνεκα οὗ — *that for the sake of which*. A motive, however, in its concrete reality, is nothing apart from the mind, — only a mental tendency.

If motives "*influence* to action," as Reid says, they must coöperate in producing a certain effect upon the agent; and the determination to act, and to act in a certain manner, is that effect. They are thus, on Reid's own view, in this relation, *causes*, and *efficient* causes. It is of no consequence in the argument whether motives be said to *determine* a man to act, or to *influence* (that is, to determine) him to determine himself to act. It does not, therefore, seem consistent to say that motives are *not causes*, and that they *do not act*.] — *Notes to Reid.*

opposite doctrines are thus at once resistless in assault, and impotent in defence. Each is hewn down and appears to die under the home-thrusts of his adversary; but each again recovers life from the very death of his antagonist, and, to borrow a simile, both are like the heroes in Valhalla, ready in a moment to amuse themselves anew in the same bloodless and interminable conflict. The doctrine of Moral Liberty cannot be made conceivable, for we can only conceive the determined and the relative. As already stated, all that can be done is to show, 1° That, for the *fact* of Liberty, we have, immediately or mediately, the evidence of consciousness; and, 2°, That there are, among the phænomena of mind, many facts which we *must* admit as actual, but of whose possibility we are wholly unable to form any notion. I may merely observe that the fact of *Motion* can be shown to be impossible, on grounds not less strong than those on which it is attempted to disprove the fact of *Liberty;* to say nothing of many contradictories, neither of which can be *thought*, but one of which must, on the laws of Contradiction and Excluded Middle, necessarily *be*.

It is proper to notice, that, as to *live* is to *act*, and as man is not free to live or not to live, so neither, absolutely speaking, is he free to act or not to act. As he lives, he is necessarily determined to act or energize — to think and will; and all the liberty to which he can pretend, is to choose between this mode of action and that. In Scholastic language, man cannot have the liberty of *freedom*, though he may have the liberty of *specification*. The root of his freedom is thus necessity. Nay, we cannot conceive otherwise even of the Deity. As we must think Him as necessarily existent, and necessarily living, so we must think him as necessarily active. Such are the conditions of human thought. When Dr. Clarke says, "*The true definition of Liberty is the Power to Act*," he should have recollected that this power is, on his own hypothesis, absolutely fatal if it *cannot but act*.] — *Notes to Reid.*

[Substance and Quality are, manifestly, only thought as mutual relatives. We cannot think a Quality existing absolutely, in or of itself. We are constrained to think it as inhering in some basis, substratum, hypostasis, or Substance; but this Substance cannot be conceived by us except negatively, that is, as the unapparent — the inconceivable, correlative of certain appearing Qualities. If we attempt to think it positively, we can think it only by transforming it into a Quality or bundle of Qualities, which, again, we are compelled to refer to an unknown substance, now supposed for their incogitable basis. Every thing, in fact, may be conceived as the Quality, or as the Substance of something else. But Absolute Substance and Absolute Quality, these are both inconceivable, as more than negations of the conceivable. It is hardly requisite to observe, that the term Substance is vulgarly applied, in the abusive signification, to a congeries of qualities, denoting those especially which are more permanent, in contrast to those which are more transitory. What has now been said, applies equally to Mind and Matter.

Space applies, proximately, to things considered as Substance; for the qualities of substances, though they are in, may not occupy, space. In fact, it is by a merely modern abuse of the term, that the affections of Extension have been styled *Qualities.* It is extremely difficult for the human mind to admit the possibility of unextended Substance. Extension, being a condition of positive thinking, clings to all our conceptions; and it is one merit of the philosophy of the Conditioned, that it proves space to be only a law of Thought, and not a law of Things.] — *Discussions.*

THE END.

LIST OF BOOKS PUBLISHED BY

JOHN ALLYN,

(LATE SEVER, FRANCIS, & CO.,)

21 Bromfield Street, Boston.

Standard College Text-Books.

The Metaphysics of Sir William Hamilton. Collected, Arranged, and Abridged for the Use of Colleges and Private Students. By FRANCIS BOWEN, Alford Professor of Moral Philosophy in Harvard University. 12mo. Cloth $2.00

A Treatise on Logic; or, The Laws of Pure Thought. Comprising both the Aristotelic and the Hamiltonian Analyses of Logical Forms. By FRANCIS BOWEN, Alford Professor of Moral Philosophy in Harvard University. 12mo. Cloth 2.00

Chemical Tables. By S. P. SHARPLES, S. B. 12mo. Cloth 2.25

First Principles of Chemical Philosophy. By PROF. J. P. COOKE, JR. 12mo. Cloth 3.50

The Phædo of Plato. With Notes by WILHELM WAGNER, Ph. D. 16mo. Cloth 1.50

Selections from the Greek Historians. Arranged in the Order of Events. With Notes, by CORNELIUS C FELTON, LL. D., late President of Harvard University. 12mo. Half morocco 2.00

Selections from Modern Greek Writers, in Prose and Poetry. With Notes, by CORNELIUS C. FELTON, LL. D., late President of Harvard University. 12mo. Cloth 1.25

The Panegyricus of Isocrates. From the Text of BREMI. With English Notes, by CORNELIUS C. FELTON, LL. D., late President of Harvard University. A Revised Edition. 12mo. Cloth. . . 1.00

The Clouds of Aristophanes. With Notes, by CORNELIUS C. FELTON, LL. D., late President of Harvard University. 12mo. Cloth 1.25

The Birds of Aristophanes. With Notes, and a Metrical Table, by CORNELIUS C. FELTON, LL. D., late President of Harvard University. 12mo. Cloth 1.25

Selections from Herodotus and Thucydides. With Notes by R. H. MATHER, Professor of Greek and German in Amherst College. 16mo. Cloth 1.00

Horace. With English Notes, by REV. A. J. MACLEANE, M. A. Revised and Edited by R. H. CHASE, A. M. 12mo. Cloth 1.50

Cicero's Tusculan Disputations. Book First: The Dream of Scipio; and Extracts from the Dialogues on Old Age and Friendship. With English Notes, by THOMAS CHASE, A. M. 16mo. Cloth . $1.25

M. Tullii Ciceronis pro A. Cluentio Habito Oratio ad Judices. With English Notes, by AUSTIN STICKNEY, A. M., Professor of Latin in Trinity College, Hartford, Conn. 12mo. Cloth . . 1.00

The Formulas of Plane and Spherical Trigonometry. Collected and arranged for the Use of Students and Computers. By E. P. SEAVER, A. M., Assistant Prof. of Math. in Harv. Coll. 16mo. Flex. cloth .80

A German Grammar. A Companion to Dr. Ahn's Method. By H. W. JUST. 16mo. Cloth 75

The Catena Classicorum.

THE FOLLOWING VOLUMES ARE NOW READY:

THUCYDIDES. Books I., II. Edited by CHAS. BIGG, A. M. 12mo. $2.00

DEMOSTHENES. The Olynthiacs and Philippics. Edited by G. H. HESLOP, A. M. 12mo. 1.50

ARISTOPHANES. The Acharnians and Knights. Edited by W. C. GREEN, A. M. 12mo. 1.50

SOPHOCLES. The Electra. Edited by R. C. JEBB, A. M. 12mo. 1.25

SOPHOCLES. The Ajax. Edited by R. C. JEBB, A. M., 12mo. 1.50

DEMOSTHENES. On the Crown. Edited by ARTHUR HOLMES 1.50

JUVENAL. Edited by G. A. SIMCOX. *In Preparation.*

Weale's Classical Series.

LATIN DICTIONARY. By GOODWIN. Part I. Latin-English. $ 1.00
Part II. English-Latin . .75

JUVENAL, Satires of. By ESCOTT 75

LIVY. Books XXI, XXII. By SMITH 75

TERENCE. Andria and Heautontimoroumenos. By DAVIES .75

PLATO. Apology and Crito. By DAVIES 1.00

GREEK DICTIONARY. By HAMILTON. Part I. Greek-English. $1.00
Part II. English-Greek . 1.00

ÆSCHYLUS. Prometheus Vinctus. By DAVIES . . .50

EURIPIDES. Alcestis. By MILNER 50

Hecuba and Medea. By SMITH .75

SOPHOCLES. Œdipus Rex. By YOUNG 50

Elegant Standard Books.

THE GOLDEN TREASURY SERIES.

A *Handy* Edition of the GOLDEN TREASURY SERIES, in 18mo., on cheaper paper, is also published, at 75 cts. per volume.

The Golden Treasury of the Best Songs and Lyrical Poems in the English Language. Selected and Arranged, with Notes, by FRANCIS TURNER PALGRAVE, Fellow of Exeter College, Oxford. 16mo. Green vellum 1.25

The Children's Garland. From the best Poets. Selected and Arranged by COVENTRY PATMORE. 16mo. Red vellum . . 1.25

The Book of Praise. From the Best English Hymn-Writers. Selected and Arranged by ROUNDELL PALMER. 16mo. Maroon vellum 1.25

The Pilgrim's Progress. From this World to that which is to come. By JOHN BUNYAN. With Illustrations by STOTHARD. 16mo. Vellum cloth 1.25

A Book of Golden Deeds of all Times and all Lands. Gathered and Narrated by the Author of "The Heir of Redclyffe." 16mo. Green vellum 1.25

The Jest-Book. The choicest Anecdotes and Sayings. Selected and Arranged by MARK LEMON. 16mo. Green vellum . . . 1.25

The Ballad Book. A Selection of the choicest British Ballads. Edited by WILLIAM ALLINGHAM. 16mo. Vellum 1.25

The Sunday Book of Poetry. Selected and Arranged by C. F. ALEXANDER. 16mo. Vellum 1.25

THE GOLDEN TREASURY JUVENILE.

Dream Children. By the Author of "Seven Little People and their Friends." Full-page Illustrations, after Designs by WHITE, with Ornamental Initials illustrating each Story. 16mo. Vellum cloth $1.25

The Poems of Thomas Gray. Illustrated. A new and elegant Edition. Small 4to. Morocco Cloth 1.75

Democracy in America. By ALEXIS DE TOCQUEVILLE. Translated by HENRY REEVE, ESQ. Edited, with Notes, the Translation revised, and in great part rewritten, and the Additions made to the recent Paris Editions now first translated, by FRANCIS BOWEN, Alford Professor of Moral Philosophy in Harvard University. Elegantly printed on linen paper at the University Press. Bound in maroon vellum. 2 vols. Post 8vo. 5.00

American Institutions. By DE TOCQUEVILLE. Being a cheap edition of Vol. I. of the above. 12mo. Cloth. 1.75

www.ingramcontent.com/pod-product-compliance
Lightning Source LLC
LaVergne TN
LVHW021232110826
845150LV00002B/310

9781425562960